P9-EML-464

Library of Congress Cataloging in Publication Data

AMLING, FREDERICK.
 Investments, an introduction to analysis and management.

 Includes bibliographies and index.
 1. Investments. 2. Investment analysis. I. Title.
HG4521.A54 1983   332.6'78   82-20438
ISBN 0-13-504324-7

*Editorial/production supervision and
 interior design: Susan Adkins*
Cover design: Ray Lundgren
Manufacturing buyer: Ed O'Dougherty

Printed in the United States of America

10 9 8 7 6 5 4 3 2 1

ISBN 0-13-504324-7

Prentice-Hall International, Inc., *London*
Prentice-Hall of Australia Pty. Limited, *Sydney*
Editora Prentice-Hall do Brasil, Ltda., *Rio de Janeiro*
Prentice-Hall Canada Inc., *Toronto*
Prentice-Hall of India Private Limited, *New Delhi*
Prentice-Hall of Japan, Inc., *Tokyo*
Prentice-Hall of Southeast Asia Pte. Ltd., *Singapore*
Whitehall Books Limited, *Wellington, New Zealand*

FREDERICK AMLING

Professor of Business Finance
The George Washington University

INVESTMENTS

An Introduction to Analysis and Management

FIFTH EDITION

Prentice-Hall, Inc., Englewood Cliffs, New Jersey

This book is dedicated to
Gwen
Jeff and Cindy
Scott and June
Terry and Ann

CONTENTS

PART II
THE INVESTMENT ALTERNATIVES

CHAPTER 5
PREFERRED-STOCK ANALYSIS AND VALUATION:
AN OWNERSHIP SECURITY   *138*

CHAPTER 6
COMMON STOCK AS AN INVESTMENT—
WITH OPTIONS AND FUTURES INDEX   *154*

PART IV
FUNDAMENTAL ANALYSIS

PREFACE

The fifth edition of *Investments* has been revised to reflect the theoretical and practical forces that have brought about dramatic changes in the investment process. A major change in the past five years has been a substantial increase in the number and type of investment outlets available to investors (brought about in part by high interest rates and inflation), including high yielding certificates of deposit, money market funds, zero coupon bonds, variable rate bonds, options and futures contracts, and tangible assets including gold, silver, diamonds, real estate, antiques, and international securities. All of these financial and tangible assets are now available to individual and institutional investors for investment and must be a part of their decisions. The overriding consideration in making decisions centers on the expected rate of return (return) from an asset versus the expected variability of the rate of return (risk). All assets purchased by investors may be classified by their return and risk characteristics.

As a consequence, return—the rate of return the investor expects to earn from an investment—and risk—the variability of the return—continue to be an integral part of the subject of investments. This focus makes the investment decision easier.

A second change has been the influence that modern portfolio theory has had upon investment decisions; MPT has made the subject more quantitative both in the method of calculating the rate of return and the way in which risk is measured. And it has given investors and advisors a better way of communicating among themselves and their clients. Even if one disagrees with MPT and its implications when applied directly to investment decisions, the logic and discipline obtained by an understanding of the theory can be appreciated.

A third change has been the institutional and international growth in investments. Institutional investors dominate the investment scene. There has also been a substantial growth in the willingness of investors to purchase international assets, including Eurodollars and Eurobonds, for example.

A fourth change has been in the growth of the options, futures, and commodity markets. These markets have existed for a long time. They are becoming more a part of the investor's decisions about investment and speculation.

A fifth change relates to technical analysis. Technical analysis, the antithesis of MPT, has been with us for some time, but now it is being used by investors to develop strategies in their investment decisions.

Another major change has been an increased emphasis on portfolio planning and measuring investment performance. Investors must plan to meet their goals by establishing expected return targets and then developing a strategy to meet these goals. Investment performance must be measured to make certain the return and risk goals are being achieved.

The book has been reorganized to reflect these changes and to make a greater distinction between fundamental analysis, modern portfolio theory, and technical analysis. These seem to be the dominant forces in investment decision-making today. Therefore, the book has been divided into seven parts to reflect these changes and emphasis.

Part I explains what investment is and how to measure rate of return and risk. It provides an overview of how an investor might decide on the selection of an investment based upon the return and risk expectation. This overview sets the stage for what will be discussed in more detail in later chapters. Sources of information which can be used in the decision-making process are presented; they include institutional sources. Who the investors are, their relative importance, and where they invest helps establish realism in the investment process.

Part II presents a description, and return and risk characteristics, of various investments available to individuals and institutions. Included are money market funds, government securities (both short and long term), federal agency securities, state and local municipal bonds, corporate bonds, international bonds, common stocks (both domestic and foreign), options, preferred stock, convertible preferred and bonds, mutual funds, tangible investments such as real estate, gold and silver, antiques, and commodities and commodity futures. A method of analysis and description is provided.

Part III provides a description and analysis of the market structure in which securities are traded. The markets, which are reasonably efficient, are divided into primary, secondary, third, and fourth markets. The role of brokers and dealers in the marketplace is explained, along with the ways in which economy and efficiency can be attained in buying and selling securities. The role of regulation and the movement toward a national market system are presented.

Part IV explains fundamental analysis and demonstrates how an investor would analyze securities for investment. The process begins when an analysis of the national economy and its expected growth over the next three years. Industries that are expected to be competitively strong are identified. The leading competitive companies in the leading industries are then analyzed to establish their attractiveness for investment.

The analysis includes: (1) competitive position of the company; (2) profitability and future earnings; (3) operating efficiency; (4) current financial position; (5) capital structure analysis; (6) management; and (7) valuation appraisal, which includes an estimate of return and risk. The use of valuation models is designed to prevent an investor from paying too much for a good common stock. The return-to-risk ratio is calculated for this purpose. The chapters on company analysis demonstrate how an investor will be able to reach a logical decision. To reinforce the analytical process, a case in the electronics industry is provided. The Modesystem computer valuation system is demonstrated in the appraisal process.

Part V presents the subject of technical analysis, showing how a technical analysis of the stock market can help in making investment decisions. The common methods of technical analysis and the psychology of the marketplace are discussed. A summary method of analysis is presented to help investors make their own decisions about the technical strength of the market.

Part VI introduces modern portfolio theory from the Markowitz quadratic program to beta analysis to the capital asset pricing model. Risk reduction, using only a few securities, is demonstrated. Where investors invest is a function of their attitude toward risky or risk-free assets. The implications of MPT for portfolio management are noted. Essentially, management under MPT is a process of reducing risk to the level of the market and then deciding how much market vs. risk-free assets should be purchased, after which a buy and hold philosophy prevails.

Part VII focuses on the problems of portfolio management, including planning for the objectives to meet an investor's goals. A discussion of diversification to reduce all risk is presented. Meeting the goals of the income and growth investor is discussed along with a strategy to direct each investment in the portfolio. The return-to-risk ratio is used as a major guide to investment selection and portfolio management. Finally, examples of portfolio management and performance measures are given as productive methods for active investment management.

This book should provide a frame of reference in which better investment decisions can be reached. Account executives, analysts, counselors, or portfolio managers, those who are called upon to manage the investment accounts of other people, must understand the needs and motivations of their clients; the text offers a background for the individual who will invest for others. Many people who achieve financial status and recognition are called upon to serve institutional investors—for example, colleges and universities—and the book familiarizes these individuals with the policies and objectives to help them solve the investment problems of these institutions. The approach, therefore, is oriented both to the person about to embark on an investments career and to the decision-making individual who is acting for himself and for others.

In many aspects this is a methodological book. It discusses investment functions, explaining the *how* of the decision-making process as well as the *why*. The investor needs a frame of reference in which to make a value jugdment based upon the returns and risks of investment. The investor's field of reference will widen and develop with experience. As knowledge grows, the investor will become a better and more sophisticated judge of investment values, and, it is hoped, a more successful investor.

The text presentation is designed to bring theory and principles to the practical decision-making process, particularly in the areas of company analysis and portfolio management. First the principles involved are discussed, and then they are demonstrated by practical cases, providing an analysis that allows a tentative decision to be reached. It is not enough to tell investors what to do; they must be shown a method of decision-making and experience the results. For many years these principles and theories have been successfully applied in the teaching of investments and in the management of substantial sums of money. Cases have been introduced to bring realism into the investment process, including fundamental analysis, technical analysis, MPT, and portfolio management.

But the process requires that work be done, and solutions found to the problems and cases, by the student so that learning can take place. In short, the book follows an old-fashioned principle—investment success comes about because it is earned.

The fifth edition of *Investments* is based on many years of experience in teaching investments at the Universities of Maine, Connecticut, and Pennsylvania, at Miami University, Oxford, Ohio, and The George Washington University; and on the author's practical experience as an investment advisor, as a member of the board of several mutual funds, as a financial advisor to the American Psychiatric Association and the AAUP, as president of Frederick Amling and Associates (involved with valuation theory and the computer), and as a consultant to the Trust Department of The Riggs National Bank of Washington, D.C., in putting to work the theory of investment analysis and portfolio management.

Many have given invaluable assistance. My sincere thanks to Dr. Jacob O. Kamm, who, by his example of stimulating teaching and productive scholarship while at Baldwin-Wallace College, provided me with the initial inspiration to enter the field of finance. Appreciation must be expressed to Dr. Willis Winn, formerly Dean of the Wharton School, and former president of the Federal Reserve Bank of Cleveland, for his continued interest in my career; to Dr. Bruce Ricks, formerly Director of Economic Research at the Federal Home Loan Bank Board; Dr. Charles Linke, Professor of Finance at the University of Illinois; Professor J. Ronald Hoffmeister of the University of Wyoming, Professor V. Ray Alford of John Carroll University, Professor Jaroslaw Konarynsky of Northern Illinois University, Professor John B. Major, Jr., of Illinois State University, and Professor Joseph Hess of Northern Illinois University for their excellent and invaluable editorial assistance. And to A. Frederick Banda, Professor, University of Akron, for his early helpful comments about the book.

A special note of thanks to Dr. Robert H. Parks, President of Robert Parks & Associates and Professor of Economics at Pace University, for his helpful notes about the investment management of life insurance company assets; Mr. William Hennig, President, Keystone Custodian Funds, for his comments on mutual funds; and Dr. William Freund, Vice President and Chief Economist, and Mr. Thomas T. Murphy of the New York Stock Exchange, for their comments on the security market.

Many of my associates and colleagues have helped me to better understand the economy, the marketplace, and investment values. A note of appreciation is given to my associates at The Riggs National Bank of Washington, D.C., who have helped to make the marketplace my workshop: Mr. William McChesney Martin, Jr., formerly Counselor to the Bank; Mr. Fred Church, formerly Executive Vice President—Trusts and Chairman of the Federal Reserve Board; Mr. Frank Lyons, Executive Vice

President—Trusts; Mr. Davis Bunting and Mr. Charles Plumb, Senior Vice Presidents; Jim Lebherz, Vice President—Fixed Incomes; Brian Schutrumpf, Vice President and Director of Equity Research, and Tina Samson, Trust Investment Officer; Mr. Bruce Wildman and Mr. Gene Pulliam, Vice Presidents; Mr. Robert T. Sweet, formerly Vice President, Investments, and now Vice President of Maryland National Bank; and to my friends in both research and portfolio management.

My thanks go to Dr. George Ellis, formerly President of Keystone Custodian Funds and now President of the Home Savings Bank of Boston, and to the members of the boards of directors of Keystone Apollo, Polaris, Keystone OTC, and Keystone International Fund for the opportunity to participate in the formation and management of four funds, and particularly to Mr. John Schroder, President, Dr. Burton Hallowell, Chairman of Keystone Custodian Funds, Mr. William Godfrey, formerly Chairman of Keystone Custodian Funds, and Mr. George Bissell, Chairman of Massco and Keystone Custodian Funds.

I would like to express my gratitude to the editors of Prentice-Hall, David Hildebrand and Susan Adkins, for their help in bringing the manuscript to completion.

A note of gratitude is extended to Jim Henry, David Butler, Joe Borrelli, Elliott Eichner, and F. Scott Amling for their help with the updating of tables, to John Balzarini for the work on technical analysis, and to Mr. Spiro Manolis, my associate, for his work in rewriting and developing the computer programs for Modesystem. Thanks also to Dr. Minor Sachlis and Mr. Charles Miller for their helpful comments about the manuscript. A special note of thanks for William Droms, Associate Professor of Finance, Georgetown University, and Tim Haight, Associate Professor of Finance, Loyola College, Baltimore, for their careful reading of the manuscript. And to Bill Margrabe, Paul Peyser, Ted Barnhill, and Neil Cohen, Assistant Professors of Finance at George Washington University, for their comments about selected chapters of the book.

Thanks, too, must go to Viv Storz, Joan Kuehling, Nancy Moore, Elizabeth McAleer, Doris Baker, Leah White and Sana Office Services of Biddeford, Maine, for typing portions of the manuscript. An expression of appreciation must be given to Professor Peter Vaill, formerly Dean, School of Government and Business, The George Washington University, for his support, and to Dean Norma Loeser of the School of Government and Business, The George Washington University, for her constant encouragement. And to my students, thanks for their questions, interest, and response that has made investments an exciting field of endeavor. A special note of thanks to Elizabeth R. Ward and David Butts, teaching assistant, for their excellent work on the final up-date and the teachers manual.

Above all, I thank my wife, Gwen, for her help, encouragement, and assistance through the time-consuming process of writing and revising.

Frederick Amling
Washington, D.C.

CHAPTER 1

INVESTMENT: RETURNS AND RISKS

Appendix with Sources of Information

OVERTURE

The countries of the world offer their citizens many investment instruments with a wide degree of return and risk. Debt and ownership securities issued by public, private, and government corporations have supplied growth capital to the business and public sectors and have simultaneously provided, through private ownership of property, the necessary outlets for the savings of Americans and all the people of the world.

The world's capital markets, where investment securities are traded, have changed dramatically. Double-digit inflation in some countries, high interest rates, double-digit federal deficit rates in the United States, a world boom-and-bust business cycle, the threat of further increases in OPEC oil prices, land wars in the Middle East, Afghanistan, and Angola, and the threat of war in other countries have taken their toll.

The stock market in the United States plummeted in 1982 under a barrage of unfavorable events. We could logically have asked, "Will the market system survive?" The answer, at the height of OPEC oil prices or when long-term bond prices in the U.S. markets reached new lows, might have been negative. Yet our economic system, along with that of other countries, *has* survived. The United States economy will recover from recession; corporate profits will increase again; and the Dow Jones Industrial Average (DJIA) probably will move above 1,100. Large corporations will once again enter the capital markets to sell funds and common stock. Indeed, all over the world the market system and the capital and money markets have survived and are working quite well.

There are new opportunities for the investor. Investors and speculators are now considering stock options and financial futures. Money market funds that invest in short-term securities, government securities, and certificates of deposit are common. Investors consider precious metals for investment, buy tax-exempt short-term mutual funds, and still consider real estate when mortgage money is available and prices are attractive. The investment arena has broadened; no longer do investors have limited options. It is important that potential investors have an intelligent way to select from among these alternatives. The major purpose of this book is to provide a framework within which investors can make the best decisions in the choice among traditional investments and the newer forms.

THE RISK-AVERSE INVESTOR

The study of investments and the principles and practices of investment are concerned with the investor's attempt to make logical decisions about alternatives that have varying degrees of return and risk.

It is assumed that the typical investor does not like risks (the possibility of loss of principal or purchasing power). For that reason, the investor is said to be *risk-averse*. That the investor is risk-averse is generally accepted as a principle to be followed in making investment dcisions, and it makes sense. Whether the investors are individuals or institutions, they are likely to choose an investment that offers the highest return with the lowest risk—that is, an investment which offers the lowest risk commensurate with any given level of return. Most individuals fall into this risk-averse class, although there are *risk takers*—those who go out of their way to maximize risk. Unfortunately, doing this does not maximize reward. Trust institutions investing for an estate, the beneficiary of a trust, or an individual are assumed to be risk-averse. They attempt to reduce risk and find the highest possible return with the lowest possible risk. The aversion to risk is not unlike that of the large business corporation which attempts through good management to maximize reward and minimize risk in making business investment decisions.

Investment return is expressed as a rate found by dividing the sum of investment into the income plus the capital gain or loss. *Risk* is the possible loss of income or capital or the unavailability or variability of expected return.

The Investor's Attempt to Maximize Wealth

It is assumed that investors attempt to maximize wealth, which is accomplished through the process of maximizing return and minimizing risk. This might be done by protecting capital, by increasing income or capital, and by reducing risk. It is also fostered in the life-style of investors, who in their daily lives attempt to make all financial, consumer, and investment decisions according to the wealth-maximization principle.

This principle can be simply demonstrated as follows: Assume that *I* represents the average future annual income from an investment, and V the present value of all future income at a capitalization rate of k. The present value of the income is calculated using the formula $V = I/k$. Note that if $I = \$1,000$ and $k = 10$ percent (.10), then V is \$10,000. Assume that the investor can increase income by 10 percent, but that to do so a 12 percent risk level must be accepted. In this case, the investor's income increases to \$1,100, and the present value, V, becomes \$9,166.67 instead of the previous \$10,000. Although the investor's expected income has increased, the present value of the assets has decreased because of the higher discount rate to compensate for the higher risk. In this case, the investor would be better off with the \$1,000, 10 percent investment, because this maximizes wealth based on the difference between the two alternatives. The new alternative of \$1,100 with a risk rate of 12 percent would be the poorer choice, primarily because of the additional risk associated with the income. The \$100 additional income does not fully compensate the investor for the additional risk of the investment. The investor might accept the alternatives if maximum income was desired.

A third principle to keep in mind is this: The higher the return, the higher the risk. If investors expect higher returns, they must accept a higher level of risk. This leads to another principle, that investors should attempt to keep risk proportional to return. An investor should not accept an additional amount of risk that exceeds the additional amount of return.

A fifth principle states that investors would rather have more wealth or return than less. The increased return a security provides offers greater wealth and utility. But for the average investor, each dollar of the increased income offers a smaller amount of utility or wealth than does a dollar of income at a lower level of income and wealth. Therefore, as an investor's income increases, a higher return for the same amount of risk is required, since the extra dollar added to income has a lower utility value than the dollar of investment that is put at risk at lower income levels.

A DEFINITION OF INVESTMENT

Investment may be defined as the purchase by an individual or institutional investor of a financial or real asset that produces a return proportional to the risk assumed over some future investment period.

The main thrust of this book has to do with the analysis of financial assets that represent claims on both real and intangible assets. We will also examine some of the more popular forms of real investment. The purchase of any asset that offers the expectation of income and capital gains may be defined, more broadly, as an investment.

The purchase of a house is a form of investment for many people. Housing prices have increased substantially in most cities in the United States and the world, and this has resulted in capital appreciation or capital gains. Even though the owner has borrowed money and is repaying the mortgage from savings from current income, and even though no current return is anticipated from the investment, there is still an element of investment involved.

Real estate may be purchased for investment or income. Many people have used real estate as a hedge against inflation. No financial securities are involved. The owner manages the property or hires a manager to undertake the chores of renting the premises, collecting the rents, and generally maintaining the property. This can be an important part of an investor's financial structure. Care and analysis are required in making this type of investment decision, since there are substantial tax problems and economic factors that must be determined before a decision is reached.

Actually, real estate is a form of real investment sometimes called *business* or *economic investment*. Economic or business investment is any investment in real assets that brings about the production of goods and services for the purpose of maximizing the present value of the owner's equity. The principle of maximization is the same as that applied to the financial investment. A business purchases assets that are used to produce goods and services, which in turn provide income to the owners of the assets. A careful and thorough analysis of each business investment is undertaken to determine the expected return and the risk involved.

Many expenditures for durable consumer goods have investment characteristics. The purchase of house furnishings in the form of antiques, art objects, oriental rugs, paintings, and prints represents a form of consumer investment that actually could result in gains, even though the purpose of the purchase appears to be a consumer expenditure. Such purchases do add to the individual's wealth, and they require special knowledge, expertise, and analysis.

The principle demonstrated by this discussion is that there are investment considerations involved in almost all individual and institutional economic and financial transactions. If investors consume less and save more, there is a possible positive effect on investment. If investors purchase durable goods that actually increase rather than decrease in value, there is an element of investment. A retirement program, an insurance policy, and expenditures for education all have elements of investment that have the effect of increasing an individual's wealth.

The fact that this book is primarily concerned with intangible investments does not mean that other alternatives of real or consumer investment are less important. For many individuals, the purchase of a house, an automobile, a diamond ring, gold jewelry or coins, or silver will be their most important investment. The discussion in the text is designed to help investors who have reached a wealth level where securities investment becomes a primary concern. Therefore, securities investments—common stock, preferred stock, and various types of bonds, including those of public corporations, governments, and government and quasi-government agencies, as well as money market funds, options, and financial futures—will be emphasized.

Elements of the Investment Definition

RETURN. The return (the reward) from the investment includes both current income and capital gains (or losses) brought about by the appreciation (or depreciation) of the price of the security. The income and capital gains are then expressed as a percentage of the beginning investment. Hence, return usually represents the total annual income and capital gain as a percentage of investment.

In bond investment, *yield* is the compounded rate of return on the purchase price of the bond over its life. Simply stated, it is referred to as *yield to maturity*. Since yield to maturity includes interest and capital gains or losses, it is also the return. The yield on a common stock, however, assumes no maturity date. Therefore, the stock yield is simply the price of the stock divided into the current dividend; there is no compounding of returns. It is known as the *current yield*. When bond yields are compared with stock yields, errors of judgment might be made, since the measures are different.

The return on a stock is calculated by including annual capital gains. If an investor receives $2 per share in dividends and earns $3 per share per year in capital gains and has an average investment of $25, the return on the stock would be 20 percent. A return measure will be presented below that allows the returns on stocks and bonds to be calculated in a comparable way.

RETURN AND RISK. There appears to be a direct correlation between return and risk; that is, the higher the reward, the higher the risk. Therefore, the investor should attempt to keep the risk associated with the return proportional. Seeking excessive risk does not ensure excessive return. Not all securities with a given level of return have the same degree of risk.

The classification of investment securities by their risk level is being explored by academic theoreticians and financial practitioners. It is not easy to establish a relationship between return and risk. A value judgment must be made by the investor as to the relationship between the perceived level of risk and the perceived level of return. Knowledge of the amount of reward and risk associated with each security will enable the investor to make better investment decisions in the long run.

THE TIME FACTOR. The time period is an important part of the definition of investment. When an investor makes a decision about investing funds, the question is often raised; "How many years in the future should I consider for investment?" or, "How far out should I go?" The investor is really asking whether long-term, short-term, or intermediate-term bonds, or stocks for the short term or long term should be purchased. The time period actually chosen is a function of the investor's expectations. The investor usually selects a time period and return that meet expectations of return and risk. Common stocks do not have a maturity date; bonds do. If an investor followed a *buy-and-hold* policy, the time period would be infinite. Yet business and economic conditions change, which suggests that investors should change. Actually, the time period for investment depends on investors' attitudes. Some professional investors think a three-year period is best—long enough to eliminate the effects of the business cycle and the market cycle on security prices, yet short enough to achieve economic results from new products, new developments, and new ideas. Often, this three-year time horizon helps investors to be successful simply because it allows them to ignore market cycles and hold for the upward trend of economic growth.

The investment period assumed in this book is three years. Since common stocks do not have a maturity date, it is necessary to estimate what the price will be three years in the future. This may be referred to as the return for a three-year holding period. The same is true for bonds that have a 20-year maturity. As investments are examined, expected return and risk are measured over a three-year period. The investment review and analysis process then becomes a succession of three-year forecast periods. As time moves on and as conditions change, investors reevaluate the expected return and risk for each investment, including bonds as well as common stocks.

The return performance of equity investment has been satisfactory over longer periods. The investor must therefore estimate the next three years but must put the analyses into a longer time frame to make the most successful decisions.

Investment and Speculation

The difference between investment and speculation is primarily a difference in the amount of return expected, the amount of risk assumed, and the length of the holding period. Usually, *speculation* is for short periods of time—say, from one week to a few months. An investment is continuous for a series of three-year periods over a longer period of time. So the emphasis in speculation, because of the shorter holding period, is solely on capital gains or appreciation rather than dividend or interest income.

The second distinction is that the expected return from a single speculative security purchase is much greater than the expected return from the purchase of an investment security. Du Pont common stock can serve as an example. During the first part of 1975, du Pont common traded at 99. An appraisal of du Pont, along with the use of valuation models, which will be discussed later, indicated that the stock was undervalued and should be purchased. Part of the analysis was based upon the correct assumption that the world economy would recover in 1976, that interest rates would decline and profits increase, and that the profits of du Pont and the chemical industry would improve along with the economic recovery.

In approximately three months, the price of du Pont increased to 132. The return for the three-month period was 33.33 percent, or 133.32 percent on an annualized return basis (33.33 percent × 4). There was a $33 gain. A person who had bought du Pont for speculation would have sold the shares at a price of 132 and would have earned the 133.32 percent annual return. The speculator would then look for other depressed securities that would offer the possibility of a large capital gain. Investors would have held for three years or longer. For the longer period, the investor would have received an annual dividend of $4.25 per share in 1975, $5.00 in 1976, $5.76 in 1977, $7.26 in 1978, $5.97 in 1979, and $8.25 in 1980. The company split the stock in 1979 on a 3-for-1 basis. The dividends per share are on the basis of the original shares.

In 1981, the price of a share of du Pont common stock was approximately $40, or $120 on a presplit basis. The investor who had held du Pont for six years and then sold it would have received dividends of $4.25, $5.00, $5.76, $7.26, $5.97, and $8.25, in each year, respectively. The average annual dividend was $6.08. The investor would have earned a total capital gain of $21 ($120 − $99 = $21). The annual capital gain was therefore $3.50. The annual total dollar return, including dividends and annual capital gain, was $9.58. The average investment for the period was $109.50 ($99 + $120/2). The average annual return was therefore 8.75 percent or $109.50 divided into $9.58. Therefore, the investor earned a much lower annual return over a longer period of time than did the speculator. Yet the investor's risks were lower, and so were transaction costs. (This assumes that the speculator traded several times during the 6 years to achieve the higher return.)

It is apparent from the example that the speculator, ignoring federal income taxes, received a greater return than the investor. Yet the principle "the higher the expected return the higher the risk" must not be ignored; certainly the speculator is taking greater risks. Once the speculator traded du Pont, another stock must be found that will provide the 133 percent annualized return. This is extremely difficult to do. In order to approximate a higher annual return, the speculator would be required to resort to short sales, trading on margin, or buying options, all of which will help to increase return (that is, if the speculator is successful). But the risk of loss soars. Also, it has been assumed that the speculator is always right. We all know that the probability of being correct on every speculation is extremely low. Therefore, the speculator must lower total-return expectations because of unsuccessful trades. And return must be lowered because of higher transaction costs, owing to the frequency of trades. Actually, the risks involved in the short-term movements of market prices are substantially greater than those of the long-term movements. The characteristics of price movement in the market, in the short run, appear to be random in character. In spite of the technical analysis of the market through the analysis of price and volume changes, the speculator is accepting substantially greater risk than the investor because the return is so varied.

Between speculation and investment there are various degrees of less-risky speculations and more-risky investments. The challenge of both investment and speculation is to make certain that the expectation of return is proportional to the risk involved. Unfortunately, the acceptance of higher risks does not lead to higher returns. If the risk is kept proportional to the return, then the investor or speculator has a clear choice between high-return, high-risk securities and low-return, low-risk securities. Under these conditions, the choices facing the investor and speculator become a continuum in the return-to-risk scale where choices are said to be efficient. *Efficient investments* are those that offer the highest return with the lowest risk or the lowest risk for a given return. Thus the principle is emphasized again—the investor or speculator must make sure that investment or speculation offers an efficient relationship between return and risk.

THE INVESTMENT PROCESS

The investment process is a series of activities that result in the purchase of real assets or securities. Attention must be given to how to investigate, analyze, and select securities that will be satisfactory investments. To this end, a summary of the steps in the process seems appropriate.

Once returns are estimated and the risks involved are understood, the investor is faced with the practical matter of obtaining funds for investment. Saving to provide such funds is really the first step in the investment process. True, some people inherit money, some marry for money, and some win it in a sweepstakes. Yet for most, the money for investment comes from a surplus of income over expenditures—that is, from savings.

Institutional investors obtain money in different ways. Commercial banks invest depositors' money; savings and loans invest depositors' money, owners' equity, and mutual owners' shares. Life insurance companies invest a portion of the premium income; credit unions invest the owners' money; businesses invest the owners' funds in assets and securities; pension funds invest money accumulated through the company's pension program; mutual funds and money market funds invest their owners' money in securities; even federal government agencies invest in government securities for the benefit of the taxpayer.

The next step in the investment process is an understanding of the investor's attitude toward risk. Each investor must be willing to accept the risk associated with investment in securities or assets, and be able to identify the return and risk combination that is acceptable. In other words, before accepting investment risks, the investor must be in a sound financial position and must be prepared to apply intelligent reason to the decision-making process.

Another part of the investment process is a thorough knowledge of each type of security or asset available for investment, including the expected returns from each as well as the risk associated with each. Return, which includes dividend and interest income and capital gains or losses as a percentage of the amount invested, represents the reward to the investor. The risk is measured by the statistical variability of past or future expected returns. Statistical analysis aids the decision process, yet a rational system could be established using the instinctive judgment of experienced portfolio managers who can rank securities according to the perceived risk.

One important ingredient is the economic and security analysis that leads to a decision as to which companies will be selected for investment based upon their indicated level of return and risk. This is sometimes referred to as the *macro-micro* approach to investment analysis, or the "top down" approach. It is also considered the fundamental approach to security analysis and selection. The focal point of the analysis is to estimate the future expected return over a three-year holding period and the variability of the return. This requires an estimate of future earnings and dividends, future price-earnings ratio, and future price. Valuation appraisal is one of the most important aspects of the investment process.

Another key ingredient is a working information system. Part of the information system centers on brokerage firms, stock exchanges, and published information sources such as Standard and Poor's, Moody's, and Value Line, as well as the financial press, including the *Wall Street Journal, New York Times*, and *Business Week*. An information system will be discussed in the appendix to this chapter. (Answering the questions at the end of each chapter and finding problem solutions is a way to use the information system.)

Another important part of the process is knowledge of the market structure in which securities are traded, by whom they are traded, how they are registered, and who are the investors. The efficient market concept must be understood, along with the mechanics of trading and the relationship of the broker to the investor. The behavior of the market itself must be understood. The variations in the market, in the short term, can be extreme. A wide degree of price variation is a function of the random character of prices subjected to unexpected events in an already uncertain world.

The brokerage community tends to be short-term-oriented, which tends to increase the variability of returns and hence the risk. Many brokers and speculators consider only short-term trading, which tends to be speculative and adds little to return but a great deal to risk. The many technical traders, who think the charts tell all, also add to the variability and uncertainty of the marketplace. Unfortunately, it is in this setting that the investor must operate. And it is difficult to be rational and logical in an irrational world.

The final stage in the investment process is to select several securities or assets that will furnish an expected return and risk that are acceptable based on the needs of the particular investor. A single-security "portfolio" is very risky. No one security is likely to meet an investor's needs. It has been demonstrated that a small amount of diversification reduces risk more than return. Therefore, it is important to understand the theory of portfolio construction as well as the steps necessary to build a portfolio.

INVESTMENT APPROACHES

The discussion of the investment process actually merged three different investment approaches. (1) the fundamental analysis approach, (2) the technical approach, and (3) the modern portfolio theory approach.

The Fundamental Approach

The fundamental approach assumes that rigorous analysis of each company will result in selecting stocks that are undervalued. The investor would select stocks based on an economic analysis, an industry analysis, and a company analysis. The stocks are held as long as they promise a high return; they are sold if the investor thinks they have become overpriced. Chances are they would be held for relatively long periods of time. Some fundamental investors follow a "buy and hold" policy by selecting quality stocks and holding them for a relatively long period. The fundamental approach is followed by the majority of financial institutions.

New evidence suggests that fundamental analysis leads to superior results. A working paper on the value of investment research has been published by the National Bureau of Economic Research. The authors, Wilbur C. Lewellan and Gary G. Schlarbaum of Purdue University and Kenneth L. Stanley of Emory University, analyzed the buy and sell recommendations of a major national brokerage house over the 1964–1970 period. The study concludes that an investor following these recommendations would have "fairly consistently" obtained an annual rate of return of two percentage points higher than the market averages, even in years when stock prices fell.[1] The conclusion the study reached was that the research reports contained new information or new analytical insights into value. This study, among others, supports the view that fundamental analysis pays off.

The Technical Approach

The technical approach to investment emphasizes that the behavior of the price of the stock and perhaps the volume of trading will determine the future price of the stock. The technical approach centers around plotting the price movement of the stock

[1] See *Economic Diary*, August 17–21, 1981, p. 18; *Business Week*, September 7, 1981.

and drawing inferences from the price movement. The technician then selects a few stocks for purchase and trades in these issues. The emphasis is on capital gains or price appreciation in the short run.

Modern Portfolio Theory (MPT)

Modern portfolio theory assumes that the market is efficient and that information is available about the market and individual stocks. New information is quickly transferred to the marketplace, and a new price is established. Since the marketplace is efficient and stock prices of one moment are independent from prices in the next moment, it is impossible to predict future prices. Information is known to all, and no one, on average, can do much better than the market. In addition, securities with the same risk level tend to provide similar return.

Investors using MPT assume that they cannot beat the market. They therefore diversify so they have enough securities to provide them with the average return of the market. Since they cannot predict, they follow a buy-and-hold philosophy. Their attitude toward risk is determined by the amount invested in riskless securities and the amount invested in risk securities, which is comparable to the return of the market as measured by some market index. In addition, if they are positive toward the market, they might establish a portfolio of risky securities that have a higher risk and return than the market. If they are successful, they will be compensated by a higher return for the higher risk assumed.

This book emphasizes the fundamental approach, as reflected in Chapters 11 to 19. It also discusses the investment implications of technical analysis in Chapter 20 and of modern portfolio theory in Chapter 21.

THE MEASUREMENT OF RETURN

The majority of investors tend to emphasize the return they expect from a security. They also tend to view both return and risk in subjective terms. Intuitive judgment is used to make decisions about risk. The reasoning, for example, goes something like this: Chrysler is more risky than GM, General Telephone is more risky than AT&T, and Polaroid is more risky than Eastman Kodak.

Return also receives subjective and intuitive analysis. The usual statement about return is something like, "The stock offers a dividend yield of 7 percent and has prospects for future price appreciation." The dividend yield, which is current price divided into the current dollar dividend, is mentioned specifically, but little or no attempt is made to estimate in a formal way the likely impact of capital gains or losses on the total return.

It is therefore appropriate to develop a measure of return that includes both dividends or interest and capital gains in the calculation. This measure will then be applied to the calculation of historic or future expected returns. The precise measure of return will make it easier to estimate and judge the magnitude of returns of various securities.

The return includes dividends and capital gains. The best proxy for return is the future expected return. This point will be developed later.

The basic equation for measuring return for a yearly period or less is:

$$\frac{P_1 - P_0 + D_1}{P_0}$$

where P_0 is the dollar beginning price of the security, P_1 is the dollar end-of-period price, and D_1 is the dollar amount of dividends paid in period 1. Assume as an example that a stock was purchased at $100 and sold at the end of the year for $110. The investor received $2 in dividends during the year. P_1 would be $110, P_0 would be $100, and D_1 would be $2. The return for the year would be ($110 − $100 + $2) ÷ $100, or 12 percent.

Quarterly Returns

The return equation may be used for quarterly periods. The P_1, P_0, and D_1 become end-of-quarter price (P_1), beginning-of-quarter price (P_0), and quarterly dividend (D_1). To avoid confusion, the symbols P_{q1}, P_{q0} and D_{q1} could be used to indicate the quarterly period. Let us apply the annual formula above to the quaterly data, assuming that the price increases $2.50 per quarter and that the quarterly dividend is $.50. The return for the first quarter would be ($102.50 − $100.00 + $.50) ÷ $100 = 3 percent; the return for the second quarter would be ($105.00 − $102.50 + $.50) ÷ $102.50 = 2.93 percent; the third-quarter return would be $3.00 ÷ $105.00 = 2.86 percent; and the fourth-quarter return would be $3.00 ÷ $107.50 = 2.79 percent. These are not annualized rates. In order to obtain the annualized return, it would be necessary to multiply the quarterly returns by 4. Thus, the annualized return for the first quarter would be 12.00 percent (3.00 percent × 4), 11.72 percent for the second, 11.44 percent for the third, and 11.16 percent for the fourth quarter, and the averaged annualized return for the year would be 11.58 percent [(12.00 + 11.72 + 11.44 + 11.16) ÷ 4].

Return Over Several Years—Approximate Method

If the return is measured over several years annually, the basic return equation must be changed to allow for compounding. Let us assume that a stock was purchased at $50, sold three years later at $80, and paid a $2 per share dividend in each of the three years. The basic equation for the approximate compounded return for the investment period is:

$$[(P_N - P_0) \div N] + D \div (P_0 + P_N) \div 2$$

where P_0 is the beginning price of the security, P_N is the price at the end of the period, N is the number of years the investment was held, and D represents the annual average dividend or interest received. Many readers will recognize this as the approximate method for calculating the yield to maturity for a bond.

Substituting values in the formula to obtain return gives:

$$[(\$80 - \$50) \div 3] + \$2.00 \div [(50 + 80) \div 2] = (\$10.00 + \$2.00) \div \$65$$
$$= \$12.00 \div \$65.00 = 18.46 \text{ percent}$$

The average annual compound return for each of the three years is therefore 18.46 percent.

Return Over Several Years—Compound Method

A more precise method of calculating return is by the use of the present-value formula, which takes into consideration compounding. In the example above, the rate of return per year can be obtained by discounting $80 received at the end of the third year from the sale of the shares of stock along with the $2 received each year in the form of dividends, until the present value is just equal to the $50 purchase price. The discount rate that allows the present value of the income stream to equal to purchase price is the return earned on the investment. The formula for determining the return is:

$$P_0 = \frac{D_1}{(1+r)^1} + \frac{D_2}{(1+r)^2} + \frac{D_3 + P_3}{(1+r)^3}$$

where P_0 is the current price; D_1, D_2, and D_3 are the dividends received in years 1, 2, and 3; P_3 is the price received in the third year; and r is the rate of return earned. The formula is solved for r.

Let's substitute numbers into the equation, as follows:

$$\$50 = \frac{\$2.00}{(1+r)^1} + \frac{\$2.00}{(1+r)^2} + \frac{\$2.00 + \$80.00}{(1+r)^3}$$

In solving for r, values are substituted until the sum of values to the right of the equals sign in the formula is equal to the sum of the values on the left of the equals sign. Starting with .18, or 18 percent, as the first value for r and substituting in the formula gives the following:

$$\$50 = \frac{\$2.00}{1.18} + \frac{\$2.00}{(1.18)(1.18)} + \frac{\$82.00}{(1.18)(1.18)(1.18)}$$
$$= \frac{\$2.00}{1.18} + \frac{\$2.00}{1.3924} + \frac{\$82.00}{1.6430}$$
$$= \$1.6949 + \$1.4364 + \$49.9087$$
$$= \$53.04$$

The dividend and price stream when discounted at 18 percent give a present value of $53.04, which indicates that the assumed r value, or rate of return, was not high enough, and a higher value must be substituted. This time, .20, or 20 percent, will be used in solving the equation, as follows:

$$\$50 = \frac{\$2.00}{1.20} + \frac{\$2.00}{(1.20)(1.20)} + \frac{\$82.00}{(1.20)(1.20)(1.20)}$$
$$= \frac{\$2.00}{1.20} + \frac{\$2.00}{1.44} + \frac{\$82.00}{1.728}$$
$$= \$1.6666 + \$1.3888 + \$47.4537$$
$$= \$50.51$$

Since the value of the right side of the formula remains above $50, the return is not high enough. If a 21 percent rate is used (.21), the present value is $49.31. This indicates the r value is too high at 21 percent. By interpolating, the exact r value is found. In this case, r becomes 20.425 percent, as follows: The interval between 20 percent and 21 percent is 1 percent. The present value for 20 percent is $50.51, and for 21 percent, $49.31, with a difference of $1.20. Since $50 is the desired present value, it is necessary to subtract $50 from $50.51 to arrive at $.51, and then divide by $1.20 to arrive at the percentage rate, which is .425. When .425 percent is added to 20 percent, the return from the investment is found to be 20.425 percent.

The compound rate of return earned on the investment is 20.425 percent. The r in the formula is the same as the compounded rate of return earned from the investment for the time period the investment was held.

In summary, it is important that both capital gains (or losses) and interest or dividend income be included in the return measure. It is also important that the length of the holding period be considered and that the return approximate the compound return over the period the asset was held or over some future period.

THE MEASUREMENT OF RISK

In addition to measuring return, it is necessary to develop a comparable measure of risk. In this text, as well as throughout the literature in the field of investments, two statistical measures of risk are employed: standard deviation and beta.

The first is the standard deviation of either past or future expected returns; where return is measured annually and/or quarterly, the results are averaged and the standard deviation of the mean average is calculated. It is the standard deviation, or variability of return, that is used to measure risk. The stock with the highest variability of return relative to the average return is the most risky. Actually, the principle to be followed is that the standard deviation, sigma (σ), or variability of return is the proxy for investment risk.

Measuring Standard Deviation

Past returns are averaged in the case of annual returns, and then the standard deviation of the average returns is calculated. Assume that for the past ten years, a common stock has had the annual returns listed in Table 1–1. The annual return was calculated using the equation $(P_1 - P_0 + D) \div P_0$, except that P_0 and P_1 represented the average of the high and low price in years 0 and 1: $(P_H + P_L) \div 2$, where P_H is the high price for the year and P_L is the low price for the year. Obviously, this represents only an approximation of the annual return, assuming that a representative price for each year is the average of the high and low price.

The standard deviation of the market return appears in Table 1–1, along with a comparison return of the stock. The standard deviation is found by using the formula $\sqrt{\Sigma X^2/N}$, where ΣX^2 is the summation of the squared differences of each return from the average. N is the number of items—in this case, 10. The differences squared total to .0384. The standard deviation of the stock in Table 1–1 is found by taking the square root of .0384 divided by 10 ($\sqrt{.0384/10}$), which equals .062. Thus, the average return was .08, with a variability of $\pm.062$, or 8 percent ±6.2 percent. The standard deviation is a simple tool for approximating risk. Obviously, the greater the standard deviation, the greater the risk.

The stock in Table 1–1 has a higher return and a higher standard deviation than

TABLE 1–1
Return* and Standard Deviation of Market (S&P 500) and Stock

Annual Return, Stock	Annual Return, Market	Mean Average, Stock	Mean Average, Market	Difference (X)		Difference Squared (X^2)	
				Stock	Market	Stock	Market
.08	.09	.08	.07	.00	.02	.0000	.0004
.10	.09	.08	.07	.02	.02	.0004	.0004
.12	.10	.08	.07	.04	.03	.0016	.0009
.12	.14	.08	.07	.04	.07	.0016	.0049
.12	.10	.08	.07	.04	.03	.0016	.0009
.08	.00	.08	.07	.00	−.07	.0000	.0049
.10	.08	.08	.07	.02	.01	.0004	.0001
−.10	−.05	.08	.07	−.18	−.12	.0324	.0144
.08	.05	.08	.07	.00	−.02	.0000	.0004
.10	.10	.08	.07	.02	.03	.0004	.0009

.80 ÷ 10 = 8%   .70 ÷ 10 = 7%

$$\Sigma = \sqrt{\frac{.0384}{10}} \qquad \Sigma = \sqrt{\frac{.0282}{10}}$$

$\sigma = 6.2\%$ $\sigma = 5.3\%$

*Yearly return, including dividends and capital gains or losses.

the market, and the return related to risk (standard deviation) is higher than the market, which suggests that the stock has performed better than the market but is somewhat riskier. The ratio of return to risk is slightly less for the security, suggesting it was more attractive than the market.

Beta

A second measure of risk is referred to as *beta analysis*, or *volatility*. The beta concept was developed from the application of statistical regression analysis to the behavior of stock prices. The percentage changes in the price of the stock are "regressed" against the percentage changes in the price of a market index, usually the S&P 500 Price Index. In the discussion that follows, returns of stocks regressed against the return of the market index will be used. This relationship can be described by the basic formula $Y = \alpha + \beta X + \epsilon$, where Y is the return from the security, α or alpha is the OY interecept, β or beta is the slope of the regression formula, and ϵ or epsilon is the unexplained or residual return, which has an average value of zero. These relationships are shown graphically in Figure 1–1. Beta is referred to as the systematic risk to the market, and $\alpha + \epsilon$ represents the unsystematic risk. Applying the concept to the data in Table 1–1, Figure 1–2 was constructed to establish the alpha and beta relationship between the stock and the market. The stock has a beta or systematic risk to the market of .99. This suggests that the stock does have as much risk as the market, but that it does have a slightly higher unsystematic risk. Based on the analysis, it could be concluded that the stock in the past has provided the investor with a return and risk comparable to the market.

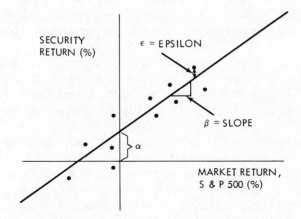

FIGURE 1–1

Regression Equation and Beta, Alpha, and Epsilon Relationships

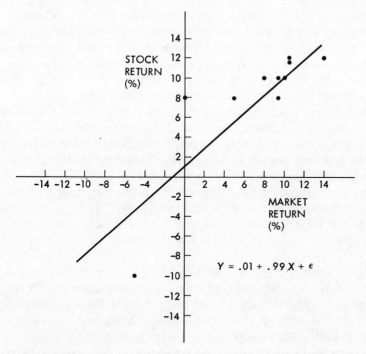

$$Y = .01 + .99X + \epsilon$$

FIGURE 1–2

Beta of Stock to Market

As the return formulas are examined, it becomes apparent that changes in price and dividends summarize the risks involved. The market price of a stock will change because of several risk elements: the market risk, business risk, interest-rate risk, and inflation or purchasing risk.

Understanding and measuring risk is fundamental to the investment process. Therefore, an understanding of the nature of investment risks will increase our awareness of the investment problem. It will also serve to unite the investment process into a logical whole until we reach the point in our discussion where we consider portfolio management and risk.

When we consider investing our money, we are immediately aware of the conflict between our desire for the safety of principal and the amount of future return we want to achieve. Virtually all our decisions revolve around this notion of reward versus risk. Certainly, we want to achieve a substantial return from our investment, but we are not always willing to accept the risk associated with the high returns we want. Under certain circumstances, we might be willing to accept the risk of a high probability that we will lose our entire investment, but speculative investments of this type should be limited to a small portion of our total investment. We next ask, "What is the probability we will lose 30 percent of our investment?" After all, the price might drop 30 percent within the next few months because of uncertain market conditions. But if we are not speculating and do not have to sell even if the stock does drop, then we do not suffer the market risk. If we can invest for one, two, or three years, the economic growth of a company with an upward trend of earnings will reduce or overcome the market risk. With earnings moving up, prices of common stock usually reflect the expected growth of earnings. It is possible in extreme circumstances to have a market drop of 30 percent. Nobody would invest in the stock market if he or she knew that tomorrow's stocks were going down 30 percent in price. However, we do not know what will happen tomorrow. Therefore, we must be prepared for the worst and also anticipate that the economic growth possible from a given investment will overcome these short-term price fluctuations.

Stated another way, we might ask, "What is the probability that a return of 10 percent will be achieved each year over the next three years?" If the variability of the expected return is 5 percent, we can assume that two-thirds of the time we will earn between 5 and 15 percent. If the variability is too high, we could reject it as being too risky.

In the day-to-day work of investing, because timing is so important to investment success, the question is repeatedly asked before a stock is purchased, "What is the downside risk associated with this stock?" We want to know the immediate risks, the quantity of risks (to the extent that we can measure them), and the variety of all the risks we face. Planning against risk minimizes investment error.

Table 1–2 indicates the broad spectrum of securities investments and savings outlets available to the investor. The investments are ranked according to risk, reward, and the amount of management decision-making ability required from the investor. It is apparent that the more speculative securities provide the highest return and variability, and therefore the risk is correspondingly high. The amount of risk and the

TABLE 1–2
Risk, Return, and Management Sophistication of Securities and Savings Outlets

Management Decision Required	Security or Savings	Reward: Approximate Returns (%) *	**	Variability—Standard Deviation (%)	Market Risk	Business or Credit Risk	Interest or Money-Rate Risk	Purchasing-Power or Inflation Risk
	Security:							
H	Speculative common stock	20	15	15	H	H	L	L
H	Speculative mutual funds	15	13	12	H	H	L	L
H	Growth common stock	15	13	12	H	H	L	L
M	High-quality common stock (blue chip)	12	10	10	M	M	L	L
M	Investment mutual funds	12	10	10	M	M	L	L
M	Income common stock	10	10	8	M–L	M–L	M	M
M	Balanced mutual funds	10	10	7	M–L	M–L	M	M
M	Convertible preferred stock	10	10	6	M–H	M–H	L	L
M	Convertible bonds	12	12	6	M–H	M–H	L	L
L	Corporate bonds, AAA	14	12	5	L	L	H	H
L	Corporate bonds, below BAA	16	13	6	M	M	M	H
L	Municipal bonds, tax-free	12	10	5	L	L	H	M
L	Government bonds	15	11	7	L	L	H	H
L	Short-term government bonds	14	8	5	L	L	L	H
L	Money market funds	15	8–9	5	L	L	L	M
	Savings:							
L	Variable annuity	9	8	1	L	L	L	M
L	Credit union	8*	8	1	L	L	L	M
L	Savings and loan associations	8*	8	½	L	L	L	H
0	Life insurance savings	7	6	1	L	L	L	H
0	Mutual savings banks	6	8	1	L	L	L	H
0	Commercial banks	6	8	½	L	L	L	H
L	Certificate of deposit	15	8	¼	L	L	L	M
L	Swiss bank account	0	0	0	L	L	L	H
0	Cashbox	0	0	0	L	L	L	H
0	Mattress, drawer, desk	0	0	0	L	L	L	H

H = High   L = Low
M = Moderate   0 = Zero
*Based on market conditions, third quarter 1981.
**Based on market conditions, first quarter 1983 (approximate).

amount of reward cannot be equated precisely. It is possible to buy a growth common stock that offers the expectation of a 12 percent return and yet has a much higher degree of risk than a speculative common stock that offers a 15 percent return. It is also apparent that some securities offer a higher return even though they are in the same investment category. Hence, there is great need for constant analysis and management of expected risk and expected returns. And this is why the standard deviation of returns is used as an estimate of risk.

As a principle, it is important to keep risk proportional to reward. The money we place in the bank account or the mattress or the cashbox is highly susceptible to the inflation risk. If we are faced with inflation, then we should deemphasize savings or fixed-income obligations. On the other hand, if we are facing a recession, the best place we can have our money would be in a savings bank or in government bonds. It is also apparent that some of the savings vehicles offer higher rates of return than do securities, but they do not offer the prospect of higher risks, because of an extremely low variability. At any given moment, the array might vary. However, the relationships among the securities, when we examine rewards and risks and the need for management, are significant points to remember as we move into a discussion of the specific securities we might purchase. Our area of study will be where the greatest amount of management decisions and sophistication are required.

Two types of risk are primarily associated with ownership securities—namely, the market risk and the business risk. Debt securities are primarily susceptible to the money-rate or interest-rate risk, yet they share in the market and business risks. Both debt and equity securities suffer from the purchasing-power or inflation risk.

The Market Risk

The market risk is the loss of capital owing to changes in common stock prices and is usually associated with changes in investor expectations about the prospects of a company. Essentially, understanding market risk is understanding price behavior. The causes of changes in market price are usually beyond the control of the corporation. An unexpected war or the end of one, an election year, political activity, illness or death of a president, speculative activity in the market, the outflow of gold—all are tremendous psychological factors in the market.

Whatever the reason, the prices of common stocks change frequently, and the conclusion we reach is that there is no one price at which a stock is traded. Prices change daily and weekly. There is substantial evidence that, since randomly generated influences cannot be predicted, stock prices are random in character and cannot be predicted in the short term. Yet careful analysis must be conducted to anticipate the future as best we can. Assume, for example, that we had bought 100 shares of stock at $40 a share just before a sharp drop in the stock market. The stock now sells at $25 a share. If we were forced to sell it, we would have a capital loss of $15 per share. A complete analysis prior to purchase indicated that the stock was a good investment, and nothing in the forecasted earnings has changed from the time the stock was purchased until the market dropped. Whatever the reason, the drop in the market is a temporary cyclical swing that caused a temporary drop in the price of the stock. Obviously, we try to avoid selling by being in a position to weather the storm until prices come back and favorable economic factors are given time to bear fruit.

The behavior of stock prices and the several types of securities can be examined to learn something of what we may expect. The price movements of a selected stock-market index—Standard & Poor's 500 Index—appears in Figure 1–3. It is apparent that common stock prices over a long period of time have had a substantial growth rate, with fluctuations around the trend. In any given year, however, there was a range in prices, with a substantial market risk. The range of price movement is a good deal

S&P 500 Stock Price Index Adjusted for Inflation

FIGURE 1–3

S&P 500 Stock Price Index Adjusted for Inflation

SOURCE: *The Outlook,*Standard & Poor's Corporation, February 9, 1983. p. 927.

wider than we might expect, indicating a much higher than expected degree of market risk. In fact, if we fitted a curve to the data and then found the standard error of the estimate by using statistical techniques, we would find the standard error of the estimate to be high. The rhythmic pattern of stock-price movements is not of the same magnitude, even though a drop in price is usually followed by an increase, except that in the decade of 1970s there was less of an upward trend and more cyclical activity. The trend of stock prices has been upward for a substantial period of time. Because price stability is a good measure of market risk, the standard error of the estimate around the trend line seems to be a good way of determining the degree of risk. If price movements are within statistical limits, we can consider them normal. If they go beyond these limits, prices are unstable and market risk is high. The greater the standard error relative to the absolute price level, the greater the market risk.

The variability of return (standard deviation) is also used as an indicator of risk. The S&P 500 earned 7.51 percent from 1971 through 1980, with a standard deviation of 13.52 percent. This suggests that the S&P 500 was less profitable and far more risky than we would have expected. A comparison of market returns and the returns of selected securities will be discussed shortly.

Figure 1–4 (a–d) shows examples of the price behavior of the traditional classes

Chrysler Corporation

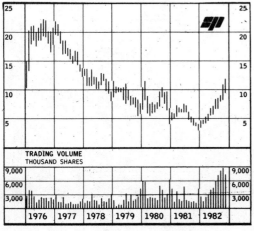

(a) Recessive—cyclical

Bethlehem Steel Corporation

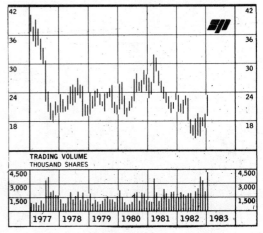

(b) Cyclical

American Brands, Inc.

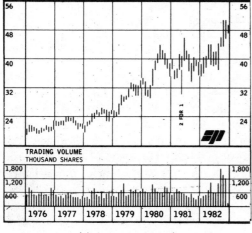

(c) Income—growth

Eastman Kodak Company

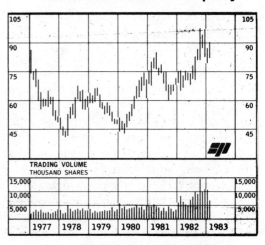

(d) Growth—cyclical

FIGURE 1–4

Price Behavior of Recessive, Cyclical, Growth and Income Stocks

SOURCE: Standard & Poor's, *Stock Report*, August 13, September 22, November 3, December 4, 1981, pp. 90, 326, 802, 532.

of common stock. The growth-cyclical company is a successful company that relies upon earnings growth and increased market price. Its performance has been better than the market generally. But even so, prices move cyclically around a trend line rather than in a straight line. Even the growth stock has a cyclical pattern, Eastman Kodak is a good example of a growth company that has cyclical characteristics.

The cyclical stock by its very nature is influenced more by the business cycle. Usually, the price movement is related to the cyclical earnings of the company and the changes in those earnings. This type of company benefits greatly from economic boom and suffers from recession, making the market risk substantial. These companies cannot be bought and held for maximum gains; they must be traded to obtain the best benefits.

The income-stock pattern looks more like that of the Standard & Poor's 500 Stock Index than do the others. These stocks offer modest growth, substantial dividend income, and movement around the norm so that one is aware of the market risks involved. They are not completely vulnerable to cyclical changes, but they are vulnerable to the money-rate risk. As interest rates go down, income stocks tend to increase in price, and vice versa.

A recessive stock is one that is declining. Earnings are usually going down and dividends are dropping. This might reflect a declining industry, poor management, or poor products. Not much interest is shown in this type of company, except by those who think it might be taken over by a stronger management and improved. In a "turnaround" situation, in which the new management turns a loss into a gain, the profits in price appreciation can be substantial. It would be possible to trade in this type of stock, if we were aware of the market risks involved. We see immediately that the prices move about a trend line downward, that the price variation from month to month is substantial, and that this type of stock should not be held for the long term. Actually, the way Chrysler has performed is somewhere between a recessive stock and a cyclical stock and has recovered.

All stocks, including those of the best quality, are susceptible to the market risk. General Motors, AT&T, Minnesota Mining & Manufacturing, du Pont, Eastman Kodak, all excellent companies, move in a rather wide price pattern. In fact, a 10 to 20 percent price movement might be considered normal for many companies. Under conditions of severe stress, such as occurred in 1981, we could expect market-price movements to be substantially greater. However, we can be more precise in our knowledge of market risk simply by using some statistical estimates and a visual reference to come up with the range of prices that will occur over time for a particular stock. In Figure 1–4c, a trend line fitted to the data visually (a very unsophisticated way to measure) provides a range around the trend line that indicates a substantial market risk.

But the historical calculation of the variability of returns points out the total level of risk, not just the market risk. So it would be wise to employ the measure to estimate total risk and not just the market risk. It might be assumed that price changes are independent from earnings change, but that assumption would be incorrect. Prices change for a multitude of reasons, not all of which are predictable or even known.

In Table 1–3, the stocks listed in Figure 1–4 are compared to the S&P 500 Index in return, standard deviation, and beta relationship. The growth-cyclical stock, Eastman Kodak, returned 10.7 percent, with a standard deviation of 22.8 percent for the ten-year period. With a ten-year beta of 1.13, the stock had a higher risk than the S&P Index, and earned a higher return.

The most profitable stock was American Brands, which gave the investor a return of 14.8 percent with a risk of 14.8 percent. The stock had a beta of .70, which suggested

TABLE 1-3

Returns and Risk of Recessive-Cyclical, Cyclical, Income-Growth, and Growth-Cyclical Stock and of the S&P 500 Index

Year	Average Price ($)	Gain of Loss ($)	Dividend ($)	Total Return ($)	Total Annual Return (%)
Chrysler (c) *					
1981	6.19	(1.69)	—	(1.69)	(21.4)
1980	7.88	(0.68)	—	(1.68)	(7.9)
1979	8.56	(2.38)	0.20	(2.18)	(19.9)
1978	10.94	(6.22)	0.85	(5.37)	(31.3)
1977	17.16	0.78	0.90	1.68	10.3
1976	16.38	5.44	0.30	5.74	52.5
1975	10.94	(2.62)	—	2.62	19.3
1974	13.56	(15.94)	1.40	(14.54)	(49.3)
1973	29.50	(5.31)	1.30	(4.01)	(11.5)
1972	34.81	5.87	0.90	6.77	23.4
American Brands (AMB)†					
1981	40.25	3.50	3.25	6.75	18.36
1980	36.75	7.77	2.95	10.72	36.99
1979	28.98	5.85	2.31	8.16	35.78
1978	23.13	0.75	1.81	2.56	11.44
1977	22.38	1.32	1.49	2.81	13.34
1976	21.00	2.42	1.40	3.82	20.05
1975	18.60	1.72	1.34	3.06	18.13
1974	16.88	(2.12)	1.28	(0.84)	(4.42)
1973	19.00	(3.25)	1.19	(2.06)	(9.25)
1972	22.25	0.56	1.14	1.70	8.09
Bethlehem Steel (BS)‡					
1981	26.88	3.00	1.60	3.60	15.08
1980	23.88	0.99	1.60	2.59	11.31
1979	22.89	(0.24)	1.50	1.36	5.45
1978	23.13	(6.18)	1.00	(5.18)	(17.67)
1977	29.31	(11.19)	1.50	(9.69)	(24.60)
1976	40.50	8.00	2.00	10.00	30.77
1975	32.50	2.69	2.75	5.44	18.21
1974	29.81	(0.37)	2.30	1.93	6.39
1973	30.18	0.22	1.65	1.87	6.24
1972	29.96	4.59	1.20	5.78	22.82

*Reward—average annual return, −3.55%, risk—standard deviation, 30%; beta—−.10.
†Reward—average annual return, 14.80%; risk—standard deviation, 14.79%; beta—.70
‡Reward—average annual return, 7.4%; risk—standard deviation, 17.11%; beta—.61.

TABLE 1–3 (Cont.)

*Eastman Kodak (EK)***					
1981	76.75	17.96	3.00	20.96	35.7
1980	58.79	1.50	3.20	4.70	8.2
1979	57.29	2.66	2.90	5.56	10.17
1978	54.63	(13.12)	2.33	(10.79)	(15.9)
1977	67.75	(33.38)	2.10	(31.28)	(30.9)
1976	101.13	14.63	2.07	16.70	19.3
1975	86.50	(1.06)	2.06	1.00	1.1
1974	87.50	(40.07)	1.99	38.08	29.84
1973	127.63	6.13	1.81	7.94	6.5
1972	121.50	35.50	1.39	36.89	42.90
Standard & Poor's 500 Index††					
1981	122.50	3.13	7.08	10.81	9.05
1980	119.37	15.67	6.55	22.22	21.14
1979	103.70	6.75	6.20	12.95	13.34
1978	96.95	(2.01)	5.07	3.06	3.09
1977	98.96	0.06	4.90	4.96	5.02
1976	98.90	16.07	3.77	19.84	23.95
1975	82.83	(1.79)	4.08	2.29	2.83
1974	81.04	(25.14)	5.25	(19.89)	(1.78)
1973	106.18	(4.22)	3.46	(0.76)	(0.69)
1972	110.40	12.92	2.67	15.59	15.99

**Reward—average annual return, 10.69—; risk—standard deviation, 22.75%; beta—1.13.
††Reward—average annual return, 8.65%; risk—standard deviation, 10%; beta—1.00.
SOURCE: Frederick Amling & Associates, Washington, D.C.

it was less risky than the S&P 500. Actually, Bethlehem Steel looked more like a growth stock than Eastman Kodak did.

The cyclically regressive stock, Chrysler, earned a negative return for the ten-year period and a negative beta. The stock went opposite to the direction of the S&P 500, since the market was up and Chrysler declined for the ten-year period. It was the least profitable among the four companies.

The cyclical income stock, Bethlehem Steel, ranked third in performance, with a defensive beta of .61 and a 7.4 percent average annual return for the ten-year period. American Brands and Eastman Kodak earned a higher return than the S&P 500 Index.

The return and risk analysis presented in Table 1–3 provides the investor with a good summary of past behavior of the stock. At least the reward and risk characteristics can be understood, even though they might change in the future. Such an analysis is better than vague generalization about the past and the future expected events and much better than a casual observation of a stock-market chart.

PROTECTION FOR MARKET RISK. There are several ways in which investors can protect themselves from the market risk. First, carefully study each security to understand its price behavior. Stocks that have demonstrated a cyclical pattern in the past will be likely to continue this pattern in the future. Stocks that have demonstrated a growth pattern in the past will continue to do so in the future unless there is some drastic change in expectations about the company. Regarding behavioral characteristics of stocks, history tends to repeat itself, but not perfectly.

Second, as a result of analysis, choose those stocks that have the lowest amount of market risk. Common stocks that are growth stocks or that offer a combination of growth and income usually do not have the same degree of market risk carried by the recessive and the cyclical stocks. Analyze market behavior and select stocks that offer growth or a combination of income and growth. Avoid the risks and penalties associated with the recessive type of stocks.

Third, be extremely careful in the timing of purchase or sale of common stock. Use the standard error of the estimate as a gauge; buy stocks when they are below the limits of one standard error of the estimate, and sell when they are above. Again, this statistical technique is not perfect. On the other hand, over long periods of time, we would be better investors if we were somewhat more mathematical in our analysis.

Fourth and last, be prepared to invest for a period of time that will allow benefits from the rising trend of market prices and avoid the cyclical activity of the market in its daily and monthly price movements. This is consistent with the definition of investment. In the process, we minimize exposure to investment risk. In Figure 1–5,

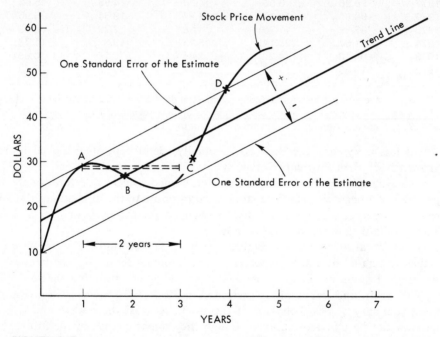

FIGURE 1–5

Two Years—A Realistic Time Period for Market-Risk Compensation for a Growth Stock

if we buy at *A* and expect to obtain the rewards over time, we must hold for at least two years before we have a chance of getting our money back. This example is not far from reality. In fact, if we bought at point *A* and held until point *C*, we would break even on our investment. It is not until we move above point *C*, more than two years after purchase, that we have made money. It would have been better for us to have purchased at *B*. If we pay too high a price for a stock, we must wait a substantial number of years to have any hope of obtaining a satisfactory rate of return. That is why a three-year time period is recommended for investment.

The Business Risk

Changes in the earning power of a company may result in a loss in income or capital to the investor. This inability of a company to maintain its competitive position and the growth or stability of its earnings, either temporarily or permanently, is referred to as *business risk*. As a result, dividends are changed, and this has an effect on the return and variability of return of a stock. Common stock, the lower-rated preferred stocks, and bonds possess business risk.

The various gradations of business risk might be exemplified as follows: First, the growth company that had expected to increase its earnings at the rate of 20 percent per year, but now only expects an increase of 10 percent per year because of a reversal in its competitive position in the industry. This results in a reassessment of the earning capacity of the company and can result in a substantial price decline and a resultant loss to the investor. Second, a company that has had stable earnings even though it was not growing very rapidly, but now finds that because of business reversals, its earnings begin to decline. This might be the recessive type of company we mentioned earlier. The third class of company has sustained a period of deficits because of its poor financial position, and its earnings are declining; there is a serious question as to whether the company will be able to remain in business. Geico, a Washington, D.C.-based insurance company, is a good example of a company whose earnings declined to a point where it was questionable whether the company would survive. Trading in Geico shares was stopped. Trading resumed later, and the stock price increased because of improved earnings. Today the company is successful, but it was touch and go for a while.

Some indication of the extent of the business risk is found in the number of company failures each year in the United States. The number varies, but in an average year, more than 15,000 business firms fail. In fact, it has become fashionable for the smaller business to go into bankruptcy. Its claims are usually forgiven, and the owners can go back into business again with a clean slate. Most of these failures are small companies that close their doors because they are unable to earn a profit. The majority of investors are probably not aware of these companies because of their size and their legal form, but they do mirror the characteristics of our business world.

These facts should give us some insight into the risk associated with the business activity of companies and help us realize the forces that have caused even large businesses to fail in the past. The causes of failure operate in the larger corporations in which we might invest our funds as well as in small companies.

The fluctuation in business activity or the business cycle that leads to a change in earnings is also an indication of business risk. A recession in industrial output will lead to a drop in profits for some companies. The effect of the decline in sales varies from company to company. Some companies might be forced to close. For others, it will simply mean a drop in earnings or a slowing down in the growth rate. The result is a drop in share price.

The Federal Reserve Board Index of Industrial Production can be used as an indicator of business health and business risk. Figure 1–6 indicates the variation in past business activity, and shows that output declined sharply in 1974–75 and 1982.

SEASONALLY ADJUSTED, MONTHLY

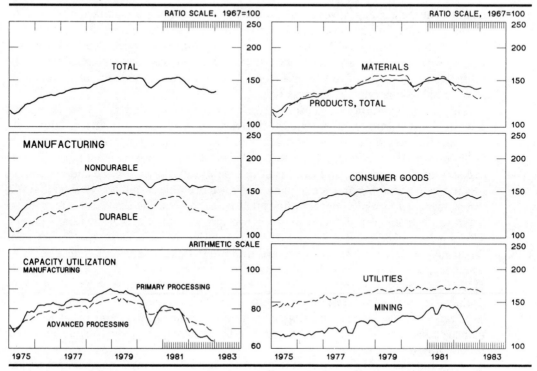

FIGURE 1–6

Industrial Production and Capacity Utilization

SOURCE: Federal Reserve Chart Book, February 1983, p. 24.

We see in Figure 1–7 that corporate profits before and after taxes began to rise after the recessions of 1974–75 and 1980, and after most other recession years as well. Certainly, greater stability in profits would lead to greater stability in share prices and lower business risk assumed by the investor.

One way to measure business risk is by measuring the stability of earnings and the stability of the growth rate of earnings. The company having the greatest stability in its growth rate of earnings and the greatest stability of earnings would have less business risk than a company that had widely fluctuating earnings. In essence, an investor would certainly be willing to pay more for the company with the stable growth earnings than for a company that had cyclical or widely fluctuating earnings. An estimate of earnings stability can be found by fitting a curve to the earnings per share of a company and finding the standard error of the estimate around those earn-

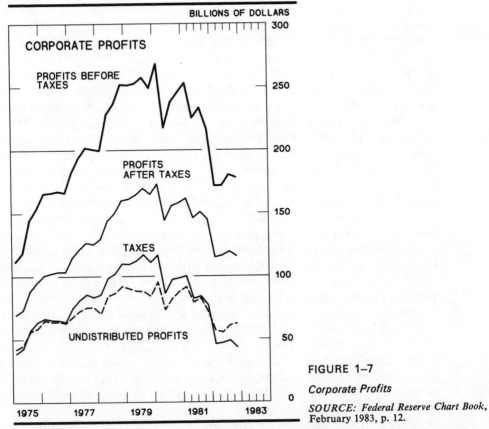

FIGURE 1–7

Corporate Profits

SOURCE: Federal Reserve Chart Book,
February 1983, p. 12.

ings. The company with the greatest stability of earnings and the lowest standard deviation would have the lowest business risk. However, visual inspection of the growth pattern of earnings, particularly when the growth rate is analyzed, will give some idea of the stability of earnings and growth rate and the amount of risk involved.

GUARDING AGAINST BUSINESS RISK. How can the investor guard against the risk of loss associated with the failure—either partial or complete—of a business firm? There are several appropriate solutions to this problem. First, a thorough analysis should be made of the competitive position of the company and its prospects for future profitability. This requires a detailed analysis of the past profit performance of the company. Careful examination of the trends and stability of the profits will indicate the degree of risk involved. The standard deviation of past returns gives an indication of the relative risk. Second, common stock should be purchased when it offers an attractive return on the investment in spite of the possible changes in profitability. In short, business risk is reduced by selecting securities carefully and knowing their return-to-risk characteristics.

The Money-Rate Risk

Many investors consider high-quality bonds or other fixed-income securities the only safe way to solve the problem of investment risk. Some institutional investors must limit their investment primarily to mortgages and investment-quality bonds. These securities, however, are subject to the money-rate risk.

The money-rate risk is the risk of loss of principal brought about by changes in the interest rates paid on new issues of securities. An example of how a change in interest rates will result in a loss to the investor will clarify this risk. Assume that a bond was purchased several years ago at par for $1,000 (quoted as 100), with an interest rate of 5 percent per year payable semiannually. The bond maturity is 25 years, and the company promised to repay the $1,000 investment at maturity. The yield to maturity is 5 percent. Now, suppose interest rates rise in five years because of a new supply-and-demand relationship for funds in the capital markets. Money is said to be tight. A tight-money policy might be followed because of the government's attempt to prevent inflation in the domestic economy and to improve the international balance-of-payments problem, such as occurred in 1981 in the United States. As a result, yields increased to 14 percent on new bonds of equal quality. What happened to the yields on bonds that were issued at 5 percent? The price of the 5 percent bonds will drop until the 5 percent interest payment results in a yield to maturity of 14 percent, which is just equal in yield to the new 14 percent bonds that are being issued. The problem, however, is serious, because a $1,000 bond with a 5 percent interest rate now has a market value of $530.80.[2] If the bond were sold, a loss would be sustained. If, on the other hand, the market yields had declined from 5 to 4 percent, then the bond would increase in price, and we would have a capital gain instead of a loss. The significant point to note is that there was a change in price and yield independent of the quality of the bond, a change brought about by external money-market conditions over which we had no control.

Another risk is assumed by investors if bonds are purchased with a very high interest rate. If bond yields fall, bond prices move to a premium. There is a tendency on the part of the corporation issuing the bonds to call the bonds and refinance at a lower rate of interest. This puts bondholders in a position where they might lose money not only through inflation in prosperous times, but also in deflationary times when yields drop, bond prices increase, and the company calls the bonds at a price lower than the market price. Most corporate bonds cannot be called for redemption before ten years.

Table 1–4 shows the yields on U.S. long-term marketable Treasury bonds since 1960. The changes reflect the changes in the bond yields. The past trend of interest rates has been upward, but down in 1983.

This is also demonstrated in Figure 1–8, which shows the pattern of yield on long-term government bonds of the United States. It also shows the pattern of bond yields in other countries. Germany and Switzerland have a similar pattern as the United States, but at lower levels, as do France and Canada. The United Kingdom suffered

---

[2]The present value of $50 at a 14% discount rate for 10 years is $50 × 5.216 = $260.80. The present value of $1,000 at 14% is .270 × $1,000 = $270. These total to $530.80. These figures may be verified by reference to Appendix A (1) and (2).

INVESTMENT OVERVIEW

TABLE 1–4

Yields on Long-Term U.S. Treasury Bonds, Indicating
Long-Term Changes in Money Rates

Year	Treasury Bond Yields (%)
1983, Jan.	10.37
1982	12.23
1981	12.89
1980	10.81
1979	8.74
1978	7.89
1977	7.06
1976	6.78
1975	6.98
1974	6.99
1973	6.30
1972	5.63
1971	5.74
1970	6.59
1969	6.10
1968	5.25
1967	4.85
1966	4.66
1965	4.21
1964	4.15
1963	4.00
1962	3.95
1961	3.90
1960	4.01

Mean = 6.67   Standard deviation = 2.58
(1960–1980)

SOURCE: *Federal Reserve Bulletin*, February 1977, p.
A27, September 1981 and February 1983, p. A28.

severely in 1975 but has managed to bring rates down to the United States level in recent years. This has meant a decrease in bond prices in the world's bond markets, with a rise in prices in 1983.

DEFENSE AGAINST THE INTEREST-RATE OR MONEY-RATE RISK. The investor must be realistic in solving the problem of a possible loss associated with changes in money rates. One solution is to hold the investment to maturity. Thus, if a debt security is purchased, it should be held until it matures. Capital losses because of money-rate changes would be avoided.

A defense against increasing or changing yields is a shortening of bond maturities. By buying 90-day Treasury bills at high interest rates, we avoid a capital loss. The bills are reinvested at the market rate.

We might be able to trade or sell the bond and take a loss, which is tax deductible, and then invest in the higher-yield bonds. This might improve yield to maturity, particularly if the investor is in a high tax bracket.

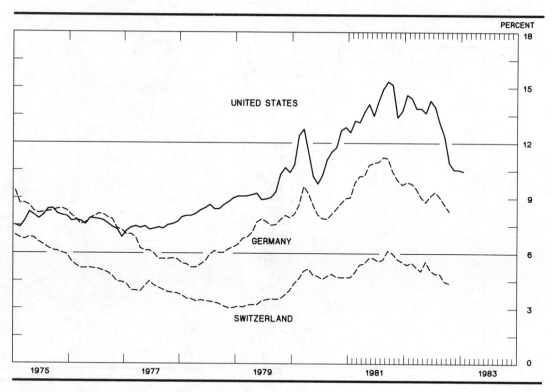

FIGURE 1–8(a)

Long-Term Government Bond Yields, Selected Countries

SOURCE: *Federal Reserve Chart Book*, February 1983, pp. 84, 85.

The best solution would be to space the maturity dates of bond investments so that the money is invested in several different maturities. As the bonds mature, the proceeds can be reinvested at the new and higher yields if the trend of yields continues to move up. It would be wise to shorten the time to maturity, unless long-term yields are very high on a historical basis, if rates are expected to rise.

In our analysis, we must remember that there is a certain degree of instability in bond yields. Bond yields do fluctuate from time to time and have a variability similar to that of common stock. Common stocks, particularly high-quality income stocks, also respond in similar fashion when interest rates change. The best defense is proper analysis of the direction of interest rates and maturity diversification.

The Inflation Risk

All securities and bank deposits suffer from the inflation risk, the risk of loss of income and principal because of the decreased purchasing power of the dollar. Figure 1–9 gives evidence of what happened to consumer and producer prices and the GNP deflator in recent years. The basic trend of inflation has been upward, with high cyclical peaks in recent years. It seems the U.S. economy is becoming less stable and more risky for investors even though inflation was lower in 1982.

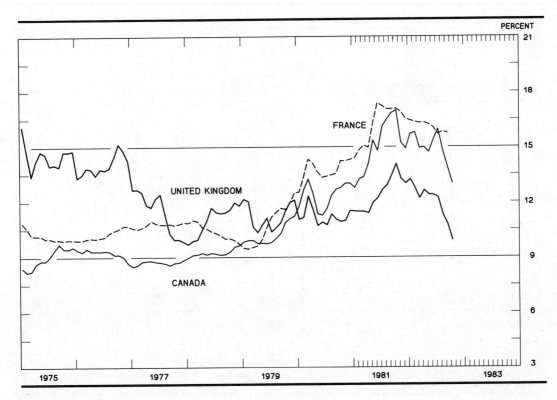

PERCENT

FIGURE 1–8(b)

The effect of inflation on the real buying power of stocks is seen in Figure 1–3. Figure 1–3 shows the growth-cyclical pattern of stock prices as measured by the S&P 500 Index in current dollars. The right side of Figure 1–3 adjusts the S&P 500 index for inflation. An investment in 1953 held until 1980 would have resulted in a sixfold increase. Yet in "real" dollars of purchasing power, as seen in Figure 1–3, there was an increase from approximately 40 to approximately 68, which was not even a onefold increase.

The United States has experienced a constant decrease in the purchasing power of the dollar, and this trend is likely to continue. A dollar today, for example, will purchase less than half of what it could purchase a few years ago. Some product improvement over the period has also increased prices. A new modern automobile might cost double what a five-year-old car would cost. Some people will say that a new auto is twice as good as an old auto, what with pollution-control, gas, and diesel economy. Yet costs have increased because of inflation. College costs have soared. Medical costs have risen rapidly. At the present time, it costs $400 a day to keep a patient in the average hospital, and forecasts for ten years hence suggest costs of twice that amount. Housing costs have moved up substantially within the last few years. These are the real aspects of inflation. We can look at composite indexes all we wish, but when we get down to the things we buy and use every day, we find that inflation constitutes a real threat to the purchasing power of our money. It is the single most

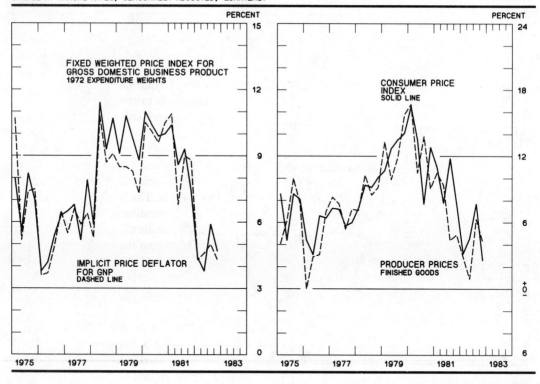

FIGURE 1–9

Comprehensive Price Measures

SOURCE: *Federal Reserve Chart Book*, November 1981, p. 20.

important threat against increasing stock prices and return on fixed-income investments. High rates of inflation lead to monetary restraint, which leads to high interest rates, which lead to lower long-term bond prices and lower stock prices.

THE INVESTOR'S SOLUTION TO INFLATION. How can the investor solve the problem of inflation with investment securities? Fixed-income securities do not solve the problem, because they do not increase in value to compensate for the rising cost of living. Not only that, but as interest rates rise, bond prices fall, and the investor loses capital. Ownership securities in the form of common stock can provide against the inflation risk.

The correlation between increasing stock prices and the consumer price index (CPI) is not perfect; stock prices tend to be more cyclical in character than consumer prices. Yet even in this tendency, they perform imperfectly. As the rate of inflation increases, interest rates increase, yields on stocks increase, and stock prices fall. With high rates of inflation, common stock is not a good hedge against inflation. Over long periods of time, however, common stocks have tended to offer higher returns, including dividend income and capital appreciation, than fixed-income securities. This suggests that if bonds yield 13 to 15 percent and have lower risk, they would be more attractive than common stock. However, the trend of stock prices tends to compensate for the trend of increasing consumer prices, and is a better way to hedge against inflation.

Under conditions of high rates of inflation, the best solution is one of defense. This defense is accomplished by investing in short-term securities and selling, to the extent possible, long-term securities, including bonds and stocks. This, however, requires careful analysis and foresight and might be difficult to accomplish.

Another defense against inflation is diversification into real assets—real estate, land, objects of art, gold and other precious materials, diamonds, oriental carpets, and similar scarce and valuable assets, which tend to rise in price along with inflation. Unfortunately, no asset is a perfect hedge against inflation. The investor simply must develop an inflation defense, which demands that all expenditures be examined for their inflation-protection ability. Under inflationary conditions, people attempt to save more of their salaries as prices rise. This tends to hasten the day when demand subsides and the rate of inflation diminishes. When consumer liquidity and confidence are restored, spending and investment begin anew. The cyclical characteristics of our economy suggest that this process will continue in the future.

In assessing the investment environment, it is important to put inflation, interest rates, market risk, and business risk into perspective. As a basic principle, stable consumer and wholesale prices, and stable interest rates, market prices, and earnings are favorable for increasing equity prices and investment values. Conversely, inflation, unstable earnings, rising interest rates, and unstable market prices are unfavorable for long-term investment.

Return and Risk of Securities

Figure 1–10 provides a graphic relationship for the securities that will be examined in the text. It represents the return-and-risk relationships for Treasury bills and other securities, including government, municipal, and corporate bonds, and several market indexes, including the Dow Jones Industrial Averages and the Standard & Poor's 500 Index. The data reflect expectations in mid-1982 and provide knowledge about what might be expected in the future from financial securities in the capital markets.

INVESTORS' ATTITUDE TOWARD RETURN AND RISK

Investors are truly "risk-averse." They must establish their attitudes about return and risk. Investors must have an understanding of return and risk from various securities. They must develop the specific return and risk characteristic they are willing to accept.

Figure 1–11 reflects what must be done and shows the return and risk available from investments in the market. The line *MM* represents various investments where

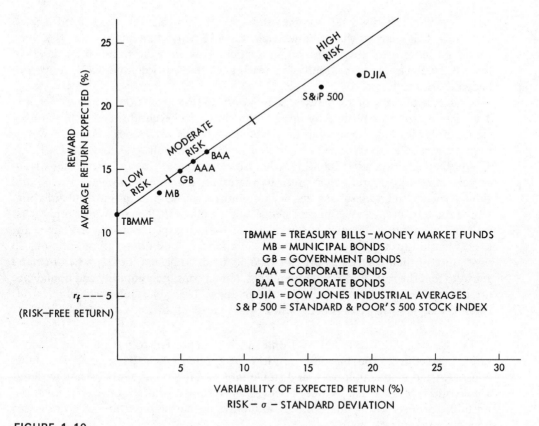

FIGURE 1–10

Return-and-Risk Relationship for Investment Securities Available to Investors

reward is proportional to risk, ranging from risk-free investment to speculative securities (up and to the right) that offer higher returns and risks.

The curves $I_{1,2,3}$ and $I'_{1,2,3}$ represent the attitudes of two different investors about the combination of return and risk they would be willing to accept. The curves represent combinations of return and risk to which investors I and I' are indifferent; that is, any place on any curve is acceptable. Unfortunately, the first investor, I, can obtain only that combination of securities at point A. That is the best the investor can do, since the market doesn't offer any more. The second investor, I', is willing to accept more risk to earn a higher return, so this investor would invest in securities in the marketplace at point B. This investor is really a risk-taker.

What this boils down to is that the investor must decide if he or she wants an investment in a group of securities that offers a 15 percent return with a variability or risk of 10 percent, or securities that offer a return of 20 percent and risk of 18 percent. All investors must have a firm idea of what to expect in the future from an investment. This is what investment is all about, and we will proceed in the next chapters to analyze the return and risk of investment to help investors achieve this goal.

INVESTMENT OVERVIEW

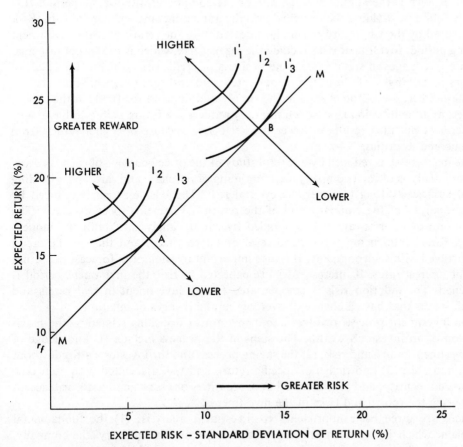

FIGURE 1–11

Investors' Attitude toward Return and Risk and Investment Opportunities

SUMMARY

The world economies offer a wide variety of securities or assets to satisfy the investor's desire for return and risk. Most investors are risk-averse, and attempt to maximize their wealth. As a principle, investors maximize wealth by maximizing return and minimizing risk. These additional principles govern investor decisions: investors prefer more to less; the search for higher returns leads to higher risk; and risk should be proportional to return.

Investment may be defined as the purchase by an individual or institution of an asset that produces a return proportional to risk over some future period. The investments available for purchase are typically financial assets, but real or tangible assets may be included among the alternative investments.

Return includes dividend or interest income and capital gains over the holding period. Return is the annual average rate or the compound rate for the period. It is usually found by dividing the principal into the annual income and capital gain. Risk is measured by the variability or standard deviation of the return over the investment holding period. Investment risks include the market risk, which is the loss of principal because of changes in stock prices; the business or credit risk, which is the result of changes in earnings or failure; the money-rate or interest-rate risk, which results in a capital loss because of the change in the supply and demand for funds in the capital market; and the inflation risk, which not only reduces the future ability to buy goods and services but also results in lower market prices because of higher return from fixed-income securities.

The market risk is reduced by a careful study of the price behavior of each security, a careful analysis of each company, careful timing of purchase and sale, and a holding period sufficiently long to cover the cyclical risk. The business risk is reduced by careful analysis of the company and of the return-risk benefits to be expected. The money-rate or interest-rate risk is avoided by careful analysis of both the money-market forces influencing the general level of interest rates and the specific credit risk involved with each company. It is also important to attempt to forecast the future level of interest rates. If interest rates are expected to rise, the investment period is shortened. The inflation risk is compensated for by investment in real assets and growth stocks that have a chance of overcoming the ravages of inflation.

The investment process revolves about investment decisions related to the maximization of an investor's wealth. The steps in the process include (1) knowledge of the investment return and risk; (2) the saving process and the investor's attitude about return and risk; (3) knowledge of specific return and risk associated with each type of financial security; and (4) the selection of securities or assets an investor will accept considering the return and risks of the investments.

There are three basic approaches to investment analysis: (1) the fundamental approach, which includes an analysis of the economy, the industry, the company, and the valuation of securities; (2) the technical approach, which analyzes the price behavior of securities; and (3) modern portfolio theory, which accepts the notion that the market is efficient and that investors cannot beat the market. The emphasis in this book is on fundamental analysis, yet we will also consider the investment implications of technical analysis and modern portfolio theory.

SUMMARY OF PRINCIPLES

1. Investors are risk-averse.
2. Investors attempt to maximize wealth.
3. There are investment implications for the purchase of most assets.
4. Return includes capital gains and dividends or interest income.
5. Risk is measured by the variability of return.
6. Inflation is the enemy of the investor.
7. Investing has become worldwide.

8. Good research and sources of information will help to improve the investment process.

1. What is risk? What is a risk-averse investor? What should be the investor's basic goal in regard to risk?
2. Distinguish between a real investment and a securities investment.
3. Explain what is meant by *return* or *reward*.
4. What elements are involved in risk? Does taking more risk always lead to more wealth?
5. Explain what is meant by a return-risk relationship.
6. What is the equation for measuring return for one year? For three years?
7. How is risk measured? Give the equation for measuring risk.
8. What is meant by the term *beta*, and how is it obtained?
9. How would you measure market risk, business risk, interest-rate risk, and inflation risk?
10. Explain how the charts of price movement of a stock can give an indication of return and risk.
11. Should an investor consider foreign securities for investment?
12. How does the investor obtain protection from risk?
13. Define the term *investment* as it relates to securities investment.
14. What part does future time play in investments?
15. List the steps involved in the investment process.

PROBLEMS

1. Miss Mary Jane Moore bought 100 shares of du Pont at $52, net of commission, in 1972. In 1973, she sold the shares at $65, net of commissions. Moore received $1.92 per share in dividends in 1973. What return did she earn for the one-year holding period? What was the current yield on the purchase?
2. Moore purchased 100 shares of du Pont in 1976 and held them through 1980. The following data reflect what happened to du Pont's price and dividends for the period:

	Average Price	Dividends
1976	$35.00	$1.75
1977	40.00	1.92
1978	39.00	2.42
1979	43.00	2.75
1980	40.00	2.75

   a. Calculate the annual return for each year.
   b. Calculate the annual average return and the standard deviation for the four-year period.
   c. Comment on the return and risk for du Pont for the period.

3. The price and dividends earned on the S&P 500 Index for the period were as follows:

	Average Price	Dividends
1977	$ 99.00	$4.90
1978	97.00	5.07
1979	104.00	6.20
1980	119.00	6.55

In 1976, the S&P price was $99 at the time du Pont was purchased. Using this price:
a. Calculate the annual return of the S&P 500.
b. Calculate the annual average return of the S&P 500.
c. Calculate the standard deviation of the S&P 500 return for the period.
d. Compare the risks of du Pont with the S&P 500. What do you conclude?

CASE

Times were difficult at the end of 1981, and Bill and Barbara knew it. The federal budget deficit was expected to increase; the rate of inflation was declining; interest rates were moving erratically lower; unemployment had risen; housing prices had declined; and auto sales were at an all-time low. In this environment, they wished to invest $100,000 to provide security of principal (they did not like to lose money), and they wanted a combination of revenue and growth. As they looked at the array of investment opportunities suggested in Figure 1–10, they knew they had to decide among the return and risk alternatives to determine where their money should be invested. Explain to them how they might establish alternatives, as suggested by Figure 1–11.

SELECTED READINGS

BAUMAN, W. SCOTT. "Investment Returns and Present Values." *Financial Analysts Journal*, March–April 1968, p. 35.

BAYLIS, ROBERT M. "The New Performance." *Financial Analysts Journal*, July–August 1974, pp. 55–63.

BERNSTEIN, PETER. "What Rate of Return Can You 'Reasonably Expect'?" *The Journal of Finance*, May 1973, pp. 273–82.

BLUME, MARSHALL E. "Betas and Their Regression Tendencies." *The Journal of Finance*, June 1975, pp. 785–96.

BURTON, J. S., and J. R. TOTH. "Forecasting Long-Term Interest Rates." *Financial Analysts Journal*, September–October 1974, pp. 73–86.

FARRELL, JAMES, JR. "Homogeneous Stock Groupings." *Financial Analysts Journal*, May–June 1975, pp. 50–61.

———, WILLIAM W. JAHNKE, and BARR ROSENBERG. "Is Beta Phlogiston?" *Financial Analysts Journal*, January–February 1974, pp. 70–81.

HASTY, JOHN M., and BRUCE D. FIELITZ. "Systematic Risk for Heterogeneous Time Horizons." *The Journal of Finance*, May 1975, pp. 659–73.

LEVY, ROBERT A. "Beta as a Predictor of Return." *Financial Analysts Journal*, January–February 1974, pp. 61–69.

MCENALLY, RICHARD W. "A Note on the Return Behavior of High Risk Common Stocks." *The Journal of Finance*, March 1974, pp. 199–202.

MODIGLIANI, FRANCO, and GERALD A. POGUE. "An Introduction to Risk and Return—Concepts and Evidence." *Financial Analysts Journal*, March–April 1974, pp. 68–80, and May–June 1974, pp. 69–86.

NORGAARD, RICHARD L. "An Examination of the Yield of Corporate Bonds and Stocks." *The Journal of Finance*, September 1974, pp. 1275–86.

ROBICHEK, ALEXANDER, and RICHARD COHN. "The Economic Determinants of Systematic Risk." The *Journal of Finance*, May 1974, pp. 439–48.

SHARPE, WILLIAM F. "Capital Asset Prices: A Theory of Market Equilibrium under Conditions of Risk." *Journal of Finance*, September 1964.

————. "Are Gains Likely from Market Timing?" *Financial Analysts Journal*, March–April 1975, pp. 60–69.

————, and GUY M. COOPER. "Risk-Return Classes of New York Stock Exchange Common Stocks, 1931–67." *Financial Analysts Journal*, April 1972.

————, and H. B. SOSIN. "Risk, Return and Yield on Common Stocks." *Financial Analysts Journal*, March–April 1976, pp. 33–42.

International

BLATTMACHR, JONATHAN G. *International Estate Planning*. New York: Practicing Law Institute, 1980.

ERRUNZA, VIHAG R. "The Effects of International Operations on the Market Value of the Firm." *Journal of Finance*, May 1981, p. 401.

European Stock Exchange Handbook, Park Ridge, N.J.: Noyes Data Corporation, 1973.

F&S International Annual. Cleveland: Funk and Scott Publishing Company. (More in F&S Index of Corporations and Industries.)

GEYIKDAGI, Y. M. "The Cost of Equity Capital and Risk of 28 U.S. Multinational Corporations vs. 28 U.S. Domestic Corporations: 1965–1978." *Management International Review*, 1981, p. 22.

Guide to World Commodity Markets. New York: Kogan Page, London/Nichols, 1979.

HENNING, CHARLES N., WILLIAM PIGOTT, and ROBERT HANEY SCOTT. *International Financial Management*. New York: McGraw-Hill, 1978.

Jane's Major Companies of Europe 1979–1980. London: Macdonald and Jane's.

MATHER, IGBAL, and MANNAGAN KYRNN. "Risk Management by MNCS." *Management International Review*, 1981, p. 22.

OECD Economic Surveys. Paris: OECD.

STOPFORD, JOHN, JOHN H. DUNNING, and KLAUS O. HABERICH, *The World Directory of Multinational Enterprises*, New York: Facts on File, Inc., 1980.

WIHLBORG, CLAS, "Economies of Exposure Management of Foreign Subsidiaries of Multinational Corporations." *Journal of International Business Studies*, winter 1980, p. 9.

World Capital Markets, London: Phillips and Drew, 1980.

World Economic Indicators, 1981 edition. New York: Business International Corporation.

APPENDIX: SOURCES OF INVESTMENT INFORMATION

The process of making an investment decision depends upon a careful analysis of the growth of the national economy and judgment concerning the implications of the trends of political events within the national economy. It includes an analysis of industries to identify those that will perform better than the national economy as a whole. A source of information must be developed that provides us with the facilities to analyze a company and to identify those companies that should do better than average. The technical forces working in the marketplace that will have an influence on share prices must be identified. Finally, we need information for developing a portfolio to meet the investor's needs and for measuring its performance. It is important to identify sources of information that will be helpful in these areas and to indicate the nature and use of the information.

We are discussing here an overall list of basic sources and a simple but sound information system for an individual or institutional investor. It is easy to be overwhelmed with the data that are available to the average investor; however, a simple and effective system of gaining information is much more useful than having complete knowledge about all sources of information but not being able to use any of them. The ideal method of obtaining information about investment opportunities is easy. First, the direction of the national economy is established; second, those industries that offer the greatest expectation of profit are chosen; and third, the most profitable companies are found. This process requires a substantial amount of time, energy, and money, which are not always available to the individual investor. They might be available to the professional investor, but even here, any one firm is limited to the number of companies and industries it can follow, unless it has an unlimited budget and staff.

INFORMATION ABOUT THE NATIONAL ECONOMY

Information about the national economy can be obtained from many sources.

Federal Sources

One of the most important basic sources of information about the national economy is the *Federal Reserve Bulletin*, published monthly by the Board of Governors of the Federal Reserve System, Washington, D.C. It contains a summary of business conditions, along with the Federal Reserve Board Index of Industrial Production and a compilation of statistics on business trends, including production capacity, construction, employment, retail sales, and prices. A breakdown of the national economy by income account, including gross national product and national income, is provided, as well as information about interest rates, yields of securities, and other valuable financial data. The information is also presented in chart form on a monthly or annual basis in the *Historical Chart Book*. The Federal Reserve Bank of New York publishes a *Monthly Review* that includes comments about the business situation. The twelve regional Federal Reserve banks also publish monthly bulletins devoted to banking and economic activity of national import. The Federal Reserve Bank of St. Louis, for example, has done substantial work with econometric models in attempting to predict the movement of the securities market and forecasting the national economy. It has also conducted research on the impact of the money supply on the national economy. The New England Federal Reserve Bank has done a considerable amount of work in specific areas of banking and regional investment problems. The Federal Reserve Bank of Richmond publishes a summary of leading economic forecasters, which is available in February of each year.

The *Survey of Current Business*, published by the U.S. Department of Commerce, presents data about basic business trends and comments on the business situation. An elaborate section on economic statistics, business activity, prices, and production is included. The charts of various economic components of the economy are very helpful.

Business Conditions Digest, issued monthly by the Bureau of the Census of the U.S. Department of Commerce, provides many economic indicators in convenient form for analysis and interpretation. The basic presentation follows work done by the National Bureau of Economic Research and provides valuable information on leading, coincidental, and lagging indicators. A particularly important series is the composite leading indicator index, which is helpful in anticipating expected future movements of the economy and the securities market. The Bureau of Economic Analysis provides timely data about the national economy.

Private Publications

Business Week, published by McGraw-Hill, is a weekly periodical that provides statistical data and a business-outlook section reviewing changes in business and economic development. The First National City Bank of New York publishes a *Monthly Economic Letter* whose major feature is the lead article on general business conditions. *Morgan Guaranty Survey*, published by the Morgan Guaranty Trust of New York and the Bank of New York, provides information on general business conditions.

The First National City Bank has tape recordings of its leading economists, available monthly, to give some insight into what is going on in the national economy. Chase Manhattan Bank publishes *Business in Brief*, sponsored by its economic research division. In addition, top investment firms, such as Merrill Lynch, Kidder-Peabody, Loeb Rhoades, and Dean Witter, employ economists who provide forecasts or expectations about developments in the national economy. Firms that provide econometric models of the U.S. economy are Wharton Associates; Data Resources Inc. (DRI), led by Otto Eckstein; and Chase Econometrics. From time to time, forecasts made from the econometric models are made available to the public through the financial press. The *New York Times* frequently provides excellent reports on the condition of the national economy and its possible direction in the next twelve months. Other business periodicals or journals that provide coverage about the state of the nation's economy are *Dun's Review and Modern Industry, Forbes, The Wall Street Journal, Money, Fortune,* and *Nation's Business.*

Most of these services include reports on the profitability of the nation's businesses as well as the outlook for the national economy. At the same time, comments are made about other segments of the money and capital markets.

INDUSTRY AND COMPANY INFORMATION

Industry and company reports are published through a wide array of sources. The leading investment houses in the United States provide information about individual securities and the industry in which they are located. Merrill Lynch provides a quarterly *Security and Industry Survey* that is made available to a large number of institutional investors, and indirectly becomes available to the investing public. The information includes a description of the industry, the outlook for the industry, and the outlook for the companies that make up the industry. Stocks are classified as growth or no growth, stable or liberal income, and good quality or speculative.

The financial press provides a wealth of information for the investor, which should be followed on a regular basis. Certainly an investor should not be without *The Wall Street Journal,* which is published each business day and provides a complete list of stocks traded on the New York, American, regional, and over-the-counter exchanges. The *New York Times* provides not only current quotations for daily stock transactions but a substantial amount of valuable information. *The Wall Street Journal* has a special column, "Heard on the Street," which provides up-to-the-minute reports of the nation's top security analysts, portfolio managers, and advisors, with advice to investors. *Barron's,* a financial weekly, carries a substantial amount of information with its weekly price quotes. Its leading article, "Up and Down Wall Street," furnishes specific information and opinions about individual companies, the market, and the study of price movements; comments about the securities market can be found in the "Trader."

Financial World, published weekly, and the *Magazine of Wall Street,* a biweekly, feature articles on the trends of the market, industry valuations, and data on individual companies.

The *Financial Analysts Journal* provides current articles about investments, portfolio management, the latest thinking in the field of investment, and developments in the academic and business community. *Business Week, Forbes,* and *Fortune* are excellent sources of information about companies and management, as well as the economy.

Periodicals containing industry statistics from trade associations include *American Gas Association Monthly, American Machinist, American Petroleum Institute's Weekly Statistical Bulletin, Automotive Industries, Baking Industry, Best's Insurance News, Broadcasting, Coal Age, Directory of National Trade Associations, Dodge* [F.W.] *Reports, Electrical Merchandising, Electrical World, Mining Record, Engineering News-Record, Paperboard Packing, Implement and Tractor, Industrial and Engineering Chemistry, Iron Age, Leather and Shoes, Oil and Gas Journal, Paper Trade Journal,*

Polk's National New Car Service, Printers' Ink, Railway Age, Rock Products, Television Digest, and *Textile Organization.*

INVESTMENT SERVICES

Three investment advisory services provide information not only about industries and companies, but also about the outlook of the national economy. These are Moody's Investors Service, 99 Church Street, New York, N.Y., owned by Dun & Bradstreet; Standard & Poor's Corporation, 345 Hudson Street, New York, N.Y., owned by McGraw-Hill; and the Value Line Investment Surveys, owned by Arnold Bernhard & Co., 5 East 44th Street, New York, N.Y.

Moody's and Standard & Poor's services are reference volumes, referred to in previous sections as Moody's *Manuals* and Standard & Poor's *Manuals.* Standard & Poor's, however, also issues a weekly magazine called *The Outlook*, and Moody's issues a weekly publication called *The Stock Survey.* Both services review market conditions and make specific recommendations about common stock. *The Outlook* contains an overall market forecast and policy recommendations.

One very valuable source of information published by Standard & Poor's is the *Stock Guide.* It is issued monthly and contains brief but essential facts about 5000 or more common and preferred stocks. Many of the stocks are given quality ratings to guide the investor. The ranks given stocks in *The Outlook*, and in the *Stock Guide* help to establish investment philosophy and policy. Moody's has a handbook of widely held common stocks, which is issued quarterly and covers more than 1000 companies. It is called *Moody's Handbook of Common Stock* and contains historical price and earnings information. In addition, Moody's publishes a weekly and monthly *Bond Guide*; Standard & Poor's issues a *Bond Outlook*, and Moody's a *Weekly Bond Survey.* Information about bonds is found in *Moody's Bond Record—Corporates, Convertibles, Governments, Municipals, and Commercial Paper Ratings, Preferred Stock Ratings.* Historical price information about bonds is difficult to find. The best source about the price of bonds is the *Wall Street Journal* or local papers that carry bond quotations. Professional brokers use the Pink Sheets to determine market makers in stocks, the Blue List for municipal offerings, and the Yellow List for corporate bonds.

One of the best sources of information, factual and interpretive, is Standard & Poor's *Stock Report.* Such a report contains up-to-date information about the company, with a recommendation, historical data, operating statistics, financial information, and facts about the officers and directors of the company. In concise form and short space, it provides a substantial amount of information as well as a rating service.

Standard & Poor's also provides an annual set of statistics and prices, entitled *Standard & Poor's Statistics.* Such information is particularly important in developing historical data that can be used for measuring the performance of individual securities. Standard & Poor's, through subsidiaries, provides *Compustat*, a computer magnetic-tape data file service that produces basic balance-sheet and income data for analysis. Another Standard & Poor's service is the *Earnings Forecaster*, which provides estimates of earnings from various sources for the next year. In midyear, for example, forecasts and estimates are made for the entire year, and some earnings estimates are obtained for the following year. This is particularly valuable in supplying data for the valuation equation discussed later in the text.

Standard & Poor's also issues an excellent series of industry surveys covering the major industrial classifications. The report is broken down into "Basic Analysis" and "Current Analysis and Outlook."

The Value Line Investment Surveys cover almost 1400 stocks in 60 industries, providing historical and factual data as well as rating stocks for appeal in the year ahead and for a three- to five-year period. All these services, both factual and advisory, are available from a good public library or a university library and should be consulted on a regular basis.

The Institutional Brokers Estimate System monitors the earnings estimates on companies of interest to institutional investors.

TALKING WITH MANAGEMENT

It is impossible to cover all information sources in a brief outline. It is more important to develop a simple yet effective source of information. Some professional analysts think it desirable to visit the management of the companies in which they plan to invest to hear firsthand about the expectations and plans for the future. Others believe that the reports from management tend to be optimistic and that any analysis based on them will be biased.

THE BASIC INFORMATION SYSTEM

Whether the investor is an individual or an institution, it is necessary to keep informed about investments. The analysis that results from the use of the information system is a continuous process of sifting and weighing information. A previous judgment or decision is confirmed or changed, which results in a basic change in investment and portfolio policy.

The Individual Investor

For the individual investor, the first step in creating a basic information system is to establish a relationship with a good brokerage firm, one that provides information and performance. The data should be factual and unbiased and should not lead to undue activity for the investor's account.

The second step is to develop a philosophy and a frame of reference for making independent analyses and judgments about individual companies. This requires being informed about the national economy, the growth of industries, and the growth of companies; this, in turn, requires that basic information be obtained on a daily and weekly basis from the financial press and from Standard & Poor's, Moody's, and Value Line. In applying valuation equations, the investor must have information about future expected earnings. These could be obtained for a one-year period from the *Earnings Forecaster*, published by Standard & Poor's Corporation. Factual reports from Standard & Poor's *Listed and Unlisted Reports*, information about next year's earnings from the *Forecaster*, and judgments based upon discussions with analysts and analysis of the financial statement of a company would determine what the earning power of the corporation is expected to be in the future. From this, future dividends and the future expected price can be estimated for the valuation equation. The expected return can be calculated. Risk, having been calculated on the basis of past data, should be used as a guide to the return-to-risk relationship.

This, then, is one of the simplest systems imaginable for making investment decisions. It consists of *Stock Reports* and the *Earnings Forecaster* from Standard & Poor's and an individual analysis of the company, and/or reports from brokerage firms indicating expectations, then value judgments and the calculation of expected return, and a final decision based on the return-risk analysis.

Individual companies would be purchased to form a portfolio, which would then be appraised monthly or weekly, based on the information obtained by the investor. In addition, the investor would read *Business Week*, *Barron's*, and other periodicals, including some of the monthly reports of the Federal Reserve Bank of New York, the Chase Manhattan Bank, and Citicorp to keep abreast of developments.

Brokerage Research for Institutional Investors

The brokerage community provides extensive and up-to-date information for institutional investors, such as mutual funds and bank trust departments. A sample of the type of research available only to the institutional investor community is listed below. The firms listed are important brokerage firms that help to make decisions easier and the marketplace for securities more efficient.

Goldman, Sachs Inc., New York

Investment Strategy Highlights
    The economy
    Monetary policy and interest rates
    Valuation model and other measures of value
    Confidence
    Supply-demand relationship
    Technical
    Stock market composition and performance
    Recommended portfolio structure and stocks

Portfolio strategy
    Risk, return, and equity valuation

Economic research
    International Economic Comment, Financial
    Market Perspective, the Pocket Chartroom

Industry and company reports

Kidder, Peabody & Co., New York

Economic perspectives—weekly

Fixed income prespectives—monthly

Monthly valuation data—quantitative research

Monthly investment review—analysts' rating of stock attractiveness

Portfolio Manager's Digest

The "Top 50"

TRAC technical review and commentary

Modern portfolio theory

Selected stock list

Trinity's Multiplex Portfolio—rankings of performance of brokerage firms and trust departments of selected firms

Merrill Lynch, Pierce, Fenner and Smith, Inc., New York

Monthly Research Review
  Industry and stock recommendations
  Recommended yield stocks
  Recommended convertible securities
  Economics
  Composite data: market
  Domestic company statistics

Performance Monitor—monthly
  Provides performance measures for market, market mix, group rotation, asset mix, and earnings.

Business Outlook
  A weekly review of the business environment

Capital Market Monitor—a bimonthly perspective
  Economic, financial, inflation, consumer, business, and international overview. Valuation summary and portfolio strategy.

Long-term Economic Outlook
  Forecast through 1991

Industry surveys

Corporate bond research

Floating rate notes
  Yankee bonds

Fixed income research
  Railroad equipment trust certificates

Salomon Bros., Inc., New York

Bond market research

International bonds and money market performance

Bond portfolio analysis
  Mortgage research
  Market analysis
  Utility bond analysis
  Portfolio analysis

Mortgage department
  Market analysis

Stock research
  Investment policy
  Industry analysis
  Strategy systems

    Bond market research
       Market performance
       International bond market analysis

Foreign Securities

Information about foreign debt and equity securities is available from the sources listed above. Specialized knowledge can be obtained from brokers and security dealers in the countries where the securities are issued.

CHAPTER 2

SAVINGS FOR INVESTMENT
Individual and Institutional Investors

The act of savings precedes the act of investment, although the two may occur simultaneously. Savings and investment are undertaken by individual investors, institutional investors, governments, and businesses. The subject of investment once focused on individual investors and how they saved and invested. But the capital formation process is much broader. Institutional investors, or *financial intermediaries* as they are called, play an important if not a dominant role in world investments. In fact, the institutional investor makes the capital and stock markets work efficiently. Foreign institutional investors and individuals also play an important role in our financial markets, just as U.S. investors do abroad. So it is important to understand who the investors are, where they get their funds, and where they invest. In this chapter we will look at individual and institutional investors. In Part II, we will examine the securities and assets they purchase; in Part III we will see how the capital markets work and how, where, and by whom shares of stock, bond options, and other assets are traded.

THE INDIVIDUAL AS SAVER AND INVESTOR

If people do not spend income for consumption goods, they save it. Personal savings of individuals represented approximately 6 to 7 percent of disposable (after-tax) personal income in the United States during the seventies. The savings rate was closer to 5 percent in the early 1980s. And personal savings rates in Japan and Western Europe historically have been twice as high as in the United States. So one aspect of current government policy is to raise the savings rate. Donald Regan, secretary of the treasury in the Reagan administration, explained the President's brand of economic development as follows:

> Reaganomics in a nutshell: the less we tax, the more we can save. The more we can save the more we can invest. The more we invest, the more we can produce. The more we produce, the more we can provide for everyone's benefit.[1]

Savings from Current Income

Purchases of durable consumer goods are usually considered consumption expenditures, even though people often think of some of them as savings. On the other hand, repayment of debts and equity purchases of real estate are considered savings. Deposits in savings institutions and savings deposits in commercial banks represent savings built up in part from current income. Money from current income given to nondeposit institutions such as life insurance companies, pension funds, and investment companies represents savings. There is an element of investment in savings accounts and life insurance reserves; however, they are usually considered savings and not investment media. Our definition of savings would also include money used to purchase securities directly. A person buying securities would be saving and investing, in the financial sense, in the same transaction.

Not all savings from current income are available for the purchase of securities by the savers themselves. In fact, the major portion of annual savings goes to such financial intermediaries as pension funds, life insurance companies and savings institutions, and for debt repayment. The institutions will purchase securities and invest. The greatest amount of funds for the purchase of securities comes from insurance and pension funds, commercial banks, and the federal and local governments. Institutional investors are much more important as direct purchasers of securities, in the aggregate, than are individuals, as we shall see below.

Accumulated Savings of Individuals

Available to the individual for direct investment in corporate securities is money from past savings that have been built up in savings and loan accounts, mutual savings banks, savings accounts with commercial banks, credit union balances, and demand deposits with commercial banks. Usually, the money held on deposit by these institutions has already been used to purchase securities—predominantly debt securities. The funds deposited in savings and loan companies are usually invested primarily in residential mortgages and partially in government securities. Mutual savings banks also make mortgage loans and invest in government securities; in addition, they buy private corporate debt and other debt instruments. The credit union, in business mainly to make loans to members, also invests in short-term government securities, but not in equity securities. In fact, most of these financial institutions—including the credit union—avoid investing in common stock. But pension funds, mutual funds, and life insurance companies do invest in common stock, and the amount has increased in recent years. If the individual chooses, he or she may draw on these balances for the purchase of securities directly.

[1] *The Washington Post*, The Federal Triangle, Friday, September 25, 1981, p. A29.

Table 2–1 provides a list of some past attractive savings opportunities for investors. The *All-Savers certificate* was created during the Reagan administration to encourage savings at savings institutions. This instrument was free from federal income taxes, was for one year only, had a one-year maturity, and a yield of 70 percent of the yield on Treasury bills. The first yield was established at 12.1 percent. The pretax yield was based on the saver's marginal tax rate. A saver with a marginal tax rate of 50 percent would actually have earned a before-tax yield of 24.2 percent. The *NOW* account (negotiable order of withdrawal) is really a checking account that pays interest at the passbook rate. *Short-term and long-term money market certificates* pay a yield based on the Treasury bill rate. The Treasury bill is issued by the U.S. Treasury to raise

TABLE 2–1
Domestic Saving Alternatives

Institution	Savings Plan	Minimum Amount ($)	Time	February 1982 Rate (%)	February 1983 Rate (%)
Savings and loan associations	All-Savers certificate[a]	$ 500	12 mo	12.1%	9.70
	NOW account	300	—	6.0	7.96
	Short-term money market certificate	10,000	26 wk	14.379	8.256
	Long-term money market certificate	100	30 mo	16.3	8.308
	Jumbo certificate	100,000		negotiated	
	Regular savings	100	—	$5\frac{3}{4}$	5.50
	3-month certificate	100	3 mo	$5\frac{3}{4}$	8.256
	1-year certificate	100	1 yr	$6\frac{1}{2}$	8.62
	3-year certificate	100	3 yr	$6\frac{3}{4}$	9.64
	4-year certificate	100	4 yr	$7\frac{1}{2}$	10.00
	6-year certificate	100	6 yr	$7\frac{3}{4}$	10.36
	8–10 year certificate	100	8–10 yr	8.0	10.46
Commercial banks	All-Savers certificate[a]	500	12 mo	12.1	9.70
	NOW account	300	—	$5\frac{3}{4}$	7.96
	Savings account	50	—	$5\frac{3}{4}$	5.50
	Certificate of deposit	100,000	1 mo	15.0	8.28
			3 mo	$15\frac{3}{4}$	8.36
			6 mo	16.3	8.46
			1 yr	16.0	9.13
U.S. savings bonds	Savings Bond EE	25	$\frac{1}{2}$–8 yr	—	—
	Savings Bond H and HH	500	20	$8\frac{1}{2}$[b]	7.50
Money market mutual funds	Any money market fund	500	—	17.1	7.80

[a]Rate based on 70 percent of Treasury bill yield at time of issuance. The first time issued, the rate was 12.1 percent. The yield was exempt from federal income taxes and from some state income taxes. This was a one-time opportunity for each saver.

[b]Interest is paid by check. There is no automatic reinvestment.

money for the U.S. government. It is backed by the full faith and credit of the U.S. government. However, if sold before maturity, money market certificates pay only the passbook rate. The *jumbo certificate* rate is negotiated between the institution and the saver but is based on Treasury bill yields. A *certificate of deposit* at a commercial bank pays an attractive yield. These are one way in which commercial banks can obtain money to lend. *U.S. savings bonds* offer two ways to save. One is by the Series EE savings bond, which has a minimum price of $25 that becomes $50 at maturity in 8 years and provides a yield of 9 percent. The rate is variable and 85 percent of the rate in 5-year Treasury notes with a minimum of 7 1/2 percent. They must be held for six months before dedemption. The Series H bond pays interest by check, has a 10-year maturity, and pays a yield of 8 1/2 percent. Both are guaranteed by the U.S. government. The Series HH bonds are also variable rate bonds paying a minimum of 7 1/2 percent every six months by check.

Money market funds have grown tremendously. Assets in 1980 were $74 billion and grew to $226 billion in 1982. A *mutual fund* purchases or invests in the securities of other companies. In the case of money market funds, they purchase certificates of deposit government securities, and commercial paper of business corporations. *Commercial paper* is a short-term IOU sold by large businesses to lenders for short periods of time. Savers thus have had very profitable savings alternatives.

Pension funds and life insurance reserves are important vehicles by which people save a portion of their income each year. The accumulated funds are invested in securities for the individual even if he or she does not elect to invest directly with them. Over a long period of time, these funds build up to large amounts of money that are eventually available for individuals to purchase securities with directly if they wish to do so. Of course, by using these funds for this purpose, we give up some, although not all, of the benefits of the pension program or the life insurance. We cannot use pension funds until we retire, at which time the proceeds will usually be taken in the form of income rather than in a lump-sum payment, although some pension funds do provide lump-sum payments that can then be invested directly. Usually, money cannot be borrowed from the pension fund, and hence it is unavailable for investment as it is being built up. Life insurance reserves can be borrowed or pledged for a loan, and this is a source of investment funds.

Business units also invest their surplus funds in government securities, mainly in short-term securities to maintain liquidity. Government units themselves follow the same pattern as corporate investors. Foreign investors also provide funds from savings for investment; they invest in debt and equity securities, and they represent a source of savings for investment in the United States.

Savings and the Individual

The amount of money anyone saves is directly dependent upon amount of income, how long they have earned that income, expectations for future income, the stability or instability of income, attitude toward saving and thrift, and how other people around them spend their income.

The fact that our nation aggregates large amounts of savings each year, as we shall see shortly, does not mean that a specific individual will invest in securities. Saving is needed to purchase securities, but a desire to invest is also needed.

THE AMOUNT OF INCOME AND SAVINGS. As incomes increase, people tend to save a greater portion and have more money available for the direct purchase of securities. A family with $15,000 disposable income after taxes might be able to save a few dollars. A family that earns $35,000 may be able to save, directly or indirectly, 15 percent of its income. A family that earns $50,000 may be able to save over 25 percent of its disposable income.

The upper-income groups do most of the saving; they could purchase securities directly. Families in the middle-income group will have larger accumulated savings if they are older and have earned income for a number of years. Some people, particularly physicians and other professionals, who have a sharp increase in income after a long period of little or none, find that because their personal expenditures and income taxes are high, it is difficult for them to save. They will undoubtedly seek a financial plan that will reduce taxes and increase net income as a percentage of total personal income. Ordinarily, people who expect their income to rise will save less from present income, anticipating saving more from future income.

SOCIAL COMPETITION AND AGE FACTORS. Careful study of budget statistics shows that the difference in the consumption patterns of additional sums of money received by the rich and by the poor is not as great as we would imagine if we accept the idea that the upper-income groups do all the saving and the lower-income groups do very little. Most upper-income groups pay more in federal income taxes. They also spend more for housing, travel, and education, making it more difficult for them to save and invest directly. Social emulation may take hold in the higher-income groups, and the attempt to keep up with the Joneses also limits savings and investing.

The age pattern of the income group is also a factor in ability to invest. The older people in the upper-income group will have had a chance to accumulate savings and funds for investment. A younger person at the same income level might not be able to invest because of the demands on the income and because of the short period of time he or she has been earning a high income. We are experiencing this phenomenon in the United States at the present time. More and more individuals and households are earning over $30,000, and this trend is expected to continue. Many, however, have just entered this income level and find it difficult to save and invest. They have to wait until they have sufficient funds to begin a direct-investment program.

ATTITUDE TOWARD SAVINGS AND INVESTMENT. The amount of money actually saved for investment will be determined by a person's attitude toward thrift in general, and by the specific goals established for the individual and the family.

People usually save with a particular purpose or goal in mind. They save to purchase a major consumer good, to provide an education for their children, to provide additional income for their retirement years, or to buy a second home, a second car, a vacation hideaway, or a mink coat. Some save for the specific purpose of buying securities to help reach financial goals. Few people today save for the sake of saving. In the inflationary recession period of 1980, many people gave up saving and borrowed to maintain a standard of living that was increasing in cost. Inflation and uncertainty caused Americans to spend more and at the same time, to invest less, since many were also disenchanted with the securities market. But savings are still vital to provide for investment.

Savings are the result of a conscious effort to save for a specific purpose, and this often means investment. The usual reason for taking large amounts of money from savings accounts is to buy stocks and bonds. Today, saving is a way to begin an investment program in order to increase a standard of living and provide greater wealth. Many people who are self-employed have Keogh plans that use savings for the purchase of securities, and IRA plans perform the same service for those whose employers provide no pension plans.

Investing Borrowed Money

Money for the purchase of securities may be obtained by borrowing, as well as from savings previously accumulated or from current income. Some investors consider it wise to borrow money to buy securities, since they reason that they can earn more from their investment than the cost of borrowing the funds. The usual sources of borrowed funds are (1) margin loans from brokers, (2) security loans from commerical banks, and (3) life insurance loans.

PURCHASING STOCK ON MARGIN. Securities may be purchased on margin through a broker by opening a margin account. The term *margin* refers to the amount of ownership we must have in each share of stock that we purchase. A 50 percent margin permits us to buy stock by borrowing 50 percent of its cost from our broker, giving us a 50 percent ownership. If a stock is selling at $50 and the margin is 50 percent, we could borrow $25 per share and would need $25 of our own money to complete the transaction. (Interest is paid, of course, on loans obtained to purchase securities.)

The margin requirement is determined by the Federal Reserve Board of Governors, which has the authority to change the requirement as monetary policy dictates. The margin requirement was 50 percent in 1983, indicating monetary ease by the Federal Reserve Board. The margin requirement applies to all margin transactions in securities on registered securities exchanges, and also to bank loans made for the purpose of carrying any security traded on such exchanges.

The major advantage of buying stock on margin is the increased amount of stock that can be purchased with the same amount of money. With $1,000, one can purchase 100 shares at $10 per share on a straight cash basis. If the margin is 50 percent, another $1,000 can be borrowed to buy a total of 200 shares of the same $10 stock. If the stock increases in value, a profit on twice as many shares is earned. On the other hand, if the price should decline, more will be lost; and more margin or equity will be required as the price falls. If the investor has no liquid assets or has borrowed so much that margin cannot be provided, the broker can sell the shares and use the proceeds to get back the amount of the loan. Speculative situations such as these have been disastrous in the past for purchasers of securities.

Security loans outstanding at any one time can be an unstabilizing influence in the securities market. When there is a great deal of stock market credit, the prices of securities are forced up by the additional demand for stock purchased with the proceeds of the loans. Under these conditions, a drop in prices may precipitate a demand for liquidity, securities may be sold, and prices may be forced down. By the same token, if money is borrowed to finance short sales, stability may result.

A *short seller* thinks the price of stock is going down. The seller borrows stock from or through a broker and sells it on the market, adding to the supply of stocks and tending to depress the price. The broker arranges to borrow the shares from other customers who have margin accounts and allow these shares to be loaned for this purpose. As the price of the stock declines, the short seller will buy stock in the market to repay the stock borrowed. Since the short seller sold at a higher price, he or she makes a profit. The act of buying adds to the demand for the stock and tends to support the price.

Short sales are usually made on margin by speculators in the stock market. In the act of borrowing to finance short sales, the market trader performs a stabilizing function. If the majority of people bought securities with borrowed money, however, the impact on the market would be unstabilizing, since there would be little support if the market should begin to drop.

COMMERCIAL BANK LOANS. Commercial banks lend money directly for the purchase of securities. When the securities are listed on a registered exchange, the amount of the loan is governed by the margin requirements established by the Federal Reserve Board. If the securities are traded in the over-the-counter market, the loan will be determined by the lender, who must meet competition from other lenders. On high-quality debt securities of private corporations, commercial banks will usually lend from 70 to 75 percent of market value, although the bank margin requirement for convertible bonds is currently 50 percent. Loans on unlisted common stocks tend to follow the margin requirements of stocks traded on registered exchanges, but the amount of the loan may vary according to the quality of the stock. Security loans are short-term or term loans, and some provision is usually made for gradual retirement.

LIFE INSURANCE LOANS. The great majority of policy owners consider life insurance a part of their retirement program and would not borrow the money for the purchase of securities. Nevertheless, the cash surrender value of life insurance may be borrowed for that purpose. Because the rate of interest charged by life insurance companies is low, it is an economical way to borrow money. National Service Life Insurance, the federal government life insurance company, charges only 4 1/2 percent annually for the money borrowed against reserves and requires that the interest be paid annually. Monthly installments are not required to retire the debt. Commercial life insurance companies typically charge 5 to 6 percent interest—and no formal repayment plan is necessary. Since the borrower has the use of the funds for a full year, the effective rate of interest is low. Usually, the interest for the first year is deducted in advance. If the loan is not paid off and the borrower dies, the amount of the loan is deducted from the proceeds of the policy. Life insurance borrowing is one of the lowest-cost methods of obtaining short-term and long-term funds for any purpose. As an example, one investor borrowed $15,100 against the cash value reserves of several life insurance policies at 5 percent to purchase 12.1 percent All-Savers certificates that were tax exempt.

The Investment Fund—Borrowed Funds and Savings

The individual investor therefore must save money to invest or be content to invest indirectly in life insurance or some form of pension plan. Obviously, small amounts of money saved and invested regularly can lead eventually to large investments. There are three plans for the small investor that can turn a savings program into an investment fund. Funds can be accumulated through a thrift plan, an annual investment plan, or an investment club.

THRIFT PLAN. Investment might begin with the monthly or quarterly purchase of common stock through a thrift plan in the company where we work. Most plans of this type offer the opportunity to put a small amount of salary into the common stock of the company or into selected investment companies. The small amounts, regularly contributed, can eventually lead to a sizable investment fund.

ANNUAL INVESTMENT PLAN (AIP). An excellent way to invest small amounts is to save for investment on a regular basis and then invest annually in common stock. One way to accomplish this would be to have monthly salary deductions for the purchase of Series EE savings bonds. When the cash value of the bonds reached $500 or more, they could be cashed in and the money used to buy common stock. There is economy involved in buying $500 worth of stock at once rather than ten purchases of $50 each, as the savings in brokerage commissions over time can be substantial. The benefits of dollar averaging are achieved by buying at different prices. Over long periods of time, it is just as advantageous to buy stock once a year as once a month. Monthly forced savings becomes a habit, and larger amounts can be invested regularly and more cheaply annually. In a short period, a sizable sum can be accumulated in a portfolio of securities.

INVESTMENT CLUB. Another alternative is to begin an investment fund in a small way by joining an investment club. The number of members in a club varies from 10 to 25. The members pool their funds and decide which stock or stocks to purchase. Typically, $10 is invested by each member each month. The purpose of the investment club is not only to invest, but to learn something about investment and the economic and financial system. It also allows the investment of small sums of money and the purchase of securities cheaply. It would be costly for one person to buy such a small dollar amount alone. The purchase of shares in quality companies over a long period of time can lead to a sizable investment fund.

The National Association of Investment Clubs has taken an active role in encouraging the growth of these clubs. Their annual and regional meetings are excellent. The information they distribute is extremely helpful for the "little investor." However, the investment club idea is not confined to the small investor with $10 a month;

several clubs of professional analysts require an initial investment of $500 and a $100 monthly contribution.

Individual Investors—Where They Invest Their Money

It is difficult to determine where any one individual investor will invest. Some invest only indirectly in a pension fund. Others put money into real estate and precious metals. Some invest in stocks for the long term. Some buy mutual funds for growth and others for income. Some speculate by trying to buy low and sell high. Some people do not save and never invest directly in securities or real assets. Some people keep their money in a passbook account, and some will "invest" in money market funds. In fact, individuals invest in many ways, depending upon their attitude toward return and risk. And they probably invest in the same securities institutional investors buy.

INSTITUTIONAL INVESTORS—WHERE THEY INVEST

Even though the investment policies of institutions differ markedly from the objectives of the individual, the process in both cases is very similar. The life insurance investment manager is limited to investment in government, municipal, and corporate bonds, real estate mortgages, and a small but growing amount of common stock. In an attempt to improve yield, life insurance companies do invest in high-yielding third- and fourth-quality bonds, and higher-yielding, higher-risk private placement bonds.[2] A casualty company, on the other hand, will invest a greater percentage of its funds in common stock. Since there are bound to be differences among institutional investors with regard to investment policies and practices, we must look in detail at institutional investment activities.

Some notion of where institutional investors invest their funds is given in Table 2–2. The greatest percentage of the assets of pension funds is invested in common stocks, the biggest percentage of assets of savings and loan associations is invested in mortgages, and state and local government retirement programs invest the greatest percentage of assets in bonds. We will take a closer look at some of these institutions in a moment.

This area of investment is growing rapidly, particularly in its new emphasis on variable annuities, and in the growth of mutual funds and of life insurance–mutual fund companies. The most dynamic growth has been in money market mutual funds.

The institutional investor represents a powerful force in our industrial and financial community, dominating the investment and financial markets. The investment managers of institutions, because of the funds they control, collectively possess a latent power over the management of the corporations owned, even though the objective is not power or control, but earning a satisfactory return with a minimum risk.

[2]Murray E. Polakoff et al., *Financial Institutions and Markets* (Boston: Houghton Mifflin, 1970), chap. 7, p. 136.

TABLE 2–2
Where Some Institutional Investors Invest

Where Funds Are Invested	Type of Institution							
	Commercial Banks	Savings and Loan	Mutual Savings Banks	Credit Unions	Life Insurance Companies	Fire and Casualty Companies	State and Local Govt. Retirement Funds	Private Pension Funds
Currency, demand deposits, time deposits, and certificates of deposit	4%*	2%	2%	3%	1%	2%	2%	6%
U.S. government securities	12	7		9		12		
Municipal securities	11					47		
Consumer loans	15							
Business loans	35							
Mortgages	19	83	59		28			
Corporate securities			16		51	31	75	78
Corporate bonds					42	16	53	24
Corporate stocks					9	15	22	54
Consumer credit				79				
All other	4	8	23	9	20	8	23	16
Total, percent	100%	100%	100%	100%	100%	100%	100%	100%

*Cash and reserves.

Life Insurance Companies

THE BUSINESS OF LIFE INSURANCE COMPANIES AND THE SOURCE OF FUNDS. The business of the life insurance company is financial protection for a person's beneficiaries if that person should die. Protection is also provided, while the insured lives, by the buildup of the cash value of the policy. Life insurance offers two promises to the purchaser: an estate if the insured should die, and an estate if the insured should live. A premium is paid in exchange for this protection.

Premiums are the major source of income of the life insurance company. The premium income is used for three purposes: First, part of it pays for the expenses of the operation of the company. In the life insurance industry, these expenses are referred to as *loading charges* and represent the first item of expense in establishing the premium.

Second, a portion of the premium is used to pay *death claims* to the beneficiaries of the insured. The payment of death claims varies from year to year. Over a period of time, the number of people out of 100,000 (or any larger number) insured who die can be determined accurately. The number of deaths per year and the amount of death claims paid is an important determinant of the amount of the premium an individual must pay. As a person becomes older, the probable amount of time for paying premiums becomes shorter, so the premium for a new policy on the life of an older person must be larger to provide funds for the costs of paying the claim.

The third major item of expense that makes up the premium is the reserve. The *reserve* is a sum of money that accumulates each year for the benefit of the life insurance policy of the insured. The amount paid into the reserve from premiums each year, plus the income earned from the investment of the reserve funds, must be sufficient to provide the face value of the policy when the policy matures. Under an ordinary life policy, maturity would be at age 100, based upon the Commissioners Standard Ordinary Mortality Table. A 10-year, 20-year, 30-year, or fully paid-up life at age 65 would also mature at age 100, but it is paid up at an earlier date. Enough money in each of these policies would be paid into the reserve so that the fund plus investment income would equal the face value of the policy at age 100. The endowment policy has a much higher premium, because it usually endows—has a cash value equal to the face value—much before age 100. Both ordinary life and endowment policies have a cash value. Term insurance has no reserve and no savings feature, so there is no investment aspect associated with this type of policy.

The reserve that is built up to allow the life insurance policy to endow at age 100 is invested at an assured rate of return. The rate varies from time to time, but for each individual policy it is guaranteed by the insurance company not to change while the policy is in force. If the rate of return earned on the premium reserve exceeds the guaranteed rate, or if management expenses are lower than estimated, or if the mortality rate is lower than expected, the surplus funds are used for the benefit of the policy owner or the stockholder. Usually, the life insurance company builds up a contingency reserve fund to compensate for the variation in management expenses, death benefits, and earnings on the reserve fund. If the contingency reserve exceeds the amount determined by management as necessary to meet its contingencies, it may be paid to the owners of a stock company as a dividend. If it is a mutual company, the policyholders are the owners, and they will receive the dividend. In a stock company, the policy owners and the stockholders are separated. The owners receive the dividends, and the policy owners receive only the contractual, guaranteed rate of return on invested reserves. This rate is usually stated in the contract. The dividends the policy owner in the mutual company receives are usually quite substantial; the premiums paid, however, are somewhat higher than those paid by the policy owner in a stock company.

Most life insurance companies offer accident and health insurance along with the various life insurance contracts. The accident and health policies provide for payment of income and medical fees while a person is disabled. The premiums must cover this risk. It is difficult to determine in advance the number of people who will become ill or disabled; each company must establish premiums for this type of business from its own experience in paying claims. The funds obtained from the premiums are invested by the company to provide additional funds to meet the risks assumed.

INVESTMENT OBJECTIVES. The investment objectives of the life insurance company reflect the source of its funds, and also the commitment the company has made about the funds placed in its custody.

Stability. Since the policy agreement states that the rate of interest on reserves will be guaranteed, and since the guarantee remains in force for the life of the policy, the life insurance company's investments must provide stable income equal to or higher than that rate. Investments that provide fixed income for a long period of time at yields of 12.0 percent and higher, such as government securities, corporate bonds, and mortgages, provide excellent outlets for the funds of the insurance company.

Liquidity. The need for liquidity in life insurance company investment management is important. Liquidity is provided through the regularity of receipt of premium income. The premium usually covers management expenses and cash disbursements in the form of death benefits and other payments. The remaining funds can be invested in securities that provide a great degree of liquidity through the flow of investment income. There are times when the flow of income is disrupted, as in recessions. During those periods, new business diminishes, policy loans increase, forward loan commitments prove too high, and mortgage repayments decline. In order to stem the outflow of funds, forward commitments are reduced by 80 percent, the companies borrow from banks, and some securities are sold at losses.

Time Period. The investment function as it exists in the life insurance company is long term, owing to the nature of reserves and the obligations of these companies. The average investment period for an insurance company is much longer than for the individual investor. Because the insurance company has a long-term investment program, it can purchase long-term bonds to hold to maturity. It can buy entire issues of bonds from small and medium-size industrial corporations raising long-term capital. The life insurance company negotiates directly with the company seeking funds. These *private placements*, as they are called, are exempt from registration with the Securities and Exchange Commission, so one of the accompanying costs of obtaining capital is eliminated. The interest on these securities tends to be slightly higher than the market rate of interest.

Regulation of Investment Objectives. Life insurance companies are limited in their investment activities by comprehensive state regulations designed to protect the policy owner. Regulation is coordinated through the commissioners of insurance within each state. The regulation of life insurance investment activities is comparable to the regulation of trusts. Some states apply the prudent-man rule to life insurance investment; others provide a list of securities that can legally be owned for investment by life insurance companies and trust funds. Most states provide some control over investment policy. The usual restrictions govern the quality and type of investment the life insurance company can make. Bond investment reflects the ability of insurance companies to assume risk, and they do invest in lower-rated and unrated obligations. Life insurance companies are also permitted to invest in real estate mortgages; these and bonds make up the bulk of their investments. The amount invested in common stock is limited to a small percentage of the total funds, expressed as a percentage of investable funds or surplus. This amount is approximately 10 percent.

In recent years, some states have allowed life insurance companies to sell variable-annuity contracts for retirement programs through life insurance rather than the fixed-annuity contract under the usual insurance-company retirement program. The fixed-income annuity provides a fixed income for life or for a certain number of years and is limited to investment in fixed-income securities. The funds under the variable-annuity contract can be invested partially in common stocks; the major advantage of this contract is its ability to provide against the risk of inflation. The correlation between the rising price level and the rising stock market level is not perfect, however, and the variable annuity is not a perfect answer to inflation. The amount invested in common stock will be determined by the contract and regulatory agency. Variable-annuity contracts are likely to increase in the future.

As shown in Table 2–3, the amount of common stock as a percentage of total investments owned by life insurance companies has increased over 1968. The increase reflects the "aggressive" investment policy of life insurance companies in recent years and the liberalization of regulatory agencies. We should also note the growth in total investments and the growth in foreign government securities.

TABLE 2–3

Assets of Life Insurance Companies
(millions of dollars and percentage of total)

	March 1968		November 1972		November 1976		November 1982	
	$000	% of Total	$000	% of Total	$000	% of Total	$000	% of Total
Government securities								
United States	4,582	2.6	4,459	1.9	5,606	1.8	14,370	2.5
State and local	3,007	1.7	3,356	1.3	5,467	1.7	7,935	1.4
Foreign	2,973	1.7	3,378	1.4	6,492	2.1	10,377	1.8
Total	$10,562	6.0%	$11,193	4.6%	$17,565	5.6%	$32,682	5.7%
Business securities								
Bonds	66,412	37.0	87,425	36.8	121,659	38.4	229,101	39.6
Stocks	9,348	5.2	25,641	10.8	32,843	10.4	54,549	9.4
Total	$75,760	42.2%	$113,066	47.6%	$154,502	48.8%	$283,650	49.0%
Mortgages	68,055	37.9	76,207	32.0	90,808	28.7	140,956	24.4
Real estate	5,263	2.9	7,272	3.1	10,310	3.3	20,480	3.5
Policy loans	10,362	5.8	17,922	7.5	25,710	8.1	52,916	9.2
Other assets	9,475	5.3	12,311	5.2	17,610	5.5	47,516	8.2
Total assets	$179,477	100.0%	$237,971	100.0%	$316,505	100.0%	$578,200	100.0%

SOURCE: *Federal Reserve Bulletin,* December 1963, p. 1687; June 1968, p. A36; February 1972, p. A39; February 1977, p. A29; November 1981, February 1983, p. A30.

Risk-Taking. The fact that bond investment dominates the policy of life insurance companies does not mean that risk is absent; the company does assume some risk in its investments. The purchasing-power risk is a real problem, and so is the money-rate risk. Money rates do, of course, change. There are two ways in which management can compensate for changes in yields on long-term bonds.

First, the investments can be allowed to reach maturity, thus preventing a loss of principal even if a loss of interest income occurs. Life insurance policies tend to reflect current interest rates. If, for example, the market rate of interest is 14 percent, a 7-percent rate is guaranteed on invested reserves of the life insurance company. Money invested at the time will earn 14 percent for a period of 20 to 25 years—long enough to cover the guaranteed rate of interest and the bonds held to maturity. If in the next year the yields go to 15 percent, a rate expected to continue in effect, the insurance companies can increase the guaranteed rate to policy owners to perhaps 8 percent. The old policies would continue to receive a guaranteed yield based on the original contractual rate, but as new policies are written, the guaranteed rate is increased. If rates later fall, the company could find itself earning less than it had guaranteed to the policy owners. Therefore, every effort is made to keep the market rate of interest earned by the insurance company and the rate guaranteed to policy owners closely correlated.

A second way to compensate for money-rate changes is to manage the bond portfolio carefully to take advantage of expected changes in yields. In this way, the portfolio manager compensates for the money-rate risk.

The business risk and the market risk are also problems for most insurance companies, since they own equity securities, which are subject to the vicissitudes of the stock market. As the amount of equity ownership by insurance companies increases, these risks will become greater. Business risk is also assumed in another way. Life insurance companies have a substantial investment in commercial and industrial mortgages.

Taxation and Investment.   Mutual life insurance companies enjoy a partial exemption from federal income taxes to prevent the investment income to the policy owner from being taxed twice. This is because all the income received by the company is eventually paid to policy owners. In the case of the stock companies, all the money earned from investment above the liability reserve and the guaranteed dividend is paid to the stockholders, so these companies are not in the exempt category.

There is some controversy over the income tax exemption of life insurance companies. The tendency at present is for taxes to be levied on their income at increasingly higher rates. In the past, these companies gave little consideration to the impact of federal income taxes on portfolio decisions, because their earnings were almost completely tax-exempt. Therefore, municipal bonds, with their tax advantage, were only a small portion of their investments.

PORTFOLIO POLICY AND MANAGEMENT.   The majority of life insurance companies follow a conservative investment policy. High-quality bonds make up the bulk of their investments, and risk-type securities such as common stock are a small but growing portion of total investment funds. Some companies trade their securities to take advantage of changes in interest rates. Some purchase bonds with lower ratings to improve investment return. But the basic policy of life insurance company investment is buy and hold. This policy is expressed in the mortgage investments and in private placements. The bonds purchased are usually held to maturity. At the same time, a few companies have become much more sophisticated in their investment practices. In addition, life insurance companies are managing pension funds in increasing amounts, and in this area, performance and results are more important than on the basic life insurance contract if the pension trusts are to be competitive. Life insurance companies have become more aggressive in competing with other institutional investors, such as mutual funds, for the savings and investment dollars of the consumer. Many life insurance companies merged or acquired mutual-fund companies in the late 1960s so that they could be more competitive. Travelers acquired Keystone Custodian Funds in 1979 for this reason.

The investment function centers on the new money and maturing investment that comes in each day, which must be invested. Diversification of corporate bond investments is maintained by industry and company. Maturities of securities investments are staggered to provide a diversification of timing of maturities related to bonds and mortgages.

Fire and Casualty Companies

NATURE OF THE BUSINESS.   Fire and casualty companies sell insurance to cover the risk of loss of property or injury to people. Most companies insure against the usual insurable risks, such as loss of property, which includes fire, windstorm, hail, explosion, riot, and civil commotion; and casualty, which includes injury to people in fire, storms, riots, and the like, and injury to workers, property damage, and auto damage. The fire and casualty insurance coverage is commonly associated with real property— homes and personal property such as automobiles. However, an extremely wide range of other real and personal property is covered. Specialty companies have been formed to provide coverage for auto insurance and marine insurance. Real property is usually insured for up to 80 percent of its value. Personal property is insured for the full amount, with the actual claim determined by the value of the property at the time of loss.

Estimating the amount of loss that will be sustained each year because of fire, windstorm, and automobile accidents is difficult. The total amount of loss was expected to decrease if "no-fault" insurance continued to spread, but this has not happened, and premiums have increased. The premium paid by the insured is usually for a short period, lasting from one to three years. The amount of the premiums must cover the losses during the period of insurance and the management expenses of the company. During some years, the premiums will be more than enough to cover all insurance costs; at the end of the year, an underwriting profit will be realized. In other years, premium income will not be adequate to cover the losses, and an underwriting loss will be suffered. To cover the years of underwriting loss, a reserve fund must be maintained from previously accumulated profits and from the funds contributed by the owners of the insurance company.

SOURCE OF FUNDS AND INVESTMENT POLICY.   The source of funds for investment by fire and casualty companies is the premiums collected in advance (the *unearned premium reserve*) and funds contributed by the owners. The investment policy is determined by the nature of the business and by the source of funds. Generally, if the equity in the fire and casualty company is high, a large proportion of the funds is invested in common stock. If the owners' equity is small, preferred stock and high-quality bonds will dominate the investment portfolio. Another factor has an impact on the investments of these companies. Fire and casualty companies can accept greater risk than life insurance companies, because they are investing their own money rather than the money of the policy owners. This refers to the policy reserves of the life insurance company; there is no comparable policy reserve in the fire and casualty company. Therefore, the casualty companies can invest more heavily in common stocks, which comprise about 15 percent of their securities investments. Their biggest investment, however, is in tax-free municipal securities.

Marketability and liquidity are important for the fire and casualty company. Securities may be sold to meet underwriting costs and losses. This is true even though underwriting profits are kept within the business and income from investment is paid out to the stockholders.

One of the risks assumed by the fire and casualty company is the risk of inflation. Inflation has had an adverse effect on underwriting costs, and these companies have had to compensate for the risk through common stock investments. State laws governing fire and casualty company investments require that a minimum proportion of investments be in high-grade bonds. The bulk of the funds may be invested at the discretion of the company.

Type of Investment Policy. The investment policy of the fire and casualty company is aggressive rather than defensive. It might be considered a managed aggressive policy, since fund managers have almost complete discretion over the investment of funds. The biggest portion of investable funds is invested in well-known, high-quality industrial common and preferred stocks, and in government and municipal bonds. The bonds act as a reserve to meet the liabilities of the company and to provide liquidity; that is the defensive portion of the investment fund. The common stocks constitute the aggressive portion, needed because of the risks assumed by the companies.

Generally, corporate debt obligations represent a small part of the total portfolio. The greatest portion is invested in federal, state, and local municipal obligations. Particularly strong interest is shown in municipal bonds because, since the fire and casualty companies do not enjoy special exemption from federal income taxes, they are interested in tax-exempt securities.

Investment Management. Most fire and casualty company portfolios are managed by a research staff and managers, much like those of a life insurance company. The size of the department will vary with the size of the casualty company. Usually, the investment department makes recommendations to the board of directors and does not assume final authority in making the investment decisions.

The quality of investment management of fire and casualty companies is difficult to determine from the limited information presented periodically by the company. The profit position of the company cannot be used as a criterion for successful management because of the impact of underwriting profits or losses. Many companies suffer annual underwriting losses and prosper only because of their investment income. Since the dividends of a fire and casualty company are determined by the investment income, an increase in dividends might reflect a better investment performance, but this can be used only as a relative indication.

Thrift Institutions—Savings and Loan Associations and Mutual Savings Banks

Recently, savings and loan associations and mutual savings banks have grown substantially. Their growth is reflected in the asset and liability positions of these institutions as shown in Tables 2–4 and 2–5. These "thrift" companies receive money

TABLE 2–4

Assets and Liabilities of Savings and Loan Associations
(millions of dollars)

	1968	1972	1976	1981	December 1982
Assets					
Mortgages	$124,306	$206,367	$323,394	$518,547	$484,297
Investment securities	9,821	21,839	35,691	63,547	83,460
Cash	2,772	2,673	—	—	—
Other	9,330	12,691	33,107	82,497	138,264
Total	$146,229	$243,570	$392,192	$664,167	$706,021
Liabilities					
Savings capital	$125,694	$207,290	$336,553	$525,061	$565,502
Reserves and undivided profits	9,556	14,749	22,027	28,395	25,853
Borrowed money	4,808	9,857	19,187	88,782	97,982
Loans in process	2,463	6,215	6,907	6,385	—
Other	3,708	5,459	7,518	15,544	16,684
Total	$146,229	$243,570	$392,192	$664,167	$706,021

SOURCE: *Federal Reserve Bulletin,* June 1968, p. A36; June 1973, p. A38; February 1977, p. A29; November 1981, February 1983, p. A30.

from depositors or owners and invest the funds for their benefit. One distinction between the mutual savings bank and the savings and loan association is the type of ownership. Mutual savings banks are owned by the depositors, making them truly mutual in character. The depositors share in the earnings of the bank after all expenses, reserves, and surplus contributions have been set aside. The mutual savings banks have no capital stock, and as in the case of mutual life insurance companies, owners and depositors are one and the same. The interest paid on the money in the mutual savings bank is not a guaranteed rate. Earnings are determined at the end of the interest period, and the board of trustees declares an interest payment on the depositors' accounts based on these earnings. Mutual savings banks operate under the laws of the state in which they are chartered. They are located primarily in the East, with more than half in New York and Massachusetts; there are a few in the Middle West.

Most savings and loan associations are also mutual corporations in which members' savings are technically invested in ownership shares. Beginning in 1972, however, a growing number of associations have been converted to stock companies comparable to the California savings and loan associations. Savings and loan associations may be federally chartered, or they may be chartered by the state. The federally chartered institution has two regular investment programs: the savings share account plan, a passbook account; and the investment share account plan, evidenced by a share certificate with a $100 par. The same dividend rate is paid on the balance in each type account. The investment share account represents ownership; the savings account represents only savings and no mutual ownership. Stock companies have only savers.

TABLE 2–5

Assets of Mutual Savings Banks
(millions of dollars and percentage of total)

	November 1968	% of Total	November 1972	% of Total	November 1976	% of Total	November 1982	% of Total
Assets								
Loans								
Mortgages	51,199	75.1	66,815	67.0	80,884	60.7	94,017	54.6
Other	1,267	1.8	3,503	3.5	5,801	4.4	16,702	9.7
Total	$52,466	76.9%	$70,318	70.5%	$87,685	65.1%	$110,719	64.3%
Securities								
U.S. government	4,303	6.3	3,419	3.4	5,836	4.4	9,456	5.5
State and local	221	.3	894	0.9	2,466	1.9	2,496	1.4
Corporate and other	9,113	13.4	21,648	21.9	33,047	24.8	35,753	20.8
Total	$13,637	20.0%	$25,961	26.2%	$41,349	31.1%	$ 47,705	27.7%
Cash	871	1.3	1,321	1.3	1,668	1.2	6,291	36.5
Other assets	1,190	1.7	1,996	2.0	3,632	2.6	7,572	4.5
Total assets	$68,164	100.0%	$99,595	100.0%	$133,361	100.0%	$172,287	100.0%
Liabilities								
Deposits	61,554	90.3	90,112	90.5	120,971	90.7	151,304	87.8
Other liabilities	1,553	2.3	2,611	2.6	3,376	2.5	11,893	6.9
Surplus accounts	5,058	7.4	6,873	6.9	9,015	6.8	9,089	5.3
Total liabilities	$68,164	100.0%	$99,596	100.0%	$133,362	100.0%	$172,287	100.0%

SOURCE: *Federal Reserve Bulletin,* June 1968, p. A35; February 1973, p. A39, February 1977, p. A29; November 1981, February 1983, p. A30.

THE FUNCTION OF THRIFT INSTITUTIONS. The principal function of both the savings and loan association and the mutual savings bank is to accumulate the savings of many people and lend these savings safely and conservatively to other people for the purpose of buying, building, or improving real estate. The loan is usually a first mortgage on the property. Sometimes the savings and loan associations are referred to as building and loan companies, which adequately describes the functions performed. These institutions provide investors and owners with safe outlets for their funds, and borrowers with an adequate source of long-term funds for the purchase of a home.

PROBLEMS. The higher cost of money through money market certificates and the low yield on their major investment—home mortgages—has created losses for many companies in the savings and loan industry. Little or no money flowed in in 1982. A profitable future was uncertain. However, mortgage rates declined in 1983 and the flow of funds into the associations improved.

Commercial Banks

THE BUSINESS OF COMMERCIAL BANKS. The primary purpose of a commercial bank is to make loans to business. The loans are mostly short-term, essentially working-capital loans, made to finance the purchase of inventory or to finance customers' receivables. The short-term commercial loan has traditionally been profit-table for the commercial bank, and at the same time it has offered the bank liquidity. Thus it fits admirably into the earning requirements of the bank, whose fundamental problem is to provide liquidity in the short run and yet to maintain long-run profit-ability. In recent years, longer-term loans have become more important to commercial banks.

Table 2–6 indicates the importance of loans in the overall assets of the commercial banks. The table also shows, however, that many of the loans are not of the commercial

TABLE 2–6

Loans and Securities of Commercial Banks, 1972, 1976, 1981, 1982
(billions of dollars and percentage of total)

	1972		1976		1981		November 1982	
	$	% of Total	$	% of Total	$	% of Total	$	% of Total
Loans								
Commercial loans	$123	22.6	$174	22.5	$ 358	27.0	$1,036	51.0
Agricultural loans	14	2.6	22	2.0	33	2.5	36	1.8
Security loans	13	2.4	12	1.6	22	1.7	23	1.1
Loans to financial institutions	23	4.2	42	5.4	30	2.3	32	1.6
Real estate loans	89	16.4	142	18.4	286	22.0	302	14.9
Other loans to individuals	80	14.7	92	12.0	185	14.2	191	9.4
Other loans	9	1.7	14	1.8	47	3.6	48	2.4
Total	$351	64.6%	$498	64.5%	$ 961	73.8%	$1,668	82.2%
Investments								
U.S. government	60	11.0	126	16.3	111	8.5	126	6.2
State and municipal	87	16.0	103	13.3	—	—	—	—
Other securities	25	4.6	9	1.2	231	17.7	236	11.6
Total	$172	31.6%	$238	30.8%	$ 342	26.2%	$ 362	17.8%
Federal funds	21	3.8	36	4.7	—	—	—	—
Total loans and investments	$544	100.0%	$772	100.0%	$1,303	100.0%	$2,030	100.0%

SOURCE: *Federal Reserve Bulletin*, June 1973, p. 22; February 1977, pp. A18, A19; November 1981; January 1983, p. A16.

variety. Collectively, loans to individuals and real estate loans are more important as an earning asset to the bank than are the traditional commercial loans. The composi-tion of earning assets reflects the change that has come about in modern commercial-banking systems. At one time, a commercial bank was thought of as a business bank. Today it is for all people, including the consumer, the stockholder, the mortgage holder, and other financial institutions. The commercial banks are really "department-store banks," since they have undertaken new endeavors to improve both their earnings and their competitive position within the industry.

The other major earning asset of the commercial banks is investment in debt securities. The business of the bank is to be liquid as well as profitable. The short-term securities in the investment account provide the degree of liquidity needed to meet demands for withdrawals from depositors, and the government securities act as a secondary reserve. Longer-term securities are purchased when the commercial bank's needs for liquidity are met.

SOURCES OF INVESTMENT FUNDS. The source of funds over which the bank management exercises control comprises primarily time and demand deposits, the sale of certificates of deposit (CDs), and the total capital retained through earnings and the sale of stock. Demand deposits are the major source of investable and loanable funds for the commercial banks; next in importance are time deposits, then certificates of deposit, borrowed funds, and finally ownership capital.

NOW accounts were introduced in 1981 and super now, or money market accounts in 1983. The growth of total deposits has come from time deposits and CDs. The increase in time deposits relative to demand deposits reflects one change our banking system has undergone in recent years. The savings function has improved in our financial system, whereas demand deposits have declined in relative importance because of the increased competition for funds. Corporate treasurers have become much more sophisticated in the handling of corporate funds; corporations that at one time retained idle funds on deposit in the commercial bank now invest instead in short-term debt securities, such as Treasury bills and the short maturities of municipal obligations, in order to improve earnings. Rising interest rates have made other outlets more attractive, savers have put their funds to work in savings type accounts, and these changes have taken their toll of demand-deposit growth.

INVESTMENT POLICY. The investment policy of commercial banks is determined both by regulation and by the nature of the banking business. The commercial banks are subject to state regulation through the state bank examiner, and/or they are regulated by the Federal Deposit Insurance Corporation (FDIC) and/or the Federal Reserve System. The regulation provides for conservative supervision of both state and national banks through bank examinations. The federal regulations allow commercial banks to own all bonds of investment quality in the top four of Moody's and Standard & Poor's ratings. Banks cannot buy common stocks or speculative bonds. Another regulation provides for diversification of loans and investments. To ensure the safety of depositors' funds and to prevent loss through poor judgment resulting from lack of diversification, a commercial bank usually cannot lend or invest more than 10 percent of its unimpaired capital and surplus in one asset.

The second important factor influencing the investment policy of the commercial bank is the nature of the banking business and the sources of funds. First, the commercial bank needs liquidity in its nonloan portfolio to protect the bank's loan position. Deposits are payable on demand, and funds to pay depositors should not come from the liquidation of commercial loans. The result would be instability in our commercial banking system. Liquidity comes usually from the investment account rather than the loan account. Funds are invested in government bonds of short maturities to provide this liquidity. Each bank must maintain legal reserves in the form of deposits with its Federal Reserve bank, with short-term investments in government securities as a secondary reserve providing funds in time of need, in addition to legal reserves.

A third determinant of investment policy of commercial banks is their limited ability to sustain loss. Banks are investing depositors' money, which leads to financial conservatism, and the reserve provided by ownership capital is small. The equity account of a bank, therefore, provides little protection for the depositors' funds. Care and conservatism must be exercised in the investment of bank funds.

The tax position of the commercial bank represents the fourth influence on its investment policy. Commercial banks are not given special consideration under the federal income tax laws; they are subject to the full impact of federal income taxes.

Bank Trust Investments

One of the services commercial banks perform is to invest funds for clients through trust investment activities. Many commercial banks have pooled-equity funds, which are much like mutual funds. In a pooled-equity fund, many small trusts are put together into one trust, and the total "pooled" fund is managed for beneficiaries. The performance of such funds is shown in Figure 2–1, which indicates that the bank-managed funds did as well as the S&P 500 Index.

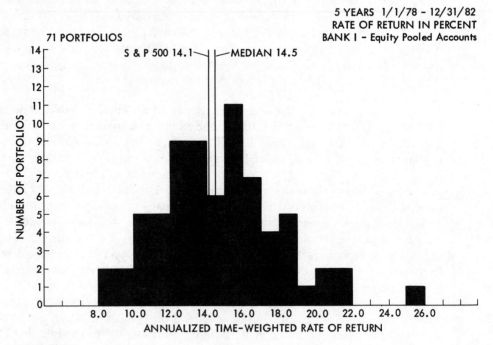

FIGURE 2–1

Distribution of Returns, Bank I—Equity Pooled Accounts

SOURCE: Frank Russell Co., Inc., Performance Charts and Statistics, Tacoma, WA. 12/31/82.

INVESTMENT OVERVIEW

The purpose of the pension fund is to provide people with income after they have retired from gainful employment. Many American businesses provide some form of retirement program to safeguard workers' financial future in their old age. The asset values of pension funds have increased dramatically in the past decade, owing to the increase in the number of pension plans and the number of workers covered by them. Most of the early pension plans were voluntarily adopted by companies to solve the problem of retirement of salaried employees on an annual contract. Today, pensions are bargained for, along with wages and working conditions, by organized labor groups. The growth of pension plans must be attributed to both union and management, and to the development of social security. The growth of old-age and survivorship benefits has stimulated the growth of private pension plans. While both systems of retirement income have grown, there have been express advantages for the government social security program, because it gives greater mobility to the worker and because it does not penalize the older worker who has no vested interest in the retirement program of the company in which he or she seeks employment or in which he or she was employed late in life.

ERISA, PENSION FUNDS, AND INDEX FUNDS. The Employee Retirement Income Security Act of 1974, ERISA, has had a substantial impact on the investment policies of pension-fund managers. ERISA requires that the fund manager be "prudent"— and if a portfolio manager, corporate administrator, or board member who guides pension investment policy is "imprudent," then he or she is liable.

The requirement of prudence applies to each security in the portfolio, not just the behavior of the portfolio. As a result, fund managers have become more cautious and conservative. Some have given up management of the funds and have gone to "insured" pension programs with insurance companies. Under such plans, the return expected is low, but the results are actually guaranteed.

In an effort to perform as well as the market, several fund managers—including Wells Fargo Bank of San Francisco, the American National Bank & Trust Co. of Chicago, and Batterymarch Financial Management Corporation in Boston—have developed index funds, which they are now selling to pension funds. Although the number of index funds is small, there seems to be a large market for them. The index followed is the S&P 500, and in recent years it has performed as well as the average pension-fund stock portfolios.

SOURCE OF PENSION FUND MONEY. Corporate or business pension programs are either contributory or noncontributory. Under the contributory plan, the employee makes a contribution to the pension fund through a paycheck deduction. Under the noncontributory plan, the entire cost of the retirement program is paid for by the employer. Either method results in an additional cost to the employer, but in the contributory plan there is a saving that goes to the employee if he or she should leave the company. Either plan results in a type of contractual saving for the benefit of the employee in the retirement years.

TYPES OF PENSION PLANS.   There are two types of private pensions plans—insured and noninsured. The insured plan is guaranteed by an insurance company; reserves are built up and invested under a program that will provide a certain income in the future for the employee, based on the amount contributed to the program and the length of time it is in force. Of the insured plans, two subtypes predominate. Deposit-administration group-annuity plans compose more than 50 percent of all insured pension plans. Under this plan, a single fund is set up for all employees in the pension group, and as an employee retires, money is withdrawn to buy an annuity. The other plan is the deferred-annuity type, in which a paid-up annuity benefit is purchased each year for each employee. Upon retirement, an employee receives income from the total annuity benefits accumulated.

The noninsured pension plan places the burden of providing retirement funds on the employer. Usually, the employer accumulates reserves for the payment of pension liabilities, in which case the fund is considered *funded*. In addition, business corporations often employ commercial banks or trust companies to manage the funds; then they are referred to as *trusteed* plans. Millions of workers in the United States are covered by noninsured private pension plans, the most important type of fund in terms of assets and people.

INVESTMENT POLICY.   The investment policy of the insured pension plan is much the same as the general investment policy of life insurance companies. The noninsured investment funds are much less rigid, and their managers have a great deal of flexibility in establishing policies. Most noninsured pension funds are not fully funded, and pension liabilities are not formally stated. Therefore, their investments can be in securities that do not assure stability of principal or income. Since they have no fixed commitment, they can accept more risk by purchasing common stock. The pension funds are long run and do not need a significant degree of liquidity. They do not need a great deal of stability of income because of the lack of a fixed contractual arrangement. The investment policy of the pension funds as a group may be summarized somewhat as follows: They assume a conservative amount of market risk, are interested in long-term appreciation as a hedge against inflation, do not need liquidity on income, are exempted from federal income taxes, and invest the majority of their money in corporate bonds and stocks.

College Endowment Funds

Colleges and universities in the United States are constantly seeking new revenue sources, public and private, to provide staff, buildings, and libraries to meet the needs of an exploding student population. For private colleges, this means active alumni fund-raising campaigns; for state-supported institutions, endless hours of discussion and reporting to state officers and state legislators to explain the need for more and more dollars of public funds. No state college, however, is supported solely by tax dollars; most states impose tuition charges on the students to meet the operating costs of the college or university. The private institution, needing operating income to raise faculty salaries, to increase research expenditures, to promote scholarly activity, and to provide scholarships for needy students, looks to endowment funds for part of its income.

SOURCE AND MANAGEMENT. Most college endowment funds come from loyal alumni and private grants, in the form of cash, proceeds from life insurance, securities, or real estate. The majority of funds are administered by the trustees of the college or university, when the trustees are knowledgeable about investment matters. One Midwestern university uses a three-man committee of the board of trustees to manage the investment fund of the university, and has appointed a three-man advisory board, all with investment experience, from the academic and administrative staff of the university to advise the trustee group. Some college endowment funds use professional investment counsel.

Most of the funds are not restricted as to how the money will be invested; some limit the investment outlets. How the money is invested is determined by the use to which the income will be put. A fund that provides annual scholarships must receive regular income to meet the conditions of the trust endowment. A fund that is to be used for future needs of the university can be invested without regard to current income, and it can be invested in growth shares to provide the greatest future benefits. The fund manager must consider restrictive covenants imposed by the donor in establishing investment objectives, and must earmark the proceeds of the investment fund. Otherwise the manager is usually unrestricted in management activities. This means that there are no restrictions on common-stock ownership or on owning real property, if it is a satisfactory and productive investment.

The fund manager must act wisely and with prudence, and should have long-range investment objectives. There is little need for liquidity and marketability. Income taxes are not a problem, since educational and charitable funds are exempt from federal income taxes.

COLLEGE ENDOWMENT FUNDS IN PRACTICE. College endowment-fund management has been somewhat conservative and defensive in character. Collectively, the funds are balanced between common stocks, fixed-income securities, and productive real estate. The advantages of a balanced fund are apparent. First, they allow a portion of the total fund to move freely with the economy and either prosper or decline. At the same time, they have a stable base of fixed-income securities that will provide a guarantee of funds for the future. The balanced fund combines the advantages of equities and fixed-income obligations.

The typical college endowment fund has almost 60 percent of its assets in common stocks; 30 percent in bonds, cash, and preferred stocks; and 10 percent in real estate. The variation among funds is substantial, however; one fund, Ohio State, has had as much as 80 percent in common stocks, and one, Toronto University, has had a similar amount in bonds, preferred, and cash. In recent years, university endowment funds have begun to focus more on return. This emphasis on "total return" is a step forward for the administration of endowment funds.

TIAA–CREF

Many college and private-school teachers invest their retirement funds in TIAA-CREF. CREF is the variable portion of the pension program called College Retirement Equities Fund. TIAA, the Teachers Insurance and Annuity Association, represents the fixed-income investment fund. In 1980, TIAA earned 9.44 percent on total invested assets, and 10.11 percent in 1981. The performance of CREF has been good; its investment results over time appear in Figure 2–2. Most investors would be happy to have done as well in a difficult period of U.S. investment history.

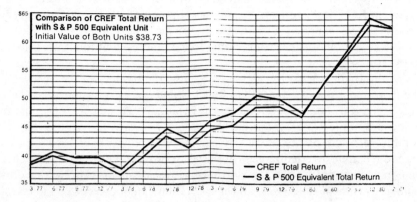

FIGURE 2–2

CREF Performance

SOURCE: TIAA-CREF Annual Report, 1981 Investment Supplement, p. 37.

TABLE 2–7

Mutual Fund Assets
(billions of dollars)

	1979	1980	Percent Change	1981	Percent Change
			Year End		
Investment objective					
Aggressive growth	$ 3.0	$ 4.7	+57.9%	$ 5.0	+6.4%
Growth	13.0	16.8	+29.3	15.2	−9.5
Growth and income	16.5	19.5	+18.6	18.2	−6.7
Balanced	3.4	3.4	—	2.8	−17.6
Income	4.5	4.8	+5.7	4.5	−6.3
Bond	5.1	5.7	+12.3	5.9	+3.5
Municipal bond	3.0	2.9	3.3	3.1	+6.9
Option-income	0.5	0.6	+19.5	0.6	—
Total	$49.0	$58.4	+19.2%	$55.3	−5.3%
Money market	$45.2	$74.4	+64.7%	$181.9	+144.5%
Short-term municipal bond	0.3	1.9	+502.5	4.2	+121.1
Total	$45.5	$76.3	+67.7%	$186.1	+143.9%
Grand total	$94.5	$134.7	+42.6%	$241.4	+79.2%

SOURCE: Mutual Fund Fact Book, Investment Company Institute, 1981 p. 7.

Mutual Funds

Because of the growth of money market funds, the growth of mutual funds has been staggering. Past growth between 1979 and 1980 was a tremendous 67.7 percent for money market funds, including tax-exempt municipal funds (see Table 2–7). Money market funds more than doubled in size before the end of 1981. Savers and investors were attracted by the daily compounding and the 17 percent return. In fact, money market funds are the dominant force in the mutual fund industry. Aside from money market funds, the dominant investment of mutual funds is in growth and income stocks.

SUMMARY

The amount of money an individual saves and eventually invests is a function of income, age, peer pressure or social emulation, and attitude toward savings, investment, and risk-taking. Aggregate savings of individuals and institutions represent sources of investment funds. Institutions that save and invest include commercial banks, mutual savings banks, savings and loan associations, life insurance companies, credit unions, pension funds, and mutual funds. Savings may be put to work in savings accounts, certificates of deposit, and U.S. savings bonds. In addition to savings, funds may be saved and invested through an annual investment plan or investment clubs. Funds may also be borrowed and invested through brokers, commercial banks, and life insurance.

As a principle, investors should diversify between real and financial assets to hedge against inflation.

The investment principles governing the management of institutional investments are the same as those applied to the management of funds for an individual. The manager must be concerned with the objectives of security of principal, income, liquidity, marketability, and tax status. In addition to the general principles, policy will be governed by legal contracts and the needs of the individuals using the services of institutional investors. Life insurance companies must be ready at any time to meet the cash value of each life insurance policy in force. The life insurance company guarantees a fixed rate of interest, and is limited in its investments by state regulation to the best-quality fixed-income investments and only a small amount of common stock, although the permissible amount of common stocks held has increased. Legal restrictions, ability to assume risk, tax position, and the insurance contract dictate investment policy for these companies.

Fire and casualty companies have flexibility in the management of their funds. They can accept more risk, since the money invested belongs to the owners of the company. They are interested in tax-exempt securities because of their high tax bracket. The insurance contract these companies issue is surrounded with uncertainty, and they attempt to improve their capital gains to meet this uncertainty.

Savings and loan companies and mutual savings banks invest primarily in real estate mortgages and only incidentally, if at all, in fixed-income obligations. Competition in the future might draw them into a wider range of investment activities.

Commercial banks are interested in liquidity and are limited by law to investment in bonds. They make longer-term loans but are governed by liquidity and security of principal in making investments. The pooled-equity fund, under bank management, offers varying rates of profitability compared to the market for trust holders.

Pension funds and college endowment funds are free to invest in a wide range of securities; they approach closely the investment function of the individual investor. College funds have the widest discretion, and many own some productive real estate as an investment. ERISA and index funds have had a substantial effect on pension fund management.

Mutual fund growth has been led by the growth in money market funds. Mutual funds invest in a wide range of equity and debt securities. MMMF growth slowed in 1983.

Institutional investors dominate the investment world. It is helpful for individual investors to learn where institutional investors invest their funds.

SUMMARY OF PRINCIPLES

1. Savings are necessary for investment.
2. Investing institutions are conservative but have varying return-to-risk problems.
3. Conservatism can be a strong force in investment success.
4. It is difficult for even professional investors to be successful.
5. Return-and-risk analysis is helpful in making investment decisions.
6. It is wise to diversify to reduce risk.
7. Institutional investors tend to dominate financial markets.

REVIEW QUESTIONS

1. In what ways do the investment objectives of institutional investors differ from those of individual investors?
2. What is the nature of business of a life insurance company? What governs its investment policies? What type of securities does it purchase? What risks can it assume?
3. What is the nature of the business of fire and casualty companies? What type of securities do they purchase? What risks can they assume? How do they differ from life insurance companies?
4. State the nature of savings and loan companies' basic investment policy. How do they meet risk?
5. Can investment take place along with saving?
6. Where would an investor borrow money to buy securities?
7. Does investment in real assets play a part in an individual investor's financial program?
8. What part do personal assets and liabilities play in the investment process?

9. What are an individual's financial prerequisites, and why are they important?

10. Discuss some of the reasons investors save at different rates. What does their attitude toward investment and saving have to do with it?

11. When does saving stop and investment begin?

12. Should investors borrow to buy investment securities? Where would they borrow?

13. Do all investors accept the same return from investment? Do they accept the same risk?

14. Discuss how an investor with modest resources can accumulate a fund to invest.

15. Do financial institutions follow different investment principles than individuals?

PROBLEMS

1. Analyze the changes in life insurance company investments from 1968 to 1983. Where had the major changes taken place? Were their investments more risky (see Table 2–3)?

2. Based on data in Table 2–4, had savings and loans become more risky?

3. Explain the major changes in commercial bank assets and liabilities from 1972 to 1983. Were the banks more or less liquid (see Table 2–6)?

4. Based on the data in Table 2–7, was the mutual fund industry more or less risky in 1981 compared to 1979 and 1980? Why?

CASES

1. Jimmy and Derrick, recent college graduates, have obtained their first jobs. They would like to accumulate money for investment but think they "can't save a cent!" Based on what you have learned in Chapters 1 and 2, suggest how they might achieve their objectives of saving and investment. How would you handle the problem of "I can't save a cent"?

2. Commercial banks, savings and loan associations, life insurance companies, and and private pension funds invest to meet different objectives. Their decisions result in different returns being earned and a different degree of risk being accepted. Based on the discussion in this chapter and Chapter 1, discuss the implied return and risk position of these institutional investors. Which one has the highest perceived expected return and risk and the lowest? Rank each on the basis of return and risk. What are the implications of the analysis?

SELECTED READINGS

BLACK, FISCHER, "The Investment Policy Spectrum: Individuals, Endowment Funds and Pension Funds." *Financial Analysts Journal*, February 1976.

———. "The Long-Run Pension Policy." *Financial Analysts Journal*, May 1980.

CALDERFIELD, STANFORD. "The Truth about Index Funds." *Financial Analysts Journal*, July 1977.

COTTLE, SIDNEY. "The Future of Pension Management." *Financial Analysts Journal*, March 1977.

ELLIS, CHARLES D. "Pension Funds Need Management." *Financial Analysts Journal*, May 1979.

HOFFLAUD, DAVID L. "A Model Bank Investment Policy." *Financial Analysts Journal*, May 1978.

KAHN, IRVING. "Lotteries Always Lose." *Financial Analysts Journal*, March 1977.

CHAPTER 3

GOVERNMENT SECURITIES
An Analysis of Federal, State, and Local and Foreign Securities

No one type of security can provide a solution to every investment problem. If high and stable income is sought, capital growth is given up. If greater current income or greater capital appreciation is sought, a greater risk is accepted. The final selection will be a delicate balance between risk and return.

For example, an investor might consider purchasing shares of an electronics company with a high growth rate that offers the hope of financial return. But the investor might not wish to accept the risks associated with a stock that is priced high in relation to current earnings. Other alternatives must be considered. This is done to minimize risk and maximize return and net worth. To do this, the investor must be familiar with all types of investments.

The safest and most riskless securities will be discussed in this chapter, beginning with long- and short-term debt securities of the U.S. government and agencies. Then securities issued by state and municipal governments and foreign debt securities will be discussed. The relative investment merits of these securities and where they fit investors' preferences will be presented.

The investment principles to be followed determine the order of the discussion. As a principle, short-term securities are less risky than long-term securities. Short-term government securities are less risky than short-term commercial paper. Another principle is that U.S. government securities are less risky than U.S. agency bonds and municipal bonds. Foreign securities, generally, would be ranked below U.S. securities from the viewpoint of the U.S. investor.

The need for money for an ever-growing federal government has provided institutional investors with an ample supply of quality securities in which to invest funds. The magnitude of the U.S. federal debt is shown in Table 3–1. Federal debt has kept pace with expanding government activities. Historically, debt has surged forward because of war expenditures and, in more recent years, because of defense efforts. In Table 3–1, we see the magnitude of debt because of record federal spending. In spite of the growth in debt, the credit position of our government is strong. The United States has never defaulted or repudiated a bond issue.

The ownership of U.S. debt is concentrated in the hands of institutional investors. Private persons do not own a very large portion of marketable U.S. government securities. Commercial bank ownership is concentrated in short-term securities. U.S. securities play an extremely important part in our financial system. Most of our financial institutions depend on government securities for investment outlets; a few invest *only* in government securities. Some individuals purchase short-term marketable government securities to meet specific and temporary portfolio needs. Short-term Treasury bills are a haven for investors who want to keep their money working for them until favorable long-term investments are available among common stocks.

Government securities are classified into several groups. The two main groups are marketable and nonmarketable securities. Marketable securities, which include Treasury bills, Treasury notes, and Treasury bonds, represent the largest portion of federal debt. Among nonmarketable issues, also a large portion of the public debt, the most important security is U.S. savings bonds. Treasury tax notes and savings notes are also included in this group. Another category of bonds closely related to the direct obligations of the government are the debt issues of government corporations and agencies, which are not direct obligations of the United States. The specific securities included in this category are issues of the Federal Land Bank, Federal Home Loan Bank, Federal Intermediate Credit Bank, Bank For Co-ops, Federal National Mortgage Association, World Bank, Inter-American Development Bank, and the Postal Service.

The marketable securities issued by the federal government are divided into short-term, intermediate-term, and long-term issues. Each has certain advantages and disadvantages for the individual investor. The demarcation between time classes is arbitrary. The majority of government securities in the short-term group have maturity dates of less than one year (Treasury bills); intermediate-term securities, of from three to five years (Treasury notes); and long-term (Treasury bonds), of greater than five years. Prices for direct government obligations and agency bonds are quoted daily in *The Wall Street Journal*. Let us take a closer look at each of the marketable securities of the federal government and its agencies, to learn how they can be used.

Treasury Bills

Treasury bills are short-term securities sold by the Treasury of the United States as a direct obligation. They have a maturity range of from 91 days to one year, are sold at a discount, and are redeemed at par at maturity. The bills are issued in bearer form

TABLE 3–1

Gross Public Debt of U.S. Treasury (billions of dollars, end of period)

Type and Holder	1977	1978	1979	1980	1981	1982 Aug.	Sept.	Oct.	Nov.	Dec.
Total gross public debt	$718.9	$789.2	$845.1	$930.2	$1,028.7	$1,109.2	$1,142.0	$1,142.8	$1,161.7	$1,197.1
By type										
Interest-bearing debt	715.2	782.4	844.0	928.9	1,027.3	1,108.1	1,140.9	1,136.8	1,160.5	1,195.5
Marketable	459.9	487.5	530.7	623.2	720.3	801.4	824.4	824.7	852.5	881.5
Bills	161.1	161.7	172.6	216.1	245.0	273.1	277.9	283.9	293.5	311.8
Notes	251.8	265.8	283.4	321.6	375.3	457.4	442.9	438.1	454.2	465.0
Bonds	47.0	60.0	74.7	85.4	99.9	100.9	103.6	102.7	104.7	104.6
Nonmarketable[a]	255.3	294.8	313.2	305.7	307.0	306.7	316.5	312.2	308.0	314.0
Convertible bonds[b]	2.2	2.2	2.2							
State and local government series	13.9	24.3	24.6	23.8	23.0	23.5	23.6	23.8	25.0	25.7
Foreign issues[c]	22.2	29.6	28.8	24.0	19.0	15.6	14.6	14.6	14.9	14.7
Government	21.0	28.0	23.6	17.6	14.9	12.5	12.2	12.2	12.5	13.0
Public	1.2	1.6	5.3	6.4	4.1	3.1	2.4	2.4	2.4	1.7
Savings bonds and notes	77.0	80.9	79.9	72.5	68.1	67.4	67.5	67.8	68.1	68.0
Government account series[d]	139.8	157.5	177.5	185.1	196.7	119.9	210.5	205.7	199.9	205.4
Noninterest-bearing debt	3.7	6.8	1.2	1.3	1.4	1.1	1.2	6.0	1.2	1.6

[a] Includes (not shown separately) : Securities issued to the Rural Electrification Administration, depository bonds, retirement plan bonds, and individual retirement bonds.

[b] These nonmarketable bonds, also known as Investment Series B Bonds, may be exchanged (or converted) at the owner's option for 1½ percent, 5-year marketable Treasury notes. Convertible bonds that have been so exchanged are removed from this category and recorded in the notes category (line 5).

[c] Nonmarketable dollar-denominated and foreign currency-denominated series held by foreigners.

[d] Held almost entirely by U.S. government agencies and trust funds.

TABLE 3–1 (Continued)

Type and Holder	1977	1978	1979	1980	1981	1982 Aug.	1982 Sept.
By holder[e]							
U.S. government agencies and trust funds	154.8	170.0	187.1	192.5	203.3	205.8	216.4
Federal Reserve banks	102.8	109.6	117.5	121.3	131.0	132.9	134.4
Private investors	461.3	508.6	540.5	616.4	694.5	n.a. ← →	n.a. ← →
Commercial banks	101.4	93.2	96.4	116.0	109.4		
Mutual savings banks	5.9	5.0	4.7	5.4	5.2		
Insurance companies	15.1	15.7	16.7	20.1	19.1		
Other companies	20.5	19.6	22.9	25.7	37.8		
State and local governments	55.2	64.4	69.9	78.8	85.6		
Individuals							
Savings bonds	76.7	80.7	79.9	72.5	68.0		
Other securities	28.6	30.3	36.2	56.7	75.6		
Foreign and international[f]	109.6	137.8	124.4	127.7	141.4		
Other miscellaneous investors[g]	49.7	58.9	90.1	106.9	152.3		

[e] Data for Federal Reserve Banks and U.S. government agencies and trust funds are actual holdings; data for other groups are Treasury estimates.

[f] Consists of investments of foreign balances and international accounts in the United States.

[g] Includes savings and loan associations, nonprofit institutions, corporate pension trust funds, dealers and brokers, certain government deposit accounts, and government-sponsored agencies.

Note. Gross public debt excludes guaranteed agency securities. Data by type of security from *Monthly Statement of the Public Debt of the United States* (U.S. Treasury Department); data by holder from *Treasury Bulletin.*

SOURCE: *Federal Reserve Bulletin*, November 1981, p. A32, and December 1982, p. A33.

in denominations ranging from a minimum of $10,000 to $1,000,000, in $5,000 increments. Individuals may purchase the bonds directly from the Treasury. The Treasury advertises the bills by public notice and invites tenders for a stated amount of bills under competitive bidding. Dealers in government securities, commercial banks, and other financial institutions are the usual bidders. An individual may also buy Treasury bills from a commercial bank or arrange the purchase through a brokerage firm.

The yields on Treasury bills in recent years have been higher than on the longer-maturity Treasury bonds. The primary reason for this unusual phenomenon was a financing policy followed by the Treasury with regard to short-term obligations. The resulting demand for short-term funds increased the interest rate on the short-term bills. In 1966–69, short-term rates were high to prevent inflation and stop the outflow of gold. William McChesney Martin, Jr., then chairman of the Board of Governors of the Federal Reserve System, announced that the discount rate was raised because of inflationary conditions in the economy brought about by the government's fiscal programs stemming from the Vietnam war. Arthur F. Burns faced the same problem in 1974. Burns, chairman of the Federal Reserve Board, was faced with an economy suffering from galloping inflation. Paul Volcker faced the same problem in 1982. As a result, the Fed was forced to follow a tight-money policy. Interest rates on short-term securities reached historical highs and then declined sharply in 1983. These are charted in Figure 3–1 and Table 3–2.

Treasury Notes

Treasury notes are really term loans made by the Treasury and are typically issued for from three to five years, although they can have maturities of from one to five years. Once the securities are issued, they can be bought and sold freely in the money market. They assume the pattern of yields of other marketable securities having the same maturities. The yield pattern is shown in Figure 3–1 and Table 3–2. Treasury notes have become, in recent years, an important source of funds for the U.S. Treasury. They give both the Treasury and the investor flexibility in their financial requirements. These bonds are short enough in maturity to offer some freedom from changes in money rates and yet, with a high variability of yield in recent years, are long enough to afford somewhat higher yields to the investor than are offered by Treasury bills or certificates. They have historically offered higher yields than long-term government bonds. But they have had higher variability of yields and must therefore be considered more risky than other government securities.

The Money Market Instruments

Treasury bills and notes are short- and intermediate-term investments that are a part of the money market. Other money-market instruments include federal funds, which are loans between commercial banks, Canadian and United Kingdom Treasury bills, 90-day Eurodollars, 91-day banker's acceptances, negotiable certificates of deposit, commercial paper of large business corporations, and other short-term securities issued by private, quasi-public, and federal corporations. These securities are a haven for short-term or temporary money. They are used by investors when substantial

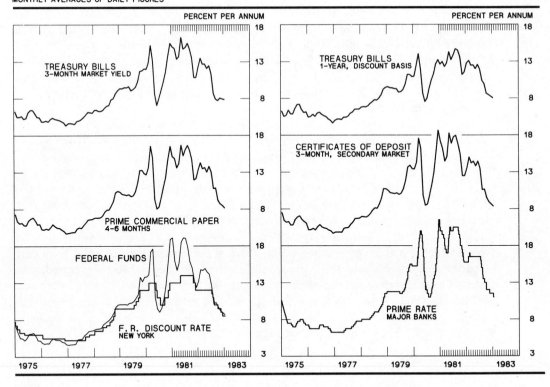

FIGURE 3–1

Short-Term Interest Rates

SOURCE: Federal Reserve Chart Book, February 1983, p. 72.

uncertainty surrounds the stock market or when short-term yields are extremely high. In part, they are competitive with savings accounts.

Investing in fixed-income securities requires a careful analysis of the money and capital markets. Money markets are influenced by the supply and demand for funds and by monetary policy as reflected in the actions of the Federal Reserve Board. Careful analysis includes the direction of the movement in the prime rate, which is directly influenced by the "fed funds" rate, the commercial-paper rate, and the rate on Treasury bills. The yields on these securities are a function of the growth of the money supply. If the rate of growth is above the Federal Reserve target growth rate, the Federal Reserve Board will tighten the money supply, and interest rates will go up. If money-supply growth is less than the Fed target, interest rates will be stable. The effect of rising money-market rates acts to depress stock and bond prices. Easy money and low interest rates tend to raise stock and bond prices.

An analysis of the money market is necessary. If an analysis of the money market indicates that interest rates are rising, then the investor would invest in short-term securities. If rates are expected to decline, the investor would tend to invest in the long-term or intermediate-term market.

The analysis of money-market yields includes a complete analysis of the current

THE INVESTMENT ALTERNATIVES

TABLE 3–2

Yields on Selected Money-Market Instruments, Short-, Intermediate-, and
Long-Term Federal Government Securities, and Long-Term Municipal Bonds
(annual average yield in percentages)

Year	Prime Commercial Paper (6 mo)	Finance Company Paper Placed Directly (6 mo)	Prime Bankers Acceptances (90 days)	*Federal Funds Rate*
1970	7.72%	7.23%	7.31%	7.17%
1971	5.11	4.91	4.85	4.66
1972	4.69	4.52	4.47	4.44
1973	8.15	7.40	8.08	8.74
1974	9.87	8.62	9.92	10.51
1975	6.33	6.16	6.30	5.82
1976	5.35	5.22	5.19	5.05
1977	5.60	5.49	5.59	5.54
1978	7.99	7.78	8.11	7.93
1979	10.91	10.25	11.04	11.19
1980	12.29	11.28	12.78	13.36
1981	14.76	13.73	15.32	16.38
1982	11.89	11.20	11.89	12.26
1983, Jan.	8.15	7.97	8.19	8.68
Mean*	9.31	8.77	9.43	9.67
Standard deviation*	2.85	2.66	3.17	3.54

*Calculated from years 1974 through 1983.

SOURCE: Federal Reserve Bulletin, August 1975, p. A26; December 1975, p. A25; May 1976,
p. A27; December 1977, p. A27; December 1978, p. A27; November 1981, p. A27; February
1983, p. A28.

U.S. Government Securities, Short Term					Government Bonds, Long Term			
3 Mo Bills		*6 Mo Bills*		*1 Year Bills*	*United States*		*State and Local*	
New	*Market*	*New*	*Market*		*5-Year*	*Long-Term*	*Aaa*	*Baa*
6.46%	6.39%	6.56%	6.55%	6.53%		6.59%	6.12%	6.73%
4.35	4.33	4.51	4.52	4.67		5.74	5.22	5.89
4.07	4.07	4.40	4.49	4.77		5.63	5.04	5.60
7.04	7.03	7.10	7.20	7.01		6.30	4.99	5.49
7.80	7.84	7.90	7.95	7.71		6.99	5.89	6.53
5.80	5.80	6.12	6.11	6.30	7.77%	6.98	6.42	7.62
4.90	4.98	5.20	5.26	5.52	7.18	6.78	5.66	7.49
5.20	5.27	5.51	5.53	5.71	6.99	7.06	5.20	6.12
7.22	7.19	7.57	7.58	7.74	8.32	7.89	5.52	6.27
10.04	10.07	10.00	10.06	9.75	9.52	8.74	5.92	6.73
11.50	11.43	11.37	11.37	10.89	11.48	10.81	7.85	9.01
14.08	14.03	13.81	13.80	13.14	14.24	12.87	10.43	11.76
10.69	10.61	11.08	11.07	11.07	13.01	12.23	10.88	12.48
7.81	7.86	7.90	7.93	8.01	10.03	10.37	9.00	10.98
8.50	8.51	8.65	8.67	8.58	9.84	9.07	7.28	8.50
2.85	2.81	2.69	2.68	2.41	2.6	2.2	2.01	2.29

supply and demand for short-term money, as well as the anticipated direction of interest rates. An analysis would be made of the supply and demand conditions in the entire money and capital markets and of U.S. fiscal policy. In addition, the international monetary condition must be examined. Yields on short-term securities abroad do have an effect on yields in the U.S. market. Such an analysis must be made to maximize yield and minimize risk on short-term investments in money-market instruments.

Repurchase Agreements

A repurchase agreement is usually a sale of a U.S. Treasury security with an agreement that the seller will buy back the security at a set price within a specified time period. The security acts as collateral. It is possible to use any money market instrument. The transaction is quite common in institutional investment, and the investment period is for one or a few days. In more recent years, the investment period has been extended to one to three months or longer. The smallest denomination is $1 million, the rate of interest is based on a 360-day year, and the transactions are settled in federal funds.

The unique character of repurchase agreements allows the investor to tailor the time period to meet investment needs at a known and certain rate of interest. They provide the seller with funds and the buyer with a liquid investment. A commercial bank may buy temporarily idle funds from a customer by selling Treasury securities on a repo basis, or a commercial bank can sell immediately available federal funds to a government securities dealer to keep funds invested. The bank earns the *full* money-market rate of interest. Repos are used by nonfinancial business corporations that have idle funds to invest. They are also used by the Federal Reserve banks in adjusting the reserve positions of commercial banks for periods usually no longer than 15 days. The rate of interest paid or earned is negotiated between buyer and seller, but is usually competitive with money-market rates.

Commercial Paper for Large Investors

For large investors, commercial paper is a competitive alternative to short-term Treasury bills. Commercial paper usually sells on a higher yield basis than Treasury bills, and for a shorter period of time. General Motors Acceptance Corporation (GMAC) and Ford Motor Corporation (FMC) commercial paper has an average maturity of 25 to 30 days. The typical commercial-paper denomination is $100,000 plus $1,000 increments. Some dealers will sell $25,000 if the maturity is at least 30 days. Commercial paper is not for the small investor, but for large investors it is sometimes a safe haven for funds.

Money-Rate Risk

Short-term government securities are not subject to the risk of loss because of changes in money rates, owing to their short maturities. However, if an investor continually invested and reinvested in Treasury bills, the risk of changes in the money rate would be solved, but the purchasing-power risk would be assumed. Investment in short-term government securities is no way to provide against the loss of purchasing power brought about by inflation, unless interest rates are extremely high, as they were in 1981.

Treasury Bonds

Treasury bonds are long-term, interest-bearing debts of the United States that represent the largest portion of publicly held marketable debt. The maturities range from six months to 35 years, with the concentration in the longer maturities. Yields on long-term bonds are provided in Figure 3–2 and Table 3–2. A greater degree of variability is assumed when these long-term bonds are purchased, because of the potential loss through the fluctuation of money rates. Treasury bonds are purchased primarily by institutional investors and others who desire a long-term, fixed-income investment with a high degree of safety and stability of income. There has been a substantial yield variability in long-term bonds, accompanying the upward trend in interest rates. Investors have tended to avoid the long bond maturities because of the growing uncertainty about the direction of yields.

A commercial bank cannot invest its depositors' money in common stock, but

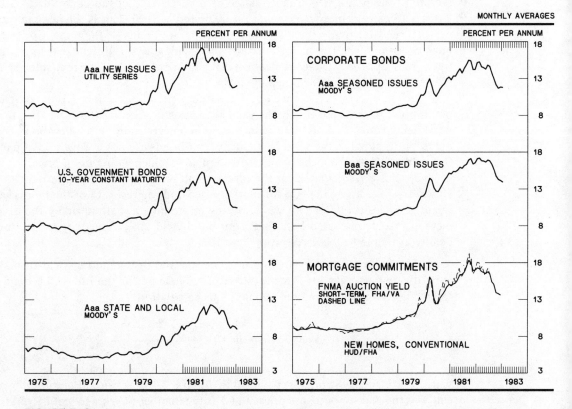

FIGURE 3–2

Long-Term Interest Rates

SOURCE: Federal Reserve Chart Book, February 1983, p. 73.

it can trade in bonds, and an astute money manager can buy low and sell high in bonds. Aggressive money managers have improved returns substantially by trading in long-term government bonds and playing the pattern of the interest-rate curve. If we buy a long-term, 15 percent bond to yield 16 percent, we are buying it at a discount. We hold it until one year before maturity when, let us assume, short-term bill rates are at 14 percent. The bond has increased in price, and we have a capital gain. By selling the bond at a profit, we can reinvest the proceeds in higher-yield long-term bonds. The results are not spectacular, but when hundreds of millions of dollars are being invested, the amount of savings and profits can be substantial.

Bonds are purchased on a yield-to-maturity basis. The equation for measuring return was introduced in the first chapter, but bond yields and prices change. Therefore, we interrupt the discussion of investment securities to discuss these changes in the calculation of bond yields.

CALCULATION OF BOND YIELDS.   If we understand how to calculate bond yields, we will understand the inverse relationship between bond prices and yields. The fulcrum around which yields vary is the interest rate, which is fixed in amount over the life of the bond. It is usually stated as a percentage of the par value of a bond. Thus, a 14 percent interest rate on a $1,000 bond is $140. This is the nominal rate, as we shall see later under the discussion of corporate bonds. If the market price of the bond drops to $900, the yield to maturity, or yield, goes up. If the market price of the bond goes up, the yield goes down. Changes in the level of current interest rates, however, provide for the change in yields.

If current interest rates move up, the market price of existing bonds or comparable bonds must go down, to equate the yield of the existing bond with the yield on the new bond being issued at a higher interest rate. The interest rate on the new bond coming out at par is equal to the yield to maturity; but bonds are not always sold at par, and the yield will vary from the coupon or nominal rate depending upon price.

The yields are calculated for the investor and reported in *The Wall Street Journal*. However, if we know the current market price and interest rate of the bond, we can calculate yield in one of two ways: by the approximate method or by the discount method. Yields may also be found from bond-yield tables, but they are not always readily available to the investor.

Approximate Method.   The approximate method of computing yield to maturity is by dividing average investment into average income for the life of the bond. The following formula can be used to make this calculation:

$$\text{Yield to maturity (YTM)} = \frac{\frac{M - P}{N} + I}{\frac{M + P}{2}}$$

where I is the periodic interest payment in dollars, M is the price at maturity or par or call, P is the issue or purchase price, and N is the number of years to maturity. Assume, for example, that we had purchased a Treasury bond in November 1981 that was to mature in November 1986. It paid interest at a rate of 13 7/8 percent. We could buy it at 93.1 or 93 1/32. (Government bonds are quoted in 32nds of a point.) What would be the yield to maturity on the bond? Substituting in the equation, we would have the following:

$$\text{Yield} = ([(1,000 - 930.3125) \div 5] + 138.75) \div [(1,000 + 930.3125) \div 2]$$
$$= (13.94 + 138.75) \div 965.16$$
$$= 152.69 \div 965.16$$
$$= .1582 = 15.82\%$$

The yield from the bond is approximately 15.82 percent, according to our calculations. This method of calculating return can be used for any type of investment, including common stock. However, for long periods of compounding, substantial error can be introduced into the results by this method.

Yield by Use of the Present-Value Table. Yield can also be approximated by use of the present-value tables, as found in Appendix Tables A–1 and A–2. Anyone who has had experience with corporate capital budgeting in business finance will recognize the applications of this technique. In using the present-value tables, we equate the present value of the future interest payments and capital repayments to the purchase price of the bond. The discount rate that equates these two amounts is the yield to maturity. The yield is found by trial and error. An example can be derived by using the figures from the approximate method demonstrated above. From A–2 we find the present value of the stream of income for 14 and 16 percent as follows:

	14%	16%	
Present value of $138.75 per year for 5 years ($138.75 × 3.43)	$475.91	$454.27	($138.75 × 3.274)
Present value of $1,000 face value due at maturity in 1986 (5 years) ($1,000 × 0.519)	$519.00	$476.00	($1,000 × 0.476)
Total present value	$994.91	$930.27	
Market price of bond	$930.3125		

The present value of the income stream at 13 7/8 percent would be $1,000. If we bought the bond at par with a 13 7/8 percent interest rate, we would enjoy a 13 7/8 percent yield to maturity. Since we paid less than par, the yield is higher. We find the present value by interpolating between the 14 and 16 percent rates, based on trial and error estimates. The present value of the income and principal at 16 percent is $930.27, which is a few pennies less than the purchase price of $930.31. The present value at the 14 percent rate is $994.91. The present-value 14 percent is too high. The difference between the purchase price and the present value at 16 percent is just a little too high, which means the yield is slightly less than 16 percent. To find the exact yield, we must interpolate between the present value at 14 and 16 percent. The dollar amount of the interval is $994.91 − $930.27 = $64.64. This $64.64 is equal to 2 percent (16 − 14). The difference in the price and the present value is $930.3125 − $930.27 = $.0425. Therefore, the 16 percent yield is too high by $.0425 ÷ $64.64, or .000657 percent.

This, multiplied by the 2 percent interval, gives us .0013 percent. This .0013 subtracted from 16 percent gives us the exact yield, which is $16.00 - .0013 = 15.9987$ percent. For all intent, the yield is 16 percent.

The basic equation represented by the bond tables is as follows:

$$P_0 = \sum_{t=1}^{n} \frac{I_t}{(1 + r_d)^t} + \frac{P_n}{(1 + r_d)^n}$$

where I is the interest per period; r_d is the yield to maturity, or holding period, or discount rate; P is the maturity value or par; P_0 is the market price; and n represents the expected number of years the bond will be outstanding. The discount table or formula gives a more accurate yield than the approximate method.

Bonds of Government Corporations and Agencies

The bonds sold by government corporations and agencies offer investment outlets for funds of individuals and of institutions. This debt is long-term, and the wide range of maturities offered would fit the portfolio requirements of most investors. These bonds are not guaranteed by the U.S. government.

We are all familiar with some of the government corporations that have been established to help certain groups in our society or to provide for assistance in our world responsibilities. Some major agencies are discussed in the following sections. A list of these bonds and the amounts issued appears in Table 3–3.

There are also a substantial number of special issues, including Washington Metropolitan Transit Authority bonds (Wash Mets). A bond trader at a bank or brokerage firm can supply details about these special issues.

FEDERAL LAND BANK OBLIGATIONS.   The Federal Land Bank system was established by the Federal Farm Loan Act of 1916. Twelve banks were established to make long-term capital loans to farmers in the form of mortgages. These loans were to be made available through the joint efforts of the government and individuals, through National Farm Loan Associations. Money was raised in the form of debt securities from private investors. Hence, Federal Land Bank bonds offer the investor an outlet for loanable funds at rates consistent with other federal obligations. Long-term financing through the Federal Land Banks provided a great deal of help to the American farmer during the 1930s and later.

FEDERAL INTERMEDIATE CREDIT BANK SECURITIES.   Federal Intermediate Credit Banks were established in 1923 in order to give further aid to farmers by providing a source of intermediate credit loans. The loans were made not directly to the individuals, but through twelve intermediate banks much like the Federal Land Banks. The banks were authorized to discount the notes given by farmers to local production credit associations and other agricultural credit associations. The money for purchasing the notes is obtained by selling bonds to the public.

BANKS FOR COOPERATIVES.   Twelve district banks were established in 1933 under the provisions of the Farm Credit Act to aid farmers' cooperatives. Cooperatives have existed for almost 150 years, helping farmers to achieve purchasing and marketing economies. The Banks for Cooperatives make commodity loans, operating-capital loans, and facility loans. The banks may issue debentures to finance their needs, and this is where individuals and institutions supply capital.

FEDERAL HOME LOAN BANKS.   The Federal Home Loan Banks were established in 1932 to assure a steady flow of savings into banking institutions organized to provide mortgage funds. The system was patterned after the Federal Reserve banking system. The banks lend money to member institutions accepting mortgages as collateral; to obtain capital for their operations, they borrow money from investors.

FEDERAL NATIONAL MORTGAGE ASSOCIATION BONDS.   The Federal National Mortgage Association (FNMA) was created in 1938 to provide a secondary mortgage market that would stimulate construction and create a market for government-insured FHA mortgages. It became a separate stock corporation in 1970. In addition to providing a market for mortgages, the association makes mortgage loans on large-scale rental projects. The funds for these activities come from the sale of notes and debentures to investors. These securities are referred to in the trade as Fannie Maes. The maturities range from short-term to long-term, and yield rates are comparable to Federal Land Bank bonds and short- and long-term Treasury bonds. The association has been successful in meeting its objectives and provides a secure investment for investors.

WORLD BANK BONDS.   The World Bank (International Bank for Reconstruction and Development) was established through the Bretton Woods Agreement of 1944. The basic purpose of the bank is to make or guarantee, in whole or in part, loans that will be used for the reconstruction or development of countries. All members of the bank must be members of the International Monetary Fund, and they contribute capital to the bank in varying amounts. The United States has contributed over $6.35 billion. The World Bank lends money and may also borrow money for the purpose of helping countries that are trying to develop their resources. The yields on World Bank bonds are somewhat higher than on other agencies' securities. World Bank bonds are not issued by a federal agency, and the higher yield reflects the greater risks in the securities compared to those of federal agency bonds discussed above.

INTER-AMERICAN DEVELOPMENT BANK.   The Inter-American Development Bank is an international institution of 23 American governments. It issues bonds to raise funds for loans to aid the economic and social development of its member countries. The United States has subscribed to $300 million of the bank's capital, with $1,697 million subject to call.

U.S. POSTAL SERVICE.   The U.S. Postal Service is an independent business of the executive branch of government; it succeeded to the business of the Post Office Department on July 1, 1971. The Postal Service is authorized to borrow funds to carry out its objectives, but the account may not exceed $10 billion. The bonds are guaranteed by the U.S. government.

TABLE 3-3

Federal and Federally Sponsored Credit Agencies, Debt Outstanding (millions of dollars, end of period)

Agency	1978	1979	1980	1982						
				Mar.	Apr.	May	June	July	Aug.	Sept.
Federal and federally sponsored agencies[a]	$137,063	$163,290	$193,229	$228,749	$232,274	$234,593	$238,787	$242,565	n.a.	n.a.
Federal agencies	23,488	24,715	28,606	31,408	31,613	31,551	32,274	32,302	32,280	32,606
Defense Department[b]	968	738	610	454	447	434	419	408	399	388
Export-Import Bank[c,d]	8,711	9,191	11,250	13,421	13,475	13,416	13,939	13,938	13,918	14,042
Federal Housing Administration[e]	588	537	477	382	376	363	358	353	345	335
Government National Mortgage Association participation certificates[f]	3,141	2,979	2,817	2,165	2,165	2,165	2,165	2,165	2,165	2,165
Postal Service[g]	2,364	1,837	1,770	1,538	1,538	1,471	1,471	1,471	1,471	1,471
Tennessee Valley Authority	7,460	8,997	11,190	13,250	13,410	13,500	13,715	13,760	13,775	14,010
United States Railway Association[g]	356	436	492	198	202	202	207	207	207	195
Federally sponsored agencies[a]	113,575	138,575	164,623	197,341	200,661	203,042	206,513	210,263	n.a.	n.a.
Federal Home Loan Banks	27,563	33,330	41,258	58,839	59,937	60,772	61,883	62,058	n.a.	n.a.
Federal Home Loan Mortgage Corporation	2,262	2,771	2,536	2,500	2,500	2,500	3,099	3,099	n.a.	n.a.
Federal National Mortgage Association	41,080	48,486	55,185	59,270	60,478	61,996	62,660	65,563	65,733	68,130
Federal Land Banks	20,360	16,006	12,365	8,717	8,217	8,217	8,217	8,217	7,652	7,652
Federal Intermediate Credit Banks	11,465	2,676	1,821	1,388	926	926	926	926	926	926
Banks for Cooperatives	4,843	584	584	220	220	220	220	220	220	220
Farm Credit Banks[a]	5,081	33,216	48,153	61,405	63,381	63,409	64,506	65,178	65,657	65,553
Student Loan Marketing Association[h]	915	1,505	2,720	5,000	5,000	5,000	5,000	5,000	5,000	5,000
Other	2	1	1	2	2	2	2	2	2	2
Federal Financing Bank debt[a,i]	51,298	67,383	87,460	113,567	114,961	117,475	120,241	121,261	122,623	124,357

TABLE 3–3 (Continued)

Agency	1978	1979	1980	1982						
				Mar.	Apr.	May	June	July	Aug.	Sept.
Lending to Federal and Federally Sponsored Agencies										
Export-Import Bank[d]	6,898	8,353	10,654	13,305	13,305	13,305	13,829	13,829	13,823	13,954
Postal Service[g]	2,114	1,587	1,520	1,288	1,288	1,221	1,221	1,221	1,221	1,221
Student Loan Marketing Association[h]	915	1,505	2,720	5,000	5,000	5,000	5,000	5,000	5,000	5,000
Tennessee Valley Authority	5,635	7,272	9,465	11,525	11,685	11,775	11,990	12,035	12,050	12,285
United States Railway Association[g]	356	436	492	198	202	202	207	207	207	195
Other Lending[j]										
Farmers Home Administration	23,825	32,050	39,431	48,681	49,356	51,056	52,346	52,711	53,311	53,736
Rural Electrification Administration	4,604	6,484	9,196	14,452	14,716	15,046	15,454	15,688	15,916	16,282
Other	6,951	9,696	13,982	19,118	19,409	19,870	20,194	20,570	21,095	21,684

[a] In September 1977 the Farm Credit Banks issued their first consolidated bonds, and in January 1979 they began issuing these bonds on a regular basis to replace the financing activities of the Federal Land Banks, the Federal Intermediate Credit Banks, and the Banks for Cooperatives. Line 17 represents those consolidated bonds outstanding, as well as any discount notes that have been issued. Lines 1 and 10 reflect the addition of this item.

[b] Consists of mortgages assumed by the Defense Department between 1957 and 1963 under family housing and homeowners assistance programs.

[c] Includes participation certificates reclassified as debt beginning Oct. 1, 1976.

[d] Off-budget Aug. 17, 1974, through Sept. 30, 1976; on-budget thereafter.

[e] Consists of debentures issued in payment of Federal Housing Administration insurance claims. Once issued, these securities may be sold privately on the securities market.

[f] Certificates of participation issued prior to fiscal 1969 by the Government National Mortgage Association acting as trustee for the Farmers Home Administration; Department of Health, Education, and Welfare; Department of Housing and Urban Development; Small Business Administration; and the Veterans Administration.

[g] Off-budget.

[h] Unlike other federally sponsored agencies, the Student Loan Marketing Association may borrow from the Federal Financing Bank (FFB) since its obligations are guaranteed by the Department of Health, Education, and Welfare.

[i] The FFB, which began operations in 1974, is authorized to purchase or sell obligations issued, sold, or guaranteed by other federal agencies. Since FFB incurs debt solely for the purpose of lending to other agencies, its debt is not included in the main portion of the table to avoid double counting.

[j] Includes FFB purchases of agency assets and guaranteed loans; the latter contain loans guaranteed by numerous agencies with the guarantees of any particular agency being generally small. The Farmers Home Administration item consists exclusively of agency assets, while the Rural Electrification Administration entry contains both agency assets and guaranteed loans.

SOURCE: Federal Reserve Bulletin, February 1983, p. A35.

GOVERNMENT NATIONAL MORTGAGE ASSOCIATION. The Government National Mortgage Association (Ginnie Mae) is a wholly owned government corporation within the Department of Housing and Urban Development and was established to take over the special-assistance, management, and liquidating functions of the FNMA.

Advantages and Disadvantages of U.S. Government Securities

The advantages of U.S. government securities as an investment are apparent. In spite of a large and increasing debt, our government enjoys an excellent credit position with domestic and foreign lenders. Most bond-rating agencies give government bonds the highest rating. So the first advantage of government securities is their obvious quality and the security they afford the investor. A second advantage is the stability of income they provide, particularly the long-term government securities. A third is their great degree of marketability. There is a broad and ready market for government securities, particularly among institutional investors. They can be sold quickly and easily in the bond market when funds are needed immediately. And government bonds eliminate the market risk and the business risk because of their security of principal and stability of income. A fourth advantage is their ability to meet the investment needs of financial institutions and institutional investors. A sophisticated financial manager can improve yields substantially by trading and by playing the pattern of rates when possible. Government securities may be used to pay estate taxes. "Flower bonds," as they are called, are credited against federal estate taxes at face value even when purchased at a much lower market price. And long-term government bonds are not callable, which is an advantage if the investor wishes to lock in high long-term yields.

There are, however, several disadvantages with investment in government securities. Unless the investor buys government bonds that are selling below par, there is no capital gain without trading in the securities. Government securities are debt instruments; the government simply guarantees to repay principal at maturity. The income is stable and secure but offers no chance for increases in the future, as the interest rate is established by contract and will not be changed over the life of the bond.

The fixed income and fixed principal lead to two major disadvantages of government bonds: (1) their inability to guard against the risks of inflation, and (2) their variability of yield and susceptibility to changes in money rate. Bonds do not provide a hedge against inflation, because income and maturity values are fixed; if the purchasing power of the dollar declines, so does the purchasing power of the bond, and there is no way to compensate for this loss. Then, if yields in the market should increase, as they have in recent years, the price of the bond existing in the marketplace will decline, and the investor will lose if the bond must be sold. Even if bonds are held to maturity, the investor will lose the difference between the low rate of interest on the existing bond and the rates on the new bonds. This risk of loss is brought about because of changes in money rates. If a person can invest in the bonds at a high rate of interest, this risk of loss is minimized. In this situation, if yields decline the price of the bond will go up and the investor will gain, owing to the inverse relationship between bond prices and bond yields. This happened in 1983.

FINANCIAL FUTURES

A financial future is a contract to buy or sell an underlying fixed-income security or financial insurance sometime in the future. Ordinarily investors buy securities in the "cash" market and are said to take a long position. Investors usually buy commercial paper, Treasury notes or bonds, and the federal agency securities listed in Table 3–4. The price of the futures contract is directly related or linked to the cash price in the case of commercial paper and other financial securities.

Financial futures began with trading in Government National Mortgage Association bonds (Ginnie Maes) in 1977. In 1981, they accounted for more than 22 percent of the combined financial, agricultural, and metals futures. The price of a financial future is found in *The Wall Street Journal* under Future Prices. The Ginnie Mae issue is listed under GNMA 8% (CBT) in Figure 3–3, along with Treasury bonds, bills, and bank CD financial futures.

There are four option periods: March, June, September, and December. After each period the opening price, high price, low price, and settlement price for the 8% GNMAs traded on the Chicago Board of Trade Exchange appears. The price is quoted in points and 32nds of 100 percent, and the trading unit is $100,000. Thus, the December 1982 settlement price was 58 and 22/32nds of $100,000, or 58.6875 times $100,000, which equals $58,687.50. The yield on this issue is 16.026 percent on the settlement price. Twelve days before, February 5, 1982, the same issue traded at 58 and 7/32 to yield 16.163 percent. The price was $58,218.75. If this future contract had been purchased, the speculator would have earned $468.75. That doesn't seem like much of a gain, but a future contract can be purchased on margin with as little as $2,000. A speculator could buy a future contract with $2,000, hold it for a short period of time, and earn an excellent return before commission. Of course, an investor could have purchased the 8% GNMA issue in the cash market at an ask price of 61.12, to yield 15.17 percent. On February 17, 1982, the ask price was 61.16, to yield 15.24.

The Participants—Buyer/Seller, Broker, and Exchange

Each financial future contract involves a buyer or seller, a broker, and a futures exchange. A buyer of a future contract, the person required to take delivery of the security or commercial paper, has a "long" position. The seller, the person required to deliver the security or commercial paper, has a "short" position. A person who buys a financial futures contract is guaranteeing a known yield at some time in the future. In such a situation, the buyer is trying to buy a higher yield in the future and is fearful that interest rates will fall. A seller takes the opposite position, is committed to deliver the financial instrument, and is said to have a "short" position.

A customer (buyer or seller) purchases or sells a contract through a broker, who as a member of a clearinghouse or an exchange will take the order to the exchange floor and buy or sell a contract sold by another broker. All such financial futures transactions are carried on the books of a clearinghouse member. Purchases and sales are conducted in an auction market with an equal amount of long and short contracts

TABLE 3–4
Cash Market Securities

	30-day Commercial Paper	90-day Commercial Paper	4- to 6-year Treasury Notes	CDR GNMA	Certificate Delivery GNMA	Long-term Treasury Bonds
Basic trading unit	Commercial paper $3,000,000 face value	Commercial paper $1,000,000 face value	U.S. Treasury notes and noncallable bonds $100,000 principal balance with a coupon rate of 8%	$100,000 principal balance of GNMA 8% coupon or equivalent balance	GNMA certificates $100,000 principal balance	U.S. Treasury bonds with $100,000 face value
Delivery method	Financial receipt backed by commercial paper in an approved vault	Financial receipt backed by commercial paper in an approved vault	Federal Reserve book entry wire-transfer system. Invoice is adjusted for coupon rates and maturity	GNMA collateralized depositary receipt (CDR)	Actual GNMA certificate; only one day per month, usually the 16th	Federal Reserve book entry wire-transfer system. Invoice is adjusted for coupon rates and maturity or call dates
Price quotation	Index: 100 minus annualized discount, e.g., 100 − 6.54 = 93.46	Index: 100 minus annualized discount, e.g., 100 − 6.54 = 93.46	Percentage of par, e.g., 94-10 or 94 10/32	Percentage of par, e.g., 94-01 or 94 1/32	Percentage of par, e.g., 94-01 or 94 1/32	Percentage of par, e.g., 94-01 or 94 1/32

```
Est vol 5,619; vol
GNMA 8% (CBT)—$100,000 prncpl; pts., 32nds of 100%
                                          Yield        Open
        Open  High  Low  Settle  Chg  Settle  Chg  Interest
Mar    59-05 59-10 58-23 59-00  +  2  15.935  —  .018  14,395
June   58-24 59-02 58-15 58-24  +  3  16.007  —  .028  13,147
Sept   58-23 59-00 58-15 58-23  +  4  16.017  —  .036   8,139
Dec    58-24 58-30 58-13 58-22  +  4  16.026  —  .036   7,155
Mar83  58-18 58-30 59-14 58-21  +  4  16.035  —  .036   6,700
June   58-22 58-22 58-20 58-20  +  4  16.044  —  .036   5,357
Sept   58-19 58-30 58-15 58-20  +  5  16.044  —  .045   4,819
Dec    58-20 58-30 58-14 58-20  +  6  16.044  —  .055   3,243
Mar84  58-17 58-30 58-17 58-20  +  7  16.044  —  .064   3,610
June   58-18 58-30 58-18 58-20  +  8  16.044  —  .073   1,483
Sept   58-18 58-30 58-10 58-20  +  9  16.044  —  .082   1,124
Dec    ..... ..... ..... 58-20  + 10  16.044  —  .091     588
Mar85  ..... ..... ..... 58-20  + 11  16.044  —  .100      56
June   58-10 58-30 58-10 58-20  + 12  16.044  —  .110      10
Est vol 14,500; vol Tue 12,309; open int 69,826, —160.
TREASURY BONDS (CBT)—$100,000; pts. 32nds of 100%
Mar    59-02 59-15 58-23 59-04  ....  14.205  ....  62,911
June   59-18 59-31 59-06 59-21  +  2  14.081  —  .014  39,301
Sept   59-31 60-12 59-21 60-03  +  2  13.980  —  .014  17,439
Dec    60-15 60-24 60-01 60-16  +  2  13.887  —  .014  19,787
Mar83  60-28 61-04 60-15 60-28  +  2  13.802  —  .014  14,077
June   61-06 61-13 60-26 61-07  +  2  13.725  —  .014  13,246
Sept   61-04 61-23 61-04 61-17  +  2  13.656  —  .014  14,438
Dec    61-28 61-30 61-24 61-26  +  2  13.594  —  .014  12,765
Mar84  62-04 62-10 62-02 62-02  +  2  13.540  —  .014  10,760
June   62-14 62-14 62-10 62-10  +  2  13.486  —  .013   5,065
Sept   62-20 62-20 62-18 62-18  +  2  13.432  —  .013   1,921
Dec    62-28 62-28 62-26 62-26  +  2  13.379  —  .013     875
Est vol 96,000; vol Tue 71,808; open int 212,585, —589.
TREASURY BONDS (NYFE)—$100,000; pts. 32nds of 100
Feb    ..... ..... ..... 65-08  +  6  14.306  —  .041       0
May    ..... ..... ..... 65-20  +  6  14.224  —  .041   1,072
Aug    ..... ..... ..... 65-31  +  6  14.150  —  .040     477
Nov    ..... ..... ..... 66-02  +  3  14.130  —  .020     365
Feb83  ..... ..... ..... 66-12  +  3  14.063  —  .020      24
May    ..... ..... ..... 67-05  +  3  13.898  —  .020      10
Est vol 0; vol Tue 119; open int 1,948, —1,188.
TREASURY BILLS (IMM)—$1 mil.; pts. of 100%
                                      Discount      Open
        Open  High  Low  Settle  Chg  Settle  Chg  Interest
Mar    85.69 85.84 85.47 85.69  +  .02  14.31  —  .02  15,473
June   86.03 86.17 85.86 86.91  —  .13  13.09  +  .13  10,435
Sept   86.32 86.39 86.12 86.13  —  .18  13.87  +  .18   3,792
Dec    86.46 86.55 86.28 86.28  —  .17  13.72  +  .17   1,907
Mar83  86.62 86.69 86.41 86.41  —  .16  13.59  +  .16   2,008
June   86.70 86.80 86.50 86.50  —  .19  13.50  +  .19     816
Sept   86.78 86.85 86.59 86.59  —  .15  13.41  +  .15     129
Dec    86.77 86.90 86.69 86.69  —  .08  13.31  +  .08       4
Est vol 29,138; vol Tue 23,928; open int 34,564, +1,304.
BANKS CDs (IMM)—$1 mil.; pts. of 100%
Mar    84.02 84.20 83.87 84.10  +  .10  15.90  —  .10   4,282
June   84.30 84.52 84.24 84.33  +  .01  15.67  —  .01   1,270
Sept   84.73 84.86 84.65 84.65  +  .01  15.35  —  .01     262
Dec    ..... ..... ..... 84.90  ....   15.10  ....        7
Est vol 6,191; vol Tue 6,121; open int 5,821, +312.
```

FIGURE 3–3

Financial Futures Quotes

SOURCE: The Wall Street Journal, February 18, 1982.

outstanding, since every transaction requires a buyer and a seller. The major exchanges are the Chicago Board of Trade and the New York Futures Exchange.

Clearinghouses were established to ensure fulfillment of the contract and to provide a standard contract. Clearinghouses require the buyer and the seller of a financial future contract to provide a cash margin that is held in deposit. The margin is typically 5 percent, so substantial leverage is involved. The margin is adjusted as the price of the financial future changes.

The buyer or seller of a financial futures contract is required to meet the terms of the contract. A financial futures contract cannot be resold and is nontransferable. A buyer or seller may cancel the obligation by fulfilling the terms of the contract or by executing an offsetting futures contract. The offsetting contract is the typical way to settle in practice.

The growing interest in financial futures has been brought about by the variability of interest rates and the willingness of speculators to provide ways to hedge this risk. Individual investors and financiers have a way of passing the risk on to someone else (hedging the risk) at a known premium or cost. The transferences of risk to speculators is the chief purpose of the financial futures contract. If an investor has bought long-term Treasury bonds at a yield of 15 percent and is afraid long rates will move higher, there is a way of being protected through the use of financial futures. The investor could sell a futures contract a quarter ahead. If interest rates rise and the price of the bond falls, the investor loses. However, if the investor has sold bonds at a specific yield, at the end of the period the long position can be delivered. If rates decline, the cost price of the bond rises. The investor continues to hold the bonds and buys out the futures contract. Even though there is a loss, the loss has been limited.

A futures market also helps the forecast process. If Treasury bill yields are 14 percent and lenders are willing to sell Treasury bills at 14 1/4 percent in 90 days, the pressure exists for higher yields. The investor thus has some idea about the direction of yields and can invest accordingly.

Prices of futures contracts on U.S. government and agency securities move in the same manner as bond prices. Rising interest rates result in falling futures prices, and falling interest rates result in higher futures prices. The purchase of a futures contract (long) at a price of 98 will result in a loss if market interest rates rise. The offsetting contract, a short, would have to be at a lower price in the month of contract expiration. Unlike the cash markets, which have no limit on the daily movement of prices, the futures exchanges put an artificial limit on the daily price movement of futures contracts. There have been occasions when people were unable to close out a contract by an offsetting contract until the exchange's daily trading limits allowed prices to "ratchet" up or down to the level of the true market.

The relationship between the cash price and the futures price of a financial security is called the *basis*. The basis is expressed as the difference between the cash price of a financial security and the price of that security in the futures market. The basis can be positive or negative, depending upon whether the futures price is under or over the cash price. In the case of financial instruments, *carrying costs* refer to the financing costs of short-term interest rates relative to the yield on the cash financial security. The normal configuration for long-term interest-rate futures will be for the futures price to be below the cash price, reflecting a positively sloped yield curve.

As a futures contract expires, the basis approaches zero—that is, the cash and futures prices tend to converge. This occurs because the supply and demand factors determining the prices of the commodity and the expiring contract become identical. Although the cash and futures prices do not always fluctuate equally, their movements do parallel one another in response to changing market conditions. This parallel movement makes the basis more predictable, and therefore less risky. The reason cash and futures prices parallel each other is the action of arbitragers. *Arbitrage* is the simultaneous purchase and sale of the same commodity in order to profit from the distortions of unusual price relationships. For example, if there is a distortion between the cash-future basis and the carrying costs and level of expectations, the futures price is either too high or too low relative to the cash price. The arbitrager would see this distortion and benefit from purchasing the futures and selling the cash or vice versa. Because of this market mechanism, movements in the cash price are reflected by similar movements in the futures. Cash and futures markets respond to the same basic supply and demand factors. The cash market tends to respond to situations in its market while the futures market tends to reflect the broader national or international trends for the months ahead. Either price may move first, but the price level in one market tends to rise or fall with the other.

The key element of the futures market to the hedger is its liquidity and to the speculator the use of leverage. For the hedger, liquidity is provided by the speculator until an offsetting hedge comes to market. In turn, the speculator is able to apply financial leverage and thus increase prospects for gains. The ability of the speculator to assume the risk by initiating positions freely and quickly gives the market the necessary liquidity it needs. The speculator's expectations relate exclusively to the direction and scope of price changes in the futures position. Speculators are interested in anticipating the direction of future price change in order to profit from the trade.

Use of Speculative Positions in Financial Futures

In September, with Treasury bills yielding 14 percent, the speculator expects interest rates to rise. The speculator is able to sell a December Treasury bill futures contract at a price of $96,500, implying a 14 percent yield. If short-term rates rise to 15 percent, the speculator will be able to buy a December contract for $96,250 at a 15 percent yield to close out the position. The gain on the transaction will be $250. The speculator is thus protected.

Hedgers seek to avoid the risk of price changes due to interest-rate fluctuations. They may take a position in the futures market approximately equal and opposite their cash market position. The losses on cash market transaction due to rate changes may be offset by gains on opposite futures transaction. An example of a long hedge is that of a corporate treasurer who in March anticipates buying $1 million in 91 days Treasury bills in June. The treasurer finds the current yields on the bills attractive, and fears a decline in interest rates. The treasurer may hedge the position by buying a September bill contract and selling that contract in June when the bills are purchased. The increased cost of the Treasury bills in June (if rates have fallen) may be offset by an appreciation in the sale of the futures contract.

STATE AND MUNICIPAL BONDS AS INVESTMENT SECURITIES

State and municipal securities possess a unique combination of investment qualities: security of principal, stability of income, and income tax advantages. Their record of experience has been good, since there have been few defaults on state and local debt historically. In the 1930s some defaults occurred, representing a small proportion of the total municipal debt outstanding. It was not until New York defaulted on its bonds, followed by a bailout by the federal government and a reduction in the rating of "Big Macs" (New York Municipal Assistance Corporation), designed in part to save New York City, that investors began to reexamine their previous unqualified acceptance of tax-exempt bonds as quality investment that served as a tax haven for the wealthy. "Big Macs" have since been issued to replace the old bonds; they carry a BBB rating from S&P.

Income from state and municipal bonds has to date been exempt from federal income taxes, so individuals and corporations in the high-income brackets have found this type of bond attractive for investment. Even though the rates of interest and yields on state and municipal bonds have been lower than those of U.S. government securities, they offered a much higher yield after taxes. An investor in the 50 percent bracket, for example, buying a 12 percent municipal bond would have the same after-tax yield as from a fully taxable bond with a yield of 24 percent. The fully taxable equivalent is found by dividing 1 minus the person's marginal tax rate into the tax-exempt's rate of interest times 100 (to convert back to percentage). In this example, $1 - .50$ is divided into $.12 \times 100$, which gives 24 percent. This is the fully taxable equivalent an investor in the 50 percent tax bracket would need to provide 12 percent after taxes.

The wealthy individual, corporate investor, or financial institution in a high tax bracket can obviously benefit from this type of investment. However, future tax reform may change or eliminate the tax-exempt status of these bonds, making them competitive with other securities. And greater care must be given in the analysis of municipal bonds so that investment in bonds that might default can be avoided. New York is not the only large city in difficulty. Cities such as Boston, Baltimore, Cleveland, Detroit, and Philadelphia have had fiscal problems, along with the state of Massachusetts.

The Growth of State and Municipal Debt

The total amount of state and municipal debt is much smaller than the total federal debt, and it has been declining somewhat. Approximately 75 percent of the total state and municipal debt outstanding has been issued by local government units, which include counties, municipalities, townships, and towns, as well as school districts and special districts. As state and local debts have increased, the number of government units has decreased. Special districts have increased, but the number of school districts has decreased dramatically because of the mergers that have taken place to finance new school facilities. Often it is uneconomical or impossible for one school district to finance a new high school, for example. Through the merger of several districts into one large one, the financing of the new facilities becomes feasible.

The changes in state and municipal debt can be visualized clearly from the figures in Table 3–5.

The growth of debt, even when for noble purposes, in many cases has outstripped the growth of revenues. It isn't difficult to find a reason for the growth of municipal debt. Since the end of World War II, the demand for public services of all types has skyrocketed. Population has expanded, and more schools, more roads, more colleges, and more utilities had to be provided. Not all communities have been successful in solving their individual problems. Most likely, the pressure for new services to meet the future growth of population will continue undiminished and compound the problems of these communities. In addition, excessive municipal expenditures result in

THE INVESTMENT ALTERNATIVES

TABLE 3–5

New Security Issues of State and Local Governments (millions of dollars)

Type of Issue or Issuer, or Use	1979	1980	1981	1982						
				May	June	July	Aug.	Sept.	Oct.	Nov.
All issues, new and refunding*	43,365	48,367	47,732	5,705	5,793	5,624	6,527	6,504	8,339	9,638
Type of issue										
General obligation	12,109	14,100	12,394	1,510	1,814	974	1,683	1,703	2,330	3,251
U.S. government loans†	53	38	34	10	16	22	25	30	30	34
Revenue	31,256	34,267	35,338	4,195	3,979	4,650	4,844	4,801	6,009	6,387
U.S. government loans†	67	57	55	38	45	49	52	54	57	57
Type of issuer										
State	4,314	5,304	5,288	601	1,074	257	835	1,077	1,010	1,086
Special district and statutory authority	23,434	26,972	27,499	3,045	2,867	3,735	3,670	3,456	5,062	5,165
Municipalities, counties, townships, school districts	15,617	16,090	14,945	2,059	1,852	1,632	2,022	1,971	2,267	3,387
Issues for new capital, total	41,505	46,736	46,530	5,574	5,703	5,438	6,099	6,301	7,175	8,932
Use of proceeds										
Education	5,130	4,572	4,547	484	727	293	516	831	562	712
Transportation	2,441	2,621	3,447	292	245	117	769	546	651	1,279
Utilities and conservation	8,594	8,149	10,037	1,363	830	1,272	685	283	1,323	1,928
Social welfare	15,968	19,958	12,729	2,102	2,307	2,745	2,515	2,542	2,665	2,157
Industrial aid	3,836	3,974	7,651	355	416	564	728	1,054	556	673
Other purposes	5,536	7,462	8,119	978	1,178	447	886	1,045	1,418	2,183

*Par amounts of long-term issues based on date of sale.

†Only bonds sold pursuant to the 1949 Housing Act, which are secured by contract requiring the Housing Assistance Administration to make annual contributions to the local authority.

SOURCE: *Federal Reserve Bulletin,* February 1983, p. A36.

part from poor management, lack of control, uncontrolled welfare, inability to deal with unions, and an inability to make hard social decisions.

The pattern of the growth of state and municipal debt will be similar in the future to the pattern that has developed in recent years. The figures in Table 3–5 reveal the purposes for which loans were raised. While the percentage spent for education has lessened as a percentage of the total, there has been a sharp increase in expenditures for other purposes.

New roads and bridges have required states and municipalities to obtain money from the sale of debt securities. As our population expands, there will be a need for repair of highways and bridges. This will require that more money be raised by local government units. The need for all types of public utilities has expanded. Large sums of money have been spent annually for new water-treatment stations, sewage plants, and trash-removal facilities. In the future, the need for this type of facility will continue and increase, and so will the expenditures. Pollution controls alone will require billions of dollars. As individuals and political leaders begin to recognize social and cultural needs not only for the minimum public utilities, but also for the amenities of life such as art and cultural centers and public recreation facilities, expenditures in this category will increase.

Housing and urban renewal projects have stimulated communities to borrow money to improve their cities and towns and to provide housing for low-income families. Many cities—New York, Philadelphia, Boston, and Cincinnati are a few—have embarked upon major redevelopment projects supported by public and private capital. In the future, we may look for greater expenditures for urban renewal, pollution control, and industrial development. Money will be needed to solve the housing problems of people living in the ghettos of our cities. The amount of money these programs will require is awesome.

Municipal and state funds raised from debt issues are used for a wide variety of other purposes. Veterans' aid, including veterans' bonuses, has received a modest but mentionable share of the funds raised. States have issued debt for mental institutions and state recreation facilities. The growth of our population—even though the rate is slowing down—and increasing social consciousness will undoubtedly create large future expenditures in all these areas. Yet in the future, these projects must be undertaken within the financial capabilities of the communities. Citizens are not in a mood to overextend their financial resources.

State and Municipal Borrowers

STATES. States may issue debt from time to time, with the consent of the people, to carry on their activities. The laws vary among the states as to how debt shall be raised. In accordance with the Tenth Amendment to the Constitution, each state is sovereign and has absolute power to issue debt without interference from the federal government. The state of Ohio, for example, can issue debt as a direct obligation subject to approval by the people of the state.

The states have been, on the whole, excellent credit risks. There have been few times in history when states were forced to repudiate their debt. When repudiation occurs, the state simply tells creditors it will not pay. Since the state is the sovereign power and the individual cannot sue for payment, an investor could suffer a substantial loss, so the creditor is in a weak position. Default is rare, however, since states have excellent revenue sources, such as taxes on sales, gasoline, motor vehicles, income, inheritance, and general property; and they have enjoyed an excellent credit rating. In recent years, the states have been taking a more active supporting role in helping schools meet their financial commitments.

New York and other states, since the early 1960s, have used a "backup fund" to protect bond issues. Invented in New York, such a fund operates to provide money to pay the first-year interest and charges on bond issues. The agency issuing the bonds sells enough bonds to cover the first year's interest and bond service, and promises to replenish the reserve so that it is always sufficient to pay debt service for the ensuing year. If the reserve is too low, this fact is reported to the state at the time the annual budget is prepared, and appropriation is made to cover the deficit in the reserve and bring it to full stated requirements. The bonds issued under this arrangement are referred to as "moral obligation" bonds, a term that is more literary than legal, since *all* state and special debt is a moral obligation upon the citizens.

MUNICIPALITIES.   The creditor may be in a stronger position in dealing with local political units, depending upon the terms of the bond indenture, but these units are limited in their source of revenues to pay for debt service and retirement. Cities, towns, and counties are heavily dependent upon property taxes to support their activities. In many cities, property taxes have not produced sufficient revenue, and the cities have resorted to income or sales taxes as a source of funds. The power to levy an income tax is given to most cities by the state, and the tax rate is usually limited by the state. The debt burden is great in many local political units, since they are constantly under pressure to increase community services, and therefore they constantly seek new sources of revenue. Even New York City, with a large tax base, has reached a limit in the amount of services it can provide. Austerity is necessary for New York to bring expenditures in balance with revenues.

SPECIAL DISTRICTS.   School districts, road districts, and park districts represent another type of borrower. These districts are almost completely dependent upon the property tax. When money is needed for special districts, the people in the district must usually approve an increase in property taxes to support the bond issue that will be used to finance the improvement. Without the approval of the voters, the project cannot be carried out. The districts that have the greatest difficulty are those with rapidly growing needs, a low tax base, and a large existing debt, where the people do not wish to or cannot extend themselves to meet the needs of the community. The dilemma for such communities is almost unsolvable without aid from the state, other districts, or even the federal government.

ASSESSMENT DISTRICTS.   Another classification of borrowers is the assessment district, usually formed to provide a single facility, such as sewage, street lighting, or paving. Usually the obligation to pay the assessment bonds is assumed by the lot owner, who is given the choice of paying the lump-sum value of the improvement or paying the debt and interest over the life of the bond issue, which varies from 10 to 20 years, depending upon the amount of the expenditure. The position of the bond issue is strong if the dollar cost of the improvement is small in relation to the property.

PUBLIC AUTHORITIES.   Public authorities also issue debt securities that are part of the heterogeneous category called *municipals*. The public authority is usually established to operate one or several businesses. The New York Port Authority, for example, is perhaps the most widely known in the United States. The Maine Turnpike Commission, the Ohio Turnpike Authority, the New Jersey Turnpike Authority, and the Pennsylvania Turnpike Authority are other examples of successful public authorities that have sold bonds to the public and have been attractive investment outlets. Where competitive economic conditions are favorable, the public authority method of financing a project is an excellent way of meeting the needs of the people and allowing them to pay as they go. The credit ratings of most public authorities have been excellent, but a few have run into financial difficulties that could result in loss to the investor. The West Virginia Turnpike and Calumet Skyway bonds experienced difficulty when revenues fell far below expectations. There is a risk that these bonds might not be paid at maturity.

Also in this category are the municipal development corporations that have been established to aid cities in their economic growth. The federal tax laws no longer provide exemption for the interest received from this type of bond, and it is likely that this change will result in diminished growth of this type of municipal activity.

Types of State and Municipal Bonds

State and municipal bonds are debenture contracts that do not have a pledge of either real or personal property. Their credit rating rests upon their ability to pay principal and interest solely from tax revenues, solely from operating revenues of a special revenue facility, or from a combination of both. The *debenture contract* is simply a long-term written promise to pay. The bonds are issued in both straight and serial maturities. *Serial* maturities have advantages for both the investor and the issuer. A portion of the debt of serial bonds is paid off every six months from income or revenues. This ensures the retirement of the debt and improves the credit rating of the bonds that remain in the hands of the public. The issuer of this type of bond meets the obligation, the investor has the contract completed, and the credit contract has been fulfilled. The varying maturities for these bonds make them attractive to many groups of investors, rather than to just a limited segment of the investment market. Investors can choose the maturity in advance, so that if we wish to invest in six-month or six-year bonds, we can select the maturity that meets our requirements.

If debt is not amortized through serial repayments, then a *sinking fund* is established to repay the debt. The sinking fund requires that the money be set aside for the retirement of the debt when it matures. The money can be invested in other securities or in the securities of the bond issue itself. The sinking-fund payments have the same effect in the retirement of the bond issue as the period retirement of the serial bonds. The right to call the bonds for retirement or sinking-fund purposes is retained in the contract of the newer issues of municipal bonds, to allow the municipality flexibility in its financial planning.

If we exclude those bonds guaranteed by the federal government, there are two basic types of state and municipal bonds: (1) general obligation bonds, and (2) revenue bonds. Even this classification is an oversimplification of state and municipal debt issues. Usually two other classifications are provided. Special-assessment bonds are considered as a separate, third class. However, these bonds are usually repaid from money received from the person assessed, and because of this, we would put them in the revenue-bond category. A fourth type is the combination bond, which is supported by revenues from a project but is also guaranteed by the pledge of revenues from tax sources. Bonds with this combined guarantee are also considered a type of revenue bond.

GENERAL OBLIGATIONS. General obligations are fully tax-supported bonds that are guaranteed by a political unit with the power to levy taxes. These bonds are sometimes called "full-faith-and-credit bonds." There is no pledge of a specific property, but the bondholder receives the unconditional guarantee that both interest and principal will be paid at maturity. As shown in Table 3–5, this type of bond represents the bulk of the debt issued by states, cities, counties, and special districts. The base for the tax that supports this debt is usually the assessed value of real estate. In cities, income tax or sales-tax receipts might be pledged as the means of debt repayment, but property taxes are still the most important source of funds for the repayment of general obligations. The investment quality of general obligations depends upon (1) their legality, and (2) the ability of the issuer to repay the debt.

The question of legality is quite important. Municipal bonds have occasionally been sold to investors when the issuing unit has absolutely no power to issue the debt. In some cases, because of legal technicalities, innocent investors have lost money. Today, legal consultants who are experts in matters pertaining to the issuance of municipal debt are employed to determine the legality of the bond issue before it is sold to the public. The municipal-bond lawyer employed by the bondholders investigates the constitution, statutes, charters, and judicial procedure to determine if the bond issue has met all the necessary legal conditions of issuance. If the bonds are legal, he or she will make an unqualified statement of the fact. This legal opinion will not prevent loss if subsequent events prove the attorney wrong; however, the statement is good evidence that everything is in order about the bond issue. When the bonds are sold, the buyer usually receives a copy of the legal opinion. It is wise for a potential purchaser of state and municipal bonds to know whether a legal opinion has been made for each bond issue in which he or she wishes to invest.

Ability to Pay Debt Coverage and Income—An Analysis

The economic and financial position of the government unit issuing the debt must be analyzed. Essentially, it must be known whether the community has a broad, strong, and growing economic base, and whether debt and taxes are reasonable in relation to the present and future income and debt of the community. This is the critical point of analysis for state and municipal bond investing. An affirmative answer must be obtained to the question, "Is it likely that the issuer will be able to pay the debt at maturity from its future tax receipts?"

Some guides to the ability of a state or municipality to pay its debt are the growth of population, economic background and trends, the debt burden, the cash balance as reported in the annual report, the rapidity of debt retirement, the record of property-tax collections, and the five-year financial plan.[1]

Population growth will have a big effect on debt-paying ability. A growing population in an affluent community will be advantageous, but a growing population in a low-income community represents a poor credit risk. Many large cities today are in this position, including Washington, D.C. Debts of these communities are suspect, whereas the more affluent suburbs are adequately taking care of their debts. The per capita income and debt figures have meaning only in the context of the growth and composition of the population.

The economic trend of the community requires special analysis, including answers to questions such as the following: Is it a one-industry community? Most people know

[1]Dell H. Stevens, "The Analysis of General Obligation Municipal Bonds," L.F. Rothschild & Co. New York June 19, 1974.

what happened to Cocoa Beach, Florida, with the cessation of the space program. Is there a diversity of industry? A stable, growing, diverse industry base is best. What are the leading sources of income in the community, and are they stable? Marathon Oil is the major employer in Findlay, Ohio. This profitable and well-run company gives financial strength to the city. Other industry plus farming adds diversity and growth to the economic base. What percentage of the tax base is represented by industry? A large, stable percentage is desirable. Is the economy subject to wide economic variation, such as in a resort community? A balanced community is best. What has been the direction in the value of the homes in the community, the income level, the relative personal wealth, and the personal savings of citizens? Obviously, growth in personal per capita wealth, including housing prices, income, and savings, with a growing population is favorable for debt repayment as long as the debt is contained within the limits of ability to pay. Is the community near the location of a major shopping area and related commercial activities? Actually, a "town-builder" type of employment is best. Town-builder employment is one that attracts money from outside the community.

An analysis of debt burden is imperative. This includes the growth and present amount of net indebtedness, which represents gross debt minus debt that is self-sustaining, minus sinking funds, and minus financial assistance from other government units. The overall growth in combined indebtedness must be estimated. This includes all debt for which the municipality is responsible. It is essential that debt per capita be estimated, along with the trend of debt per capita. This is then related to the market valuation of the property in the community on a per capita basis and the assessed valuation on a per capita basis. Debt per capita can also be compared to income per capita, providing a good idea of the burden of debt.

Most municipal units have a limit on their taxing ability. The limit may be expressed as a percentage of the assessed value of the property or as a maximum tax rate. Under this limit, the government unit can raise only a certain amount from general assessment—say, 10 mills per $1,000 of valuation. Anything beyond this figure must be specially approved by the people. Where the debt is expressed as a percentage of the assessed property value, the rate has actually ranged from 1 to 20 percent of value, 7 percent being a common limit. These limits must be known to the investor when he or she makes an analysis of a particular debt, so that the investor knows whether the community has exceeded its debt capacity. There is no standard or uniform guide as to when debt is excessive, and the investor must make a decision upon a relative rather than an absolute criterion.

Often, a certain type of debt will be excluded from the debt limits. Special-assessment bonds, although secured by revenues, are often secured also by a pledge from the municipality. These revenue bonds are not included as a part of the debt, and yet they should be added, since the municipality has pledged its security. Investors must be certain that the debt limits include all the obligations that have been issued or pledged by a municipality. Where the debt is secured by taxes other than property taxes, the investor must determine whether the revenue will be sufficient to service the debt. More and more cities are levying income taxes to meet the costs of government. This revenue may be pledged to support full-faith-and-credit obligations. Where income taxes or other sources of revenue are used, a careful analysis must be made to determine whether these sources are adequate. Again, the standard of comparison is relative. The best way is to compare debt-service costs to the amount of revenue expected from the tax. The greater the coverage of income over debt costs, the more secure the debt issue. Conservative opinion suggests, however, that debt service should not exceed 20 percent of the annual budget from all sources.

The cash balance at the end of each fiscal year is an indicator of financial difficulty. If a community has recurring and accumulating cash deficits, it is in trouble. A trend in cash balances can be obtained from the annual report of the state or municipality.

The rapidity of debt retirement must be examined. A community might try to repay debts too quickly and, in the process, find that the ability of citizens to pay is exceeded. On the other hand, communities like New York, unable to pay current debts, push to the future an operating deficit by borrowing for too long. Eventually there is a day of reckoning, at which time the debt is paid or the community defaults.

The record of tax collection is important. As a guide, 97 percent of taxes should be collected, with most of the development taxes collected within three months after being listed. A collection rate of 90 percent is clearly unacceptable; such a community is in trouble.

Knowledge of the five-year financial plan of the community is important. This assessment indicates future strains and stresses. The future should not be ignored in establishing creditworthiness. A clear indication of trends must be sought.

Standard & Poor's has listed a number of early warning signals that might be helpful in the analysis of municipal bonds. These are listed below:

1. Current-year operating deficit
2. Two consecutive years of operating-fund deficit
3. Current-year operating deficit that is larger than the previous year's deficit
4. A general-fund deficit in the current-year—balance-sheet—current position
5. A current general-fund deficit (two or more years in the last five)
6. Short-term debt outstanding (other than BAN) at the end of the fiscal year, greater than 5% of main operating-fund revenues
7. A two-year trend of increasing short-term debt outstanding at fiscal year-end
8. Short-term interest and current-year debt service greater than 20% of total revenues
9. Property taxes greater than 90% of the tax limit
10. Net debt outstanding greater than 90% of the debt limit
11. Total property-tax collections less than 92% of total levy
12. A trend of decreasing tax collections—two consecutive years on a three-year trend
13. Declining market valuations—two consecutive years, three-year trend
14. Overall net debt ratio 20% higher than previous year
15. Overall net debt ratio 50% higher than four years ago[2]

As minimum data necessary to establish a municipal bond rating, the following information is required:

1. Debt statement, including maturities, with bonds segregated as to security, over-lapping debt, which is this unit's share (on the basis of proportionate valuations) of the debt of overlapping taxing units.

[2]Standard & Poor's, *Fixed Income Investor*, March 6, 1976, p. 849.

2. Assessed valuation for the last four years, segregated as to realty and personalty, and as to industrial, commercial, utility, and residential basis of assessment.

3. Tax collection statement for four years, including amount of current levy, amount collected on that levy in ensuing year, and amount collected to some recent date. Statement of this unit's tax rate and the overall tax rate for the past four years.

4. Recent population estimate.

5. Copies of the past two annual reports and the latest budget.

6. List of the ten leading taxpayers with their assessed valuations, including the number of employees for industrial taxpayers.

7. Brief description of the economy of the area, including the character of development, the level of building activity, and the value of homes (for residential areas).

8. School enrollment for the past ten years (where applicable).

9. Future borrowing plans by this unit and overlapping units.

10. Five-year proposed capital improvement program.

11. Statement regarding current status of pension funds of unit's employees.[3]

Unfavorable features in municipal-bond analysis include the financing of mass transit, excessive leasing of facilities, limits on use of new revenues, bonds financed from revenues that restrict funds for general-obligation bonds, lack of priority in receiving funds, changes in administrative management, and a small community. Favorable features include extra backing for local bonds, new construction, new industry, and rising economic values.

REVENUE BONDS. Revenue bonds are bonds of a political subdivision, government unit, or public authority whose debt service is paid solely out of revenues from the project. They are not solely general tax revenues, but some revenue bonds may have the additional support of a pledge of tax revenues.

Revenue bonds fall into three categories: utility, quasi-utility, and nonutility. Utility bonds include (1) bridge, tunnel, or toll highway; (2) electric light and power; (3) gas; (4) public transportation; (5) off-street parking facilities; (6) water; and (7) multiple-purpose, the more common combinations being electric and water, and sewer. Quasi-utility include (1) airport, (2) dock and terminal, (3) hospital, (4) public market, and (5) public garage. Nonutility include (1) gasoline tax, cigarette tax, beer tax, utility excise tax, or similar tax; and (2) rentals of public buildings.

Revenue bonds possess certain advantages over other forms of municipal debt from the viewpoint of the municipality issuing them. First, they enable the municipality to avoid an increase in debt that is payable out of general revenues. Second, revenue bonds can be issued when the legal limit of debt has been reached by the municipality, as they do not ordinarily come under legal debt limits. Third, revenue bonds follow closely one principle of good taxation—the benefits-received theory—since the debt is repaid by those who use the service. Presumably, revenue bonds also represent ability to pay, which is another tenet of good taxation. Fourth, revenue-bond financing does not require approval from the citizens, and projects can be undertaken that ordinarily would not come under the responsibility of the local government. Fifth,

---

[3]Ibid., p. 850.

some communities do not have the revenue to support debt from general taxes and must look to revenue bonds to finance the improvement. In principle, therefore, revenue bonds are an ideal way to finance needed projects.

The basic criterion for the valuation of a successful revenue-bond issue is the economic feasibility of the project. If a project is economically sound and will produce revenues adequate to service the debt, it must be considered a successful venture. We must be aware that equity securities as such do not exist when revenue projects are started. Thus, debt repaid from revenues of community projects is subject to the business risk. Each project must be examined to determine its likelihood of success and whether revenues will be adequate. There are many examples of issuance of revenue bonds by authorities. A partial list of these bonds appears in *The Wall Street Journal*, with current price quotes. Many of the issues have suffered because of the general increase in money rates. A few, as cited before, have done poorly because the projects were unsuccessful. The Mackinac River Bridge bonds, in contrast, were economically sound. The bridge replaced a ferry service whose revenues were adequate to provide debt service for the bond issue, and so the project was successful from the beginning.

Even though care is taken in establishing the economic value of a project, errors may be made that lead to financial loss. Not all financing is as economically sound as the Mackinac Bridge bonds. Complete bond quotations and information about state and municipal bonds may be obtained from a municipal bond dealer, or from Standard & Poor's weekly *Bond Outlook* or Moody's weekly *Bond Survey*. Quotes may be obtained from the "pink sheet" of over-the-counter-market bond prices in brokerage offices. (The quotes are printed on pink paper—hence the name.)

Bond Ratings

It is difficult for an individual to determine independently the legality and financial and economic position of a municipal bond issue. For this information, bond-rating services are available that can be consulted when an evaluation is made of a specific bond issue. *Moody's Municipal and Government Manual*, a factual, interpretative rating service, provides ratings for virtually all state and municipal bonds. Occasionally ratings are omitted, or are changed if new information is available. The bonds are rated from Aaa to C. The Aaa (Triple A) bond issues are defined this way:

> Bonds which are rated Aaa are judged to be of the best quality. They carry the smallest degree of investment risk and are generally referred to as "gilt edge." Interest payments are protected by a large or by an exceptionally stable margin, and principal is secure. While the various protection elements are likely to change, such changes as can be visualized are most unlikely to impair the fundamentally strong position of such issues.[4]

The Baa bonds, representing the lowest quality that institutional investors may buy, are defined this way:

> Bonds which are rated Baa are considered as lower medium grade obligations, i.e., they are neither highly protected nor poorly secured. Interest payments and principal security appear adequate for the present but certain protective elements may be lacking or may be

[4] *Moody's Municipal and Government Manual* (New York: Moody's Investors Service, 1981), p. vi.

characteristically unreliable over any great length of time. Such bonds lack outstanding investment characteristics as well.[5]

Bonds in the A and Baa groups that Moody's believes possess the strongest investment attributes are designated by the symbols A1 and Baa1.

The C bonds are defined this way:

Bonds which are rated C are the lowest rated class of bonds, and issues so rated can be regarded as having extremely poor prospects of ever attaining any real investment standing.[6]

Beginning today, April 26, 1982, five of Moody's nine corporate bond rating symbols will include numerical modifiers 1, 2, and 3. These modifiers have been added to each rating symbol from Aa through B in order to give investors a more precise indication of relative debt quality in each of the historically defined categories.

An Aa1 rating, for example, now indicates that the security meets all of Moody's criteria for a double-A rating and that it ranks at the high end of that rating category. The modifier 2 indicates that the security is in the mid-range of its category and a 3 indicates that the bond is nearer the low end of its generic category.

A triple-A rating will have no numerical modifier; it remains Moody's highest corporate bond rating. Also, generic ratings Caa, Ca, and C will not have numerical modifiers. The new system comprises the following symbols:

Aaa	Baa1, Baa2, Baa3	Caa
Aa1, Aa2, Aa3	Ba1, Ba2, Ba3	Ca
A1, A2, A3	B1, B2, B3	C

In effect, Moody's has increased the number of possible corporate credit ratings from nine to 19. We emphasize, however, that the numerical modifiers are only refinements of the defined categories. The relative positions of all of Moody's corporate bond rating symbols, and their definitions, remain unchanged—as do all procedures for bond ratings (see complete description below). Moody's rating symbols and their meanings for commercial paper issuers have not changed.[7]

Reference to the bond rating will quickly provide a close approximation of quality. Before we purchase municipal bonds, we should determine the rating to verify our independent analysis and thus be able to balance the risks with the possible rewards. Standard & Poor's is a similar well-known information source that rates municipal and corporate bonds. Its bond ratings may be obtained in the *Bond Guide*.

Yields and Risk Associated with Municipal Bonds

The yields on state and municipal bonds are usually lower than the yields on comparable federal government bonds and others that are subject to federal income taxes. We must not assume that because their yield is lower, they are a better risk. They sell on a lower yield basis because their interest is exempt from federal income taxes, and interest and principal are usually exempt from the taxes levied by the state in which they are issued. The pattern of yields follows very closely the movement of yields in the money market. The yield at any one time will depend upon two factors: (1) the supply of bonds, which is determined by the demand for funds from the municipalities and states; and (2) the demand for the securities, which is determined by the

[5]Ibid.

[6]Ibid.

[7]Ibid., 1982

rates for other high-quality taxable bonds, the number of investors who will benefit from tax exemption, and the money-market conditions in general. The pattern of yields on the Aaa-quality municipal bonds is presented in Figure 3–2 and compared there with yields on U.S. government and corporate Aaa and Baa bonds. The money-market crisis, the Vietnam war, the outflow of gold, and the inflationary fiscal deficits brought about a sharp increase in long-term interest rates from 1966 through 1970, and a subsequent decline in 1971–72 followed by a slight rise in 1973. Municipal bond yields increased substantially in 1975 at the height of New York City's financial problems. Rates rose to new highs again in 1981 but declined again in 1983. The main restraint during 1981–1982 was the monetary policies of the Federal Reserve banks, which were, of necessity, restrictive because of inflationary pressures.

The variability of the yield of municipal bonds is apparent from the data presented in Figure 3–2 and Table 3–2. Analyze the variability of yield of municipal bonds compared to Treasury bills and long-term government bonds. The risk associated with municipal bonds is clearly indicated by the trend of yields and the variability, and there is substantial risk in all bonds as revealed by the variability of yields.

To help understand the factors that influence the height and ranges in bond yields, the equation $r_b = r_f + r_I + r_c$ is provided. The first component of the yield on bonds (r_b) is r_f, the risk-free yield, usually assumed to be 3 percent, which is comparable to the long-term real growth of capital. The second part of the yield relates to the inflation rate, r_I, which is currently 5 to 6 percent. The final part of the yield is r_c, which is a function of the credit risk. Thus, with a 3 percent risk-free return, an 8.5 percent inflation rate, and prime credit, a bond would yield 11.5 percent. A lower-rated bond would sell on a 12.5 percent yield basis, the 1 percent increase accounted for by the credit risk. Lower tax rates, however, reduce the tax advantage of municipal bonds.

The Reagan administration, early in 1981, succeeded in reducing corporate and personal federal income tax rates. Personal taxes were lowered to a 50 percent maximum. The tax reduction made tax-exempt bonds less attractive to wealthy individuals and corporations, and somewhat more comparable to fully taxable bonds. It had the effect of raising the cost of state and municipal financing. With the lower tax rate, the rate of interest would have had to be increased on these bonds in order to make them as attractive as they were before the rate reduction. Municipal bonds therefore tend to sell more and more like fully taxable obligations. If the tax exemption were eliminated, as has been suggested in many reform proposals, the bonds would sell on a yield basis allowed by the credit position of the issuing authority operating in a competitive capital market, just like other bonds.

The Place of Municipal Bonds in the Investor's Portfolio

State and municipal bonds are unique because of their exemption from federal income taxes and, usually, from taxes imposed within the state of issue. Only five states impose an intangible tax on bonds issued within the state (Arkansas, Illinois, Missouri, Montana, and Texas); Pennsylvania exempts state bonds but taxes local bonds. Where personal income taxes are levied against bond interest income, most states exempt the income from their own state and municipal bonds. Colorado, Idaho, Indiana, Iowa, Kansas, Montana, Oklahoma, and Wisconsin, however, consider all bond interest income subject to personal income taxes. Ohio and Utah include local but not state bonds as taxable for income tax purposes. Warrant interest is considered income in Arizona. However, the important exemption from federal income taxes makes municipal bonds attractive for investors in the upper income tax brackets, particularly commercial banks and wealthy individuals.

The highest-rated bonds possess a great degree of quality. They are readily marketable, and the short maturities have a high degree of liquidity. Wealthy people seeking stability of income and security of principal should look carefully at the advantages of state and municipal bonds to meet their needs. An individual, institutional, or corporate investor in a high tax bracket should consider municipal bonds. Even those in a lower tax bracket can benefit from tax exemption. If an investor in the 20 percent tax bracket bought a 12 percent tax-exempt bond, it would give the equivalent of a fully taxable yield of 15 percent. A 15 percent rate of return for a long period of time on a safe and secure investment is an attractive return. As a further advantage, state and municipal bonds are not subject to the amount of market risk that accompanies the purchase of common stock.

The municipal bond does not offer an opportunity for future growth, however, and this must be considered when investment is contemplated. And municipal bonds do not provide against the possible loss of purchasing power from inflation. They are subject to the money-rate risk too, since the yields fluctuate with the pattern of yields in the money market. Municipal bonds have the same degree of variability as federal government bonds. Revenue bonds bear still another risk, the business risk. Since revenue bonds are supported by the revenues from quasi-competitive business ventures, the risk of failure always exists.

FOREIGN SECURITIES

Securities issued by foreign governments are also available for the investor. Canadian Treasury bills have from time to time provided investors with a higher yield than American securities. However, the investor would be required to accept the exchange risk between the American and the Canadian dollar. If, for example, the value of the Canadian dollar falls relative to the American dollar, the investor loses. On the other hand, if the Canadian dollar increases in price relative to the American dollar, the investor obtains a profit on the currency as well as a higher yield from the Canadian Treasury bill. This principle can be applied to securities issued by the governments all over the world.

For those not interested in accepting the exchange risk, dollar-denominated securities are available. The best known are *Eurodollars*, sold for dollars in Europe, and *Yankee bonds*, which are Canadian securities sold in the U.S. market. The advantage of investing in such securities is the higher yield and lack of exchange-rate risk.

Obviously, longer-term securities are available for investment. In making such an investment, an investor must examine:

1. The creditworthiness of the government
2. The yield

3. The exchange-rate risk
4. The liquidity

If all are satisfactory, an investor might profit from the purchase of the short-term and long-term securities of foreign governments.

SUMMARY

The securities issued by the U.S. government are excellent investment-grade securities. They provide the investor with marketability and liquidity and possess a high degree of safety of principal and stability of income with a modest yield. Marketable securities are sometimes used by individual investors to achieve liquidity and maintain a defensive position in their investment portfolios. The short-term securities are particularly adaptable to the temporary needs of the investor. Short-term bills and commercial paper are useful as a temporary haven for funds and are used by corporations and financial and institutional investors. The long-term government securities may be used as the conservative portion of an investor's securities holdings. Federal securities are fully taxable and do not offer the investor complete protection from the purchasing-power risk or the money-rate risk. Business risk and market risk are minimal, but there is a variability in yield, which suggests that some risk is present.

There is a growing interest and market in financial futures. Speculators use them to trade, and some investors use them to hedge their position.

Municipal bonds are unique. They possess the features of safety of principal and stability of income, and they are exempt from federal income taxes and the majority of state taxes. They are usually referred to as "tax-exempts." Some market risk is assumed with general-revenue bonds, particularly if they are associated with economically unfeasible projects. The business risk is present in revenue bonds, and they offer no protection from the purchasing-power risk or the money-rate risk.

Careful analysis of municipal bonds must be conducted, including trends, growth of population, economic background, debt burden, annual cash balance, rapidity of collection of taxes, and the five-year financial plan.

Foreign government securities might be purchased by investors for a higher yield and a possible gain because of changes in the exchange rate. Careful analysis must be made of the country, the security, and the future of exchange rates.

SUMMARY OF PRINCIPLES

1. Short-term securities are less risky than long-term securities.
2. U.S. government securities are less risky than other debt securities.
3. Long-term government securities have substantial risk based upon their variability of yields.
4. Municipal bonds must be carefully analyzed for quality, yield, and the trends of interest rates in the capital markets.
5. Money-market analysis, along with Federal Reserve Board policy, is important to consider before any investment is made in government securities.

6. Foreign securities have the additional risk of exchange-rate changes.

7. Financial futures have speculative appeal.

REVIEW QUESTIONS

1. What is the difference between a U.S. Treasury bill, a Treasury note, and a Treasury bond?
2. How would we judge the basic value of a government security?
3. What are the basic risks inherent in the purchase of government securities?
4. How variable and risky are yields on governments?
5. What are the advantages and disadvantages of the ownership of long-term and short-term government securities?
6. What does the term *state and municipal bonds* mean?
7. What feature of state and municipal bonds makes them unique?
8. Will tax exemption always apply to the tax-exempt bonds?
9. Explain a financial future contract.
10. Indicate the basic types of state and municipal obligations. Be sure to contrast general obligation with revenue bonds.
11. What factors determine the investment quality of a state or municipal obligation? Explain in detail.
12. What part do legality and debt limits play in the valuation of municipal securities?
13. To what extent can we rely on the bond ratings of the various investment services as an indicator of value? Be sure to differentiate between Aaa and Baa ratings.
14. What are the major risks inherent in the purchase of state and municipal bonds?
15. What type of investor would use municipal bonds?

PROBLEMS

1. Eileen bought a five-year government bond in 1976 to yield 7.18 percent to maturity in 1981. The coupon on the bond was 7.18 percent. What yield did she earn annually over the life of the bond, assuming she held it to maturity? How much income, in dollars, did she receive annually? What price did she receive at maturity? What price did she pay for the bond? What was the current yield from the investment?

2. In 1977, the bond Eileen purchased was selling to yield 6.99 percent to maturity. Assume the bond was issued in 1976. What was the purchase price of the bond in 1977? What was the annual income from the bond? What was the current yield earned on the bond?

3. If Eileen sold the bond in 1977 on a 6.99 yield basis after holding the bond for one year, what return would she have earned from the bond?

4. Scott bought a long-term government bond in 1976 to yield 6.78 percent to maturity in 2006. In 1977 the yield on the bond rose to 7.06. What happened to the price of the bond? What return did Scott earn from the bond from 1976 to 1977? The yield on the bond rose to 7.89 percent in 1978, 8.74 in 1979, and 10.81 in 1980. Based on

the change in yield and the change in years to maturity, calculate the price of the bond in 1978, 1979, and 1980. Now calculate the return earned in 1978, 1979, and 1980, which takes into consideration price change and interest income. (The interest or coupon each year is at the same rate as the 1976 yield of 7.18 percent.) Summarize the annual return for each year 1976 through 1980. Find the average of the returns and the standard deviation. Comment on the return and risk of the bond. What conclusion can you come to?

CASE

Jeff looked at the data in Table 3–2 to determine where he would invest $10,000. He wanted a bond with a high yield and a low risk. Jeff was in the 30 percent tax bracket and wanted income. He also wanted low risk. Examine Table 3–2 carefully and advise Jeff.

SELECTED READINGS

ANG, J. S., and K. A. PATEL. "Bond Rating Methods: Comparison and Validation." *The Journal of Finance*, May 1975, pp. 631–40.

AYRES, H. F., and J. Y. BARRY. "Dynamics of the Government Yield Curve." *Financial Analysts Journal*, May–June 1979.

DILLER, STANLEY. "Analyzing the Yield Curve: A New Approach." *Financial Analysts Journal*, March–April 1981.

HOFFLAND, DAVID L. "NYC and the Municipal Bond Market." *Financial Analysts Journal*, March–April 1979.

PARCEY, ROBERT W., and STUART K. WEBSTER. "City Leases: Up Front, Out Back, In the Closet." *Financial Analysts Journal*, September–October 1980.

CHAPTER 4

PRIVATE
CORPORATE BONDS
Usual and Unusual Analysis

We turn now to a consideration of the investment characteristics of the debt securities of private corporations. Greater yields are anticipated from private corporate bonds, but with only slightly greater risk, than from fully taxable U.S. government securities. Many corporate bonds offer the investor a high degree of stability of income and safety of principal. Several special types of corporate bonds, such as convertible bonds and bonds with warrants, will be examined for investment opportunities. Some individual investors might not show enthusiasm for the usual form of corporate bonds, but bonds with profit-sharing features, such as convertibles, can be attractive to individual and institutional investors alike. Unfortunately, long-term bond yields have risen in past years, along with interest rates in general. This forced bond prices lower and made investors wary of purchasing long-term bonds. This appears to be their major weakness.

THE SIGNIFICANCE OF CORPORATE DEBT SECURITIES

Bonds have been the most important source of funds for business. There are two basic reasons for the heavy reliance on debt financing to raise corporate funds. First, the sale of bonds is less expensive in terms of interest and issuance costs than the sale of any other form of security. Under present tax laws, bond interest is deductible as an expense, reducing the cost of financing to the corporation. For a corporation in the 46 percent tax bracket, for example, the after-tax cost of issuing a 16 percent bond is 8.64 percent (.16 × .54). This is because the company receives a tax credit of 46 percent of the interest expense, and so the net cost to the company is 54 percent of the interest cost.

The second major reason for the issuance of debt securities is the ready market that exists for them. Debt securities are an important investment outlet for all institutional and some individual investors. Some of the financial institutions, as we pointed out previously, are permitted to own nothing but debt securities. A commercial bank, for example, can buy only bonds rated Baa and higher. This requirement is imposed by law and by these institutions' own financial conservatism.

THE NATURE OF CORPORATE BONDS

A corporate bond issue is a long-term debt of the corporation. It is a long-term written promise to pay a certain sum of money at a certain time for a specified rate of interest. Since the amount of money borrowed is usually large, and since no one investor would be able to lend the entire amount to the corporation, the loan is divided into a large number of parts or pieces and sold to many investors. These parts are bonds, and in their entirety they constitute the bond issue.

Debt and equity securities issued by a corporation are sources of long-term capital, and they are listed on the liability side of the firm's balance sheet. Debt for investment must be understood in relation to the assets as well as the ownership of the corporation. Long-term debt in most industrial corporations must be less than shareholders' investment and smaller than fixed assets. (At this point, it would be wise for the reader to review accounting and corporation finance to refresh his or her understanding of basic balance-sheet and operating-statement relationships.)

A corporation issuing bonds is in effect selling its credit to the individual or institution that is willing to lend money by investing in its debt securities. The corporation agrees to pay interest on the money borrowed and to repay the loan at maturity. The interest paid represents compensation to the investor for the risk assumed. The greater the risk, other things being equal, the higher the interest and the greater the cost to the corporation that is selling its credit. The lower the risk, the lower the interest and the lower the cost to the company.

When a corporation borrows money, it promises to do two things for the bondholder. It promises, first, to repay the money on a specified date; and second, to pay the interest on the money borrowed at a specified rate and at specific times. The issuing company will make further commitments, each of which is designed to improve the promise of repayment, the security of principal, and the promise to pay the interest. The degree of uncertainty surrounding the repayment of the borrowed money and the payment of interest determines the risk involved and the rate of return that investors receive. Some bonds offer a third promise to the investor—the promise of sharing in the growth of earnings. The type of bond sold obtains its identity from the nature of the promises made by the company.

The Bond Indenture

The specific promises made to the bondholder are set forth in the *bond indenture*—an agreement between the corporation issuing the bonds and a corporate trustee, usually a commercial bank or trust company, representing the bondholder. The trustee is necessary because it would be impractical and economically unfeasible for the corporation to enter into a direct agreement with each of the many bondholders. Having a single trustee who represents all bondholders is also helpful for the purpose of working out any financial difficulties that might arise in the future.

The usual items found in the indenture are these: the authorization of the issue; the exact wording of the bond; the interest or coupon rate; the trustee's certificate; the registration and endorsement; the property pledged as security, if any; and the agreements, restrictions, and remedies of the trustee and the bondholders in default. If there is a conversion right or a redemption right, this is usually stated. Correct legal language is used to avoid misunderstanding. The information contained in the indenture relates to the promises made by the corporation to the bondholders. Each of these promises will be discussed to indicate the usual features of a bond issue as well as to present the various types of bonds that may be issued.

The Repayment of Principal—The First Promise

The first promise the corporation makes is to repay the borrowed money at a specified time and for a stated amount. The usual value of a bond is $1,000. This is referred to as the *par value*, *face value*, or *maturity value*. Corporate bonds can be and are issued in larger denominations. Some are issued in units of $5,000 or $10,000 if they go to institutional investors; and there is nothing to prevent a large institutional investor who buys $1,000,000 worth of bonds from having one $1,000,000 security.

MATURITY DATE. The time of repayment of the principal of the bond is a part of the pledge of repayment. When each issue is sold, its maturity date is established. The maturities vary, much like those of government bonds. The length of time to maturity for long-term bonds is from 20 to 100 years. Short-term bonds have a maturity of less than a year, and intermediate-term bonds mature in from 5 to 10 years. The actual time will be established in the bond indenture. A bond issue with a 20-year maturity is actually a bond with many different maturity dates. As it approaches maturity, it becomes first an intermediate-term bond and then a short-term bond. A long-term bond is in reality, then, a bond with varying maturity dates and yields.

CALL FEATURE. Most modern corporate bonds are callable at the discretion of the issuer. The *call feature* is designed to solve two problems facing the corporation. First, it allows bonds to be purchased by the corporation for retirement piecemeal, year by year, by reserving for the corporation the right to call the bond before maturity for sinking-fund purposes. This assures corporation and creditors of the eventual retirement of the debt. Second, the call feature is used to allow the bond issue to be retired in total before maturity, perhaps to permit the issuing corporation to take advantage of lower interest rates in the money market, or to make way for new financing. When a company calls the debt outstanding, the investment maturity is changed. The maturity value is also changed, because the bonds are usually called at a higher price than the par value, to compensate the investor for the risk of reinvesting.

A higher call price and a shorter time to maturity tend to increase the yield on bonds. The time at which the bonds can be called and the amount for which they can be called are stated in the bond indenture. When purchasing a bond, the investor should examine the indenture carefully to determine if and when it can be called for redemption. If a call feature were exercised, it could change the investment period and yield by a change in the maturity date and the maturity price, and thus affect the bond yield. In purchasing a bond, compute the yield to maturity and the yield to the first call date to determine what impact an early call would have on the yield. Many bonds cannot be called for a stated number of years, and this could be a disadvantage at high interest rates if yields are expected to decline.

SERIAL BONDS. Some bond issues are retired serially, just like municipal bonds. A schedule of yields, interest rates, prices, and maturity dates is announced before the bonds are purchased. The investor selects the maturity of the bond issue that is best for him or her. If a long-term investment is needed, then bonds that mature in later years will be purchased; for a short investment period, short-term securities will be purchased. The basic purpose of the serial bond issue is to provide for the retirement of the debt in an orderly, easy, and direct fashion. It assures the eventual elimination of debt, and it tends to improve the credit rating of the remaining outstanding bonds.

A serial bond issue meets the needs of many investors because of the range of maturities; it is actually a series of bond issues, with an issue maturing every six months. A 20-year serial bond of $20,000,000, for example, is really 40 different bond issues of $500,000 each, with different yields to maturity ranging in time from 6 months to 20 years. Serial bond issues, like bond issues with a sinking fund, have an effect on yields. The shorter maturities of serial bonds, under normal circumstances, have lower yields than the longer maturities.

THE PLEDGE OF SECURITY. The third feature of the promise to repay the principal relates to the security of the pledge. Actually, the pledge to repay made by a corporation to the trustee who represents the bondholders is a formal promise, in writing and signed under seal. However, the promise to pay, without further comment in the bond contract, is simply a pledge. To assure the investor that the principal is secure, the corporation sometimes offers security in addition to a simple promise to pay. Several types of bonds are classified by this additional pledge of real or personal assets.

Debenture Bonds. The pledge to repay takes its highest form in the debenture bond, which is a full-faith-and-credit obligation. When a corporation issues a debenture bond, it says to the creditor, "I [the corporation] promise to repay the money you have lent me at the maturity date. I give you my bond that I will repay, but I do not pledge a tangible, specific asset as security for the loan. I simply pledge my good faith and credit that I will repay the loan." The company, in making the pledge to repay, actually pledges its assets, its earnings, and its character to fulfill its obligation to the bondholder. If the company did not pay interest or repay principal at maturity, its assets could be sold to satisfy the claims. Debenture bonds are typically issued by corporations that have an unquestioned credit rating and by those that do not have a large amount of assets to pledge as additional security. The debenture bond bears the same relationship to the corporation as long-term government bonds bear to the federal government.

Subordinated Debentures. A subordinated bond is usually junior to all existing bond issues and actually reduces the investor's security of principal. It is sometimes junior to current liabilities or to bank loans. The exact relationship of the subordinated bond to other debt will be found in the bond indenture. Subordinated bonds usually have a claim on assets superior to that of preferred and common stock. They are often used with the conversion feature, in which the final security will be an ownership claim that is junior to a debt issue. Subordinated debentures may offer greater income for the investor and other features, even though they offer less security of principal.

Mortgage Bonds. Some bond issues pledge additional security to support the pledge of principal repayment. A mortgage bond issue not only agrees to repay the principal at maturity, but also pledges real property as additional security. All the customary features of the bond issue are the same except for the pledge of general or specific assets. The strict interpretation of the indenture states that if the company defaults, the general or specific asset pledged can be sold to pay creditors. If this is not sufficient, the creditor can sue the corporation.

A mortgage on real property has substance only if the property is relatively marketable and if there are no claims on it that take precedence over the claim that is being satisfied. Real property that has more than one use would be a superior security to an asset having only one use. The Marathon Oil Corporation, for example, has an excellent group of office buildings in Findlay, Ohio. But if they were pledged as security for a bond issue, their value would be questionable. If Marathon Oil failed, it would be difficult to sell the buildings to pay the claims. No other industry in Findlay is large enough to afford or to use the office facilities, and for a corporation outside of Findlay, the costs involved in relocation and the adjustments in method such a move would involve might be prohibitive. In practice, it is rare that assets are sold to satisfy creditors. Usually, the assets are kept in the business and the claims of the creditors are adjusted downward. As the claims are scaled down, it is possible that the junior bondholders or the stockholders might end up with nothing, or only a modest share in the future earning power of the enterprise.

The type of mortgage is also an important consideration. A first mortgage on a property is usually more desirable than a second mortgage, since it has first claim on the specific asset pledged. If the company did not pay its interest or principal and the property were sold to pay the claim, not enough money might be left to pay the second mortgage, or junior claim. Possibly the higher interest rate on the second mortgage would compensate for the added risk, but it is difficult to determine in advance if a 20 percent increase in yield is adequate compensation for the potential loss of the entire principal. Without balancing risk of loss with added compensation, we must conclude that a second or third corporate mortgage is less secure than a first mortgage. (However, a second mortgage on a valuable property might be relatively better and more secure than a first mortgage on a poor piece of property.) When we look for security of principal and expect repayment of principal in a mortgage bond issue, we must determine to what extent the property pledged adds materially to the fulfillment of the pledge of repayment of principal.

Collateral Trust Bonds. Some bond issues pledge stock or bonds as additional security for the money borrowed. This type is referred to as a collateral trust bond.

The collateral is usually the personal property of the corporation issuing the bonds. This type of bond enables the investor to sell the property pledged to pay the claim should the corporation fail to pay interest or principal when it is due, thus adding to the security of the bond issue and providing something beyond a written promise to pay. A collateral bond issue usually arises out of the relationship between a parent company and its subsidiary. Let us assume, for example, that a parent company owns $10 million of debt securities of a subsidiary company. The parent company needs money but does not wish to sell the bonds. Instead, it sells collateral bonds to the public by pledging the securities of its subsidiary and giving a "full-faith" commitment to repay the debt if the collateral is not sufficient. The parent company has a well-secured loan and still retains its ownership of the bonds of the subsidiary company. The quality of the collateral trust bond is determined by the credit position and asset and earnings positions of both the company issuing the debt and the company whose securities are being pledged. Both common stocks and bonds can be used as collateral.

Equipment Trust Bonds. Another way in which the principal of a bond issue is secured is through the pledge of equipment. The title to the property or machinery usually remains in the hands of the trustee until the debt is repaid. The best example of this type of debt issue is the equipment trust bonds commonly used in railroad finance. Railroads since the end of World War II have financed almost their entire purchase of new equipment through the sale of equipment trust certificates based on the Philadelphia lease-plan method. Assume that the Union Pacific wanted to purchase a new diesel locomotive, but did not have the full purchase price. The company would put up 20 percent of the equity and would borrow the remaining 80 percent through the issuance of equipment trust certificates that would be retired serially every six months over the next ten years. The title to the equipment would remain in the hands of the corporate trustee. Each six months after the purchase of the equipment, a principal and interest payment would be made to the trustee. The trustee in turn would retire some of the equipment trust certificates and pay the interest on the outstanding debt. If the Union Pacific could not make the principal payment, the trustee could sell the property and pay off the creditors. The equipment is usually readily salable, and the trustee has the title and can sell it if necessary. The equity put up by the issuing corporation serves as a reserve to protect the lender, should the market value of the asset drop.

These bonds have served their purpose well. They have generally provided the institutional investor a safe and secure principal with an excellent yield to maturity. They have been subject to the money-rate risk, however. The ratings of several equipment trust obligations may be found in Standard & Poor's *Bond Guide*.

Bonds with Supplemental Credit. Some bond issues have an additional or supplemental pledge as added protection for the creditor. No specific asset or security is pledged, but the principal is secured by something more than the general credit of the company issuing the bonds. *Guaranteed bonds* are an example of this type. They are secured by the corporation issuing the bonds, and the principal, interest, or both are guaranteed by another corporation. This type of bond might be issued in a situation where the entire assets of a company are leased. The company leasing the assets guarantees that the interest and principal of the debt outstanding will be paid.

Joint bonds are another type of supplemental credit bond jointly secured by two or more companies. Two companies that use a common facility and have raised money to finance it through the sale of debt provide a good example of a situation where the bonds might be jointly secured. The investor has the additional security of another corporation's pledge. *Assumed bonds* are another type of bond with the pledge of additional security. The assumed bond results from a merger or a consolidation of two companies. Let us assume that company A is merged into company B. Company A has a bond issue that has been issued prior to the merger. Once the merger has been completed, company B assumes the obligations of company A. The bondholder now has the pledge of two companies as security for a bond issue.

RECEIVER'S CERTIFICATES.   Receiver's certificates are debt instruments that arise out of reorganization. When a corporation in reorganization needs capital, the receivers or the trustees have the power to raise additional funds. The securities issued are known as receiver's certificates, and the principal value of these claims ordinarily takes precedence over any other debt outstanding. The risk of loss is still present, however, since the company may not be able to solve the problems that have resulted in loss. Any additional pledge of security in the form of real, personal, or intangible assets, or any additional pledge or guarantee by another corporation, will be covered in the indenture.

REGISTERED BONDS.   One other safeguard might be indicated in the indenture to assure the basic security of the bond. A bond may be registered as to principal to protect the owner from loss. When the bond principal is registered, the name and address of the bondholder are recorded with the issuing company. The method of transferring a registered bond is much the same as that of transferring stock. The interest on a registered bond is usually paid by check. The registration of the principal does not guarantee that investors will receive principal repayment at maturity, but it does provide protection from loss should the bond certificate be lost or destroyed.

The Payment of Interest—The Second Promise

The second promise made to the purchaser of corporate debt securities by the issuing corporation, the promise to pay the interest on the debt, is of perhaps greater importance to the investor than the promise of repayment of principal. The rate of interest that is paid and the time of payment are stated in the indenture. Usually, the interest is paid semiannually, in an amount based upon the stated rate of interest, and by check directly to the bondholder or by coupon. When the interest is paid by check, the bond is usually registered as to principal; the coupon bond is usually registered as to interest. The coupons are numbered, and each coupon represents one interest-payment period. As each coupon comes due, it is presented to a designated paying agent—usually a commercial bank or trust company. Unfortunately, if the bond should be lost or stolen it would be difficult to recover, since coupon bonds are usually *bearer bonds*, which are negotiable. The coupons are negotiable when due and payable, and proof of ownership is not needed to cash them in. Coupon bonds, then, require special care and safekeeping to prevent loss.

The rate of interest on coupon bonds—the *coupon rate*—is based on the par value of the bond. (*Interest rate* and *coupon rate* are often used interchangeably.) The rate, of course, establishes the number of dollars of interest, the nominal rate, that will be paid to the bondholder. Whether the interest is paid by check or coupon, the amount is fixed for the life of the bond. Since the interest rate of the bond cannot be changed, the price is the only variable. As this changes, as we noted earlier, the yield on the bond changes.

The interest on bonds issued in the United States is paid in dollars. At one time prior to 1933, bond principal and interest were sometimes payable in gold. These clauses were nullified by Congress in 1933 when the United States went off the gold standard. Since 1975, it is again legal to own gold in the United States, and it is conceivable that "gold bonds" could emerge. Some foreign securities may be payable either in the currency of the issuer or in American dollars.

If interest is not paid when it is due, the bond issue is in default, and all interest and principal become due and payable. It is then the job of the trustee to act for and protect all bondholders. This clause, which is a standard part of the bond agreement, is referred to as the *acceleration clause*. It does not ensure repayment of principal, but it does protect the creditor and establishes his or her claim to assets. Where payments of interest and principal are made together, it accelerates all future payments and eliminates the need for selling on each defaulted payment.

In any debt instrument, the interest payment is secure only if the corporation issuing the debt has adequate income to cover all its expenses, including the interest cost on the debt. In determining the quality of the bond issue and ability to pay interest, the best guide is the number of times the interest is covered by net operating profit or by net income after taxes. The lower the interest charges and the higher the net operating profit or net income after taxes, the more secure the interest payment. There are other assurances that are offered to increase the security of the interest payment. Often, a corporation is required to maintain a minimum cash or working capital position. Occasionally, further guarantees of interest payment come from additional pledges to be found in a guaranteed, joint, or assumed bond.

INCOME BONDS. Bonds are sometimes issued that require the interest to be paid only if there are sufficient earnings to pay. These are called *income bonds*. In some income bonds, the interest payment must be approved and declared by the board of directors, in much the same way that dividends are paid on preferred stock. If the interest on the bond is not paid, it may be cumulative and payable at a later time. Income bonds are still debt instruments, but they are closely related to stock in the essential characteristic of interest payment. In the past, income bonds arose out of reorganization and were sometimes referred to as *adjustment bonds*. Today they are used for several purposes, one of which is to recapitalize a company by replacing preferred stock with tax-deductible income bonds. The effect is to lower the after-tax cost of financing the company by substituting for a nondeductible dividend a deductible interest payment that need not be paid if no earnings are present.

PROTECTIVE COVENANTS. The dual promises of the corporation to repay principal and to pay current interest are also protected by other covenants in the bond indenture. The protective covenants, as they are called, do not pledge specific or additional assets, but they do bind the corporation to certain agreements that control its operations and protect bondholders. One such agreement limits the dividends on common stock, in order to protect the cash and working capital position of the company, which in turn protects the bondholder. If cash or working capital drops below a certain limit, no dividends can be paid. Other protective covenants are associated with specific types of bonds. Mortgage bonds usually include a protective provision that limits debt to a certain percentage of the value of the new property. It might say that debt cannot be placed upon new properties in excess of 50 percent of value. These are only a few examples of the many possible protective covenants. Each covenant helps to improve the creditor's security position and increases the possibility that the two main promises, of principal repayment and interest payment, will be met.

EVALUATING CORPORATE BONDS

The ultimate investment quality of a corporate bond issue depends upon the company's ability to repay the debt, pay the interest, and provide additional security or covenants to assure that the financial commitments will be met. In debt analysis, therefore, ability to repay, interest coverage, and overall credit position of the company must be examined. In addition, the rating services are used as a guide to investment quality. In general, the following principles should be followed in the selection of a bond for investment:

1. Emphasis should be placed on the ability of a company to pay its obligations as they come due against income.
2. The rules of interest coverage, the ability to repay principal, and the ability to meet all obligations should be based upon the assumption of recession conditions rather than the value of property.
3. Lack of safety and security cannot be made up for by increased yield. The higher the yield, usually, the higher the risk.
4. Specific quantitative tests should be used for bond analysis, including the nature and size of the company, terms of the issue, record of solvency, interest coverage, value of assets, and equity base of the company.[1]

Ability to Repay the Debt

The first step in analyzing a bond issue is to determine the ability of the company to repay the debt whether the company fails or continues to prosper. Assume that the company fails and is required to pay creditors from the assets that remain. In the absence of prospects for earnings, the first consideration is whether the assets of the company are sufficient to pay the debt. The value of the assets and their relation to the specific debt issue and the total debt outstanding must be examined. A company with a small amount of debt in relation to the market value of its assets is in a much better position, other things being equal, to repay the debt than a corporation with a high

[1] Based upon Benjamin Graham, David L. Dodd, and Sidney Cottle, *Security Analysis*, 4th ed. (New York: McGraw-Hill, 1962), chap. 22.

THE INVESTMENT ALTERNATIVES

debt relative to the market value of its assets. Market value and not book value must be stressed. An asset cannot always be sold for its book value or original cost.

Two tests are used to determine the ability to pay should the company fail. One is the ratio of debt to net worth; the other, debt to fixed assets. In industrial finance, debt of all types should not exceed net worth. If railroads or public utility companies are being analyzed, the debt ratio can be higher. In regard to the second ratio, long-term debt should generally not exceed 50 percent of the market value of the fixed assets of the company. If debt does not exceed this limit, it is not excessive and would be properly secured. Practical debt limits for companies in a wide range of industries appear in Figure 4–1. It is obvious that in practice few industrial, public utility, or railroad companies have a ratio of debt to net worth or equity of 1 to 1, even in the case of public utilities, which usually have a large amount of debt in the capital structure.

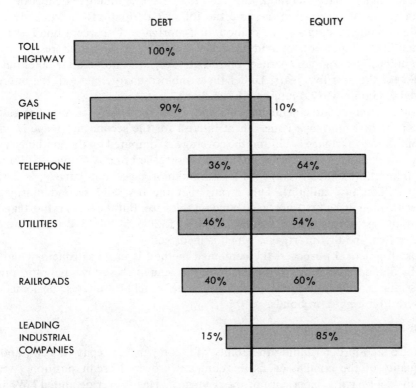

FIGURE 4–1

Approximate Division of Capital Structures between Equity and Debt Financing, Selected Industries

Ability to Pay the Interest

The company must also be able to pay its interest, usually every six months, from its current earnings. Cash flow and earning power are both used as measures of capacity to pay interest. These measures do double duty, since they indicate if the company can pay principal as well as interest. Without sufficient earnings or cash flow, or the prospect for earnings and cash flow, the bond interest is not secure, nor is the bond issue. On the other hand, if interest is adequately covered, the bond issue is secure and interest will be paid according to the agreement. What is adequate coverage, of course, depends upon the company and the industry. Net income after taxes in normal years should cover interest payments at least three times in the case of industrial companies, and two times in the case of railroads or public utilities. If the interest rate is historically low, however, the coverage limits should be raised. During World War II, for example, long-term interest rates were below 3 percent. The interest coverage ratios should be higher in this situation—perhaps five times interest payments—than when interest rates are 15 percent. The higher coverage will compensate for future situations when financing charges might be higher.

There are two acceptable methods of computing the interest coverage ratio. One is the combined-charge method, and the other is the cumulative-deduction method. For purposes of illustration, assume the following situation: A company has two bond issues outstanding—a $20 million, first-mortgage, 15 percent bond issue, and a $10 million, 17 percent, second-mortgage bond issue. Total interest charges are $4.7 million. The company earned, on the average, $12 million after taxes but before interest for the past five years. Under the combined-charge method, the interest was covered 2.55 times ($12.0 million/$4.7 million).

Using the cumulative-deduction method, the fixed-charge coverage is calculated first on the first-mortgage issue. Then, interest for the second mortgage is added to that of the first-mortgage issue, and the coverage is computed on the combined amount. Using this method, the coverage on the first-mortgage bond is 4 times ($12.0 million/ $3.0 million), and the coverage on the second mortgage, cumulatively, is 2.55 times ($12.0 million/$4.7 million). This means that the first and second mortgages are less secure than just a first-mortgage bond, in this case. But the second mortgage alone has an interest coverage of 5.3 times ($12.0 − $3.0 ÷ $1.7 = 5.3) which suggests it is better than the first mortgage, which is incorrect.

For all practical purposes, the combined method is more satisfactory and is that used by Standard & Poor's *Bond Guide*. In fact, the interest-coverage ratio presented (times interest and miscellaneous charges earned) includes interest on loans as well as interest on long-term bonds.

Credit Position of the Company

The third step in determining the ability of a company to repay its debt, and hence the quality of the bond issue, is the company's overall credit position. What has been the debt-paying experience of the company? Has it ever defaulted? What is the character of the issuing corporation? Is it in a strong financial position, and has it always been strong financially? These questions are subjective, but the answers will reflect a good credit position for a company or a poor one. If the credit record has been good, then a bond issue might be considered satisfactory. Generally, a strong company—competitively and financially—with a strong equity position and a management that has proved its ability to manage debt has the best credit position. The Dun and Bradstreet reports can serve as an excellent guide; a good rating by Dun and Bradstreet would be an adequate indication of the overall credit position of the company.

THE INVESTMENT ALTERNATIVES

Where debt is secured by the pledge of other corporate securities, as in the case of collateral trust bonds, or when another corporation guarantees an issue of bonds, the securities pledged and the credit position of the company that has issued them, or of the company that has given its additional pledge, must be carefully analyzed. This analysis is exactly the same as the credit analysis that would be performed on the company issuing the debt securities.

Bond Ratings and Investment Quality

Independent analysis by an investor to determine the quality of a bond is important. Some analysts are expert at making these valuation judgments; however, even under the best of circumstances, it is difficult to judge the quality of private corporate bonds. It is therefore desirable to enlist the aid of professional services that provide investment ratings for bond issues. Moody's and Standard & Poor's are two well-known companies in this field. These services rate corporate bonds just as they do municipal bonds, ranging from those of high and unquestionable investment quality to speculative bonds that might be unsuitable for investment. The ratings and the language of the ratings are almost identical with those used for municipal bonds, shown in the preceding chapter.

In *Moody's Industrial Manual*, the Aaa bonds are defined as "Judged to be of the best quality." They carry the smallest degree of investment risk and are generally referred to as "gilt-edge" securities. Interest payments are protected by a large or an exceptionally stable margin of earnings, and the principal is secure.[2] The rating service usually states also that "while the various protective elements are likely to change, such changes as can be visualized are most unlikely to impair the fundamentally strong positions of such issues."[3] The rating schedule applies to all types of private corporate obligations. The higher the investment rating, the more secure the bond issue. The investment quality of bonds diminishes in stages until ratings of C are reached. Standard & Poor's uses a similar rating system, which is shown in Figure 4–2. Using such ratings and the analysis of interest and asset coverage of debt, the investment quality of a bond issue can, within limits, be judged.

Bond Yields and Investment Quality

The yields on long-term private corporate bonds, shown in Figure 3–2, are higher than those for fully taxable government securities. The pattern of the yields is much the same. In fact, most bond yields follow the same pattern if they are high-quality, money-rate bonds. The movement of long-term yields for all debt securities is variable, and the bonds do not remain as stable as the fixed interest rate suggests. The variability of yields reflects the amount of risk in bond investment. Bonds, therefore, have a certain instability of price just as common stocks do; so analysis and timing of purchases are as important for bonds as for common stocks.

Bond yields vary with changes in yields in the long-term bond and money markets. Yields differ also because of quality differences in the rating of bonds, and according

[2]*Moody's Industrial Manual* (New York: Moody's Investors Service, 1976), p. vi.
[3]Ibid.

CORPORATE BONDS

BANK QUALITY BONDS—Under present commercial bank regulations bonds rated in the top four categories (AAA, AA, A, BBB or their equivalent) generally are regarded as eligible for bank investment.

AAA Bonds rated AAA are highest grade obligations. They possess the ultimate degree of protection as to principal and interest. Marketwise they move with interest rates, and hence provide the maximum safety on all counts.

AA Bonds rated AA also qualify as high grade obligations, and in the majority of instances differ from AAA issues only in small degree. Here, too, prices move with the long term money market.

A Bonds rated A are regarded as upper medium grade. They have considerable investment strength but are not entirely free from adverse effects of changes in economic and trade conditions. Interest and principal are regarded as safe. They predominantly reflect money rates in their market behavior, but to some extent, also economic conditions.

BBB The BBB, or medium grade category is borderline between definitely sound obligations and those where the speculative element begins to predominate. These bonds have adequate asset coverage and normally are protected by satisfactory earnings. Their susceptibility to changing conditions, particularly to depressions, necessitates constant watching. Marketwise, the bonds are more responsive to business and trade conditions than to interest rates. This group is the lowest which qualifies for commercial bank investment.

BB Bonds given a BB rating are regarded as lower medium grade. They have only minor investment characteristics. In the case of utilities, interest is earned consistently but by narrow margins. In the case of other types of obligors, charges are earned on average by a fair margin, but in poor periods deficit operations are possible.

B Bonds rated as low as B are speculative. Payment of interest cannot be assured under difficult economic conditions.

CCC-CC Bonds rated CCC and CC are outright speculations, with the lower rating denoting the more speculative. Interest is paid, but continuation is questionable in periods of poor trade conditions. In the case of CC ratings the bonds may be on an income basis and the payment may be small.

C The rating of C is reserved for income bonds on which no interest is being paid.

DDD-D All bonds rated DDD, DD and D are in default, with the rating indicating the relative salvage value.

NR—Not Rated.

Canadian corporate bonds are rated on the same basis as American corporate issues. The ratings measure the intrinsic value of the bonds, but they do not take into account exchange and other uncertainties.

MUNICIPAL BONDS

Standard & Poor's Municipal Bond Ratings cover obligations of all states or sub-divisions. In addition to general obligations, ratings are assigned to bonds payable in whole or in part from special revenues.

AAA-Prime—These are obligations of the highest quality. They have the lowest probability of default. In a period of economic stress the issuers will suffer the smallest declines in income and will be least susceptible to autonomous decline. Debt burden is not inordinately high. Revenue structure appears adequate to meet future expenditure needs. Quality of management would not appear to endanger repayment of principal and interest.

AA-High Grade—The investment characteristics of bonds in this group are only slightly less marked than those of the prime quality issues. Bonds rated AA have the second lowest probability of default.

A-Upper Medium Grade—Principal and interest on bonds in this category are regarded as safe. This rating describes the third lowest probability of default. It differs from the two higher ratings because there is some weakness, either in the local economic base, in debt burden, in the balance between revenues and expenditures or in quality of management. Under certain adverse circumstances, **any one such weakness** might impair the ability of the issuer to meet debt obligaitons at some future date.

BBB-Medium Grade—This is the lowest investment grade security rating. Under certain adverse conditions, several of the above factors could contribute to a higher default probability. The difference between A and BBB ratings is that the latter shows **more than one** fundamental weakness, whereas the former shows only one deficiency among the factors considered.

BB-Lower Medium Grade—Bonds in this group have some investment characteristics, but they no longer predominate. For the most part this rating indicates a speculative, non-investment grade obligation.

B-Low Grade—Investment characteristics are virtually non-existent and default could be imminent.

D-Defaults—Interest and/or principal in arrears.

FIGURE 4-2

Standard & Poor's Bond Ratings

SOURCE: Standard & Poor's *Bond Guide*, May 1981.

to type of industry. Table 4–1 indicates the yields of AAA and BAA bonds.[4] Bonds with the lowest rating, which are still in the top investment categories for purchase by institutional investors, have a higher yield than the highest-rated bonds.

Over the entire period covered by Table 4–1 the AAA bonds sold on a lower yield basis than did the BAA obligations. Such relationships, however, vary over time, and cannot be counted on to remain the same in the future.

The bond issues in Table 4–1 are varying-quality investment-grade debt securities that might be considered attractive outlets for investment funds. Most of the debt issued was either debenture bonds backed by the full faith and credit of the corporations, or mortgage bonds secured by a first mortgage on real property. Some of these issues might continue to meet investment needs today. Certainly, the very high yields on all these bonds are impressive.

The bonds in the highest rating classes (AAA and AA) are often called money-rate bonds, because their yields fluctuate with changes in the money rates. The lower-grade bonds do not offer as high a degree of security, but they do offer a higher yield. These bonds, however, possess the credit risk or the business risk. In the purchase of bonds below BAA or BBB rating, a greater risk of loss of capital is assumed. It is possible that the company could not pay the debt at maturity or pay the interest, and hence the bond is generally in a lower category. These bonds would fluctuate with changes in the market yield and shifts in their overall credit position.

Table 4–1 provides an insight into the return and risk characteristics of corporate

[4]Moody's rates bonds Aaa and Baa, whereas Standard & Poor's rates bonds AAA and BAA.

THE INVESTMENT ALTERNATIVES

TABLE 4–1

Annual Yields of Long-Term Corporate Bonds,
Average Return and Standard Deviation

Year	All Industries	AAA	BAA
1970	8.51	8.04	9.11
1971	7.94	7.39	8.56
1972	7.63	7.21	8.16
1973	7.80	7.44	8.24
1974	8.98	8.57	9.50
1975	9.46	8.83	10.39
1976	9.01	8.43	9.75
1977	8.43	8.02	8.97
1978	9.07	8.73	9.49
1979	10.12	9.63	10.69
1980	12.75	11.94	13.67
1981	15.06	14.17	14.75
1982	14.92	13.79	14.41
Mean	9.98	9.40	10.40
Standard Deviation	6.02	5.16	4.97

SOURCE: *Federal Reserve Bulletin,* May 1976, p. A27; September
1978, p. A27; November 1981; February 1983, p. A28.

bonds as well. Yields have tended to rise over the past 10 years, with recurring periods of very high yields followed by a decline in yields, and then higher yields again. Yields on lower-rated BAA or BBB bonds, on the average, were 80 to 100 basis points higher than for AAA-rated bonds. The standard deviation of the average yields was higher with BAA bonds than with AAA bonds. The standard deviation relative to the average yield was higher for BAA bonds than for AAA bonds. In principle, lower-rated bonds are more risky than higher-rated bonds and offer a higher yield.

RISK AND HOLDING-PERIOD YIELDS. The variability of bond yields as indicated by data in Table 4–1 can be used to the investor's advantage. Yields are not constant. It pays the investor to buy bonds when yields are high and sell when yields are low. Assume, for example, that an investor bought an 8 percent AAA bond in 1970 and sold it in two years when it was yielding 7 percent. The bond had a 1990 maturity with an 8 percent coupon. The investor would receive $80 per year interest for the two years and would sell the bond at a higher price in 1972. The price in 1972 would be found by using the equation:

$$P_{1972} = \sum_{t=1}^{18} \frac{I_t}{(1+r)^t} + \frac{P_{18}}{(1+r)^{18}}$$

Since r is 7 percent and I_t is $80, it is a simple matter to find P_{1972} by substituting the numbers in the equation. The sum of the present value of $80 at 7 percent for 18 years is $784(9.800 × $80), from Appendix A2. The present value of P_{18}, $1,000, is $321(.321 × $1,000), from the Appendix A1. The total present value is $1,105, which is the price in 1972, or P_{1972}.

The investor bought the bond at $1,000, sold it for $1,105, and received $80 a year interest. The approximate yield is [($1,105 — $1,000)/2 + $80] ÷ [($1,105 + $1,000) ÷ 2] = ($52.50 + $80) ÷ $1,052.50 = $132.50 ÷ $1,052.50 = 12.59 percent. Therefore, an investor could have purchased a bond yielding 8 percent that provided a total return for the holding period that was more than 50 percent higher. So bonds and stocks have something in common: Buying bonds or stocks when expected yields are relatively high and selling them when yields are relatively low over some holding period of two or three years can enhance profitability. The Salomon bond index earned over 40 percent in 1982 because of this action.

However, let's assume the investor just held the bond until the end of 1981. What would the investor have earned for the period? At the end of 1981 the yield on an AAA bond would have been approximately 15 percent. In this case the bond price would be much lower. The present value of the $80 interest income at 15 percent for 9 years would be $381.76 ($80 × 4.772). The present value of the $1,000 maturity value of the bond would be $284.00 ($1,000 × .284). The price of the bond would therefore be $665.76 ($381.76 + $284.00). The investor purchased the bond at $1,000 and during the 11 years held suffered a total loss of $334.24. This amounts to an annual loss of $30.39; it would reduce the $80 interest income to $49.61 and would have provided only 4.96 percent return on original investment. Since the investor actually lost money, the average investment would have been lower. The investor's yield on average investment would have been 5.96 percent ($49.61 ÷ $832.88). This was not a satisfactory return considering inflation. The example points out clearly why investors have been wary of buying long-term bonds.

Advantages and Disadvantages of Corporate Debt Securities

Corporate debt securities of private businesses offer certain definite advantages for the investment of funds. They provide a high degree of safety of principal and stability of income, comparable to those of government securities. The highest-quality bonds, above a BAA rating, are excellent investments for institutional investors too, particularly for those who can invest only in debt securities. Yields are higher than those offered by government securities. For this reason, this type of security is attractive if income is needed. Bonds rated BAA offer the individual investor a still higher yield and represent an attractive investment without a substantially higher risk.

The major disadvantages of corporate bonds are much the same as those for other debt securities. They do not offer the promise of capital gain, nor are they a hedge against inflation unless the bonds are traded or held for a shorter period. Corporate bonds are also susceptible to changes in money rates. Yields fluctuate in sympathy with yields in the money market, and these fluctuations can be as severe as in the stock market. Poor timing in the purchase or sale of bonds or buying long-term bonds when interest rates are rising could result in financial loss. Some low-grade bonds do not provide security of principal, and are susceptible to business or credit risk. These factors might force us to ignore debt as an outlet for our funds.

The nature of corporate debt securities—their security of principal and stability of income—makes them attractive to institutional investors only when bond yields are historically high. Generally, the small investor is not a major purchaser of long-term bonds. Corporate bonds might be attractive for the investor in the moderate income tax bracket who seeks a higher yield than would be afforded on government bonds, and who is willing to give up some security of principal to achieve the greater income.

ZERO-INTEREST-RATE BONDS. In the past few years, some corporations have issued zero-interest-rate bonds. These bonds sell at a discount and are repaid at maturity—a 15 percent, 10-year bond would sell at an approximate price of $247 per $1,000 face value of the bond. This allows investors to build assets over time. Taxes must be paid annually if the bond is private. Municipal bonds are tax free. Such bonds could be attractive for investors who do not need current income.

VARIABLE-RATE BONDS. Some corporations have begun to issue variable-rate bonds. The price of these bonds remains stable. The income or interest is changed to reflect changes in market yields. Their main advantage is price stability and better return performance for the investor.

Keeping Abreast of Corporate Bonds

In addition to the sources of information presented in this chapter, *The Wall Street Journal* provides a daily review of up-to-date bond information. Bonds listed on the New York Stock Exchange are quoted daily, and price and volume relationships are summarized. *The Wall Street Journal* also carries "Bond Markets" and "Financing Business" columns that help keep the investor abreast of current events in the money and capital markets. Invaluable factual and advisory data are presented in Standard & Poor's *Bond Guide*, which also provides a coded reference to underwriters who handle specific issues, in case more information is needed by an investor. Moody's is also an excellent source.

CONVERTIBLE BONDS

The majority of corporate bonds offer two promises to the investor; convertible bonds offer a third—the promise of sharing in capital growth—by giving the bondholder the right to exchange bonds for common stock of the company. If the stock increases in price, the bond will also increase in price. If the stock price remains the same, the bond will still provide a good yield. The right to convert the bond into common stock is stated in the bond indenture. It may be expressed in terms of the price at which the shares of stock may be exchanged for the bond; it is then referred to as the *conversion price*. Or it can be expressed as the number of shares into which each bond may be converted—the *conversion rate*. It makes little difference how conversion is established; whether it is stated as a price or in a number of shares per bond, the effect is the same. Let us assume, for example, that a bond can be converted into common stock at a conversion price of $50 per share. Since the par value of a bond is usually $1,000, this means that each bond may be converted into 20 shares of stock. The rate could therefore be expressed as a conversion rate of 20.

The common stock price of a convertible bond is found by multiplying the number of shares of stock into which the bond is convertible by the market price of the stock. Xerox 6s of 1995, for example, are convertible into 10.87 shares of common stock. The price of the bond in October 1981 was 60. The stock was at 43, which gives the bond a stock price of $464.41 (10.87 × $43). In this case, the price of the bond was higher than the price of the stock into which it could be converted. Note that prices of bonds are usually higher than common stock prices. The reason for this is the expectation by the investor, at the time of the initial offering of the bond, of a price rise in the stock.

When a convertible bond is sold originally, the conversion rate is set below the value of the bond. This encourages investors to hold the bond for appreciation. As the price of the stock increases, the price of the bond moves above par, and expectation of a future price increase by the investor continues. So once again, the bond sells higher than the equivalent value in stock. Under normal circumstances, the bond will continue to move up and sell above its conversion value in terms of common stock. Convertible bonds with quality ratings, therefore, offer a satisfactory investment, with income and a chance to share in company growth.

A representative list of investment-grade and convertible bonds can be found in S&P's *Bond Guide*. Standard & Poor's also publishes a selected list of convertible bonds in *The Outlook* from time to time, as a source of up-to-date information.

Calculating Return and Risk

A convertible bond must be analyzed as a bond and as a stock. In analyzing it as a bond, the investor must be keenly aware of debt-to-asset and interest-to-income ratios, as in the analysis of ordinary bonds. As a stock, its future earnings, dividends, and price must be analyzed. In making a decision about the expected return of a convertible bond, the investor can use the equation:

$$P_0 = \sum_{t=1}^{n} \frac{I_t}{(1 + r)^t} + \frac{P_n}{(1 + r)^n}$$

In this case, P_n represents the expected price of the convertible bond for some year or holding period in the future. P_n is some function of the price per share of the common stock times the conversion rate, plus a premium for future expectations of growth of earnings. If the stock price is expected to be $55 in three years, the conversion ratio is 25, a 5 percent price premium is expected over the conversion price, $65 a year is paid in interest, and the present price of the convertible bond is $1,100 (110), then the approximate yield is ([($1,375.00 + $68.75 − $1,100.00) ÷ 3] + $65.00) ÷ [($1,443.75 + $1,100.00) ÷ 2] = [($343.75 ÷ 3) + $65.00] ÷ ($2,543.75 ÷ 2) = ($114.58 + $65.00) ÷ $1,271.88 = $179.58 ÷ $1,271.88 = 14.12 percent.

If the three-year price of $55 is realistic, the investor will earn a yield of 14.12 percent, which is almost twice as high as the interest rate on the bond. If the price in the future is higher or lower, the return will be higher or lower. Such estimates might be within 30 percent of the average, which means that the investor expects a return of 14.12 ± 4.24 percent. The average return, then, is 14.12 and the risk 4.24 percent. This will help in making a final decision about purchasing the security.

The Advantages of Convertible Bonds

The major advantage of convertible bonds is their defensive-aggressive characteristic. They provide security of principal and interest income, and they offer the possibility of an increase in capital value. If the common stock of the company increases in price, the price of the convertible bond will increase also. If, on the other hand, the price of the stock drops, then the price of the bond will drop. However—and this is a further advantage of this type of security—if the stock price drops and the bond declines in price, it will sell like a bond rather than a stock. When it sells as a debt instrument, the price is supported, which puts a floor under the price and reduces the possibility of complete loss.

A second advantage of convertible bonds is their strength as collateral for loans. Commercial bankers tend to lend the same percentage amount of the convertible bond as the margin requirement for common stock, but the amount is negotiable. Borrowing on margin permits the purchase of a larger amount of bonds with a given amount of dollars. This leverage will help improve returns if the investor's decision is correct.

A third advantage is the regularity and security of income from these bonds. Many are convertible into stock that pays only a small dividend, or none at all. The income from such common stock would be small or nonexistent, and the current yield low. The interest income from the convertible bonds could be substantially higher than that from the common stock. To attract capital, some convertible bonds that have a low B rating will pay a high rate of interest. The risk involved in this type of security is greater, however, and should be thoroughly studied before a commitment is made.

A fourth advantage is that convertible bonds may protect people who wish to speculate by selling stock short. Assume a stock is sold short at 100. It declines to 80. Selling it at 100 and buying it back at 80 gives 20 points per-share profit. At the same time, sufficient convertibles could be purchased so that if the stock should rise in price, the bonds could be converted to stock and delivered to the person from whom the stock was borrowed in the first place. If the price of the stock should decline, profit is made on the short sale and interest is earned on the bonds. When the bond price moves back up the bonds can be sold, and profit is made from both a falling and a rising stock market.

A fifth advantage of convertibles is to institutional investors and financial institutions. Convertibles offer such investors an opportunity to share in the growth of common stock even though they cannot, by law, own a large amount of common stock or a non-dividend-paying common stock.

The Disadvantages of Convertible Bonds

The major disadvantage of convertible bonds is in the loss that might occur if they are purchased at too high a price. In order to be attractive for investment, they should provide a fair return in terms of the bond or the stock price, and the risk of a sharp drop in price should be small. A convertible bond purchased at 160, for example, might have a negative yield to maturity. This implies that the stock is overpriced. A person buying a convertible at this price loses the advantage of a price increase, and at the same time accepts the possibility of a sharp decrease should the market price of the stock fall because of a decline in earnings or because of the market risk. If the bond offers a satisfactory return in terms of the common stock value, then it may be purchased for investment. If there is little chance for the stock price to decline because earnings are strong, then the bond could be purchased at these levels.

A second disadvantage of convertibles is their relative lack of security compared to other corporate debt. Most are rated lower than comparable nonconvertible bonds. Many convertible bonds are subordinated to other debts, giving them a junior claim to assets in case of failure. In essence, a convertible bond is a debt that serves as equity, and it must be considered such when analyzed.

Most convertible bonds are callable, too; the corporation may call the bonds at its discretion. Should this happen, bondholders would be forced to convert or to sell and take a profit if a capital gain exists. In a bond call, the decision to convert is taken away from the bondholder through the act of calling, which forces conversion. This might come at an inappropriate time for the investor and represents a third disadvantage of convertible bonds. The bond issue is usually protected from a call for 10 years, but this must be verified at the time of purchase. A fourth disadvantage is that such bonds are subject to the money-rate risk. As yields rise, the price will fall. And this was the trend in past years through 1981.

BONDS WITH WARRANTS

The warrant bond is a type of security that offers the investor some of the same advantages as convertible bonds. One warrant is associated with one bond, but a warrant attached to the bond gives the owner the right to buy a specified number of common shares at a stated price—called the *subscription price*—for a limited period of time. The time period might be as long as five years. The warrant may be exercised separately from the bond, in which case it is called a *detachable warrant*. A bond having a detachable warrant could benefit the investor in one of two ways if the warrant increased in value because of an increase in price of the common stock: (1) The warrant could be sold and the gain realized; (2) the warrant could be exercised and the stock bought at the option price, then sold at the market price. If the stock were held and ownership of the bond retained, the investment position would change. The investor would be a bondholder *and* a stockholder. The warrant, however, might be nondetachable, in which case it would be necessary to send the bond to the company's agent. The agent would detach the warrant and return the bond at the time the option was to be exercised.

Bonds with warrants allow investors to share in the growth of the company without undue risk by participating in the potential increase in value of the common stock. If the market price of the common stock remained below the subscription price set in the bond agreement, then the bond would be held without exercising the warrant. If the stock increased in price, the warrant could be sold and the bond retained. A profit on the warrant would be earned, and a safe debt-type security would be held for investment.

Bonds with warrants, however, are not as common in present-day markets as the more popular convertible bonds. The market price of the bond plus the market value of the stock from the warrant, compared with the market price of the bond plus the cash cost of exercising the warrant, will help decide the relative advantage of buying the bond or the stock. Bonds with warrants selling on a high current-yield basis might be attractive because of the expected profit potential of the growth in common stock price.

The ability to share in price increases by means of warrants is not as great as it is for convertible bonds. The warrant bond offers protection against the purchasing-power and the business risk. The quality of each bond issue must be judged by the tests used for other bonds—namely, ability to repay the debt, ability to pay interest, and overall credit position of the company. Bonds with warrants offer a higher return and a higher risk than ordinary bonds.

FOREIGN BONDS

Foreign corporations raise money by selling bonds to investors in their country. BMW might wish to sell bonds to German investors to raise money for expansion. These bonds, from the viewpoint of German investors, are domestic bonds denominated in *Deutch marks*. From the viewpoint of American investors who might wish to buy the German bonds of BMW, they are considered *indigenous foreign bonds*. If BMW wished to sell bonds in the United States denominated in *marks* and sold for *marks* held in the United States, they would be called *external foreign bonds*. Actually Eurobonds are a good example of this type of bond. Assume IBM sold dollar-denominated bonds in Europe to holders of American dollars. This would be an example of Eurobonds. If Sony sold Japanese bonds in Europe denominated in *yen*, they also would be called Eurobonds.

Investors might wish to invest in foreign bonds for several reasons:

1. The yield might be higher than from American corporate bonds.
2. Foreign currency deposits might be available.
3. The investor might profit from changes in the exchange rate which would provide higher return.
4. International bond investment might reduce the risk or variability of the portfolio.

The disadvantages are the added risk of currency fluctuations, lack of information, and the creditworthiness of a specific bond issue.

The pattern of yields of long-term government bonds issued by selected countries is presented in Figure 1–8 in Chapter 1. These yields reflect the behavior of yields in foreign bonds, compared to U.S. bonds. Although the levels differ, the patterns are similar.

SUMMARY

As a basic principle, short-term corporate investments are less risky than long-term investments; and intermediate-term securities offer the investor a higher yield and greater risk than short-term securities. As another basic principle, lower-rated bonds are more risky than higher-rated bonds. Convertible securities, as a general principle, are more risky but can be more rewarding than ordinary private corporate bonds.

As a basic principle, a careful analysis must be made of all debt securities. The analysis centers on the ability of the company to pay interest charges and the debt when it is due. In addition, the ratio of total debt to capital and assets must be calculated to determine whether debt is excessive. The analysis should include interest coverage currently and in the future; fixed charges relative to income available for charges, where charges include debt retirement as well as interest; and the change expected in the ratios in the future. In determining debt limits, it is important to estimate future earning power and the overall credit position of the company. Norms and trends for interest-coverage ratios vary, and judgment must be exercised to determine adequacy.

The yield and variability should be estimated. Measuring return and variability for a long-term bond requires several estimates of the holding-period return. The average return and standard deviation will establish these figures. The equation for estimating return for a three-year holding period is:

$$P_0 = \sum_{t=1}^{3} \frac{I_t}{(1 + r)^t} + \frac{P_3}{(1 + r)^3}$$

This can be compared to other bonds and stocks for a similar period. In using this equation, it is necessary to estimate future price at the end of the holding period. This, of course, requires a forecast of bond yields to determine the future bond price. Return to first call and yield to maturity may also be calculated.

The same process is undertaken for convertible bonds. In the case of convertible bonds, the future price of the bond must be estimated. Future price is determined by multiplying the price of the common stock by the conversion rate and adding any premium to the bond that exists because of the attractiveness of the privilege. The average of several estimates establishes the expected return and the variability. This provides the investor with return-to-risk figures. A convertible bond must be examined both as a bond and as a common stock.

Bonds with warrants must be analyzed in a way similar to that for convertible bonds. The return expected is a function of the future value of the bond and the stock relative to the present price and future option price. Zero-interest-rate bonds might be attractive for some investors, since they stress certain capital growth. For investors interested in protecting principal, a long-term variable-rate bond might be attractive.

Foreign corporate bonds might be attractive, but they have additional risk created by lack of information and exchange-rate fluctuations.

SUMMARY OF PRINCIPLES

1. Corporate bonds are generally more risky than governments.
2. The basic principle of debt analysis is to assure interest and debt repayment.
3. The higher the yield, the greater the risk and the lower the bond rating.
4. Long-term bonds are more risky than short-term bonds.
5. Intermediate-term bonds are more risky than short-term bonds.

6. All long-term bonds have substantial variability of returns, which in some cases is comparable to common stock variability.

7. All bond prices must be forecasted to estimate return for a holding period.

8. Convertible bonds usually have lower current yields but higher expected return and are more risky than nonconvertible bonds.

9. Foreign bonds might offer higher returns because of the increase in returns from changes in currency exchange rates and higher risk.

REVIEW QUESTIONS

1. When a corporation borrows money, what are the promises it makes to the investor who purchases the bond or bonds?

2. What do the terms *maturity*, *call*, and *serial* have in common, and how do they differ?

3. Discuss ways in which the security of the pledge to repay may be enhanced or weakened.

4. The company issuing bonds agrees to pay the interest, on a regular basis, to the bondholder. Distinguish between *interest rate*, *coupon rate*, and *current yield*.

5. What are protective covenants designed to do for the bondholder?

6. Explain how yield to first call is calculated.

7. Explain how yield for the bond holding period is calculated.

8. Explain how the variability of yield for a bond or convertible bond is estimated.

9. Discuss the ways in which we can assess the investment quality of a corporate bond.

10. Discuss the relationship among bond quality, bond ratings, and bond yields.

11. What risks are assumed when high-grade and/or speculative-grade bonds are purchased by the investor?

12. What advantages and disadvantages do foreign bonds hold for the investor?

13. How variable are returns on long-term corporate bonds and on convertible bonds?

14. Which are more risky, corporate bonds or convertible bonds? Explain.

15. How would you define zero-interest-rate bonds and variable-rate bonds?

16. What are the advantages and disadvantages of an investment in convertible bonds? Where and when would they be most apt to be used by the investor?

17. What is meant by a bond with warrants, and what advantages does such a bond hold for the investor?

PROBLEMS

1. In June 1976, AT&T bonds maturing in June 1985 had a coupon of 4 3/8 percent (4 3/8s 85) and were selling at 78.
   a. Calculate the current yield of the bond.
   b. Calculate the yield to maturity, using the approximate method.
   c. Calculate the yield to maturity, using the discount method.

d. The bond price in 1981 was 81. With four years to maturity, what would be the yield of the bond?

e. If an investor had sold the bond in 1981, what would have been the annual return of the bond for the period held?

f. How did the bond perform over the investment period?

2. A First Bank System convertible bond was issued in June 1976 and due in the year 2000, paid 6 1/4 percent, and was rated AA. The bond was convertible into 20.62 shares of common stock. The bond sold at 82 in 1981, and the common stock sold at 40. The stock paid a dividend of $2.44 a share to provide a current yield of 7.1 percent.

a. Calculate the yield to maturity of the bond in 1981 (assuming it was not converted).

b. Now assume that the common stock sold at 56 in 1981. The bond should sell at an 8 percent premium. Calculate the expected return of the bond, assuming the bond is converted in four years.

c. Comment on the return and risk characteristics of the convertible bond.

3. The zero-interest-rate, 10-year bond sold at a 15 percent yield to maturity. One year later, the bond sold on a yield basis of 13 percent. What was the price of the bond? What return did an investor earn for the one-year holding period?

4. A 30-year variable-rate bond sold on a 15 percent yield basis. The following year the rate declined to 13 percent. What happened to the bond price? What was the return for the period?

CASE

Terry examined the yields from foreign bonds listed in Figure 1–8. He thought he would like to invest in some foreign bonds that would provide him with a high yield and low risk. He also thought he might earn an added return because of rising currency values relative to U.S. currency. From the data in Figure 1–8, estimate the annual yield for the past five years for the bonds of each country represented. Average the annual yield and calculate the standard deviation. Without considering the change in currency values, which foreign bond has been most profitable? Which most risky? Which bond issue(s) would you recommend Terry purchase, and why?

SELECTED READINGS

BIERMAN, HAROLD, JR. "Convertible Bonds as Investments." *Financial Analysts Journal*, March–April 1980.

BURTON, J. S., and J. R. TOTH. "Forecasting Long-Term Interest Rates." *Financial Analysts Journal*, September–October 1974, pp. 73–86.

FINDLAY, M. C., and E. E. WILLIAMS. "Better Debt Service Coverage Ratios." *Financial Analysts Journal*, November–December 1975, pp. 58–62.

GROSS, WILLIAM H. "The Effects of Coupons on Yield Spreads." *Financial Analysts Journal*, July–August 1979.

GUSHEE, CHARLES H. "How to Immunize a Bond Investment." *Financial Analysts Journal*, March–April 1981, p. 44.

HALL, J. PARKER IV. "Shouldn't You Own Fewer Long-Term Bonds." *Financial Analysts Journal*, May–June 1981.

HOMER, SIDNEY. "Total Money Management with Specific Illustrations from the Bond Market." New York: Salomon Brothers, 1973.

JENKINS, JAMES W. "Taxes, Margining, and Bond Selection." *Financial Analysts Journal*, May–June 1980.

LEIBOWITZ, MARTIN L. "Understanding Convertible Securities." *Financial Analysts Journal*, November–December 1974, pp. 57–68.

———. "A Yield Basis for Financial Futures." *Financial Analysts Journal*, January–February 1981.

LENDERMAN, RICHARD. "The Sinking Fund Bond Game." *Financial Analysts Journal*, November–December 1980.

LOVELL, ROBERT JR. "Alternative Investments." *Financial Analysts Journal*, May–June 1980.

MACAULAY, FREDERICK R. *Some Theoretical Problems Suggested by the Movement of Interest Rates, Bond Yields and Stock Prices in the U.S. since 1856.* New York: National Bureau of Economic Research, 1938.

MALKIEL, BURTON G. *The Term Structure of Interest Rates.* Princeton, N.J.: Princeton University Press, 1966.

MAYER, KENNETH R. "Yield Spreads and Interest Rate Bonds." *Financial Analysts Journal*, November–December 1978.

MERTON, ROBERT. "On the Pricing of Corporate Debt: The Risk Structure of Interest Rates." *The Journal of Finance*, May 1974, pp. 449–70.

ROLL, RICHARD. "Investment Diversification and Bond Maturity." *The Journal of Finance*, March 1971, pp. 51–66.

SHARPE, WILLIAM F. "Bonds versus Stocks—Some Lessons from Capital Market Theory." *Financial Analysts Journal*, November–December 1973, pp. 74–80.

SOLDOFSKY, R. M. "Yield-Risk Performance Measurements." *Financial Analysts Journal*, September–October 1968, pp. 130–39.

———. "Yield-Risk Performance on Convertible Securities." *Financial Analysts Journal*, March–April 1971, pp. 61–65.

———, and R. L. MILLER. "Risk-Premium Curves for Different Classes of Long-Term Securities, 1950–66." *The Journal of Finance*, March 1966, pp. 429–45.

WALTER, J. E., and A. V. Que. "The Valuation of Convertible Bonds." *The Journal of Finance*, June 1973, pp. 713–32.

CHAPTER 5

PREFERRED-STOCK
ANALYSIS AND VALUATION
An Ownership Security

Preferred stock, an ownership security, has certain risks not associated with a fixed-income debt security: Dividends are contingent upon earnings rather than being mandatory, as is the interest on bonds; and the preferred stock's claim on corporate assets is subordinate to that of bonds. Yet the dividends on preferred stock are usually fixed in amount, just as with bonds. It suffers along with bonds from the interest-rate risk. In this chapter, the unique characteristics of preferred stock will be examined, along with its virtues and limitations for an investment program.

THE GENERAL NATURE OF PREFERRED STOCK

Historically, corporations have not relied heavily on preferred stock as a major source of funds. New preferred issues have represented only a small portion of the money raised by corporations through the sale of securities, because preferred stock does not possess the tax advantages of bonds, yet the payment of dividends is almost as binding as the interest payment on bonds. There are, however, attributes that make preferred of interest to certain investors. The first and primary attribute is the preference of their dividends on the earnings of the company. The second is the preference to a claim on assets over common stock in the unusual case of liquidation and in the more usual case of reorganization, refinancing, or adjustment of a company's capital account. A third is the partial (85 percent) tax exemption of preferred dividends if owned by another corporation.

The First Attribute—First Preference to Dividends

Cash dividends on preferred stock have priority over those on common stock. This is of primary importance to preferred-stock owners. If a dividend is declared (even when earnings are adequate and cash is available, dividends must be declared by the board of directors) and the corporation does not have sufficient earnings to pay the dividend on both preferred and common stock, it is required to pay the dividend on preferred first. If any funds remain after payment of the preferred dividend, one may be paid on the common stock. This priority of dividends is in contrast to the interest payment on bonds, which is a fixed claim upon earnings and must be paid or the corporation will be in default. Dividends on preferred are subordinate to both federal income taxes and bond interest. Dividends on preferred stock are paid from net income after taxes; bond interest is paid before taxes. This subordination tends to make preferred stock somewhat weaker than the dividend priority suggests.

The Second Attribute—Preference to Assets

Most preferred stocks have a par or stated value. The *par value* is stated in the charter of the corporation and may be changed by consent of the corporate stockholders. When preferred stock has no par value, the directors may, at their discretion, assign a value to it, called the *stated value*. In the event of failure of the corporation, the preferred stockholder has the right to receive the par or stated value of the shares before any money is distributed to the common stockholders. The assets are usually not liquidated and distributed; rather, the corporation is reorganized, and claims against the assets are scaled down. Preferred stock purchased in the market is entitled in liquidation, reorganization, or recapitalization to only the par or stated value, even though the purchase price was higher.

Preferred stock is attractive to those who desire greater security of principal and a higher current income than is supplied by common stock. Should the company fail, the investor is assured of a superior position with respect to owners of common stock.

The Third Attribute—Partial Tax Exemption

Corporations that invest in preferred stock pay federal income taxes on only 15 percent of the dividend income. Eighty-five percent of the dividend is exempt. A corporation in the 46 percent tax bracket would pay only a 6.9 percent tax on the total preferred-dividend income. This would appeal to insurance companies or private corporations.

The Usual Features of Preferred Stock

Several other features are typically associated with preferred stock. The classes of stock a corporation has issued are described in the corporate charter; so is preferred stock. If the charter were silent and common law were allowed to rule, the preferred stock of a company would not be significantly different from the common stock, except that it would be cumulative and nonparticipating. The charter and the preferred-stock agreement are not silent, however, and detailed characteristics are clearly set forth.

VOTING. Preferred stock is usually nonvoting. Its owner does not vote to elect the company directors. However, it does have *contingent voting rights*. That is, in times of financial trouble, preferred stockholders would be given the right to elect some of the directors. The New York Stock Exchange will not list a preferred stock for trading unless it carries the contingent right to vote. The exchange rule states that if six quarterly dividends have not been paid, the preferred stockholders have the right to elect a minimum of two directors. Also, preferred stockholders usually have the right to vote approval on the issuance of additional preferred stock, mergers and consolidations with other companies, and charter amendments.

MATURITY AND CALL. Typically, preferred stock has no maturity date. In this respect it is similar to common stock. The usual preferred stock is callable, however, at the option of the company. The call or redemption feature allows the company to retire all or part of the issue at a price stated in the original agreement. This provides flexibility for corporate management, but it may be detrimental to the investor. The discussion of bonds disclosed that a change in maturity date caused by activation of the call option will have an impact on yield. The change might be advantageous or harmful to the investor. The effect is the same for callable preferred stock. The effect of the call date on return must be calculated.

SINKING FUND. A sinking fund is customarily provided in 40 percent of the modern preferred-stock agreements. Stock may be called for sinking-fund purposes to ensure the retirement of the preferred stock. Such a provision is most often found in industrial and public-utility preferred stock, where there might be some desire to eliminate the stock from the capital structure. If a sinking fund is included, it is a small percentage of the total issue.

DIVIDENDS. Dividends on preferred stock are stated as a percentage of par value or as a dollar amount. Usually, when the par value is low or when there is no par value, the dividend is stated in dollars. The $5 preferred stock of General Motors is a good example of this type of dividend. When the par value is above $50, the dividend is stated as a percentage of par.

The dividends of a company may be *cumulative* or *noncumulative*, but the usual preferred-stock dividend is cumulative. This means that if a payment is missed, the dividend accumulates and is added to future dividend payments. The accumulation of dividends, or dividend arrearage because of inability to earn enough to pay dividends, has caused financial difficulty for some companies. Dividends in arrears often force the company to change its capital structure or to recapitalize to eliminate past unpaid dividends. When recapitalization is completed, the company will once again be in a position to pay dividends on the common stock. When dividends on preferred stock are in arrears, no dividends can be paid on common stock.

Preferred-stock dividends can be *participating* or *nonparticipating*; usually they are nonparticipating. A participating preferred stock will share, beyond its stated dividend rate, in earnings with the common shares. Participation might be equal with common stock, or there might be a limit. Most participation features allow preferred stock to share equally with common stock after a similar amount of dividend has been paid on the common stock. This is unlimited participation. Details of participation are not rigid, and, based upon the judgment of the corporation's directors, they can be set to meet the needs of investors.

Participating preferred would be an ideal security in which to invest, offering the same security of principal as regular preferred, together with an opportunity to share in future growth of the company. Few outstanding preferred issues, however, combine both quality and the participating feature.

CONVERTIBILITY. Preferred stock is typically nonconvertible. Only about one-third of the issues outstanding enjoy the conversion privilege—a feature that makes convertible preferred an attractive investment security. This conversion feature is almost identical with that of bonds. In each case, there is an additional privilege of sharing in the potential increase in common stock value, plus some security of principal and stability of income. Convertible preferred, however, does not usually have security equal to that of convertible bonds. The corporation's subordinated convertible debentures have a claim senior to that of convertible preferred stocks. If a convertible preferred stock were the senior security with no debt outstanding, then it could be as strong as a senior convertible bond issue. With preferred stock, the conversion ratio is usually protected from dilution by stock splits and stock dividends in the same manner as with convertible bonds.

Tables 5–1 and 5–2 provide lists of high-grade noncallable, callable, and convertible utility and industrial preferreds that possess most of the characteristics of preferred stock. The list of preferreds with the special convertible feature could offer advantageous investment opportunities. The convertible feature makes them more attractive than ordinary preferred for individual investment requirements.

YIELDS ON PREFERRED STOCK

The yield on preferred stock is different from that on bonds in that there is no maturity value for preferred. The yield is a current yield, found by dividing the current price or purchase price into the dollars of dividend income paid on the stock. The yield on the $6 Pacific Telephone & Telegraph preferred in Table 5–1, for example, is obtained by dividing the price of $56\frac{1}{2}$ into $6, which gives a current yield of 10.6 percent. In the case of a bond, the purchase price and maturity price might differ, resulting in a gain or a loss for the investor that would affect yield to maturity. In the case of preferred stock, there will be no capital gain or loss if the stock is held forever. Dividend income, then, is the only income received, and it will be paid perpetually—assuming, of course, that there is no call feature or sinking fund.

As yields change in the marketplace, however, the price of the preferred stock will change. The change in price will change the return the investor earns for the period the stock was held if the preferred stock is sold at a price different from the purchase price. If the price rises, the investor will earn a higher return than the dividend yield. If the price declines, the investor will earn a lower return than that indicated by the current yield. Yields on preferred stocks rose during the period 1979 through 1981. Since prices declined, investors lost money even though the dividend was stable for the period. This is illustrated in Figure 5–1. Notice how the price declined as market

TABLE 5–1

Selected Noncallable and Callable Preferred Stock

Issue	Par Value ($)	Price High	Range Low	Rating	Approx. Value ($)	Current Yield (%)
Noncallable Preferred						
Amstar Corp., 5.44%	12.50	$5\frac{7}{8}$	$4\frac{3}{4}$	BBB	5	13.6
Celanese Corp., 4.5%	100.00	$38\frac{3}{8}$	$31\frac{1}{2}$	BBB	$32\frac{1}{2}$	13.9
Consolidated Edison of NY, 6%	100.00	104	73	A	103	5.8
Detroit Edison, 5.5%	100.00	$58\frac{1}{4}$	$51\frac{3}{4}$	BB	$54\frac{1}{2}$	10.1
Ingersoll-Rand, 12.35%	No par	48	$32\frac{3}{4}$	BBB	35	6.7
Kaiser-Aluminum, 4.75%	100.00	103	61	No rank	61	7.8
Pacific Gas & Electric, 6%	25.00	$12\frac{1}{8}$	10	A	10	15.0
Pacific Tel. & Tel., 6%	100.00	$56\frac{5}{8}$	$45\frac{1}{2}$	BBB	$56\frac{1}{2}$	10.6
Uniroyal, 8%	100.00	$44\frac{3}{4}$	30	C	$39\frac{1}{2}$	—
Callable Preferred						
American Tel. & Tel., $4	1	$62\frac{7}{8}$	50	AA	62	6.5
Consolidated Edison NY, $5	No par	$38\frac{5}{8}$	$32\frac{7}{8}$	A	$33\frac{1}{4}$	15.0
Consumers Power, $4.50	No par	33	$26\frac{1}{4}$	BB	$27\frac{1}{2}$	16.4
General Motors, $5.00	100	$45\frac{3}{8}$	37	AAA	$37\frac{3}{8}$	13.4
Ohio Edison, 4.56%	100	$34\frac{1}{2}$	28	BB	28	16.3
Philadelphia Elec., 4.68%	100	$33\frac{1}{4}$	28	BBB	28	16.7
Public Service Elec. & Gas, 6.8%	100	$50\frac{3}{8}$	42	A	$42\frac{1}{4}$	16.1

SOURCE: *Barron's*; S&P *Stock Guide,* August 1981.

TABLE 5–2

Convertible Preferred

Issue	Call Price ($)	Common Shares, Each Pfd.	Recent Price Common ($)	Value Pfd. in Common	Recent Price Pfd. ($)	Price Range Pfd. High	Low	Yield (%)	Rating
Amerada Hess, $3.50	150	4.35	$24\frac{7}{8}$	108.20	97	186	97	3.6	A
Atlantic Richfield, $3.00	82	6.80	$48\frac{1}{8}$	327.25	325	450	$285\frac{1}{2}$	0.9	AA
Eaton Corp., 4.75%	25	1.50	$30\frac{3}{4}$	46.13	45	57	42	2.6	A
Lockheed Corp., $11.25	111.25	2.874	$41\frac{1}{4}$	118.55	127	$130\frac{3}{4}$	97	8.9	No rating
Monsanto Co., $2.75	73	1.12	$63\frac{1}{2}$	71.12	$71\frac{1}{8}$	$90\frac{1}{2}$	$77\frac{1}{2}$	4.0	No rating

SOURCE: *Barron's;* S&P *Stock Guide,* August 1981.

THE INVESTMENT ALTERNATIVES

yields on preferred stocks increased. Also note that because of the decline in price, the average annual return earned on the preferred stock was negative for each year from 1979 through 1981. The current yield as a percentage of purchase price remained constant for the period. If the investor held the preferred stock until 1983 the annual return would have averaged 4.89 percent for the five-year period.

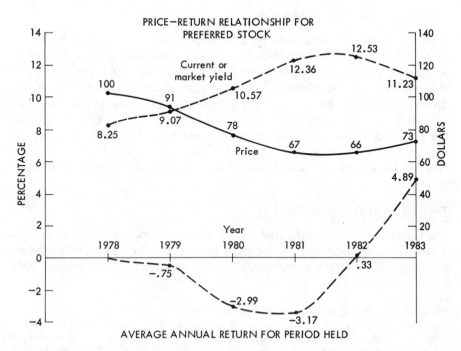

FIGURE 5–1

Price-Return Relationship for Preferred Stock

When a preferred stock has a call date and a call price and can be called for sinking-fund purposes, return is calculated the same way as bond yield. This calculation allows a valid comparison about the expectations of a preferred stock return for a period of time, compared with bond yield for the same period. This should enable investors to make better decisions. Let us assume, for example, that the preferred stock as illustrated in Figure 5–1 was called at 100 in 1982. What return did the investor earn, assuming it was purchased at 100 in 1978? The average investment is (100 + 100)/2 = 100. The average annual income is $8.25 (the average dividend over the period). The yield to call date, then, is 8.25 percent.

If an investor had purchased the preferred stock at $78 per share, the results would have been much different. The average investment would have been $89 per share. The average annual gain would have been $11.00 ($100 − $78)/2). The average income would have been $8.25, and the total average annual dollar income would have been $19.25. The annual average rate of return would have been 21.6 percent ($19.25 ÷ $89). The current yield at $78 would have been 10.57 percent ($8.25 ÷ $78). In the case of the call, the investor would have earned an excellent return. Therefore the investor must be careful in making a decision about preferred stock. The return will vary depending upon changes in yields, the period held, and whether the stock is expected to be called and when. Yields on preferred stock quoted in the financial press are current yields, found by dividing the current price into the dividend paid by the company, not the yield to first call date, or to maturity if there is a maturity date.

Yields Compared with Bond Yields

Yields on preferred stock have usually been higher than on government or private corporate bonds; preferreds offer the investor a comparatively attractive yield with reasonable quality and security. This varies, of course, with the quality of the stock. It is possible that a high-quality preferred stock issue of one company would have a higher credit rating than a bond of a company with substantial debt, and particularly when the preferred is the senior stock issue of the company. Under these conditions, the preferred stock would offer a lower yield than the bond. Dividend income of preferred stock, however, may be offset by the 85 percent dividend credit under present IRS regulations, which would make for lower rates than for bond interest that is fully taxable.

The Pattern of Preferred Yields

The pattern of yields on preferred stock is almost identical with that of yields on other fixed-income obligations. Higher-quality preferreds sell on a lower yield basis than do medium- and lower-grade preferreds. This is apparent from the average yield figures

TABLE 5–3
Preferred Stock Yields, Industrials—Moody Averages

Year	Medium Grade, High Dividend	Speculative Grade, High Dividend	High Grade, Low Dividend	Medium Grade, Low Dividend
1982, June	13.82%	15.39%	11.91%	15.00%
1981	13.12	14.08	11.64	13.07
1980	11.14	11.91	10.11	10.63
1979	9.64	10.36	8.54	9.16
1978	8.71	9.37	7.76	8.12
1977	7.79	8.16	7.12	7.44
1976	7.92	8.48	7.37	7.81
1975	8.47	9.04	7.83	8.18
1974	8.37	8.72	7.48	8.14
1973	7.29	7.58	6.65	7.01
1972	7.03	7.46	6.56	6.85
1971	7.11	7.63	6.55	6.84
1970	7.70	8.35	7.03	7.25
1969	6.62	7.11	6.15	6.38
1968	5.83	6.33	5.62	5.83
1967	5.34	5.70	5.13	5.39
1966	5.03	5.53	4.67	4.95
1965	4.60	4.93	4.07	4.38

SOURCE: Moody's Industrial Manual, vol. k, 1981, A-I, pp. A40–44, Vol. I, 1982, A-I, pp. a36–a38.

THE INVESTMENT ALTERNATIVES

in Tables 5–3 and 5–4. Yields on speculative-grade preferreds averaged almost 1 percent, absolute, above the yields on the highest-quality preferreds. Yields on industrial and public-utility preferreds differ in an interesting way. High-grade industrial preferreds sold on a lower yield basis than the public-utility preferreds. Likewise medium-grade industrial preferreds sold on a lower yield basis than medium-grade public-utility preferreds. This information is useful only to the investor who needs income and is willing to give up some security of principal and accept more risk to obtain it. Such an investor should buy medium-grade utility preferreds rather than medium-grade industrial preferreds. The lower-quality preferreds do not follow the money-rate pattern as closely as do the high-quality; they are also influenced by the business risk.

Variability of Preferred Yields—Return and Risk

Yields on high-grade preferred stocks have been relatively unstable, even though dividends have been stable. A careful comparative analysis of yields on bonds and preferred stocks would reveal that preferred yields are as variable as bond yields.

TABLE 5–4

Preferred Stock Yield, Public Utilities—Moody Averages

Year	High Grade, Low Dividend	Medium Grade, Low Dividend
1982, July	14.28%	15.03%
1981	13.96	14.89
1980	11.84	13.12
1979	9.53	10.56
1978	8.59	9.33
1977	8.12	8.74
1976	8.71	9.41
1975	9.45	10.64
1974	9.26	9.88
1973	7.56	7.78
1972	7.23	7.43
1971	7.10	7.36
1970	7.56	7.78
1969	6.76	6.91
1968	6.07	6.28
1967	5.54	5.77
1966	5.19	5.41
1965	4.53	4.72

NOTE: Yields are based on the closing prices for the last Friday of each month. Averages are not available prior to 1946 because of the lack of suitable issues. Starting with July 1975 the "aa" yield average replaced the high grade, low dividend series and the composite average of the "a" and "baa" replaced the medium grade, low dividend series. These new averages are reasonably comparable to the old series.

SOURCE: Moody's Public Utility Manual, vol. 2, 1981, p. A10; Vol. 2, 1982, p. 10.

The variability of preferred stock yield suggests a degree of risk with preferred stock investment higher than that for bond investment. In principle, preferred stock investment would be more risky than bond investment because of the higher variability of yield, particularly with the speculative-grade preferreds. Before a specific preferred stock is purchased, it would be wise to calculate the historic yield and variability to assess the degree of reward and risk involved, as was done in the analysis related to Figure 5–1.

ANALYSIS OF PREFERRED STOCK

An analysis of preferred stock must emphasize security of principal and security of income. Both attributes—the earnings and the assets of the preferred stock—must be carefully examined on a per-share basis. Most preferred stocks have preference to assets in liquidation; hence, it must be known if the net assets per share are adequate to cover the par or stated value of the stock should the company fail. Since dividends are declared and paid before common dividends, the amount of earnings per share available for the preferred stock must be determined, and also the extent to which earnings cover the preferred dividend requirements.

Assets per Share

Assets per share of preferred stock are significant in determining liquidating value. The book value, or amount of net assets per share, is found by subtracting all debt from the total assets of the company and then dividing by the number of shares of preferred outstanding. Assume, for example, that a company has total assets of $110 million and short- and long-term liabilities of ,$50 million, leaving a net asset balance of $60 million. Assume further that there are 1 million shares of $10 par preferred stock outstanding. The net asset value per share would be $60; this would cover par value six times, providing sufficient assets to repay preferred stockholders par value should the company be liquidated.

If book value covers par value two or three times, this is adequate asset protection under normal circumstances. The marketability of the assets owned by the company, however, will determine whether the preferred stock is adequately secured. Therefore, not only the number of times net assets per share will cover par value must be estimated, but also whether the book-value figure is realistic in terms of the actual market value of the assets owned by the company. In the assumed case, the assets were valued at $110 million; however, assume that in liquidation they would bring only $80 million. The liquidating value of the company, then, is actually lower than the balance sheet value. The liquidating value of the preferred stock would also be less. It would drop to $30 million, or $30 per share ($80 − $50 million, divided by 1 million shares of $10 par value). Asset coverage remains more than adequate, but it is much less than the book-value figures indicate.

If there is adequate asset coverage, preferred stock will be more secure. Asset coverage is adequate when the dollar amount of preferred stock is small in relation to total assets, when net assets are liquid and marketable, and when there is a small amount of debt with prior claim on the assets of the company.

Dividend Coverage

The investor who buys preferred stock is interested in stability of income, and for this reason might be more interested in the safety of dividend than in net assets per share. If the company is able to maintain adequate earnings on each share outstanding, the dividend will be secure. The dividend-coverage ratio, a guide to the security of preferred stock dividends, is found by dividing the dollars of dividend into the net income per share after taxes. It may also be computed on a total basis, but before common dividends have been paid. It is expressed as the number of times contingent charges are earned. In the case mentioned above, 1 million shares of preferred stock had been issued. Let us assume that the company had a net income of $2.5 million after taxes. The preferred stock has a dividend rate of 5 percent, or $.50 per share, for a total dividend requirement of $500,000. Net income per preferred share was $2.50, and the dividend requirement of $.50 per share would result in a dividend-coverage ratio of five times. Under normal circumstances, a 2- or 3-to-1 dividend-coverage ratio is entirely adequate for preferred stock. Thus, the times-contingent-charge earned ratio of 5 to 1 is adequate.

When preferred stock represents only a small part of the capital structure, earnings per share will be extremely high and will provide adequate coverage for the investor's dividend. In 1979 for example, General Motors earned $1020.10 per AAA preferred share on the $5 preferred. The dividend on the preferred was adequately secured. Standard & Poor's *Stock Guide* computed the dividend-coverage ratio on $5 GM preferred for the investor as 204 times in 1979. Few companies that issue preferred stock are in as good a financial position as that. A lesser coverage, however, will provide sufficient protection, and this has been achieved by many companies.

When two issues of preferred stock are outstanding, the preferred dividends should be added together and then the dividend-coverage limit may be applied. If one preferred stock requires a dividend of $200,000 and another a dividend of $300,000, the dividends should be combined, and the net income after taxes should adequately secure both dividends equally. This method would be used even if one preferred stock had a prior claim over net income after taxes. The dividend-coverage limit, when computed in this manner, provides a conservative measure of coverage.

Debt interest takes priority over preferred and common dividends. When both bonds and preferred stocks are issued, interest charges and preferred dividends should be added together. The total is divided into net income after taxes to determine the number of times fixed charges and contingent charges have been earned. This is referred to as the times-fixed-and-contingent-charge earned ratio. Investment manuals such as Moody's and Standard & Poor's provide these figures for the investor, although they sometimes compute the ratio before taxes. Most quality nonconvertible preferreds have adequate coverage; most of these companies earned the charges at least three times. The company must demonstrate an ability to cover adequately all charges against income.

Interest and preferred-dividend coverage, and then preferred-dividend coverage alone, should be calculated to determine how secure the preferred dividend will be. The computation should be made for several of the most recent years; one year is not sufficient to judge whether dividends are secure. An inadequate dividend-coverage ratio or a ratio that fluctuates widely would not be satisfactory. The advantage of preferred stock ownership is its stability of income; if dividends are in jeopardy, or yields are expected to rise, the investor will lose this advantage. In analyzing preferred stocks, those that do not meet the dividend-coverage requirements should be rejected.

Preferred Stock Ratings

Standard & Poor's has developed quality ratings on preferred stocks similar to their bond ratings. The ratings represent a considered judgment of the relative security of dividends and the prospective yield stability of the stock. The ratings are AAA, prime; AA, high grade; A, sound; BBB, medium grade; BB, lower grade; B, speculative; and C, submarginal. This is shown in Figure 5–2.

STANDARD & POOR'S PREFERRED STOCK RATING DEFINITIONS

A Standard & Poor's preferred stock rating is an assessment of the capacity and willingness of an issuer to pay preferred stock dividends and any applicable sinking fund obligations. A preferred stock rating differs from a bond rating inasmuch as it is assigned to an equity issue, which issue is intrinsically different from, and subordinated to, a debt issue. Therefore, to reflect this difference, the preferred stock rating symbol will normally not be higher than the bond rating symbol assigned to, or that would be assigned to, the senior debt of the same issuer.

The preferred stock ratings are based on the following considerations:
I. Likelihood of payment—capacity and willingness of the issuer to meet the timely payment of preferred stock dividends and any applicable sinking fund requirements in accordance with the terms of the obligation.
II. Nature of, and provisions of, the issue.
III. Relative position of the issue in the event of bankruptcy, reorganization, or other arrangements affecting creditors' rights.

"AAA" This is the highest rating that may be assigned by Standard & Poor's to a preferred stock issue and indicates an extremely strong capacity to pay the preferred stock obligations.

"AA" A preferred stock issue rated "AA" also qualifies as a high-quality fixed income security. The capacity to pay preferred stock obligations is very strong, although not as overwhelming as for issues rated "AAA."

"A" An issue rated "A" is backed by a sound capacity to pay the preferred stock obligations, although it is somewhat more susceptible to the adverse effects of changes in circumstances and economic conditions.

"BBB" An issue rated "BBB" is regarded as backed by an adequate capacity to pay the preferred stock obligations. Whereas it normally exhibits adequate protection parameters, adverse economic conditions or changing circumstances are more likely to lead to a weakened capacity to

make payments for a preferred stock in this category than for issues in the "A" category.

"BB," "B," "CCC" Preferred stock rated "BB," "B," and "CCC" are regarded, on balance, as predominately speculative with respect to the issuer's capacity to pay preferred stock obligations. "BB" indicates the lowest degree of speculation and "CCC" the highest degree of speculation. While such issues will likely have some quality and protective characteristics, these are outweighed by large uncertainties or major risk exposures to adverse conditions.

"CC" The rating "CC" is reserved for a preferred stock issue in arrears on dividends or sinking fund payments but that is currently paying.

"C" A preferred stock rated "C" is a non-paying issue.

"D" A preferred stock rated "D" is a non-paying issue with the issuer in default on debt instruments.

NR indicates that no rating has been requested, that there is insufficient information on which to base a rating, or that S&P does not rate a particular type of obligation as a matter of policy.

Plus (+) or Minus (−) To provide more detailed indications of preferred stock quality, the ratings from "AA" to "B" may be modified by the addition of a plus or minus sign to show relative standing within the major rating categories.

The preferred stock rating is not a recommendation to purchase or sell a security, inasmuch as market price is not considered in arriving at the rating. Preferred stock *ratings* are wholly unrelated to Standard & Poor's earnings and dividend *rankings* for common stocks.

The ratings are based on current information furnished to Standard & Poor's by the issuer, and obtained by Standard & Poor's from other sources it considers reliable. The ratings may be changed, suspended, or withdrawn as a result of changes in, or unavailability of, such information.

Standard & Poor's Corporation receives compensation for rating securities. Such compensation is based on the work done and is paid either by issuers of such securities or by the underwriters participating in the distribution thereof. The fees generally vary from $1,500 to $20,000 for corporate securities.

FIGURE 5–2

Standard & Poor's Preferred Stock Rating Definitions

SOURCE: Standard & Poor's Stock Guide, December 1982, p. 6.

PREFERRED STOCK AS AN INVESTMENT

When the subject of preferred stock is brought up in investment discussions, someone will always say it is not a satisfactory investment for the individual investor, that it should be purchased only by institutions. When challenged, the argument will be supported in the following way: "Preferred stocks are really a hybrid security. They do not possess the major advantage of common stock, which is the ability to share in the earnings of the company. Nor do they possess the major advantage of bond investment, which is security of principal and stability of income. Therefore, I cannot recommend them for the individual investor, and I'm not certain that institutions should invest a great deal of money in preferred stock either." Less charitably, the case might be stated negatively by saying that preferred stocks possess all the disadvantages of common stocks and bonds and few of the advantages.

In many respects, the critic is right. Preferred stock *is* a hybrid; it does not share in earnings of the company, nor does it have the security of a bond. However, these are simply its limitations for investment; its use is not completely precluded and, under some conditions, is wholeheartedly encouraged. Preferred stock might fit into an investor's portfolio if yields are high, if there is a tax advantage, and if yields are expected to decline.

Ordinary Preferred

Ordinary preferred stock is attractive to investors if they can earn more income than they could receive from bonds. The yield on high-grade preferred stocks is usually greater than that on investment-grade bonds above the BAA rating, and there is a comparable degree of price stability. These stocks would offer the investor somewhat more income with only a modest decrease in security. A high-quality preferred stock of a sound company with adequate assets-and-earnings coverage will be attractive for the investor having an immediate need for maximum current income and desiring stability of yield as well. The high-grade preferred fluctuates in yield but follows the pattern of money rates closely. The major advantages of high-quality preferreds are (1) partial security from the business risk, and (2) security from the market risk. Their major disadvantages lie in their inability to compensate adequately for the money-rate risk and the purchasing-power risk.

Lower-grade preferred stocks offer larger income but also greater yield variability. If the demand for current income is high, then lower-grade preferreds will satisfy the need. Additional income will partially compensate for the additional risk involved. Dividends on preferred stock do have a minor tax advantage over interest income. Preferred dividends can be offset by the dividend credit, whereas bond interest cannot be.

The variability of preferred yields suggests that there is risk involved in the ownership of preferred stock. It is important for this reason to estimate expected return for the preferred stock for some holding period. A three-year holding period seems to be appropriate. If the period is actually to be longer, then the investor should use the longer period. Since the dividend rate is fixed, as demonstrated above, the only estimate to be made is for the future price at the end of the holding period. Since the price of high-quality preferreds is affected by capital-market conditions, it will be necessary to forecast some level of yields in the future and determine what impact this will have on price. If interest rates are expected to be lower, then the preferred-stock price will be higher, and vice versa. The business and credit position of the company and the level of the stock market will also affect the price. Once a price is estimated, the return can be calculated using the basic equation:

$$P_0 = \sum_{t=1}^{3} \frac{D_t}{(1+r)^t} + \frac{P_3}{(1+r)^3}$$

where P_0 is the price of the convertible preferred, D_t is the dividend of the preferred per year for three years, and P_3 is the expected price of the preferred in three years. Based upon this estimate, the investor can decide if the return is acceptable.

Actually, the investor should make several attempts to estimate return. In this way, several estimates of (r) will be obtained, these results can be averaged, and a standard deviation calculated. With this information, the investor has a knowledge not only of return, but of risk as well. The fact that yields and return do change was demonstrated by our discussion of Figure 5–1.

Convertible Preferred

Convertible preferred stock enjoys the advantage of being able to share in the profits of the corporation through capital growth of common stock. Such stocks offer the investor greater stability and security of income than common stocks and, at the same time, an opportunity to hedge against loss of purchasing power caused by inflation if the common stock increases in price. The investor retains the risk of loss, however, because of yield variability. Convertibles provide a good aggressive-defensive security for the investor and are an attractive instrument when unusual uncertainty surrounds the market. This condition has existed several times in the immediate past, and high-grade convertibles offered an ideal solution to the dilemma. In such cases, if the common stock price rises, the price of the preferred will increase. The preferred investor will share in the gain, and the investor's return will be increased. Should the market decline, and along with it the price of common stock, preferred stock will then sell as regular preferred, offering greater security of price than the common stock.

The investor must be careful about the price paid for convertible preferred. If it is purchased at a substantial premium, it is vulnerable to the downward movement of prices. It is best to purchase a convertible preferred stock close to the original price or par value, or on an attractive yield basis, or fairly priced in relation to common stock expectations. Preferred stock will have more stability and security under these conditions, and will produce a higher return because of the opportunity for capital gains.

Here again, the investor is faced with the need to estimate future return and its variability. In the case of convertible preferred stock, the investor must estimate future price. The future price of the convertible preferred is some function of the price of the common stock. It is suggested that several estimates of the future price be made, the return calculated, and the variability of return should also be calculated. In this way, the investor has both an estimate of return and an estimate of risk. In the basic equation:

$$P_0 = \sum_{t=1}^{3} \frac{D_t}{(1 + r)^t} + \frac{P_3}{(1 + r)^3}$$

P_3, the expected price of the preferred in three years, is some function of the price of common stock in three years—that is, the price of common stock times the conversion rate. Therefore, the price of the common stock must be estimated.

A danger of convertible preferred stock is that it might be called for redemption. Most preferred stock issued today, particularly convertible preferred, is callable at the option of the company. If it is called, the investor has the option of accepting the call or redemption price or converting the preferred stock into common stock. By that time, the benefits anticipated from preferred ownership may have been achieved. Of course, if a profit were earned in the process of converting or in accepting the redemption price, the investor had a satisfactory investment. If the price of the preferred increased because of the increase in the price of common stock, the investor would make a profit and need not convert the stock. All the investor need do is sell the stock.

Preferred with Dividends in Arrears

Some investors consider preferred stock with large dividend arrearages an attractive outlet for funds. They reason that the unpaid dividends might eventually be paid in cash, or the capitalization of the company might be changed and the arrearages eliminated by issuing stock to replace the dividends. This type of reasoning may be true in certain unusual situations, but it does not generally hold. A company that has not paid current dividends from past earnings has not had sufficient earnings to meet its claims. The circumstances that created the arrearages in the first place often continue, so that these claims cannot be paid off in the future, and current dividends may not be paid. This is true of the majority of companies that have dividends in arrears. The investor who purchases preferred with arrearages is speculating on the possibility of a windfall that is unlikely to occur.

If the preferred dividend is eliminated by a recapitalization of the company, the investor continues to be in a relatively poor position. In the recapitalization process, preferred dividend arrearages are exchanged for either common or preferred stock. In some cases, both preferred stock and dividends are exchanged for a new preferred or a combination of preferred and common stock, on the theory that the company will be able to afford to pay the new dividend rate on a regular basis. One typical arrangement is to exchange the old preferred for common stock on which there is no dividend requirement. These changes help the company meet its immediate problem of being unable to pay dividends, but they usually impose more severe requirements on future dividends. The net effect is that the investor is in a junior position and does not receive any greater income than he or she would have if the recapitalization had not taken place. Preferreds with dividend arrearages are weak speculative securities that offer the investor the possibility of high returns along with high risks.

SUMMARY

The preference concept arises from the nature of the agreement between the corporation and the preferred stock owners. Preferred stock has preference to the assets of the corporation over the common stock should the company be dissolved, liquidated, or merged. Preferred stock also has preference over common stock to the earnings of the company, and dividends on it must be paid before those on common stock. Preferred stock offers two promises: (1) a return of par or stated value in liquidation, and (2) a secure dividend superior in claim to the common dividend. In addition to its preference features, it is usually nonparticipating in the earnings of the company, but the dividends are usually cumulative. Preferred is nonvoting and has no maturity date, but a sinking fund and call feature are often provided for possible retirement of the stock.

Some investors consider preferred stock a hybrid security, possessing all the disadvantages of debt and none of the advantages of common stock. However, high-grade preferred stocks have stability of income and security of principal. They do not share in the business or market risks to the extent of common stock. They do share the money-rate and purchasing-power risks. High-grade preferreds offer higher current yields than both common stock and bonds and would be satisfactory to meet needs for stability of income. Lower-grade preferreds offer higher income and are less affected by changes in the money rates, but are more susceptible to the business and market risks. Yields on preferreds tend to be as variable as bond yields. Preferred dividends are stable, but yields vary, and annual average return can be negative in a period of rising yields. In general, preferred stock investors lose as market yields rise and profit as dividend yields fall.

Convertible preferred stocks offer not only income but the opportunity to share in the profits of the company. They usually pay a higher dividend than common stocks. They offer the possibility of appreciation and possess greater return variability than ordinary preferred. Preferred stocks with dividends in arrears offer a speculative opportunity for gain. It is important in purchasing preferred or convertible preferred to estimate expected return and variability of expected return.

SUMMARY OF PRINCIPLES

1. Preferred stock is more risky than corporate bonds.
2. Convertible preferred is more risky than preferred stock and offers the prospect of a higher return than preferred stock.
3. Preferred stock must be analyzed to establish investment quality and risk and return for the holding period.
4. Preferred stock is highly susceptible to the money-rate risk.

REVIEW QUESTIONS

1. Discuss the nature of preferred stock and indicate the attributes that make it unique.
2. Describe the usual features of a preferred stock with respect to the typical rights given to it in the stock agreement.
3. Contrast the stability or variability of yields on preferred stock with those of government, municipal, and corporate bonds.
4. Comment upon the stability of the current yield on preferred stock.
5. Discuss the advantages and disadvantages of a convertible preferred stock for an investor.
6. How can we determine whether the preferred dividend is secure?
7. What would we emphasize in an analysis of preferred stock?

8. Under what circumstances would a preferred stock with dividends in arrears be an attractive investment?

9. What risks are associated with the purchase for investment of preferred stock, and how can they be estimated?

PROBLEMS

1. An investor purchased the Duke Power $8.70 preferred stock at $100\frac{1}{2}$ on March 28, 1977. The investor thought the stock would be an excellent investment because dividend rates were expected to decline over the next five years. Rates for similar-quality preferreds were expected to decline to 8 percent.
   a. Calculate what the price of the preferred would be in five years.
   b. Based upon the price expected in five years, what return would the investor earn?

2. Assume that the investor made a wrong estimate, and preferred yields increased to 13 percent. What effect would this have on future price and annual return for the five-year period?

3. An investor owns 100 shares of RCA $4 convertible preferred. The price as of March 28, 1977, was $71\frac{3}{4}$. The preferred is convertible into 2.11 shares of common stock. The common stock was selling on the market for $28.75. The common stock price in the preferred stock was $31.81, which means the convertible preferred was selling at a premium of almost 18 percent. Assume that the price of the stock in five years was expected to increase 20 percent, and the preferred stock was to continue to sell at an 18 percent premium.
   a. What annual average return would the investor earn?
   b. What annual average return would the investor earn if the increase in common stock price was only 10 percent and the premium remained at 18 percent?
   c. What annual average return would the investor earn with a 5 percent decrease in the stock price? The premium remains at 18 percent.
   d. Based on your answers to (a), (b), and (c) above, calculate variability of return and comment on the riskiness of the investment.

SELECTED READINGS

CURRAN, WARD S. "Preferred Stock for Public Utilities." *Financial Analysts Journal*, July–August 1969, p. 112.

DONALDSON, G. "In Defense of Preferred Stock." *Harvard Business Review*, 40 (July–August 1962). Reprinted in *Foundations for Financial Management*, ed. James Van Horne, pp. 194–218. Homewood, Ill.: Irwin, 1966.

PINCHES, GEORGE E. "Financing with Convertible Preferred Stocks, 1960–1967." *The Journal of Finance*, March 1970, p. 53.

SCHWARTZ, WILLIAM. "Convertibles Get Realistic Image." *Financial Analysts Journal*, July–August 1967, p. 55.

SOLDOFSKY, R. M. "Convertible Preferred Stock: Renewed Life in an Old Form." *The Business Lawyer*, July 1969, pp. 1385–92.

CHAPTER 6

COMMON STOCK
AS AN INVESTMENT—
WITH OPTIONS
AND FUTURES INDEX

Studies of common stock returns indicate that they offer the investor the highest return and the highest risk of all investment securities over long periods of time. Because of these risks, attitudes toward common stocks have varied from extreme optimism to extreme pessimism. In this chapter, we will examine the advantages and disadvantages of owning common stock, the returns that can be earned, the risk, and the part they might play in an investment program.

THE CHANGING ATTITUDE TOWARD COMMON STOCK

The attitude of individuals and institutions toward common stock ownership has followed a cycle. During periods of pessimism and rampant inflation, as in 1974–75 and 1979, investors avoided common stocks. In periods of optimism with expected low interest rates, as in 1983, investors bought common stocks. Today over 30 million investors own common stock.

Why the interest in common stock? First investors have recognized the returns of common stock ownership in spite of recurring dips. Many now believe that the returns overshadow the risks. Second, the government has taken a more active role in maintaining a high level of economic activity and employment, and a fight against inflation which has strengthened the economy and the securities market. Third, corporate earnings in the United States are expected to increase and are more stable than in past periods. Fourth, there has been greater emphasis by mutual-fund managers on performance and the measurement of performance. Fifth, the outlook has been more favorable for common stock ownership—that is, less inflation, rising profits, and the possibility of relatively lower interest rates, compared to 1979–80, with its high inflation, rising interest rates, worsening international situation, and declining dollar.

THE NATURE OF COMMON STOCK

Common stock is an ownership security. It guarantees to the owner the right to share in the earnings of the company. If earnings do not materialize or if losses are sustained, then the stockholder loses. It is important to understand the significance of this statement. There is nothing certain about earnings on common stock, and the investor can lose as well as earn a high return.

Evidence of Ownership

Ownership of common stock is evidenced by a *stock certificate*, which is freely transferable by the owner. Established channels for transfer include the broker, who brings together buyer and seller, and the transfer agent, who transfers the stock of a company for a bona fide buyer or seller of securities and keeps an up-to-date list of the stockholders on the books of the company.

When common stock is purchased, the broker can keep the certificate "in street name" for convenience and safety. This means that the certificates will be held by the brokerage firm for the account. When dividends are paid, the broker must credit the account; when annual reports or rights are received, the investor must be notified. When the stock is to be sold, the investor merely calls the broker, and the broker credits the proceeds to the account. If the investor wishes, he or she may receive the stock certificate directly. When the stock is sold, the form on the back of the certificate must be completed or a separate power of attorney signed. If it is sold through a broker, the broker will be appointed as attorney to transfer it. This is done by placing the broker's name on the appropriate line on the back of the certificate. The certificate is signed and dated and sent to the broker, usually by registered mail. If the broker wishes to transfer the stock to a buyer, the broker need only fill in the name of the person to whom it will be transferred and send it to the transfer agent.

Several companies have now automated the process of transferring ownership shares. The computer prints the name and number of shares owned on the face of each nondenominational security. Some day, the stock certificate will be eliminated altogether, and the stockholder's ownership will be a statement of holdings supplied by the company's transfer agent, much like the statement provided by mutual funds.

Many people lose securities each year or have them stolen. Since it is costly and time-consuming to replace them, certificates should be kept in a safe place. If they are lost, stolen, or otherwise destroyed, the transfer agent should be notified immediately. A new share may be obtained by filling out an evidence-of-loss form and posting bond obtained from a casualty insurance company.

Maturity of Common Stock

Common stock has no maturity date; its life is limited by the length of time stated in the corporate charter. The corporate life might be for a stated or limited period, or it might be perpetual; most corporations have a perpetual charter.

For investment purposes, common stock can be purchased and sold at any time. The date the stock is sold by the investor is the "maturity" date, and the price at which the stock is sold is the "maturity" price. The investor is vitally concerned with the return earned over the period that the stock is owned, since the return for the holding period represents the total income to the investor and is a measure of performance to be compared to those of other securities investments.

Investors are interested in the future dividends and price appreciation from a common stock. Therefore, expected return must be calculated based on some time in the future. If an investor plans to hold the stock forever, then the yield is reflected in all future dividends related to the present price. However, stocks do become overpriced and underpriced and can be sold to improve return to investors. Therefore, the appraisal of stock values is a continuous process, and will be discussed under company analysis.

Voting in the Modern Corporation

Granting stock options for management, approving mergers, issuing debt securities, waiving the right to subscribe to new shares, changing the par value of the stock, and increasing the authorized capital of the company are all matters upon which owners may—indeed, should—vote. In some cases, the right to vote is taken away from a portion of common stock. A company might issue Class A and Class B common, for example, one class with complete voting rights and the other with limited rights, or none at all.

Historically, the nonvoting class of common stock was issued to allow the original voting stockholders to maintain control; nonvoting stock could be sold to raise additional money without losing control of the company. Nonvoting shares are seldom used today for this purpose, as certain institutional changes have tended to work against their use. One of the conditions for listing on the New York Stock Exchange, for example, is that all common shares have voting rights.

Florida Telephone, traded over-the-counter, is an example of a company having two classes of stock outstanding. Its Class B common stock has limited voting rights, while Class A has full voting rights. The same is true of the Westgate-California Corporation, whose Class B stock does not have voting rights. Sometimes, however, Class B stock has the right to vote and Class A does not.

What impact does the nonvoting feature have on the market price of the stock? This question cannot be answered with certainty, but there is a tendency for nonvoting shares to sell for a lower price than voting shares.

ORDINARY AND CUMULATIVE VOTING. Typically, each share of common stock has one vote. This is referred to as ordinary voting. One hundred shares of common stock would have 100 votes on corporate matters. In electing directors at the annual stockholders' meeting, the owner would have the right to cast 100 votes for each of the directors to be elected. Some corporations allow cumulative voting, which would confer the right to vote the 100 shares for each director or, if one wished, to cast all the votes for one. In electing fifteen directors, for example, the stockholder could cast 100 votes for each director, or 1,500 for one director, or divide the total 1,500 votes among the candidates in any way desired. The advantage of this type of voting is that it allows a minority group of shareholders or an individual holding a large amount of stock to be represented on the board of directors. Under ordinary voting, a person with 49 percent control fighting a group with 51 percent control would be unable to elect a single director. With cumulative voting, the minority would be able to elect slightly less than half the number of directors. This is not a point of great concern for most small investors in large American corporations. It is important, however, to a large minority group of stockholders seeking control of the company. In any case, the right to vote should not be ignored, nor should its importance be minimized by any stockholder.

Par Value

Like preferred stock, common stock can be par or no-par. If it is no-par, it can have a stated value at which it is carried on the company's books. Most corporations tend to place a low par value on their shares. This gives them the advantage of paying low state excise and franchise fees when these are based on the par value of the stock. But many states tax no-par shares at $100 par, which makes it costly to issue no-par shares. Another advantage of low-par shares is the flexibility they provide in issuing new shares. Shares must be sold at or above par value. A low par value permits them to be sold at a price related to their market price. A high par value of, say $100 might make it difficult or impossible to sell the stock if the market price was $80, whereas a par value of $2 would allow the shares to be sold at $80 without any difficulty.

A low par value also dispels the idea that the common stockholder will receive a fixed amount of money if the company is liquidated. As residual owner, the common stockholder cannot expect to receive a fixed dollar amount, but a $100 par value on common stock gives the impression that $100 should be available for distribution to the stockholder. This might not be the case. In any event, a low par value focuses attention on earning power or earnings per share rather than on a par value that has little significance.

Book Value

A figure that has much more significance than par is the book value per share. The *book value* of common stock is found by dividing the number of common shares outstanding into the total assets minus all debt and minus the value of preferred stock, when it exists. Some investors prefer to consider book value the net worth available for common stock. The figure obtained by using either method is divided by the number of shares of common stock outstanding. The book value figure provides some idea of the dollars per share that have been invested. Of course, book value has little to do with valuation, since the proceeds obtainable from assets sold in the market-place might differ greatly from the book value or the earning power of the assets.

Book value is usually a poor guide to market value. The productivity of assets and a specific combination of assets and entrepreneurial ability often create greater earnings and greater values than the book value of the assets suggests.

DIVIDENDS ON COMMON STOCK

Owners of common stock have the right to receive dividends. The amount and manner of payment will be decided by the company management and approved by the board of directors, based upon the needs of the company. The amount and type of dividend will depend upon the earnings of the company, its financial position, and the need for funds for investment in new plant and equipment. An established dividend policy suggests a fixed dividend rate. Under these conditions, a dividend is said to be "certain." A company that pays a regular cash dividend can be said to have a fixed dividend policy of paying cash, even though the amount of the dividend will vary. One of the single most important characteristics of most common stock is the variability of the dividend and the variability of the factors that contribute to dividend policy over a long period of time. The dividend might increase as the company prospers or it might decrease with a decline in earnings.

The Cash Dividend

The cash dividend is the most familiar and expected type paid on common stock. Ordinarily, the word *dividend* is synonymous with *cash*, unless a company follows a different practice. If another type of dividend is paid, it is identified as a stock dividend or a property dividend. In an ordinary year, more than 80 percent of the common stocks listed on the New York Stock Exchange will pay some cash dividend. More than a dozen companies have paid dividends for over a century, in the form of either stock or cash; the majority have paid in cash. Citicorp, for example, has paid a dividend every year since 1813.

The amount of the cash dividend is usually established in relation to earnings and cash flow per share. The portion of the dividend that is a percentage of current earnings is called the *payout ratio*. This ratio varies over time, from company to company, and from industry to industry. American corporations, as represented by the companies in the S&P 500 Index, have paid out from 40 to 50 percent of their earnings in dividends.

Payout rates vary in accordance with economic conditions, the growth of the company—rapidly growing companies pay out less—and the expectations of the stockholders. During periods of economic recession, many companies maintain dividend payments even though they have no earnings. This results in a payout ratio of over 100 percent—a situation that occurred in the early 1930s. In times of financial adversity, a company will not pay a dividend. Consolidated Edison omitted its common stock dividend at the height of the credit crunch in 1974.

The cash flow of a company can also be used as a guide to dividend policy. Cash flow is computed by adding depreciation, depletion allowances, and other noncash costs to the company's net income after taxes. This figure represents the return of profits from the company's investments, and it includes the return of capital as measured partially by investment in plant and equipment. The cash flow of companies, along with profits, has increased steadily and become more stable in recent years. Dividends tend to bear a more stable relationship to cash flow than to earnings after taxes, which tend to be cyclical in character. Therefore, when common stock is purchased for investment, cash flow as well as earnings per share must be considered to anticipate the future level of dividends. As a matter of principle, stocks that pay a cash dividend have a relatively higher value than stocks that do not pay a dividend.

The outstanding advantage of common stock is the potential growth of dividends per share. Dividends of the S&P 500 Index grew 9.20 percent between 1971 and 1980. In contrast, bond interest and preferred dividends were stable.

Stock Dividends

The stock dividend is usually stated as a percentage of the value of the stock. A 2 percent stock dividend would give the holder of 100 shares of common stock two additional shares. Stock dividends are given in the same type of share owned by the stockholder. If another type of security is given as a dividend, it is technically considered a property dividend or an unlike stock dividend, and is therefore fully and immediately taxable as income, whereas the tax on like dividends is paid when the stock is sold, and then only as a capital gain.

Stock dividends are frequently issued by smaller companies and growth companies. Stock of such companies is more likely to be traded on the over-the-counter market and on the small stock exchanges than on the New York Stock Exchange, where the majority of the companies listed pay cash dividends. Approximately 8 percent of the companies covered in Standard & Poor's *Stock Guide* pay some form of stock dividend, whereas only 3 percent of the companies listed on the New York Stock Exchange do so.

Stock dividends are issued by companies that wish to conserve cash for the purchase of equipment and plant facilities, or investment in inventory and receivables, in order to ensure continued growth of the enterprise. A rapidly expanding, profitable growth company can use every dollar of cash it can generate to finance increasing sales. If a growth company did pay out dividends in cash obtained from cash sales and the collection of receivables, it would have to turn to the capital markets for funds, either borrowing them or selling equity securities. The cost of capital, particularly through the sale of common stock, is high, and the expenses of registration and selling are substantial. So rather than incur additional expenses, the company simply retains its earnings. These earnings are acknowledged by issuing new shares of stock in an amount equal to the total dividend. The effect is to increase the amount of outstanding stock, which capitalizes the retained earnings. The stock dividend gives the shareowner tangible evidence that earnings have been permanently retained in the business.

STOCK DIVIDENDS AND STOCK SPLITS. The percentage rate for the usual *stock dividend* is below 10 percent, 2 to 5 percent being typical. A stock dividend above 25 percent is usually referred to as a *stock split*. There is, however, a technical difference between a stock dividend and a stock split. In both cases, the number of shares of stock outstanding increases, and so the book value per share is reduced. But a stock dividend is reflected in the company's balance sheet by an increase in the amount of capital stock items and a decrease in the amount of retained earnings in the ownership or capital account; in a stock split, the dollar amount of the capital stock account remains the same. A 25 percent stock dividend and a 5-for-4 stock split, for example, have the same effect on book value, and the number of shares increases by 25 percent. However, the 25 percent dividend increases the value of the capital account as well as the number of shares; the value of the capital account in a stock split remains the same, so there is a lower capital value per share. Typical rates for stock splits are 3 for 2, 2 for 1, and 3 for 1. IBM, for example, has used a 2-for-1, a 3-for-2, and also a 5-for-4 rate. Riggs National Corporation split 2 for 1 in 1981. The immediate effect of a stock split or a large stock dividend is to lower the price per share. The long-range effect is to provide a wider distribution of the shares at a more marketable price. Stock splits are helpful and profitable for the investor, however, only if earnings and dividends continue to grow.

STOCK DIVIDENDS AND FEDERAL INCOME TAXES. The Internal Revenue Code states that a stock dividend is exempt from federal income tax until the stock is sold. A 10 percent stock dividend on 100 shares lowers the per-share cost and the tax base on the original 100 shares. If, for example, an investor paid $50 per share for 100 shares of stock, for tax purposes the cost basis per share would be $50. After the 10 percent stock dividend is declared, the investor spreads the cost over 110 rather than 100 shares, and the cost basis, $45.45 ($5,000 ÷ 110) per share, becomes the tax basis from which the investor's taxable gains or losses are determined when the stock is sold. There is no immediate tax effect when the stock dividend is paid, and its holding period is assumed to be the same as that of the shares for which it was issued.

If an investor sells the stock dividend shares or fractional shares, there will also be a change in the tax base. The stock dividend will then be taxed as a gain or a loss, depending on the basis of computing the fractional interest, and long term or short term, depending on the holding period of the stock upon which it was paid. Assume, in the example above, that the investor sold ten shares at $55. Would federal income taxes be paid on $550, or on a fraction of that amount? The investor's cost basis was calculated to be $45.45 per share, and it would be necessary to pay a capital gains tax on the per-share difference between $55 and $45.45. A tax would be paid on $9.55 per share times ten shares, or $95.50. If the original stock had been held for more than one year, the gain would be taxable as a long-term capital gain. If it had been held for less, the gain would be a short-term capital gain and taxed as ordinary income.

SIGNIFICANCE OF STOCK DIVIDENDS. Some controversy exists over the importance and significance of stock dividends. If the company's stock maintains its market price, then payments of stock dividends offer several distinct advantages to the stockholder. They allow a dividend to be received without the burden of paying income tax on it, as would be necessary with cash dividends. A wealthy investor would not have the current dividend income taxed at high rates. Or if, after having held the original stock long enough, the investor sold the shares representing the dividends, a capital gains tax, lower than the ordinary tax rate, would be paid. The maximum long-term capital gains tax rate in 1983 was 20 percent.

Another advantage of greater share ownership is that it allows the investor's capital to grow at a compounded rate if the current dividend is maintained. Some people argue that stock dividends merely give the stockholder something that was already received—that is, retained earnings that will be invested and allowed to grow to improve and build up equity. Why then, they ask, is it necessary to pay any dividend at all? It is difficult to come to a definite conclusion about the value of a stock dividend; but a company that manages to continue its growth will, through a policy of stock dividends, allow investors to improve their financial and their tax positions as well.

No amount of stock dividends will turn a company with declining earnings into an investment success. In principle, a stock dividend is valuable only if the company continues to grow and prosper. Stock dividends are desirable, however, when a company must conserve cash or is experiencing rapid growth, where per-share earnings and price will not be diluted, and when the investor is in a tax bracket where cash dividends are not wanted. Table 6–1 lists some companies that paid only stock dividends.

TABLE 6–1

Selected Companies That Paid Stock Dividends in 1981

Price Range January 1– August 1, 1981						Earnings,
High	Low	Company	Last Record Date	Last Payment Date	Dividend Rate (%)	Latest Fiscal Year ($)
$53\frac{7}{8}$	$37\frac{1}{4}$	Borg-Warner	7/20/81	8/15/81	5.0%	$5.02
$55\frac{3}{8}$	$35\frac{7}{8}$	Burroughs	10/1/81	11/7/81	7.0	3.68
$29\frac{1}{4}$	$22\frac{5}{8}$	Grumman	8/4/81	8/20/81	5.7	2.23
$31\frac{1}{4}$	$22\frac{3}{4}$	Hudson Bay	5/11/81	6/1/81	5.2	1.69
25	$19\frac{3}{8}$	Kellogg	5/20/81	6/15/81	7.0	2.44
$63\frac{7}{8}$	$49\frac{1}{4}$	Morgan (J.P.)	6/16/81	7/15/81	5.7	8.65
$37\frac{3}{4}$	$28\frac{1}{4}$	Safeway Stores	5/26/81	6/30/81	8.1	4.42
$72\frac{3}{4}$	$42\frac{3}{8}$	Standard Oil (Ohio)	8/10/81	9/10/81	4.7	7.76

SOURCE: Standard & Poor's *Stock Guide,* August 1981.

Cash and Stock Dividends

Some companies pay both cash and stock dividends. The company recognizes that a policy of paying some dividends is desirable, and that some people desire stock dividends for tax advantages. The company itself might wish to conserve cash for reinvestment in plant or working capital. Georgia Pacific and Metromedia, Inc., are good examples of companies that pay both cash and stock dividends. In 1978, Acme Electric paid a cash dividend of $.32 per share along with a 1.1 percent stock dividend. Crane paid a $1.60 cash dividend along with a 2 percent stock dividend. Many corporations listed on the New York Stock Exchange pay some cash and some stock. Next to cash dividends alone, this is the second most important form of dividend.

Special Dividends and Dividend Policies

Some companies do not pay dividends at all, because they wish to retain the funds for expansion. They do not think it necessary to formalize the retention of earnings by declaring a stock dividend, and would argue that there were no advantages in issuing more shares, thereby imposing a burden on management to maintain future earnings. If earnings could not be maintained, the dilution effect would take place. (The retained earnings, when invested, earn a smaller amount than do previously invested funds; hence, earnings are said to be *diluted*.) Or companies may not pay dividends because they cannot afford them with their present and future expectations of profit. Perhaps the company is in receivership or is being reorganized.

PROPERTY DIVIDENDS. Although the practice is uncommon, some companies from time to time declare property dividends. Usually this type of dividend consists of the personal property of the company and takes the form of securities of other companies, or of one of the company's own products. A typical property dividend would be the stock of a subsidiary owned by the parent company. Rather than pay a dividend in its own stock, the parent company distributes to its shareholders stock of the subsidiary company, to conserve cash and to effect a permanent change in the company structure.

Occasionally, a company will pay a property dividend in the form of its product. During World War II, one liquor company gave each shareholder some of the liquor it had produced. Alcoholic beverages were scarce, and this made the dividend attractive to many shareholders. However, this was not a regular dividend and could not be continued as a permanent practice.

Property dividends are taxable as income to the investor. They are treated, for tax purposes, as cash dividends. The tax basis is the stated value of the dividend at the time it is given.

LIQUIDATING DIVIDENDS. The liquidating dividend is a return of capital to the owners of the business. If the company is going out of business, it may distribute its assets to the owners as a liquidating dividend. A mining company that uses up its minerals and an oil company that uses up the oil in the ground are both engaged in business requiring that an asset be "wasted" to render its service to the final consumer. Depletion allows such a business to recover the expense of the wasted asset. If the funds retained because of depletion are no longer needed, they can be paid out to the owners. Since they represent a return of principal, they may be free from ordinary income taxes and subject only to capital gains taxes. Some public utility companies, financial institutions, and investment companies distribute capital and capital gains to their shareholders, and these are also subject to capital gains taxes. A real estate company, by the same token, might distribute a dividend based upon a depreciation allowance that retains within the business funds that are not needed for current operation. A dividend of this type would not be subject to ordinary income taxes but would be taxed as a long- or short-term gain, depending on the tax base of the property distributed. These examples represent a partial liquidation of company assets.

SCRIP DIVIDENDS AND BOND DIVIDENDS.   A scrip dividend may be given to owners of common stock when a company is short of cash. It is in the form of a transferable promissory note that may or may not be interest-bearing. The scrip continues as a liability of the company until it is paid. Scrip is justified when earnings exist to pay a dividend but the company does not have the money to pay it. It is not used frequently.

In some instances, bonds or notes are used to pay a dividend on common stock. The weakness of this practice is that a stockholder receiving the dividend actually changes the relationship to the company: He or she becomes a creditor rather than an owner. Both scrip and bonds may be used to pay a dividend when, as a matter of conservative financial policy, none should be paid. An investor could interpret both types of dividends as a sign of financial weakness rather than as a benefit.

REGULAR AND EXTRA DIVIDENDS.   Dividends may be classed as regular or extra. Regular dividends are the usual amount paid on a regular (most often quarterly) basis. Some companies, like GM, make it a practice to pay a regular dividend plus an extra, declared at the end of the year. The latter is based on earnings and will be paid if the amount of earnings permits. If earnings are not much greater than expected, then probably no extras will be paid.

DIVIDEND POLICY.   Whatever type of dividend it distributes, a corporation should establish a stable dividend policy. Such a policy, as a principle, tends to result in a greater maximization of the present value of the owners' equity than does a haphazard policy. The policy should reflect the needs of the company and of its shareholders. It should relate closely to the earnings or cash flow of the company. It should be changed infrequently, and then only to reflect a change in the economic position of the company and the needs of its shareholders. A haphazard policy of dividend payments will not allow a company or its stockholders to reach their financial objectives. And the company that consistently pays a regular cash or stock dividend tends to have greater appeal than one that has no stated policy about dividends, or has an irregular policy.

The Declaration of Dividends

Dividends are declared by the board of directors. The date of announcement usually precedes the date of record by several weeks. After the date of record, the stock sells *ex dividend*; that is, a person buying it after this date does not receive the declared dividend. A person who buys stock in anticipation of receiving a dividend must make certain to become a stockholder of record before the stock goes ex dividend. He or she must buy the stock with the dividends "on." The actual date of payment will be some time after the date of record.

Dividend Information

Current information about dividends may be found in *The Wall Street Journal* under "Dividend News." Information about rate, regularity, and type of dividend can be found in Standard & Poor's *Stock Guide*. An examination of the explanatory footnotes for price quotations in *The Wall Street Journal* will show the variety of dividends.

THE PREEMPTIVE RIGHT

In addition to receiving dividends and voting on corporate matters, the stockholder has the right, called the *preemptive right*, to maintain a proportionate share in the assets, earnings, and voting power of the corporation. When additional common stock of the corporation is to be sold to raise capital, the preemptive right gives the present stockholder the opportunity to subscribe to the new issue of stock, in an amount based on the number of shares he or she owns. Selling stock to current stockholders is known as a *privileged subscription*, or a *preemptive rights offering*.

Common Law

The preemptive right is a matter of common law doctrine rather than of statutory law; half the states in the United States permit this right to be limited or denied by statute. Raising money by first offering the stock for sale to the shareholders is common among U.S. corporations. If shareholders do not elect to participate in the rights offering, they may sell the privilege in the marketplace. Not all stock is permitted to share in the preemptive right. If the stock issue is part of a continuing sale of stock, if it is treasury stock (stock issued, then reacquired by the company), or if it is issued to buy property or settle a debt, it will not be subject to the preemptive right.

The Value of Rights

The value of the right depends on the market value of the stock, the subscription price the company establishes for the shares that are to be sold, and the number of rights necessary to buy one new share of stock. The right attached to each share of stock owned is called a New York right, and several New York rights are usually required to buy one new share of stock. The shares are offered at a price below the existing market price to make them attractive purchases. If a stock were selling in the market for $50 a share, for example, it might be offered to existing shareholders at $42.50 per share—a discount of 15 percent. If the discount were much smaller than 15 percent, it would be difficult to sell the stock. If it were larger, the total number of shares sold would not increase, and the total amount of money raised by the company would be reduced. Assume, in the example above, that ten rights are required to buy one new share of stock. The value of each right would be approximately $.75. Simply divide the number of rights needed to buy one new share into the difference between the market and subscription prices to arrive at the value of the right. If the market price changed after the conditions of the right offering had been determined, the value of the right would also change.

The Time Period of the Rights Offering

The investor must keep in mind three dates that may have an effect on the value of the right—the announcement date, the record date, and the expiration date. On the announcement date, the board of directors gives details of the privileged subscription;

these include the number of rights needed to buy one new share of stock, the price of the stock, and the record date—the day on which the list of stockholders is established. Owners of stock on the date of record receive the right to subscribe to new shares according to their proportional share in the company. From the announcement date to the date of record, the stock sells with rights attached, or *cum rights*. After the date of record, it sells *ex rights*, or without rights.

In some cases, an investment banker assists with the sale of any unsold shares of new stock, through what is called a *standby underwriting syndicate*. When a syndicate is used, the investor may sell rights owned to a member of the syndicate. These rights may then be sold to *shareowners* who wish to acquire enough rights to buy a full share of stock or other investors who wish to purchase shares. It is the underwriter's responsibility to make certain that all the rights are exercised, in order to ensure the success of the offering. Between the date of record and the expiration date, the rights are traded; if the company is listed on the New York Stock Exchange, they will be traded there along with the stock of the company. The market price of the right will be quoted daily until the rights expire.

The last important date is the expiration date—on this date, rights no longer have value. The period between the date of record and the expiration date varies; two weeks to a month is typical. The time is sufficient for all shareholders to take the necessary steps to use their rights. Occasionally, stockholders do not exercise their rights. In one case, a person purchased rights to buy shares in a company but neglected to act before the rights had expired. The time period was adequate; the investor simply misunderstood the nature of the preemptive right and was careless in the details of the transaction. Therefore, there is real meaning in the principle that any rights received as part of common stock ownership should be sold or exercised.

The Theoretical Value of the Right

The theoretical value of the right can be calculated by using a simple formula. If the stock is selling with rights—that is, between the announcement and date of record—the formula is $Vcr = (M - S)/(R + 1)$, where Vcr is the value of the right when the stock is selling *cum rights*, M is the market price of the stock, S the subscription price, and R the number of rights needed by buy one new share of stock. The one in the formula compensates for the value of the right in the market price of the stock after the announcement date; theoretically, the market price of the stock goes up to include the value of the right on the day the privileged subscription is announced.

Assume that a stockholder is given the right to subscribe to one new share of stock for each five shares owned, at a price of $25 per share. The announcement date is May 1, the record date May 30, and the expiration date June 15. The market price after the announcement is $31. What then is the value of the right? We find it by substituting in our formula: $Vcr = (M - S)/(R + 1) = (\$31 - \$25)/(5 + 1) = \$6/6 = \$1$. The theoretical value of the right, therefore, is $1. If the market price should drop before the rights are issued, the value of the right also drops. A sharp drop in prices in the market might result in a right's having little value.

On the date of record, when the stock sells *ex rights*, other things being equal, the price of the stock in the market should drop by the value of the right. In our example, the stock would drop from \$31 to \$30—assuming there has been no price change. How do we calculate the theoretical value after the date of record? We use the same basic formula; but since a right is no longer attached to the shares in the market, we remove the one from the denominator and express the formula as $Vxr = (M - S)/R$, where Vxr is the value of the right *ex rights*: $Vxr = (\$30 - \$25)/5 = \$1$. As before, the theoretical value of the right is \$1.

THE MARKET VALUE AND THE THEORETICAL VALUE OF THE RIGHT. The actual value of the right in the market will vary from the theoretical value, depending on demand for the rights and interest in the new issue of stock. Given strong market conditions, a small issue of stock, and an ownership group that wishes to buy the new shares, the market for rights will be limited, and the only trading engaged in will be the purchase and sale of fractional shares. Occasionally, a strong demand for rights forces their price higher than their theoretical value.

Advantage to Investors

The investor is in a favorable position when new shares can be purchased because of a preemptive rights offering. An opportunity is provided to buy stock at an attractive price, with minimum effort and minimum brokerage cost. This is true as long as the future prospects of the company seem to promise a satisfactory rate of return. Purchasing stock through a rights offering has the added advantage of lower margin rates. The actual margin requirements for a rights offering vary; the specific margin requirement must be determined at the time of purchase.

RETURNS, INVESTMENT EXPERIENCE, AND INVESTOR EXPECTATIONS

When a bond or preferred stock is purchased, the yield to be received by the investor is known, within narrow limits. But what will be earned if common stocks are purchased? One often hears how Joe Smith bought Moon Rocket common at 2 1/2 and it is now selling at 81. This suggests a rather high yield. And IBM was selling at 196 in 1951; in 1973, after it had split several times, it was selling at above 300. The latest split was 4 for 1 in 1979. An investor who purchased one share in 1951 would have owned approximately 120 shares, with a market value of about \$13,000 in 1983. This represents an increase in value of over 60 times the original investment, or a compound return well above 15 percent without considering current dividends. Is this usual? The answer is an emphatic *no*! Such growth is not usual, but some companies have achieved similar results. Let us examine what can reasonably be earned on common stocks.

Current Yield

Current yields on the stocks in the Dow Jones Industrial Average offer a clue to what might be expected in terms of current income from a common stock investment. Table 6–2 presents dividends on the industrial, transportation, and utility averages.

TABLE 6–2

Prices and Yields on Dow Jones Averages

	Mar. 21, 1983	Feb. 1, 1982	Jan. 25, 1982	Feb. 1, 1981
30 Industrials	$1,117.74	$851.03	$871.10	$952.30
	4.88%	6.50%	6.35%	5.75%
20 Transportation	$506.27	$357.17	$356.14	$408.64
	2.74%	4.30%	4.32%	3.13%
15 Utilities	$126.25	$106.95	$107.51	$112.20
	9.89%	11.20%	11.14%	9.23%

SOURCE: *Barron's*, February 8, 1982, p. 109, and March 21, 1983, p. 116.

Low current yields, it would seem, should make common stock unattractive to individual investors; however, common stocks have been good investments over long periods of time. Current yields do not reveal the growth in capital value in common shares, but this growth can be established indirectly.

Assume that an investor bought one share of an industrial common stock in 1952 on a current-yield basis of 7.5 percent. Assume further that the company's earnings have doubled since then. In 1983, the stock sold on a current-yield basis of 2.5 percent. The price of the stock in 1983 was actually four times higher than in 1952. If earnings had remained constant and current yield had been reduced by two-thirds, the stock would have tripled in value. Because earnings doubled, there was a sixfold increase in price. It appears that the investor, on this current-yield basis, is losing each year. Actually, an increasing price provided an exceptional rate of return. Therefore, the *total return* or return for the holding period is more important as a guide to profitability.

Historic Return and Risk from Common Stock

Current yield does not take into consideration the price appreciation that many stocks traded on the New York Stock Exchange have experienced. The market has risen over the period 1950–83 in spite of cyclical drops. The trend of the market has brought about capital gains, which must be considered in measuring investment success.

Studies have been undertaken to determine what a person would earn through common stocks, considering both dividend income and capital gains. A major study sponsored by Merrill Lynch, Pierce, Fenner & Smith found that an average of all common stocks listed on the New York Stock Exchange earned, between 1926 and 1960, 9.01 percent compounded annually. The rate earned between 1950 and 1960 was 14.84 percent.[1] In a later study, Lorie found that stocks earned an average of 9.3 percent before taxes for the period 1926–65.[2] Fisher and Lorie found in a later study covering

[1] Lawrence Fisher and James H. Lorie, *Rates of Return on Investments in Common Stocks*, pamphlet, The Center for Research in Security Prices, Graduate School of Business, University of Chicago, 1963.

[2] James H. Lorie, "Rates of Return on Investments in Common Stock: Year by Year Record, 1926–1965," *Journal of Business*, 39 (January 1966), 296.

the period 1925–76 that the return earned was 9.0 percent annually. This assumed no taxes and with dividends reinvested.[3] The "real" rate of return deflated by the price index was 6 percent. Ibbotson and Sinquefield found that stocks earned an annual compound return of 9.0 percent for the period 1926–79. In the return calculation 4.0 percent represented capital appreciation and 5.0 percent represented current yield.[4]

A study on yields, based upon random selection and random timing of purchases of stocks listed on the New York Stock Exchange during the period 1950–62, was conducted in 1963.[5] The study dealt with 50 investors who had bought an average of 5.6 different securities—mostly common stocks of industrial companies—and held them for an average of 4.5 years. The results were significant. They had earned an average return of 13.8 percent, with a standard deviation of from 33.04 to −12.67 percent. When stocks comparable to the Dow Jones Industrial Averages were purchased for the same time period, the average was 13.14 percent, with a standard deviation of from 32.01 to −2.80 percent. This study, of course, reflects only one time period in the history of the stock market.

The study did reveal that random selection would allow the investor to earn, on average, a return comparable to that of the market index. Yet the standard deviation was higher in the randomly selected stocks, which suggests that the risks were greater for random decisions than for the market as a whole. It is for this reason that the random-selection process should be avoided and that decisions should be based on intelligent analysis of the data, particularly the expected return and variability of return.

More recent studies based upon computer programs developed at The George Washington University provide some insight into past total returns of the S&P 500 Index, the DJIA, and the individual companies included in the DJIA. The computer output also includes the standard deviation of past total returns, which is used as a measure of risk. It is important to realize that only one-third of the DJIA stocks earned 5 percent or higher for the ten-year period 1966–75. Only two out of thirty earned above 9 percent, which is considered the total return to be expected from common stock investment over long periods of time. The decade 1971–81 was a little better for stock returns. The average annual return for the S&P 500 Index was 7.51 percent. The high standard deviation of returns, however, persisted.

Another observation is warranted. The variability of the ten-year total returns for all the stocks in the DJIA in Table 6–3 was very high. This indicates the substantial amount of risk associated with common stock and the need for careful analysis.

It is necessary to have a measure of performance that provides comparability in return for both common stock and bonds. The return formula presented in Chapter 1 provides a way to measure return and can also be used as a standard of performance. Assume that a stock was bought at $25, held for seven years, and sold at $60. During

[3]Laurence Fisher and James H. Lorie, *A Half Century of Returns on Stocks and Bonds* (Chicago: The University of Chicago, Graduate School of Business, 1977), p. 24.

[4]Roger G. Ibbotson and Rex A. Sinquefield, *Stocks, Bonds, Bills and Inflation: Historical Returns (1926–1978)* (Charlottesville, Va.: Financial Analysis Research Foundation, 1979).

[5]Frederick Amling, "Random Investment Decisions and Portfolio Yields," *Miami Business Review*, April 1963.

TABLE 6-3

Average Total Return and Standard Deviation of Market Index and Individual DJIA
Companies, 1971–1980 and 1972–1981

Stock or Index	Price 6/30/81	Average Annual Return 1971–1980[a]	Risk (Standard Deviation) 1971–1980[b]	Price 1/1/83	Average Annual Return 1972–1981[a]	Risk (Standard Deviation) 1972–1981[b]
Alcoa	$ 32.87	10.57	16.62	$ 26.13	11.29	15.96
Allied Chemical	53.75	12.28	18.62	N.A.	N.A.	N.A.
American Brands	42.63	13.27	14.08	44.88	14.15	13.72
American Can	40.13	6.02	12.25	30.38	10.24	13.08
AT&T	56.87	8.50	9.43	56.25	9.73	9.58
Bethlehem Steel	24.75	7.45	19.27	15.38	4.93	17.02
Chrysler	6.75	NEG.	254.10	N.A.	N.A.	N.A.
DJIA	N.A.	N.A.	N.A.	N.A.	N.A.	N.A.
du Pont	53.00	3.44	14.55	34.75	0.36	13.03
Eastman Kodak	76.37	1.89	26.75	81.38	-8.13	19.31
Esmark Inc.	—	—	—	55.25	18.22	32.47
Exxon	67.00	14.00	15.89	28.00	12.75	16.67
IBM	58.37	4.29	18.33	73.50	1.36	17.04
General Electric	66.00	3.20	13.24	74.63	3.88	14.02
General Foods	31.75	3.55	15.40	38.38	8.47	12.99
General Motors	56.25	4.09	21.56	46.63	4.35	21.52
Goodyear Tire	17.75	-1.44	18.69	24.38	2.85	22.62
International Harvester	18.13	8.05	15.38	73.50	1.36	17.04
International Nickel	20.87	1.95	21.62	N.A.	N.A.	N.A.
International Paper	48.00	7.16	20.28	39.00	8.09	20.66
Johns-Manville	19.75	1.57	24.04	N.A.	N.A.	N.A.
Minnesota Mining/Mfg.	60.50	2.11	16.73	63.63	-0.04	11.98
Owens-Illinois	30.75	4.72	21.94	24.50	9.02	21.52
Procter & Gamble	71.50	6.42	17.85	23.13	20.58	36.34
S&P 500 Index	132.50	7.51	13.52	151.26	6.87	13.18
Sears	19.25	-6.10	15.73	22.38	-12.52	11.74
Standard Oil (Cal.)	38.13	19.77	21.84	28.50	15.98	24.51
Texaco	34.25	10.18	21.87	29.13	8.05	23.57
Union Carbide	57.50	7.16	22.50	47.00	7.14	22.50
U.S. Steel	30.75	8.53	25.94	17.75	13.42	29.35
United Technologies	56.87	20.22	29.48	46.25	19.14	29.70
Westinghouse	32.37	2.73	27.16	31.13	3.98	27.67
Woolworth	34.75	-2.06	34.07	24.88	4.07	30.13

[a] $\frac{P_1 - P_0 + D}{P_0}$, where P_0 is $(H_0 + L_0) \div 2$, and P_1 is $(H_1 + L_1) \div 2$. This is the formula for the annual return.
The calculation is made for each of the 10 years and averaged.
[b] Standard deviation of 10 years of annual returns.

SOURCE: Frederick Amling & Associates, Washington, D.C.

the seven years, the following annual dividends were received:

Year:	1	2	3	4	5	6	7
Dividends:	$.50	$.50	$.60	$.65	$.65	$.75	$.80

What return was earned, and was the performance satisfactory?

The return can be calculated by the approximate method. The average investment was $42.50, or ($25 + $60)/2, and the average annual income was $5.64, where $5, or ($60 − $25)/7, was the average annual taxable capital gain and $.64 the average annual dividend income. The return from the investment before federal income taxes was 13.3 percent ($5.64 ÷ $42.50). Assume that the investor was in the 50 percent tax bracket; then, dividend income, ignoring any dividend credits, would have been $.64 minus $.32 ($.64 × 50 percent), or $.32 after taxes. The average annual capital gain after taxes was $5 minus $1.00 ($5 × 20 percent), or $4.00. The final investment value was $53.00 ($60 − $7.00), and therefore the average investment after taxes was $39.00 ($53 + 25)/2. (The $7.00 is the tax on the capital gain of $35 over the seven-year period; tax rate was 20 percent.) The after-tax return for the seven-year period was 11.1 percent, or ($.32 + $4.00)/$39. The use of present-value tables would provide a more precise answer, as would the equation:

$$P_0 = \sum_{t=1}^{7} \frac{D_t}{(1 + r)^t} + \frac{P_7}{(1 + r)^7}$$

The yield of 13.3 percent before taxes or 11.1 after taxes should be considered satisfactory, since the investor had anticipated a return of 10 percent and since, according to the Fisher and Lorie study, 9 percent would have been acceptable as a return over long periods of time. Both criteria suggest that the stock's performance was favorable. Without these criteria, the investor would not know how well the investment program had performed.

Common Stock Ratings

Bond and preferred-stock ratings emphasize the basic security of the issue, particularly with respect to interest and dividend coverage. The question of the security of principal is also important in the valuation and rating process employed by independent rating agencies, such as Standard & Poor's *Bond Guide* and *Stock Guide*. The ratings for common stocks are presented in Figure 6–1. Note the caution that the ranking code is not a recommendation to buy or sell.

Total Return Potential from Buying and Selling Stocks, 1970–1981

Many investors think they can improve the return from common stock by buying stocks at the low point in the market and selling them at the high point. Investors engaged in this activity attempt to buy low and sell high, the age-old panacea for investment success. They shun the buy-and-hold strategy. If an investor were to trade in the market, what returns would be possible if the investor purchased stocks at the cyclically low point and sold at the cyclically high point? It would be assumed that investors would put their money into Treasury bills after they sold at the market peaks and then awaited the market lows before reinvesting in common stocks. It is impossible to determine what rate of return all investors would have earned by purchasing all stocks, but some indication of potential return can be obtained by using the S&P 500 Index as the proxy for the market and learning what rate could have been earned by being a perfect market trader. A *perfect market trader* is one who buys at the cyclical lows and sells at the cyclical highs and never makes a mistake.

EARNINGS AND DIVIDEND RANKINGS FOR COMMON STOCKS

The investment process involves assessment of various factors—such as product and industry position, corporate resources and financial policy—with results that make some common stocks more highly esteemed than others. In this assessment, Standard & Poor's believes that earnings and dividend performance is the end result of the interplay of these factors and that, over the long run, the record of this performance has a considerable bearing on relative quality. The rankings, however, do not pretend to reflect all of the factors, tangible or intangible, that bear on stock quality.

Relative quality of bonds or other debt, that is, degrees of protection for principal and interest, called creditworthiness, cannot be applied to common stocks, and therefore rankings are not to be confused with bond quality ratings which are arrived at by a necessarily different approach.

Growth and stability of earnings and dividends are deemed key elements in establishing Standard & Poor's earnings and dividend rankings for common stocks, which are designed to capsulize the nature of this record in a single symbol. It should be noted, however, that the process also takes into consideration certain adjustments and modifications deemed desirable in establishing such rankings.

The point of departure in arriving at these rankings is a computerized scoring system based on per-share earnings and dividend records of the most recent ten years—a period deemed long enough to measure significant time segments of secular growth, to capture indications of basic change in trend as they develop, and to encompass the full peak-to-peak range of the business cycle. Basic scores are computed for earnings and dividends, then adjusted as indicated by a set of predetermined modifiers for growth, stability within long-term trend, and cyclicality. Adjusted scores for earnings and dividends are then combined to yield a final score.

Further, the ranking system makes allowance for the fact that, in general, corporate size imparts certain recognized advantages from an investment standpoint. Conversely, minimum size limits (in terms of corporate sales volume) are set for the various rankings, but the system provides for making exceptions where the score reflects an outstanding earnings-dividend record.

The final score for each stock is measured against a scoring matrix determined by analysis of the scores of a large and representative sample of stocks. The range of scores in the array of this sample has been aligned with the following ladder of rankings:

A+ Highest	B+ Average	C Lowest
A High	B Below Average	D In Reorganization
A− Above Average	B− Lower	

Standard & Poor's present policy is not to rank stocks of most finance-oriented companies such as banks, insurance companies, etc., and stocks of foreign companies; these carry the three-dot (...) designation. NR signifies no ranking because of insufficient data or because the stock is not amenable to the ranking process.

The positions as determined above may be modified in some instances by special considerations, such as natural disasters, massive strikes, and non-recurring accounting adjustments.

A ranking is not a forecast of future market price performance, but is basically an appraisal of past performance of earnings and dividends, and relative current standing. These rankings must not be used as market recommendations; a high-score stock may at times be so overpriced as to justify its sale, while a low-score stock may be attractively priced for purchase. Rankings based upon earnings and dividend records are no substitute for complete analysis. They cannot take into account potential effects of management changes, internal company policies not yet fully reflected in the earnings and dividend record, public relations standing, recent competitive shifts, and a host of other factors that may be relevant to investment status and decision.

FIGURE 6–1

Common Stock Ranking

SOURCE: Standard & Poor's *Stock Guide*, October 1981, p. 7.

We will assume that the trader-investor started the process at the low point of the S&P 500 Index at 68 in 1970 and continued trading until 1981 when the S&P 500 Index reached 114. (These figures are approximate.) If the investor had purchased at the low point and held until 1981, the annual average return would have been 14 percent. If the investor had bought at the average price of the market in 1970 and held for the period, the annual average total return would have been 7.51 percent. But back to the question of the possible annual average total return if the investor were a perfect trader.

During the approximately 11-year period, the investor would have had 8 trading opportunities. This can be seen in Figure 6–2. After having bought at the low in 1970, the investor would then sell when the first high point was reached and purchase Treasury bills until the market reached a new low point. During the period, the investor would have been invested in stocks for approximately 6.2 years and would have held Treasury bills for 4.5 years. It was assumed that the investor would have earned 6 percent on average from the Treasury bills and 4 percent from dividends while the stocks were owned.

The total average annual return earned for the period would have been 27.7 percent. This annual average return includes capital gains, dividends, and interest earned on the Treasury bills. The return includes transaction costs. If we assume a 4 percent transaction cost, the annual average return is reduced to 23.7 percent. By being a perfect trader, the investor could have earned 23.7 percent rather than 14 percent, which would have been almost a 70 percent improvement in the annual rate of return. But the investor would have had to be perfect.

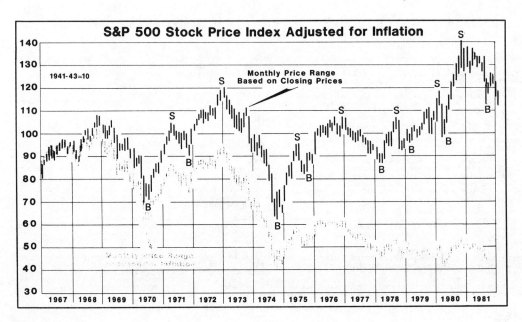

FIGURE 6–2

*High and Low Points for S&P 500 Index with Trading Periods and Months Held per Period.
Dollar and "Real" S&P 500 Index Compared*

SOURCE: *The Outlook*, p. 570.

The investor would have more than doubled the return earned from buying the average of the market by being a successful trader. By buying stocks at the average market price, the return would have been 8 percent compared to the trading return after transaction costs of 23.7 percent. The improvement in this case would have been almost 200 percent. The potential return from trading stocks might seem low, but we considered only the S&P 500 Index. If the investor had purchased only the best-performing common stocks, the returns would have been much higher. But the investor would not only have to be a perfect trader, but a perfect picker. Here are the conclusions from this "what if" question for the period 1970 through 1981:

1. Significantly higher returns could have been earned from common stocks if the investor were a perfect picker and a perfect trader.
2. Substantially higher returns could have been earned if the investor were a perfect trader of stock as a whole, using the S&P 500 Index as a proxy for the market.
3. Higher returns could have been earned if the investor had bought at the market low in 1970 and had held for the period.
4. The lowest returns would have been earned if the investor had purchased stocks at the average of the market in 1970 and had held for the period.

The conclusion is obvious. The investor must be a perfect picker and perfect trader to outperform the market significantly.

THE INVESTMENT ALTERNATIVES

And Let's Not Forget Foreign Securities

Investment in foreign securities when combined with American securities tends to reduce the risk of the portfolio. At least this was one conclusion reached by Donald R. Lessard in a *Financial Analysts Journal* article.[6] This is because securities in foreign markets move differently from other securities. The exchange rate risk might make the securities more risky, but the returns might be higher to offset the risk.

Table 6–4 summarizes the returns from equities in selected foreign markets for the

TABLE 6–4

Average Returns for Selected Countries, 1970–79
Before and After Currency Valuation Adjustment

Country	Money Market %	Bond Market %	Equity Market %
Before adjustment (local currency)			
USA	7.3	4.4	5.7
Japan	7.5	8.0	12.6
UK	8.6	8.2	10.1
Canada	7.2	6.2	11.8
Germany	6.1	7.7	2.5
France	8.7	7.0	6.7
Switzerland	2.1	6.0	2.0
Australia	7.0	4.3	4.2
Netherlands	6.3	6.9	4.4
After adjustment (U.S. $)			
USA	—	7.3	4.4	5.7
Japan	4.1	11.9	12.4	17.2
UK	−0.8	7.8	7.4	9.2
Canada	−0.9	6.2	5.2	10.8
Germany	7.9	14.5	16.1	10.0
France	3.3	12.2	10.5	10.2
Switzerland	10.5	12.8	17.1	12.7
Australia	−0.1	6.9	4.1	4.1
Netherlands	6.7	13.3	14.0	11.4

SOURCE: *World Capital Markets—A Review of the Past Decade,* Phillips & Drew, Lee House, London Wall, London EC2Y5AP.

period 1970–79 before and after adjustments for changes in the relative value of the currency. The money market returns and returns on bonds are also provided. An investor would have profited by investing in Japanese, United Kingdom, Canadian, and French stocks during the period. In fact, the investor would have been better off investing in money market securities, except for Switzerland, rather than purchasing common stock in the United States. This is before adjustment for changes in the value

[6]Donald R. Lessard, "World, Country and Industry Relationships in Equity Returns," *Financial Analysts Journal*, January–February 1976.

of currencies. And investors would have been better off buying bonds (except for American and Australian) during the period.

After adjusting for currency transactions, all money market returns were higher than the return in the U.S. equity market. Except for Canada and Australia, all bonds earned a higher return than the return of the U.S. equity markets. And only Australia earned a lower equity return than the United States. All other countries earned a higher after-currency adjustment rate of return than the U.S. equities. In fact, just by holding the currency, Germany, Switzerland, or the Netherlands would have provided a higher return than the U.S. equity market.

ADVANTAGES AND DISADVANTAGES OF COMMON STOCK

The major disadvantages of common stock are its lack of earnings and price stability, and the variability of returns, all of which create substantial risk. When common stock is purchased, there is no guarantee or contractual agreement that the dividend will remain fixed, or even that a dividend will be paid. Since income is unstable and uncertain, the stock price will fluctuate widely, and both principal and current income might be lost. Another disadvantage is the difficulty of estimating future earnings and price, particularly by those who do not understand the nature of common stock. Because price fluctuates and forecasting earnings is difficult, it is an undesirable investment for certain investors, particularly some institutional investors who require stability of income. The low current dividend yield at present tends to make it unattractive to people who need substantial current income. Investors who buy common stocks must accept the market and business risks associated with such investment.

The advantages of common stock should also be apparent. First, the potential for profit is greater than with any other investment security. The current dividend yield is low, but potential for capital gain is great. The return can be substantial over a period of time. Common stock also offers tax advantages. The larger return on some common stocks results from an increase in principal or capital gains, which are taxed at a lower rate than ordinary income. The maximum capital gains tax rate was 20 percent in 1983; the rate was lowered by ERTA (Economic Recovery Tax Act) in 1981. And some common stocks are a good hedge against inflation—even though not compensating perfectly for the diminished purchasing power of the dollar. When interest rates are high, stocks tend to be less attractive and prices tend to be depressed. The major advantage of investment in common stock is its ability to increase in value by sharing in the growth of earnings over the long term.

Sources of Information about Common Stock

Earnings, dividends, price, and time are the focal points for the decision-making process, and one of the most frustrating aspects of investment analysis and management is the difficulty of obtaining up-to-date information about the earnings and dividends of a company. What we need is a relatively simple, reliable, available, and inexpensive information source. Standard & Poor's *Stock Guide* is an excellent source of up-to-date facts. The annual report of the company, news in *The Wall Street Journal* under the subject "Digest of Earnings Reports," and reports mailed to shareholders by the company provide basic sources of sales and earnings information.

A primary source of factual information is Standard & Poor's *Standard Listed Stock Reports*, available in most libraries. The *Value Line Investment Surveys* and *The Outlook*, another publication of Standard & Poor's, offer good information.

Portfolio Needs and Common Stock

Common stock is looked upon as an aggressive type of investment. If the economy is expanding, with increasing profits, stable prices, and relatively low interest rates, then common stock is an excellent investment. It is versatile and can provide income, growth, or a combination of both to meet the needs of almost any investor. The risks are greater than with either bonds or preferred stock, for in periods of rapidly increasing prices, high interest rates, and low real economic growth, common stock prices fall. In addition, the returns or holding period returns of common stock are highly variable. Common stock fits admirably into an investor's program when there is little need for current income and when a favorable tax status and capital growth are desired. More will be said about common stock in the portfolio in later chapters.

OPTIONS

The purchase of a warrant or a right gives the investor a way to participate in the ownership of common stock for a fraction of the cost of buying shares outright. Unfortunately, warrants and rights do fluctuate in value, do not pay dividends, and may expire before the investor achieves any financial gain. Investors ordinarily buy warrants and rights when they anticipate a gain through a rise in price. Actually, besides warrants and rights, there are many other different types of options by which common stock may be bought.

Rights or warrants may also be used as a method to protect a speculative transaction. There are times when even conservative investors will attempt to take advantage of a stock that is overpriced by selling the stock short. In a short sale, the investor sells stock he or she does not own—stock borrowed from another investor—in the hope that its price will decline so the investor can purchase the stock at the lower price and repay the owner from whom the stock was borrowed. Obviously, if 100 shares of a stock are sold at 30 and the price drops to 25, the investor will make a profit of $500 before brokerage commissions and other expenses necessary to complete the transaction. But what if the price doesn't decline, but goes up? Assume that the price rises to 35. The investor or speculator can't keep the short position (arranged with the help of a broker) open forever, and it may be costly to continue to wait until (or if) the stock declines below 30. If the stock is sold at 35 to cover the short sale, the investor will lose $500 plus commissions. He or she may protect the short sale by buying a warrant or right that fixes the purchase price and limits the possible loss on the trade. Assume rights or warrants are purchased to buy 100 shares of stock at a price of $28 per share, and the cost of buying the options is $400—$4 or 4 points a share. This means that the investor is, in effect, buying the stock at $32 per share and has limited the total loss to $2 per share if the stock should go up.

Unfortunately, warrants and rights are issued infrequently, are not available for all stocks, and—rights, particularly—have a short life of approximately one month. Other options are available in the marketplace that can be used in the same way as a right. A *call* option, for example, can be purchased by the short seller to minimize losses. A call is a contract, negotiable in form, giving the purchaser the privilege of purchasing a given number of shares of stock for a certain period of time at a certain price. Assume that the cost of the option is $2 per share, or $200, to buy the stock at 30. The short seller has the privilege of buying 100 shares of stock at 32 for 90 days. If the stock dropped to 25 within 90 days, the short seller would buy the stock and return it to the person from whom it was borrowed. Under the circumstances, the short seller receives a smaller profit per share ($30, the sale price, minus the $25 per share repurchase price, minus the $2 per share cost of the option), but the potential loss has been limited to $2 per share. A limit on losses is obviously an advantage.

Call-Option Terminology

It might be helpful to introduce first the terminology associated with a call option to purchase common stock. The *buyer* is the person who acquires the option for a *premium*, which is the price the buyer pays the *writer* who sells or creates the option. If the writer owns the stock, it is referred to as a *covered writer*, and if the writer does not own the stock, it is an *uncovered writer*. The *striking price* or *exercise price* is the price per share at which the buyer may buy, in the case of a call, 100 shares of the underlying stock. On an options exchange, the exercise price is set in advance and does not change during the life of the option. If the stock changes price, new exercise prices will be introduced for trading to reflect the price of the underlying stock. The *expiration date* is the last day on which the buyer can exercise the option. The length of the option varies from 30 days to one year, with quotes reported for various maturities. The 60-, 90-, and 180-day options are most typical. Options are traded on listed options exchanges, referred to as *secondary markets*, that enable investors to buy and sell options. Secondary markets include the Chicago Board Options Exchange, the American Stock Exchange, Philadelphia Options, and Pacific Exchange. Such markets allow buyers to acquire and sell options and allow writers an opportunity to *buy back* an option, which liquidates the writer's position.

Purchasing a Call Option

It is unnecessary to be a short seller of stock to use the call option. Assume that the price of a stock is expected to rise from $30 to $35 a share. An investor or speculator could buy the stock or buy an option contract to purchase 100 shares at $30 per share. Assume as before that the cost of the option, without brokerage commissions, is $200. The speculator, for $200, has the privilege of buying 100 shares at 30. If the stock increases to $35 per share before the option expires, the speculator can exercise the option and sell the shares in the market for a gain of $300—($35 − [$30 + $2]) × 100. On the other hand, if the stock increases to $35 and the option has not expired, the option will increase in price. Therefore, the speculator need not exercise the option but merely sell it in the marketplace. If the investor is successful, he or she can profit by exercising the option and selling the stock or by selling the option. If the speculator is unsuccessful and the stock does not increase in price, the only loss is the cost of the option, $200, in addition to the brokerage costs.

The effect of the purchase of the call option, in the example above, is to allow the speculator to buy 100 shares of stock worth $3,000 for $200 for a 90-day period. An investor could actually put $2,800 in a savings account for 90 days and buy a $200 call option and be in the same position as if he or she bought 100 shares of stock at 30, ignoring brokerage costs, except that there would be no dividends from the stock, since the investor does not actually own the stock. In this way, the speculator earns interest from the investment and can benefit if the stock should increase in price.

The purchase of a call option has speculative appeal. If market timing is correct, gains of 20 to 100 percent are possible. Yet the buyer of a call option assumes the speculative risk of a total loss of the premium paid for the option. The return-to-risk ratio is low, and the purchase of a call is a speculation rather than an investment. Risks are high. In other words, the variability of return is high in the purchase of call options, which indicates that the risks are high. As a matter of principle, the risks associated with the purchase of a call option for speculative gains exceed the rewards that can be achieved. On the other hand, call options used to minimize losses involving speculative trades tend to limit losses and improve the return-to-risk ratio for the speculator.

Writing Call Options

An investor might not be willing to buy call options because of the speculative risks involved. On the other hand, writing options in a stable-to-risky market can be profitable.[7] Assume, for example, that an investor has purchased 100 shares of XYZ Corporation for investment. She plans to hold the stocks, as an investment for income and capital gains, for a three-year period. By selling call options against the stock, the investor receives the premium income, which is added to the return of the stock. The effect of writing the option is to increase the investor's return without substantially increasing the risk of investment. If the investor bought XYZ common stock at $50 per share against which a call option was written for a $4 premium per share, the effect is similar to selling the stock at $54 per share. If the stock price remained at $50 per share until the expiration date, the call would most likely not be exercised. The investor would remain fully invested in the stock and would have added $4 per share to total return.

If XYZ stock increased in price to $58 per share before the call expired, there would be a good chance that the call would be exercised at the striking price. In that event, the investor would not share in the full rise in the price of the stock, but at least the premium income would have increased the total return. This simply illustrates that the investor must be prepared to have the shares "called" out of her portfolio if she undertakes a program of writing options. If the market price should decline to $45 per share, the call would not be exercised and the investor would continue to hold the stock. In this case, the investor suffers a $5 per share loss (temporary, of course), but

[7]Wilford J. Eiteman, Charles A. Dice, and David K. Eiteman, *The Stock Market*, 4th ed. (New York: McGraw-Hill, 1966), chap. 16.

the option premium has made up 80 percent of the loss if it does not decline further. The loss on the stock would have been greater if the investor had not written the option contract.[8]

The subject of call options is complex, but in principle it is to the investor's advantage to write options against stock held in the investment portfolio. This is primarily because more than half the option contracts written are never exercised. The premium received from call options therefore tends to increase return and reduce risk.

Puts, Straddles, and Spreads

Other options, such as puts, straddles, and spreads, may be purchased by an investor or speculator to help achieve the goal of maximizing return and minimizing risk. Such options are not traded on listed exchanges as calls, rights, and warrants are, but are available through brokerage houses and members of the Put and Call Brokers and Dealers Association.

A *put* option is a negotiable contract giving the holder the right to sell stock to the writer—usually 100 shares—at a specified striking price for a specified period of time at a set premium. This option is useful in declining markets, where it would be desirable to sell a stock at, say, 30 to the writer of the put after the stock price declines to 25. The premium paid for the put, as for all options, is a function of market conditions, the supply and demand for the stock, and the length of the option. A *straddle* is a contract that combines a put and a call. A *spread* is similar to a straddle, but with the call option exercised at a price higher than a put. Straddles and spreads are designed for speculators who are trading on both sides of the market. By buying puts, calls, straddles, and spreads, speculators tend to limit the total loss on any one or a series of trades.

An Example of Put, Call, and Straddle Options in Practice

An example of how options work can be understood from the quotes provided for Cessna. Cessna options were traded on the Chicago Board, and Figure 6–3 provides option price information for February 5 and 17, 1982. On February 5, the premium for the May option was 1 3/4 or $175 for the contract at a striking price of 20. The February premium was 3/8, and there was no trade for the August call. The last is the premium price. The May call option on Cessna would give the purchaser the right to buy 100 shares at $20 per share through May 1982. Essentially the speculator is buying Cessna at 21 3/4 and is optimistic that the price of the option will increase or that the price of the stock will increase, or the purchaser is protecting a short sale—Cessna was sold short at 19 1/4, expecting it would drop. If it went up and Cessna was not owned, the speculator would be required to buy the stock on the market at whatever price it was being traded. If the price moved sharply higher to 25, the speculator would have lost $675 ($25 − 19 1/4 × 100). Therefore, having a call option contract would allow the speculator to buy 100 shares at 20 per share plus 1 3/4 premium or a 21 3/4 per share price. This would limit losses to $250 ($21 3/4 − $19 1/4 × 100).

[8] Merrill Lynch, Pierce, Fenner & Smith, Inc., *The Merrill Lynch Guide to Writing Options*, New York, June 1975.

42 THE WALL STREET JOURNAL, Monday, February 8, 1982

Chicago Board

Option & NY Close	Strike Price	Calls—Last Feb	Calls—Last May	Calls—Last Aug	Puts—Last Feb	Puts—Last May	Puts—Last Aug
Amdahl	. 25	2	4	4¾	9-16	1 15-16	2½
26½	... 30	¼	1⅞	r	3¾	4⅝	5
26½	... 35	r	¾	1⅞	r	r	r
A E P	...15	1 3-16	1⅜	1 11-16	r	r	r
16¼	... 20	1-16	r	⅛	r	r	r
Am Hos	35	7	8½	8½	r	r	r
42⅜	... 40	2⅞	4¼	5	3-16	1⅛	r
42⅜	... 45	r	1¼	2	r	r	4
A M P	.. 45	r	r	r	⅛	r	r
48⅞	... 50	5-16	r	r	r	3¼	r
48⅞	... 55	r	1	r	r	r	r
Baxter	.. 25	10⅞	r	s	r	r	s
35¼	. 27½	8	r	s	r	r	s
35¼	... 30	5⅜	6⅜	7½	1-16	7-16	1
35¼	... 35	15-16	2⅜	3¾	¾	2¼	r
35¼	... 40	s	¾	1⅜	s	r	r
Blk Dk	..15	¼	1¼	1 13-16	½	1 1-16	r
14¾	... 20	r	5-16	9-16	r	r	r
Boeing	.. 20	⅞	2	2⅞	¼	1⅛	1⅝
20⅜	... 25	1-16	7-16	1 1-16	4¾	4¾	r
20⅜	... 30	1-16	⅛	s	9½	r	s
Bois C	...30	1	3	r	r	r	r
30⅞	... 35	r	1⅛	2½	r	4	r
C B S	.. 45	r	r	4	1	2½	r
45	 50	r	¾	r	r	r	r
Cessna	.. 15	4⅜	r	r	r	r	½
19¼	... 20	⅜	1¾	r	1⅛	1⅝	r
19¼	... 25	1-16	½	r	r	r	r
Coke	 30	2	3	3½	1-16	1	1¼
32⅛	... 35	1-16	11-16	1½	r	r	r
32⅛	... 40	r	r	½	r	r	r
Colgat	.. 10	r	r	8¼	r	r	r
18⅛	... 15	3⅜	3¾	4⅛	r	¼	⅜
18⅛	... 20	7-16	1⅜	1¾	r	r	3
Cmw Ed	20	5-16	⅝	⅞	3-16	⅝	r
20	 25	r	1-16	⅛	r	r	r
C Data	..30	6⅛	7⅛	r	1-16	13-16	1¼
36	... 32½	3¼	s	s	3-16	1 5-16	s
36	 35	1 9-16	3⅞	5¼	⅝	2¼	3
36	 40	1-16	1½	2⅝	4¼	4⅝	5½
36	 45	r	½	s	r	r	s

46 THE WALL STREET JOURNAL, Thursday, February 18, 1982

Chicago Board

Option & NY Close	Strike Price	Calls—Last Feb	Calls—Last May	Calls—Last Aug	Puts—Last Feb	Puts—Last May	Puts—Last Aug
Amdahl	. 25	2⅛	3⅞	5	1-16	1⅜	1 11-16
27¼	... 30	1-16	1 11-16	2⅞	2⅞	4	4⅝
27¼	.. 35	1-16	½	1½	r	r	r
A E P	..15	1¼	r	1 13-16	r	r	r
16¼	.. 20	r	r	⅛	r	r	r
Am Hos	35	7¼	8⅜	r	r	r	r
42⅛	... 40	2¼	3⅞	5¼	1-16	⅞	1½
42⅛	.. 45	r	1⅛	2⅛	r	r	r
A M P	.. 45	r	r	r	r	1	r
49¾	... 50	⅝	3⅜	r	r	2¼	r
49¾	.. 55	1-16	1⅛	2¾	r	6	r
Bally	... 25	1	r	4	r	r	r
Baxter	.. 25	11	r	s	r	r	s
36	 30	6	7¼	8	r	7-16	r
36	... 32½	3¾	5	s	r	r	s
36	 35	1	2⅝	4¼	⅛	1⅜	2
36	 40	s	⅞	r	s	4⅜	r
Blk Dk	..15	1-16	⅞	1¼	1	r	1¾
14¼	... 20	r	3-16	7-16	r	r	r
Boeing	. 15	s	4½	4¾	s	¼	½
18¾	. 20	1-16	1	1¾	1¼	2	2 7-16
18¾	... 25	1-16	¼	11-16	6¼	6¼	6¼
18¾	... 30	1-16	⅛	s	11¼	r	s
Bois C	...25	r	r	r	r	⅜	r
28¼	... 30	⅛	1¾	r	2	2¼	r
28¼	.. 35	r	r	1½	6⅜	r	r
C B S	.. 45	1-16	2⅛	r	2	r	r
43½	... 50	r	⅝	r	r	r	r
Cessna	.. 15	3⅜	r	r	r	⅜	¾
18	 20	⅛	¾	1⅝	2	2¼	r
18	 25	r	¼	9-16	r	r	r
Coke	 30	1¾	2¾	3¼	1-16	¾	r
31⅜	. 35	r	⅝	1 1-16	3⅞	r	r
31⅜	. 40	r	⅛	⅛	r	r	r
Colgat	.. 15	2 15-16	3⅜	3⅞	r	5-16	½
18	 20	1-16	15-16	1⅜	r	2 5-16	r
Cmw Ed	15	5	5¼	r	r	1-16	⅛
20	 20	⅛	9-16	13-16	1-16	⅝	r
20	 25	r	1-16	⅛	r	r	r
C Data	..30	3¾	5⅜	r	r	1	r
33½	. 32½	1¼	s	s	¼	1⅞	s
33½	.. 35	⅛	2⅜	4	1¾	3	r
33½	. 40	r	15-16	2	6	6¾	r
33½	. 45	r	¼	s	11¼	r	s

FIGURE 6–3

Chicago Board Option Prices, February 5 and 17, 1982

SOURCE: The Wall Street Journal, February 8, 1982, p. 42, and February 18, 1982, p. 46.

Let's see what would have happened by February 17, 1982. The price of Cessna dropped to 18, and the premium for the May option at a striking price of 20 declined to 3/4. The result is that the speculator lost \$100 on the option contract. If 100 shares of Cessna common were owned, a loss of \$200 would have resulted. If the stock were sold short, at 19 1/4, and the February 17 price was 18, the speculator would have had a profit of \$125. Probably the speculator would not have exercised the option, since the price had not dropped far enough to provide a profit. Since \$175 was paid for the option, the speculator would have lost \$50 on the option plus the cost of the commission to buy the option and the cost to sell the stock short.

If the speculator had purchased a put on February 5, 1982, the results would have been different. The May put option sold at a 1 5/8 premium, which gave the speculator the option to sell 100 shares at 20 until the option expired in May. Since the stock price declined to 18 on February 17, the speculator could buy stock at 18 and deliver at 20 and earn $200 less the cost of the premium of 1 5/8. The net result would be a profit of 3/8 or $37.50 before commissions. After commissions, there would be a loss. The other alternative would be to sell the put option contract. The put premium was quoted at 2 1/4 on February 17, 1982. If the put had been sold, the speculator would have earned a profit of 5/8 per share or $62.50 on the 100-share option. After commission, a small profit would have been earned.

The straddle is a put and a call combined. The discussion above would represent the description of how a speculator would have behaved had a straddle (a call plus a put option) been purchased on February 5, 1982, on Cessna at a striking price of 20. If a speculator had purchased a straddle, no profit would have been made, as the cost of the straddle premium would have been $337.50, $175 for the call plus $162.50 for the put. The options had until May 1982 before they expired. For the 12 days between February 5 and 17, only the put would have been profitable. The options might become profitable later in the period. The call could be used for several short sales before the period ended. And there was the possibility that the price could rise later in the period.

The sharp change in the price of Cessna and the price of the Cessna options points to the major risk of purchasing options—the risk of sharp price changes. The price of Cessna common declined from 19 1/4 to 18, a 6.5 percent drop. The May call declined from 1 3/4 to 3/4, for a 57 percent decline. The leverage in calls is spectacular, and a small change in the price of the stock can lead to a significantly higher rate of decline in the price of the option. The speculator must understand this phenomenon and the risks involved. The speculator also must realize that the price of the option is independent of the price of the common stock. The two are related, but not perfectly. It is possible to buy a stock that is underpriced with the option of the same stock overpriced. Therefore, the speculator must be aware of paying too much for an option. In addition, the market for options has become more perfect, with huge profits unlikely.

INDEX FUTURES

Trading in stock index futures began February 24, 1982, in Kansas City, with over 2000 contracts in futures changing hands. The futures contracts were based on the Value Line Index of stock prices. The June 1983 contract closed at 137.50, 8 percent higher than the March 1982 contract, which was 126.65. Each point of the index has been assigned a value of $500.

A trader who thinks the index will fall below 130 could sell a contract that would mature in March, June, September, or December. If a June contract were sold at 125 and the market fell to 120 before June, the position could be *sold out* by purchasing a contract at 120. The trader would realize a profit of $2,500, or $500 a point, on an initial investment of $6,500. The original investment would have been 10 percent of the index at 130. The market price was $130 \times \$500 = \$65,000$. Ten percent of this was $6,500. If the market went up instead of down, the speculator would lose.

Other markets are thinking of starting competing stock index contracts even though it is not known how successful the new index futures contract will be. It is thought that institutional investors will be heavy users. The Commodity Futures Trading Commission (CFTC) is considering several applications for such contracts. The New York Futures Exchange wishes to trade all the Big Board Indexes. The Chicago Mercantile Exchange and the New York Commodities Exchange, Inc., want to trade the S&P 500 Index. The Chicago Board of Trade made application to trade ten indexes.[9]

At the time trading started, some members of Congress thought the trading in indexes was premature and irresponsible. They suggested that it was like legalized gambling: No securities changed hands, and all transactions were in cash. It was not certain that the index futures market would be a success.

SUMMARY

In the past few years, common stock ownership, with its inherent risks and potential rewards, has offered varying degrees of returns. In distinct contrast to the case of bonds or preferred stock, the earnings and dividends on common stock are not fixed by contract or indenture but are determined by the success of the business and changes in yield and risk in the capital markets. The common stockholder is the residual owner—the risk-taker—and receives profits but also assumes the risk of loss. The stockholder has the right to receive a certificate as evidence of ownership, to receive dividends, to vote on corporate matters, and to maintain a proportional share in the earnings, assets, and voting control through the preemptive right granted in many states. Dividends received on common stock are in the form of cash or stock, or both. Type of dividend will have an important effect on the investor's tax position. A stock dividend, for example, is not taxable until sold. A cash dividend is taxable in the year paid. Investors in the high tax brackets are interested in companies that pay a stock dividend.

The success of common stock investment is determined by timing and by certainty of earnings. A company offering growth of earnings and a high degree of certainty of earnings will bear less risk than one that promises little growth and a great deal of uncertainty. Current yields on common stock have been low but have moved upward over the past decade; but are now less than bond yields. Current yield, however, has been only a small portion of investment return on many common stocks; the total return, or holding period return, is more important.

Investment returns over time have varied in magnitude and degree of risk. Investors are wise to use total return from a historical investment as a measure of performance. A total return of 9 percent over long periods is possible. But variability of total return as measured by the standard deviation is high; therefore, common stocks are riskier than bonds or preferred stock. As a matter of principle, common stocks are riskier than bonds, and some are more profitable than bonds even when bond yields are 15 percent or higher.

[9] *The New York Times*, February 25, 1982, pp. 1, 14.

Common stock owners must assume the business, money-rate, and market risks, but they do not assume completely the purchasing-power risk. When money rates are high, stock prices tend to decline. Common stocks appear in portfolios that are aggressively seeking gains and need growth and income.

The major advantage of common stock is the capital gains that can be earned because the stock shares directly in the growth of the company. The major disadvantage is the greater risk of loss. Foreign securities, based upon past experience, offer investors the possibility of higher returns and lower risks when combined with U.S. securities.

Options represent a way in which common stock can be owned without as large an investment as required by direct stock ownership. Call options, however, are risky and might offer high returns for short periods of time with a high degree of risk. More than 50 percent of call options are unexercised. This suggests that as a principle, call options and put options are too risky for the average risk-averse investor. On the other hand, writers of options tend to increase total return without accepting substantial risk. As a principle, investors should consider the possibility of writing options against securities in which they maintain an investment position.

An index futures market allows speculators to hedge, trade, and buy claims on which profits and losses may occur.

SUMMARY OF PRINCIPLES

1. Common stock offers the highest return and the highest risk of all securities.
2. The investor must estimate the total return and risk of common stock for some future holding period in order to make a decision about purchase.
3. Stocks that pay a cash dividend are more valuable than those that do not.
4. Stock dividends and stock splits might not add value unless earnings increase.
5. A stable dividend policy is considered valuable.
6. Total return, including dividends and capital gains or losses, is more important than dividends alone as a measure of profitability.
7. Investor expectations usually underestimate risk.
8. Risks of buying calls usually outweigh rewards.
9. It is sometimes profitable for the investor to sell call options against securities owned.
10. Foreign securities tend to reduce the risk and improve the return of a portfolio.

REVIEW QUESTIONS

1. Common stock represents the residual ownership of the corporation. Explain.
2. How do ordinary voting and cumulative voting differ?
3. What is the significance of book value, and how does it differ from par value and market value?

4. What are the typical forms of dividend payments?

5. What is the tax advantage in stock dividends? Is this true of dividends paid in the securities of companies not held by the investor?

6. Some people think stock dividends are unrealistic and unnecessary, since they give the investor what he has already received. Comment.

7. Do preemptive rights have value? Discuss.

8. Might the market value and the theoretical value of a right differ? Discuss.

9. Explain the difference between current yield on common stock and total return for a period.

10. What has been the trend of current yields over the past ten years?

11. What has been the level of total return in that period?

12. How variable are returns on common stock, and what does this imply about riskiness?

13. What are the advantages and disadvantages of common stock?

14. Explain the advantages and disadvantages of a call option and a put.

15. An investor would be wise to write options. Comment.

16. Should an investor consider foreign common stocks for investment? Why or why not?

17. How does an index futures work?

PROBLEMS

1. As an owner of American Widget Company common, you are given the right to subscribe to a new issue of stock that is being sold to raise capital to expand plant facilities. The announcement of the offering was made on January 1 for owners of record January 30. The rights expire February 15. Subscription price for the new stock was set at $45 per share. Each stockholder is allowed to buy one new share at the subscription price for each eight shares of stock owned. The market price January 7 was $54.
   a. What was the theoretical value of the right on January 7?
   b. If nothing disturbed the price, what would the value of the right be on February 1?
   c. What value would the right have on February 16?
   d. Would we expect the market price and theoretical price to be the same in this case? Why, or why not?

2. Dr. H. I. Low bought 100 shares of Safe and Sound at $100 per share. He held the stock for three years and sold it at 160. The company paid $2.50 per share in dividends in each of the three years. What total return did Dr. Low earn from his investment?

3. Three years ago, Robert Riskey bought 100 shares of stock at $10 per share. The company has paid no dividends during the period. Riskey is interested in knowing

the total return he earned and the indicated risk he assumed. The quarterly prices were as follows:

Year	Quarter	Price
1	1	$10
1	2	11
1	3	12
1	4	13
2	1	14
2	2	15
2	3	14
2	4	11
3	1	13
3	2	14
3	3	16
3	4	15

a. What was the average quarterly return over the investment period? (Use the formula:

$$\text{Yield} = \frac{(P_1 - P_0) + D_Q}{P_0}$$

where P_1 is the ending price, P_0 is the beginning price, and D_Q is the quarterly dividend in dollars.)

b. What was the annual return earned on the investment?

c. What was the standard deviation of the annual average return?

d. Should Riskey continue to invest in the stock of the company? Why or why not?

5. The S&P 500 Index had the following high price, low price, earnings per share, and dividends for the years 1966 through 1976:

Year	High Price	Low Price	EPS	DPS
1966	94.06	73.20	5.55	2.87
1967	97.59	80.38	5.33	2.92
1968	108.40	87.72	5.76	3.07
1969	106.20	89.20	5.78	3.16
1970	93.46	69.29	5.13	3.14
1971	104.80	90.16	5.70	3.07
1972	119.10	101.70	6.42	3.15
1973	120.20	92.16	8.11	3.38
1974	98.80	60.96	8.88	3.60
1975	95.61	86.82	8.10	3.75
1976	108.00	90.00	10.00	4.50

SOURCE: Standard & Poor's *Stock Reports.*

a. Calculate the annual return for each year, using the equation $[(P_1 - P_0) + D_0] \div P_0$, where P_0 is the average of the high and low price in year zero, etc.

b. Calculate the average annual return for the period 1966 through 1976.

c. Calculate the standard deviation of the annual return.

THE INVESTMENT ALTERNATIVES

d. What conclusions do you draw about the return and risk of the S&P 500 stocks?

e. Compare these figures with the S&P 500 Index return and risk shown in Table 1–3. What conclusions do you draw?

CASE

Helen had heard that if an investor purchased different common stocks, it would be possible to reduce risk but not reduce the return. Actually, an investor in combining stocks is constructing a portfolio and engaging in diversification to reduce risk. In Chapter 1, there were four common stocks in Table 1–3. Combine the two stocks with the highest returns. The act of combining actually assumes that you add one share of stock A to one share of stock B. After combining the two shares, calculate the average annual return and the standard deviation of the return for the period.

Explain what happened to return and risk. What conclusions would Helen draw from this example? Would it uphold her original assumption? Explain.

SELECTED READINGS

BLACK, FISHER. "Fact and Fantasy in the Use of Options." *Financial Analysts Journal*, July–August 1975, pp. 36–41.

———. "The Ins and Outs of Foreign Investment." *Financial Analysts Journal*, May–June 1978.

———. "The Dividend Puzzle." *The Journal of Portfolio Management*, winter 1976.

———, and MYRON SCHOLES. "The Valuation of Option Contracts and a Test of Market Efficiency." *The Journal of Finance*, May 1972, pp. 399–418.

COLE, JAMES F. "What About the Anatomy of the Stock." *Financial Analysts Journal*, November–December 1977.

DIMSON, ELROY. "Instant Option Valuation" *Financial Analysts Journal*, May–June, 1977.

EISEMAUN, PETER C., and EDWARD A. MOSES. "Stock Dividend: Management View." *Financial Analysts Journal*, July–August 1978.

ELTON, E. J., and M. J. GRUBER. "The Economic Value of the Call Option." *The Journal of Finance*, September 1972, pp. 891–902.

Exchange-Traded Put and Call Options. The Options Clearing Corporation, 1980.

Financial Instruments Markets: Cash Futures Relationships. Chicago Board of Trade, 1980.

FISHER, LAWRENCE, and JAMES H. LORIE. *A Half Century of Returns on Stock and Bonds.* Chicago: The University of Chicago School of Business, 1977.

GASTINEAU, GARY L. "An Index of Listed Option Premiums." *Financial Analysts Journal*, May–June 1977.

GRAHAM, BENJAMIN. "The Future of Common Stocks." *Financial Analysts Journal*, September–October 1974, pp. 20–32.

HAWKINS, DAVID F. "Toward an Old Theory of Equity Value." *Financial Analysts Journal*, November–December 1977.

IBBOTSON, ROGER, and JEFFREY JAFFE. " 'Hot Issue' Markets." *The Journal of Finance*, September 1975, pp. 1027–42.

KAPLAN, R., and R. W. ROLL. "Accounting Changes and Stock Prices." *Financial Analysts Journal*, January–February 1973, pp. 48–53.

LEVY, ROBERT A. "On the Safety of Low P/E Stocks." *Financial Analysts Journal*, January–February 1973, pp. 57–63.

LINTNER, JOHN. "Distribution of Incomes of Corporations among Dividends, Retained Earnings and Taxes." *The American Economic Review*, May 1956.

MALKIEL, B. G., and R. E. QUANDT. "The Supply of Money and Common Stock Prices: Comment." *The Journal of Finance*, September 1972, pp. 921–26.

NIEDERHOFFER, VICTOR B., and RICHARD ZECKHAUSER. "Market Index Futures Contracts." *Financial Analysts Journal*, January–February 1980.

POZEU, ROBERT C. "When to Purchase a Protective Put." *Financial Analysts Journal*, July–August 1978.

PRICE, LEE H. "Choosing Between Growth and Yield." *Financial Analysts Journal*, July–August 1979.

RADCLIFFE, R. C., and W. G. GILLESPIE. "The Price Impact of Reverse Splits." *Financial Analysts Journal*, January–February 1979.

RODRIGUEZ, RITA N. "Measuring Multinationals Exchange Risk." *Financial Analysts Journal*, November–December 1979.

SHARPE, W. F., and H. B. SOSIN. "Risk Return and Yield on Common Stocks." *Financial Analysts Journal*, March–April 1976, pp. 33–42.

SLIVKA, RONALD T. "Risk and Return for Option Investment Strategies." *Financial Analysts Journal*, September–October 1980.

WALTER, JAMES E. "Dividend Policies and Common Stock Prices." *The Journal of Finance*, March 1965.

"What Investors Should Know about the Options Market." *Changing Times*, December 1975.

CHAPTER 7

MUTUAL FUNDS
AND
INVESTMENT COMPANY SHARES

More and more we find both individual as well as institutional investors interested in mutual funds. Investors have found mutual funds to be a viable investment alternative. Institutional portfolio managers are adapting the mutual fund approach to meet trust clients' needs. They comingle the assets of many trusts into specially designed common stock or bond funds. They then buy shares in these funds for individual accounts.

INVESTMENT COMPANY SHARES AS AN INVESTMENT

Investment companies offer a partial solution to portfolio management by providing expert research advice and professional management. The growth of mutual fund assets (see Table 7–1) has been remarkable but cyclical, particularly that of the money market funds. Closed-end funds have grown in recent years at the same pace as mutual fund assets, but they represent only 20 percent of the amount. In many respects, investment companies resemble industrial corporations that invest their money in land, machinery, and buildings; but investment companies invest in bonds, preferred stock, and common stock of other corporations and in municipal securities.

The balance sheet of a typical investment company would list the securities owned on the asset side of the sheet. On the liability side would be the shares sold to investors. The earning assets of an investment company are the same as those of an individual investor who chooses to invest money directly in securities. The earning assets—the securities purchased by the investment company—produce income from two sources: dividends and interest, and capital gains.

TABLE 7–1

Mutual Fund Assets
(millions of dollars, December 31)

Investment Objective	1978		1979		1980		1981	
	Dollars	% of Total	Dollars	% of Total	Dollars	% of Total	Dollars	% of Total
Aggressive growth	2,329.9	5.2	2.964.8	6.0	4,681.3	8.0	4,925.9	8.9
Growth	11,380.9	25.3	13,010.4	26.4	16,823.4	28.8	15,122.5	27.5
Growth and income	15,237.9	33.9	16,462.3	33.4	19,522.6	33.4	18,186.6	33.1
Balanced	3,722.5	8.3	3,438.0	7.0	3,389.2	5.8	2,778.3	5.1
Income	4,557.8	10.1	4,542.1	9.2	4,801.7	8.2	4,455.5	8.1
Bond	4,700.2	10.4	5,086.5	10.3	5,712.6	9.8	5,894.2	10.7
Municipal Bond*	2,631.6	5.9	3,324.0	6.7	2,908.3	5.0	3,051.5	5.6
Option Income	418.9	0.9	469.0	1.0	560.4	1.0	551.3	1.0
Total	44,979.7	100.0	49,297.1	100.0	58,399.6	100.0	54,965.8	100.0

*1977–79 includes short-term; thereafter, only long-term.

SOURCE: Standard & Poor's *Industry Survey—Investment Funds,* February 28, 1981, p. 164; and January 14, 1982, p. 164.

Funds invested by investment companies are obtained in much the same way as capital is obtained by industrial corporations. The manufacturing company sells preferred stock and common stock and borrows money through the issuance of debt. Investment companies, as a group, raise capital in much the same way, although the methods of individual companies vary. If the company is a mutual fund, it sells only ownership shares. A closed-end company raises capital, both common and debt, exactly like an industrial company. In the final analysis, how an investment fund raises its capital depends on the nature of the company and the policies established by its management.

Closed-End Investment Companies

There are two basic types of investment companies—*closed-end* and *open-end*. The closed-end investment company, sometimes referred to as an *investment trust*, operates in much the same way as any industrial company. It issues a fixed number of shares of common stock, which may be listed on an exchange and may be bought and sold just like any other corporation's stock. The stock of the Tri-Continental Company, a large closed-end investment company, is traded on the New York Stock Exchange, for example. When the stock of a closed-end investment company is purchased through a broker, the purchaser pays the broker a commission, computed in the same way as for any other listed security. The management of the closed-end investment company may from time to time issue additional common stock, but for the most part, the number of shares of stock outstanding is constant. If management desires, it may raise capital by selling preferred stock or bonds. The majority of closed-end investment companies have bonds and preferred stock outstanding as a part of their capital structure.

LEVERAGE. The use of fixed-income securities to obtain capital for a closed-end company results in leverage for the common-stock owners of the fund, affecting both the assets and the net income of the investment company. The closed-end company that issues debt or preferred stock is said to have both *asset leverage* and *earnings leverage*, because preferred stock and bonds represent a fixed claim against the assets of the company. The interest on debt and the dividends on preferred also represent a fixed and contingent charge against the company's earnings. Since both income and asset claims are fixed, any increase in asset values, and any increase in earnings over the interest payments or dividend requirements, go to the common stockholders. As long as the closed-end company earns more on its assets than is necessary to pay the fixed claims and a similar amount to the common stockholder, the owners will benefit. As earnings go beyond the point where bonds and preferred earn their guaranteed rate of return, the additional earnings are left to be paid to the common stockholders. As earnings increase, the rate of increase of the return to the common stockholders increases faster than the rate of increase of the return on the total assets.

Asset leverage occurs when the prices of the common stock owned by the investment company increase or decrease. If the value of the total assets increases, there is a greater proportional increase in the value of the common stock of the investment company. Since the debt issued is a fixed claim against assets, any increase in assets goes to the common stockholders. Thus, as the value of the investments increases, the company's common stock actually increases faster. Table 7–2 demonstrates asset leverage. In time period 1, the closed-end investment company had assets of $200, all invested in common stock. The capital was raised by the sale of $100 worth of bonds and $100

TABLE 7–2
Asset Leverage of a Closed-End Investment Company

	Time Period 1			Time Period 2 (20% increase in common stock)			
Assets		Liabilities		Assets		Liabilities	
Common stock	$200	Debt	$100	Common stock (+20%)	$240	Debt	$100
		Common (100 shares)	100			Common (+40%)	140
	$200		$200		$240		$240

of common stock. In time period 2, after the value of the investments in common stock has increased 20 percent, the leverage is reflected in the change in the ownership account. The $40 increase in common stock value results in a 40 percent increase in the common equity account. None of the increase goes to the bondholders, because they have a fixed claim against the assets of the company. The result of the 20 percent increase in the assets of the closed-end company is a 40 percent increase in the value of its common stock—asset leverage, which can be expressed as the following ratio:

% increase in common stock ÷ % increase in asset value

Thus, at a given volume of assets, a percentage increase in assets will be greater when it is related to the common equity account. As the assets increase in value without a corresponding increase in debt capital, the leverage effect is diminished. The asset leverage in the case given would diminish as the assets continued to increase in value.

The asset-leverage effect of the closed-end investment company also operates when assets decline in value. Assume that the assets in time period 1 in Table 7–2 decrease by 20 percent in time period 2 instead of increasing. The decrease would be magnified in the decline in the price of common stock of the company. In this case, the decrease would be 40 percent. This is a disadvantage of the closed-end investment company that should be taken into account. Unfortunately, the leverage factor does not follow through to the market price on a one-to-one basis. Some closed-end funds sell at a discount and some at a premium over book price, which suggests that the leverage effect is unstable because the funds are unstable.

Closed-end investment companies that raise a substantial portion of their capital with debt may be susceptible to wider fluctuation in value than investment companies with a relatively small amount of debt. If they invest the funds obtained from debt in common stocks, the result would be a more volatile market action. If the money were invested in debt securities, there would be little or no effect on market action of the shares of the fund.

The earnings leverage and the asset leverage of the closed-end investment company tend to accentuate the cyclical price movement of the stock. This can be an important advantage if the investor can anticipate changes in the market or if the investor is able to buy the stock at attractive prices. On the other hand, a serious loss could result if the investor purchased shares in a heavily leveraged investment company at the wrong time. Closed-end companies tend to sell at a discount below net asset value. Actual discounts for the years 1975–80 are displayed in Table 7–3. Part of the discount is reflected in the costs of acquiring assets. The remainder must be attributed to attitudes in the marketplace. In order to bolster the price of the shares in the marketplace, some funds have repurchased these shares in the market.

When shares are repurchased at less than book value, it tends to bolster market price and adds to the book value of the remaining shares. An investor buying at a deep discount a closed-end fund that has a stated policy of repurchasing shares has an excellent chance of outperforming the competition.

Open-End Investment Companies

In contrast to that of the closed-end company, the stock of the open-end investment company is not traded on an exchange; it is traded in the over-the-counter market by specific dealers who handle its purchase and sale. The open-end investment company is usually called a *mutual fund*. The concept of mutuality is in the fact that there is only one class of owner, who shares the gains or losses of the fund with all the other owners. No leverage occurs in the open-end fund, unless the fund can borrow money to invest, as some funds do. The money obtained from the sale of shares is invested directly in the securities of other companies.

Table 7–4 shows the balance sheet of a typical open-end investment company, or mutual fund. In part A, owners of the fund have contributed $2,400,000, or at least

TABLE 7–3

*Percentage Discount Below Net Asset Value:
Closed-End Investment Companies

Company	1975	1976	1977	1978	1979	1980
Publicly Traded Funds						
ASA Limited	+58	+35	+9	+3.6	−26	−7
Adams Express	−23	−21	−12	−22	−21	[1]−18
General American Investors	−26	−18	−17	−27	−17	−3
Japan Fund	−16	−22	−29	−24	−16	[2]−23
Lehman Corp.	−20	−18	−20	−29	−20	−15
Madison Fund	−30	−28	−20	−25	−20	−11
Niagara Share	−3.7	−15	−15	−23	−19	+2
Petroleum & Resources	+2.2	+2.3	+7.7	−5.7	−11	[3]Nil
Source Capital	−45	−18	−23	−20	−21	−14
Tri-Continental	−22	−21	−12	−22	−23	[4]−25
U.S. & Foreign Securities	−26	−25	−27	−27	−24	[4]−21
Dual-Purpose Funds						
Gemini	−36	−25	−27	−9	−12	−13
Hemisphere	+178	+10	+95	NM	+132	+30
Income & Capital Shares	−40	−33	−32	−27	−20	−12
Scudder-Duo Vest	−32	−27	−22	−20	−16	−12

*Percentage difference of net asset value to year-end price. 1981 fiscal yr. data: [1]−15. [2]−18. [3]−11. [4]−20.

SOURCE: Standard & Poor's *Industry Survey—Investment Funds,* February 28, 1981, p. 166; and January 14, 1982, p. 167.

have a claim on this amount of assets, for the 240,000 shares of stock outstanding have a value of $10 per share. If we ignore the costs of selling the assets, this $10 figure is the net asset value per share of the fund. The mutual fund stands ready, through its agents or representatives, to buy or sell shares at this price, which is usually computed once a day at the close of the market.

Part B of the table shows the impact of a purchase of 100 mutual fund shares by an investor at a price of $10 per share, the net asset value at the time. The number of shares outstanding increases by 100, and the purchase adds $1,000 to the cash account. Eventually the $1,000 will be invested in bonds and common stock of other companies, in an attempt to meet the long-range objectives of the investor. If the market price of the investments owned by the mutual fund increases, then the fund shares owned by the investor will increase by the same proportional amount. There is no leverage in this relationship. All owners mutually share the profits and losses of the fund.

The illustration above did not consider the cost of selling or purchasing open-end shares. There is a cost involved, however, since sales costs in distributing the shares must be met. This charge, or commission, is usually called the *loading charge,* and it is paid only when shares are purchased. It is usually added to the net asset value per share and goes to the salesperson or dealer and to the company handling the distribution of the fund. The maximum commission under the National Association of Secu-

TABLE 7–4

Balance Sheet of a Small Balanced
Mutual Fund Investment Company

A

Assets		Liabilities and Ownership
Cash	$ 100,000	
Bonds	500,000	Shares outstanding 240,000
Preferred	600,000	Value $2,400,000
Common	1,200,000	
	$2,400,000	

B

Assets		Liabilities and Ownership
Cash	$ 101,000	
Bonds	500,000	Shares outstanding 240,100
Preferred	600,000	Value $2,401,000
Common	1,200,000	
	$2,401,000	

rities Dealers schedule is $8\frac{1}{2}$ percent on the first $15,000, down to 4 percent on $100,000 or more.

The price for a mutual fund is usually quoted on a bid-and-asked basis. The bid price is the price an investor would receive if he or she sold the shares; it is the same as the net asset value. The asked price represents the net asset value (bid price) plus the loading charge (the charge that covers the cost of selling). The selling charge must be large enough to compensate the distributor adequately for services; this encourages wider distribution of the fund. The price ranges for investment companies are quoted daily in *The Wall Street Journal.*

A few funds are listed in *Forbes*'s fund ratings for 1981 in Figure 7–1. Ratings are provided, as well as the relative growth rate, asset size, sales charges, and annual expenses. Similar lists can be found in Standard & Poor's *Industry Surveys*, and in the *Mutual Fund Performance Monthly*, published by Wiesenberger Services, Inc., One New York Plaza, New York, N.Y. 10004.

The cost of purchasing mutual fund shares may be high. This has long been a criticism of mutual fund ownership. The commission, however, does cover the cost of the purchase and the cost of the sale. Securities may be purchased on an exchange at a cost of less than 1 percent; including the selling cost, the round-trip commission would be about 2 percent. But in some cases, the cost of purchasing mutual funds is more than four times as great as in the purchase and sale of stock.

To invest small amounts of money on a regular basis is expensive in buying either mutual funds or common stock listed on an exchange. On stock purchases of $500 or less, the round-trip commission might equal or exceed the cost of purchasing the same dollar amount of a mutual fund. Large dollar purchases of mutual funds do have the disadvantage of a high commission. But small dollar purchases of mutual funds are comparable to small dollar purchases of common stock with respect to the commission paid.

1981 Fund Ratings

Performance			Investment results							
			Average annual total return 1968-81	Latest 12 months		Total assets		Maximum sales charge	Annual expenses per $100	
in UP markets	in DOWN markets			return from capital growth	return from income dividends	6/30/81 (millions)	% change '81 vs. '80			
		Standard & Poor's 500 stock average	5.7%	14.9%	4.9%					
		FORBES stock fund composite	5.8%	25.2%	3.4%					
		FORBES balanced fund composite	4.7%	3.0%	8.3%					
		FORBES bond and preferred stock fund composite	3.6%	–13.4%	12.5%					
		Stock funds (load)	Group averages							
			5.6%	24.6%	3.7%					
D	D	Affiliated Fund	7.5%	14.8%	6.2%	$1,736.5	10.5	7.25%	$0.38	
A	B	AMCAP Fund	10.0	26.3	3.8	254.1	91.2	8.50	0.80	
•C	•A	American Birthright Trust	—*	14.8	none	129.7	77.2	8.50	1.32	
B	B	American General Comstock Fund[1]	10.0	33.0	4.3	179.5	39.7	8.50	0.90	
B	F	American General Enterprise Fund	4.2	44.2	1.0	605.0	20.9	8.50	0.75	
A+	•C	American General Pace Fund[2]	—*	51.7	2.7	59.6	210.4	8.50	1.05	
•B	•C	American General Venture Fund	—*	34.5	2.9	60.4	205.1	8.50	1.12	
C	A	American Growth Fund	8.4	14.8	5.1	28.2	26.5	7.25	1.49	
C	B	American Insurance & Industrial Fund	9.6	13.1	6.3	15.1	5.6	8.50	1.00	
D	•D	American Leaders Fund	—*	9.1	7.9	48.1	0.4	6.50	1.37	
D	B	American Mutual Fund	9.1	22.7	4.7	508.0	30.5	8.50	0.54	
C	C	American National Growth Fund	8.0	23.0	4.3	57.7	41.4	8.50	0.79	
D	F	Anchor Growth Fund	0.1	23.9	4.4	139.0	7.3	8.50	0.65	
D	C	Axe-Houghton Stock Fund	4.4	25.2	1.4	122.4	64.7	8.50	0.88	
B	•D	BLC Growth Fund	—*	37.0	2.3	14.6	40.4	8.50	1.04	
D	•B	BLC Income Fund	—*	25.3	5.2	16.4	32.3	8.50	0.94	
C	C	Broad Street Investing Corp	7.9	20.3	4.8	377.0	17.1	7.25	0.45	
C	D	Bullock Fund	6.4	17.5	4.0	140.4	5.5	8.50	0.78	
C	D	The Cardinal Fund	4.5	16.2	4.0	13.5	4.7	8.50	0.93	
C	D	Century Shares Trust	6.5	16.9	4.6	71.9	10.8	7.25	0.99	
B	F	CG Fund	5.7	23.4	3.9	152.2	28.8	7.50	0.68	
A+	A	Charter Fund	13.5	26.2	3.1	40.6	60.5	8.50	1.35	
B	C	Chemical Fund	6.2	21.2	3.0	1,032.6	20.0	8.50	0.62	
B	F	Colonial Growth Shares	2.8	24.5	2.1	67.0	11.1	8.50	1.18	
C	F	Common Stock Fund State Bond & Mortgage Co	3.1	17.3	3.2	33.8	5.3	8.50	1.15	
D	D	Commonwealth Fund Indenture Trust Plans A & B	2.8	5.5	7.8	10.2	–5.6	7.50	0.40	
D	C	Commonwealth Fund Indenture of Trust Plan C	4.2	6.5	6.5	35.4	0.6	7.50	0.75	
D	D	Composite Fund	4.8	24.6	3.8	26.0	21.5	7.00	0.91	
C	C	Corporate Leaders Tr Fund Certificates, Series "B"	6.7	14.8	6.3	49.6	7.1	†	0.10	
C	D	Country Capital Growth Fund	3.7	26.0	2.7	47.0	16.3	7.50	0.85	
D	C	Decatur Income Fund	8.4	13.6	6.3	376.3	29.5	8.50	0.69	
D	D	Delaware Fund	6.0	25.5	4.1	255.9	7.8	8.50	0.77	
D	D	Delta Trend Fund	2.2	46.9	2.7	10.3	27.2	8.50	1.60	
D	C	Diversified Fund of State Bond and Mtge Co	6.1	12.7	4.9	7.4	17.5	8.50	1.00	
D	C	Dividend Shares	5.1	11.0	5.4	251.8	1.7	8.50	0.80	
C	C	The Dreyfus Fund	6.4	26.8	3.9	1,752.2	15.9	8.50	0.74	
B	•C	The Dreyfus Leverage Fund	—*	9.4	4.4	322.4	1.9	8.50	1.00	
		Eaton & Howard Funds								
A	F	Growth	4.2	41.3	1.0	36.5	21.7	7.25	0.95	
D	F	Stock	1.1	7.2	4.7	73.2	–5.6	7.25	0.67	
A+	F	Fairfield Fund	3.2	48.3	0.6	32.8	36.7	8.50	1.13	
•B	•B	Fidelity Destiny Fund	—*	33.4	2.9	233.1	48.0	‡	0.75	
A+	D	Fidelity Magellan Fund[3]	13.0	67.9	2.7	104.4	161.7	2.00	1.23	
C	•F	First Investors Discovery Fund	—*	48.2	0.3	6.0	42.9	8.50	1.50	
A	F	First Investors Fund for Growth	3.7	31.3	2.2	69.9	16.3	8.50	1.01	
D	C	First Investors Natural Resources Fund[4]	2.5	–4.8	10.0	11.1	–9.0	8.50	1.30	
D	B	First Investors Option Fund	3.4	14.3	4.7	81.8	97.1	7.25	1.10	
C	C	Founders Mutual Fund	4.5	16.3	4.5	132.8	5.1	4.00	0.52	

• Fund rated for two periods only; maximum allowable rating A. *Fund not in operation for full period. †Fund not currently selling new shares; existing shares traded over-the-counter. ‡ Available only through contractual plan. [1]Formerly Comstock Fund. [2]Formerly Pace Fund. [3]Formerly Magellan Fund. [4]Formerly First Investors Fund.

FIGURE 7–1

Forbes 1981 Fund Ratings

SOURCE: Forbes, August 31, 1981, p. 64.

No-Load Funds

Several funds do not charge a purchase fee or commission. These funds are *no-load funds*. Two such funds are Loomis-Sayles Mutual Fund and Scudder Stevens & Clark Balanced Fund. The manager of the fund is compensated by a management fee that varies from $\frac{1}{2}$ to 1 percent. No-load funds have grown because of their economy of cost and because they have performed as well as the mutual load funds. Part of the reason for growth has been the record of the T. Rowe Price funds, and part has been that some of the open-end funds have been converted to no-load funds.

CRITICISM OF MUTUAL FUNDS—
THE WHARTON SCHOOL STUDY AND THE SEC

Criticism has been leveled against mutual funds as a result of the Wharton Study of 1962 and the Special Study by the SEC. Because the performance of no-load funds has been as good as that of load funds, we must look at these criticisms very carefully.

The Wharton Study, authorized by the SEC, made the following statements about the mutual fund industry:

1. The performance of mutual funds did not differ greatly from what would have been achieved by an unmanaged portfolio.
2. The turnover rate of the stock holdings of mutual funds was greater than the average turnover rate of all stocks on the New York Stock Exchange.
3. The growth of mutual funds contributed significantly to the increase in stock prices in the preceding ten years.
4. The funds had little bargaining power in the creation of advisory-fee rates.
5. There might be a conflict of interest between management and shareholder in selling fund shares.
6. The sale of mutual fund shares was the determining factor in the allocation of buying and selling the funds' securities.
7. The structure of rates for large transactions was largely inflexible because of the "give-up."

The mutual fund industry answered the Wharton criticisms in the following manner:

1. While it was true that Standard & Poor's 500 had outperformed the mutual funds, if similar indexes were selected for comparison with the average common stock fund or balanced fund, the latter had outperformed on a fractional basis.
2. While the funds had a higher (15.2 percent to 14.4 percent) turnover rate than the New York Stock Exchange, the exchange figure included highly inactive preferred stocks and did not include "off-board" trading, so that conjecture about mutual funds' increasing short-term market volatility was unfounded.
3. Furthermore, the share of the market controlled by funds was 4.5 percent [December 1961], so that many other factors must have had a greater role in influencing the rise in stock prices. [The volume had risen to over 15 percent by 1976.]
4. Since the Investment Company Act of 1940 did not mention fee rates for advisory services, the fees charged by the funds varied; the shareholder could decide on any of a number of funds to select and would eventually have to approve future management contracts.

5. There was no evidence that selling efforts by mutual funds diluted the performance of the management; additionally, shareholders benefited from fund growth via lower per-share operating costs and from "sliding-scale" fee reductions.

6. Transactions were placed according to the best price and most efficient service; if these characteristics were similar, then it was natural for a fund to favor a broker who sells shares.

7. The "give-up" per se did not influence commissions on large or small orders. The rates charged by the brokers were set for them by the NYSE, which had not allowed for discounts for large-volume transactions.[1]

Hugh A. Johnson, creator of Johnson's Charts, made the following statement in his analysis of the Wharton School report:

> ... I hope that everyone can appreciate the sum and substance of the Wharton Report, which actually says that you cannot get diversification to compare with funds at a comparable cost; that the record of doubling the original investment in 5 3/4 years is excellent; that growth stock funds appreciate faster than the S&P Index in rising markets; that balanced funds are more stable than the market; that income funds produced more income in the last four years than a representative index of the market; that mutual funds faithfully dispatched their stated investment objectives; that their tremendous growth gives no evidence of affecting their performance; that, in short, they are doing exactly what they say they can do and doing it better than the individual investor can do it for himself.[2]

The SEC continued its study of the mutual fund industry and, in a surprisingly tough report in December 1966, asked for legislation to curb the industry in the following ways:

1. Put a 5 percent ceiling on mutual-fund sales charges, which currently averaged 9.3 percent.

2. Enact a standard of "reasonableness" for management fees, which currently averaged 1/2 of 1 percent of a fund's assets.

3. Ban "front-end-load" plans. The front-end-load contractual plan provided that half the buyer's first-year payments go to the salesman.

4. Ban mutual-fund holding companies.

5. Prohibit "give-ups" of brokerage fees.

6. Grant volume discounts.

7. Police insider trading, so that fund managers would not take advantage of the fund's trades.

8. Take a more active interest in portfolio companies by prohibiting the sale of any company that managed a mutual fund if the ownership charge might burden the fund's shareholders or limit the fund's future action.[3]

The sales charges or loads have by now been reduced, lower management fees have resulted, front-end-load funds have been eliminated, brokerage give-ups have been stopped, volume discounts are now available, and greater emphasis has been placed on fund performance and its measurement. The changes have resulted from the efforts

[1]"Mutual Funds Look at Wharton Study," *Banking*, November 1962, pp. 8ff.

[2]Hugh A. Johnson, quoted in John A. Straley, *What About Mutual Funds* (New York: Harper & Row, 1967), p. 76.

[3]"SEC vs. Mutual Funds: Congress Will Decide," *Business Week*, December 10, 1966, p. 147.

of the SEC, the Banking and Currency Committee of Congress, the Farrar Report to the SEC in 1971, and the efforts of the individual mutual funds that have been voluntarily responsive to the criticisms. In addition, the sale of no-load mutual funds has increased substantially, and load funds have declined in investor interest. The public mood suggests unwillingness to pay what it thinks are high loads on the load-type mutual funds.

MANAGEMENT OF THE INVESTMENT COMPANY AND THE MUTUAL FUND

A major reason for purchasing open-end or closed-end shares is for the professional management provided. There is a slight difference in how the two types of companies are managed. Closed-end companies are usually managed by their officers, who are partners or officers in a brokerage or investment banking firm. Research for the closed-end company is done by analysts employed by the partners' firms. The open-end investment company usually has a specialized investment-management company manage the portfolios of the fund, and compensates it on a fee basis for services performed. The management of the open-end trust is then free to concentrate on the distribution of the shares of the fund to the public. The management of investment companies and mutual funds is considered to be professional. Its degree of excellence, of course, is not constant and varies with each company and fund.

Cost

The cost of management of an investment company is indirectly paid by the owners of the shares outstanding, since it is directly deducted as an expense from the income of the fund.

A familiar way of expressing the cost of management services is to relate it to the total value of the company assets. Practically all trust and counseling fees are presented as a percentage of the value of the investment fund. A typical fee charged by the management of an open-end investment company is $\frac{1}{2}$ of 1 percent of the investment fund. In less than 15 percent of the funds under $25 million in size, the amount of the fee increases with good performance and decreases with poor performance, compared to the performance of a market average. The expense ratio, cents per $100 of assets—also a way of judging the efficiency of a fund—is used as a measure of management expense for any mutual fund.

Objectives

When management of an investment fund is undertaken, a basic portfolio policy is established. The first concept considered in shaping company policy is the concept of management itself. In most modern investment companies, managers have complete discretionary power to buy and sell securities for the fund according to their judgment of the market and economic conditions.

Many investment companies established earlier in American financial history were not managed funds but fixed or semifixed companies. *Fixed* and *semifixed* referred to the securities that were purchased: Once the basic list of securities was established, there was little or no change made. Even when economic and market conditions suggested a change, no action could be taken by the originators or managers of the fixed fund. The fixed-investment company provided diversification, but little or no management. Most investment companies today, both open-end and closed-end, are completely managed. Some are always fully invested; some have restrictions that prevent a fully managed posture.

An important consideration in the management of an investment company is the type of securities that will be purchased and the portfolio policy that will be emphasized. In accordance with the wishes of the managers, a specific type of fund will be established. The classification of closed-end and open-end funds is generally broken down into eight distinct areas: (1) common stock fund, (2) balanced fund, (3) bond fund, (4) preferred stock fund, (5) specialty fund, (6) exchange or swap fund, (7) foreign investment fund, and (8) dual fund.

COMMON STOCK FUND. The common stock fund is made up of a diversified list of common stocks, although it may be limited to a particular industry or group of industries. This type of fund, whose net assets account for about 60 percent of total mutual fund assets, is the oldest and most numerous in closed-end and open-end investment companies. The management of the common stock fund can be defensive or aggressive, depending on the condition of the stock market, and policy can stress growth or income, depending on the discretion of management. Keystone S3 and S4 and Massachusetts Investors Growth Stock Fund are examples of common stock funds.

THE BALANCED FUND. The balanced fund takes a conservative approach to the risks of investment—with a balance among bonds, preferred stocks, and common stocks in several different industries and companies. Balanced funds account for about 25 percent of total mutual fund assets. Some well-known balanced funds are the Boston Foundation Fund, Eaton & Howard Balanced Fund, the George Putnam Fund, and the Scudder, Stevens & Clark Balanced Fund.

THE BOND FUND AND THE PREFERRED STOCK FUND. The bond fund and the preferred stock fund are devoted to fixed-income types of securities. Investors Selective Fund, Inc., and several of the Keystone Custodian Funds are examples of the complete bond fund. Preferred stock funds include National Securities' Preferred Stock Series. Bond and preferred stock funds offer a high degree of security for the investor. They have not grown as fast in popularity as common stock or balanced funds.

THE SPECIALTY FUND. The specialty fund is one segment of the general category of common stock funds. Specialty funds frequently invest in the common stocks of one industry, usually the stocks of the larger, quality companies in the industry. The electronics industry has been the focus of several specialty funds. Some funds are considered specialty funds because they base the selection of securities on special selection techniques or investment situations. Special-situation funds grow out of reorganized, merged, or rejuvenated companies that offer the investor considerable opportunity for growth.

The small business investment company (SBIC) is an example of a specialized closed-end investment company. In 1958, the Small Business Investment Act authorized the formation of investment companies to invest solely in small business concerns, and accorded them favorable tax treatment. The objective of practically all these companies is long-range capital growth. Some SBICs have done extremely well; others might be considered short-run failures.

DUAL-PURPOSE FUNDS. The dual-purpose fund was introduced to the stock market in 1967. This type of investment company offers stock in two classes: income, providing a return of between 10 and 12 percent in 1983, and capital gains for those who seek growth. Income shareholders receive all the investment income from the portfolio, while the capital shareholders receive the capital appreciation. In a sense, you have two dollars working for each dollar invested; one investor gets the income and the other the appreciation. A leverage effect is at work, best understood by thinking of a convertible preferred stock with a variable dividend and a variable capital growth 12 to 18 years hence.[4] Putnam Duofund and Scudder-Duo Vest Fund have been quite successful dual funds.

EXCHANGE FUNDS AND FOREIGN INVESTMENT FUNDS.   Exchange funds are designed to allow an investor to trade a set of investment securities for a different type of productive asset. Assume that an investor has held a stock for many years and has a large capital gain. If she sells, she must pay a substantial capital gains tax. However, if she exchanges her investment for a share of an exchange fund, she need not pay the tax now, and the fund managers can invest as they see fit. Foreign investment can be achieved by purchasing a fund such as the Canadian Fund International Investors, and KIF, a Keystone Custodian Fund.

Choice of a Fund

In considering a fund, investors must tailor the choice to meet their special needs. Generally, the needs of most investors would be met by a general common stock fund emphasizing growth or income or both. Diversified common stock investment companies invest in leading companies and industries; their funds should provide long-range growth comparable to the growth of the market and the national economy. Some investors, such as corporate executives who already have a high-risk position in equity securities of their own, might not be wise to buy mutual fund equities.

In the final analysis, the classification of an investment company is determined by the securities selected by the managers. The portfolios of two funds with the same stated objectives will emphasize different companies and different industries. Utilities and oils are widely held industry classifications, and IBM is held by most investment

---

[4]Armon Glen, "Two Mints in One," *Barron's*, January 3, 1967, pp. 5ff. A later article points out the obvious advantages of dual funds: Armon Glen, "Double Trouble," *Barron's*, September 2, 1968, p. 3.

THE INVESTMENT ALTERNATIVES

companies. Some funds emphasize chemicals; some, office equipment. A degree of likeness exists in the quality of each portfolio, but there are individual differences in emphasis on specific industries and companies. The same type of analysis would reveal the similarities and differences in the portfolios of closed-end funds.

INVESTMENT COMPANIES AND FEDERAL INCOME TAXES

Under the Internal Revenue Act of 1942, many investment companies enjoy tax privileges not shared by the typical industrial, public utility, or railroad company. The 1942 act provided that an investment company will not be taxed on its dividend or interest income or on any realized capital gains if it is a regulated investment company:

> A *regulated investment company* is defined as a domestic corporation which at all times during the year is registered under the Investment Company Act of 1940 as a management company and satisfies the following prerequisites: (1) at least 90 percent of its gross income is derived from dividends, interest, and gains from the sale or other disposition of securities; (2) less than 30 percent of its gross income is derived from the sale of securities held less than three months; (3) its investments have the requisite diversification (among other things, at least 50 percent of assets must be in cash, government securities, or a diversified list of securities); (4) it distributes to its stockholders as taxable dividends at least 90 percent of its net investment income, exclusive of capital gains; and (5) it elects to be treated as a regulated investment company. Once the latter election is exercised, it is binding in all subsequent years. . . .
>
> Under an amendment to the Internal Revenue Code that became effective on January 1, 1957, a regulated investment company may elect to retain long-term capital gains and pay a 25 percent tax on the same for the account of its stockholders. In that event, each shareholder must (1) include his share of the capital gain in his federal income tax return, (2) take credit for the 25 percent tax paid for his account by the company, and (3) add to the cost basis of his stock 75 percent of his share of the undistributed capital gain.[5]

The Tax Reform Act of 1976 allowed municipal bond funds to pass on tax-exempt income to the owners of the funds.

By purchasing the shares of a regulated investment company, the investor retains his own tax position and does not suffer a tax on both the investment company's income and his own. An investor in a high income tax bracket would look for a fund that concentrated on capital growth; one in the lower brackets would probably be indifferent to the capital gains treatment of income from an investment company unless, for other reasons, he or she desired growth or income from the investment account. Almost all investment companies are regulated; they pay to investors the entire investment earnings and net capital gains and therefore pay no federal income taxes.

PERFORMANCE OF INVESTMENT COMPANIES

The current income from investment companies varies widely from company to company, depending on objectives. Where the current returns are above average, one generally finds below-average market volatility, and vice versa. The performance of

[5]Standard & Poor's *Industry Survey—Investment Companies*, September 11, 1969, p. 142.

TABLE 7–5

Mutual Fund Performance: 25 Large Funds

	Net Assets Per Share (% Change from Previous Dec. 31)[a]					S&P Perfor-mance Score[b]	Objec-tive[c]
Fund	1978	1979	1980	1981	2 mo. 1982		
Keystone Custodian S-4	+18.2	+44.4	+58.0	−19.8	−14.9	186.3	G
Technology	+18.5	+28.3	+45.5	+16.3	−7.5	171.3	GI
National Investors	+6.9	+25.2	+29.0	+14.3	−6.6	138.2	G
Putnam Growth	+7.7	+15.9	+29.5	−7.3	−5.2	126.7	GSI
American Mutual	+6.8	+15.2	+19.0	+2.4	−6.3	140.5	ISG
Oppenheimer Fund	+4.0	+34.3	+38.7	−12.2	−11.1	168.2	G
Dreyfus Fund	+7.2	+18.9	+23.2	−3.2	−8.7	141.3	GIS
Investment Company of America	+10.7	+14.7	+15.9	−3.6	−2.9	137.7	GI
Affiliated	−1.8	+21.8	+17.9	−6.2	−5.9	133.8	GI
Mass. Inv. Growth Stock	+10.5	+23.0	+37.0	−8.3	−4.8	144.8	G
Putnam Investors	+8.1	+15.2	+38.3	−10.6	−8.2	141.3	GIS
Fidelity Trend	+7.3	+15.4	+22.4	−7.7	−7.9	128.8	G
Investors Variable	+6.2	+17.4	+24.5	−3.9	−7.7	137.7	G
United Accumulative	+5.3	+12.0	+29.1	−6.4	−6.8	132.8	G
S&P 500 Stock Index	+1.1	+12.3	+25.8	−9.7	−7.7	120.4	
Mass. Investors Trust	+3.3	+16.4	+24.7	−9.7	−5.9	128.8	IR
Fidelity Fund	+4.3	+13.0	+27.4	−7.5	−3.7	133.8	GI
Price (T. Rowe) Growth	+8.5	+8.1	+25.5	−15.6	−10.8	110.8	G
Investors Stock	−0.1	+14.3	+19.7	−12.3	−3.9	77.3	IS
Hamilton Ser. HDA	+1.3	+11.1	+19.8	−11.9	−8.8	108.3	GI
Chemical	+8.2	+20.4	+26.2	−7.3	−6.3	165.8	G
Fundamental Investors	+2.0	+10.6	+15.1	−6.2	−5.1	115.6	GI
State Street Investment	—	—	+22.0	−5.6	−6.6	123.4	GI
Investors Mutual	−2.8	+4.2	+11.0	−9.5	−3.5	98.2	GIS
United Income	−4.1	−0.7	+3.8	−4.0	−2.3	100.8	IS
Wellington	−0.9	+5.7	+13.6	−5.6	−4.8	106.9	GIR

[a]Adjusted for capital gains distribution.

[b]For six years and 1 month through January 1981 computed by compounding annual performance data, with January 1, 1974 as 100.

[c]G—Growth; I—Income; R—Return; S—Stability, in order of importance.

SOURCE: Standard & Poor's *Industry Survey—Investment Funds,* February 26, 1981, p. 165; and January 14, 1982, p. 165.

the leading mutual funds can be seen in Table 7-5. As the chart shows, most funds did well in 1980 but did not do well in 1982.

The net-asset comparison for the leading closed-end investment companies in Table 7–6 tells a similar story. Compared to the market as a whole, as measured by Standard & Poor's 500 Index, the closed-end investment companies have followed the action of the market. Most of those presented exceeded the results obtained by the market as a whole over the period.

THE INVESTMENT ALTERNATIVES

TABLE 7–6
Closed-End Fund Performance

Company	Net Asset Record (% change)*				
	1976	1977	1978	1979	1980
S&P Stock Index	+19.1	−11.5	+1.1	+12.3	+25.8
Publicly Traded Funds					
ASA Limited	−15.1	+16.9	+14.9	+99.1	+102.0
Adams Express	+24.6	−5.6	+3.9	+15.5	+26.2
General American Investors	+17.6	−1.3	+15.4	+35.3	+36.4
Japan Fund	+22.7	−5.8	+49.2	−22.5	+22.9
Lehman Corp.	+14.0	−6.5	+8.7	+25.3	+21.9
Madison Fund	+33.3	−2.2	+11.4	+28.3	+41.2
Niagara Share	+16.3	−5.8	+11.5	+47.5	+35.1
Petroleum & Resources	+35.3	−3.1	+6.1	+51.7	+52.1
Source Capital	+33.1	+13.6	+27.3	+26.7	+12.1
Tri-Continental	+19.6	−11.2	+1.4	+18.2	+27.0
U.S. & Foreign Securities	+21.8	−9.2	+6.9	+21.3	+21.0
Dual-Purpose Funds					
Gemini	+67.1	+1.5	−5.7	+21.0	+16.0
Hemisphere	+302.2	−64.6	NM	NM	NM
Income & Capital Shares	+43.0	−19.9	−12.8	+27.3	+37.0
Leverage Fund of Boston	+60.0	−5.8	+15.0	+22.0	+34.1
Scudder-Duo Vest	−5.0	−11.3	+20.0	+1.3	+59.3

*% change per common share from prior year, assuming reinvestment of capital gains
paid in year; years end Dec. 31 except ASA Ltd. ends Nov. 30.
SOURCE: Standard & Poor's *Industry Surveys—Investment Funds,* January 14,
1982, p. 166.

Studies of the performance of mutual funds are conflicting. Farrar's study indicated that portfolios selected at random showed sharply lower expected returns than the funds, and only moderately lower risk.[6] Friend and Vickers concluded that mutual funds as a whole clearly do no better than random portfolios in their common stock industry selection.[7] If mutual funds do no better than random selections, then the fund managers are not using methods that would lead to results at least equal to the market. They should utilize random statistical techniques to assure owners that they will "get the market," rather than ignoring the concept of statistical randomness in stock selection. Funds are certainly large enough to offer this service to their investors.

Williamson concluded from one of his studies that fund managers have not been

[6]Donald E. Farrar, *The Investment Decision under Uncertainty* (Englewood Cliffs, N.J.: Prentice-Hall, 1962.)

[7]Irwin Friend and Douglas Vickers, "Portfolio Selection and Investment Performance," *The Journal of Finance,* September 1965. See also Irwin Friend, Marshall Blume, and Jean Crockett, *Mutual Funds and Other Institutional Investors: A New Perspective* (New York: McGraw-Hill, 1970).

able to predict the market, that they cannot change the volatility of their funds, and that they cannot outperform the market year in and year out. He noted too a marked change toward higher volatility and performance in the funds and wondered if this was correct.[8] Kim found that in the seven-year period from 1969 through 1975, mutual funds did not earn as much as the market averages. He also found that high-risk portfolios did not produce high returns and that fund managers did not outperform the market averages.[9] Table 7–6 suggests that for the period 1975–80 the performance of investment companies is similar on average to the market as measured by the S&P 500 Index.

Performance of Mutual Funds—Alpha and Beta

Wiesenberger provides a service entitled *Mutual Fund Performance Monthly*. It includes an alphabetical listing of mutual funds and gives ranked alpha and beta values for ten years, five years, and the latest twelve months. Net asset values for the past two years, the year to date, and the most recent month are also provided.

The mutual funds are also ranked by the percentage of change in net-asset value, providing easy comparisons with the S&P 500 Index. One is impressed with the range in both alpha and beta values, the variability of both alpha and beta over time, and the number of funds that do not perform as well as the market.

MONEY MARKET FUNDS

Money market funds have grown substantially, as we noted in Chapter 2. Table 7–7 provides a list of such funds and their performance over time. The rates earned vary with the level of interest rates in the marketplace. In addition forty U.S. money market mutual funds had 21.9 billion dollars invested in Eurodollar-CDs as of May 28, 1982. The large investment is considered to be a confirmation of the safety of carefully selected Eurodollar-CD investment instruments. A much greater fraction of total money market mutual fund assets invested in Eurodollar-CDs would be beneficial to increasing the returns to investors with a negligible change in risk levels.[10]

Tax-Exempt Money Market Funds

Investors in the 50 percent tax bracket might achieve liquidity and a high tax-free return by investing in tax-exempt money market funds. A list of such funds appears in Table 7–8. Their relative attractiveness is determined by the need for liquidity and the investors' marginal tax bracket.

[8]J. Peter Williamson, "Some Observations on Mutual Fund Performance, 1961–70," working paper, Dartmouth College, February 1971.

[9]T. Kim, "Investment Objectives, Policies, and Performance of Mutual Funds, 1969," unpublished report, College of Business Administration, Memphis State University, delivered at Eastern Finance Association, April 23, 1976.

[10]Park, Yoon S. and Anckonie, Alex, "The Contribution of Eurodollar Assets to the Profitability of U.S. Money Market Mutual Funds," a George Washington University School of Government and Business Administration working paper presented at the annual meeting of the Academy of International Business, Washington, D.C., Oct. 1982.

TABLE 7-7

Money Market Funds (assets of $100 million or more, available to individual investors, period ended March 16, 1983)

Money Market Fund	Assets	Average Maturity	7-day Average Yield (%)	30-day Average Yield (%)
AARP US Gov't M.M.T.	3,613.7	38	7.8	7.7
Alex. Brown Prime	612.0	32	8.0	8.0
ALLIANCE GROUP				
Capital Reserves	1,072.7	41	7.6	7.7
Gov't Reserves	198.1	25	7.5	7.5
American General	272.3	32	7.7	7.9
American Liquid Trust	273.3	24	7.4	7.4
Boston Company Cash Mg.	306.2	38	8.1	8.2
Capital Cash Mgt Trust	181.1	12	7.9	7.9
Capital Preservation	1,820.0	29	7.1	7.2
Capital Preservation Fund II	701.3	3	7.5	7.6
Cardinal Gov't Securities	323.8	24	8.1	8.0
Carnegie Gov't Securities Tr	198.7	20	7.6	7.7
Cash Equivalent Fund	4,456.4	38	8.3	8.4
Cash Equivalent Gov't Only	461.9	29	7.8	7.8
Cash Management Trust	519.6	18	7.8	8.0
Centennial Money Market Tr	152.9	29	7.7	7.7
Columbia Daily Income	548.8	25	7.6	7.6
Composite Cash Mgt Co.	199.7	25	7.6	7.6
Current Interest M.M.F.	1,418.0	36	7.6	7.8
Daily Cash Accumulation	3,948.7	28	7.8	7.8
Daily Income	571.2	33	7.8	7.9
DEAN WITTER				
Active Assets Gov't Sec.	134.7	19	7.6	7.6
Active Assets M.T.	1,311.7	39	8.2	8.2
InterCapital Liquid Assets	6,995.5	43	8.1	8.1
Delaware Cash Reserve	1,596.0	33	7.9	7.9
Dollar Reserves	105.2	15	8.0	7.9
DREXEL BURNHAM LAMBERT, INC.				
Cash Fund Gov't Sec.	181.3	45	7.7	7.8
Cash Fund M.M. Port.	1,010.3	28	8.0	8.0
DREYFUS				
Liquid Assets	9,216.0	58	8.1	8.1
M.M. Instrmts Gov't	959.2	82	8.2	8.2
Dreyfus Money Market	1,690.0	50	8.1	8.1
ED Jones Daily Passport	678.1	34	7.6	7.6
EGT Money Market Trust	115.7	32	7.6	7.6
Eaton Vance Cash Mgt Fund	211.6	26	7.7	7.7
Equitable Money Mkt Acct	323.9	40	7.8	7.8
Fahnestock Daily Income	155.2	34	7.8	7.9
FIDELITY GROUP				
Cash Reserves	3,608.4	39	8.1	8.1
Daily Income	2,941.9	36	7.9	8.0
U.S. Gov't Res.	342.1	43	7.6	7.6
Financial Daily Income	206.6	18	8.2	8.2
First Investors Cash Mgt	447.8	26	7.7	7.7
First Variable Rate	1,003.8	x30	7.9	7.9
Franklin Federal M.F.	123.3	3	7.6	7.6
Franklin Money Fund	858.8	20	8.2	8.0

Money Market Fund	Assets	Average Maturity	7-day Average Yield (%)	30-day Average Yield (%)
Fund/Gov't Investors	1,038.8	21	7.8	7.7
General M.F. Inc.	190.9	53	7.8	8.0
Gov't Investors Trust	524.4	24	7.7	7.6
Gov't Sec Cash Fund	102.0	40	7.8	7.8
Gradison Cash Reserves	531.6	31	7.7	7.7
Hilliard Lyons G.F., Inc.	155.7	31	7.5	7.5
HUTTON, E.F.				
Cash Reserves Mgt	5,337.7	35	8.2	8.1
Hutton AMA Cash Fund	117.1	48	8.1	8.1
Hutton Gov't Fund	664.6	44	8.1	8.2
IDS Cash Management	1,031.7	44	8.4	8.4
John Hancock Cash Mgt	523.8	42	7.6	7.6
Kemper Money Market	3,726.7	42	8.4	8.5
Legg Mason Cash Rsrv Tr	249.8	33	7.6	7.6
LEHMAN				
Cash Management	711.9	24	7.9	7.9
Gov't Fund Inc.	131.4	23	7.6	7.6
Lexington Money Market	270.9	29	8.1	8.1
Liquid Capital Income Trust	1,604.2	25	8.0	8.0
Liquid Green Trust	127.4	36	7.6	7.6
Lord Abbett Cash Reserve	252.7	25	7.8	7.8
Mass Cash Mgmt Trust	802.5	34	7.6	7.6
McDonald Money Market	168.0	23	7.8	7.8
MERRILL LYNCH				
CMA Gov't Securities	1,459.6	47	7.8	7.6
CMA Money Fund	13,448.8	43	8.2	8.0
Government	1,765.9	44	7.6	7.6
Institutional	1,252.9	40	7.9	7.9
Ready Assets	16,279.3	47	8.3	8.1
Retirement Res.	1,030.1	49	7.9	7.5
Midwest Income St Gov't	186.6	32	7.3	7.3
Money Market Management	187.9	33	7.5	7.5
Money Market Instruments	357.7	32	7.6	7.6
Mutual of Omaha M.M.A.	370.8	38	7.9	8.0
NEL Cash Mgt Trust	742.7	38	8.0	8.0
National Liquid Reserves	1,772.3	49	8.2	8.3
Nationwide M.M.F.	429.1	33	8.0	8.0
Oppenheimer M.M.F. Inc.	1,199.0	24	8.1	8.1
Paine Webber Cash Fund	5,142.7	30	7.9	7.9
Parkway Cash Fund	554.2	22	7.7	7.8
PRUDENTIAL-BACHE SECURITIES				
Chancellor Gov't Sec. Tr	250.1	56	7.7	7.7
Command Money Fund	449.8	30	8.0	8.2
MoneyMart Assets	2,866.9	29	8.1	8.0
Putnam Daily Div. Trust	358.9	37	8.0	8.1
Reserve Fund-Gov't	355.2	12	7.4	7.5
Reserve Fund-Primary	2,403.9	27	7.9	8.0
Rothschild (L.F.) Earnings & Liquidity	370.0	26	8.0	8.0

Money Market Fund	Assets	Average Maturity	7-day Average Yield (%)	30-day Average Yield (%)
St. Paul Money Fund Inc.	129.8	19	7.6	7.6
SCUDDER				
Cash Inv. Trust	1,085.0	35	7.5	7.5
Gov't Money Fund	166.5	35	7.4	7.3
Sears U.S. Gov't M.M.T.	389.5	23	7.3	7.8
Seligman C.M. Fund Prime	523.1	31.	7.6	7.6
SHEARSON/AMERICAN EXPRESS				
FedFund	1,487.4	35	8.0	8.0
Daily Dividend	4,748.1	39	7.9	7.9
FMA Cash	394.4	49	7.9	7.9
Government & Agencies	1,031.5	52	7.9	7.9
T-Fund	799.8	32	8.0	8.0
TempFund	3,812.6	31	8.2	8.2
Short Term Income Fund	210.9	32	7.8	7.9
Standby Reserve Fund	205.4	30	7.9	7.9
SteinRoe Cash Reserves	763.8	30	7.8	7.9
Summit Cash Res.	469.0	49	8.0	7.8
Sutro Money Market Fund	114.7	32	7.6	7.6
T. ROWE PRICE				
Prime Reserve	2,744.4	45	8.1	8.1
U.S. Treas. M.F.	136.4	34	7.5	7.5
Transamerica Cash Rsrv	255.4	37	8.2	3.2
Trinity Liquid Assets Tr	127.7	15	8.0	8.0
Trust/Cash Reserves	182.5	33	7.5	7.5
Tucker Anthony Cash Mgt	366.6	38	7.7	7.7
USAA M.M.F.	130.5	32	7.8	7.8
United Cash Management	388.7	37	7.9	7.9
Value Line Cash Fund	541.9	29	8.0	8.1
Vanguard M.M.T. Federal	410.5	33	7.7	7.8
Vanguard M.M.T. Prime	1,019.1	36	8.1	8.1
Webster Cash Reserve	1,301.1	31	7.9	7.9
Donoghue's MONEY FUND AVERAGE[e] (Averages for all 236 taxable funds)		38	7.8	7.8

Yields represent annualized total return to shareholders for past seven- and thirty-day period. Past returns not necessarily indicative of future yields. Investment quality and maturity may vary among funds. (x) Average term to next rate adjustment date. (e) Figures given as estimate because of computer problems.

Reprinted in condensed form with permission from Donoghue's MONEY FUND REPORT® of Holliston, MA.

COMMENTARY: Assets of the 236 money funds reported by Donoghue's declined $1.6 billion to $182.3 billion for the week ending March 16, 1983. The funds' 7-day average yield increased slightly, to 7.77% from 7.71%. The funds' 30%-day average maturity yield fell slightly, to 7.77% from 7.78%. The funds' average maturity figure dropped one day to 38 days following two weeks at 39. days.

SOURCE: Barron's March 21, 1983. p. 113.

TABLE 7–8

Tax-Exempt Money Market Funds

Fixed Net Asset Value	Assets (mil.)	7-Day Yield-%	Average Maturity (days)
Calvert Reserves	130.8	4.72	65
Centennial Trust	39.2	4.30	90
Chancellor Money Fund	169.0	4.30	88
Daily Cash Exempt	85.0	4.18	94
Daily Tax Free Income	140.7	4.81	60
Dean Witter Reynolds:			
Active Assets	172.0	4.21	57
Intercapital	274.0	4.37	57
Delaware Money Fund	30.0	4.45	83
Dreyfus Money Market	1,523.3	4.59	90
Eaton Vance Reserves	6.4	4.49	90
Federated Trust	3,808.0	4.40	72
Fidelity Money Market Tr	2,285.0	4.54	79
Fourth St. Trust MM Port.	25.7	4.35	101
Franklin	58.8	4.53	80
IDS Money Fund	52.8	4.74	98
Lehman Money Market	100.7	4.14	80
Lexington Daily Income	39.6	5.04	80
Merrill CMA	2,900.0	4.35	62
Mun. Cash Res. Manag.	687.3	4.62	89
Nuveen Money Market	829.0	4.74	47
Parkway Reserve Fund	30.0	4.14	70
Prov/Mun. Temp. Inv.	1,237.0	4.21	52
Scudder Money Fund	168.6	4.00	64
Shearson FMA Mun. Fund	126.0	4.07	69
T. Rowe Price Money Fund	614.0	5.00	113
Tax-Free Money Fund	262.0	4.30	86
Tucker Anthony	26.6	4.10	85
Vanguard Mun. Money Mkt	267.2	4.69	74
Variable Net Asset Value			
Calvert	46.9	6.01	528
Federated	103.0	6.02	596
Fourth St. Tax Free	16.2	6.01	4 yrs
Merrill Lynch	NA	NA	NA
Vangd Mun. Bnd Sh Term	345.4	5.74	355

NA—Not Available.

SOURCE: Bank of Boston. *Barron's,* March 17, 1983, p. 113.

Mutual Funds That Do Not Pay Dividends

Tax-managed mutual funds reinvest income and never pay dividends. These funds concentrate on utility stocks. Since income is not distributed, no income tax is paid. Only when the shares are sold does the investor pay taxes, and then the maximum tax is based on the tax rate for long-term capital gain, which is a maximum of 20 percent.

THE INVESTMENT ALTERNATIVES

By returning their income, these funds could be subject to the corporate income tax at ordinary federal tax rates. Such funds use the "dividends received deduction," which allows corporations to deduct from their taxable income 85 percent of the dividends they receive. The funds, therefore, are liable for taxes on only 15 percent of their dividend income. This obligation is offset by deducting operating expenses. The performance of these funds has been erratic, judging from the results in Table 7–9.

TABLE 7–9
Performance of Tax-Managed Mutual Funds

Funds	Assets (millions of dollars)	1980	1981†
American Birthright Trust, Palm Beach, Fla.	$122.7*	−14.10%	+48.67%
Foster, Hickman & Zaenglein Tax-Managed Fund, Rochester	1.1*	+18.41	+36.65
Colonial Tax-Managed Trust, Boston	101.0*	+17.12	+11.14
Chancellor Tax-Managed Utility Fund, New York	88.8*	N.A.‡	N.A.
Eaton Vance Tax-Managed Trust, Boston	121.0	N.A.‡	N.A.
Tax-Managed Fund for Utility Shares, Palm Beach	146.0	+2.17	+1.72
Average Equity Mutual Fund	—	−1.69	+33.48

*As of Sept. 30, 1981

†For period Dec. 31, 1980, through Dec. 23, 1981. Assumes all dividends are reinvested.

‡Fund begun in 1981.

SOURCE: The New York Times, January 3, 1982, p. 14.

The Dart Board Fund

You can't buy the Dart Board Fund, but *Forbes* magazine constructs one just to see how the random walk hypothesis works. Table 7–10 shows the fund and how it performed against the market leaders. It didn't do badly. In fact, it did a lot better than the DJIA and S&P 500. But, of course, it had much more risk!

Commodity Pools

The number of commodity futures funds grew to 827 in 1981, compared to 532 in 1979, and these are just the funds registered with the Commodity Futures Trading Commission (CFTC). Pools with fewer than 15 members or assets of less than $200,000 need not register with the CFTC. There are probably 900 unregistered funds or pools.

In a pool, the investor-speculator buys shares, usually in minimum amounts of 5 units, at $1,000 per unit. A one-time commission is paid for each unit. Gains and losses are distributed to each unit and are realized when the investor sells one or all units. The initial payment represents the maximum amount the investor-speculator

TABLE 7–10

The Dart Board Fund

Present Portfolio	Value of Portfolio 2/5/80	12/31/81	Change in Value Since 2/5/80	6/30/67	Price 12/31/81
Allegheny Intl—$11.25 pfd	$ 600.80	$ 791.29	+32%	−21%	$76\frac{3}{4}$
Allied Corp—$6.74 pfd	1,213.40	2,176.74	+79	+118	$52\frac{1}{8}$
Arvin Industries	1,181.44	1,361.21	+15	+36	$14\frac{7}{8}$
Baker International	3,957.72	4,695.66	+19	+370	38
Carolina P&L	439.09	522.86	+19	−48	$20\frac{1}{4}$
Chase Manhattan	1,003.03	1,339.33	+34	+34	$53\frac{7}{8}$
Checker Motors	2,191.78	1,846.08	−16	+85	$27\frac{1}{2}$
Cooper Industries	2,836.60	5,515.65	+94	+452	$51\frac{1}{2}$
Federal Paper Board—common	940.30	795.69 ⎫			27
$1.20 pfd	775.52	618.66 ⎬ −9		+115	$31\frac{1}{2}$
Rexham*	652.43	736.80 ⎭			15
Firestone Tire & Rubber	404.46	571.28	+41	−43	$12\frac{5}{8}$
Florida Steel	2,830.71	4,560.71	+61	+356	$19\frac{1}{4}$
General Dynamics	2,666.41	1,683.64 ⎫ −34		+87	$24\frac{1}{2}$
Houston Natural Gas†	184.50	183.79 ⎭			$44\frac{1}{2}$
Helene Curtis	504.17	798.96	+58	−20	12
INCO Ltd.	762.47	387.32	−49	−61	$14\frac{1}{4}$
INCO (originally ESB)	1,807.72	918.13	−49	−8	$14\frac{1}{4}$
International Paper	1,303.49	1,347.07	+3	+35	$39\frac{1}{8}$
Interpace	1,508.96	1,222.64	−19	+22	17
MacAndrews & Forbes Group	2,765.95	5,937.37	+115	+494	$12\frac{1}{8}$
Pacific Tin Consol	2,000.05	1,549.98	−23	+55	$17\frac{1}{8}$
JC Penney	779.63	907.99	+16	−9	$28\frac{5}{8}$
Pittston	4,172.44	4,021.26	−4	+302	$25\frac{5}{8}$
Singer—common	75.74	124.46 ⎫ +8		−74	$13\frac{7}{8}$
$3.50 pfd	169.26	140.52 ⎭			$22\frac{3}{8}$
Standard Oil Indiana	4,873.50	5,372.12	+10	+437	52
Texas Oil & Gas	20,036.98	41,986.37	+110	+4,099	35
Textron	772.30	723.40	−6	−28	$26\frac{5}{8}$
Thorn-EMI Ltd—ordinary	685.71	563.85 ⎫ +26		−14	$8\frac{3}{4}$
pfd		300.33 ⎭			$2\frac{1}{4}$
Tyco Labs	547.73	1,197.90	+119	+20	$12\frac{3}{8}$
Total	65,400.99	94,899.06	+45	+239	
Wilshire 5000	1,176.99	1,286.24	+9	—	
S&P's 500	114.66	122.55	+7	+35	
DJIA	876.62	875.00	0	+2	

*Shareholders of Riegel Paper received both Federal Paper Board common and preferred shares and Rexham common.

†General Dynamics divested Liquid Carbonic, which was subsequently acquired by Houston Natural Gas.

SOURCE: Forbes, February 1, 1982, p. 99.

THE INVESTMENT ALTERNATIVES

can lose. A pool usually will be disbanded if and when the assets fall to 50 percent of their original value. The remaining assets are apportioned among the participants. About $500 million was invested in public pools in 1982, with 40,000 participants. An individual commodity trading account requires $10,000 to $15,000 from the investor-speculator. The investor pays all commissions and must meet margin calls.

Some pools do well; some do poorly. Table 7–11 provides some gainers and losers in a list of traded pools. Looking at the results, it is easy to see that this is a risky endeavor even for speculators.

TABLE 7–11

Commodity Funds

Fund	Start Date	Offer Value/ Share	Unit Value 12/31/81	Unit Value 1/31/82	Mo. % Change	12 Mo. % Change
Aries Commodity Fund	2/80	$1,000	$ 920	$ 951	+ 3.4	−18.2
Saturn Commodity Fund	2/81	1,000	781	796	+1.9	−20.4
(A.G. Edwards & Sons)						
Boston Futures Fund I	1/80	957	992	1,059	+6.8	+0.6
Boston Futures Fund II	8/80	957	955	1,019	+6.7	−2.4
Western Capital Fund I	11/81	1,000	923	905	−2.0	−9.5
(Eastern Capital Corp.)						
Chancellor Financial Futures Fd	3/81	1,000	752	785	+4.4	−21.5
Chancellor Fin. Futures Fd II	10/81	1,000	894	906	+1.3	−9.4
Chancellor Futures Fund	2/80	942	1,277	1,252	−2.0	+42.2
(Bache Halsey Stuart Shields)						
Commodity Trend Timing Fd	1/80	963	1,468	1,481	+0.9	+19.1
Commodity Venture Fund	11/80	1,000	1,375	1,409	+2.5	+40.8
Matterhorn Comdty Partners	6/81	950	955	949	−0.6	−0.1
Vista Futures Fund	4/81	934	1,034	1,053	+1.8	+12.7
(Shearson/American Express)						
Galileo Futures Fund	3/79	1,000	819	917	+12.0	−19.8
(Clayton, A.E. Edwards, B.E. & L.)						
Financial Futures Fund	7/81	8.08	6.71	6.69	−0.3	−17.2
(Dunn & Hargitt, Inc.)						
The Future Fund	7/79	1,000	3,128	3,266	+4.4	+26.6
The Resource Fund	8/78	1,000	3,412	3,569	+4.6	+30.7
(Heinold, Blyth Eastman Dillon)						
Harvest Futures Fund I	6/78	1,000	2,987	2,804	−6.1	−10.2
Harvest Futures Fund II	2/80	970	492	494	+0.4	−2.8
Heinold II. Commodity Fd	1/78	1,000	2,853	2,530	−11.3	+35.6
Heinold Recovery Fund I	3/78	465	771	681	−11.7	−27.5
Heinold Recovery Fund II	3/78	189	270	224	−17.0	−40.1
Global Fund	9/81	994	1,033	1,044	+1.1	+5.0
(Heinold Commodities Inc.)						
Horizon Futures Fund	10/80	1,000	1,095	1,179	+7.8	+11.0
(Heinold & Smith Barney Upham)						
Hutton Commodity Partners	2/80	1,000	1,058	1,102	+4.2	+4.2
Hutton Partnership II	12/80	1,000	1,107	1,167	+5.4	+27.0
(E F Hutton & Co.)						

TABLE 7–11   (Continued)

La Salle St. Futures Fund (A.G. Becker & Co.)	9/81	937	975	963	−1.2	+2.8
McCormick Fund I (McCormick Commodities, Inc.)	1/82	92	—	92	0	—
Enterprise Fund	11/81	1,000	997	979	−1.8	−2.1
Lake Forest Fund	1/81	1,000	599	601	+0.3	−36.8
Midwest Commodity Fund I (Filler, Weiner, Zaner)	6/81	1,000	866	841	−2.9	−15.9
Peavey Commodity Futures Fd I	10/80	876	895	886	−1.0	+20.0
Peavey Commodity Futures Fd II (Peavey/Dain Bosworth Inc.)	4/81	847	892	885	−0.8	+24.6
Princeton Future Fund	3/81	989	1,069	969	−9.4	−2.0
Princeton Future Fund II (Paine Webber)	11/81	985	973	934	−4.0	−1.2
Sceptre Futures (Dolphin Securities Inc.)	2/81	90	65	66	+1.5	−26.7
Thomson McKinnon Futures Fd	11/78	942	1,686	1,547	−8.2	+6.1
Thomson McKinnon Cmdty Partners (Thomson McKinnon Securities)	8/81	1,000	1,124	992	−11.7	−0.8
Dean Witter Reynolds Comm. Ptnrs (Dean Witter Reynolds Inc.)	3/81	1,000	968	1,022	+5.6	+2.2
Average performance this month and last 12 months:					−0.4	+0.7

SOURCE: *Barron's,* March 1, 1982, p. 108.

ADVANTAGES AND DISADVANTAGES OF INVESTMENT COMPANIES

The major advantages to the investor of investment company shares are management and diversification: portfolio management is provided for the investor, as well as more diversification than he or she could obtain by a small common stock account.

Investment in mutual fund shares also gives the investor a sense of security that allows a long-run perspective. Without this attitude, investment success would not be great. Purchasers of a single stock may change their position and sell in the short run because they think they have made a mistake, when in the long run they would have done well if they had held.

The disadvantages of investment company stock must also be considered. First, the round-trip cost of buying and selling a mutual fund is usually greater than that of buying and selling common stock. Second, the cost of management is high—between $\frac{1}{2}$ of 1 percent and 1 percent of the net asset value of the fund. Third, it is difficult for the investor to ascertain the quality of the management of an investment company. And fourth, many investment companies cannot do as well as the market.

As much care must be exercised in selecting investment companies as in selecting common stocks. We must examine quality of management, portfolio policy, price, and cost of management. At best, investment company shares offer a partial solution to the problem of the complete management of an investment fund for an individual or institution.

The best way to select and analyze a mutual fund is by its persistence of performance. An investor should have his or her objectives clearly in mind, and choose a fund that consistently meets these objectives.

SUMMARY

Investors have an additional investment opportunity in mutual funds. The wide variety of funds available for purchase will meet the needs of most or all investors. The spectrum ranges from money market funds to venture capital funds. Mutual funds are as risky or as safe as the financial assets they purchase. They therefore must be analyzed in the same way as a single financial asset. The advantage of mutuals is the diversification of assets they purchase and the ability of the investor to buy small amounts at regular intervals. Mutual funds should be carefully analyzed to make certain the fund's objectives are consistent with the investor's objectives. Then funds meeting the investor's objective must be judged on the basis of performance. Funds should be selected that offer the lowest cost of management and the highest performance.

Institutional investors follow the same principles of diversification as do mutual funds. Both manage their portfolios to obtain the highest return with the lowest risk.

SUMMARY OF PRINCIPLES

1. The same principles that apply to securities investment apply to the selection of investment companies.
2. Investment in investment company shares is not a panacea for an investor's problems.
3. Shares in investment companies have return-to-risk characteristics similar to those of other securities.
4. The purchase of investment company shares can help in the portfolio management problem by fostering dollar averaging and investing small amounts of money regularly.
5. Institutional investors employ the same principles as mutual fund managers.

REVIEW QUESTIONS

1. What are the advantages and disadvantages of a mutual fund investment?
2. What are the advantages and disadvantages of a closed-end investment company as an investment?
3. What accounts for the cyclical nature of the growth of mutual funds and closed-end investment companies?
4. Explain what is meant by *leverage in the capital structure* of the closed-end investment company.

5. Why have no-load investment companies grown more rapidly than closed-end investment companies in recent years?

6. Is the cost of buying mutual funds excessive? Why have mutual funds been criticized?

7. What type of mutual fund or investment company can an investor buy?

8. What is the indicated quality of mutual fund management?

9. What has been the performance of mutual funds? Has it been better than that of the market? How should we measure the performance of a mutual fund?

10. What are the *alpha and beta characteristics* of a mutual fund portfolio compared to the S&P 500 Index?

11. Do institutional investors follow mutual fund principles? Explain.

PROBLEMS

1. Compare the growth of the mutual funds listed in Table 7–1. Which funds have grown the most? Which have grown the least? What conclusions do you draw from these trends?

2. Table 7–5 provides the net asset performance for 25 large mutual funds. Using a regression analysis format, compare the indicated alpha and beta of Keystone Custodian S-4 and Putnam Investors for the period 1978, 1979, 1980, and 1981. Although four data points are statistically inadequate, what conclusions would you draw about the risk and return characteristics of each company?

3. Compare the annual percentage price change of the S&P 500 Index and the investment companies charted in Table 7–6. Plot the annual percentage change of the investment companies' return against the returns of the S&P 500 Index. Were the investment companies more profitable than the S&P 500 Index? Were they riskier? Explain.

CASE

Mary Jane and Don wanted to purchase a mutual fund that would have a small amount of risk but would provide the highest possible growth of principal and income. You have been asked to recommend a fund for them. Your source of information is found in Table 7–5. Select from the mutual funds that have growth and income as a goal the one that best meets their objectives.

SELECTED READINGS

BLACK, F., M. C. JENSEN, and MYRON SCHOLES. "The Capital Asset Pricing Model: Some Empirical Tests." In *Studies in the Theory of Capital Markets*, ed. M. C. JENSEN. New York: Praeger, 1972.

BLUME, M., and I. FRIEND, "A New Look at the Capital Asset Pricing Model." *The Journal of Finance*, March 1973, pp. 19–33.

ELLIS, CHARLES D. "Performance Investing." *Financial Analysts Journal*, September–October 1968, p. 117.

FAMA, E. F., and J. D. MACBETH. "Risk, Return and Equilibrium: Empirical Tests." *Journal of Political Economy*, May–June 1973, pp. 607–36.

FISHER, LAWRENCE. "Analysts' Input and Portfolio Changes." *Financial Analysts Journal*, May–June 1975, p. 73.

FRANCIS, J. C., and S. H. ARCHER. *Portfolio Analysis*. Englewood Cliffs, N.J.: Prentice-Hall, 1971.

FRIEND, I., and M. BLUME. "Measurement of Portfolio Performance under Uncertainty." *American Economic Review*, September 1970, pp. 561–75.

FRIEND, I., M. BLUME, and J. CROCKETT. *Mutual Funds and Other Institutional Investors*. A Twentieth Century Fund Study. New York: McGraw-Hill, 1970.

JENSEN, MICHAEL C. "Capital Markets: Theory and Evidence." *Bell Journal of Economics and Management Science*, autumn 1972, pp. 357–98.

———. "Problems in Selection of Security Portfolios: The Performance of Mutual Funds in the Period 1945–1964." *The Journal of Finance*, March 1968, p. 389.

———. "Risk, the Pricing of Capital Assets and the Evaluation of Investment Portfolios." Doctoral dissertation, University of Chicago, 1968.

LEVY, HAIM, and MARSHALL SARNAT. "The Case for Mutual Funds." *Financial Analysts Journal*, March–April 1972, p. 77.

MCDONALD, J. G. "Objectives and Performance of Mutual Funds, 1960–69." *Journal of Financial and Quantitative Analysis*, June 1974, pp. 311–33.

MENNIS, EDMUND A. "An Integrated Investment System." *Financial Analysts Journal*, March–April 1974, p. 38.

Securities and Exchange Commission. *Institutional Investor Study, Report of the Securities and Exchange Commission*. Vol. 2. 92nd Cong., 1st Sess., House Document No. 92–64. Washington, D.C.: Government Printing Office, 1971.

SHARPE, W. F. "Mutual Fund Performance." *Journal of Business*, January 1966, pp. 119–38.

———. *Portfolio Theory and Capital Markets*. New York: McGraw-Hill, 1970.

SOLDOFSKY, ROBERT M. "Yield-Risk Performance Measurements." *Financial Analysts Journal*, September–October 1968, p. 130.

TREYNOR, J. L. "How to Rate Management of Investment Funds." *Harvard Business Review*, January–February 1965, pp. 63–75.

Wharton School of Finance and Commerce, University of Pennsylvania. *Study of Mutual Funds*. Washington, D.C.: Government Printing Office, 1962.

WILLIAMSON, PETER J. "Measuring Mutual Fund Performance." *Financial Analysts Journal*, November–December 1972, p. 78.

CHAPTER 8

INVESTMENT IN REAL ESTATE, PRECIOUS METALS, FUTURES, AND ART OBJECTS

Until the commodity price boom of 1980, most Americans had not invested in assets such as gold, silver, coins, antiques, and objects of art. This is not true of people in other countries of the world. In many countries, individuals hold their wealth in the form of gold coins, silver, or jewels. When, for example, some Vietnamese refugees reached the United States, they brought with them their most valuable possessions, which mostly were gold in all forms, including coins and gold leaf, and jewels. Only diamonds could have had a higher value and still have been as portable. Only a minority of Americans, historically, have been coin, stamp, or antique collectors, and from 1933 until 1975, Americans could not legally own gold. Now, however, it is common for Americans to own gold in the form of coins and other precious metals. In fact, some financial institutions arrange for the purchase of gold for clients. There seems to be a growing institutional interest in all real assets as a hedge against inflation, even though that interest has been dampened by sharply declining prices of these assets throughout most of 1981–82.

Americans have been interested along with the rest of the world in investing in real estate. Home ownership has been profitable because of the favorable tax treatment and the increase in housing prices, which began to rise in earnest in the early 1960s. Figure 8–1 demonstrates the past increase in prices, along with one estimate of the future increase in the average price of an American house or condominium.

This chapter is based on Chapter 15, "Investment in Real Assets," Amling, Frederick, and Droms, William G., *Personal Financial Management*, Richard D. Irwin, Inc., Homewood, Illinois, 1982, with permission of the publisher.

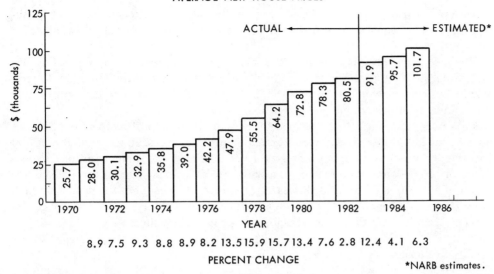

AVERAGE NEW HOUSE PRICES

FIGURE 8–1

Average Price of New Houses in the United States, 1970–1982 with Estimates 1983–1985

SOURCE: U.S. Bureau of the Census, National Association of Realtors.

A substantial number of financial institutions have made mortgage loans in the past. Typically savings and loan associations, commercial banks, mortgage companies, and life insurance companies have made mortgage loans. Because of the high rate of inflation and high interest rates, some institutions have purchased real estate directly as an investment, or have obtained a share of the profits when making mortgages on commercial ventures. The reasons for these arrangements are to protect themselves from inflation and to provide a reasonable mortgage rate for the borrower. The speculative surge in 1981 prices softened in 1982 and might not return, but it has raised the consciousness of investors to the problems of inflation and the mobility of securities to protect them against rapid inflation.

The long-run solution for inflation in part requires a bundle of constraints, including monetary restraint, a balanced federal budget, more private capital investment, more private saving, less dependence on imported energy, greater worker productivity, and no indexing of wages to prices. But until a utopian environment is reached, an investor should seek protection from inflation. Individuals and financial institutions might consider investment in real assets to protect the purchasing power of their investment dollars. In this chapter, we will examine the investment characteristics of real estate and precious metals and other real assets.

REAL ESTATE INVESTMENT: AN INFLATION HEDGE

In most areas of the United States, there has been a substantial increase in the prices of real estate because of the substantial demand for housing. In Hawaii, California, and Washington, D.C., housing prices have increased at annual rates in excess of 15 percent per year or more. In Georgetown, a fashionable and expensive area of Washington, it was not uncommon for an investor to buy a house for $100,000 and sell it six months later for $125,000.

The speculative fever in housing—and it is speculation—was so bad in Los Angeles, California, in 1979, that builders, flooded with buyers, sold their houses by lottery. The lucky winners would then buy the house and move in or sell the option at a profit and get in line for the next auction.

In Washington, D.C., there has been a substantial amount of renovation of houses on Capitol Hill, close to the Congress, and in other areas of the city. It was not uncommon for investors to buy a house for $30,000, renovate for an additional expenditure of $15,000, and then rent the house for $6,000 a year or sell it for $70,000, for a gain of $25,000 in six months. Prices at the end of 1982 were not rising at these high rates. However, a long-range price increase remains a possibility, and the lure of profits and tax incentives continues to attract investors into real estate.

Factors to Consider in Real Estate Investment

Potential real estate investors must understand how to make a profit in real estate. Several factors must be considered.

LOCATION. The first step is to locate a property that has the potential of maintaining or increasing its value. This requires that the investor study the trends in real estate prices. An analysis of the prices of houses or commercial property in various sectors of the city will reveal the trend and magnitude of price changes as well as the stability of prices. This may require a bit of work, but it will pay off in the decision-making process. One U.S. metropolitan neighborhood, for example, experienced an 8 percent annual increase in price over a five-year period. Houses increased in price from $50,000 to $73,500. In another section of the same city, slightly more expensive houses increased from $60,000 to $96,700, for a 10 percent annual increase. Such an analysis suggests that the more expensive area was more desirable, financially, than the first area. Obviously, the past is not going to repeat exactly in the future, but such a trend analysis will reveal clues to the better investment areas in the community. Remember, as the two neighborhoods were rising in value, there were also neighborhoods in the same city where houses were being abandoned. Therefore, it pays to look carefully at neighborhood trends.

The price analysis suggests that the three most important factors in selecting real estate are: (1) location, (2) location, and (3) location. A careful price analysis will reveal the best location. This means buying a well-constructed house on an attractive lot that meets all living requirements, both physically and esthetically. Investors should buy in a neighborhood that is close to public transportation, stores, schools, and recreational facilities. The neighborhood should be quiet, properly zoned, protected by police and fire departments, and a pleasant place to live. The location analysis applies to the purchase of commercial as well as residential real estate.

In most large American cities, the city center has declined, unless massive efforts have been made for redevelopment. Where these efforts have been made, there has been a trend toward increased values in the city center. Baltimore, Boston, and New

York are examples of this turnaround situation. Certainly, investors can find opportunities for investment in these areas. The trend is now back to the city in some areas. As the cost of energy increases and public transportation improves, the trend should continue. If there are any doubts about the value of a neighborhood, lot, or house, it would be wise to consult with a real estate agent, a developer from a reliable and reputable firm, or a mortgage banker, all of whom are familiar with the trend of property values in their area.

BUY AT A FAIR PRICE.   As real estate investors, we should try to buy the property at a fair price, and the property must be affordable. Whether the price is fair or realistic can be determined by the selling price for comparable properties. In the real estate sales business, these are referred to as *comparables*. The real estate agent can supply a list of comparable sales in the neighborhood and advise about the price per square foot of a commercial property.

Once armed with a comparable list, we make an analysis to determine if the price is realistic. Sellers establish the price in the same way. A fair price is determined, then 6 percent real estate commission is added, and then an additional amount for bargaining. For example, assume that six houses in the same neighborhood, all slightly different, sold, respectively, for $54,500, $53,500, $56,000, $55,000, $57,500 and $53,000, within the past six months. The house the investor likes sold for $55,000 six months ago. The current sale price is 5 percent higher, which means $57,750. A real estate commission of 6 percent ($3,465) makes the offering price $61,215. With an amount added for negotiation, the price probably moves to $62,500. The investor could begin the negotiation for the house by making a written offer to buy through an agent. If the market is *tight* (that is, few houses are available), it would be wise to offer close to the asking price. In that case, the investor might offer $62,500. If the house has been on the market for a few months, if the market is slow, and if there are other similar houses on the market, the investor might offer only $59,000. Eventually, a price is agreed upon between buyer and seller.

UNDERSTAND THE CONTRACT FOR PURCHASE.   The contract for purchase requires an offering price, usually a good faith deposit of 10 percent of the offering price, and the settlement date, which is the date when title and ownership of the property will transfer to the buyer. A "clean" contract in the above case would be an offer to purchase the house for $62,500, with a deposit of $6,250 and a statement that the balance will be paid when title passes in 60 days. An "unclean" contract would be one where the contract is contingent upon some future event happening, such as a proviso that the seller paint the house inside and out or that the offer is subject to parents' approval. Putting these conditions with the purchase contract is proper if market conditions warrant. If the market is tight and the investor wants the house, the simpler and cleaner the contract, the better.

UNDERSTAND THE CREDIT STATEMENT.   In addition to supplying the signed contract and deposit money, the purchasor-investor will also be required to provide a credit sheet. This requirement tells the seller of the financial position (assets and liabilities and income) of the purchaser-investor. Obviously, the seller wants to learn whether the purchaser has the financial ability to purchase the house. The seller can then make a reasonable judgment about whether or not the investor will be able to obtain a mortgage on the property and carry through on the transaction. This is particularly important for the seller when the seller is taking back a mortgage as part of the price of the house. The seller must know if the purchaser will be able to afford the house.

ANALYZING THE INVESTMENT

Before a decision is made to buy the house, it must be determined if it will be a good investment. In order to do this, the investor must estimate the future growth of income and expenses, rents, property taxes, insurance, management, and maintenance. A realistic set of assumptions would be as follows: As the situation is analyzed, it is learned that property taxes have increased 8 percent per year, rents have increased 10 percent every two years, maintenance expenses have increased 7 percent per year, and insurance costs have increased 5 percent per year. The insurance rate must be adjusted periodically because of increased property value. The insurance cost will increase an additional 10 percent in three years because the property increases in value at the rate of 12 percent per year. In addition, there is the mortgage interest, taxes, and depreciation expense, which is an important part of the rate of return estimates. President Reagan's Economic Recovery Act of 1981 provided that real estate investments could be written off over 15 years using a 1.75 declining balance depreciation method.

The depreciation schedule would be as follows: a normal depreciation rate would be one-fifteenth per year, or 6.67 percent. The law allows 1.75 times that amount in the first year. The first year's depreciation is therefore 11.67 percent, or 12 percent rounded. The second year's depreciation is 6.67 times 100 percent minus 11.67. That is, 6.67 times 88.33, or 5.89. The depreciation rate in the second year is therefore 5.89 × 1.75, which is 10.31 percent, or 11 percent rounded. This process continues until the asset is fully depreciated.

Since this is a commercial investment, the lending institution will provide a 25-year mortgage loan for 75 percent of the value of the property. The interest rate is assumed to be 11 percent, which is higher than that for a loan on an owner-occupied house. Obviously, if the mortgage rates are 17 percent, the investor will face a different and higher cost. If the house is purchased for $57,000, then the mortgage would be $42,750 (75 percent), and the down payment would be $14,250 (25 percent). The monthly cost of the mortgage payment, including principal and interest, would be $419. This payment will remain constant over the 25-year life of the mortgage. Depreciation of the house is assumed to be accelerated based upon the 1981 Economic Recovery Act. The land value is $10,000, and the value of the building is $47,000.

Closing Costs

Investors must think about closing costs as well as the amount of down payment and the monthly mortgage and tax payments. Closing costs can be sizable. For example, the approximate closing costs for a $57,000 house with a mortgage of $42,750 in Montgomery County, Maryland, in 1978, are listed in Table 8–1.

TABLE 8–1

Sample Closing Costs

Recording fees	$ 12.00
Revenue stamps	250.80
Transfer tax	
State	285.00
County	245.00
Tax certificate: County	5.00
Survey: Minimum—$60	60.00
Plat	2.50
Notary fees	4.00
Title examination	132.50
Settlement fee	57.00
Preparation of papers: Note and deed of trust	65.00
Title insurance	166.50
Subtotal	$1,285.30
Taxes, real estate (county and state) prorated from June 31 to July 1; assume January 1 settlement and six months' taxes	400.00
Total taxes and closing costs	$1,685.30

The closing costs represent more than 10 percent of the down payment, when the real estate taxes are included. Some of the fees and taxes associated with closing costs are tax deductible. Certainly the real estate taxes are deductible, along with the state and county transfer taxes, revenue stamps, settlement fees, and possibly title insurance. For purposes of illustration, it is assumed that all settlement costs are deductible as a business expense, but in an actual case, a tax expert should be consulted.

Making the Income and Expense Estimate

In the purchase of the investment property, it will be assumed that the investor is in the 50 percent tax bracket and that the after-tax cost of the settlement expense is half of $1,685.30, or $842.65. The after-tax amount must be added to the initial investment. The total amount of $1,685.30 is paid at settlement. Once the house is purchased, the rental income and expense data are as depicted in Table 8–2. There is an operating loss of $7,186 in the first year, $6,794 in the second, $5,963 in the third, $4,695 in the fourth, and $4,722 in the fifth year. This results in a reduction of ordinary income taxes and results in an after-tax loss of $3,593 in the first year down to $2,361 in the fifth year, with varying amounts in each of the other years. In effect, this reduces the ordinary taxes the investor pays and adds to cash flow. Table 8–3 recaps the cash flow effect. No depreciation is deducted in calculating the cash flows because depreciation is a noncash charge. The net effect is a savings in after-tax dollars that produces a positive net cash outflow. The net cash gain after taxes is estimated to be $1,670 in the first year and $1,348, $1,246, $386, and $747 in the next four years. This means that the investor would have a positive return after taxes in each of the forecast years. If the investor bought the house as an investment, the investment schedule would be

TABLE 8–2

Income and Expense Estimate of Investment Property

	Base Year	Annual Rate of Increase (%)*	Year 1†	Year 2	Year 3	Year 4	Year 5
Gross annual rental income	$5,400	(10)‡	$ 5,400	$ 5,400	$ 5,900	$ 5,900	$ 6,400
Real estate agent fee			540	540	590	590	640
Net rental income	4,860		4,860	4,860	5,310	5,310	5,760
Annual expenses							
Taxes	800	(8)	800	864	933	1,008	1,008
Insurance	200	(5)	200	210	221	232	243
Additional value						23	24
Maintenance	750		750	802	859	919	983
Depreciation**	5,640		5,640	5,170	4,700	4,230	3,760
Interest	4,704		4,656	4,608	4,560	4,512	4,464
Total tax expense			$12,046	$11,654	$11,273	$10,005	$10,482
Operating loss*			(7,186)	(6,794)	(5,963)	(4,695)	(4,722)
After-tax operating loss*			(3,593)	(3,397)	(2,982)	(2,348)	(2,361)

*Assumes 50 percent tax bracket.
†Assumes no change the first year.
‡Every two years.
**Approximate; based on 15-year, 1.75 declining balance method.

TABLE 8–3

Cash Income and Expense of Investment Property*

	Year 1	Year 2	Year 3	Year 4	Year 5
Cash income	$4,860	$4,860	$5,310	$5,310	$5,760
Cash expenses					
Taxes	800	864	933	1,088	1,088
Insurance	200	210	221	232	243
Maintenance	750	802	859	919	983
Principal repayments plus interest	5,033	5,033	5,033	5,033	5,033
Total expenses	6,783	6,909	7,046	7,272	7,347
Cash gain (loss)	(1,923)	(2,049)	(1,736)	(1,962)	(1,614)
Annual tax saving†	3,593	3,397	2,982	2,348	2,361
Net cash gain (loss) after taxes	1,670	1,348	1,246	386	747

*With tax effect.
†After-tax operating loss from Table 8–2.

as follows:

$$\text{Base year } \$14,250 + \$843 = \$15,093$$

Table 8–4 shows the investor's net worth at the end of five years, assuming the property increases in value as shown in the table. For this investment, net worth is simply the difference between the value of the property and the amount of the outstanding mortgage. The net worth represents the investor's equity in the property. The after-tax cash revenue is also shown.

TABLE 8–4
Property Value and Net Worth*

	Base Year	1	2	3	4	5
Property value	$57,000	$63,000	$71,501	$80,081	$89,691	$100,454
Mortgage value	42,750	42,323	41,896	41,469	41,042	40,615
Net worth in property	$14,250	$21,477	$29,605	$38,614	$48,649	$ 59,839
Plus closing costs	(843)					
After-tax cash	$15,093	$ 1,620	$ 1,348	$ 1,246	$ 386	$ 747

*With tax effect.

The maximum capital gains tax effect in 1981 was 20 percent. The investor declares 50 percent of the long-term gain and pays a maximum of 40 percent on this amount. If the house is sold in five years at $100,454, less 6 percent sales commission, the net sales price is $94,427, and the gain on the sale is $60,927 ($94,427 − $33,500). The $33,500 is the adjusted cost basis for the property, i.e. $57,000 − $23,500 which is the amount of depreciation taken over the 5 year period. A maximum tax of 20 percent of this amount would be $12,185, leaving a net profit of $48,742. In addition to this net profit, the investor would also recover the $14,250 original investment. The total cash proceeds for the sale to the investor would then be $62,992 ($14,250 + $48,742).

In summary, the investor would put down $15,093, receive income of $1,670 in the first year, $1,348 in the second, $1,246 in the third, $386 in the fourth, and $747 in the fifth. The amount of money returned to the investor after taxes in five years is $62,992, assuming the house is sold at the end of the fifth year.

Estimating the Rate of Return

The rate of return from the investment can be estimated by discounting the income or revenue back to the original investment. To do this, we need the present value tables in Appendix A1. In this case, the discounted value of the annual income and the value of the investment in five years is discounted back to the present at a discount rate. When the discounted present value of the cash flow equals the present value of the investment of $15,093, the rate of return on the investment has been determined.

In the case of the purchase of the real property described above, the after-tax investment flows are shown in Table 8–5, along with the present value of the flows.

TABLE 8-5

Present Value of Real Estate Cash Flows

		Present Value of One Dollar at 40%	Present Value at 40%
Initial investment	$15,093		
Annual income			
Year 1 = $1,670		.714	$ 1,192
Year 2 = $1,348		.510	687
Year 3 = $1,246		.364	454
Year 4 = $ 386		.260	100
Year 5 = $ 747		.186	139
Sum of present value of income at 40%			$ 2,572
Present value of $62,992 at 40% (based on gain in five years of $62,992 discounted at 40%— .186, all figures rounded)			$11,717
Total present value			$14,289

The present value of the investment at the end of five years discounted at 40 percent is slightly lower than the present value of the original investment. If you made the calculation using the discount rate table from Appendix A1, the rate would be 38.4 percent, found by interpolating between the present value rates for 35 and 40 percent. This is an attractive rate of return. It was high because the mortgage interest rate was low compared to 1982–1983 mortage rate levels. Obviously, the return would have been lower by perhaps 4 or 5 percentage points if a higher rate of interest was paid.

Can You Avoid Taxes on the Capital Gains?

It is impossible to avoid paying taxes on income from a real estate venture forever. However, it is possible to postpone taxes for a long time. Before the Economic Recovery Act, many real estate ventures had an annual loss (a negative cash flow) after taxes. The investor was required to supply an additional annual amount of money that was added to the investment capital. Capital gains taxes would be paid when the asset was sold, but it is unnecessary to sell real estate to enjoy the increase in price. As the property increases in price, the investor can increase the size of the mortgage on the property by refinancing the mortgage. (This assumes a lending institution is willing to make the mortgage loan.) In the case of the investment under discussion, the value of the property is assumed to have increased to $80,081 (see Table 8–4) at the end of three years. This property can be mortgaged with a mortgage value of 75 percent of the amount, or approximately $60,000. By increasing the mortgage to $60,000, the investor would have an additional $17,250 available for the purchase of another house.

The only problem with this plan is that the investor is increasing indebtedness and increasing the monthly mortgage costs in the process of increasing the debt. In addition, the mortgage rate might increase, which reduces the investor's advantage. Money from rental income or other income must be available to pay the increased borrowing costs. Some lending institutions might be unwilling to increase the mortgage on the property, particularly in times of tight money. Lending policies of financial institutions do change, and they might decide to make loans only to owner-occupants, rather than to investors. This means that the real estate investor must be certain that the money borrowed will be reinvested in profitable investment outlets.

The possibilities of borrowing an increased amount of money from mortgages for additional real estate investment suggest substantial profits and represent a form of pyramiding. Let's see how this would work. It is based on the idea that there is enough equity to buy a new house every three years for every house that is owned. The schedule is shown in Table 8–6. The table reflects the condition where one house

TABLE 8–6
How to Pyramid a Real Estate Investment

	Years				Total
	0	3	6	9	
First house	First house	Second house	Third house	Fourth house	4
Second house		Second house	Third house	Fourth house	3
Third house			Third house	Fourth house	2
Fourth house				Fourth house	1
Total houses	1	2	3	4	10

is purchased the first year. In the third year a second house is purchased by increasing the mortgage on the first house, which is used to make the down payment. The investor now owns two houses. Assuming that prices continue to increase, the investor can buy another house in the sixth year using the money obtained from the two houses. (Theoretically two houses could be purchased in year 6 and eight in year 9, but we assume only one house is purchased every three years.) In order for this system to work, an investor must realize a constant increase in prices and the ability to borrow the mortgage money.

The only limit is that the amount of income from rents and other sources must carry the mortgages or that the investor will be able to make up the difference from other sources. If an investor is successful in buying houses, it would be possible to have assets valued at $100,000 in year zero with a mortgage of $80,000 and equity of $20,000 eventually become $569,000 with a mortgage of $455,000 and equity of $114,000. That isn't a bad outcome when the investor only invested about $20,000 to begin the real estate program. But all the gain will not go to the investor, since taxes have not been paid. But the gain potential is substantial.

What Can Go Wrong?

The description of the real estate investment pyramid is excitingly profitable. The projections seem reasonable. Values have gone up in the past more than the rates assumed. The debt as a percentage of the value is not excessive. The only thing that could go wrong is that the estimates could be wrong or that the United States could have another recession or that the investor might not be able to borrow the money.

A RECESSION MIGHT CAUSE LOSSES.   The American economy tends to be cyclical. Every three or four years, an economic slowdown disrupts business and results in losses to real estate investors, businesses, and workers who become unemployed. It happened in 1969, in 1974–75, and in 1981–82. Unemployment rose above 9.8 percent, the inflation rate was in the 12 percent range, and the mortgage interest rate increased to as high as 17.5 percent. There were several quarters of negative growth in the economy, and corporate profits declined.

In the 1974–75 recession, billions of dollars were lost by institutions. Mortgage lenders borrowed cheap funds in the money market to invest in high-priced mortgages, only to find later that the cheap short-term money cost 20 percent, and they couldn't make a profit by investing in 17 percent mortgages. Real estate investment trusts (REITs) did the same thing and lost millions of dollars. Many investors thought they could make money in real estate by buying the common stock of REITs. Some even borrowed heavily against the common stock, thus increasing their leverage and the amount of the hoped-for profit. To their dismay, the shares declined in price. Their sought-after fortune became a millstone around their necks. Financial embarrassment was followed by collapse and, for some, financial failure. If an investor asks "What can go wrong?" just remember the recessions of 1974–75 and 1981–82, and the answer will be clear.

POOR ESTIMATES. Since all the conclusions are based on estimates, the more practical answer to the question "What can go wrong?" is that the estimates can be wrong. The market price of property might not increase as rapidly as expected. In fact, something might happen that could cause a substantial loss—an uninsured mud slide, flood damage, or a blight in the neighborhood created by a change in zoning. An example of this would be the placement of a landfill garbage and trash collection area near the property. This actually happened in one affluent county in Potomac, Maryland. Fortunately for the county residents, it was found that a landfill attracts birds. Since the birds are a menace to air navigation and since the landfill site was in the path of commercial and general aviation, the courts would not allow development of the site. Instead, county authorities planned a sewage treatment plant that could cause a reduction in property values.

RENTS LOWER THAN EXPECTED.   Rents might not increase as expected because of market limits. And, of course, the investor could be plagued by instability of lease income because of high tenant turnover. This is one of the major risks of owning rental property. The investor may have to suffer through periods when rental properties are vacant. This applies to commercial as well as residential real estate ventures.

THE INVESTMENT ALTERNATIVES

Since rental income could cease altogether, there will be no cash inflows to offset mortgage and other costs. For example, one investor owned four single-family rental properties. One year, all four properties were vacant for four consecutive months. The investor had to pay all four mortgages from ordinary income, thus increasing the investment much faster than anticipated and calling on income from other sources to carry the property. The investor might be unable to pay and could have the mortgage foreclosed. If an investor does invest in real estate, it is critically important to establish a reserve fund to cope with such unexpected contingencies.

EXPENSES HIGHER THAN EXPECTED. Expenses could also be higher than originally expected, and real estate taxes could increase more than anticipated. Maintenance expenses might be higher, particularly if there is high turnover of tenants. Insurance costs increase with inflation and could reduce profits. One or all these expense increases might result in lower profits and an unfavorable investment.

In principle, then, real estate investment offers relatively high rates of return. However, there are risks involved. Caution must be exercised, or else the investor could turn the lure of high profits into a loss. This applies to commercial real estate investments as well as to apartment buildings.

INVESTMENT IN LAND OR FARMS

One investor bought a farm in northern Maine several years ago. It wasn't his new home; it was an investment in land for the future. It was a form of protection against inflation. It was an improved property, and a working farm. Not only would it be likely to increase in value in the future, it could also serve as a vacation retreat and a profitable hobby. Many investors are interested in land because it is scarce. And the value of land has increased in the last decade, in spite of a deep recession in the mid-1970s. Even though land has appreciated generally, it is important to choose the right piece of land, in the right location, at the right time. In addition, the carrying costs of ownership, including taxes and interest on loans used to purchase the property, can mean a substantial burden. Therefore, investors should keep carrying costs to a minimum if they decide to purchase land.

The Selection Process

In the selection of land as an investment, there are several well-known principles to follow. First, it is wise to buy land well ahead of the path of development. There are two dangers in applying this principle: The investor might buy too far ahead of development and carrying costs will eat up the profit, or the wrong path may be chosen and development might never take place. The second principle concerns the time over which the land is to be developed. The shorter the time, the higher the return. A third principle is to be patient. In order to ensure that patience will be rewarded, make certain that all payments on the property, including taxes, interest, insurance, and development costs, can be met. The fourth principle is to obtain adequate financing. Often, an owner will sell the land with a 29 percent down payment and a mortgage of 71 percent to be paid over several years. (This follows current IRS rules.) This is usually done to stretch out the capital gains, since capital gains must be paid only when the property is sold. Each time a payment is made on the mortgage, a part of the property is "sold" and some of the gain is taken. In this way, the seller does not pay all the tax in a single year, and the investor has a built-in financing arrangement.

The unit of land investment is high. In large metropolitan areas, large tracts of land with 200 acres close to the city will sell for as high as $10,000 per acre, or $2 million for the tract. Smaller tracts closer in may sell for $18,000 an acre for future residential development. A small tract of land well beyond ordinary metropolitan commuting boundaries might sell for less.

LAND PARTNERSHIPS.   One of the big problems in land investment is that it takes a lot of money and the right financing. Unless the investor can afford to finance a purchase, it might be difficult to play the game. It also forces the smaller investor into other avenues; for example, buying developed lots and holding for later resale. Often, this requires a long holding period, since the lots are often overpriced to begin with. Another way to invest is to become involved in a land syndicate or partnership. Before entering into a syndicate arrangement, make certain it is legitimate, fraud-free, and economically sound. Make sure the principals are known, or else don't play the game.

AN IMPORTANT RULE TO FOLLOW.   Don't borrow large sums of money with short-term repayment agreements. It's a great idea to borrow at low short-term rates and renew every 180 days. Yet in periods of high and rising interest rates, the cost of borrowing short term will increase. The loan might be renewed, but at very high and unprofitable rates. Therefore, arrange for financing so that costs and income are in balance, which means that long-term financing should be arranged.

Investment in Real Estate Investment Trusts (REITs)

REITs, or real estate investment trusts, are another way to participate in real estate investment. The REIT is a form of closed-end investment company. The real estate investment trust sells a limited number of shares to investors and borrows heavily to obtain maximum leverage. The funds obtained are invested in real estate ventures, including the purchase of buildings and mortgages.

SOME ADVICE ABOUT REITS.   Be careful in selecting a REIT and buy into more than one company to provide adequate diversification. The shares of REITs must be analyzed like any other security. Avoid ventures that invest only in mortgages if an inflation hedge is desired.

Several REITs failed in the mid-1970s because the cost of borrowed money was higher than the earnings from real estate mortgages. Ordinarily, long-term mortgages pay a higher interest than short-term loans. In periods of "tight" money, or when there is a credit crunch, short-term rates rise much higher than mortgage rates. In a time of high interest rates, business turns bad, and firms fail. Mortgage holders cannot make their payments, and the mortgage lenders fail. It isn't a cheerful thought, but it did happen in 1973–74 and 1982–83.

Individual investors have been lured to assets that increase in value at a greater rate than inflation. They appreciate that precious metals are not subject to taxes as real estate is, and yet they increase in value. Of course, investors must pay capital gains if the real asset is sold at a profit. Investors also appreciate the rise in the prices of the real asset (of course, investors or speculators do not like it very much when prices drop sharply, as they did in 1981–82).

More and more, there is a growing interest on the part of insititutional investors in real assets that will protect their clients from the loss of purchasing power created by inflation. Some institutional investors are prohibited from owning "unproductive" assets—assets that do not produce current income. The majority have considered investment in gold and silver, but most have chosen not to accept the risks associated with ownership of any commodities because the prices vary due to changes in supply and demand. The risks are real, but the returns are commensurate with the risks. The returns are generally greater than the returns on common stock. We will examine a few ways in which investors may share in the growth in value of precious metals and objects of art.

In Gold We Invest and Speculate

Gold, that soft, lustrous, yellow metal, has served at various moments in history as primitive people's wealth; as a material for artistic expression; as a lure for those in search of riches; as a monetary system (based upon gold coins); as the basis for the world's monetary systems (the gold standard); and today as a valuable commodity that serves as a private store of value, a hedge against inflation, and a substitute for a depreciating paper currency. It seems that the acceptability and love for gold is so universal that the more gold is produced, the more it is demanded.

The reason for owning the metal in modern times has been the lure of profits. As the rate of inflation rose, speculators rushed to buy gold, and the price rose. The pattern of the price of gold is seen in Figure 8–2. It rose to a new high in 1980, only to drop dramatically in 1981. Depending on when gold was purchased, an owner could have made money or lost a fortune. Figure 8–2 demonstrates the variability of the price of gold and silver and the risk involved in its ownership. There was a tremendous speculative surge in the price of gold and silver in early 1980. Buying in such an environment was very risky.

How to Invest in Gold

Investors can own gold by buying gold jewelry, gold coins, gold bullion, and the shares of gold mining companies.

GOLD JEWELRY. The easiest way to buy gold is to buy gold jewelry, including necklaces, bracelets, rings, chains, earrings, watches, medallions, and art objects. Unfortunately, it is the poorest way to buy gold if the main thought is maximum return on investment. There are two basic value components in jewelry. First, there is the

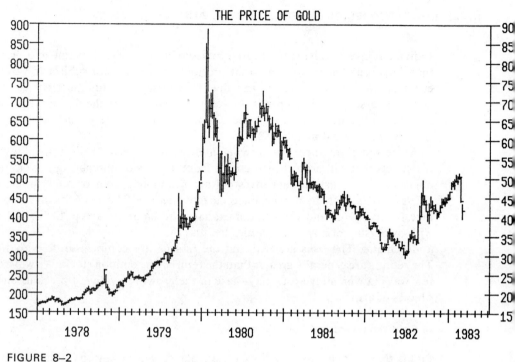

FIGURE 8–2

The Price of Gold (Week Ending Prices, Spot New York)

SOURCE: Courtesy of J. Aron and Company, a division of Goldman Sachs.

purity of the gold and second, the artistic value of the gold object. The purity of gold is measured in karats, with 24-karat gold the purest and most expensive. Pure gold is soft and is mixed with other metals to increase strength and reduce the karat content. Therefore, 12-, 14-, and 18-karat jewelry is quite common. Solid gold jewelry is more valuable than gold plate or gold-filled jewelry. Since an investor is interested in the value of pure gold in a piece of jewelry by weight (31.1 grams equals 1 Troy ounce), it is important when buying to know the pure gold equivalent.

The second factor in the value of jewelry is in the design or artistic merit. This is difficult to determine and usually requires expert opinion as to value. Certainly, investors should obtain expert opinion and an appraisal before a major expenditure for gold jewelry.

The price of gold jewelry has increased with the dramatic increase in the price of gold and has declined equally as dramatically. It is instructive to compare the price of the same gold watch or chain today with its price a few years ago. A gold necklace purchased for $125 in 1976 was worth over $460 in 1983. This rate of growth is unlikely to continue in the future at the same rate, and the gold price will fluctuate. Yet it is gratifying that the asset purchased and used will have lasting value and increase the owner's net worth. Ordinarily, buying jewelry is an inefficient way of buying gold. Yet gold continues to be a store of value; over a long period of time, it could prove to be a satisfactory investment.

GOLD COINS. One way for an investor to enjoy gold and profit from it is to purchase jewelry items made from gold coins and bars. Both gold coins and 5-gram wafers of pure gold can be purchased as pendants with gold chains. The 5-gram wafers can be made into attractive cufflinks that will increase and decrease in value with the price of gold. And, of course, such items are beautiful and interesting to wear or use. Twenty-, 10-, and 5-dollar gold pieces also make attractive bracelets and pendants but might lose value, as the coins wear from exposure.

GOLD COINS TO OWN. The United States Treasury has minted a new gold coin that has become another way to own gold. In the past, "gold bugs" could own gold only by buying coins from dealers as numismatists. One of the most popular coins among collectors and investors has been the South African Krugerrand, which contains 1.00 Troy ounce of gold that is 916.66/1000 fine. The coin itself is sold for its gold content rather than its value as a collector's item. Investors may also buy a 2 Rand South African coin which has about one-fourth the gold content of the Krugerrand.

The $20 U.S. "Double Eagle" of both the Liberty and St. Gaudens types have been popular as collectors' items. Each contains .9675 Troy ounces of gold that is 900/1000 fine. The circulated coins make fine pieces of jewelry and are beautiful as a collector's item. In 1974, a coin of this type sold for $90. In 1983, the coin sold for over $600 if it was in reasonable condition. The $10 and $5 gold coins are also an easy way for an investor to own gold. The following coins are also considered appropriate for purchasing gold:

Coin	Fineness	Weight (Oz)
Mexican 50 peso	900/1000	1.2056
Austrian 1 ducat	986.66/1000	.1109
Austrian 4 ducat	986.66/1000	.4438
Austrian 100 corona	900/1000	.9802
Hungarian 100 korona	900/1000	.9802
English old sovereign	916.66/1000	.2354

Each coin will vary in price, depending upon quality and gold content. If an investor contemplates a major purchase, expert advice should be sought.

GOLD BARS. Gold bars or bullion may now be owned by Americans. This is the cheapest and most direct way of owning gold. The price of gold has risen and fallen erratically since it has been legal for Americans to own gold. On December 31, 1974, American citizens were given the right to own, buy, and sell gold bullion. This was the first time since the U.S. went off the gold standard in 1933, 41 years before, that Americans could own gold. During the period 1933 to 1975, gold could be owned by individuals only in coins, jewelry, and objects of art. The federal government owned the gold, and for a period, gold served as a monetary base and reserve for U.S. currency.

Historically, the price of gold was fixed by the U.S. government. Even under regulation, the price moved from $20.66 an ounce before 1934 to $42.22 in 1974. The free market price of gold rose to $175 an ounce during this time. On January 6, 1975, the

Treasury of the United States sold 2 million ounces of the country's 276-million-ounce stockpile. After the initial offering, the price of gold declined steadily until it reached a low point of $116.50 per ounce. It then began a dramatic rise in 1978, moving to $197.50 per ounce. It went to $230 in the fourth quarter of 1978. The price of gold finally rose to over $860 per ounce in 1980, in a speculative flurry not seen for many years. By the middle of 1980, the price had declined to $630 per ounce. The price dropped further in 1982, falling below $400. Thus, investors could have made substantial profits in gold or, alternatively, tremendous losses, depending on when the asset was purchased. Investors can check the local newspaper or *The Wall Street Journal* for the latest gold price. Figure 8–4 provides the prices of gold and other commodities.

The erratic price movement of gold since it became legal in the United States is seen in Figure 8–2. If gold had been purchased and held for the five-year period from 1976 to 1981, the price would have increased from $175 to approximately $400. The approximate annual compound rate of growth would have been 15.6 percent but with a high degree of variation, which indicates a high degree of risk.

The rate of return on gold tends to move in the opposite direction of the rate of return on common stocks. That is, if common stock returns are high, the return on gold will be low. Actually, this is a good quality. What it really means is that gold is a good inflation hedge and compensates for a stock market that declines with inflation and high interest rates. Buying gold, an unproductive asset, is risky. The price changes quickly, sharply, and erratically, because it is susceptible to international money market speculation and the whims of the supply and demand in the world markets. But gold is somewhat of a hedge against inflation.

GOLD BARS TO OWN.   Swiss banks sell gold bars in denominations from 5 grams to 10 ounces. U.S. dealers also sell gold bars. One of the best-known dealers, the Deak-Perera Group, sells its own gold bars in 1.5- and 10-ounce sizes, 999/1000 fine. Each bar is numbered and sealed in a clear plastic package. The Deak-Perera Group offers a repurchase agreement. The statement on the back of each package reads:

> Should the Deak-Perera Group repurchase this bar, we will do so at the prevailing spot price of gold. We will charge the customer no assaying or refining costs provided that the packaging or the security paper within is not disturbed, altered, or damaged in any way. January 1975   (Signed) N. L. Deak.

This provides Deak's customers with a simple, inexpensive, and safe way of buying gold bars.

GOLD MINING SHARES.   Gold mining shares are another way of participating in the potential profit of owning gold. The process is indirect, and the price of gold shares does not always follow the price of gold. The unfortunate part about buying the shares in mining companies is that it is not easy to translate a rise in gold price into a dollar of common stock profits. When an investor buys a share in the company, profits are being purchased, and not so many ounces in gold. An investor must examine the financial position of the company and its competitive position before making an investment.

How to Own Silver

Silver has been an inflation hedge over the years. Anyone who owns silver coins, sterling silver flatware, tea services, or sterling silver jewelry has been protected from inflation and has enjoyed the beauty and use of the item during the period of ownership. Investors can buy silver in much the same way as they can purchase gold. In order to give some idea of the price inflation in silver, note that the price of silver bullion increased from $1.79 per ounce in 1969 to $5.40 per ounce in 1978. On January 21, 1980, the price increased to a record high of $50 per ounce. By the middle of 1980, it had declined to about $15 per ounce. The price of silver reached a two-year low of $8.52 an ounce on July 31, 1981, and then rebounded to $9.60 on August 21, 1981. In early 1983 it sold for $14 per ounce. The price pattern is seen in Figure 8–3.

It is almost impossible to keep up with the price changes in all silver objects. But a few examples can give an investor a notion of what has happened to prices over the past 30 years. One four-place International Sterling pattern cost $34 a setting in 1950. In 1980, the same pattern sold for over $500. A sterling tea service purchased for $600 in 1960 had a retail price of $4,000 in 1980. And a U.S. silver dollar, which cost $1 in 1950, sold for $15 or higher in 1980 just because of its silver content.

Owning sterling silver flatware increases an investor's wealth and provides daily enjoyment if it is used. This is certainly an excellent combination. It is interesting to examine the attitude of colonial families toward silverware. A wealthy family in colonial Deerfield, Massachusetts, for example, would have several silver mugs, one perhaps made by Paul Revere (priceless now). A poor family might have only one mug or dish, but it represented a major part of the family assets. Therefore, an investor need not buy 12 place settings of silver to enjoy and profit. A collection can begin with the purchase of one spoon.

An investor must understand the dynamics of the silver market. People sold their silver coins at the peak of the market in 1980. This set the stage for the decline that followed. At least through 1981, refiners had been busy melting down coins, flatware, and jewelry to make into silver bars. Owners of bags of coins can obtain a premium price and can switch into bars and wafers without paying a tax on the gain, if one exists. The bars and wafers are .999 fine.

Investors can buy bags of coins. A 55-pound bag of 90 percent silver coins issued before 1964 contains 712 ounces of silver. This has a market value of $6,835.20 at a market price of $9.60 per ounce. The bag of coins has a face value (as money) of $1,000 each. Investors can also purchase 40 percent bags with 295 ounces of silver dollars weighing 760 ounces, each bag with a face value of $1,000. The standard silver bar is 1,000 ounces and is the global trading unit. Cash prices of silver are reported in the financial press. Figure 8–4 provides a list of commodity prices, including the Troy ounce price of silver in the New York market. The price of silver was $10.73 on Friday, March 11, 1983. It dropped $.44 in price from Thursday's price. The price quoted is the Handy and Harman base price.

A smaller trading unit, the 100-ounce silver bar, has also become popular. And the two bars will sell at different prices. On August 23, 1981, a 100-ounce silver bar closed at $10.20 per ounce, while the standard 1,000-ounce bar was quoted at $9.70 an ounce.

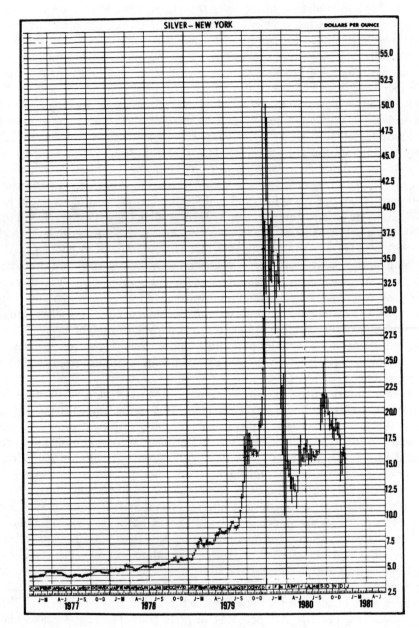

FIGURE 8–3

SOURCE: Deak-Perera, Washington, D.C.

230

Cash Prices

Friday, March 11, 1983
(Quotations as of 4 p.m. Eastern time)

	Fri	Thurs	Yr.Ago
GRAINS AND FEEDS			
Alfalfa Pellets, dehy, Neb., ton ...	98.00	98.00	78.00
Barley, top-quality Mpls., bu	2.40-2.45	2.40-2.45	3.02½
Bran, (Wheat middling) KC ton ..	77.00	76.0-77.0	73.16
Brewer's Grains, Milw. ton	92.00	92.00	78.00
Corn, No. 2 yellow Cent-Ill. bu	bp2.68½	2.69	2.43
Corn Gluten Feed, Chgo., ton	110.00	110.00	110.33
Cottnsd Meal, Clksdle,Miss. ton .	145.00	145.00	130.00
Flaxseed, Mpls., bu	n5.20	5.20	7.40
Hominy Feed, Ill., ton	85.00	84.00	60.00
Linseed Meal, Mpls., ton	130.00	130.00	151.00
Meat-Bonemeal 50%-pro, Ill. ton	217.5-222.5	217.5-222.5	206.25
Oats, No. 2 milling, Mpls., bu	n1.55-1.65	1.55-1.65	2.14
Rice, No. 2 milled fob Ark. cwt	117.-118.	117.-118.	18.25
Rye, No. 2 Mpls., bu	n2.30	2.30	3.75
Sorghum, (Milo) No. 2 Gulf cwt ..	5.43	5.52	5.12
Soybean Meal, Decatur, Ill. ton ..	174.00	174.50	178.00
Soybeans, No. 1 yel Cent.-Ill. bu ..	bp5.62½	5.64½	5.85
Sunflower Seed, No 1 Mpls. cwt ..	n9.05	9.05	11.50
Wheat, Spring 14%-pro Mpls. bu .	r4.03½	4.04	4.12¾
Wheat, amber durum, Mpls. bu ..	3.95-4.45	3.95-4.45	4.62
Wheat, No. 2 sft red, St.Lou. bu ...	h3.26½	3.27	3.36
Wheat, No. 2 hard KC, bu	r4.11¾	4.13¾	4.22
FOODS			
Beef, 700-900 lbs. Mid-U.S.,lb.fob	.99	.98	1.04
Beef, boxed, gross, Mid-US cwt ..	f101.98	101.65	105.18
Broilers, Dressed "A" NY lb	x.4473	.4470	.4581
Butter, AA, Chgo., lb.	1.47	1.47	1.47
Cocoa, Ivory Coast, $metric ton ..	g1,970	2,021	z
Coffee, Brazilian, NY lb.	n1.28	1.28	1.45
Eggs, Lge white, Chgo doz.	.64½-.65	.64½-.65	.76¾
Flour, hard winter KC cwt	11.05	11.10	10.30
Hams, 17-20 lbs, Mid-US lb fob	.77½	.80	.83
Hogs, Iowa-S.Minn. avg. cwt	51.00	52.00	48.50
Hogs, Omaha avg cwt	e52.00	52.65	48.85
Orange Juice, frz con, NY lb.	b1.115	1.16	1.16
Pepper, black, NY lb.	a.66	.66	.78
Pork Bellies, 12-14 lbs Mid-US lb .	.66	.67	.67½
Pork Loins, 14-17 lbs. Mid-US lb ..	1.11	1.10	.93
Potatoes, rnd wht, 50 lb., fob	y1.25	1.20-1.25	2.47½
Steers, Omaha choice avg cwt	63.56	63.56	66.75
Steers, Tex.-Okla. ch avg cwt	e64.00	z	66.75
Steers, Feeder, Okl Cty, av cwt ..	73.25	73.25	65.50
Sugar, beet, ref. Chgo-Wst lb fob .	.2890	.2890	.2840
Sugar, cane, raw NY lb. del.	.2178	.2179	.1689
Sugar, cane, raw, world, lb. fob ..	.0617	.0610	.1094
Sugar, cane, ref NY lb. fob	.3210	.3310	.2760
FATS AND OILS			
Coconut Oil, crd, N. Orleans cif ..	a.21½	.21⅜	z
Corn Oil, crd wet mill, Chgo. lb. ..	.21½	.22	.24½
Corn Oil, crd dry mill, Chgo. lb. ..	n.24	.24	.25¾
Cottonseed Oil, crd Miss Vly lb. ..	n.17	.17	.19
Grease, choice white, Chgo lb.	a.15	.15	.16¾
Lard, Chgo lb.	n.16½	.16½	.19½
Linseed Oil, raw Mpls lb.	.24	.24	.29
Palm Oil, ref. bl. deod. N.Orl. cif	a.18¾	.18¾	z
Peanut Oil, crd, Southeast lb.	a.25	.25	.22½
Soybean Oil, crd, Decatur, lb.	.1706	.1707	.1839
Tallow, bleachable, Chgo lb.	.15	.15	.16⅞
Tallow, edible, Chgo lb.	n.16½	.16½	.20
FIBERS AND TEXTILES			
Burlap, 10 oz. 40-in. NY yd	n.2555	.2545	.2275
Cotton 1 1/16 in str lw-md Mphs lb	.6493	.6464	.6035
Print Cloth, cotton, 48-in NY yd ..	s.60	.60	.70
Print Cloth, pol/cot 48-in NY yd ..	t.46½	.46½	.47½
Satin Acetate, NY yd	.62	.62	.62
Sheetings, 60x60 48-in. NY yd	.73	.73	.78
Wool, fine staple terr. Boston lb ..	2.13	2.13	2.65
METALS			
Aluminum ingot lb	p.76	.76	.76
Copper cathodes lb	p.78-.80	.78-.80	.73½
Copper Scrap, No 2 wire NY lb	k.58	c.57½	.52
Lead, lb.	p.20-.23	.20-.23	.28½
Mercury 76 lb. flask NY	337.00	337.00	390.00
Nickel plating grade lb	p3.29	3.29	3.29
Steel Scrap 1 hvy mlt Chgo ton	85.00	85.00	77.00
Tin Metals Week composite lb. ...	6.6642	6.6582	6.6359
Zinc High grade lb	p.38-.40	.38-.40	.40
MISCELLANEOUS			
Hides, hvy native strs lb fob	.39½-.40	.38½-.39½	.42½
Newspapers, old No. 1 Chgo ton ..	35.00-40.0	35.00-40.0	27.50
Rubber, smoked sheets, NY lb. ...	n.57½	.57¼	.47¾
PRECIOUS METALS			
Gold, troy oz			
Engelhard indust bullion	420.50	434.75	323.25
Engelhard fabric prods	441.53	456.49	339.41
Handy & Harman base price ...	420.50	434.75	323.25
London fixing AM 424.00 PM ..	420.50	434.75	323.25
Krugerrand, whol	a442.00	445.00	330.50
Platinum, troy ounce	p475.00	475.00	475.00
Silver, troy ounce			
Engelhard indust bullion	10.825	11.150	6.970
Engelhard fabric prods	11.583	11.931	7.511
Handy & Harman base price ...	10.730	11.170	7.020
London Fixing (in pounds)			
Spot (U.S. equiv. $10.870)	7.2300	7.2665	3.9150
3 months	7.4105	7.4590	4.0350
6 months	7.6040	7.6275	4.1615
1 year	7.9505	7.9625	4.2340
Coins, whol $1,000 face val	a8,610	8,655	6,710

a-Asked. b-Bid. bp-Country elevator bids to producers. h-Terminal elevator truck bids to producers. c-Corrected. d-Dealer market. e-Estimated. f-Carcass equiv. value. g-Main crop, ex-dock, warehouses, Eastern Seaboard, north of Hatteras. k-Dealer selling prices in lots of 40,000 pounds or more, f.o.b. buyer's works. n-Nominal. p-Producer price. r-Rail bids. s-Thread count 78x76. t-Thread count 78x54. x-Less than truckloads. y-Maine origin; varies seasonally. z-Not quoted.

FIGURE 8–4

Cash Prices of Commodities and Precious Metals

SOURCE: The Wall Street Journal, March 14, 1983, p. 46.

Thus, there was a $.50 per ounce premium for the smaller bar. The price of silver will also vary from market to market and from dealer to dealer.

There is a futures market in silver, with prices quoted in cents per 5,000 Troy ounces. Figure 8–5 provides a list of future contract prices for various commodities, including silver contract prices. A *futures contract* is a commitment to buy or sell a commodity at some future specified time and place. The price is established when the contract is made in the open market on a futures exchange. "Only a small percentage

Futures Prices

Friday, March 11, 1983

Open Interest Reflects Previous Trading Day.

—METALS & PETROLEUM—

COPPER (CMX)—25,000 lbs.; cents per lb.

Mar83	72.20	72.70	72.70	72.60	− .85	107.00	59.35	957
Apr	....	....	....	72.80	− .95	79.50	73.00	18
May	73.20	73.70	72.80	73.55	− .95	108.30	60.80	47,329
July	74.90	75.25	74.40	75.00	− 1.00	103.00	62.60	30,658
Sept	76.10	76.45	75.75	76.30	− 1.00	93.60	64.15	11,311
Dec	77.60	78.20	77.30	77.90	− .95	93.00	66.30	10,169
Jan84	78.60	78.60	78.60	78.45	− .95	89.50	66.90	833
Mar	79.20	79.75	79.00	79.50	− .95	90.40	68.00	6,350
May	80.20	80.50	80.10	80.50	− .95	88.40	69.00	2,406
July	81.20	81.50	81.20	81.50	− .95	89.20	70.70	2,095
Sept	82.10	83.00	82.00	82.50	− .95	90.40	73.20	2,725
Dec	83.70	84.50	83.70	84.00	− .95	92.00	82.10	605
Jan85	85.00	85.00	84.40	84.50	− .95	90.50	83.20	58

Est vol 12,000; vol Thu 10,582; open int 115,514, +262.

GOLD (CMX)—100 troy oz.; $ per troy oz.

Mar	421.00	429.00	420.50	427.50	− 3.50	515.50	396.00	564
Apr	424.00	430.00	420.50	429.30	− 3.70	604.00	327.00	42,610
May	429.50	430.50	429.50	432.30	− 3.70	436.00	411.00	8
June	428.50	436.00	426.00	435.30	− 3.80	596.00	334.00	23,986
Aug	434.00	443.00	434.00	441.70	− 3.90	545.40	348.00	7,202
Oct	442.50	444.00	441.50	448.40	− 4.00	548.50	362.00	7,448
Dec	451.20	457.00	447.00	455.20	− 4.10	554.70	370.00	10,498
Feb84	457.00	462.00	454.00	462.20	− 4.20	562.50	389.00	5,373
Apr	465.00	465.00	462.00	469.40	− 4.30	572.00	385.50	3,582
June	480.00	480.00	480.00	476.80	− 4.40	580.00	409.00	3,549
Aug	479.00	479.00	479.00	484.40	− 4.50	588.00	469.00	4,723
Oct	486.00	486.00	486.00	492.30	− 4.60	597.00	472.00	2,802
Dec	498.50	498.50	496.00	500.40	− 4.70	608.00	481.00	2,214

Est vol 38,000; vol Thu 47,032; open int 114,559, −2,148.

GOLD (IMM)—100 troy oz.; $ per troy oz.

Mar83	419.00	428.00	419.00	427.50	− 2.80	887.20	323.00	102
June	430.00	436.00	426.00	435.40	− 3.40	674.50	336.00	4,421
Sept	437.90	445.50	435.90	445.00	− 3.70	626.20	350.00	432
Dec	....	....	....	455.00	− 4.00	554.00	426.50	203
Mar84	....	....	....	465.40	− 4.30	567.80	438.60	16
June	....	....	....	476.20	− 4.60	574.60	528.70	11

Est vol 3,550; vol Thu 2,957; open int 5,185, −230.

PLATINUM (NYM)—50 troy oz.; $ per troy oz.

Mar	408.20	408.20	408.20	410.30	−11.70	497.00	362.00	35
Apr	414.50	415.00	409.50	412.30	−11.70	502.00	263.00	10,362
July	420.00	421.00	416.00	418.90	−11.90	505.00	276.50	4,921
Oct	426.00	428.00	424.00	426.40	−11.70	511.00	298.50	2,295
Jan84	436.00	436.00	433.50	433.90	−11.50	518.60	325.00	331
Apr	440.00	445.00	440.00	441.40	−11.30	528.50	381.00	452

Est vol 4,235; vol Thu 5,002; open int 18,396, +148.

PALLADIUM (NYM) 100 troy oz.; $ per troy oz.

Mar	95.50	97.50	95.50	97.10	− 3.50	136.00	50.50	144
Apr	....	....	....	97.35	− 3.50	134.60	110.00	9
May	....	....	....	97.35	− 3.50	100.00	100.00	13
June	99.50	100.00	97.00	99.10	− 3.50	137.75	54.00	4,000
Sept	99.00	100.00	98.50	100.60	− 3.50	137.00	58.00	990
Dec	101.50	101.50	101.00	102.15	− 3.50	138.00	66.00	466
Mar84	102.00	104.00	102.00	102.90	− 3.50	142.00	86.00	264
June	104.10	104.10	104.10	103.65	− 3.50	110.00	104.10	1

Est vol 564; vol Thu 382; open int 5,877, −43.

SILVER (CMX)—5,000 troy oz.; cents per troy oz.

Mar	1073.0	1095.0	1068.0	1091.5	− 21.5	1493.0	553.0	1,610
Apr	1070.0	1090.0	1070.0	1095.0	− 22.0	1503.0	1005.0	62
May	1090.0	1108.0	1078.0	1104.0	− 22.0	1518.0	1016.0	22,123
July	1095.0	1124.0	1095.0	1121.7	− 22.6	1543.0	550.0	8,563
Sept	1112.5	1137.0	1112.5	1139.4	− 23.1	1580.0	563.0	5,188
Dec	1150.0	1170.0	1141.0	1165.8	− 23.7	1607.0	587.0	3,220
Jan84	....	....	....	1174.5	− 23.7	1605.0	615.0	127
Mar	1170.0	1185.0	1170.0	1192.0	− 23.7	1640.0	628.0	2,124
May	1215.0	1215.0	1193.0	1209.5	− 23.7	1675.0	700.0	920
July	....	....	....	1227.0	− 23.7	1680.0	962.0	712
Sept	1235.0	1235.0	1235.0	1244.5	− 23.7	1715.0	1075.0	702
Dec	1247.0	1260.0	1247.0	1270.5	− 23.7	1755.0	1170.0	137
Jan85	....	....	....	1279.2	− 23.7	1314.5	1285.0	5

Est vol 23,000; vol Thur 21,203; open int 45,493, −1,495.

SILVER (CBT)—1,000 troy oz.; cents per troy oz.

Mar	1080.0	1095.0	1070.0	1088.0	− 24.0	1498.0	995.0	267
Apr	1067.5	1098.0	1067.5	1093.0	− 24.5	1509.0	545.0	8,657
May	1080.0	1108.0	1080.0	1102.0	− 24.0	1405.0	1016.0	122
June	1090.0	1115.0	1087.0	1110.5	− 24.5	1536.0	560.0	12,141
Aug	1105.0	1130.0	1105.0	1128.0	− 24.5	1560.0	575.0	2,320
Oct	1121.0	1145.5	1121.0	1145.5	− 24.5	1586.0	590.0	624
Dec	1140.0	1165.0	1137.5	1163.0	− 24.5	1620.0	625.0	5,012
Feb84	1175.0	1180.5	1160.0	1180.5	− 24.5	1645.0	639.5	321
Apr	1180.0	1205.0	1172.5	1198.0	− 24.5	1675.0	654.0	2,428
June	1200.0	1215.5	1200.0	1215.5	− 24.5	1700.0	1120.0	211

Est vol 7,389; vol Thur 9,032; open int 32,103, −492.

CBT—Chicago Board of Trade; CME—Chicago Mercantile Exchange; CMX—Commodity Exchange, New York; CSCE—Coffee, Sugar & Cocoa Exchange, New York; CTN—New York Cotton Exchange; IMM—International Monetary Market at CME, Chicago; KC—Kansas City Board of Trade; MPLS—Minneapolis Grain Exchange; NOCE—New Orleans Commodity Exchange; NYFE—New York Futures Exchange, unit of New York Stock Exchange. NYM—New York Mercantile Exchange; WPG—Winnipeg Commodity Exchange.

FIGURE 8–5

Futures Prices of Selected Commodities and Precious Metals

SOURCE: The Wall Street Journal, March 14, 1983, p. 46.

of futures trading actually leads to a delivery of a commodity, for a contract may change hands or be liquidated before the delivery date. Participants comprise commercial hedgers who use futures to minimize price risks inherent in their marketing operations, and speculators who, employing venture capital, seek profits through price changes."[1] Speculators and marketing operators purchase contracts on margin, that is, by making a partial payment, the margin, and borrowing the difference.

Figure 8–5 shows the December price of silver as 1,165.8 cents per Troy ounce, based upon a 5,000-ounce contract. The total cost of the contract would be $58,290 on the Commodity Exchange in New York (CMX). The purchaser, in one situation, expects that the cash price in December will be more than $11.66 per ounce. If he or she is correct, the price of the futures contract will rise, and the purchaser can sell the contract. If the price does not rise, the purchaser loses and allows the contract to expire.

Investors can buy silver contracts with the idea of holding the silver, expecting the price to rise. If delivery is taken, the silver must be stored, insured, and protected, which increases the cost. In an inflationary environment, silver should increase in price. Ownership of silver will therefore be an inflation hedge and compensate for possible losses in common stock investments.

Coin and Stamp Collecting

Coin collecting can be an interesting, educational, and profitable way for an investor to invest. A dean of a leading U.S. school of business once said that he knew of no other hobby where he could always keep the money he spent and had the prospect of beating inflation. It is impossible to indicate how all coins have changed in price. Popular denominations of coins have only monetary value. Old coins, like the Eisenhower dollar, have a high silver content and are valuable as silver and as a collector's item. Early in 1980, silver dimes sold for over $1.50 each, quarters for $3.75, half-dollars for $7.50, and Kennedy half-dollars (1965–69) for $2.50 each. Individual collector's items sell for higher prices. A 1909 SVDB penny sold for $45 in 1969 and $130 in 1978. A 1955 Double Die penny sold for $100 in 1969 and $220 in 1978. Certainly, these would have been profitable investments.

Stamps have had a similar increase in value. A 1925 Norse American sold for $2.25 in 1969 and $4.25 in 1968. Even when a dollar was a dollar in 1969, most investors could have afforded to pay $2.25 for a stamp. A higher-priced stamp is the 1892 $5 Black Columbian. It sold for $235 in 1969 and $650 in 1978. This stamp is an example of a good investment. However, an investor would be required to study the subject area carefully before making a commitment, and seeking professional advice would be wise. It would be smart to limit the amount of money invested in this area, since stamps and coins tend to be risky investments.

Diamonds—An Investor's Best Friend?

Most people like diamonds. They're beautiful, and they have been a good hedge against inflation in the past until 1982 when prices declined sharply. Diamonds

[1] *The New York Times*, Tuesday, August 25, 1981, under "Futures Prices."

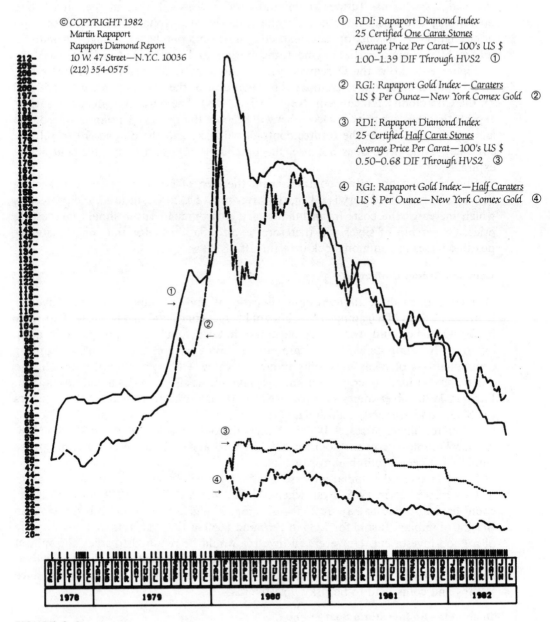

Rapaport Diamond Report
Polished Diamond Prices—Cash New York

© COPYRIGHT 1982
Martin Rapaport
Rapaport Diamond Report
10 W. 47 Street—N.Y.C. 10036
(212) 354-0575

① RDI: Rapaport Diamond Index
25 Certified One Carat Stones
Average Price Per Carat—100's US $
1.00–1.39 DIF Through HVS2 ①

② RGI: Rapaport Gold Index—Caraters
US $ Per Ounce—New York Comex Gold ②

③ RDI: Rapaport Diamond Index
25 Certified Half Carat Stones
Average Price Per Carat—100's US $
0.50–0.68 DIF Through HVS2 ③

④ RGI: Rapaport Gold Index—Half Caraters
US $ Per Ounce—New York Comex Gold ④

FIGURE 8–6

Rapaport Diamond Corporation (Polished Diamond Prices-Cash New York)

SOURCE: © Copyright 1982, Martin Rapaport, Rapaport Diamond Corporation, 10 W. 47 Street, N.Y.C. 10036.

purchased through a retail jeweler might not have the best investment potential, since the markup on diamonds is high and exceeds 100 percent. Yet a top-quality gem will increase in value over a ten-year period. If an investor wishes to invest in diamonds, the best way would be to buy diamonds at wholesale. This can be done in the gem markets of New York, London, and Amsterdam. The only problem with diamonds is that the unit of investment is high. A 1/2-carat diamond might range in price from $500 to $2,000, and a 1-carat might range from $2,500 to $7,500, depending on quality. Figure 8–6 shows a price history of diamonds. The carat, divided into points, 100 points to the carat, is the unit of measure. The bigger the stone, the more valuable per carat. As a general rule, the best stones have been the most profitable investment over time. Since investors might only buy one diamond in a lifetime, perhaps the best advice for the individual is to buy the biggest, highest-quality stone that can be found at the lowest possible price, and within the individual's budget. Buying a diamond engagement ring wholesale would also be a good idea. In the long run, this type of ring will bring more statisfaction and monetary value. The most valuable stones are clear and flawless.

Usually, finished gemstones of one carat or larger are sought for investment purposes. The value of the stone is based on color and flaw characteristics. F is a flawless stone and D is colorless. A one carat D Flawless sold for $6,700 in 1976 and $63,000 in March 1980. Since then prices have fallen 30 to 40 percent.

Paintings and Antiques

Almost anything that is scarce, attractive, and useful in the art and antique world has increased in value. Two examples will suffice to indicate the monetary gain in these assets. Andrew Wyeth is a successful, living artist. One of his paintings sold for $5,500 in 1969; the same painting sold for $16,000 in 1978. The amount of the investment is high, but the gains can be substantial.

Antiques offer investors an almost boundless way to invest, but they require a great deal of study. Money can even be made in utilitarian objects that can be used daily. An antique O.G. clock, for example, could have been purchased for $20 in 1955. Today, prices range from $250 to $350. The clocks keep good time, must be wound every eight days, and are attractive. It isn't a bad way for an investor to keep track of time. Antiques seem to be an investment that appeals to most of us.

THE SOTHEBY INDEX.   The Sotheby Index was created by *Barron's* in November 1981 to track the prices of art and antiques. Figure 8–7 indicates how prices have behaved. An investor who purchased the Sotheby Index would have earned an average return of 17.7 percent with a standard deviation of 12.5 percent for the period 1976 through 1981. This compares favorably with the stock market and other real assets. A complete list of the content of the Sotheby Index can be found in the February 15, 1982 issue of *Barron's*.

Category	Weights	Mar. 15 1983	Feb. 9 1982	Sept. 1981	Sept. 1980	Sept. 1979	Sept. 1978	Sept. 1977	Sept. 1976
Old Master Paintings	17	210	204	199	255	224	173	131	105
19 Century European Paintings	12	185	179	176	225	215	160	118	99
Impressionist & Post-Impressionist Paintings	18	267	248	239	206	175	133	114	107
Modern Paintings (1900–1950)	10	245	249	232	204	178	132	108	105
American Paintings (1800–pre-WW II)	3	450	450	424	350	315	255	171	129
Continental Ceramics	3	266	293	299	336	261	213	154	121
Chinese Ceramics	10	440	445	459	462	353	241	181	159
English Silver	5	209	175	160	205	165	124	95	89
Continental Silver	5	139	140	143	179	146	113	92	89
American Furniture	3	239	209	209	172	150	134	120	109
French & Continental Furniture	7	239	228	218	232	197	148	121	104
English Furniture	7	267	279	270	256	244	195	156	125
Weighted Aggregate		**256**	**250**	**244**	**253**	**217**	**164**	**128**	**111**

Sept. 1975 = 100.

FIGURE 8–7

The Sotheby Index

© 1982 Sotheby Parke Bernet Inc.

SOURCE: Barron's, February 15, 1982, p. 62, and March 21, 1983, p. 98.

TABLE 8–7

Rate of Return and Risk of Selected Real Assets, 1969–1978*

	Return† %	Risk‡ %
Gold	21	28
VDB penny	13	11
Silver	13	30
$5 Black Columbian stamp	12	9
Paintings	10	14
Diamonds	10	14
Double Die penny	9	5
Norse American stamp	7	7
Standard & Poor's	6	14

*Based on a graduate study of Barton Rapkin, George Washington University, June 5, 1979.

†Rounded to significant whole number. The return is the ten-year annual average rate of return.

‡This is the variation of the annual return around the average and is the standard deviation.

THE INVESTMENT ALTERNATIVES

Just what can an investor expect to earn from investments in real assets such as coins, stamps, and precious metals? That is, what rate of return and risk would an investor accept in buying such assets? In an attempt to estimate historic rates of return and risk, a study was undertaken to provide a partial answer to the question. Table 8–7 provides estimated rates of return for selected real assets from 1969 through 1978.

Table 8–7 presents the ten-year average rate of return and risk, which is the variability of the ten-year rate of return. During the period, gold, the VDB penny, silver, the paintings, and diamonds were more profitable than the stock market, but they all had the same amount of risk or greater risk. The $5 Black Columbian, the Double Die Penny, and the Norse stamp were more profitable than the Standard & Poor's Index, and less risky.

Gold and diamonds were found to have a small negative correlation to the Standard & Poor's 500 Index, which means that some gold and diamonds would balance the rate of return from common stock and tend to reduce risk. In other words, it is a good idea to diversify and invest in a combination of real assets and common stock.

SUMMARY

Real estate as an investment has been profitable over the past 15 years and is an excellent hedge against inflation. Prices have risen between 10 and 15 percent on average. Prices, however, are expected to increase less rapidly in the future. Depreciation, the write-off of taxes and interest expense, and rising rentals have provided investors with an attractive after-tax rate of return. Investors seeking a real estate investment should focus on location and value. Careful estimates of rental income and expense should be made, along with an estimate of future price for each property considered. An investor should strive for a 10 to 15 percent after-tax rate of return, which is possible under the 1981 tax laws. The risks of investment, lack of cash income from rents because of recession, or simply inaccurate estimates and lack of pure appreciation are real.

An investor may borrow money against the increase in price of real estate, and this money can be used to purchase additional real estate. The danger in the pyramid strategy is that the investor might become overextended. Financial institutions and corporations can benefit from investment in residential, commercial, or industrial real estate as well as individuals.

Land, at the right price and in the right location, might be an attractive investment. Investors might also buy REITs and participate in the expected growth of real estate values. Some investors are able to provide mortgage money at high rates on commercial properties and maintain a share in the future expected price increases. Location is just as important here as it is in buying residential properties.

The purchase of precious metals, art objects, and antiques has proved to be a way in which investors can protect themselves from inflation. Generally speaking, such assets have done better than the securities market in some recent years. However, the purchase of gold and silver in 1980 proved to be unprofitable. If an investor had purchased gold and silver in 1980, at the peak, and held it until mid-1983, substantial losses would have been incurred.

The problem with some precious metals is price volatility and cost of safekeeping, if the asset is actually purchased. Also, the assets produce no income. This prohibits use by some institutions. The major advantage of purchasing precious metals is their potential for beating inflation. Thus, in an inflationary environment, such assets are recommended. Yet if the investor anticipates a declining price level, such assets should be avoided. That is why in 1982–83 investment sentiment shifted to bonds and common stock.

Another advantage is that the rate of return on precious metals tends to move against the movement of the rate of return on common stock. As the returns on stocks increase, there is a tendency for returns on precious metals to decrease, and vice versa. Therefore, investors might reduce risk by diversifying into precious metals or works of art after careful investigation.

SUMMARY OF PRINCIPLES

1. Physical assets or real assets tend to provide a better hedge against inflation than financial assets.
2. Some diversification among real assets seems appropriate.
3. Except for a house, real assets tend to be risky because of their price volatility.
4. For most investors, except for real estate, the amount of real assets owned for investment purposes will be relatively small.

REVIEW QUESTIONS

1. What has been the direction of housing prices for the past ten years?
2. Has real estate been a good investment? Comment.
3. Explain the analytical process of selecting real estate for investment.
4. How would an investor estimate the rate of return on a real estate investment?
5. Explain how an investor can expand an investment in real estate after the first property is purchased.
6. What are the risks involved with real estate investment?
7. What are the advantages and disadvantages of farm or land investment?
8. What are the advantages and disadvantages of Real Estate Investment Trusts (REITs) for investment?
9. What are the advantages and disadvantages of gold and silver as an investment?
10. Were stamps a good investment between 1969 and 1978? Comment.
11. Have diamonds been a good investment and a hedge against inflation?
12. Have paintings been a good investment?
13. What are the advantages and disadvantages of antiques as an investment?

THE INVESTMENT ALTERNATIVES

14. What seems to be the most profitable and least risky real asset in which to invest?

15. Will real assets always be an inflation hedge? Comment.

PROBLEMS

1. The real estate investment shown in Table 8–4 assumed that the property increases in price to $100,454. Let's change that assumption and assume that the price increased 5 percent per year for the five-year period. Also assume the mortgage rate was 18 percent. What would happen to the investor's rate of return? Would it still be an attractive investment?

2. Figure 8–2 provides the monthly average spot gold prices for the period 1975 to 1980. From the chart, find the price of gold in May of each year from 1975 to 1980. The price of gold was near $400 in May of 1981. What was the annual rate of return each year for the period? What was the average rate of return? What was the standard deviation of the rate of return? Comment on the investment attractiveness of gold.

3. Figure 8- 2 provides the monthly average prices for silver. From the chart, find the price for silver each May and calculate the annual rate of return earned. The price in May of 1981 was approximately $9 per ounce. What was the average annual rate of return for the period 1975 through 1981? What was the standard deviation of the rate of return? Comment on the investment attractiveness of silver.

4. Clay and Marsha want to buy a house as an investment. They can buy a $180,000 house net of real estate fees by assuming the existing 14 3/8 percent mortgage and paying $65,000 to the owners. The PIT amounts to $1,550, with virtually all of it tax deductible for the next five years. They can rent the house for $1,100 per month. They are in the 50 percent marginal tax bracket. They think the price of the house will increase 5 percent a year for the next five years. Assuming that they sell the house in five years at the inflation-increased price less real estate commissions, what rate of return will they earn on their $65,000 investment? Should they invest in the house assuming the tax breaks under ERTA 1981?

5. Analyze the price changes of gold and silver in Figure 8–3. Which appears to be the more risky asset? Why?

6. Analyze the price changes of diamonds in Figure 8–6. What has been the average price increase? What is the standard deviation of past prices? Have diamonds been a profitable investment? Have they been risky?

7. Assume an investor could have bought the assets listed in the Sotheby Index in Figure 8–7. What rate of return would the investor have earned in each year starting in the base year 1975? Assume that 1982 was a full year. What was the average rate of return for the period? Would it have been a good investment? Comment.

CASE

Mike and Betsy were sent a copy of *Gold Investment Handbook*, a guide for institutional portfolio managers. In it they found the table below, which ranked gold as the most profitable investment for the ten-year period through May 1980. They own their own home, worth $150,000, with a $100,000 15 percent mortgage. They have $60,000 invested in a retirement plan, $15,000 in Treasury bills yielding 13 percent, and a checking account with $1,000. Betsy owns gold jewelry worth $5,000 and a diamond wedding ring worth $5,000. It is the end of 1981, and they would like your advice about how they are doing. They also would like some direction on what to do with the money invested in Treasury bills. What advice would you give them?

Compound Annual Rate of Return (Percent) Periods Ending May 1980

	10 Years	Rank	5 Years	Rank	1 Year	Rank
Gold	31.6%	1	28.4%	3	104.0%	1
Oil (Saudi Arabian Light)	31.6	2	17.7	7	92.4	2
Silver	23.7	3	27.3	4	76.8	3
U.S. stamps	21.8	4	31.0	2	43.2	4
Chinese ceramics	18.8	5	38.7	1	13.1	11
Rare books	16.1	6	12.7	10	14.0	10
U.S. coins	16.0	7	21.9	5	25.3	5
Diamonds	15.1	8	18.3	6	25.0	6
Old Masters	13.4	9	15.2	8	17.4	7
U.S. farmland	12.6	10	13.4	9	14.3	9
Housing	10.2	11	11.6	11	10.4	13
Consumer Price Index	7.7	12	8.9	12	14.5	8
Foreign Exchange (index of several currencies)	7.5	13	8.4	13	4.5	14
Stocks (S & P 500)	6.8	14	6.4	14	12.5	12
Bonds (Salomon Brothers Index)	6.4	15	5.8	15	(3.1)	15

SOURCE: *Gold Investment Handbook—A Guide for Institutional Portfolio Managers* (New York: International Gold Corporation Limited).

SELECTED READINGS

CASE, FRED E. *The Investment Guide to Home and Land Purchase.* Englewood Cliffs, N.J.: Prentice-Hall, 1978.

CAVELTI, PETER C. *How to Invest in Gold.* Chicago: Follett Publishing, 1979.

CREEDY, JUDITH, and NORBERT F. WALL. *Real Estate Investment by Objectives.* New York: McGraw-Hill, 1979.

ENGLISH, WESLEY JOHN, and GREY EMERSON CARDIFF. *The Coming Real Estate Crash.* New Rochelle, N.Y.: Arlington House, 1979.

GREENEBAUM, MARY. "A Golden Opportunity to Pass Up." *Fortune,* September 1981.

INTERNATIONAL GOLD CORPORATION, LTD. *Gold Investment Handbook—A Guide for Institutional Portfolio Managers.* New York.

KIMMEL, KENNETH M. *Real Estate Investment.* New York: Cornerstone Library, 1980.

PRICE, IRVING. *How to Get Top Dollar for Your Home in Good Times or Bad.* Time Books: New York, 1980.

REGAN, PATRICK J. "The Shattering of the Diamond Market." *Financial Analysts Journal,* July–August 1981.

THE INVESTMENT ALTERNATIVES

CHAPTER 9

SECURITIES MARKETS, BROKERS, AND DEALERS

Securities are bought and sold in the marketplace just like any other product or service. Autos are sold in dealer showrooms, insurance is sold in the agent's office or customer's home, and real estate is sold in the client's home or in the agent's office. Individual investors usually call upon brokers and dealers to buy and sell their shares. Ordinarily a telephone call is made to the office of a brokerage firm to place the order, and a customer representative employed by the firm makes certain the order is executed. A commission or brokerage fee is charged for the service. The order is executed in that segment of the marketplace appropriate for the type of asset traded.

The market is divided into the primary, secondary, and third and fourth markets. The primary market is the place where new offerings of bonds and stocks originate and in reality is a part of the over-the-counter market. Once the shares of stock or bonds are sold by members of the investment banking industry, they are traded on a registered exchange or in the over-the-counter market. Financial institutions will trade securities in the third and fourth markets. In fact, they are the third and fourth market participants.

In this chapter we will examine the securities market, identify the participants in the process, and look at the goal of a national market system.

THE MARKET CONCEPT

In theory, our economy thrives on the freely competitive marketplace to establish prices on the basis of supply and demand. The price mechanism in the market allocates resources. This is also true of securities markets. Securities markets are considered to be competitive and efficient even though there is government regulation by the Securities and Exchange Commission (SEC) and self-regulation by the National Association of Securities Dealers (NASD), and the Chartered Financial Analysts program (CFA). As a reminder, a *competitive* market is one in which (1) there are a large number of buyers and sellers; (2) no single buyer or seller can control the price; (3) buyers and sellers have complete knowledge and information about each security traded; (4) the product is relatively homogeneous; and (5) the price is established freely within the market structure. A moment's reflection will suggest that securities markets are competitive and becoming more competitive. The reasons for this observation are the changes that have taken place in the past, including the establishment of competitive brokerage fees (May 1, 1975), the automation of over-the-counter trading (NASDAQ), and the automation of trading on the New York Stock Exchange and American Stock Exchange with the regional exchanges. The direction of change has been toward a national market system.

THE SECURITIES MARKETS

What are the securities markets, and where are they located? Most people would agree that New York is the financial center of the United States and perhaps of the world. They would say that the securities market is the New York Stock Exchange, located on Wall Street. Others might include the American Stock Exchange as part of the securities market, and still others would say that the Midwest Exchange in Chicago or the exchange in Los Angeles or Philadelphia represents the securities market.

Actually, a securities market is *any place* where buyers and sellers come together to trade in securities. A person who buys U.S. Treasury bonds from or through a commercial bank is part of the securities market. Residents of a village who buy bonds issued to build a new high school are part of the securities market, even though the bonds are not traded on an exchange and negotiations are conducted in the village offices and in the offices of the municipal bond dealer. A man purchasing the shares of a company traded on a local exchange is part of the securities market. And, of course, the woman who buys Procter & Gamble stock through a brokerage office doing business on a national exchange or from the company directly is part of the securities market. Even the casual sale of securities by one person to another without the aid of a broker is part of the securities market. These examples demonstrate the breadth of the market. It is not confined to Wall Street, even though that is its center. Its location is any Main Street in any community in the United States.

The securities markets are divided into four major classifications: (1) the *primary market*, which includes sales of securities to investors by investment bankers who raise capital for business and government; (2) the *secondary market*, which includes the trading of existing shares in the organized or over-the-counter market; (3) the *third market*, which represents trading in listed securities among institutional investors off the exchange; and (4) the *fourth market*, which represents large block sales among institutional investors linked by computer terminals. Let's look at each classification.

Primary Markets

The primary market for securities results from the sale of securities by public or private corporations and governments directly to individual and institutional investors. Figure 9–1 shows graphically how the market operates. Securities sold by businesses and governments (the capital raisers) to investors with the help of investment bankers are a part of the primary market.

Investment bankers, a group of firms whose members help companies raise capital, form an underwriting (risk-taking) syndicate (group) to guarantee the sale of the shares.

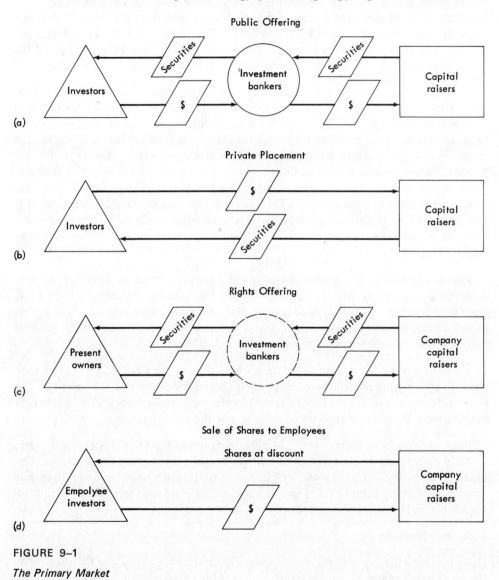

FIGURE 9–1

The Primary Market

The members of the syndicate are compensated for the function of selling, risk-taking, and management. If an investment banker sold the shares at a price of $20 a share, perhaps $1 would represent the underwriting commission or fee. Approximately $.50 would go to the salesperson, $.40 would be paid for the risk of guaranteeing a price of $19 to the company, and $.10 would be paid to the managing underwriter who put the syndicate together. This process is part of the new issues market or underwriting. The new issues market was very active early in 1983.

Federal, state, and local and foreign governments who sell bonds to the public are a part of the primary market for securities. New York bond houses such as Salomon Brothers, First Boston, and Kidder Peabody form syndicates to underwrite the sale of government bonds to institutional investors. They make what are known as competitive bids to buy the bonds for resale to investors. These bonds later trade on the over-the-counter market, which is part of the secondary market.

PUBLIC OFFERING OR NEW ISSUES.   A company that raises capital by selling common stock to the public is a part of the primary market. When Gentech (a human engineering firm) sold its shares to the public with the aid of several investment bankers, this was an example of trading in the primary market. In this case, the capital raiser was Gentech, which was selling common stock to provide capital to develop its sophisticated genetic products. The investors were people with money to put at risk to buy the shares. The investment bankers were a group of brokerage firms that agreed to sell the shares to the public for a fee known as the underwriting commission. It is also known as the underwriting spread, which is the difference between what the investor pays the investment banker and what the investment banker pays the company issuing the security.

PRIVATE PLACEMENT.   A private placement happens when a company or government raises capital by selling securities to one institutional investor such as a life insurance company. In the typical private placement, the insurance company agrees to buy an entire bond issue of a company. The terms of the agreement are negotiated between issuer and lender (seller and buyer).

RIGHTS OFFERING.   A rights offering is where the company sells shares of common stock to the existing owners based upon their proportional share of the business. The rights offering was discussed earlier in the chapter on common stock. An underwriter —investment banker—is sometimes used to sell the unsold shares.

SALE OF SHARES TO EMPLOYEES.   Many companies in the United States sell shares to their employees. These sales are a part of the primary market for securities. The amount of equity capital raised by corporations through sales to executives and employees is an important part of the primary market. And such sales are an important source of funds for business corporations.

Secondary Markets

Once businesses, governments, and agencies issue securities, they are then traded in the secondary market by brokers and dealers. Many businesses are listed on a securities exchange where the shares are traded. In order to trade on an exchange, the company must meet the listing requirements established by the exchange. The largest and most important stock exchange is the national stock exchange—the New York Stock Exchange. The second national stock exchange is the American Stock Exchange, which deals in smaller companies than the New York Stock Exchange.

There are several regional registered exchanges that trade listed shares in local or regional companies. Trading on the regional exchange is reported under Amex-Composite Transactions, which include trading on the American, Midwest, Pacific, Philadelphia, Boston, and Cincinnati exchanges, as reported by the National Association of Security Dealers.

Shares of foreign corporations are traded on foreign stock exchanges and reported daily in *The Wall Street Journal*. Figure 9–2 provides a list of foreign market transactions for selected issues on foreign exchanges. The Toronto exchange is reported separately in *The Wall Street Journal*.

The over-the-counter market represents the other part of the secondary market. In dollar volume, it is more important than the registered exchanges. Any trading of existing shares of companies and government securities not on an exchange is done in this market.

Functions of Stock Exchanges

The functions of national exchanges have grown over the years; they now include far more than furnishing an area for trading and providing information about price and sales. National exchanges also assure the investor of basic financial information and protection. For example, they require a company to provide its shareholders with a statement of earnings and a balance sheet that summarizes assets and liabilities. The fact that national exchanges must register with the Securities and Exchange Commission (SEC), under the Securities Exchange Act of 1934, affords added protection for stockholders; and this protection has been improved even further as a result of the Special Study of 1963 and the Martin Report of 1971, to be discussed later.

Several other functions performed by exchanges are important. Let us examine them.

CONTINUOUS MARKET.   The exchange provides a continuous market for individual securities issues. This is perhaps its most important function. A continuous market is predicated on a large volume of sales and a narrow price range between the bid and the asked price, and between the previous sale and the sale taking place at the moment. It also depends on rapid execution of orders. These conditions are fostered by the trading rules of the exchange. There are also a sufficient number of buyers and sellers of shares of stock of each company traded, and a sufficient number of brokers and other members of the exchange transacting orders, to assure a broad and active market.

FAIR PRICE AND COLLATERAL VALUE.   The price of a share of stock is established in an auction market. It is not set by the traders on the floor of the exchange, or by negotiation off the floor. It is established by a bidding process not only among the traders on the floor of the exchange, but through computers which link the exchanges

Foreign Markets
Closing Prices of Selected Issues

Friday, March 11, 1983

LONDON (in pence)

	Close	Prev. Close
Allied Lyons	140	142
Babcock	137	140
Barclays Bk	503	506
B A T Indust	655	660
Bass Ltd	317	321
BOC Group	208	214
British GE	205	210
Cadbury Sch	122	121
Charter Con	228	233
Coats Patons	68	69
Consol Gold	487	499
Dalgety	338	338
Distillers Co	232	233
EagleStarHd	368	372
Glaxo	695	700
Grand Metro	349	353
Guest Keen	146	149
HansonTrust	197	200
ICL Plc	82	82
Johnson Mat	326	330
Legal Gen	406	412
Lonhro	83	85
Lucas Indust	169	163
MIM Hold	242	237
Nat'l WestBk	593	591
Nrthrn Food	198	200
Racal Elect	477	467
Reed Int'l	300	304
Rio Tinto	519	524
Tate&Lyle	296	294
Thorn EMI	493	500
Thos Tilling	147	145
Trust House	168	168
T I Group	168	170
Ultramar	467	472
Utd Biscuit	143	143
Vickers	118	117

South African Mines (in U.S. currency)

	Close	Prev. Close
Bracken	3.80	4.05
DeelKrael	4.95	5.15
Doornfontein	25.75	26.75
DurbanDeep	35.00	37.00
East Rand	d20.25	22.25
Elandsrand	11.875	12.125
Elsburg	4.15	4.55
Ergo	8.13	8.50
General Mng	25.00	25.50
Grootvlei	14.625	15.625
Harmony	19.25	21.25
Hartebeest	74.50	78.50
Johannesb C	112.00	112.00
Kinross	21.00	22.50
Leslie	4.50	4.70
Libanon	31.50	34.00
Loraine	7.00	7.15
Randfontein	127.50	133.50
Rustnbg Plat	6.8125	6.8125
Southvaal	60.00	62.00
Stilfontein	16.50	17.75
Unisel	14.50	15.25
West Areas	5.95	6.45
Winkelhaak	38.25	40.25

d-Old shares. z-Not quoted.

FRANKFURT (in marks)

	Close	Prev. Close
AEG-Tele	55.50	55.20
Allianz Vers	548.70	545
BASF	129.20	128.90
Bayer AG	128.70	128.70
BMW	288	290
Cont'l Gummi	78.80	78.50
Commerzbnk	147.70	147.80
Daimler-Benz	446.00	450.50
Degussa	253	257
Deutsche Bk	291.50	289.50
Dresdner Bk	161.80	161.90
Hoechst AG	134.50	134.50
Lufthansa	108	106.50
Schering AG	332	332
Siemens	299.70	299.80
Thyssen-Hut	77.30	76.30
Veba	129.50	128.00
Volkswagen	170	171.50

TOKYO (in yen)

	Sat. Close	Prev. Close
Ajinomoto	868	868
Asahi Chem	279	279
Bk of Tokyo	291	291
BridgestnTire	475	475
C. Itoh	307	306
Calpis Food	535	528
Daiwa House	535	535
Daiwa Secur	418	416
Eisai	1,290	1,280
Fuji Bank	500	500
Fujitsu	937	937
Isuzu Mot Ltd	344	345
Kajima Corp	325	324
Kansai Elec	1,010	1,010
Komatsu Ltd	484	484
MaruiDeptStr	886	895
MitsubishiEst	460	451
MitsubishiInd	216	216
Mitsui & Co	365	369
MitsuiRealE	770	769
Nikko Secur	403	403
NipponKogaku	718	722
NipponMusicI	652	656
NipponSteel	163	164
NomuraSecur	660	657
Ricoh	700	705
Sekisui House	700	696
SumitomoBk	500	500
SumitomoCh	158	164
SumitM&F	230	225
Taisei Const	227	228
Taisho M&F	235	233
Takeda Chem	857	857
Teijin	234	232
Tokyo Elec	1,120	1,120
Toshiba	320	318
Toto Ltd	490	496
Toyo Kogyo	391	393
YamaichiSec	390	390
Yasuda M&F	240	240

z-Not quoted.

PARIS (in French francs)

	Close	Prev. Close
AirLiq	455	460
Aquitaine	122.50	125.50
BSNGrD	1,503	1,510
CieFrPet	151.80	152.50
Club Med	560	541
Imetal	48.50	50.20
L'Oreal	1,292	1,302
Hachette	785	781
MachBull	44.80	44.40
Michelin	844	852
MoetHen	917	921
PeugtCtn	171	180.50

SWITZERLAND (in Swiss francs)
Zurich

	Close	Prev. Close
Brown Bov	1,110	1,100
Ciba-Geigy	1,755	1,755
Credit Suisse	1,955	1,950
Nestle	3,940	3,940
Sandoz	4,875	4,900
Sulzer	275	273
Swissair	795	796
Swiss Alum	618	629
Swiss Bancp	323	323
Union Bank	3,170	3,175

Basel

	Close	Prev. Close
vHoffmn-LaR	8,000	8,025
Pirelli Intl	251	251

v-1/10 share.

HONG KONG (in Hong Kong dollars)

	Close	Prev. Close
Cheung Kong	10.50	10.30
Hang Seng Bk	63.00	61.00
Hong Kong El	5.95	5.60
Hong Kong Lnd	4.50	4.42
HongkongShBk	9.20	9.20
Hutchsn Whmp	14.30	14.30
Jardine Mathsn	14.70	14.90
SunHungKaiP	6.85	7.00
Swire Pacific	12.00	12.50
Swire Prop	6.25	6.40
Wheelock Mard	3.80	3.80
World Intl	1.67	1.66

z-Not quoted.

SYDNEY (in Australian dollars)

	Close	Prev. Close
ANZ Bk	3.38	3.40
Coles GJ	2.40	2.40
CRA	4.45	4.37
CSR	2.68	2.57
Nicholas	1.90	1.90
RensnGoldFlds	3.80	3.80
Repco	.94	.95
Santos	4.50	4.40
SouthrnPacPet	.16	z
Westrn Mining	4.13	4.12
Woodside Pete	.69	.68

AMSTERDAM (in guilders)

	Close	Prev. Close
AKZO	51.60	52.90
Ahold	142	146.50
Algemene Bk	359.20	361.50
Amst-Rot Bk	52.50	53
Elsevier-NDU	242.50	248.50
Fokker	27.80	28.10
Heineken's	127.30	129.70
Holec	47.20	46
Hoogovens	23.50	23.80
Nation Neder	139.20	138.50
Robeco	266	267
Rolinco	249.30	250.80
Rorento	185	185
Royal Dutch	97.90	98.20
Wessanen	114.50	115

a-Ex-dividend.

BRUSSELS (in Belgian francs)

	Close	Prev. Close
ARBED	1,260	1,256
EBES	2,140	2,130
Gevaert	2,050	2,065
GB-Inno-Bm	2,825	2,800
GrpBrLambrt	1,750	1,750
Metal Hobokn	4,280	4,180
Petrofina	4,670	4,655
SocGenerale	1,500	1,484
Solvay	2,470	2,450

MILAN (in Lire)

	Close	Prev. Close
Ciga	4,645	4,661
Fiat	2,599	2,594
Generali	128,000	123,500
La Centr	2,588	2,599
La Rinas	357.25	357.25
Mont Ed	142	139
Olivetti	2,859	2,829
Pirelli	1,714	1,699
Snia Visc	1,018	981

z-Not quoted.

FIGURE 9–2

Foreign Market Transactions on Foreign Exchanges

SOURCE: *The Wall Street Journal*, March 14, 1983, p. 46.

together, and therefore the price at any one time tends to reflect a fair market appraisal of the stock. The price is established by supply and demand. A specific price may or may not be fair when long-range investment values are considered. All that we can expect from a market is a price established freely by competitive forces. The broad auction market tends to improve marketability, and this makes securities better collateral for loans.

AID IN FINANCING INDUSTRY. A continuous market for shares competitively priced provides a favorable climate for raising capital. Even if the securities are sold by investment bankers off the exchange, the securities traded on the exchange establish a price pattern that serves as a standard of value. Such a comparison should aid in corporate financing. Since there will still be a continuous market available after the securities have been sold, the new offering is more readily salable to investors.

THE NEW YORK STOCK EXCHANGE

Certainly the best-known, largest, and most important stock exchange in the United States is the New York Stock Exchange. It does the greatest volume of business of the organized exchanges, and its activities have a far-reaching impact on financial centers in all parts of the world. The New York Stock Exchange is both national and international in character and operation. The exchange itself neither buys, sells, owns, nor sets the prices of securities. All these are activities of members of the exchange, initiated by investors who can express their needs quickly and economically through the members, using the facilities provided by the New York Stock Exchange.

History

Securities were traded in Wall Street long before the first official document was signed by 24 brokers on May 17, 1792, establishing an exchange. The agreement, known as the Buttonwood Tree Agreement, clearly established a commission of one-quarter of 1 percent and obligated the brokers to buy and sell only from each other. Before the agreement, trading took place under a buttonwood tree at 68 Wall Street. Afterward, until 1817, the business of the exchange was conducted in an office in the Tontine Coffee House. In 1817, the name New York Stock and Exchange Board was adopted, and it moved to new quarters at 40 Wall Street. The name was changed in 1863 to the present one, and in 1903, the exchange moved to its present headquarters at Broad and Wall Streets.

The first stock tickers, introduced in 1867, were replaced in 1930 by a high-speed ticker service. In 1963, new equipment was installed that could handle 16 million shares a day. On April 10, 1968, the New York Stock Exchange for the first time recorded more than 20 million shares. The continuous market was developed in 1871, and in 1920 a stock-clearing corporation was established to facilitate the sale of stock on the exchange.

The Depository Trust Company was established in 1973. It succeeded the Central Certificate Service, which was fully activated in 1969; in 1970, the public ownership of member firms began and the Securities Investor Protection Act was signed. The

New York Stock Exchange was incorporated in 1971, and in the same year, negotiated commission rates were effective, Merrill Lynch was listed, and the Securities Industry Automation Corporation was authorized.

The NYSE reorganization, based on the Martin Report, was approved in 1972, and the Securities Industry Automation Corporation was established. The consolidated tape was begun in 1974. The fixed-commission system was abolished, and the full consolidated tape begun in 1975.[1]

The Designated Order Turnaround (DOT) system was begun in 1976.[2] Under this system, market orders of up to 299 shares are transmitted electronically from member firms' offices to the appropriate trading post on the floor of the New York Stock Exchange through the exchange's electronic message switch. When the order is received, it is presented to the trading crowd by the specialist and executed promptly.[3] Specialists began handling odd lots in 1976. Foreign broker-dealers were permitted to obtain membership in 1977, and the fully automated bond system was put into effect in 1977.

The Intermarket Trading System (ITS) was begun in 1978. The purpose of this system was to move toward a national market system called for by Congress that would eventually link all markets together. The New York, American, Boston, Midwest, Pacific, and Philadelphia exchanges are all linked electronically by the ITS. Video screens report the prices and volume of shares offered for sale and purchased. Trades are made through computer terminals.[4] Here is how it works:

> Assume that a floor broker on the New York Stock Exchange holds an order to buy 100 shares of AT&T stock for a customer at the prevailing market price. If, on checking the Composite Quotation display on the NYSE floor, he sees that a broker or market-maker on, say, the Pacific Stock Exchange—where AT&T stock is also traded—is offering it at 1/8-point less than any of his counterparts on the NYSE or elsewhere, the NYSE floor broker can try to get that better price for his customer.

> All he has to do is key into the system a commitment to buy 100 shares on the Pacific Exchange. Within seconds, that commitment is printed out on the West Coast and, if the quote has not changed during those few seconds, he should receive, within another few seconds, a print-out confirming that an execution has taken place on the Pacific Exchange —which means that his customer has, in fact, bought 100 shares of AT&T stock at that better price.[5]

The New York Futures Exchange started trading in 1981.[6]

Organization and Management

The New York Stock Exchange is an incorporated association of members, so its existence is not affected by the death of one of its members. The "seats" owned by members may be transferred subject to the approval of the board of directors. The

[1] *Fact Book 1981*, New York Stock Exchange, p. 62.

[2] Ibid.

[3] John J. Phelan, *The New York Stock Exchange Looks to the Future: Report to the Subcommittee on Telecommunications, Consumer Protection and Finance of the Committee on Energy and Commerce, United States House of Representatives*, June 17, 1981, p. 11.

[4] *Fact Book 1981*, p. 62.

[5] *New York Stock Exchange Looks to the Future*, p. 6.

[6] *Fact Book 1981*, p. 62.

exchange is governed by a 21-man board of directors—a chairman and twenty directors, ten from industry and ten representing the public. The chairman and executive staff manage the exchange, and the NYSE and its subsidiaries employ about 3,000 people, who are paid out of revenues obtained from services performed by the exchange.

Membership

In 1980, the New York Stock Exchange had 1,416 members, including 1,366 members who own seats. In 1980, seat prices ranged from $175,000 to $270,000. The highest price ever paid for exchange membership was $625,000 in February 1929, and the lowest in the twentieth century was $17,000, in 1942.[7]

A member organization doing business with the public must maintain a minimum net capital, as prescribed by SEC Rule 15c-3-1a. The purpose of the capital requirements is to protect the public from financial loss.

The member must pay 1 percent of net commissions to the exchange, in addition to an initiation fee of 10 percent of the cash purchase price, with a maximum of $7,500, or if the purchase was not for cash, 5 percent of the last sale. Also, each exchange member, upon the death of another member, contributes $15 to a fund of approximately $20,000 that is provided for each deceased member's family.

A member of the exchange may conduct business as an individual, a partnership, or a corporation. If an individual member combines with other individuals to form a partnership or corporation, the member must have prior approval of the board of directors. No one may become a partner or stockholder of a member company without permission and approval of the board; and each member firm must have one partner or stockholder who is an exchange member. At the end of 1980, there were 207 partnerships and 363 corporations operating as member organizations. The remaining seats were held by individuals; a dozen were held by the estates of deceased members. Corporate memberships were not allowed originally, because of the limited-liability aspect of the corporate firm.

Types of Members

The members of the exchange are divided into classes based on the nature of their activity. The classes are (1) commission broker, (2) odd-lot dealer or broker, (3) specialist, (4) floor broker, (5) floor trader, and (6) bond broker.

COMMISSION BROKER. From the investor's viewpoint, the commission broker is the most important member of the exchange, because he or she trades primarily for the public. Certainly, commission brokers are the most numerous exchange members. It is the commission broker's main function and responsibility to buy and sell stock for the firm's customers, and to act as agent for the customer. A commission is earned for the service performed. Most of the business conducted on the floor of the exchange by the commission broker is obtained through the registered representatives of the member firm. The registered representative is an employee of a member firm who is engaged in soliciting, handling, buying, selling, or trading in securities on behalf of his

[7]*Fact Book 1981*, p. 53.

or her employer. At the end of 1980, there were 48,435 registered representatives in 4,421 brokerage offices.[8] Each member firm must have one partner or stockholder who is an exchange member.

SPECIALIST. It is the basic responsibility of the specialist to make a fair, orderly, and continuous auction market in assigned stocks. The specialist can buy and sell for his or her own account as a dealer, or for the accounts of other members or member organizations. The specialist does not do business with the public directly but handles transactions on a commission basis for other brokers who are acting for their clients. There are 67 specialist units on the trading floor of the exchange. Essentially, the specialist must buy when stock is offered for sale and must sell when stock is requested for purchase, in order to maintain an orderly market. The specialist also handles odd-lot purchases and sales. (An odd lot is from 1 to 99 shares.)

There are three measures to determine specialist performance. One measure is the participation rate obtained by dividing purchases and sales by the specialist by *all* purchases and sales. Specialists had a participation rate of 12.4 percent in 1980. The second measure is the stabilization rate, measured by the number of purchases at prices above or below the market. The stabilization rate was 90.9 percent in 1980, indicating the specialists' stabilizing price action of selling above the market price and buying below the market price. Price continuity is the third measure. Price continuity is determined by the number of transactions taking place at the same price as the preceding transaction. In 1980, 98.7 percent of transactions took place within $\frac{1}{4}$ point of the preceding sale.[9]

In order to become a specialist, a member notifies the exchange of a willingness to be a specialist, and registers for that function subject to approval by the board. There are one or more specialists for each company listed on the exchange. The average specialist handles three or four stocks and is a member of a specialist organization that handles a dozen or more stocks. Specialists account for about 15 percent of market volume for their own accounts as dealers, and for more than that if transactions for other brokers are added. Orders of other brokers take precedence over the specialist's own orders as a dealer.

The board of directors selects specialists on their ability and also on the basis of sufficient capital. Effective May 1, 1976, the specialist must have enough money to buy 5,000 shares of each 100-share-unit common stock and 100 shares of each 10-share-unit stock, and must also be able to purchase 1,000 shares of each convertible preferred stock and 400 shares of each nonconvertible preferred stock.

The specialist can "take orders away from the market," that is, receive orders to buy and sell at prices different from the existing market price. Orders are kept in a book and executed when possible. The specialist makes an orderly and continuous market; opens the market; and operates in the capacity of both dealer and broker. The specialist is in a unique position, and performs an important function in the market. Because specialists could take advantage of market knowledge or improve their own position to the detriment of customers, they are closely regulated by the exchange and the Securities and Exchange Commission.

[8] *Fact Book 1981*, p. 74.
[9] Ibid., p. 13.

FLOOR BROKER. The floor broker buys and sells shares for other brokers on the floor of the exchange. They ordinarily do not belong to a member firm but own their own seats and receive a commission on the orders executed. Floor brokers were once called "$2 brokers," because this was their commission for executing an order. Today, the commission averages closer to $4 per 100-share transaction and is negotiable. There are about 200 floor brokers on the exchange.

FLOOR TRADER. Floor traders buy and sell for their own account. Some floor traders depend for income exclusively upon trading; others engage in trading as a part-time activity and devote the major portion of their time to commission work. Most full-time traders are members of a firm. When active, the floor trader helps to make a continuous market and stabilize prices. The floor trader has been criticized, however, as performing no important economic function, and it has been suggested that traders' activities increase market instability. Since there are few full-time traders today, their direct impact on the market is not very important. In 1964, the management of the exchange and the SEC were caught up in a bitter public argument over the Special Study recommendation to abolish floor trading. Differences were finally settled by an SEC ruling allowing it to continue under greatly circumscribed conditions.[10]

BOND BROKER. About twenty members of the exchange are bond brokers who handle the almost 2,600 bond issues traded on the exchange. Bonds are divided into two classes, free bonds and cabinet bonds. Free bonds are actively traded issues; all other listed bonds are called *cabinet* bonds, since trading involves using metal cabinets where records of bids and offers are kept. All trading in these issues takes place on the bond-trading floor and has been automated.

Listings

To be traded on the New York Stock Exchange, a security must meet the exchange's requirements for listings. At the end of 1980, 1,570 companies were listed and a total of 2,228 different issues were traded, including preferred and common stock of American and foreign companies.[11] In addition, 3,057 separate issues of bonds were traded, including those issued by U.S. corporations, foreign companies, the U.S. government, the International Bank, and foreign governments. About half of those listed were U.S. government bonds. A total of 188 foreign securities were listed at the end of 1980.[12]

CONDITIONS OF LISTING. Each company applying for initial listing is selected on its own merits. In general, it must be large enough, profitable enough, and with sufficient public ownership to meet the listing requirements established by the exchange. The company must agree to provide an earnings statement to the public,

[10]Lee Silberman, "Critical Examination of SEC Proposals," *Harvard Business Review*, November 1964, p. 121.

[11]*Fact Book 1981*, p. 32.

[12]Ibid., p. 34.

must send out dividend notices, must solicit proxies for all meetings of the stockholders, and must provide other information that may affect security values or influence investment decisions. All listed common stock must give its owner the privilege of voting. The requirements for continued exchange listing are less stringent than the initial requirements; however, should a company no longer be worthy of listing, should it fail, or should there be too few investors in it, then for the good of the exchange community—the members, the companies listed, the customers, and the public—its stock would be delisted.

Trading

On the New York Stock Exchange, only members can transact business at the posts where securities are traded. An investor wishing to buy 100 shares of GM would call a registered representative, who in turn would either wire or telephone the broker on the floor of the exchange to buy the shares, or the DOT system would be used.

As a GM buy order was received, it would be given to the broker, who would go to post 3, where General Motors stock is traded. The brokers and specialists would quickly convey price information about the GM stock. The Intermarket Trading System (ITS) terminals would be viewed to find the market with the best price. The best price would be entered onto the terminal or, verbally, a short auction would take place. The buyer would offer a price that was either accepted or rejected by the other brokers. This bargaining or auctioning takes place in a matter of seconds and continues until the buying broker and selling broker agree upon a price. Upon completion of the transaction, the broker wires a confirmation of the sale to the registered representative, who notifies the customer.

A summary of the daily stock transactions in New York Stock Exchange issues on all markets is reported in *The Wall Street Journal*. The "NYSE Composite Transactions" reflect stock issues on the NYSE, on other exchanges, and in the over-the-counter market (Figure 9–3). The consolidated tape along with the ITS represents a significant step toward a national market system for trading securities, which should lead to a more efficient market.

A word of explanation is in order for those not familiar with the stock market page. The first two columns represent the high and low price per share for the period indicated. Next appears the name of the company in abbreviated form, then the type of stock, the dividend, and the percent dividend yield. Next is the P/E ratio, based on current price and current-year earnings; then the number of sales for the day in round lots of 100 shares, followed by the high, low, and closing price for the day. The last column gives the net change from the previous day's closing price.

If you visit a brokerage office, you'll find at the desk of the registered representative one of the modern methods for obtaining price information and a great deal of additional knowledge. The Stockmaster, introduced by Ultronic Systems Corporation, provides immediate access to price, volume, dividends, and earnings information. Teleregister Corporation has a telequote device that provides price data; Scantlin Electronic's Quotron provides similar information. Since 1965, the New York Stock Exchange has used a computer-based quotation-processing system developed by IBM.

52 Weeks High	52 Weeks Low	Stock	Div.	Yld %	P-E Ratio	Sales 100s	High	low	Close	Net Chg.
9¾	7⅜	CurrInc	1.10	12.	..	9	9⅜	9¼	9⅜	+ ⅛
52	32⅝	CurtW	1.20	2.7	10	53	45½	45¼	45¼	– ¼
26¾	13⅝	Cyclops	1.10	4.2	..	57	26	26	26	.....
		– D–D–D –								
3⅝	2⅛	DMG		..	..	324	3½	3⅜	3⅜	.....
26	5¾	Damon	.20	.8	..	356	25	24⅝	25	+ ⅛
21⅜	10½	DanRiv	.56	2.6	..	39	21⅜	21⅜	21⅜	.....
36	21⅞	DanaCp	1.60	4.6	24	107	34¾	34⅛	34¾	+ ¼
17	8⅝	Daniel	.18b	1.6	7	302	11⅛	10⅞	11	– ⅛
72¼	48¼	DartKr	3.84	5.8	10	1413	67	65½	66	–1
61½	20¼	DataGn		..	48	1320	56¾	54⅞	55¾	– ⅝
10⅝	4½	DatTer		..	..	206	7⅛	7	7⅛	+ ⅛
26¼	10⅞	Datpnt		..	..	1266	22⅝	22⅛	22⅜	+ ⅛
12	6¼	Dayco	.16	1.4	147	192	11¾	11½	11¾	– ⅛
64¼	31¼	DayHud	1.20	1.9	14	608	62	61	61¾	– ¼
19	14⅜	DaytPL	2	12.	7	1536	17½	17¼	17⅜	– ⅛
46¼	15½	DeanFd	.76	1.8	14	22	42⅝	42	42¼	– ¼
35⅜	22	Deere	1	3.1	..	1301	33	32⅛	32½	– ⅜
16⅞	13¼	DelmP	1.64	10.	8	101	16½	16⅛	16¼	– ¼
49½	25⅜	DeltaAr	1	2.1	..	434	47⅜	46⅝	47	.....
12¾	4¾	Deltona		..	..	119	12	11⅝	11⅞	+ ⅛
45½	18½	DixChk	1.12	2.6	15	71	43⅝	43¼	43½	+ ¼
29½	16¼	DenMfg	1.44	5.0	14	63	29⅛	28¾	28¾	– ½
36⅞	22⅜	Dennys	.64	2.0	13	160	32½	31¾	32½	+ ⅛
30½	11¼	DeSoto	1.12	3.9	22	121	29¼	29	29	.....
15¼	11	DetEd	1.68	12.	8	970	14½	14⅜	14⅜	.....
80¾	58⅝	DetE	pf5.50	6.9	..	1	79½	79½	79½	.....
60½	45¾	DetE	pf7.68	13.	..	z50	58	58	58	–1½
60	44½	DetE	pf7.45	13.	..	z500	57½	56½	56½	–1
58	43¾	DetE	pf7.36	13.	..	z190	56	56	56	+ ¼
22⅝	17⅛	DE	pfF 2.75	12.	..	9	22¼	21⅞	22¼	+ ½
23	17	DE	pfB 2.75	13.	..	16	22⅛	22	22	.....
27	23⅞	DE	pfO 3.40	13.	..	45	25⅞	25½	25¾	+ ⅛
27⅞	24	DE	pfM3.42	13.	..	269	26	25⅛	26	+ ⅜
32	24⅝	DE	prL 4	13.	..	16	30¼	30	30⅛	– ½
33	24⅝	DE	pfK 4.12	13.	..	52	31⅜	30¾	31	– ⅛
19	14	DetE	pr2.28	13.	..	11	18	17¾	17¾	– ¼
34	18⅜	Dexter	1.10	3.1	14	399	u35⅝	34	35⅝	+1⅝
13⅜	8¼	DiGior	.64	4.8	12	884	u13⅝	13⅛	13¼	+ ⅛
25⅞	18¼	DiGio	pf2.25	8.6	..	13	u26⅛	25⅜	26⅛	+ ¾
26⅜	16½	DiamS	1.76	7.4	10	1012	24⅛	23⅝	23⅞	+ ¼
95⅜	42½	Diebld	1	1.1	18	150	89¾	88¼	88¼	+ ½
132⅛	61¾	Digital		..	20	2637	127⅜	125½	125⅝	–2
24¾	10	Dilingh		..	18	58	u24⅞	24¾	24¾	.....
78¾	47	Disney	1.20	1.6	26	688	77¾	77⅛	77⅛	– ½
25⅛	18¼	DEI	2.28	9.7	6	166	24	23½	23½	– ⅝
3¾	1⅞	Divrsln		..	..	47	3¾	3⅝	3⅝	.....
16⅝	10⅞	DrPepp	.84	6.7	22	1536	12¾	12½	12⅝	+ ⅛
22¼	5	Dome	g .10	..	..	1507	17⅛	16⅝	17⅛	.....
24¼	8⅜	DonLJ	.24	1.1	16	177	22⅜	22	22⅛	– ½
70⅞	38½	Donnly	1.60	2.4	14	645	66½	65	66½	+1½
44¼	18⅜	Dorsey	1.10	2.7	..	28	41½	41¼	41½	+ ¾
32	17¾	Dover	.70	2.5	11	129	28	27⅛	27⅞	+ ¼
32¾	19⅝	DowCh	1.80	5.7	18	2565	32⅛	31⅜	31½	.....
39⅝	17⅞	DowJn	s .60	1.5	28	188	39¼	38¾	39	.....
14¼	9¼	Dravo	.50	3.7	..	108	13⅞	13½	13⅝	– ¼
24⅞	12¼	Dresr	.80	4.8	8	1658	16⅞	16½	16⅝	– ⅜
19⅜	14¼	DrexB	2	11.	..	18	19	18¾	19	.....
55¾	24¼	Dreyfus	.60a	1.4	7	98	44⅝	44¼	44⅜	– ¼
44⅜	30	duPont	2.40	5.9	11	2269	41⅛	40⅝	40¾	– ⅝
45½	35	duPnt	pf4.50	9.9	..	2	45½	45	45½	.....
24	20¼	DukeP	2.28	10.	7	2737	22⅞	22⅝	22¾	+ ¼
75½	58¼	Duke	pf8.70	12.	..	z1610	75½	74¾	75½	+1¼
71¼	55	Duke	pf8.20	12.	..	z260	70½	69½	70½	+1
25	19¾	Duke	pf2.69	11.	..	5	24⅞	24¾	24¾	– ⅛
33	25½	Duke	pf3.85	12.	..	24	32¾	32¼	32¾	+ ¼
83¼	65	Duk	pfN8.84	12.	..	z20	76¼	76¼	76¼	+ ¼
77	57¼	Duk	pfM8.84	11.	..	z2200	u77½	77½	77½	+1¼
122	58½	DunBr	2.76	2.4	23	202	115½	114	114	– ½
17	13	DuqLt	2	12.	9	404	16½	16⅜	16½	+ ⅛
16¼	12½	Duq	pf 2	13.	..	z220	15⅝	15½	15½	– ½
19½	14¼	Duq	pr 2.31	12.	..	z650	18¾	18⅛	18¾	+ ⅝
24⅛	20⅜	Duq	pr 2.75	11.	..	z250	24	24	24	.....
20⅝	11½	DycoPt	.24	1.9	6	119	12¾	12⅜	12½	.....
15⅛	5⅝	DynAm	.15	1.0	27	108	14⅞	14⅜	14¾	+ ⅜
		– E–E–E –								
32½	14¾	EGG	.36	1.3	21	757	29⅞	28⅜	28¾	–1
58¾	21¾	E Syst	.70	1.2	24	137	58⅜	57¾	58⅜	.....
20⅜	9⅝	EagleP	.96	4.9	17	148	20⅛	19¾	19¾	– ¼
26⅝	16⅜	Easco	1.32	5.2	9	23	25½	25¼	25¼	.....
10¼	4½	EastAir		..	..	761	9⅛	8⅞	9	+ ⅛
69¼	33⅞	GenRe	s1.28	1.9	15	424	68⅝	68⅛	68⅛	– ¾
6⅝	2⅜	GnRefr		..	..	124	u 6¾	6¼	6⅜	– ⅛
48½	28	GnSignl	1.68	3.8	11	274	45¼	43	44	–1½
11⅝	8	GTFl	pf1.25	11.	..	z100	11½	11½	11½	.....
12	8¾	GTFl	pf1.30	11.	..	z200	11½	11½	11½	.....
73⅝	53⅛	GTFl	pf8.16	11.	..	z100	72	70	72	–1⅝
35¼	17⅞	GTire	1.50b	4.7	40	327	34¼	32	32¼	–1⅞
6⅛	3⅝	Gensco		..	..	210	5½	5⅜	5⅜	.....
30¾	10½	GnRad	s .08	.3	47	102	30½	29¼	29½	–1¼
20½	7⅛	Genst	g .60	..	..	51	18¼	18	18	– ⅛
47⅜	29¾	GenuPt	1.38	3.2	16	185	44⅛	43⅝	43¾	+ ¼
28	13¼	GaPac	.60	2.3	54	1060	26⅛	25¼	25¾	– ¼
28⅞	25⅜	GaPw	pf3.44	13.	..	169	27½	27⅛	27¼	.....
31¼	23⅞	GaPw	pf3.76	13.	..	67	29¾	29⅜	29½	.....
22	16⅛	GaPw	pf2.56	12.	..	16	21¼	20¾	21¼	+ ¼
21½	15½	GaPw	pf2.52	12.	..	21	20⅞	20¼	20½	.....
24¾	18½	GaPw	pf2.75	12.	..	10	23¾	23¾	23¾	.....
64	48	GaPw	pf7.72	12.	..	z20	62	62	62	.....
28¼	17¾	GerbPd	s1.36	5.3	9	93	26	25¾	25¾	– ¼
17¾	6½	GerbSc	.12	.8	28	39	16	15⅝	15⅝	– ¼
64⅞	41¼	Getty	2.60e	4.5	7	716	58⅝	56½	57¾	–1
8¼	4½	GiantP		..	..	20	7¼	7⅛	7⅛	.....
12	2¾	GibrFn		..	..	560	11¼	9¾	9¾	–1⅜
21⅛	10	GiffHill	.52	2.6	280	8	19¾	19½	19⅝	.....
49	30¾	Gillette	2.30	5.0	10	738	46¼	45¾	45¾	– ¼
13½	8⅛	GleasW		..	..	44	13¼	12⅞	13	+ ⅛
15⅝	7¼	GloblM	.24	2.9	3	575	8⅝	8¼	8¼	– ¼
46	20	GldNug		..	12	247	44½	43¾	44½	+ ½
18½	4½	GldWF		..	..	166	u18⅝	18⅜	18⅝	+ ¼
37½	16⅝	Gdrich	1.56	4.5	..	527	35⅞	34¾	34⅞	–1
9¼	7	Gdrch	pf.97	11.	..	z400	8⅞	8⅞	8⅞	.....
34	21⅝	Gdrch	pf3.12	9.4	..	5	33¼	33¼	33¼	.....
36⅞	20	Goodyr	1.40	4.7	9	6206	30	29⅝	30	.....
21	13⅛	GordnJ	.56	2.8	8	87	20	19¾	19⅞	– ⅛
39½	19¾	Gould	1.72	5.4	15	1343	32¼	31	31⅞	+ ½
43¾	28½	Grace	2.80	6.5	6	1660	43⅜	42⅝	43	– ⅜
56	33⅞	Graingr	1.16	2.2	15	817	52½	51½	51⅝	– ¾
13	8½	Granitv		..	..	55	12⅜	12⅛	12⅛	– ¼
11	4⅜	GtAtPc		..	..	316	10⅝	10⅛	10⅜	+ ⅛
30½	17⅛	GtLkIn	.80a	2.7	11	8	29⅞	29⅝	29⅞	.....
28¼	15¾	GNIrn	1.50e	7.9	7	10	18⅞	18¼	18⅞	+ ⅝
49	29	GtNoNk	2	4.3	10	413	47½	46¾	46⅞	– ⅛
29⅞	9¾	GtWFin	.40	1.6	30	314	25⅞	25	25¼	– ⅝
15	7	GWHsp	n	..	46	227	11⅛	10⅞	11	– ⅜
15	11⅞	GMP	1.56	11.	11	6	13¾	13¾	13¾	.....
25⅜	12⅝	Greyh	1.20	4.9	10	1359	25	24½	24⅝	– ¼
2⅜	9-32	Grey wt		..	..	871	2¼	1⅞	2⅛	.....
4⅝	1⅞	Groler n		..	10	37	4	3⅞	3⅞	.....
15	6⅛	GrowG	.36b	2.6	17	318	14¼	14	14	– ⅛
4	2¼	GthRty		..	..	11	3¼	3¼	3¼	.....
54¾	21	Grumm	1.60	3.2	22	590	51	49⅞	50¼	– ¼
23⅞	18½	Grum	pf2.80	12.	..	8	23⅜	23⅛	23⅛	– ¼
39	11½	Guardl	.36	.9	17	204	u39⅛	38⅝	38⅝	– ⅜
27	11½	GlfWst	.75	2.9	13	4711	26	25⅛	26	+ ½
57¾	49¼	GlfW	pf 5.75	10.	..	1	57¾	57¾	57¾	.....
158½	68¾	GlfW	pf 3.87	2.5	..	2	155	155	155	+1
64	28¾	GlfW	pf 2.50	4.2	..	14	60¼	60⅛	60⅛	– ⅜
35¾	24¼	GulfOil	2.80	8.9	6	3439	31⅝	31⅛	31⅜	– ¼
20¼	9⅝	GulfRs		2.2	..	608	17⅛	16	17⅛	+ ⅝
25½	14¾	GulfR	pf1.30	6.3	..	1	20¾	20¾	20¾	.....
14⅞	11¼	GlfStUt	1.56	11.	7	1231	13⅞	13⅝	13¾	– ⅛
37½	29	GlfSU	pf4.40	12.	..	z60	35½	35½	35½	– ½
31⅛	27½	GlfSU	pr3.85	13.	..	97	30¾	30	30½	– ⅛
35⅛	27¼	GlfSU	pr4.40	13.	..	23	35⅛	34⅞	35	– ⅛
29¾	15½	GulfUtd	1.32	4.7	9	2132	28½	28¼	28⅜	– ⅛
59	36	GlfU	pf 3.78	6.7	..	15	56½	56½	56½	–2
17	7½	Gulton	.60	3.6	63	16	16⅝	16¼	16½	.....
		– H–H–H –								
13¾	7	HMW		..	26	76	11¾	11	11¾	– ⅛
10⅝	2¼	vjHRT		..	11	139	5¼	5	5	.....
21½	12⅞	HackW	s1.84	9.0	9	52	20⅝	20¼	20⅜	– ⅛
35⅜	23⅛	HallFB	1.70	5.4	15	190	33	31⅝	31⅝	–1⅛
39½	21	Halbtn	1.60	4.7	8	3080	34⅞	33½	33¾	–1½
35⅞	21½	HamrP	1.84	5.4	11	26	34⅜	34⅛	34⅜	– ⅛
13⅞	10¾	HanJS	1.47a	11.	..	37	13⅝	13½	13½	.....
18⅛	14	HanJI	1.84a	10.	..	15	17⅞	17½	17¾	+ ⅛
26¼	10¼	Hndlmn	1	4.0	13	13	25⅛	25	25	– ⅛
24	12¼	HandH	.60	2.9	33	127	20⅜	19⅝	20⅜	+ ½
38⅝	16½	Hanna	.40	1.7	..	115	23⅞	23⅜	23½	– ⅜
25¼	12½	HarBrJ	1	4.2	66	143	24⅜	23¾	23¾	– ½
41⅞	15⅝	HarInd	.76	1.9	20	27	40	39	40	+ ¾

FIGURE 9–3

NYSE Composite Transactions

SOURCE: The Wall Street Journal, March 11, 1983.

In 1980, the reported total volume on the New York Stock Exchange, including both round-lot and odd-lot transactions, was 11.6 billion shares; the daily average was 44.9 million.[13]

THE AMERICAN STOCK EXCHANGE

The American Stock Exchange is the second largest exchange in the United States. Before the Civil War, it began operations outdoors on Wall and Broad Streets. It did not move indoors until 1921. The American Stock Exchange has had a colorful history; from 1929 until 1953, it was known as the New York Curb Exchange, from the curb on Broad Street where brokers had met to trade shares. At the earlier time, one would have found brokers decked out in colorful garb trading in the street. Their clothing identified them to their staffs in nearby offices above the street. When an order was telephoned to a broker's office, it would be transmitted from the office window by hand signals or sign language to the broker below. Communication with brokers on the floor is done electronically today.

Organization

The American Stock Exchange is an association of individuals, with a board of governors consisting of 32 members. This board represents regular exchange members, associate members, the general public, and the administrative group. The executives of the exchange are salaried. The chief executive officer is the president, who carries out policies established by the board of governors.

Membership

There are 499 seats or regular memberships on the American Stock Exchange that are accorded the full privileges of membership. A member must be an American citizen, 21 years or older, and have the approval of two-thirds of the board of governors. The cost of membership and the annual dues are lower than comparable costs on the New York Stock Exchange.

In addition to regular members, there are approximately 400 associate members. These enjoy the privilege of conducting their business through a regular member at a substantial saving in commissions. The number of associate members on the exchange must be approved by the board of governors. An associate member pays approximately 10 percent of the market price of a seat for the privilege of using the facilities of the exchange. This is considered an initiation fee.

CLASSES OF MEMBERS AND LISTING. The three classes of floor members on the American Exchange are (1) specialists, who are the most numerous; (2) commission brokers; and (3) floor traders. They trade in both listed and unlisted securities.

[13] *Fact Book 1981*, pp. 63, 64.

Trading

Securities traded on the exchange vary from old, established companies to new, highly speculative issues. Often, companies list first on the American Stock Exchange and then move to the New York Stock Exchange, the "Big Board"; General Motors and du Pont did this. Prentice-Hall and Cinerama are well-known companies that are actively traded on the American Exchange.

The American Exchange is the nation's leading market in foreign securities. It originated and uses American Depository Receipts for trading in these securities. ADRs, as they are known, are certificates issued by New York banks and trust companies against foreign shares deposited in the foreign branches of American banks.

REGIONAL AND LOCAL EXCHANGES

Regional and local stock exchanges provide a marketplace for a wide variety of securities with varying degrees of public participation and support. Such exchanges conducted approximately 10 percent of the market value of the total securities traded on exchanges in the United States. The Midwest Exchange in Chicago, the Pacific Stock Exchange in Los Angeles and San Francisco, and the Philadelphia Stock Exchange generate the largest portion of the total business done by all the regional and local exchanges. The remaining business is done by the following local exchanges: Boston, Cincinnati, Honolulu, Spokane, Salt Lake City, the Chicago Board Options Exchange (CBOE), and Colorado Springs. All these exchanges are registered with the SEC, except for the Honolulu exchange, which is exempt primarily because its volume of business is so small.

Regional and local exchanges are organized along the lines of the New York Stock Exchange. The companies listed are usually small local or regional companies, but they may have their stock traded on a national exchange in addition to one or more local exchanges. In recent years, member firms of the New York Stock Exchange have listed on the regional exchanges to combat the growth of the "third market," and the broker handles the purchase or sale of a stock listed on the NYSE on a regional exchange at a reduced commission. Many trades are reported on the composite tape of the NYSE and the AMEX.

The price of shares traded on local exchanges is usually low, the volume of trading is small, seats and membership fees are inexpensive, and there are few members of each exchange. Commission schedules for stocks traded on the regional and local exchanges, like those on the New York Stock Exchange, are now negotiable. The type of securities traded and the listing requirements vary among regional and local exchanges. Stocks that enjoy listed trading privileges on the American Stock Exchange or the New York Stock Exchange often enjoy *unlisted* trading privileges on local and regional exchanges.

The Cincinnati Stock Exchange (CSE) has developed a pilot facility for trading shares which might become a part of the national market system mandated by Congress and the SEC.[14] The CSE became a part of ITS early in 1981. The NSTS is a fully

[14]Securities and Exchange Commission, *The Securities Industry in 1980: Economic and Policy Analysis*, September 1981, p. 105.

automated electronic trading system. Members can participate by entering bids and offers for securities into computer terminals without going on the floor of the exchange. A specialist on the floor of the exchange can enter bids and offers into the system as principal or agent. Orders that are entered are stored and queued by the system's computer and then executed based on programmed priorities. The priorities are established by price first and then time, but non-broker-dealer customer orders are given priority regardless of time.[15]

FOREIGN STOCK EXCHANGES

The Toronto Stock Exchange, the London Stock Exchange, and the Japanese stock exchanges have been important in world finance. The Toronto Stock Exchange has over 1,100 issues listed, with nearly all of them trading every month. The London Stock Exchange lists and trades more than twice the number of issues listed on the New York Stock Exchange, and it has three times the number of members.

The stock exchanges in Japan are young compared with those in the United States. They have become important since World War II. There are eight stock exchanges in Japan; the Tokyo Exchange clearly dominates in stock volume, trading about two-thirds the total transactions. This exchange has both listed and unlisted securities. Average prices of shares traded on both the London and the Tokyo exchanges are lower than those on the New York Stock Exchange. Average volume on the Tokyo Exchange is high in comparison with the New York Stock Exchange.

Trading on foreign exchanges is similar to trading on exchanges in the United States. Purchasing stocks on foreign exchanges, however, adds new risk for the investor. Information about securities traded on foreign exchanges is somewhat limited but has improved in recent years. Because of fluctuations in foreign exchange rates among the various currencies, the risk is greater. The market for foreign stock is narrow, and the instability of some foreign governments provides an unfavorable climate for buying and selling securities. Also, shares of foreign corporations that would appeal to conservative investors are available through exchange facilities in the United States. American Depository Receipts, mentioned earlier, which can be purchased through the New York and American stock exchanges and in over-the-counter markets, in most cases allow investors to participate in the benefits of ownership of foreign securities without trading on foreign exchanges. The more actively traded foreign securities are reported in *The Wall Street Journal*. The brokerage and transfer costs are usually higher for foreign securities.

ADVANTAGES AND DISADVANTAGES OF A NATIONAL EXCHANGE

The investor achieves several advantages in dealing in securities listed on a national exchange. The largest, best-known industrial companies are listed on the American and New York stock exchanges. Shares traded on a national exchange have liquidity, marketability, and a continuous and fair market, and information about them is

[15]Ibid., pp. 107–08.

readily obtainable. Such companies tend to be well regulated and offer protection for the investor—although not from loss. The national market, in short, tends to be more efficient and less costly. On the other hand, a disadvantage to the investor of listing is the public scrutiny that might result in a too-rapid transition of bad news. In addition, many young, rapidly growing companies are not listed and must be purchased in a less regulated and monitored environment. The registered exchanges are moving toward a more efficient national market system.

THE OVER-THE-COUNTER MARKET

An important part of the secondary market is the OTC market. Securities traded in the over-the-counter market include bank stocks, insurance company stocks, government securities, municipal bonds, mutual funds, equipment trust certificates issued by railroads, most corporate bonds except those listed on the New York Stock Exchange, and stocks of a large number of domestic and foreign industrial and public utility companies. The over-the-counter market includes all securities markets except the organized exchanges. Business is not conducted at any one place designated as the marketplace, although New York is the center of the over-the-counter market. Dealers and brokers do business directly with each other by telephone, telegraph, or teletype. The Wharton study indicated that almost 90,000 different corporate and government securities could be traded in these markets; the number actually traded was 40,000.[16] A typical trading day, according to the study, involved transactions of 3,000 different issues. Approximately three-fourths of these transactions were in corporate stock issues and one-fourth in corporate and government bond issues. The OTC markets do 100 percent of the U.S. government, state, and municipal bond business. They do over 80 percent of the corporate bond business and 18 percent of the corporate stock business.

Some stocks trade in the OTC market because the company is small or unknown, the stock is closely held by one family, the security is unseasoned or its price is high, it offers little or no investment or speculative interest, or the company simply does not wish its security to be listed on an exchange. The trading that takes place in such securities is done by negotiation, with the dealers or brokers bargaining directly to establish a price.

Approximately 4,200 broker-dealers are registered with the SEC and engage in interstate commerce to effect securities transactions. The bulk of the business is handled by broker-dealers who are members of the National Association of Securities Dealers. These broker-dealers fall into six main classifications: (1) the OTC house that deals mainly in OTC issues and does not usually belong to an exchange; (2) the investment banking house that deals heavily in underwriting new issues of stocks and bonds; (3) the dealer bank, a commercial bank that makes a market for government securities; (4) the municipal bond house; (5) the government bond house; and (6) the stock exchange member house. Major functions of these broker-dealers are to

[16]Irwin Friend, G. Wright Hoffman, Willis J. Winn, Morris Hamburg, and Stanley Schore, *The Over-the-Counter Securities Markets* (New York: McGraw-Hill, 1958).

make a market for securities outstanding, distribute new issues of securities, and help distribute large secondary offerings of stock in over-the-counter markets.[17]

Prices in the OTC Market

Many OTC stocks are quoted daily in *The Wall Street Journal* and other national daily papers. Price quotes are obtained through the NASDAQ system. These are representative prices supplied by the brokerage firms that offer or wish to buy shares of a particular stock. The prices do not include retail markup, markdown, or commissions. The NASDAQ system does not include all shares traded in the OTC market; many unlisted stocks are quoted in local markets. The availability of price quotes is taken for granted by most investors, who are then surprised to learn that sometimes price quotes of certain stocks are unavailable, and hence a continuous market does not exist. The automated OTC market is a step in the right direction, however, along with the composite tape and DOT. When ITS and NASDAQ are combined, we will have a national market system.

Commissions

Shares traded in the OTC may be done on a dealer or an agent basis. If the shares are traded on a dealer basis, the broker is selling them as a principal and must add a markup to the price to cover a "commission." A profit can be made if the shares were purchased at a lower price. The shares may be traded on an agent basis where the broker is acting as the investor's agent and the broker receives a commission. The commission charged is negotiable, and no odd-lot fee is charged for sales of fewer than 100 shares.

Automation in the OTC

One former criticism of the OTC market concerned the system of price quotes. Before NASDAQ, it was difficult to determine if the investor was getting a fair price. Not only was the price structure inadequate, but no one knew for sure the extent of the market. The broker is obligated to obtain the best price at the time of the trade, but since many investors, brokers, and dealers did not actively compete in providing bids and offers, it could not be ascertained if a completely liquid market existed. NASDAQ has gone a long way to correct this problem through its system, and a more nearly perfect market now seems to exist. The volume that has developed through the NASDAQ system has added depth and liquidity to the marketplace. At the same time, the system has narrowed the spread between the bid and asked prices and has improved the "fairness" of the marketplace.

Advantages

The OTC market is the only place where certain stocks can be purchased. Small local companies and good national companies that do not meet exchange listing requirements are traded OTC. Many of the OTC securities are top-quality, investment-grade

[17]George L. Leffler and Loring C. Farwell, *The Stock Market*, 3rd ed. (New York: Ronald Press, 1963) p. 467.

senior securities of federal, state, and local governments that fit into the investor's portfolio, particularly the institutional investor and the wealthy investor desiring fixed-income securities. The market for these securities is stable and continuous, providing marketability comparable with that of securities traded on a registered exchange. Securities that provide growth potential are also traded in this market, as are some local issues that are attractive for long-term investment. With the passage of the Securities Acts amendments of 1964, and with the improvement of self-regulation and of reporting requirements of corporations, stocks and companies in the over-the-counter market have been given a new dimension, making them more attractive for investment. A given dollar of earnings or rate of return of an OTC company would therefore have greater value than before the Securities Acts amendments were passed. This increased regulation of the over-the-counter market has removed some of the disadvantages of purchasing securities there.

The NASDAQ (National Association of Securities Dealers Automatic Quotation) system was adopted in response to a congressional mandate based on recommendations of the Special Study.[18] The automation of the OTC market has led to better and faster quotes, resulting in a more marketable and liquid continuous market. Also, steps have been taken to improve the supervision of selling activities and to strengthen the self-regulatory agencies, so that clearer standards and stronger enforcement procedures will ensure supervision of member firms.

Disadvantages

The disadvantages of OTC trading, by contrast, are imposing. Generally, the quality of securities, aside from municipal and federal government obligations, is not as high as of those traded on the New York Stock Exchange. Until the advent of NASDAQ, it was more difficult to obtain information about price and the financial affairs of companies. In general, the OTC market consists of smaller companies that have limited marketability and liquidity. The market is less well organized, and the companies are smaller, leading to a lower degree of marketability for equity securities.

THE THIRD MARKET

The "third" or "off-the-board" market refers to over-the-counter trading in listed stock and is made up of firms that are not exchange members and that do not charge regular commissions on large block sales. Shares traded are the same as those traded on the New York Stock Exchange. Prices are established by negotiation, and dealers have no responsibility for maintaining a market. Clients of the third market are the large institutional investors who are price-conscious in buying and selling securities and seek out broker-dealer firms outside exchange facilities. Third-market volume was equal to 4.6 percent of total New York Stock Exchange volume in 1976.[19]

The institutional market is substantial, and institutional investors have a tremen-

[18]Securities and Exchange Commission, *31st Annual Report* (Washington, D.C.: Government Printing Office, 1965), p. 18.
[19]New York Stock Exchange, *Fact Book 1976*, p. 16.

dous effect on the stock market. The brokerage community is "painfully aware that institutional investors, pension funds, insurance companies and the like—with large blocks of stock to buy and sell—are attracted to larger, nonmember, broker-dealer firms not only because those firms offer more advantageous net prices involving no commissions, but also because they usually are willing to quote a firm bid for the whole block. It is the rare portfolio manager who does not appreciate the convenience of being able to launch a sizable transaction with but one telephone call!"[20]

The New York Stock Exchange's principal approach to competing against the third market has been to develop techniques for handling large-block transactions quickly and with a minimum of price fluctuation. In fact, large-block trade represented 30 percent of the NYSE volume, in 1980. In addition, brokerage firms have taken out membership on regional exchanges that trade in stocks also listed on the Big Board. This makes the brokerage firms competitive with third market firms.[21]

THE FOURTH MARKET

Large-block sales of securities may be arranged by brokerage firms that link their customers by computer terminals. The customers of these specialized firms are large institutional investors, including pension funds, commercial banks, and mutual funds. In essence, a group of large institutional investors thus trade with each other through a computer terminal, obviating the need for a broker. The advantages of trading in this way—sometimes referred to as the "fourth market"—are the economy of trading in large units of at least 500 shares per month, and the speed of the transaction. Instinet is one company that provides this service. Companies of this type offer inexpensive buying and selling fees but few of the research and advisory services provided by the large brokerage houses.

A CENTRAL MARKET

Several suggestions have been made by members of the New York Stock Exchange, Congress, and the SEC, as well as by William McChesney Martin and members of the brokerage community, to establish a central market. The assumption is that a central marketplace would result in a more efficient marketplace—one that was both more liquid and more marketable. The result would be lower costs and fairer prices. The consolidated tape in NYSE-listed stocks has been implemented as a result of the efforts of the NYSE, the Martin Report, and the SEC. Such automation is welcome, beneficial, and long overdue. Unfortunately, it will take time to automate fully.

CHICAGO BOARD OPTIONS EXCHANGE (CBOE)

The Chicago Board Options Exchange was set up in 1973 as the first securities exchange in the world established expressly for the purpose of providing a market in put and call options. A call option gives the buyer the right to buy 100 shares of stock at a

---

[20]Silberman, "Critical Examination," pp. 121–22.
[21]Ibid., p. 122.

specified price. The put option gives the buyer the right to sell 100 shares of stock at a specified price. The options are sold by a "writer" or "maker" of the option contract at an exercise price for a fee. The price of the option is quoted on the Chicago Board Options Exchange.

The CBOE is said to offer the following improvements:

1. Standardized option contract and trading practices
2. Continuous reporting
3. Appointment of market makers to maintain a fair and orderly market
4. Assumption of self-regulatory responsibility
5. Provision for a clearing corporation to facilitate trading

The advantage of an options market appears obvious. It provides liquidity and marketability to a trading activity that was once more informal. The CBOE has brought market efficiency to the options market, along with increasing volume as a result. An investor or speculator may limit risks, and trading may take place against the options, which was difficult before.

SECURITIES MARKET REGULATION

Blue-Sky Laws

A number of regulations have been imposed on stock market institutions to protect the investing public. They are carried out at the federal level through the Securities and Exchange Commission (SEC), and at the state level through departments, usually called securities commissions, established to regulate the sale of securities within each state. The laws they enforce, referred to as *blue-sky laws*, deal with the intrastate sales of securities to the public. Blue-sky laws were first enacted in Kansas in 1911. Often, issues that are approved for sale by registration with the SEC are denied the privilege of sale in a specific state because of these laws.

Securities and Exchange Commission Regulation

Established under the Securities Exchange Act of 1934, which also provided for the registration of national securities exchanges, the SEC consists of five members appointed by the President of the United States. The commission is assisted in its regulatory and investigative work by more than 1,000 accountants, engineers, examiners, lawyers, securities analysts, and administrative and clerical employees. SEC headquarters are in Washington, and there are ten regional offices. The activities of the SEC are designed to protect the investment public from losses owing to fraud, unfair competition, or unethical acts. It is the duty of the SEC to inform but not to advise the public about the investment worth of an individual company's securities.

The Securities Act of 1933, administered by the SEC, requires corporations selling new issues of stock to the public to provide the purchaser with a complete statement of all pertinent financial and nonfinancial information relating to operations of the company. The 1933 act is sometimes referred to as the "Truth in Securities Act," since companies selling stock to the public are required to tell the truth, the whole truth, and nothing but the truth about their past, present, and expected future activities, by means of a statement known as a *prospectus*. This act was the first important federal legislation regulating the stock market.

The SEC also administers the Public Utility Holding Company Act of 1935, which limits the scope and growth of public utilities by controlling the number of holding companies that can be pyramided upon an operating utility, and by limiting company systems to well-defined geographic areas.

The Investment Company Act of 1940 and the Investment Advisers Act of 1940, also administered by the SEC, provide for the registration and regulation of activities of investment companies and investment advisers. Chapter X of the National Bankruptcy Act, providing for the reorganization of industrial companies, is also under the administration of the SEC.

The seven major purposes and objectives of the SEC may be summarized as follows:

1. SEC insures that the public will receive adequate information about securities traded in the various securities markets. All securities being sold to the public must be registered with the SEC except for certain exempt issues. Exempt securities include (a) the direct obligations of the federal government and the direct and indirect obligations of state and municipal governments, (b) other securities issued or guaranteed by corporations in which the United States has an interest, (c) securities issued by railroads, (d) security issues below $300,000 in amount, (e) security issues sold to one or a few institutional investors and not to the public at large, and (f) any other securities that the SEC may deem necessary to exempt, such as unregistered securities and those of an intrastate character.[22]

   The matter of disclosure, including financial and accounting data, has been the major focus of the SEC activities in the past several years. The basic objective seems to be to provide full and complete information to the investor so that the best possible decision can be made. This effort has helped create an efficient market environment.

2. SEC provides for the registration of exchanges to regulate the activities of these markets.

3. Information is required by the SEC about inside trading and the activities of officers and directors in the securities of their company, with the aim of preventing manipulation in the securities market.

4. SEC attempts to regulate the activities of investment companies and investment advisers by requiring their registration with the SEC.

5. SEC regulates the activities of the brokers and dealers that operate in the market.

6. SEC provides for regulation to limit the amount of credit that is involved in the stock market. The control over margin requirements for stock-market credit is exercised by the Federal Reserve Board of Governors from time to time, to help maintain an orderly stock market.

7. SEC is given the right of supervision over the NASD. The National Association of Securities Dealers is the only self-regulatory association of brokers and dealers. The Special Study conducted by the SEC upheld the principle of self-regulation and broadened its scope to include nonmember firms and firms involved in the over-the-counter market.

A breach of the securities acts may result in a criminal penalty, with fines of up to $10,000 for individuals and $500,000 for exchanges, and imprisonment for up to two

[22]Securities Exchange Act of 1934, Section 3 (12).

years for individuals. The SEC may also suspend a member, an exchange, or a company from trading activities or from the privilege of trading.

One amendment to the securities acts, the Securities Acts amendments of 1964, was the result of the SEC's Special Study. It has had far-reaching implications for the securities business. The four-part Special Study was conducted by 65 lawyers, economists, and staffers under the direction of Milton H. Cohen. The first part of the study cited several abuses in the securities market: "(1) Some companies give only the scantiest information to stockholders. (2) Many securities salesmen are trained only poorly, if at all. (3) Many investment advisers are irresponsible. (4) Even the biggest and most reputable of brokerage houses are at times extremely careless. (5) Some publicity men and newspaper, magazine, and broadcasting journalists are carefully cultivated by companies, usually by receiving allotments of hard-to-get 'hot' new issues that go up in price just after coming out. (6) 'A considerable number' of public relations men artificially pump up their employer's or client's stock by issuing fantastic announcements of expected earnings, mergers, new products. (7) Some public relations men profit directly from trading in shares of client companies, a practice frowned on by the SEC because the public may not be aware that the 'information which it receives comes from an interested source.' "[23]

The second part indicated other abuses: "Investigators for the SEC reported that these men [insiders] often overcharge and insufficiently protect the small investor, and called many of the rules by which they work outmoded, ineffective, and in need of reform. . . . The SEC recommended that trading in stock issues that are 'unlisted' on any exchange be automated and perhaps made cheaper for the investor, and that the cost of trading in 'odd lots' of fewer than 100 shares be lowered. It asked for closer regulation of the stock exchange specialists and bearish 'short sellers' and suggested that the exchanges' anachronistic floor traders be abolished altogether."[24]

The third part of the Special Study dealt with the obligations of the issuers of publicly held securities and brought important changes in the over-the-counter market. It recommended that unlisted securities come under regulation of the SEC and the original Securities Exchange Act, and that companies with 500 or more security holders and $1 million worth of securities should come under the jurisdiction of the Securities Act. "The recommended legislation should not exempt any category of issuers merely because they file reports or are otherwise regulated under other laws, unless such reports or other regulations are clearly designed for the protection of investors."[25] It was indicated that insider trading activities of brokers should be regulated, and no further exemptions should be provided for OTC companies.[26] The principle was followed that the widest disclosure of information is fundamental to federal securities regulation and that the disclosure of information and control of companies in the over-the-counter market would best be fulfilled by filing and providing the information required.[27]

[23]"Taking Stock," *Time*, April 12, 1963, pp. 91–92. Copyright Time, Inc., 1963.
[24]"Modernizing the Market," *Time*, July 26, 1963, p. 71.
[25]*Report of Special Study*, Part III, p. 63.
[26]Ibid.
[27]Ibid., p. 64.

The fourth part of the Special Study covered the subject of security credit, open-end investment companies, mutual funds, and the regulatory pattern of the SEC.

The Securities Acts amendments of 1964, considered the most significant statutory advance in federal securities regulation relevant to investor protection since 1940, were a major boost to regulation in the over-the-counter market. The principal objective of the 1964 amendments was to provide investors in securities traded over-the-counter the same fundamental disclosure and protection as previously afforded by the Securities Exchange Act of 1934 to investors in listed securities.[28] The act was designed to strengthen the standards of the securities business and to make more effective the disciplinary controls of the SEC and the self-regulatory rules of the National Association of Securities Dealers that concern securities brokers and dealers and persons associated with these groups. Companies with total assets of $1 million or more and 750 stockholders became subject to regulation, as were listed corporations. Regulation of OTC securities dealers was increased by requiring standards of training and rules for producing information and retail quotations, and by broadening the SEC's power to alter NASD rules and giving it the power to regulate both NASD members and nonmembers. The non-NASD firm must meet the same qualification standards as the NASD firm.

Not all the recommendations of the Special Study have been carried out. But the SEC continues to protect the investor from fraudulent acts of unscrupulous operators in the securities market. In addition, the New York Stock Exchange continues to strengthen the normal regulatory procedures, both self-imposed and those existing under the acts administered by the SEC.

SIPC: The Securities Investor Protection Act

In 1969, the securities industry weathered a financial storm of a severity not witnessed since the market breaks of 1937 and 1929. The professional and amateur alike were hurt. Many brokerage firms failed, and others suffered financial crises. As a result, the Securities Investor Protection Act was passed in December 1970, establishing the Securities Investor Protection Corporation (SIPC), to afford $50,000 protection per customer against broker-dealers that fail. When a firm fails, a trustee is appointed, and control of the liquidation process is carried out by the SIPC. After all assets are distributed, funds from the SIPC are used to pay for losses to the firm's customers—up to $50,000 for securities and up to $20,000 for cash accounts held for customers of the firm.

Money to build up the fund is contributed annually by SIPC members. During the period 1971–80, members were assessed $203.5 million, and $55.9 million was paid to 143 firms. The total paid from 1963 through 1980 for assistance to customers of about 200 firms was $96.8 million.[29]

[28]Securities and Exchange Commission, *31st Annual Report*, p. 1.

[29]*Fact Book 1981*, p. 58.

A market is said to be efficient if prices always fully reflect available information. This means that new information—what is knowable and relevant for judging securities —must be widely, quickly, and cheaply available to investors, and that it is rapidly reflected in securities prices.[30] Market conditions sufficient to ensure that prices fully reflect what is knowable include free availability of information, homogeneous investor expectations, and zero transaction costs.[31]

Transaction costs are most clearly related to internal securities market efficiency. And high transaction costs or a poorly organized market exchange structure can lead to inefficiencies. "Exorbitant transaction costs, such as those arising from a monopoly in the market making function, tend to inhibit capital movements"[32] that result in an externally efficient set of securities.

In an attempt to develop a national market system, the National Market System Committee of the New York Stock Exchange provided recommendation for an automated market system. The committee recommendations meet SEC objectives of a national market and a Consolidated Limit Order Book (CLOB). The SEC's objectives for a central market are these:

1. To maintain depth and liquidity by concentrating trading in a central market system in which
   —competing market makers will generate the best prices
   —comprehensive disclosure will show how and where to obtain the best executions
   —professionals acting as agents will put customer interests before their own
   —all qualified broker-dealers will have access.

2. To maximize market-making capacity to increase depth and liquidity, by encouraging dealer competition without artificial restraints between component markets.

3. To deal with the growing institutionalization of the market. It is alleged that the auction market and specialist system have been unable to absorb the pressure of block trading without help from other dealers.

4. To preserve and strengthen the network of securities firms providing public services and mobilizing capital.

5. To maintain high standards of fiduciary responsibilities for most securities firms.

6. To maximize the opportunity for public orders to match each other and be executed in classic auction market fashion.[33]

The SEC's objectives for CLOB are:

1. To help create a national market system.

2. To enhance competition.

3. To modify existing exchange mechanisms for the storage and execution of limit orders, to meet the requirements of member firms and investors for expeditious handling of

[30]Eugene F. Fama, "Efficient Capital Markets: A Review of Theory and Empirical Work," *The Journal of Finance*, May 1970, p. 383.

[31]Richard R. West, "On the Difference between Internal and External Market Efficiency," *Financial Analysis Journal*, November–December 1975, p. 30.

[32]Ibid., p. 32.

[33]"A National Market System," a report by the National Market System Committee, The New York Stock Exchange, Inc. (July 1, 1976), p. 76.

order flow in a national market system, to provide for multi-market protection of limit orders regardless of origin, and to cope with an increasing volume of transactions.

4. To ensure integration of the markets and preserve an opportunity for public orders to meet without the participation of a dealer.

5. To permit the effective integration of existing market makers (both exchange and third market) by ensuring continuation and extension of the public's ability to obtain priority in competing for executions.[34]

The overriding principle motivating the Securities and Exchange Commission is to create an efficient market, "one in which prices always reflect available information."[35] One reason why stock market prices might be inefficient is market frictions; a second is incomplete dissemination of new information. An automated national market system, combined with the complete disclosure of financial information required by the SEC, would go a long way toward creating an efficient market.

The Martin Report also recommended that a national market system be created. In addition, it recommended an improvement in the specialist's role, prohibition of institutional membership on the exchange, prohibition of the management of mutual funds by member firms, elimination of the practice of providing services for institutional investors in return for directed commission dollars, greater use of modern communications, and the elimination of the stock certificate.[36] Eventually the merger of NASDAQ and NSTS and ITS will result in a national market system where *all shares traded will be reflected in the price.*

SUMMARY

Securities are traded in a competitive and efficient marketplace. The market is divided into the primary, secondary, and third and fourth markets. The primary market handles all new issues by private businesses or governments. The secondary market is the place where securities trade after they are issued in their primary offerings. The secondary market is divided into registered exchanges and the over-the-counter market, all of which are now linked by computer. The primary and secondary markets account for 95 percent of the market. The "third" market represents off-market trade among institutional investors, and the "fourth" market represents large block trades among institutional investors via computer terminals.

The option market has become an important market. Options are traded on the NYSE and CBOE.

Foreign securities are traded on the NYSE and on foreign exchanges.

The market is regulated by the SEC, the exchanges, and self-regulated to protect the investor. Direct financial protection comes from the SIPC.

The market is efficient and competitive. Yet the thrust of efforts by the SEC, the NYSE, the Special Study, Congress, and the Martin Report have all stressed the need

[34]Ibid.

[35]Fama, "Efficient Capital Markets."

[36]*The Securities Markets, A Report with Recommendations Submitted to the Board of Governors of the New York Stock Exchange,* August 5, 1971.

for a national market system. When NASDAQ, ITS, and NSTS are merged, we will have a national market system and a more efficient and competitive marketplace.

SUMMARY OF PRINCIPLES

1. An efficient market is necessary to make certain that prices reflect fully what is knowable about a stock, including freely available information and investor expectations, and to permit low transaction costs.
2. A market has internal efficiencies if its transaction costs are low.
3. A central market system or a national market system will increase market efficiency.
4. The investor should seek the lowest transaction costs in purchasing and selling securities.
5. An options market tends to increase market efficiency.
6. The SEC's insistence on "full and complete" disclosure leads to a more efficient market.
7. Foreign markets tend to be less regulated and perhaps less efficient than U.S. markets.

REVIEW QUESTIONS

1. Where is the securities market, and what are its logical divisions?
2. What is the relative importance of the primary, secondary, and third and fourth markets in terms of number and value of shares traded? Define each market.
3. Explain the function of the organized stock exchange. Can you propose an alternative method of exchanging shares and raising capital for a corporation?
4. Discuss briefly the concept of the efficient market.
5. What effect have NASDAQ, ITS, and NSTS had on market efficiency?
6. Do the listing requirements of the New York Stock Exchange reduce market efficiency?
7. Who can buy and sell securities on the floor of the exchange?
8. Why is the OTC market a safer place to buy stocks today than it was in 1963?
9. Explain how foreign securities are traded.
10. What are block sales? How are they related to regional exchanges, the third market, and the fourth market?
11. How important are foreign stock exchanges compared with American stock exchanges?
12. Explain how securities market regulation in the United States by the SEC will lead to a more efficient market.
13. Relate marketability and liquidity to the concept of market efficiency.
14. What did the Martin Report recommend? Do you agree with the recommendations?
15. What were the SEC's objectives in seeking a "national market system"?

1. The ten companies listed below are traded in different areas of the securities market.

Share Sales	Company	Price
54,315	Bonanza Oil	325c
6,300	Burmah Oil	$2\frac{1}{2}$
2,100	Hitachi Ltd.	$61\frac{3}{8}$
54,100	DeBeers Mining	$6\frac{3}{4}$
100	Cape Cod Banking	$51\frac{1}{2}$
1,200	Alaska Gold	$2\frac{3}{4}$
1,100	Modine	$19\frac{1}{2}$
4,800	Grolier	2
1,800	Hechinger	$17\frac{3}{8}$
1,000	Moog B	$16\frac{1}{8}$

   a. Identify the markets in which they are traded.
   b. Which stock seems to be most marketable?
   c. If you wished to purchase 1,000 shares of each of these companies, what problem would you face?
   d. Are any of these markets more efficient than others? Comment.

2. Based on the information in problem 1 above, identify each company as to whether it is a part of the listed or over-the-counter market.

3. Using Figure 9–3, explain the meaning of the Disney quotes. In which market would you buy Disney, and is it marketable?

CASE

Hilary Smith wished to invest in foreign securities to diversify her investment portfolio. She was concerned that she would not be able to obtain information about the companies, that the shares would not be readily marketable, and that there would be the exchange-rate risk. From among the foreign markets listed in Figure 9–2, select three markets that would most likely meet and solve the problems she raised. Give reasons for your choices.

SELECTED READINGS

BAKER, GUTHRIE. "The Martin Report—Blueprint for Constructive Reform." *Financial Analysts Journal*, November–December 1971, p. 20.

BAYLIS, ROBERT. "The Growing of U.S. Investment Business." *Financial Analysts Journal*, November–December 1977.

BLACK, FISHER. "A Fully Computerized Stock Exchange." *Financial Analysts Journal*, November–December 1971, p. 24.

———. "Towards a Fully Automated Exchange." *Financial Analysts Journal*, July–August 1971, p. 28.

FARRAR, DONALD E. "Implications of the Martin Report." *Financial Analysts Journal,* September–October 1971, p. 14.

FEUERSTEIN, DONALD M. "The Third and Fourth Markets." *Financial Analysts Journal,* July–August 1972, p. 57.

GEYER, CARTER T. "The Abrogation of Rule 390." *Financial Analysts Journal,* January–February 1978.

LOGUE, DENNIS. "Market-Making and the Assessment of Market Efficiency." *The Journal of Finance,* March 1975, pp. 115–24.

PEAKE, JAMES W. "The National Market System." *Financial Analysts Journal,* May–June 1978.

SCHAEFER, J. M., and A. J. WARNER. "Concentration in the Securities Industry." *Financial Analysts Journal,* November–December 1977.

TREYNOR, JACK L. "Efficient Markets and Fundamental Analysis." Editorial, *Financial Analysts Journal,* March–April 1974, p. 14.

WEST, RICHARD. "Two Kinds of Market Efficiency." *Financial Analysts Journal,* November–December 1975, pp. 30–34.

CHAPTER 10

BUYING AND SELLING SHARES
The Investor and the Broker

In principle, an investor attempts to trade securities at the best possible price and the lowest possible cost. The investor must be sure that the broker has provided the best possible execution of the order—that is, achieved the highest price on a "sell," or the lowest price on a "buy," consistent with the market price at the time of the trade. The investor must also be aware of the competitive commission structure under which brokerage firms now operate. Since May 1, 1975—"May Day" in Wall Street jargon— the New York Stock Exchange commission structure is no longer the standard charge for all brokers and brokerage firms. The broker is free to negotiate the cost of a trade or commission with the customer and establish a set of fees for trading securities. It is therefore important to be aware of the negotiation process and be able to obtain the lowest cost per transaction or per dollar of shares traded. In this fashion, the investor will tend to maximize the investment return after the transaction costs are deducted. This can be an important part of the investor's strategy, particularly if stocks are frequently traded.

The typical retail securities transaction is handled first by a registered representative who is an employee of a commission brokerage firm. This is depicted graphically in Figure 10–1. Notice that the registered representatives are a part of the brokerage firm. The commission brokerage firm, as mentioned in the preceding chapter, is a member of the New York Stock Exchange and other national, regional, and local exchanges. Commission brokers also deal in securities that are traded only in the over-the-counter markets. In this chapter we will discuss the functions performed by commission brokers, the factors involved in selecting a broker, how to open an account with a

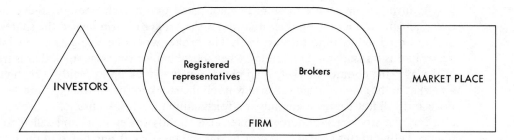

FIGURE 10–1

Relationships between Investors and the Marketplace

broker, the types of securities orders given to brokers, and the commissions and fees involved in purchasing securities.

THE FUNCTIONS OF A BROKER

The function of a broker or a brokerage firm is to buy and sell securities for customers and to obtain the best possible price at the lowest cost to the customer. The broker acts as an agent when trading in securities listed on a national, regional, or local stock exchange. The broker is asked to buy or to sell a certain number of shares of stock and is compensated for this service by a commission.

The Broker's Obligation

As an agent representing a customer, the broker is first obligated to execute the customer's orders and, in the process, to exercise due care and demonstrate a reasonable amount of skill. The broker may be held liable for any losses resulting from mistakes. The care with which orders are executed is determined by what is reasonable practice in the brokerage business at the time. The exercise of care and skill requires that the broker follow instructions and place the order in the market where the security is customarily traded. The existence of the composite tape and the electronic quote and price information systems makes it relatively easy for the broker to seek out the best price in the market. And the broker must at all times extend to the customer the right to cancel the order before it has been executed.

The broker is also obligated to refrain from making secret profits on the transaction, from crossing orders, and from acting as both broker and dealer in the same transaction. Secret profits might arise when a broker is asked to sell 100 shares of stock for $40 a share but instead sells them at $41 and pockets the $100 difference. Crossing orders come about when a trade is made between buyer and seller without going through the exchange, thus violating the principle of the auction market. The broker cannot act as broker and dealer in the same transaction. A conflict of interest could develop or a double commission would result, which would be unethical. Any case in which a dispute about the actions of a broker arises is governed by the law of agency and can be settled in a court of law.

The investor may trade in securities not listed on an exchange but traded in the over-the-counter market. In this situation, if the broker or firm owned the shares, the broker would sell them to the customer. The broker would be acting as a principal or dealer in this transaction. Sometimes, when a brokerage firm owns stock that is traded in the over-the-counter market, it specializes in the stock and is said to be "making a market in the stock." Then the firm will sell the stock to the customer at the "asked" price and will not charge a commission for handling the transaction. The broker may also buy the stock from another broker at a slightly lower price and sell it to customers, acting in this case also as a principal. When stock is purchased in the market, the customer is charged the going price plus a commission and possibly other fees.

The SEC and the brokerage firms have been vitally concerned with the ability of the customer's representative to act honestly and legally in dealings with investors. One of the basic concerns of the Special Study was to establish standards for brokers and broker-dealer firms and to control their activities. Under the Securities Acts amendments of 1964, the SEC was for the first time authorized to proceed directly against persons associated with broker-dealer firms and to impose sanctions on them, including censure and suspension of registration for up to twelve months, and statutory disqualification from being registered as a broker-dealer or from being associated with the broker-dealer. The sanctions were later expanded to cover certain additional types of injunctions, convictions, and violations.[1]

Nonmembers of the NASD who are brokers, and dealers who engage in over-the-counter business, also came under scrutiny of the Special Study and of the Securities Acts amendments. The rules were amended to include the requirement that "persons associated with nonmember broker-dealers in certain capacities must successfully complete qualifications examinations; that nonmember broker-dealers file with the commission a personal form for each of their associated persons engaged in securities activities; and that they pay fees to defray the additional costs of regulation."[2]

The NASD also established new rules to supervise its members. These "require an establishment and enforcement of written supervisory procedures and designation of a partner or officers responsible for their execution. Internal procedures must include periodic review of customer accounts and at least an annual inspection of each branch office. The rule governing discretionary accounts [such accounts treated later in this chapter] is also being amended to require written customer authorization and supervisor review and approval of activity in such accounts."[3] The NASD has prepared and distributed to its members a comprehensive supervision manual that contains detailed guidelines for effective procedures. New rules for research and investment advice have been adopted. These now generally provide that recommendations must have a basis that can be substantiated as reasonable; firms must accurately describe their research facilities and staff; and existing proprietary poistions or other interests must be disclosed. In addition, many firms have adopted training programs for their registered representatives, which include a great amount of information about the

[1] Securities and Exchange Commission, *31st Annual Report* (Washington, D.C.: Government Printing Office, 1965), p. 11.

[2] Ibid., p. 12.

[3] Ibid., p. 14.

rules and regulations of the SEC and NASD and also grounding in the fundamentals of economics and finance.

The net effect of these activities is to ensure that the broker performs the basic functions honestly and fairly, that brokers are under supervision, and that there are rules of conduct to protect the investing public. Of course, even with these restraints and guides, firms do lose money, and investors lose as a result.

Information and Research

As we learned in the first chapter, the brokerage firm supplies information and research as well as buying and selling securities for customers. Although the primary task of the broker is to buy and sell shares, the information provided helps investors to make better decisions. Investment banking and brokerage firms therefore make a valuable contribution by providing information about the economic outlook, industry analysis, company analysis, market letters and basic information found in Standard & Poor's *Stock Guide* and *Stock Reports*. Often brokers provide advice to clients who open accounts with registered representatives. And they provide formal investment management services.

Chartered Financial Analysts

Most brokerage firms employ analysts who belong to analyst societies. Such societies are found in the major cities in the United States. New York City's is the most active, and it meets almost daily. At luncheon meetings, analysts gather to hear the presidents or top executives of prominent companies speak on their companies' economic and financial history and future. Not only do these meetings provide up-to-date information about the progress of the firms, but they give analysts an opportunity to assess the abilities of management.

In recent years, the Financial Analysts Federation has established a formal training program with three stages of requirements for the analyst. The first level, Part I, provides a thorough understanding of security analysis and the fundamentals of finance, investments, and the securities market. Part II has to do with applied security analysis. Topics included are practical applications of financial analysis, economic growth, business fluctuations, and industry analysis. Part III covers the subject of portfolio management for individuals and institutions. The analyst must develop competence, judgment, and experience in answering questions presented in written form. Upon completing the training program and passing the required examinations, the analyst is designated a Chartered Financial Analyst (CFA).

The Chartered Financial Analysts have also established a code of ethics, and guidelines to the code. These form the basis of the ethical standards of 11,000 members of the Financial Analysts Federation in the United States and go a long way toward creating an ethical environment for decision-making. The statements of the code of ethics of the CFA organization indicate both the aspirations and the integrity of the members, who are professionals highly oriented toward their discipline.[4]

[4]The Institute of Chartered Financial Analysts, *Study Guide Examination to Applied Security Analysis* (Homewood, Ill.: Irwin, 1981).

Brokerage houses and dealers in securities can be classified in several distinct groups. First is the firm that performs the brokerage function but to some extent also helps companies sell new stock issues to the public. When it does the latter, the brokerage firm is acting as an underwriter and engaging in the activities of the investment banker by selling securities directly to the investing public without using the facilities of the exchange. Merrill Lynch, Pierce, Fenner & Smith and Bache Halsey Stuart Shields, Inc., are excellent examples of this type of firm. These firms deal with both the public and investing institutions.

A second type of firm is predominantly engaged in underwriting new securities issues, handling buying and selling orders for its customers only to a limited extent. These firms tend to underwrite the issues of the leading companies in the United States. Morgan Stanley and the First Boston Corporation are examples of underwriters handling large, quality companies.

A third classification of brokerage house is the smaller firm outside New York that trades in listed securities and underwrites the securities issues of small, local companies. This type of firm provides an excellent service for the investor and for the small company that wishes to go public because it needs additional equity capital. Alex Brown and Sons in Baltimore and Washington, Ferris & Company, Folger Nolan Fleming Douglas, and Johnston Lemon & Co. in Washington, D.C., Robinson-Humphrey in Atlanta and Rotan Mosely are excellent examples of this type of regional firm.

The fourth class of brokerage firm deals only in over-the-counter stocks, or only in government securities. This type of firm helps the small company sell its stock, and it deals in other securities of the same type and size. Some of these firms become specialists in a particular company's stock, and "make a market" for it.

Figure 10–2 shows the distribution of industry revenues among the various types of firms. The national full-line firms, large investment banking houses, and regional carrying firms account for almost 75 percent of aggregate industry revenues, which amounted to $18 billion in 1980.

Investment Banking

The large investment banks act as managers of, or participate in, underwriting syndicates. When a company wishes to raise capital by selling to the public or its own stockholders, it usually enlists the aid of an investment banking house. The investment banker or brokerage house advises the company on the type of security to offer and the price it should charge, then brings together other firms to help sell the issue. Each member of the underwriting syndicate is given a portion of the total amount of shares to sell; each usually assumes the risk involved in selling the stock. The underwriter guarantees that the stock will be sold and a specific sum of money paid to the corporation. If any shares remain unsold after the initial sale, each participating underwriter will take a portion of them based upon its original participation in the total number of shares.

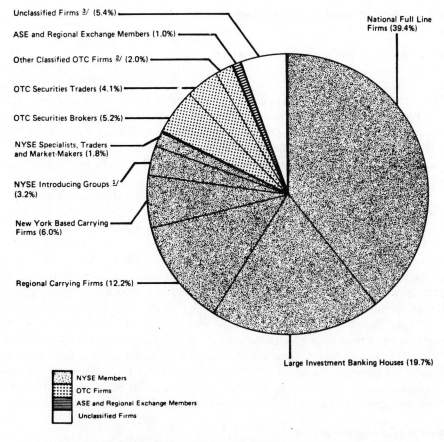

Unclassified Firms 3/ (5.4%)

ASE and Regional Exchange Members (1.0%)

Other Classified OTC Firms 2/ (2.0%)

OTC Securities Traders (4.1%)

OTC Securities Brokers (5.2%)

NYSE Specialists, Traders and Market-Makers (1.8%)

NYSE Introducing Groups 1/ (3.2%)

New York Based Carrying Firms (6.0%)

Regional Carrying Firms (12.2%)

National Full Line Firms (39.4%)

Large Investment Banking Houses (19.7%)

NYSE Members
OTC Firms
ASE and Regional Exchange Members
Unclassified Firms

1/ Includes New York Based Introducing Firms, Regional Introducing Firms and Commission Introducing Firms.

2/ Includes Investment Advisers, Securities Underwriters and Investment Company Retailers.

3/ Consists of NYSE members and OTC firms that were not categorized.

FIGURE 10–2

Distribution of Aggregate Industry Revenues Among Classified Securities Firms, 1980

SOURCE: FOCUS Report Directorate of Economic and Policy Analysis, U.S. Securities and Exchange Commission, November 1982.

All new issues sold in interstate commerce, except those specifically exempt, must be approved by the SEC. To accomplish this, a preliminary prospectus—called a *red herring*—is issued. It contains all pertinent information about the sale of the stock. A final prospectus that includes the stock's selling price must be seen by the investor. The prospectus is an excellent source of complete, recent, and objective facts.

Securities offered through investment syndicates consisting of brokers and dealers give the investor an opportunity to purchase securities without paying the usual commission. The underwriting commission, however, may be 10 percent or higher. When a brokerage firm offers its customers an opportunity to participate in these new issues, it is offering them an additional service for a fee.

SELECTING A BROKER AND A BROKERAGE FIRM

Selecting the Customer's Representative

As a matter of principle, the investor must select a broker with a great deal of care. Many people who ask, "Where can I find a good broker?" are really asking, "Where can I find a reliable person in a reliable brokerage firm who will provide me with adequate service?" This question might seem naive to the sophisticated investor, but it represents a very real problem for many people who are investing their savings for the first time. The following advice is offered in regard to selecting a broker (customer representative):

First, select a person who can give prompt and efficient service. This means he or she must be able to confirm a purchase or sale within minutes and provide price quotes quickly. A broker who cannot give prompt service is not doing the basic job.

Second, select a person who has unquestioned integrity. This requires that both the brokerage firm and the registered representative or dealer have an excellent reputation in the community. A lawyer, a banker, or an independent investment counselor can provide a list of brokers or dealers in the community who have a good reputation in the brokerage industry.

Third, choose a person who has experience in the brokerage business and who is working for a firm with an established record of good service over a period of time.

Fourth, the broker should not bother the customer or attempt to change the customer's mind after a decision is reached. Overactive trading or excessive switching from one stock to another should not be tolerated. At all times the broker should have, and give evidence of having, the best interest of the investor uppermost.

Selecting a Brokerage Firm

In selecting a brokerage firm, the investor should choose one that has an unquestioned credit rating. This is difficult for the average investor to assess. Discreet questioning in the financial community can determine the relative financial position of a brokerage firm.

Second, select a brokerage firm that can provide information and research facilities. General economic information and data about companies and industries, along with economic forecasts, should be supplied to the investor. A research staff of financial analysts should be available to analyze the investor's portfolio and make unbiased recommendations to help the investor meet investment objectives.

Third, the brokerage firm should be able to deal in securities listed on the major national and regional exchanges and, with equal facility, shares traded in the over-the-counter market. This requires membership in an exchange and in the National Association of Securities Dealers. The brokerage firm should also participate in underwriting syndicates, to give its clients the opportunity to purchase new stock issues.

In the final analysis, select a broker and a firm with a philosophy compatible with your aims and objectives. Investigate various brokers' experience and qualifications to find the person and the firm that will provide the best combination of qualities to meet your needs.

Institutional Investors and Broker Selection

Institutional investors have a somewhat different set of criteria for selecting a broker, depending upon their needs and the capability of their research staffs. The first criterion is the broker's ability to transact business quickly and at a favorable price, sometimes referred to as execution. Ability to handle a larger order is also important. A brokerage firm that can handle block sales on the stock exchange and large "off-the-board" sales will have the competitive advantage in dealing with the large institutional investor. The second criterion for selecting a brokerage firm is the *quality* of the information it supplies. To be competitive, the brokerage firm must provide good information.

The ability to transact the business and to provide research are the two main criteria used by the institutional investor in selecting a brokerage firm. The firm's proximity to the investor—whether it is a local firm—and its proximity to the over-the-counter market are also considered in the selection process.

AN ACCOUNT WITH THE BROKER

Opening an account with a brokerage firm is no more difficult than opening a checking account with a local commercial bank. To open an account, you fill out a signature card and an information card, giving information about the type of account you wish. Credit references are always required.

The simplest type of account is the cash account. In a *cash account*, no credit will be extended, no short sales will be made. All transactions must be settled within the time period given to the purchaser. The settlement date is stated on the confirmation-of-sale notice sent to the customer after an order has been executed. Another type is the *general* or *margin account*, which allows the investor to borrow when purchasing securities. Stock may be sold short, and the broker will provide securities for the transaction. The investor is required to sign a *margin agreement*, or *customer's agreement*. This permits the broker to sell the securities if the margin requirement calls for such action. It also gives the broker the right to loan your shares. The cash and margin accounts are the most usual.

You must be of legal age to open an account with a brokerage firm, because minors cannot enter into legally binding contracts. Parents may buy securities for a minor child, however, and hold them in a custodian account until the child reaches legal age, which may be 18 or 21, depending on the state or district. Many states have legislation that allows the stock to be carried in the name of the minor, with the parent acting as custodian. The adult retains management rights over the investment until the minor comes of age.

Orders are transacted through the registered representative, and a monthly statement of the results of transactions is sent to the investor. As a matter of principle, it is wise to have the securities registered in the name of the investor and have the custody remain with the investor. This protects the investor from the financial failure of the brokerage firm, and also facilitates the pledging of security collateral for a loan. But some investors leave the securities with the broker—known as keeping the securities in "street name." Since the broker's name appears on the books of the corporation as the owner, all the dividend notices, dividends, price statements, annual reports, notices of the annual meetings, and so on, are sent to the broker. The broker must notify the investor of information or dividends received. Keeping securities with the broker is convenient; the shares are available for sale at a moment's notice. This arrangement is advantageous when securities have more than one owner. An investment club, for example, would most likely leave its shares with the broker. It is the broker's responsibility and obligation to make certain that the owner enjoys all the rights of ownership when the stock is held in the name of the brokerage firm.

When the securities are sold, the proceeds of the sale, after all expenses and commissions have been deducted, can be sent to the owner by check, or they can be held by the broker for the account of the owner.

TYPES OF BROKER'S ORDERS

The investor must clearly communicate orders to the broker when buying or selling securities. It is to the investor's advantage to understand the type of orders that can be given to the broker. This information can reduce costs and misunderstandings, and improve the broker's ability to execute. For most investors, the market order is the ideal order once the investor has made the decision to buy or sell.

THE MARKET ORDER.   The market order is the simplest and most straightforward order to a broker to buy or sell a security. It is also the most common order carried out on the exchange. In receiving this order, the broker is expected to obtain the best possible price at the time the order is given. When the order reaches the floor of the exchange, it is executed promptly. The investor is certain that a market order will be completed. This is not the case with some other types of orders.

THE LIMIT ORDER.   A limit or limited order specifies the price at which stock is to be bought or sold. This is in contrast to the market order, in which no price is specified. If the price of General Motors common is 55, and a limit order is given to sell a round lot of it at 57, the limit order becomes effective when the market reaches 57. A limit order given to buy 100 shares of GM at 53, when the market price is 55, will become effective at 53 and will be exercised then by the broker or perhaps by the specialist.

The disadvantage of a limit is that it might never be completed. For example, if an order was given to buy GM at 53 and the price dropped from 55 to $53\frac{1}{2}$ and then went up again, the order would not be executed; the stock would not be bought. The price would have to drop to 53 before the order became effective and was exericsed. And it is possible that when the market reached the limit price, sufficient stock would not be available at that price. Under these circumstances, it would be better to wait until the price of GM dropped. When it was close to the desired price, a market order could be placed that would ensure the purchase of the stock. When the price of a limit order is established, it should be realistic and consistent with the current price range of the stock.

STOP ORDERS.   The stop order, or stop-loss order is essentially a combination of a limit order and a market order. An order is placed to buy or sell stock at a specified price. When the limit price is reached, it puts into effect a market order. A stop order to sell becomes a market order at or below the stop price, and a stop order to buy becomes a market order at or above the stop price. The stop order may be used to protect profits and also to limit losses in an investment purchase or in a short sale.

As an example of how the stop order may be used, assume that an investor has purchased a stock for investment purposes and is said to be "long" in the stock. (This means that the investor is maintaining a long-term position and is not selling short.) The stock was purchased at 50 and the price is now 65. The investor has a substantial profit and wishes to protect it. A stop order is placed with the broker to sell at 60. If the stock should decline to 60, this order becomes a market order, and the stock will be sold at 60 or below, as the market allows. The investor still has a good profit and is protected from a greater drop in price.

The investor could have put in a stop-loss order when the stock was purchased. Assume, for example, that the stock is purchased at 50 and the investor is apprehensive about a possible drop in price. A stop-loss order at 45 will protect the investment in case the market declines. The investor's position is "long" in this case; by putting in a stop-loss order, the loss is limited to five points. The premise from which the investor is working is that if the market price drops five points, it will probably go lower.

A speculator can use the stop-loss order to advantage when a "short" position in the stock market is taken. Assume that the speculator sells Procter & Gamble short at 70, hoping that it will drop so it can be bought back at a lower price—say, 60—and the borrowed stock returned, making a handsome profit. If the price should go to 80, the speculator would lose an amount equal to the hoped-for gain. In order to limit the loss, the speculator could place a stop-loss order with the broker at 75. When the market reached 75, the shares needed would be bought and the loss would be limited to five points per share instead of a larger amount. If the stock dropped to 60, however, and the speculator thought it might go down further, he or she could place a stop-loss order at 65. If the stock did rise instead of dropping, the shares would be bought out at that level, and the investor would still have almost a 10 percent profit on the transaction. Thus, whether the investor is "long" or "short" in a particular stock, a stop-loss order might be of benefit.

DISCRETIONARY ACCOUNTS AND ORDERS.   A discretionary account is one that gives the broker a great deal of authority in making decisions. The assumption made with a discretionary account is that, because of the broker's knowledge and experience, a better job can be done by having the customer's representative make decisions. Under a completely discretionary account, the customer's representative decides what stock to buy or sell, when to buy or sell, and the number of shares. Each order of this type must be approved by a partner of the brokerage firm, and the investor must give written approval prior to execution of the order. This type of account and order is not widely used. Many people in the financial community do not favor it or want the responsibility. Its best use is for people who are ill, out of the continental United States, or away from home for an extended period of time.

TIME ORDERS.   In some cases, time orders can be used when making purchases or sales. A time order is usually associated with a limit order. Time orders are for a day, week, or month, or are good until canceled (GTC). A day order is good until the end of the day, as the market order is. The week order is good for one week, the month order for a month. The GTC order simply remains in force until it is completed or canceled. The reason for time orders is that economic and market conditions may change and make it possible to buy or sell at a more attractive price. This order is usually given to the specialist in the stock to put into the order book.

Size of Order

In addition to classifying an order as either a buy or a sell, or as "long" or "short," it could also be a *round-lot* order, consisting of 100 shares of stock, or an *odd-lot* order, of from 1 to 99 shares. The usual unit of trading, unless otherwise stated, is a round lot of 100 shares or multiples of 100. The unit of trading for institutional investors might be as high as 1,000 shares.

THE COST OF BUYING AND SELLING SECURITIES

It is important to know how to compute the costs of buying and selling securities and to understand the impact of costs on investment decisions. The investor must keep transactions costs to a minimum and be able to verify the accuracy of commissions charged by members of the brokerage community.

Brokerage Commissions

Since May 1, 1975, each brokerage firm has been free to establish a set of commission charges based upon the competitive market environment and not by rates established by the New York Stock Exchange. Therefore, the commission for buying and selling is negotiated between the investor and the broker. The largest investors, the institutional investors, have achieved substantial discounts, ranging from 54.2 percent to as high as 57.1 percent. Individuals have experienced a decline in commission paid from 19.6 percent to 15.7 percent. These relationships are seen in Figure 10–3.

Since commissions are a trade secret, an investor should follow these principles in buying and selling shares:

1. The larger the number of shares traded, the lower the commission.
2. The higher the principal value, the lower the commission.
3. Institutions pay substantially less in commissions than do individuals.
4. The more the individual trades, the lower the negotiated rate.
5. Discount brokers usually offer low rates on small trades to individuals, but their institutional rates are not lower.

The impact of size of order and number of shares is shown in Figure 10–4 (a) and (b).

Other Costs

ODD-LOT COMMISSIONS. If the investor bought only 10 shares of a 100-share round-lot stock, computing the commission would be somewhat different. An odd-lot fee or differential is charged when less than a round lot is purchased; this is in addition to the odd-lot brokerage commission.

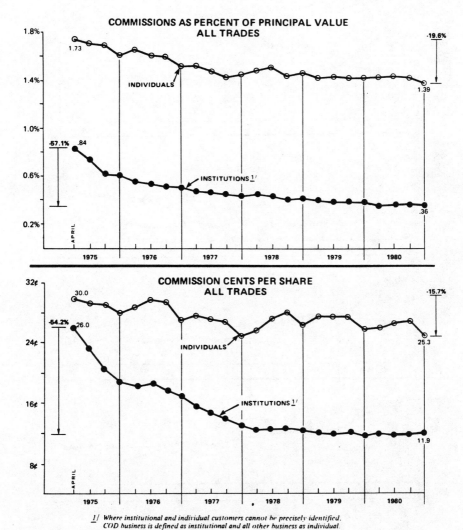

COMMISSIONS AS PERCENT OF PRINCIPAL VALUE
ALL TRADES

COMMISSION CENTS PER SHARE
ALL TRADES

1/ Where institutional and individual customers cannot be precisely identified.
COD business is defined as institutional and all other business as individual.

FIGURE 10–3

Effective Commission Rates—NYSE Member Firms, April 1975 through 4th Quarter 1980

SOURCE: *Survey of Commission Charges on Brokerage Transactions*, Directorate of Economic and Policy Analysis, U.S. Securities and Exchange Commission, November 1982.

New York State Transfer Taxes. The state of New York imposes a transfer tax on all stock sales and transfers of stock not involving a sale. It is a small tax, easy to compute, and levied only on the seller.

The SEC Fee. The Securities and Exchange Commission imposes a transfer fee on all sales of securities on a registered exchange. It is paid by the seller and amounts to 1 cent per $500 or fraction thereof of the value of the transaction. The SEC fee is is a small charge to the seller of the security for using the facilities of a registered

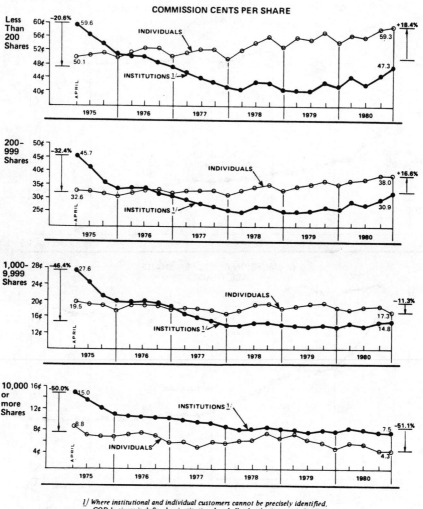

COMMISSION CENTS PER SHARE

FIGURE 10–4   (a)

Effective Commission Rates—NYSE Member Firms, April 1975 through 4th Quarter 1980

SOURCE: Survey of Commission Charges on Brokerage Transactions, Directorate of Economic and Policy Analysis, U.S. Securities and Exchange Commission, November 1982.

exchange; yet it provides over three-quarters of a million dollars a year to the U.S. Treasury in years of active trading.

MAILING AND REGISTRY.   There are also miscellaneous costs involved in transferring the shares from one owner to the new owner. Included are the costs of mailing and registering the letter containing the shares.

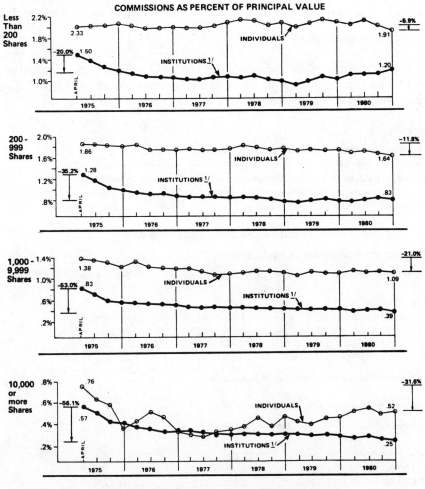

COMMISSIONS AS PERCENT OF PRINCIPAL VALUE

Less Than 200 Shares

2.33 — INDIVIDUALS — 1.91   -5.9%
-20.0% 1.50 INSTITUTIONS 1/ APRIL — 1.20

1975 1976 1977 1978 1979 1980

200 - 999 Shares

1.86 — INDIVIDUALS — 1.64   -11.8%
-35.2% 1.28 INSTITUTIONS 1/ APRIL — .83

1975 1976 1977 1978 1979 1980

1,000 - 9,999 Shares

1.38 — INDIVIDUALS — 1.09   -21.0%
-53.0% .83 INSTITUTIONS 1/ APRIL — .39

1975 1976 1977 1978 1979 1980

10,000 or more Shares

.76 — INDIVIDUALS — .52   -31.6%
-56.1% .57 INSTITUTIONS 1/ APRIL — .25

1975 1976 1977 1978 1979 1980

*1/ Where institutional and individual customers cannot be precisely identified.
COD business is defined as institutional and all other business as individual.*

FIGURE 10–4   (b)

Discount Brokers

A new type of brokerage firm—the retail discounter—has sprung up in the years
since the securities industry has gone to competitive rates. "These firms offer cut-rates
to individual investors, large and small, who are interested mainly in getting their
trades done cheaply without the usual brokerage-house frills of research reports and
stocktip phone calls."[5] There are about 50 of these firms and they have been luring

[5]Richard E. Rustin, "Cut-Rate Trading," *The Wall Street Journal*, April 5, 1977, p. 1. Reporting
done by Bruce F. Freed, Bernard Wysocki, Jr., and Earl C. Gattochalk, Jr.

business away from larger brokerage houses. Three retail discounters are Quick & Reilly, Inc., Daley, Coolidge & Co., and Letterman Transaction Services, Inc.

Commissions on Options

With the formation of the Chicago Board Options Exchange, investors and speculators have taken a great interest in options, and option volume has expanded greatly. A typical minimum commission fee is $24 or $25 (see Table 10–1).

TABLE 10–1
A Typical Commission Rate Structure for Options

An order is defined as the total executions, regardless of price, in the same option of the same class on the same side of the market (buy or sell) in one account on the same business day.

Options selling $1 and above—Listed CBOE or AMEX

Orders for purchase or sale of single options:

Principal Amount	Commission Rate	Surcharge
Under $100.00	10.0%	—
$ 100.00 to $ 2,499.99	1.3% + $12*	10.0%
$2,500.00 to $ 4,777.77	0.9% + $22	10.0%
$4,777.78 to $ 5,000.00	$71.50	—
$5,000.01 to $29,999.99	$80.73	—

*With a minimum commission of $24 per order.

Orders for purchase or sale of multiple options:

Principal Amount	Commission Rate	Surcharge
Under $100.00	10.0%	—
$ 100.00 to $ 2,499.99	1.3% + $12*	10.0%
$ 2,500.00 to $ 5,000.00	0.9% + $22	10.0%
$ 5,000.01 to $19,999.99	0.9% + $22	24.2%
$20,000.00 to $29,999.99	0.6% + $82	24.2%

Plus:　1st to 10th options:　$6 per option
　　　　11th option and over:　$4 per option

*With a minimum commission of $25 per order.

Options selling below $1—Listed CBOE or AMEX

Principal Amount	Commission Rate
$　　　0–$ 1,000.00	10.0%
$ 1,000.01–$10,000.00	6.0% + $40
$10,000.01 and over	5.0% + $140

SOURCE: Thomson & McKinnon Auchincloss Kohlmeyer, Inc.

Commission on Bonds Traded on the New York Stock Exchange

When an investor purchases or sells bonds, a commission must be paid to the broker. The rates on U.S. government bonds, bonds of Puerto Rico and the Philippines, bonds of the International Bank, bonds maturing in from six months to five years, and bonds maturing or called for redemption within six months are determined by mutual agreement between the broker-dealer and the customer, except where the exchange sets the rates. The commission on bonds traded on the New York Stock Exchange for nonmembers and allied members was, prior to negotiated rates, based upon the price of the bond; members dealing with each other charged a lower commission. Rates for nonmembers were $.75 for bonds selling at less than $10; $1.25 for bonds selling above $10 but less than $100; $2.50 for bonds selling at $100 and above; and $1.25 as a special rate for bonds maturing in from six months to five years. These commissions were based upon the selling price of a bond with a principal of $1,000. Under negotiated rates, commissions charged are generally $2.50 to $10, depending on the number of bonds in the transaction.

Commissions on Over-the-Counter Stocks

Commission charges on stocks traded over-the-counter are computed in the same way as those for listed securities. When a commission is charged, it is based on the schedule established by the firm. The customer buys on a net basis from the broker-dealer acting as a principal. The price quotation in the over-the-counter market is on a bid-and-asked basis. When buying on a net or dealer basis, the customer pays close to the asked price and would sell close to the bid price. The final price of the transaction depends upon the condition of the market when the transaction is completed.

Quotes for OTC securities are provided in major newspapers and by the National Quotation Bureau, which provides bid and asked prices daily for 7,000 stock issues and 2,000 bond issues. Brokers make these quotes available to their customers. The method of presenting bid-and-asked quotes on the OTC market has improved substantially because of the NASDAQ systems.

SUMMARY

The broker's basic function is to buy and sell securities for customers. The modern brokerage house, however, offers more than this basic service. Most large brokerage firms provide investment information for customers through their investment research departments.

In selecting a brokerage firm, the investor should consider the firm's reputation, size, credit standing, service, and information and research facilities. In selecting a customer representative, one must determine the honesty, integrity, and general experience of the representative. Institutional investors have two criteria for selecting a brokerage firm: first, the ability to buy and sell at favorable prices and volume; second, the facilities to provide profitable information and research.

Opening an account with a broker is a simple matter. The customer must give the order to buy or sell. The most frequently used order is the market order, which allows the stock to be bought at the best price in the market at the time. A limit or limited order, frequently used by investors, directs the broker to buy or sell the stock at a specific price. Stop-loss and stop orders are used to protect profits or limit losses. Time orders may be thought of as market orders suspended until the market reaches the price the customer desires. In principle, the market order is best.

As a matter of principle, the investor should keep commission costs to a minimum. This is accomplished by following two principles: (1) keeping order size and number of shares as high as possible, and (2) shopping among brokerage firms to find one that will give the best service at the lowest possible price in the long run.

Fully negotiated commission rates have reduced commission fees for institutional and retail sales. A national market system, now under development, including ITS, NSTS, and NASDAQ, will eventually lead to greater market efficiency.

SUMMARY OF PRINCIPLES

1. The investor should negotiate with the broker for the lowest possible commission over the long term.
2. The larger the value and number of shares in the transaction, the lower the commission.
3. An investor should select a broker with great care to provide efficient execution, information, experience, and integrity, and should select a firm that has an unquestioned credit rating.
4. The market order is the most efficient order for the investor to give.
5. The automated securities market is becoming more efficient.

REVIEW QUESTIONS

1. What are the primary and basic functions performed by a broker?
2. To what extent do brokerage firms engage in investment and investment banking?
3. How would you classify brokerage firms?
4. What are the factors you should consider in selecting a broker and a brokerage firm?
5. What criteria do institutional investors use to select a broker?
6. What principles should be followed to reduce the cost of buying and selling securities?
7. What principles should be followed in giving a buy or sell order to the broker?
8. What are the costs and commissions involved in the purchase of a round lot of a security and a 1,000-share order at the same price?
9. What commission would an investor pay in buying and selling bonds? Do the same principles apply to bond commissions as to stock commissions?
10. How has "May Day" affected brokerage commissions?
11. Are option commissions lower than brokerage commissions? Explain.

PROBLEMS

1. Mrs. William Pearce would like to purchase 400 shares per year of First National City Corporation stock. The money to buy the stock would come from an inheritance paid to her quarterly. The broker suggested she buy 100 shares of FNC each time she receives the money. She has heard that it is cheaper to buy stock in larger dollar amounts.
   a. What would it cost to buy 100 shares of stock four times a year compared to one purchase of 400 shares?
   b. Assuming the money was to be saved and invested at the end of the year or invested at the end of each quarter, what else would Mrs. Pearce need to consider before making her decision?
   c. What would you advise?

2. John Anderson is a trader for a large commercial bank. He is faced with making a decision about participating in a "fourth-market" firm's block-trading facilities by means of a computer terminal. He must provide a minimum of 500 shares per month, and his cost will be $\frac{1}{4}$ point per share.
   a. Assuming that the average price per share is $50, what would Anderson save in dollars by using the "fourth-market" firm? Use the data provided in Figure 10–4.
   b. What other factors would Anderson consider before making a final decision?

3. I. M. Lucky is certain he can buy 100 shares of Xerox at 53 and sell it in seven days at 56. This would be a profitable trade, and if he could do this every week, he thinks he would earn an annual return of over 100 percent. However, Lucky has not considered his commission costs.
   a. What dollar profit will Lucky have after his costs of trading?
   b. What will be his annual rate of return after commissions, assuming he doesn't make a mistake?

4. Bob Randolph is a broker for a leading national brokerage firm. He averages orders amounting to 3,000 shares a week, and the average price of a share is $50. Most of his trades are in 300-share units.
   a. What dollar volume of commissions does he generate for his firm annually? (See Figure 10–4.)
   b. If Randolph were on a strict commission basis and was paid 40 percent of gross commissions, what would he earn as an annual salary?

CASE

Angela Smith had $100,000 to invest to meet her investment objective, which was income. She had a good business sense but she did not have regular access to investment information. She had heard about discount brokers and quantity discounts in the brokerage community. She would probably trade $10,000 a year in her account at most. She didn't know a broker or customer representative. What advice would you give her?

SELECTED READINGS

BAYLIS, ROBERT M. "Business Strategy for the Securities Investment." *Financial Analysts Journal*, May–June 1980.

BAUMAN, W. SCOTT. "The C. F. A. Candidate Program." *Financial Analysts Journal*, November–December 1974, pp. 68–70.

BEUSTON, G. J., and R. L. HAGAMAN. "Risk, Volume, and Spread." *Financial Analysts Journal*, January–February 1978.

CLOSE, NICHOLAS. "Price Effects of Large Transactions." *Financial Analysts Journal*, November–December 1975, pp. 50–58.

ELLIS, CHARLES D. "The Loser's Game." *Financial Analysts Journal*, July–August 1975, pp. 19–28.

FRIEND, I., and M. BLUME. "Competitive Commissions on the New York Stock Exchange." *The Journal of Finance*, September 1974, pp. 795–820.

GEYER, CARTER T. "A Primer on Institutional Trading." *Financial Analysts Journal*, March–April 1969, pp. 16–25.

GROTH, JOHN C., WILBUR G. LEWELLEN, GARY G. SCHLARBAUM, and RONALD C. LEASE. "How Good Are Broker Recommendations?" *Financial Analysts Journal*, January–February 1979.

I.C.F.A. "Professional Standards for Financial Analysts." The Institute of Chartered Financial Analysts, 1975 (adopted May 6, 1973).

KORSCHAT, BENJAMIN. "Measuring Research Analysts Performance." *Financial Analysts Journal*, July–August 1978.

LOOMIS, PHILIP A., JR. "Broker Research after May Day." *Financial Analysts Journal*, July–August 1975, pp. 14–18.

MCENALLY, RICHARD W., and EDWARD A. DYL. "Risk of Selling Short." *Financial Analysts Journal*, November–December 1969, p. 73.

MURRAY, ROGER F. "Let's Not Blame the Institutions." *Financial Analysts Journal*, March–April 1974, pp. 18–23.

CHAPTER 11

AN ECONOMIC ANALYSIS

The first step in fundamental analysis is to determine the state of the economic environment in which we invest. Essentially we must determine the current condition of the economy, where it is headed, and the implications for investment decisions. Such an analysis allows us to select the sectors of the economy that appear to offer profitable opportunities. The analysis will also help establish what type of investment should be undertaken among real assets, riskless investments, intermediate or long-term bonds, or common stocks.

AN ANALYSIS OF THE ECONOMY

Investment in fixed-income and ownership securities is intimately associated with the economic activity of the nation. An investment in the common stock of any company is likely to be more profitable if the economy is strong and prosperous; so the expectation of the growth of the economy is favorable for the stock market. By the same token, strength in an industry that has evidenced rapid growth in the past suggests that companies within that industry and on the periphery of it will benefit from this growth and that, in the end, they will provide substantial rewards. This has been true in the past of telephone, computer, television, office-equipment and health-care industries.

Not all industries grow at the same rate, nor do all companies. The growth of a company or an industry depends basically on its ability to satisfy human wants through production of goods or performance of a service. How people earn their living and where they spend their money will, in the last analysis, determine which companies and industries will grow and prosper and which will decline.

In contrast, if expectations of a decline in the national economy are strong, the overtones and implications for investment in common stock or debt instruments are serious. If we could be certain that the next five years would bring a recession, this fact would be reflected in our investment position. Certainly it would suggest greater attention to fixed-income obligations, because these would offer considerably more safety than common stock. It is important, therefore, to analyze the national economy, attempt to determine its course over the next twelve months to three years and—to obtain some investment perspective—determine what the longer-term possibilities are.

Once this has been accomplished, the growth of the national economy can be used to forecast the growth of an industry or company and thus to determine those areas offering good opportunities. This process will also help to point out industries and companies that should be avoided because they appear to offer less attractive opportunities. As a principle, a strong and stable economy with real growth is favorable for investment.

Determining the Current State of the Economy

For investment perspective, the current state of the nation's economy must first be determined. Even the process of determining the state of economic development at the moment is not easy, simply because not all the facts and figures are available. Reporting methods provide an automatic lag in data and information. At best, the investor has only estimates. The improvement in reporting techniques from computerization of the data collected for the government by private enterprises that predict the future will help to tell where the economy is with greater certainty. If the economy is expected to grow in the future at a substantial rate compared with that of the past decade, then one course of action is obviously to invest in common stocks. If one segment of the economy is expected to grow faster than the economy as a whole, then the investor will attempt to concentrate in this rapidly growing area.

If, on the other hand, the economy is expected to begin a period of cyclical or secular decline, the investor must be more defensive. Under these conditions, bonds would be much more appealing than common stocks.

THE GNP AND COMPONENTS.   GNP stands for *gross national product*, the broadest measure of economic activity used to determine where the national economy is, where it has been, and where it is going. It represents the aggregate amount of goods and services produced in the national economy for a period of time, usually one year. Economists and investors deal in terms of the GNP, and have developed the game of "growthmanship" using GNP as a measure of economic activity.

The overall growth of GNP is reflected in Figure 11–1, based upon data developed by the Department of Commerce economists. The chart shows the past growth of the economy in current dollars and in constant 1972 dollars. A major problem of the U.S. economy surfaces from this data. First, nominal growth has been substantial, but real growth in 1972 dollars has been modest because of inflation. In making an analysis, it is wise to examine what is happening in real terms. The economy is no better off if there has been a dollar increase in output but no real growth.

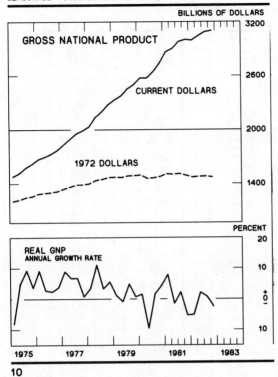

FIGURE 11-1

Gross National Product

SOURCE: Department of Commerce as found in the Federal
Reserve Chart Book, February 1983, p. 10.

Table 11–1 provides data on the past growth of the economy in current and 1972
dollars by major sector. Notice that GNP declined slightly in the fourth quarter of
1982 in 1972 dollars, indicating weakness in the economy. Personal consumption
expenditures increased because of an increase in durable goods. Personal consumption
expenditures account for approximately two-thirds of GNP. Gross private domestic
investment decreased. But notice that the reason for the decrease was because of a
decrease in nonfarm inventories; the rest of the items were stable in real terms.

Another sign of weakness was a decline in net exports. Exports declined and
imports too, which produced a decline in net exports, a further sign of weakness.
Government expenditures increased because of a slight increase in state expenditures
and a good increase in nondefense expenditures.

Thus the economy was weak based on an analysis of GNP components. The strongest parts of the economy were durables, services, residential investments, and nondefense expenditures. The weak areas were nondurable goods, business investment,
nonfarm inventories (which is reflected in manufactured goods), defense federal
spending, and state and local expenditures.

TABLE 11-1

Gross National Product and Disposition of Personal Income

	Line no.	1980	1981	1982ʳ	1981 IV	I Seasonally
					Billions of current dollars	
Gross national product (GNP)	1	2633.1	2937.7	**3057.6**	3003.2	2995.5
Personal consumption expenditures	2	1667.2	1843.2	1971.3	1884.5	1919.4
Durable goods	3	214.3	234.6	242.5	229.6	237.9
Nondurable goods..................................	4	670.4	734.5	762.0	746.5	749.1
Services	5	782.5	874.1	966.8	908.3	932.4
Gross private domestic investment	6	402.3	471.5	420.5	468.9	414.8
Fixed investment	7	412.4	451.1	443.3	455.7	450.4
Nonresidential	8	309.2	346.1	347.6	360.2	357.0
Structures	9	110.5	129.7	141.4	139.6	141.4
Producers' durable equipment	10	198.6	216.4	206.2	220.6	215.6
Residential	11	103.2	104.9	95.8	95.5	93.4
Change in business inventories.....................	12	-10.0	20.5	-22.8	13.2	-35.6
Nonfarm	13	-5.7	15.0	-23.1	6.0	-36.0
Farm	14	-4.3	5.5	.3	7.2	.4
Net exports of goods and services	15	25.2	26.1	18.5	23.5	31.3
Exports	16	339.2	367.3	349.2	367.9	359.9
Imports	17	314.0	341.3	330.7	344.4	328.6
Government purchases of goods and services	18	538.4	596.9	647.3	626.3	630.1
Federal	19	197.2	228.9	257.7	250.5	249.7
National defense................................	20	131.4	153.7	178.6	166.9	166.2
Nondefense.....................................	21	65.8	75.2	79.1	83.6	83.5
State and local	22	341.2	368.0	389.6	375.7	380.4
Addenda:						
Final sales (GNP less change in business inventories)	23	2643.1	2917.3	3080.4	2989.9	3031.1
Gross domestic product (GNP less rest-of-world sector)	24	2587.0	2888.5	3012.0	2949.8	2949.6

SOURCE: United States Department of Commerce News, Washington D.C., 20230. Bureau of Economic Analysis, February 22, 1983.

THE FEDERAL RESERVE BOARD INDEX OF INDUSTRIAL PRODUCTION. Another measure of economic activity is the Federal Reserve Board Index of Industrial Production. This monthly index, published by the Federal Reserve Board in the *Federal Reserve Bulletin*, is perhaps the best-known and most widely used index of industrial activity. Its purpose is to indicate the current amount of industrial production relative to a base-year period. The base year used is 1967. If the index was 151.0 in 1981, then the level of industrial production in real terms was 51.0 percent higher than in 1967. The FRB Index is made up of many segments of the industrial economy that reflect the total economy. As seen in Table 11-2, it is composed of market groupings (which are divided into products and materials, with products divided into final consumer goods and final equipment and intermediate products) and industry groupings. The data in Table 11-2 indicate a decline in industrial production in 1983, but not too far below 1982. The consumer area in the category "market groupings" seems to have been the strongest segment of industrial activity, but still below 1981 levels. The data seem to demonstrate no real growth in the industrial sector. The data in

FUNDAMENTAL ANALYSIS

TABLE 11–1

(Continued)

1982 II adjusted at annual rates	III	IV^r	1980	1981	1982^r	1981 IV	1982 I	II	III	IV^r	Line no.
						Seasonally adjusted at annual rates					
					Billions of 1972 dollars						
3045.2	3088.2	3101.4	1474.0	1502.5	1476.0	1490.1	1470.7	1478.4	1481.1	1473.9	1
1947.8	1986.3	2031.5	930.5	947.6	957.0	943.4	949.1	955.0	956.3	967.5	2
240.7	240.3	251.2	137.1	140.0	138.7	134.1	137.5	138.3	136.4	142.6	3
755.0	768.4	775.3	355.8	362.4	365.0	363.1	362.2	364.5	365.9	367.5	4
952.1	977.6	1005.0	437.6	445.2	453.3	446.2	449.5	452.2	454.0	457.4	5
431.5	443.3	392.4	208.4	225.8	197.0	218.9	195.4	202.3	206.3	183.8	6
447.7	438.6	436.6	213.3	216.9	205.7	214.1	210.8	206.7	202.9	202.6	7
352.2	344.2	336.9	166.1	172.0	165.5	174.2	172.0	166.7	163.4	160.0	8
143.6	141.3	139.2	48.5	51.6	53.1	53.3	53.5	53.7	53.0	52.2	9
208.6	203.0	197.7	117.6	120.4	112.4	120.9	118.5	113.0	110.4	107.9	10
95.5	94.3	99.8	47.2	44.9	40.2	39.9	38.9	40.1	39.5	42.5	11
-16.2	4.7	-44.2	-5.0	9.0	-8.8	4.8	-15.4	-4.4	3.4	-18.7	12
-15.0	3.7	-45.3	-2.9	6.8	-8.9	1.6	-15.6	-3.8	2.9	-19.2	13
-1.2	1.0	1.1	-2.1	2.1	.2	3.2	.2	-.6	.5	.5	14
34.9	6.9	.8	50.6	42.0	30.9	36.5	36.9	35.7	27.5	23.3	15
365.8	349.5	321.5	159.2	158.5	147.3	156.9	151.7	154.4	147.5	135.5	16
330.9	342.5	320.7	108.6	116.4	116.4	120.4	114.7	118.7	120.0	112.2	17
630.9	651.7	676.7	284.6	287.1	291.2	291.3	289.2	285.3	291.1	299.2	18
244.3	259.0	277.9	106.5	110.4	116.2	116.0	114.4	110.3	116.2	124.1	19
176.2	182.7	189.4	70.1	73.5	78.6	76.1	74.5	78.2	80.6	81.2	20
68.2	76.3	88.5	36.4	36.8	37.6	39.9	39:8	32.1	35.5	42.9	21
386.6	392.7	398.9	178.1	176.7	175.0	175.3	174.9	175.0	174.9	175.1	22
3061.4	3083.5	3145.6	1479.0	1493.7	1484.8	1485.3	1486.1	1482.7	1477.8	1492.6	23
2995.7	3041.6	3061.0	1447.9	1477.2	1453.8	1463.3	1448.0	1454.1	1458.6	1454.6	24

Table 11–2 indicate a general weakness in capacity utilization and slightly lower figures than 1982, which was a year of weak activity.

Construction Contracts. Construction contracts were strong through December 1982, indicating strength in this sector of the economy.

Nonagricultural Employment. Total employment was weak because of the decrease in goods-producing employment. The service sector continued to do well. At the time, the outlook for manufacturing employment was optimistic because of the increase in the durable goods sector and housing.

Retail Sales. Retail sales continued to move ahead in dollar terms through 1983. However, these figures were adjusted for inflation in consumer prices, and there was some real growth. The index seems to be consient with a relatively slow-growing economy.

Prices. Both consumer and producer finished goods prices decelerated in the period through 1983. Notice how prices in Table 11–2 have risen through 1981. Consumer prices rose 11.3 percent in 1979, 13.5 percent in 1980, and 9.9 percent

TABLE 11–2
Nonfinancial Business Activity, Selected Measures

Measure	1980	1981	1982	1982								1983
				May	June	July	Aug.	Sept.	Oct.	Nov.	Dec.	Jan.
Industrial production[a]	147.0	151.0	138.6	139.2	138.7	138.8	138.4	137.3	135.7	134.8	135.0	136.2
Market groupings												
Products, total	146.7	150.6	141.8	142.3	142.1	142.6	142.0	140.8	139.3	139.0	139.8	140.6
Final, total	145.3	149.5	141.4	142.2	142.1	142.5	141.2	140.0	138.7	138.2	139.2	140.0
Consumer goods	145.4	147.9	142.6	143.6	144.8	145.8	144.1	143.4	142.2	141.1	142.0	143.3
Equipment	145.2	151.5	139.7	140.4	138.4	138.0	137.3	135.2	134.0	134.3	135.2	135.5
Intermediate	151.9	154.4	143.4	142.6	141.9	142.8	144.7	143.7	141.6	141.9	142.0	143.0
Materials	147.6	151.6	133.7	134.3	133.5	133.0	132.8	132.0	130.0	128.5	127.7	129.4
Industry groupings												
Manufacturing	146.7	150.4	137.6	137.9	137.7	138.1	138.0	137.1	135.0	134.0	134.2	135.4
Capacity utilization (percent)[a,b]												
Manufacturing	79.1	78.5	69.8	70.2	70.0	70.0	69.8	69.2	68.0	67.4	67.3	67.8
Industrial materials industries	80.0	79.9	68.9	69.4	68.8	68.5	68.2	67.7	66.6	65.7	65.2	65.9
Construction contracts (1972 = 100)[c]	107.0	111.0	111.0	94.0	111.0	98.0	112.0	117.0	105.0	122.0	131.0	n.a.

[a] The industrial production and capacity utilization series have been revised back to January 1979.
[b] Ratios of indexes of production to indexes of capacity. Based on data from Federal Reserve, McGraw-Hill Economics Department, and Department of Commerce.
[c] Index of dollar value of total construction contracts, including residential, nonresidential, and heavy engineering, from McGraw-Hill Information Systems Company, F. W. Dodge Division.

TABLE 11–2 (Continued)

Measure	1980	1981	1982	1982								1983
				May	June	July	Aug.	Sept.	Oct.	Nov.	Dec.	Jan.
Nonagricultural employment, total[d]	137.4	138.5	136.2	137.0	136.5	136.1	135.7	135.7	135.1	134.9	134.5	135.1
Goods-producing, total	110.3	109.3	102.5	104.1	102.9	102.3	101.5	101.0	99.7	99.0	98.6	99.2
Manufacturing, total	104.3	103.7	96.9	98.3	97.3	96.7	96.0	95.5	94.2	93.5	93.2	93.4
Manufacturing, production worker	99.4	98.0	89.3	90.9	89.8	89.2	88.4	87.8	86.2	85.3	85.1	85.3
Service-producing	152.6	154.4	154.7	155.1	154.9	154.6	154.5	154.7	154.4	154.5	154.3	154.8
Personal income, total	342.9	383.5	407.9	405.7	407.3	410.8	411.4	412.3	414.5	416.1	418.5	
Wages and salary disbursements	317.6	349.9	365.4	365.4	366.0	367.6	367.8	367.7	368.0	368.0	368.6	
Manufacturing	264.3	288.1	284.9	288.1	288.4	287.7	286.4	284.5	281.3	280.1	279.3	
Disposable personal income[e]	332.9	370.3	396.5	392.9	393.4	400.6	400.9	402.0	404.0	405.5	407.9	n.a.
Retail sales[f]	303.8	330.6	326.0	347.1	336.4	341.8	338.2	341.3	345.0	353.6	349.6	349.9
Prices[g]												
Consumer	246.8	272.4	289.1	287.1	290.6	292.2	292.8	393.3	294.1	293.6	292.4	
Producer finished goods	247.0	269.8	280.6	277.8	279.9	281.7	282.4	281.4	284.1	284.9	285.1	

[d] Based on data in Employment and Earnings (U.S. Department of Labor). Series covers employees only, excluding personnel in the Armed Forces.

[e] Based on data in Survey of Current Business (U.S. Department of Commerce).

[f] Based on Bureau of Census data published in Survey of Current Business.

[g] Data without seasonal adjustment, as published in Monthly Labor Review. Seasonally adjusted data for changes in the price indexes may be obtained from the Bureau of Labor Statistics, U.S. Department of Labor.

NOTE: Basic data (not index numbers) for series mentioned in notes d, e, and f, and indexes for series mentioned in notes c and g may also be found in the Survey of Current Business.

Figures for industrial production for the last two months are preliminary and estimated, respectively.

1967 = 100; monthly and quarterly data are seasonally adjusted. Exceptions noted.

SOURCE: Federal Reserve Bulletin, February 1983, p. A46.

through July 1981. The data seem to indicate that the rate of growth of prices lessened in 1983 over 1982 which was good news.

PRIVATE FORECASTS.   Private economists provide comments about the state of the economy. The forecast in Table 11–3 of selected economic indicators provides some additional data helpful in analyzing the direction of the economy. This reflects the consensus of economists. A review of the data in Table 11–3 indicates that real GNP growth is expected to be higher, inflation lower, personal income modestly higher, FRB Index higher, expenditures for new plant lower, and the Federal government suffering from a high deficit. Housing starts will be up substantially, auto sales will be higher, unemployment will be higher, and corporate profits will be higher from 1982 and 1983 levels. The data suggest general strength in the economy through 1983.

INTEREST RATES.   An analysis of the economy would not be complete without an analysis of interest rates and bond yields. Data are provided in Figure 11–2. Here we see why we have slow growth. Interest rates rose to new highs in mid-1981 and declined in 1983. This was because of a restrictive monetary policy by the Federal Reserve Board to bring the rate of inflation lower. High interest rates eventually reduced inflation, and later brought about lower interest rates that would provide a new base for renewed economic growth.

Current Data

All the data about the economy from published sources must be updated from news releases published in the financial press. The best sources are *The Wall Street Journal* and *The New York Times. Business Week* also provides a running commentary about the economic health of the nation. News is released by the Bureau of Economic Analysis, which is a division of the U.S. Department of Commerce. The Federal Reserve Board issues data about changes in the money supply and industrial activity. The Sunday *New York Times* publishes "Data Bank," which provides data on the current state of the economy.

The World Economies

It is important for investors to take a global view of investment opportunities. If a foreign country demonstrates economic success, investors might look there for opportunities. Table 11–4 provides information about selected world economies. Notice the weakness in West Germany, France, the United Kingdom, Italy, and Canada. At a time when the U.S. economy was weak, so were those of several other industrial nations.

The strongest economy among those presented was that of Japan. This suggests that investors might search for investment opportunities in Japan. The real growth in the Japanese economy has been better—a higher real growth rate of real GNP with stability—than any other country listed in Table 11–4.

TABLE 11-3

Consensus Economic Forecast, Eggert's Blue Chip Indicators

	Percent Change 1983 from 1982								AVG for Year—1983			Total Units—1983	
	1 Real GNP (Con. '72$) (Output)	2 GNP Deflator (Prices)	3 Total GNP (Cur $)	4 Personal Income (Cur $)	5 Profits Pretax/1 (Cur $)	6 Non-Resi. Fix. Inv./2 (Cur $)	7 Consumer Price Index/3	8 Indust. Prod. Total/4	9 Treas. Bills 3 mo/5	10 Aa New Utility Bonds/6	11 Unemploy. % Labor Force	12 Housing Starts (Mil)/7	13 Auto Sls. Inc. Imp. (Mil)/8
Econoviews International Inc.	4.9H	5.8H	10.7H	6.5	22.0	9.0H	4.1	3.6	9.0H	12.0	10.2	1.70H	10.5H
Bostian Research Assoc.	4.5	5.4	10.1	10.0H	32.0	8.5	5.2	6.2H	8.0	12.0	9.5L	1.60	10.0
Morris Cohen & Associates	4.0	4.8	9.0	8.2	34.0	1.5	5.2	5.0	8.1	11.0	9.5L	1.50	9.5
Wayne Hummer & Co.	3.9	5.0	9.1	10.0H	24.0	6.6	4.8	4.3	7.6	11.5	10.1	1.51	10.1
EGGERT ECONOMIC ENTERPRISES	3.6	4.7	8.5	9.0	22.5	0.2	4.7	5.3	8.1	12.0	9.6	1.42	10.0
W. R. Grace Co.	3.5	5.5	9.1	8.8	20.0	2.7	5.3	3.2	7.5	11.7	10.0	1.43	9.1
Harris Trust & Savings Bank	3.5	5.2	8.9	8.9	22.7	7.0	4.6	3.4	8.2	12.3	10.2	1.51	9.8
Metropolitan Insurance	3.0	5.2	8.3	8.8	21.4	-0.3	4.7	3.5	7.6	11.6	10.4	1.40	9.8
Chamber of Commerce of USA	3.0	4.7	7.8	7.0	14.8	-5.3	4.2	3.4	7.0	10.5	10.4	1.50	9.2
Cahners Publishing Co.	2.8	5.6	8.4	10.0	22.0	-1.7	5.5H	2.4	8.5	—	10.5	1.40	9.6
Arthur D. Little	2.8	5.5	8.5	8.5	15.0	0.5	5.5H	4.5	7.5	12.0	10.5	1.50	10.0
CitiBank	2.8	5.0	8.0	8.3	10.9	-0.5	4.8	1.7	7.2	12.0	9.9	1.50	9.4
1st Nat. Bank–Chicago Ec. Dep.	2.8	4.7	7.6	6.3	17.4	-2.4	3.9	1.8	7.3	12.6	10.2	1.49	9.7
Conference Board	2.7	5.0	7.9	7.0	22.8	-3.1	4.5	1.9	8.4	13.3H	10.2	1.33L	9.3
Philadelphia National Bank	2.7	5.0	7.9	7.0	20.0	-1.2	4.3	1.5	8.1	12.0	10.5	1.50	8.9
Univ. of Michigan M.Q.E.M.	2.7	4.8	7.7	5.5	22.6	-1.5	3.3L	3.4	8.2	11.7	10.4	1.61	9.0
Dean Witter Reynolds & Co.	2.7	4.6	7.3	7.8	18.0	0.4	4.0	1.9	7.2	12.4	10.7	1.50	9.3
Peter L. Bernstein, Inc.	2.7	4.4	7.2	6.9	35.0H	-3.0	4.4	4.5	6.9	11.0	10.1	1.50	9.5
Arnold & S. Bleichroeder	2.6	4.0L	6.7	9.0	21.0	-1.0	4.0	3.0	8.0	10.0L	10.1	1.42	9.5
Goldman, Sachs Co.	2.5	5.2	7.8	6.9	34.2	-3.8	5.0	3.5	—	—	10.6	1.53	9.2
Nat. City Bank of Cleveland	2.5	4.6	7.2	7.7	22.0	-3.4	3.5	3.0	9.0H	13.0	10.2	1.45	9.8
La Salle National Bank	2.5	4.5	7.1	6.8	22.0	1.5	4.5	6.1	8.7	12.4	10.1	1.49	9.3
Merrill Lynch	2.4	5.1	7.6	6.2	15.7	-2.6	4.0	3.0	7.6	11.4	10.6	1.44	9.3
Bank of America, N.A.	2.4	4.9	7.5	7.2	12.4	-3.5	4.6	2.5	—	—	10.5	1.44	8.9
Wharton Econometric Forecast	2.4	4.5	7.0	6.7	8.0	-4.0	4.3	1.6	7.5	11.0	10.6	1.58	9.7

TABLE 11-3 (Continued)

| | Percent Change 1983 from 1982 | | | | | | | | AVG for Year—1983 | | | Total Units—1983 | |
| | 1 | 2 | 3 | 4 | 5 | 6 | 7 | 8 | 9 | 10 | 11 | 12 | 13 |
	Real GNP (Con. '72$) (Output)	GNP Deflator (Prices)	Total GNP (Cur $)	Personal Income (Cur $)	Profits Pretax/1 (Cur $)	Non-Resi. Fix. Inv/2 (Cur $)	Consumer Price Index/3	Indust. Prod. Total/4	Treas. Bills 3 mo/5	Aa New Utility Bonds/6	Unemploy. % Labor Force	Housing Starts (Mil)/7	Auto Sls. Inc. Imp. (Mil)/8
Irving Trust Co.	2.4	4.4	6.9	8.0	24.1	-1.4	4.4	2.2	8.8	12.4	10.1	1.40	9.0
Brown Brothers Harriman, Co.	2.3	5.0	7.4	7.5	17.7	-4.0	4.7	2.1	—	—	10.5	1.47	8.8
Pennzoil Company	2.2	5.1	7.5	7.4	13.9	-2.4	5.1	2.1	7.6	11.5	10.3	1.42	9.0
Bankers Trust	2.2	5.0	7.3	6.8	13.8	-4.9	3.9	1.9	—	—	10.3	1.49	9.0
Chase Econometrics	2.1	5.0	7.1	6.5	16.5	-2.7	4.0	1.4	7.0	11.3	10.9	1.39	9.3
Equitable Life Assurance	2.1	4.9	7.1	7.0	15.6	-5.0	4.9	2.4	8.0	10.9	10.5	1.46	8.6
Security Pacific Nat. Bank	2.1	4.8	7.0	7.0	17.5	-4.6	4.6	1.8	6.9L	11.6	10.6	1.42	9.1
Monsanto Company	2.0	5.0	7.1	7.0	10.0	-3.0	5.2	2.3	8.4	11.9	10.6	1.40	8.5L
Marine Midland Bank	2.0	4.7	6.8	7.0	3.2L	-0.5	4.0	-0.6L	7.1	12.0	10.3	1.40	9.2
Manufacturers Hanover Trust	2.0	4.3	6.3	5.6	10.4	-6.8L	3.9	1.7	7.7	12.8	10.6	1.47	9.0
Prudential Insurance Co.	1.9	5.0	7.0	7.2	20.0	-3.0	5.0	2.0	—	—	10.6	1.42	8.8
Morgan Guaranty	1.9	4.5	6.6	5.4L	12.6	-3.4	3.7	0.8	—	—	11.2H	1.51	9.1
Chase Manhattan Bank	1.9	4.5	6.5	5.9	18.1	-1.5	4.3	-0.2	—	—	10.9	1.41	8.7
E.I. Du Pont Co.	1.9	4.2	6.2	6.1	22.6	-5.0	4.0	3.5	7.0	11.3	10.0	1.40	9.0
Shearson/American Express	1.8	5.0	6.9	6.8	12.9	-0.2	4.1	2.3	7.9	12.3	10.8	1.44	9.3
UCLA Business Forecast	1.8	4.8	6.7	6.6	6.2	-4.5	4.4	1.1	8.5	12.0	10.6	1.40	8.9
U.S. Trust Co.	1.7	5.0	6.8	7.1	11.1	-6.2	5.0	1.3	7.1	11.0	10.4	1.40	8.7
Business Economics, Inc.	1.7	4.9	6.7	7.0	15.0	0.0	5.3	4.0	7.0	12.7	10.9	1.40	9.1
Siff, Oakley, Marks, Inc.	1.3	5.3	6.6	6.0	12.0	0.3	4.2	3.0	7.8	11.6	11.0	1.40	8.8
Evans Economics	1.1L	4.7	5.9L	5.5	12.9	-5.3	4.6	-0.3	7.2	12.2	11.2H	1.43	8.8
1983 CONSENSUS This month	2.5	4.9	7.5	7.3	18.2	-1.4	4.5	2.6	7.8	11.8	10.4	1.46	9.3
Last Month	2.5	5.1	7.8	7.6	18.2	-0.6	5.0	2.8	7.7	11.6	10.3	1.45	9.2

BASIC DATA SOURCES: [1]Total—Without Inventory Valuation and Capital Cons. Adj, BEA; [2]Non-Residential Fixed Investment, BEA; [3]All Urban (Copyright 1982, Capitol Publications, Inc.) Consumer Items, BLS; [4]Federal Reserve Board; [5]Bank-Discount Basis, New Issues Dept. of Treasury; [6]Moody's (new issue); [7]Bureau of Census; [8]Includes Imports, Bureau of Economic Analysis

SOURCE: Blue Chip Economic Indicators, February 10, 1983, p. 2.

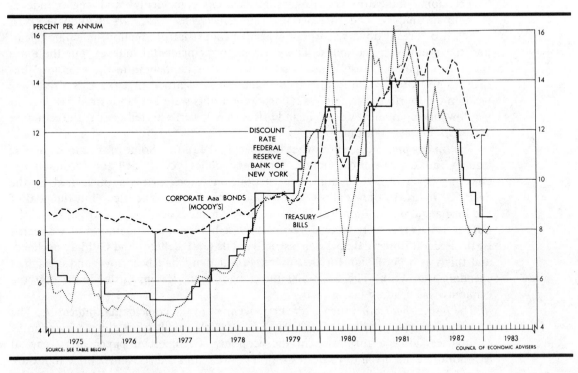

PERCENT PER ANNUM

SOURCE: SEE TABLE BELOW

COUNCIL OF ECONOMIC ADVISERS

FIGURE 11–2

Interest Rates and Bond Yields

SOURCE: Economic Indicators, February 1983, p. 30.

TABLE 11–4

Gross National Product, Selected Countries*

Country	1979	1980	1981	1982	1982 1st Qtr	2d Qtr	3d Qtr	4th Qtr
United States	2.8	−0.4	1.9	−1.8	−5.1	2.1	0.7	−1.9
Japan	5.2	4.2	4.5		1.5	8.0	2.5	
West Germany	4.0	1.8	−0.2	−1.1	−2.1	−1.3	−4.5	−0.3
France	3.3	1.1	0.2	1.6	−0.3	3.6	−1.7	2.8
United Kingdom	1.0	−1.4	−2.2		3.8	−0.1	−1.0	
Italy	4.9	3.9	−0.2		5.1	−5.9	−11.5	
Canada	2.9	0.5	3.1	−4.8	−8.5	−7.6	−3.9	

*Percent change from previous period (constant market prices; seasonally adjusted at an annual rate).

SOURCE: International Economic Statistics. Legg Mason, Washington Service. Legg Mason Wood Walker, Inc., 1747 Pennsylvania Ave, NW, Washington, D.C. 20006, March 18, 1983, p. 1.

Leading, Coincidental, and Lagging Indexes[1]

The economic indicators are grouped into leading, coincidental, and lagging indexes to help in analysis and forecasting. The *coincidental indicators* include GNP in constant or "real" dollars, corporate profits, industrial production, unemployment, and the producer price index. There are many coincidental indexes, but these are the most common. These indicators tell us what is happening in the economy, but they do not forecast the future. In our analysis we learned that the U.S. GNP was weak in the fourth quarter of 1982; corporate profits were low, industrial production was low, unemployment was high, and prices were lower. This tell us that the economy was weak but at a bottom.

The *leading indicators* tell us what to expect in the future. Some of the more popular leading indexes are fiscal policy, monetary policy, GNP deflator, productivity, consumer spending, residential construction, and stock prices as measured by the S&P 500 Index. In our analysis, fiscal policy was expansive in effect, but the goal of the Reagan administration was to reduce government expenditures and get rid of the budget deficits that were "crowding out" private borrowers. Monetary policy directed by the Federal Reserve Board was restrictive. The GNP deflator and CPI had declined, and this was a good sign for the future. Productivity had been low, and consumer spending was weak. The S&P 500 Index had risen, leaving little doubt that the economy was heading into a recovery.

The *lagging indicators* turn after the movement in the coincidental indicators. The best-known lagging indicator is the prime rate, which usually turns down a few months or quarters after a turndown in the economy. Commercial paper rates, capital expenditures, the inventory sales ratio, retail sales, and the consumer price index are other important lagging indicators. In our analysis, the prime rate and commercial paper rates began to turn down; capital expenditures were moderate; the inventory sales ratio was increasing; retail sales had been modestly higher, but not robust in real terms. And the CPI and sensitive commodity prices, another lagging indicator, had declined. The high unemployment rate confirmed the weakness in the economy early in the fourth quarter of 1981. With the announcement of a decline in the FRB Index in September 1981, most economists determined that the United States was in a mild recession.

The behavior of the leading, coincidental, and lagging indexes is seen in Figure 11-3. Notice how the lagging index declined in 1983 confirming a weak economy. Notice also the turn up in the leading index in 1983, a positive sign.

Significance and Interpretation of the Economic Indicators

The investor makes an analysis of the economy primarily to determine an investment strategy. It is not necessary for investors to make their own economic forecasts. The primary responsibility is to identify the trends in the economy and adjust the investment position accordingly. Many of the published forecasts are excellent and provide the necessary perspective. We will discuss the forecasts in a moment.

[1] An excellent article on the use of leading, lagging, and coincidental indicators is Robert S. Sobek, "A Manager's Primer on Forecasting," *Harvard Business Review*, May–June 1973.

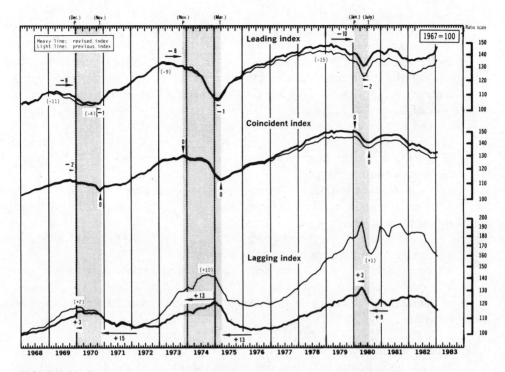

FIGURE 11–3

Composite Indexes

NOTE: P (peak) indicates the end of general business expansion and the beginning of recession; T (trough) indicates the end of general business recession and the beginning of expansion. Thus, the shaded areas represent recessions. The numbered arrows indicate the length of leads (−) and lags (+), in months, from business cycle turning dates.

( ) When the turning point of the previous index differs from that of the revised index, the lead or lag of the previous index is shown in parentheses.

SOURCE: U.S. Department of Commerce, Bureau of Economic Analysis, Washington, D.C., March 2, 1983.

The variables for analysis have their own significance. The GNP in dollar and real terms is a useful economic indicator. An expected growth rate of 5 percent in real terms would be very attractive for long-term investment and would affect the stock market positively. If the economy is expected to expand at 5 percent in real terms next year, the DJIA should be expected to behave well this year.

Inflation and price increases are detrimental to equity prices. Therefore, a real growth of GNP without inflation is favorable and desirable. Rates of 9 percent or higher are unfavorable for investment in both bonds and most equities; if inflation is expected to be that high next year, this fact will have an unfavorable effect on the stock market now.

Business investment is a key economic variable to watch. The expectation of an increase in business investment is an optimistic condition for the stock market and the economy.

The leading indicators index is very useful. A rising indicator is bullish for the economy and the stock market. A Federal Reserve Bank of Dallas economist, Wallace H. Duncan, has developed what he considers to be a better leading indicator. He divides quarterly GNP minus business inventories into consumer durables plus residential and business fixed investment. As the ratio rises, this is a sign that the economy will strengthen and that the stock market should turn up.

A high level of housing starts is a good indicator of business conditions. A high level of auto production and the expectation of growth are favorable indicators. The figures must be interpreted realistically, however: In inflationary conditions, a decline in housing starts and auto production would be a welcome sign, for it would signal reduced pressure on prices.

An increase in business inventories is good for the economy under conditions of inflation. But under stable conditions, it signifies the economy is slowing down, which would be unfavorable.

An increase in employment and a decrease in unemployment are favorable for the economy; the opposite situation is unfavorable.

An increase in personal income, coupled with substantial consumer confidence, is a favorable economic indicator.

An increase in savings is a negative indicator in depressed times, but positive under inflationary conditions.

A federal deficit is positive for a depressed economy, but negative for an inflationary economy.

Another indicator that should be examined is the balance of trade and the price of the dollar in the foreign exchange market. A deficit in our trade and balance-of-payments position is negative. Weakness in the dollar in foreign exchange markets is a negative influence on the economy and the securities markets.

High short-term interest rates, federal-fund rates, and long-term interest rates are unfavorable for the economy under normal conditions. They are quite unfavorable for equity prices. High interest rates, then, would be a negative influence on the stock market.

A high level of corporate profits and the expectation for increased corporate profits are favorable for the economy and the stock market. Generally, corporate profits are low when the GNP in real terms is low, and vice versa.

A rising stock market suggests that the economy, nine months to a year ahead, will be growing. A declining stock market suggests the economy will not grow substantially in the year ahead.

An examination of these variables will give an investor a handy reference in interpreting the direction of the economy and the stock market. This, coupled with professional economic opinion, should lead to the establishment of a sound investment policy. Consider this analysis as you read about the future of the economy and the econometric models discussed in the next sections.

Where is the economy of the United States going? This question must be answered before an investment evaluation of a company is made or an investment portfolio established. It is a difficult question to answer. Yet the evidence of the past is available as a guide. From 1976 to 1982, the annual average rate of growth of the GNP was 8.5 percent—an inflation of 7.4 percent and a real growth of 2.5 percent. Expectations for the period from 1983 through 1985 were an average annual growth rate of 9.7 percent in current dollars—a 6.0 percent increase in inflation and a real growth of 3.7 percent. At these rates, the GNP figures in Table 11–5 might result.

TABLE 11–5
Gross National Product, Forecast for 1983–1985

Year	Current GNP ($ billion)	Real GNP (1972 $ billion)	Growth Rate (%)	
			Current	Real
Forecast				
1985	$4,033	$1,644	10.0%	4.0%
1984	3,667	1,581	10.0	4.0
1983	3,333	1,520	9.0	3.0
Actual				
1982	3,058	1,476	4.1	−1.7
1981	2,938	1,503	11.6	1.8
1980	2,633	1,474	8.9	−0.4
1979	2,369	1,432	11.3	2.3
1978	2,128	1,399	12.0	4.3
1977	1,900	1,341	11.6	5.3
1976	1,702	1,271	11.3	5.6
1975	1,529	1,202	8.2	−1.3
1974	1,413	1,218	8.1	−1.4
1973	1,307	1,235	11.6	5.4
1972	1,171	1,171	10.2	5.8
1971	1,063	1,107	8.2	3.0
1970	982	1,075	5.0	−0.3

Table 11–3 provides a consensus of the future economic and investment environment into 1982. The expectation was for a modest real growth rate in 1983. The rate of inflation was expected to be lower, the FRB Index higher, government deficits lower, growth in the money supply slower; there was an expected improvement in housing starts, higher retail sales and auto sales, and higher corporate profits, with lower unemployment. This economic environment seemed attractive for stocks, with the DJIA below 850, and for bond investment, with taxable corporate rates in the 15 to 17 percent range.

TABLE 11-6

Economic Indicators (Seasonally adjusted annual rates—dollar figures in billions)

	Annual			Annual % Change			1982		E1983				E1984	
	1982	E1983	E1984	1982	1982	1983	IIIQ	PIVQ	IQ	IIQ	IIIQ	IVQ	IQ	IIQ
Gross National Product														
GNP (current dollars)	$3,057.5	$3,265.1	$3,612.3	4.1	6.8	10.6	$3,088.2	$3,101.3	$3,157.7	$3,218.4	$3,298.0	$3,386.3	$3,479.1	$3,566.6
Annual rate of increase (%)	4.1	6.8	10.6	...	...	...	5.8	1.7	7.5	7.9	10.3	11.2	11.4	10.4
Annual rate of increase—real GNP (%)	-1.8	1.7	4.9	...	...	...	0.7	-2.5	2.4	2.4	4.9	5.3	5.2	5.0
Annual rate of increase—GNP deflator (%)	6.0	5.0	5.5	...	...	...	5.0	4.3	5.0	5.3	5.1	5.5	5.9	5.2
Components of GNP														
Personal Consumption Expenditures	$1,972.0	$2,130.4	$2,325.0	7.0	8.0	9.2	$1,986.3	$2,034.6	$2,062.4	$2,103.7	$2,152.6	$2,202.9	$2,251.4	$2,302.3
% change	7.0	8.0	9.2	...	...	...	8.1	10.1	5.6	8.2	9.6	9.7	9.1	9.3
Durable goods	242.7	265.8	301.1	3.5	9.6	13.2	240.3	251.7	252.5	258.6	270.4	281.9	288.0	297.8
Nondurable goods	762.7	798.4	846.6	3.8	4.7	6.0	768.4	778.3	782.2	793.5	803.5	814.5	827.8	840.0
Services	966.6	1,066.2	1,178.1	10.6	10.3	10.5	977.6	1,004.5	1,027.8	1,051.6	1,078.7	1,106.5	1,135.6	1,164.5
Gross Private Domestic Investment	$ 421.9	$ 451.1	$ 543.0	-10.5	6.9	20.4	$ 443.3	$ 397.9	$ 442.9	$ 437.7	$ 461.3	$ 482.6	$ 512.0	$ 530.3
Nonresidential fixed investment	347.5	327.4	368.7	0.4	-5.8	12.6	344.2	336.6	323.6	322.4	326.7	337.2	350.1	362.4
% change	0.4	-5.8	12.6	...	...	...	-8.8	-8.5	-14.6	-1.4	5.4	13.5	16.2	14.8
Residential structures	95.8	124.0	150.9	-8.8	29.5	21.7	94.3	99.8	111.8	120.0	128.7	135.3	140.8	147.0
% change	-8.8	29.5	21.7	...	...	...	-4.9	25.5	57.6	32.7	32.0	22.4	17.1	18.9
Net change in business inventories	-21.4	-0.3	23.5	...	...	...	4.7	-38.5	-12.5	-4.7	6.0	10.1	21.1	20.9
Government Purchases of Goods & Services	$ 647.1	$ 699.1	$ 757.7	8.4	8.0	8.4	$ 651.7	$ 675.7	$ 683.0	$ 690.7	$ 702.1	$ 720.5	$ 733.5	$ 749.4
Federal	257.3	286.2	317.0	12.4	11.2	10.8	259.0	276.1	279.6	280.8	285.9	298.4	304.4	312.8
Nondefense	78.8	85.5	88.4	4.8	8.5	3.4	76.3	87.2	87.1	84.2	83.1	87.6	87.5	88.1
Defense	178.5	200.7	228.5	16.1	12.4	13.9	182.7	188.9	192.5	196.6	202.8	210.8	216.9	224.7
State & local	389.8	412.9	440.7	5.9	5.9	6.7	392.7	399.6	403.4	409.9	416.3	422.1	429.2	436.6
Net Exports	$ 16.6	$ -15.5	$ -14.2	-36.5	...	8.7	$ 6.9	$ -6.9	$ -10.6	$ -13.7	$ -18.1	$ -19.7	$ -17.8	$ -15.4

TABLE 11–6 (Continued)

	Annual			Annual % Change			1982		E1983				E1984	
	1982	E1983	E1984	1982	1983	1984	IIIQ	PIVQ	IQ	IIQ	IIIQ	IVQ	IQ	IIQ
Income & Profits														
Personal Income	$2,569.6	$2,745.2	$3,018.0	6.4	6.8	9.9	$2,592.4	$2,623.0	$2,658.6	$2,706.2	$2,773.2	$2,842.7	$2,909.7	$2,983.4
Disposable personal income	2,172.6	2,333.2	2,569.9	7.1	7.4	10.1	2,198.1	2,223.5	2,250.9	2,292.3	2,365.6	2,424.0	2,482.4	2,542.8
Savings rate (%)	6.5	6.0	6.8	...	...	...	6.9	5.8	5.6	5.5	6.3	6.5	6.6	6.8
*Corporate profits before taxes	176.1	193.3	234.7	−24.1	9.8	21.5	180.3	180.6	184.4	187.2	195.4	206.0	214.3	228.4
*Corporate profits after taxes	117.8	127.9	154.5	−21.9	8.6	20.8	119.4	120.4	122.3	124.1	129.2	136.1	141.6	150.5
†*Prices & Interest Rates*														
Consumer Price Index	6.1	4.9	5.3	...	...	...	7.6	2.6	4.5	5.6	5.4	5.3	5.7	4.8
Treasury bills	10.6	7.5	7.8	...	...	...	9.3	7.9	7.6	7.4	7.4	7.6	7.6	7.8
3–5 year notes	13.0	9.4	9.1	...	...	...	13.0	10.3	9.9	9.5	9.2	9.1	9.1	9.0
20 year bonds	12.9	9.9	9.4	...	...	...	12.9	10.7	10.3	10.0	9.6	9.6	9.5	9.4
Prime rate	14.9	10.6	10.8	...	...	...	14.7	12.0	10.8	10.6	10.5	10.7	11.1	10.8
New issue rate—New corporate bonds	13.9	10.4	10.0	...	...	...	14.1	11.1	10.9	10.6	10.2	10.0	9.9	9.8
Other Key Indicators														
Industrial Production Index (1967 = 100)	138.6	140.4	153.4	−8.1	1.3	9.2	138.2	135.1	136.2	138.4	141.6	145.4	148.7	152.2
Capacity utilization rate (%)	69.8	69.5	75.1	−11.0	−0.4	8.1	69.7	67.6	67.7	68.6	70.0	71.7	73.1	74.7
Housing starts (1,000 units)	1,060.3	1,447.2	1,646.1	−3.6	36.5	13.7	1,118.3	1,250.7	1,349.8	1,434.8	1,490.4	1,514.0	1,557.9	1,610.4
Auto sales (1,000,000 units)	8.0	8.8	10.1	−6.8	10.5	14.4	7.7	8.7	8.3	8.4	9.0	9.5	9.6	10.0
Unemployment rate (%)	9.7	10.3	9.5	...	...	...	10.0	10.7	10.4	10.4	10.3	10.0	9.8	9.6
‡U.S. dollar	9.4	−1.4	−3.3	...	...	...	3.6	0.7	−3.4	−0.3	−0.9	−1.2	−0.6	−1.2

*Year-to-year comparisons may not be valid due to impact of Economic Recovery Tax Act of 1981.

†Average for period.

‡Quarterly % changes at quarterly rates.

NOTE: E, estimated; P, preliminary. Figures may not add because of rounding.

SOURCE: Trends and Projections, Standard & Poor's *Industry Surveys*, March 2, 1983, p. 6.

305

Standard & Poor's Forecast

Standard and Poor's forecast portrays a slowly growing economy in 1983, followed by recovery in 1984 (see Table 11–6). Interest rates decline somewhat, inflation improves, corporate profits are higher, and unemployment gets better. Since this forecast was done in early 1983, it probably should be changed to reflect a better economic situation in the second quarter of 1983. In this type of economy, fixed-income investments at high levels of dividends or interest yields would be attractive, along with common stock.

Econometric Models and Economic Forecasting

Several firms prepare economic forecasts based on elaborate mathematical models of the economy. Wharton Associates, Chase Econometric Associates, and Data Resources, Inc., are three well-known services that do this. A forecast based on the Data Resources, Inc., model developed by Otto Eckstein, Harvard economist and member of President Johnson's Council of Economic Advisers, was made late 1981, and forecasted the period 1982 through 1986. It estimated that the economy was expected to expand in real terms through 1985, and fixed investment was expected to expand faster than the economy.

The consumer price index was expected to improve, which brings it back closer to acceptable levels. This was a favorable development for investment.

Production and housing continued to improve in the forecasted period, which was helpful in creating an environment favorable for investment. The unemployment rate continued to improve, which helped to ensure an expansion in the demand for goods and services.

Long-term and short-term interest rates tended to decrease slightly along with recovery, and would have a slight positive effect on common stock prices.

Personal income and savings continued to expand at close to normal rates. This reflects favorable consumer response to an expanding economy.

Auto sales improved in the forecasted period. Profits after taxes continue to expand but at a lower rate. This set of conditions was also favorable for common stock investment.

It would seem that the outlook for the economy was favorable for investment. With long-term bond yields relatively high and declining it would seem that the investor should diversify among bonds and stocks, investing in those areas expected to offer strong growth over the next few years. A selection of econometric estimates for 1983 and 1984 appears in Table 11–7.

Political Economic Forecasts

The Economy Recovery Tax Act of 1981 provided a stimulus to move the real growth of the economy forward with less inflation, less government, lower interest rates, and a balanced budget. The expectations of the Council of Economic Advisers appears in Table 11–8 and provides a summary of the economic views on which the budget estimates were based. A growing GNP is expected at trend levels through 1984 and then declining slightly in 1985–87, to reflect the reduced level of inflation. Real GNP

TABLE 11–7

A Sample of Econometric Forecasts

I What Are the Following Large Econometric Services Now Forecasting for 1983?

	Percent Change (1983 over 1982)			Full Year Percent Unemployment
	Real GNP	GNP Deflator	Consumer Prices	
Wharton Econometric Forecasting	2.4%	4.5%	4.3%	10.6%
Merrill Lynch	2.4	5.1	4.0	10.6
Chase Econometric	2.1	5.0	4.0	10.9
UCLA	1.8	4.8	4.4	10.6
Data Resources Inc.	1.7	5.0	4.9	10.7
Evans Economics	1.1	4.7	4.6	11.2
Compare:				
BLUE CHIP CONSENSUS	2.5	4.9	4.5	10.4

Additional Indicators:
Industrial Production 2.6%   Housing Starts 1.46 mil.   Auto Sales 9.3 mil.

II And Let's Look at Their Forecast for 1984:

	Percent Change (1984 over 1983)			Full Year Percent Unemployment
	Real GNP	GNP Deflator	Consumer Prices	
Wharton Econometric Forecast	5.1%	5.4%	4.9	9.5%
Data Resources Inc.	4.5	5.5	5.4	9.6
Chase Econometric	4.4	6.1	5.4	9.8
UCLA	4.3	4.7	4.2	9.7
Merrill Lynch	4.2	5.8	5.4	9.6
Evans Economics	3.9	5.4	5.4	11.0
Compare:				
BLUE CHIP CONSENSUS	4.5	5.4	5.3	9.3

Additional Indicators:
Industrial Production 7.6%   Housing Starts 1.68 mil.   Auto Sales 10.2 mil.

SOURCE: Blue Chip Economic Indicators, February 10, 1983, p. 3.

growth was expected to increase to the 3.9 percent level in 1982 and then to the 4.0 percent level thereafter. The GNP deflator is expected to improve by declining to the 4.4 percent level in 1988. The CPI is expected to improve even more dramatically to the 4.6 percent level in 1988. The most dramatic assumption is that the U.S. federal budget is reduced toward 1988. The level of national defense expenditures increases dramatically in the 1983 to 1988 period. Yet the annual increase in the rate of total federal expenditures declines over the period. In this environment, corporate profits increase at a

TABLE 11–8a

Short-Range Economic Forecast Underlying the Reagan Budget (billions of $)

Item	Actual 1981	Forecast		
		1982[1]	1983	1984
Major Economic Indicators:				
Gross national product, percent change, fourth quarter over fourth quarter:				
Current dollars	9.6	3.3	8.8	9.2
Constant (1972) dollars	0.7	−1.2	3.1	4.0
GNP deflator (percent change, fourth quarter over fourth quarter)	8.9	4.6	5.6	5.0
Consumer Price Index (percent change, fourth quarter over fourth quarter)[2]	9.4	4.4	5.0	4.4
Unemployment rate (percent, fourth quarter)[3]	8.1	10.5	10.4	9.5
Annual Economic Assumptions:				
Gross national product:				
Current dollars:				
Amount	2,938	3,058	3,262	3,566
Percent change, year over year	11.6	4.1	6.7	9.3
Constant (1972) dollars:				
Amount	1,503	1,476	1,496	1,555
Percent change, year over year	1.9	−1.8	1.4	3.9
Incomes:				
Personal income	2,416	2,570	2,727	2,935
Wages and salaries	1,494	1,560	1,640	1,780
Corporate profits	232	175	177	206
Price level:				
GNP deflator:				
Level (1972 = 100), annual average	195.5	207.2	218.1	229.4
Percent change, year over year	9.4	6.0	5.2	5.2
Consumer Price Index:[2]				
Level (1967 = 100), annual average	272.3	288.6	302.9	316.8
Percent change, year over year	10.3	6.0	4.9	4.6
Unemployment rates:				
Total, annual average[3]	7.5	9.5	10.7	9.9
Insured, annual average[4]	3.5	4.7	5.3	4.7
Federal pay raise, October (percent)[5]	4.8	4.0		6.1
Interest rate, 91-day Treasury bills (percent)[6]	14.1	10.7	8.0	7.9
Interest rate, 10-year Treasury notes (percent)	13.9	13.0	10.2	9.8

[1] Preliminary actual data.

[2] CPI for urban wage earners and clerical workers. Two versions of the CPI are now published. The index shown here is that currently used, as required by law, in calculating automatic cost-of-living increases for indexed Federal programs. The figures in this table reflect the actual CPI for December 1982, released January 21, 1983, which was 0.7% lower than had been projected; consequently, the cost-of-living adjustments estimated in the budget are higher than the actual adjustments will be.

[3] Percent of total labor force, including armed forces stationed in the U.S.

[4] This indicator measures unemployment under State regular unemployment insurance as a percentage of covered employment under that program. It does not include recipients of extended benefits under that program.

[5] General schedule pay raises become effective in October—the first month of the fiscal year. Thus, the October 1984 pay raise will set new pay scales that will be in effect during fiscal year 1985. The October 1981 pay raise for military personnel was 14.0%.

[6] Average rate on new issues within period, on a bank discount basis. These projections assume, by convention, that interest rates decline with the rate of inflation. They do not represent a forecast of interest rates.

SOURCE: Budget of the United States Government, Fiscal Year 1984, Office of Management and Budget, pp. 2–9, and 10.

TABLE 11–8b

Long-range Economic Forecast Underlying the Reagan Budget (billions of $)

	Assumptions			
	1985	1986	1987	1988
Major Economic Indicators:				
Gross national product, percent change, fourth quarter over fourth quarter:				
Current dollars	9.0	8.7	8.7	8.6
Constant (1972) dollars	4.0	4.0	4.0	4.0
GNP deflator (percent change, fourth quarter over fourth quarter)	4.8	4.5	4.5	4.4
Consumer Price Index (percent change, fourth quarter over fourth quarter)[1]	4.7	4.5	4.5	4.4
Unemployment rate (percent, fourth quarter)[3]	8.5	7.8	7.0	6.2
Annual Economic Assumptions:				
Gross national product:				
Current dollars:				
Amount	3,890	4,232	4,599	4,995
Percent change, year over year	9.1	8.8	8.7	8.6
Constant (1972) dollars:				
Amount	1,617	1,682	1,749	1,819
Percent change, year over year	4.0	4.0	4.0	4.0
Incomes:				
Personal income	3,142	3,377	3,661	3,956
Wages and salaries	1,921	2,090	2,281	2,483
Corporate profits	246	296	316	329
Price level:				
GNP deflator:				
Level (1972 = 100), annual average	240.6	251.7	263.0	274.7
Percent change, year over year	4.9	4.6	4.5	4.4
Consumer Price Index:[1]				
Level (1967 = 100), annual average	331.4	346.6	362.2	378.3
Percent change, year over year	4.6	4.6	4.5	4.4
Unemployment rates:				
Total, annual average[2]	8.9	8.1	7.3	6.5
Insured, annual average[3]	4.2	3.8	3.5	3.2
Federal pay raise, October (percent)[4]	6.0	5.7	5.6	5.5
Interest rate, 91-day Treasury bills (percent)[5]	7.4	6.8	6.5	6.1
Interest rate, 10-year Treasury notes (percent)	9.0	8.0	7.4	6.7

[1] CPI for urban wage earners and clerical workers. Two versions of the CPI are now published. The index shown here is that currently used, as required by law, in calculating automatic cost-of-living increases for indexed Federal programs. The manner in which this index measures housing costs will change significantly in 1985.

[2] Percent of total labor force, including armed forces stationed in the U.S.

[3] This indicator measures unemployment under State regular unemployment insurance as a percentage of covered employment under that program. It does not include recipients of extended benefits under that program.

[4] General schedule pay raises become effective in October—the first month of the fiscal year. Thus, the October 1985 pay raise will set new pay scales that will be in effect during fiscal year 1986.

[5] Average rate on new issues within period, on a bank discount basis. These projections assume, by convention, that interest rates decline with the rate of inflation. They do not represent a forecast of interest rates.

rate almost twice that of the 91-day Treasury bill rate, which is expected to decline during the period to reach the 6.1 percent level in 1988.

There was a great deal of skepticism about whether the economic goals of the Reagan administration could be accomplished. Actually, the goals were not unrealistic when compared to recent economic history. The annual growth rate of GNP, real and current, is consistent with the past; in fact, it is actually a little higher and perhaps a bit optimistic. The level of unemployment, the growth rate of corporate profits, the Treasury bill yield rate, and the real GNP deflator are all within the realm of possibility based on historical norms.

There were two statistics among the data where the administration was too optimistic. One is in the permanent reduction of the annual rate of increase in the CPI from 9.3 percent to 4.6 percent. The second is the reduction of the annual fiscal deficit from almost $150 billion annually for the period 1982–83 to only $60.0 billion in the period 1983–88. Both estimates were unrealistic. Yet the proposed tax reductions might stimulate the economy to reach the point where the CPI will decline to 6 percent, on average, with the federal budget not quite balanced but at least reduced.

The Tax Program Might Do the Job

The tax program put together by President Reagan that produced a bipartisan tax bill could be successful. The Economic Recovery Tax Act of 1981 is highlighted and summarized in Table 11–9. The actual Reagan tax bill approved by the House and Senate will differ in detail. Indexing of taxes will begin after 1984. The fiscal stimulus to the private sector reflected in the tax bill might bring about a balanced budget with less inflation and lower rates of interest.

TABLE 11–9
Highlights of President Reagan's Tax Cut Program in 1981.

The Conable-Hance bipartisan tax bill includes the following:

Marginal tax rate cuts. 5% on October 1, 1981; 10% on July 1, 1982; 10% on July 1, 1983.
Marriage penalty. 5% exclusion up to $1,500 in 1982 and 10% exclusion up to $3,000 in 1983 and thereafter.
Accelerated cost-recovery system. 10–5–3 year writeoff with 150% declining balance method through 1984. 175% and 200% declining balance method, 1985 and 1986, respectively.

    15 year audit proof cost recovery period—200% declining balance method for all real estate.

    Liberalized leasing role to facilitate transfer of ACRS tax benefits.

    No deductions for qualified progress expenditure.

Top marginal rate on investment income cut from 70% to 50%.

IRAs. Maximum contributions increased to $2,000 from $1,500, up to 100% of individual's earnings per year. Spousal IRA maximum contribution boosted to $2,250 from $1,750.

    Participants in employer-sponsored retirement plans can deduct $1,000 per year from IRA contributions. Spousal IRAs can be established with contributions up to $1,125 for active participants.

TABLE 11-9

Highlights of President Reagan's Tax Cut Program in 1981 (Continued)

Keoghs. Maximum deductible contribution raised to $15,000.

R&D. Tax credit equal to 25% incremental R&D wages.

$200/$400 interest and dividends exclusion made permanent.

Foreign workers. $50,000 exclusion plus half of the next $50,000 of foreign earned income, plus housing allowances.

Windfall profits tax. Tax credit raised for royalty owners to $2,500.

Rehabilitation tax credit. 15% tax credit for buildings over 15 years, 20% credit for buildings over 40 years, 25% credit for certified historic structures.

Estate and gift tax. Tax credit increased to $192,800, marital deduction unlimited, annual gift tax exclusion raised to $10,000 per donee.

H.R. 3849 and deficits. Will reduce deficits in 1981–83 and produce greater surpluses in 1984 and beyond. Revenue costs less than administration's original program: $7 billion difference in 1981, $17 billion in 1982, $9 billion in 1983, and $2 billion in 1984.

SOURCE: Department of the Treasury, Ann Dare McLaughlin, Assistant Secretary for Public Affairs, June 24, 1981.

The Reagan economics program had taken hold by early 1983 but at substantial cost in 10.2 percent unemployment and a tremendous budget deficit. The federal budget was not balanced. The deficits were greater than expected. There was a major disagreement between President and Congress as to a proper solution. The administration's revised forecasts indicated a less optimistic future, with higher unemployment and no balanced budget. This would imply higher interest rates. The revised forecast appears in Table 11-8 with further evidence of economic growth presented in Table 11-10.

The Record of GNP Forecasting

Before we accept any forecast of the gross national product, however, we should know something of its reliability. Victor Zarnowitz found that the average error in forecasting GNP during the period 1953–64 was approximately $10 billion, or about 2 percent of the gross national product during that period of time.[2] Maurice W. Lee suggests that these seemingly accurate projections are not very good when compared to changes in GNP[3]. When this comparison is made, the error amounts to approximately 40 percent, and the range of the error is between 28 and 56 percent of the change

[2]Victor Zarnowitz, *Appraisal of Short-Term Economic Forecasts* (New York: National Bureau of Economic Research, 1967).

[3]Maurice W. Lee, *Macroeconomics: Fluctuations, Growth and Stability*, 4th ed. (Homewood, Ill.: Irwin, 1967), p. 638.

TABLE 11–10
Actual and Projected Economic Indicators

Economic Indicator	Quarterly Data											Annual Data		
	Actual							Projected				Actual		Proj.
	1981:2	1981:3	1981:4	1982:1	1982:2	1982:3	1982:4	1983:1	1983:2	1983:3	1983:4	1981	1982	1983
Gross national product	2,902	2,981	3,003	2,996	3,045	3,088	3,101	3,194	3,263	3,343	3,430	2,938	3,058	3,307
GNP implicit price deflator (index, 1972 = 100)	193.2	197.4	201.6	203.7	206.0	208.5	210.7	213.9	216.6	219.7	222.9	195.5	207.2	218.2
Corporate profits after taxes	146.2	150.8	144.9	115.0	116.3	119.4	NA	123.0	127.0	133.0	142.1	150.9	NA	130.3
Unemployment rate (percent)	7.367	7.400	8.300	8.800	9.400	9.967	10.67	10.30	10.10	9.800	9.600	7.617	9.708	9.900
Industrial production (index, 1967 = 100)	152.5	153.0	146.3	141.8	139.4	138.2	135.1	139.0	141.0	144.0	146.0	150.9	138.6	143.0
New private housing units started (millions)	1.173	0.962	0.865	0.920	0.952	1.118	1.251	1.210	1.300	1.400	1.460	1.100	1.060	1.340
Consumer price index (% change from prior quarter or year)	7.8	11.8	7.8	3.2	4.6	7.6	2.6	5.0	5.5	5.5	5.9	10.3	6.1	5.2
90-day treasury bill rate (%)	14.83	15.09	12.02	12.90	12.36	9.71	7.94	7.85	8.00	8.00	8.25	14.08	10.72	8.10
New high-grade corporate bond yield (percent)	15.22	16.33	16.01	16.14	15.65	14.72	NA	12.00	11.70	11.50	11.50	15.48	NA	11.78
GNP in 1972 dollars	1,502	1,510	1,490	1,471	1,478	1,481	1,472	1,494	1,506	1,522	1,537	1,503	1,475	1,514
Personal consumption expenditures (1972 $)	944.6	951.4	943.4	949.1	955.0	956.3	968.0	972.0	979.0	987.0	997.0	947.6	957.1	982.0
Nonresidential fixed investment (1972 $)	170.1	173.9	174.2	172.0	166.7	163.4	159.6	156.0	156.0	158.0	161.0	172.0	165.4	158.0
Residential fixed investment (1972 $)	47.3	42.9	39.9	38.9	40.1	39.5	41.7	44.0	46.1	49.0	50.5	44.9	40.1	48.0
Change in business inventories (1972 $)	12.1	16.5	4.8	−15.4	−4.4	3.4	−17.7	0.0	2.0	3.1	5.0	9.0	−8.5	2.7
Net exports (1972 $)	44.2	39.2	36.5	36.9	35.7	27.5	21.1	28.0	28.0	27.5	27.5	42.0	30.3	28.0
Federal government purchases (1972 $)	107.0	110.7	116.0	114.4	110.3	116.2	123.7	118.0	119.0	120.0	121.0	110.4	116.2	120.0
State & local government purchases (1972 $)	176.9	175.7	175.3	174.9	175.0	174.9	175.4	174.0	174.0	175.0	175.0	176.7	175.1	174.1

TABLE 11–10 (Continued)

Series from the Current-Dollar GNP Accounts

Economic Indicator	Quarterly Data												Annual Data		
	1980:1	1980:2	1980:3	1980:4	1981:1	1981:2	1981:3	1981:4	1982:1	1982:2	1982:3	1982:4	1980	1981	1982
Gross national product	2,576	2,573	2,644	2,739	2,865	2,902	2,981	3,003	2,996	3,045	3,088	3,101	2,633	2,938	3,058
Personal consumption expenditures	1,619	1,622	1,682	1,746	1,800	1,819	1,869	1,885	1,919	1,948	1,986	2,035	1,667	1,843	1,972
Gross private domestic investment	424.0	391.0	384.1	410.3	455.7	475.5	486.0	468.9	414.8	431.5	443.3	397.9	402.3	471.5	421.9
Net exports	14.0	24.2	39.0	23.5	31.2	23.7	25.9	23.5	31.3	34.9	6.9	-6.9	25.2	26.1	16.6
Government purchases	519.2	536.0	538.5	559.8	578.1	583.2	600.2	626.3	630.1	630.9	651.7	675.7	538.4	597.0	647.1
Disposable personal income	1,767	1,781	1,846	1,903	1,959	1,997	2,060	2,101	2,117	2,152	2,198	2,224	1,824	2,029	2,173
Personal saving rate (% of disposable income)	5.5	6.1	6.1	5.5	5.4	6.1	6.5	7.5	6.6	6.7	6.9	5.8	5.8	6.4	6.5

NOTE: (1) All data are at annual rates and in billions of current dollars unless otherwise indicated. (2) To facilitate comparison and evaluation of forecasts, both actual data, released in late January, and projected data, released by ASA-NBER in December, are displayed for fourth quarter 1982.

SOURCES: Projections: American Statistical Association—National Bureau of Economic Research panel of forecasters. Actual Data: U.S. Departments of Commerce and Labor, Board of Governors of the Federal Reserve System.

SOURCE: Economic Outlook USA, Vol. 10, no. 1, Winter 1983.

in GNP. Lee also points out that the declines are less often underestimated than are the increases. A study done by Rozen Cole at the National Bureau of Economic Research indicated that it was difficult to be precise with measures of GNP. However, very few of the year-end forecasts miss the *direction* of change in the year ahead.

The use of the forecast, then, is primarily for the purpose of finding the direction of the national economy for the next year and planning investment actions accordingly. The investor should not be upset that estimates are in error by as much as $10 billion, for the fact that business is expected to be good—or bad—for the next six to twelve months gives enough information to check investment policy periodically and make any adjustments that seem to be needed, based on the projection of aggregate growth.

Recent Evidence on Economic Forecasting

An economist at the Federal Reserve Bank of Boston, Stephen K. McNees, has kept track of the performance of economic forecasters since the early 1970s. He has measured, in particular, the accuracy of predictions of the three major econometric forecasters, Chase Econometric Associates, owned by Chase Manhattan; Data Resources, Inc., owned by McGraw-Hill; and Wharton Econometric Forecasting Associates, Inc., owned by Ziff-Davis. McNees' study may be found in the September–October 1981 issue of the *New England Economic Review*. He found that "a tally of the results in 13 of the categories . . . shows that Wharton came closest to the mark most often, followed by DRI, with Chase a distant third. Of the forecasters that issue predictions early in the quarter, a group that includes the Big Three, Wharton out-predicted the rest 40 times; DRI five times; and Chase, three times. Wharton erred more than the other only twice; DRI, 21 times; and Chase, 67 times. Among the five outfits that issue mid-quarter predictions, Wharton did best 44 times and worst 19 times. The next-best performer was Townsend-Greenspan & Company, which came closest 40 times. Manufacturers Hanover Trust came in last, issuing the worst forecast 38 times, even though it did not look more than five quarters ahead."[4]

DRI and Chase both revise their figures toward the end of the quarter. DRI did the best 61 times and the worst 75 times; Chase was best 14 times and worst 75 times. There has been a change in management at Chase and the results have improved. "Victor Zarnowitz, an economics professor at the Graduate School of Business, University of Chicago . . . suggests that corporations relying on a few key statistics can predict the future about as well as econometricians feeding thousands of variables into a computer."[5]

What did the leading econometric forecasters predict for 1983–84? Table 11–7 provided an answer to that question. Keep track and let's see who was right.

INVESTMENT IMPLICATIONS

There are two areas in which we draw conclusions about investment implications. First, areas for investment, and then the types of securities. Broadly speaking, the most attractive sectors seem to be in defense, services, nondurables, business invest-

[4]Jaye Scroll, "To Divine Is to ERR," *Barron's*, March 22, 1982, p. 30.
[5]Ibid., p. 35.

ment, and imports. The most attractive economies in the world for investment seem to be Japan, Germany, and the United States. The areas for investment seem to be longer-term bonds or fixed-income investment. This is based on the notion that interest rates will decline and inflation will be less. The second area is common stocks in a depressed stock market but caution should be the word in a historically high stock market. Commodities or tangible assets are relatively unattractive, and real estate is less attractive because of pressure on prices and high mortgage rates.

SUMMARY

The first step in fundamental analysis is to determine the present state of the economy in the United States and other industrial nations. We need answers to questions such as these: What are present economic conditions? Where is the economy headed; is the economy expanding or contracting? What are the investment implications?

The current state of the economy is determined from data published by the Department of Commerce through its Bureau of Economic Analysis. In early 1983, the U.S. economy was weak, along with those of other industrial countries, but showing signs of recovery. The strongest parts of the U.S. economy were nondurables, services, and national defense, based upon data presented. The Federal Reserve Board Index of Industrial Production indicated, along with the other indexes, that the economy was weak, capacity utilization was low, construction contracts moving up, unemployment growing, retail sales increasing modestly, and the rate of price increase slowly declining. Interest rates were declining. Current data also indicated a recovering economy. Many of the world economies were also weak.

The leading, coincidental, and lagging indexes pointed to a rising economy. The leading indicators tend to signal the future. A weak leading index today means a weak coincidental index in the next period. As an example, a rising stock market indicates a strong economy ahead. The prime lending rate tends to lag behind the economy and can be rising even as the economy declines.

A growing economy with stable prices, profits, and interest rates is the best investment environment for common stock investment.

The forecasts suggested that the economy would grow at an annual rate of around 4 percent, which was below the rate of growth expected by the Reagan administration. The goal of balancing the federal budget seems a bit optimistic. And the record of GNP forecasting is not very accurate.

The implications for investment appear to be clear: Invest in the American, German, and Japanese economies; invest in the defense, services, and nondurables of the U.S. economy; invest in fixed-income securities with high current yields and some common stock but watch out for over-priced stock in a market at its peak.

SUMMARY OF PRINCIPLES

1. A strong and stable economy with real growth is favorable for investment.
2. The investor should select the strong areas of the economy for investment.

3. The investor should take a global view in estimating the future growth of the domestic economy.
4. The investor should attempt to estimate the future growth of the economy.

REVIEW QUESTIONS

1. Distinguish between the gross national product and the Federal Reserve Board Index of Industrial Production as a measure of economic activity.
2. Explain how the FRB Index of Industrial Production is used as a measure of economic activity.
3. What has been the trend of the growth of the national economy as measured by the GNP and the FRB Index?
4. Is this growth trend likely to continue? Explain why or why not.
5. Examine the major sectors of the economy and determine their growth.
6. Are all sectors of the economy growing at the same rate? Discuss.
7. What sectors appear to be attractive for investment? Comment.
8. Explain what is meant by a lagging, leading, or coincidental indicator.
9. Is it true that interest rates are a lagging indicator and that the stock market is a leading indicator?
10. Make a list of the most important leading, lagging, and coincidental indicators.

PROBLEMS

1. Analyze the data in Table 11–1 and indicate those sectors of the economy that seem to be growing rapidly.
2. Examine Table 11–2 carefully and indicate which sectors of the FRB Index appear to be growing must rapidly.
3. Table 11–3 data provide a forecast of the economy. Based on the forecast, how would an investor modify, change, or direct his or her investments?
4. The data in Figure 11–5 provide the past yield pattern of bonds, Treasury bills, and discount rate. How would you describe these past patterns? What are the implications for investors?
5. The data in Table 11–5 are provided by Standard & Poor's. Identify each statistic as a leading, lagging, or coincidental indicator. Analyze each group that is leading, lagging, and coincidental and comment on the significance for the economy and the investor.
6. Analyze carefully the economic forecasts in Tables 11–7, 11–8, and 11–10. Based on these forecasts, which sectors of the economy appear to be most attractive for investment? What are the implications for investment diversification between bonds and stocks?

CASE

Tony Cook received an update of statistics on the behavior of the economy. The data appear below. Based upon these data, what appears to be the direction of the economy? What are the implications for the investor? Assume conditions at the end of June 1983 as your point of departure.

Actual and Projected Economic Indicators (seasonally adjusted)

Economic Indicator	Quarterly Data												Annual Data		
	Actual							Projected					Actual		Projected
	1981:3	1981:4	1982:1	1982:2	1982:3	1982:4	1983:1	1983:1	1983:2	1983:3	1983:4	1984:1	1982	1983	1984
Gross National Product	2,981	3,003	2,996	3,045	3,088	3,108	3,177	3,160	3,225	3,297	3,379	3,460	3,059	3,265	3,578
GNP implicit price deflator (index, 1972 = 100)	197.4	201.6	203.7	206.0	208.5	210.4	213.4	212.9	215.3	218.0	221.0	223.5	207.1	216.7	228.1
Corporate profits after taxes	150.8	144.9	115.0	116.3	119.4	117.9	NA	122.0	127.2	135.0	142.0	145.7	117.2	131.0	156.4
Unemployment rate (percent)	7.400	8.300	8.800	9.400	9.967	10.67	10.37	10.50	10.30	10.10	10.00	9.800	9.708	10.20	9.400
Industrial production (index, 1967 = 100)	153.0	146.3	141.8	139.4	138.2	135.3	138.0	137.0	139.6	142.0	145.3	148.0	138.6	141.0	152.0
New private housing units started (millions)	0.961	0.870	0.903	0.950	1.122	1.261	1.693	1.350	1.450	1.500	1.540	1.600	1.059	1.470	1.645
Consumer price index (% change from prior quarter or year)	12.0	7.2	3.0	5.3	7.8	2.0	-0.4	2.9	4.1	4.3	4.6	5.0	6.2	4.1	5.2
90-day treasury bill rate (%)	15.09	12.02	12.90	12.36	9.71	7.94	8.08	7.88	7.50	7.65	7.95	8.00	10.72	7.80	8.00
New high-grade corporate bond yield (percent)	16.33	16.01	16.14	15.65	14.72	12.22	NA	11.65	11.50	11.40	11.30	11.50	14.68	11.50	11.20
GNP in 1972 dollars	1,510	1,490	1,471	1,478	1,481	1,477	1,489	1,485	1,495	1,510	1,527	1,541	1,477	1,503	1,565
Personal consumption expenditures (1972 $)	951.4	943.4	949.1	955.0	956.3	967.0	972.4	974.0	980.5	990.0	998.0	1,007	956.8	985.2	1,019
Nonresidential fixed investment (1972 $)	173.9	174.2	172.0	166.7	163.4	160.9	162.0	156.0	154.6	154.3	156.0	159.9	165.8	155.0	163.0
Residential fixed investment (1972 $)	42.9	39.9	38.9	40.1	39.5	42.9	49.9	44.0	47.0	49.6	51.8	53.3	40.4	48.1	55.7
Change in business inventories (1972 $)	16.5	4.8	-15.4	-4.4	3.4	-20.3	-12.4	-5.0	0.9	2.9	5.0	7.0	-9.2	0.5	9.0
Net exports (1972 $)	39.2	36.5	36.9	35.7	27.5	27.2	24.0	20.0	18.8	18.5	19.4	19.1	31.8	19.0	20.0
Federal government purchases (1972 $)	110.7	116.0	114.4	110.3	116.2	124.7	117.5	121.0	120.0	122.0	124.0	124.8	116.4	122.0	126.0
State & local government purchases (1972 $)	175.7	175.3	174.9	175.0	174.9	174.8	175.1	175.0	175.0	175.0	175.0	175.0	174.9	175.0	176.0

TABLE (Continued)

Series from the Current-Dollar GNP Accounts

Economic Indicator	Quarterly Data												Annual Data		
	1980:2	1980:3	1980:4	1981:1	1981:2	1981:3	1981:4	1982:1	1982:2	1982:3	1982:4	1983:1	1980	1981	1982
Gross national product	2,573	2,644	2,739	2,865	2,902	2,981	3,003	2,996	3,045	3,088	3,108	3,177	2,633	2,938	3,059
Personal consumption expenditures	1,622	1,682	1,746	1,800	1,819	1,869	1,885	1,919	1,948	1,986	2,031	2,054	1,667	1,843	1,971
Gross private domestic investment	391.0	384.1	410.3	455.7	475.5	486.0	468.9	414.8	431.5	443.3	391.5	430.6	402.3	471.5	420.3
Net exports	24.2	39.0	23.5	31.2	23.7	25.9	23.5	31.3	34.9	6.9	9.1	16.6	25.2	26.1	20.6
Government purchases	536.0	538.5	559.8	578.1	583.2	600.2	626.3	630.1	630.9	651.7	676.8	675.5	538.4	597.0	647.4
Disposable personal income	1,781	1,846	1,903	1,959	1,997	2,060	2,101	2,117	2,152	2,198	2,224	2,247	1,824	2,029	2,173
Personal saving rate (% of disposable income)	6.1	6.1	5.5	5.4	6.1	6.5	7.5	6.6	6.7	6.9	6.0	5.9	5.8	6.4	6.5

NOTE: (1) All data are at annual rates and in billions of current dollars unless otherwise indicated. (2) To facilitate comparison and evaluation of forecasts, both actual data, released in late April, and projected data, released by ASA-NBER in March, are displayed for first quarter 1983.

SOURCES: Projections: American Statistical Association—National Bureau of Economic Research panel of forecasters.
Actual Date: U.S. Departments of Commerce and Labor, Board of Governors of the Federal Reserve System. Reprinted by permission.

ALLOME, FRED C., and DANIEL E. O'NEIL. "Stock Market Returns and the Presidential Election Cycle." *Financial Analysts Journal*, September–October 1980.

AMBACHTEHER, KEITH P. "Investment Income during Inflation." *Financial Analysts Journal*, March–April 1978.

BABIN, CHARLES E., and DAVID R. RAMSON. "What's Holding Up Capital Investment." *Financial Analysts Journal*, July–August 1978.

BANKS, STEPHEN J. "The Origins of the Great Inflation." *Financial Analysts Journal*, May–June 1977.

BERKMAN, NELL G. "A Rational View of Rational Expectations." *New England Economic Review*, January–February 1980.

BREALY, RICHARD A. "Government Assets: Key to Inflation?" *Financial Analysts Journal*, January–Ferbruary 1979.

FAND, DAVID I. "The Reagan Economic Program." *Financial Analysts Journal*, July–August 1981.

FREUND, WILLIAM C. "Productivity and Inflation." *Financial Analysts Journal*, July–August 1981.

GRAY, WILLIAM S. "Long Term Outlook for Stock Market." *Financial Analysts Journal*, July–August 1979.

GUTMAN, PETER M. "Are the Unemployed, Unemployed." *Financial Analysts Journal*, September–October 1978.

HOWARD, GODFREY G. "A Second Look at Inflation." *Financial Analysts Journal*, September–October 1977.

IBBOTSON, R. G., and R. A. SINQUEFIELD. "Stocks, Bonds, Bills, and Inflation: Updates." *Financial Analysts Journal*, July–August 1979.

KAISER, RONALD W. "Kondratieff's Gloomy News for Investors." *Financial Analysts Journal*, May–June 1979.

LADD, EDWARD A. "Thoughts on Long Term Implications of Inflation: A Look at American Inflation from a British Perspective." *Financial Analysts Journal*, July–August 1981.

LEUTHOLD, STEVAN. "Interest Rates, Inflation and Deflation." *Financial Analysts Journal*, January–February 1981.

McCONNELL, WALTER S., and STEPHEN D. LEIT. "Inflation, Stock Price, and Job Creation." *Financial Analysts Journal*, March–April 1977.

MEIGS, A. JAMES. "The Fed and Financial Markets: Is It Killing Them with Kindness." *Financial Analysts Journal*, January–February 1981.

MENNIS, EDMUND A. "New Tools for Profits Analysis." *C.F.A. Readings in Financial Analysis*, 1981.

MEYERS, STEPHEN L. "A Re-examination of Market and Industry Factors in Stock Price Bahavior," *The Journal of Finance*, June 1973, pp. 695–706.

MILLER, EDWARD M. "Portfolio Selection in a Fluctuating Economy." *Financial Analysts Journal*, May–June 1978.

MODIGLIANI, FRANCO, and RICHARD A. COHN. "Inflation and the Stock Market." *Financial Analysts Journal*, March–April 1979.

MOOR, ROY E. "Economics and Investment Analysis." *Financial Analysts Journal*, November–December 1971, p. 63.

MOORE, GEOFFRY H. "Stock Prices and the Business Cycle." *The Journal of Portfolio Management*, spring 1975.

OKUN, ARTHUR M. "The Invisible Handshake and the Inflating Process." *Challenge*, 1980.

PICCINI, RAYMOND. "Stock Market Behavior around Business Cycle Peaks." *Financial Analysts Journal*, May–June 1980.

RANDALL, MAURY R. "Investment Planning in an Inflationary Environment." *Financial Analysts Journal*, January–February 1981.

ROCKWELL, ARTHUR E. "Long-term U.S. Economic Outlook: Issues and Methodology." *Economic Report*, March 1980.

SMAISTRLA, CHARLES J., and ADRIAN W. TROOP. "A New Inflation in the 1970's." *Financial Analysts Journal*, March–April 1980.

SOMMERS, ALBERT T. "Inflation and Domestic Economic Policy." *Financial Analysts Journal*, January–February 1975, pp. 18–23.

TERBORGH, GEORGE. "The Decline of Fiscal Discipline." *Financial Analysts Journal*, July–August 1981.

———. "Inflation and Profits." *Financial Analysts Journal*, May–June 1974, pp. 19–23.

TONGUE, WILLIAM W. "How Money Matters." *Business Economics*, May 1974, pp. 31–28.

TREYNOR, JACK L. "The Coming Revolution in Investment Management." *Methodology in Financial Investments*, (Lexington, Mass.: D. C. Heath, 1972.)

———. "Unemployment and Inflation." *Financial Analysts Journal*, May–June 1975, pp. 21–29.

———. "What Professor Galbraith Failed to Say on TV." *Financial Analysts Journal*, March–April 1978.

VOLCKER, PAUL A. "Domestic Expansion and External Responsibilities." *The Journal of Finance*, May 1971, p. 243.

WALLICH, HENRY C. "Investment Income during Inflation." *Financial Analysts Journal*, March–April 1978.

———. "Techniques of Monetary Policy." *Financial Analysts Journal*, July–August 1981.

WANNISKI, JUDE T. "Economic Policy and the Rise and Fall of Empires." *Financial Analysts Journal*, January–February 1980.

WEIDENBAUM, MURRAY I. "Matching National Goals and Resources." *Financial Analysts Journal*, July–August 1972, p. 17.

WICKERSHAM, GRACE. "The Latest Tools for Profit Analysis." *C.F.A. Readings in Financial Analysis*, 1981.

CHAPTER 12

INDUSTRY ANALYSIS

The industries that contribute to the output of the major segments of the economy vary in their growth rate and in their overall contribution to economic activity. Some have grown more rapidly than the GNP and offer the expectation of continued growth. Others have maintained a growth comparable to that of the GNP. A few have been unable to expand and have declined in economic significance. If we are to succeed as investors, we must analyze the economic significance of industries and invest in those that offer continued success, measured by the industry's ability to compete for its appropriate share of the GNP.

Seeking industries that are expected to grow at faster than the "real" rate of GNP for the future seems to be a logical starting position. We can find successful companies in industries that are not growing. On the other hand, investment success is more likely to be found in growing and strongly competitive industries. The danger in this thesis is that investors tend to bid up the price of these assets in the marketplace. An overenthusiastic investor might pay too much for a share of stock in such industries.

THE CONCEPT OF AN INDUSTRY

In a broad sense, an industry might be considered a *community of interests*. This concept would reflect the idea of a group of people coming together because they do a certain type of work or produce a similar type of product. Such groups would include agriculture as well as manufacturing, mining, and merchandising. In an economic sense, these groups form into industries because of the nature of what is produced and the processes involved in its production. We tend to think of an industry as a product- or process-oriented unit. The automobile industry, for example, reflects both the concept of the end product—the automobile—and the method of production—the manufacturing process. The banking industry also illustrates the industry concept. It consists basically of commercial banks that make business and consumer loans. The product, of course, is money, and the process is the lending process.

The classes of industries are unlimited. If we classify industries by the process of manufacture, then we can divide them according to the nature of their function; for example, the manufacturing industry, the transportation industry, and the public utility industry. These broad functional groups can then be further broken down by end product. The manufacturing industry, for instance, would include such diverse products as autos, pianos, tin cans, shoes, and cribs. It would include all products that are manufactured. The transportation industry would include railroads, airlines, trucks, ships, and possibly pipelines. Automobiles would be excluded because, although they are a form of transportation, they are not available as a common carrier except as taxis. However, private transportation competes via the auto with other forms of transportation. In this case, the auto would fall into two classes of industry: the manufacturing class and the transportation class. For practical purposes, autos would be placed in the manufacturing industry.

The classification of an industry is important when we analyze its growth. Each industry takes its share of the GNP and competes with every other industry. Thus, the manufacturing industries compete with agriculture, transportation, and public utilities. This interindustry competition is important. And within each major industry classification, the product- or service-oriented segments compete for a share of the GNP. We are mainly interested in these service- and product-oriented industries. When we define an *industry*, then, as a limited set of productive functions or activities measured by the output of an end product or service, we can observe changes much more easily than if we used a broader classification. These changes and the expectation of change should cause the investor to react favorably or unfavorably toward an industry for investment.

For careful analysis, each industry is broken down into its logical product classes. The drug industry, for example, is usually divided into proprietary drugs and ethical drugs, the auto industry into passenger autos and trucks, and the rubber industry into tires and rubber products. The *Federal Reserve Bulletin* publishes monthly production index figures for the various industries that make up the major groupings. These are useful in determining the level of economic activity of each industry group.

Howard B. Bonham, Jr., indicates the importance of input-output analysis on the demand for various products in the several industry groups. (An input-output system for the U.S. economy reflects in dollar terms the demand on our industries caused by certain amounts of final demand as represented by the national income accounts.) He considers such analysis "one of the most useful macroeconomic tools available for measuring the effects on equity investments of dynamic product flows within an economic structure."[1] Input-output analysis evolved from the work of Wassily Leontief

---

[1] Howard B. Bonham, Jr., "The Use of Input Economics in Common Stock Analysis," *Financial Analysts Journal*, January–February 1967, p. 19.

of Harvard University and continues with research sponsored by the Office of Business Education. The OBE tables are the first to be integrated with the national income accounts.[2]

THE CHARACTERISTICS OF INDUSTRY GROWTH

The growth of an industry usually begins with a major technological change. In the early years of the twentieth century in the United States, the automobile, the airplane, the radio, and the electric light were major technological developments that created new industries. In more recent years, robots, personal computers, electronic equipment and communication devices, office equipment, automated control equipment, and ionic propulsion have created new industries and rapid technological change, resulting in rapid industrial growth. As an industry expands, the following growth pattern emerges, according to Simon Kuznets:[3] In the beginning, rapid growth takes place at extremely high rates. As the industry expands over long periods of time, the percentage rate of growth diminishes. Industries never experience unretarded or accelerated growth for long periods of time.

Kuznets gives several reasons for the decreasing rate of growth of an industry. First, the major technological changes that created the industry are concentrated in the early stages of the life of the industry. These major changes are reinforced by minor changes and improvements, also made early in the development of the product as the bugs are being worked out. If we have a limited number of production functions to use in the industry and their use is changed rapidly, strong economic pressures bring about rapid upward growth. A good illustration of this is the auto industry, whose rate of growth was extremely high in the early years of its development, between 1900 and 1920. Production rates increased rapidly, and the percentage rate of change was extremely high as techniques and products improved. After the early period of development, the growth rate subsided. In 1981, although the number of autos and trucks produced was far greater than in the formative years of the industry, the rate of increase on a percentage basis was much less. The industry has become a cyclical growth industry, as well. And the Japanese became a dominant force in the industry.

A second reason for a diminution in the industry growth rate is the nature of the technological change itself. The basic types of major technological changes help to produce an old product more cheaply or a completely new product on a mass basis. This has happened in the pocket-calculator field and in the production of digital watches. A high-priced commodity or service is changed into a low-priced one, making it available to a larger market. A luxury good might be changed into a necessity good. Using the auto industry as an example, both changes increase the immediate demand for the product. In the early years of technological development, these changes have a remarkable impact on growth. Beyond the early years and the immediate reduction in

[2]Ibid.

[3]These comments are based on class notes from Dr. Kuznets's course in economic development at the University of Pennsylvania. See also Simon S. Kuznets, *Capital in the American Economy* (Princeton, N.J.: Princeton University Press, 1961); *Modern Economic Growth* (New Haven, Conn.: Yale University Press, 1966); and *Economic Growth and Structure* (New York: Norton, 1965).

costs and price, the changes have little effect on the growth of the market and the output of the industry.

The relative growth of other industries tends to reduce the impact of cost reductions, which, in turn, tends to limit the continued growth of a market. If other industries do not grow as fast as that in which the rapid expansion takes place, prices will not drop in the other industries. This will limit the decline in price in the rapidly expanding industry. Assume, for example, that a technological innovation occurs, such as the development of automated equipment, that permits a reduction in the price of transistors from $2 to $.90 per unit. The demand for transistors expands, and the number produced increases dramatically. However, germanium, a raw material for the transistor, does not undergo a corresponding expansion in demand, since there are no new economies or developments that will allow germanium to be produced at a lower price, and the amount used in producing transistors is not sufficient to bring about mass-production economies. Since the raw material cannot be lowered in price, there is also a lower limit to the price of the transistor. Any price changes that would help increase output in the future will be negligible, and the accompanying rate of expansion will be diminished. The general effect of this example can be transferred to the economy as a whole: An industry growing at a rapid rate, faster than the national economy, will eventually have its growth dampened because of the slower growth of the economy.

A third factor that tends to limit the growth of an industry is competitive pressure from other industries. The industry that first experienced a technological change may be restrained by the development of a new industry, competing directly for raw materials and thus tending to raise costs for the original industry and limit its expansion potential. Sometimes new industries are directly competitive with the old product or original product. For example, one material becomes a substitute for another, as aluminum was substituted for steel, stainless steel for chromium, and plastics for aluminum or metal. For that matter, all metals can be substituted for each other, depending upon their use. One type of power can be substituted for other types of power, depending upon the cost-price relationship involved. Nuclear power is even now being substituted for oil-generated steam to produce electricity. The woolen industry lost part of its market to cotton. Then cotton lost part of its market to silk and rayon. Then rayon and silk began losing their market to nylon, and so on. The net of these changes is that the competitive position of one product or service is often lost to a rival product that indirectly or directly does a better job than the old one. This competition tends to diminish the growth of the industry.

Another manifestation of this competition is international competition that develops for a national product. Television set production can be used as an illustration. The Japanese developed production techniques allowing TV sets to be cheaply mass-produced. Virtually overnight, the market price was reduced and the competitive position of the industry in the United States was diminished.

A fourth and final factor that might reduce the rate of growth of an industry is a decrease in population growth. In order for a product to expand its output at an increasing rate, per capita output would have to grow at an increasing rate. For this to occur, consumers would have to spend more of their income. The consumer's income does not increase as fast as the growth of the product, because the economy grows more slowly than an industry experiencing rapid growth, and so it is unlikely that the industry's growth rate can be sustained. If we have declining population growth, the industry's growth will slow down even more quickly.

The diminishing percentage rate of growth of the output of an industry is depicted in Figure 12-1. The solid curved line on the semilog graph represents a constantly decreasing rate of growth. If the same data were plotted on regular graph paper, the line would be straight. If the line in Figure 12–1 were straight, the growth rate would be constant. A constant growth rate is possible over short periods of the growth life of an industry, but not over long periods. The time intervals in the chart do not represent any specific number of years, since the life cycle of an industry cannot be shown in uniform time periods.

The Industry Growth Cycle

The growth of an industry is sometimes divided into stages. Grodinsky, in his book on investments,[4] and Mead and Grodinsky, in a previous book,[5] divided the growth cycle into the pioneering stage, the expansion stage, and the stagnation stage—a division quite similar to Kuznets's concept. Figure 12–1 demonstrates the growth of an industry graphically by the dotted line, which is divided into the three stages. Grodinsky, however, relates the stages of growth more to the characteristics of the company than to the industry as a whole. His concepts should be of interest to the investor.

THE PIONEERING STAGE. The pioneering stage, as presented by Grodinsky, is comparable to Kuznets's discovery stage, the stage when the technological development takes place. Its primary characteristics are a rapid increase in production and rapidly expanding demand for the product. Many companies enter the market to produce the product, and the market is extremely competitive. Profits are large for those firms that first introduce the product, but as competition increases, prices decline rapidly and profits fall. This tends to force out the less efficient firms. There is little price stability in the pioneering stage, and risk capital is supplied more by speculators and promoters than by investors.

As competition forces out some of the firms, they are acquired by the competitively strong companies. As a result, at the end of the pioneering stage, only a few leading companies remain in the industry. In Figure 12–1, the dip in sales at that point represents the circumstances that force many firms out of the industry. Numerous examples of this competitive struggle can be found in American industry. The auto, radio, television, and electronic industries offer excellent illustrations of the pioneering stage as part of the growth cycle.

THE EXPANSION STAGE. The expansion stage in the growth cycle is characterized by an expanding demand for the product, but the rate of growth is less than in the pioneering stage. There is greater stability of prices, products, and production during this phase. Competition is keen, and a small number of larger firms dominate the

---

[4]Julius Grodinsky, *Investments* (New York: Ronald Press, 1953).

[5]Edward S. Mead and Julius Grodinsky, *Ebb and Flow of Investment Values* (New York: Appleton-Century-Crofts, 1939).

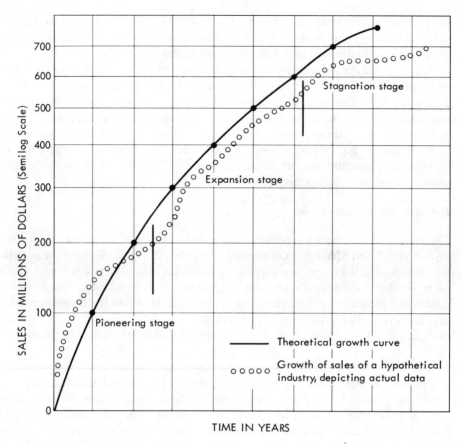

FIGURE 12–1

The Industrial Growth Curve

industry. These large firms have been put together through merger and acquisition and by their competitive superiority. The companies that remain have successfully weathered the financial adversity of the later phases of the pioneering stage and remain in business. They are well financed, they have strong financial structures, and their current financial position is excellent. They have an established dividend policy and are able to expand from internally generated funds, making them independent of the long-term capital markets except for major capital-expenditure programs.

Investors can invest funds during the expansion stage in the knowledge that substantial growth potential remains in the industry. Yet there is safety and security, since the larger companies have been able to retain a sizable share of the market. The competitive position of the firm is not automatically ensured by its initial success, but it is in a strong position to maintain its status in the industry. Investors have some assurance that they will profit from investment without the threat of a complete loss of principal. This stage of industry growth is sometimes referred to as the period of investment maturity, because of the stability and status of the firms within the industry.

FUNDAMENTAL ANALYSIS

THE STAGNATION STAGE. In the later phase of the growth cycle of an industry, the rate of growth subsides. For some industries there is no growth at all in this phase, and output actually declines. One example among many can be found in the passenger and transportation segment of the railroad industry. The number of railroad passengers has declined, and the revenues generated have not been sufficient to allow some railroads to earn a profit. Even some freight railroads are not profitable. Unless costs can be reduced through eliminating unnecessary labor and operating costs, even the more successful railroads will become profitless. In this phase, the industry simply loses its power to expand. When the national economy shows economic strength, the growth of an industry in the stagnation stage does not keep pace, and its output falls faster than the economy increases. The transition from the expansion to the stagnation stage comes about gradually, and unless investors are aware of the changes taking place in an industry, they will be taken by surprise.

Reasons for Decline in the Competitive Position of an Industry

In the stagnation stage, demand for the product is reduced by competition from other products or by factors that influence the profits of the industry by increasing costs. Grodinsky refers to these as factors of latent obsolescence that tend to destroy the competitive position of an industry.[6] Included in this category are increasingly high labor costs, changes in social habits, changes in government regulation, and improved technology or automation.

HIGH LABOR COSTS.   High labor costs might force an industry out of a profitable existence. With a lessening of demand for a product, prices must be reduced to keep the product competitive. However, if prices cannot be reduced because of relatively high production costs, and labor costs in particular, the industry will decline in economic significance.

CHANGES IN SOCIAL HABITS.   The tobacco industry suffers from latent obsolescence because of a change in social habits. Cancer and cigarette smoking have been closely linked, as demonstrated by several studies in the United States and England. When results of the early studies became known to the public, a change occurred in demand from regular to filter-tip cigarettes. In 1969, the U.S. government released the results of a study on the positive link between cigarette smoking and cancer. While this has not yet had a significant effect upon cigarette sales, the relationship between lung cancer and other fatal diseases and smoking has become more positive. The long-range result should be a diminishment in smoking. There are indications that the per capita rate of use has declined in spite of the increase in total use of cigarettes.

CHANGES IN GOVERNMENT REGULATION.   A change in government regulation, or new regulations, might operate against an industry and cause it to lose its competitive position. The outstanding example of this was Prohibition, which made an industry obsolete almost overnight. Price-support programs undertaken by the government will also influence the competitive position of an industry. The enactment of minimum-

[6]Grodinsky, *Investments*, p. 71.

wage legislation will affect an industry's wage costs and reduce its competitive effectiveness. A tax on foreign investment was enacted by the federal government as a partial solution to the outflow of gold and the worsening of our balance of payments. This had a detrimental effect on the competitive position of foreign companies such as Royal Dutch-Shell and Aluminium, Ltd. A change in the method of depreciating or depleting an asset, as in the oil industry, or a change in costing an asset, as in the cement industry, will also affect the economic position of an industry. And, of course, protecting the environment has caused some chemical companies to go out of business.

AUTOMATION. Because it can bring about changes that will influence the competitive position of an industry, automation is a problem; it is a social problem as well, and demands an answer to the question, "What can we do with workers who are displaced by the robot?" Robotics could lead to tremendous benefits for the nation and for specific industries, because it allows us to be competitive in world markets. At present, the United States is undergoing a technological explosion in the field of automated equipment. One automated machine, for example, can take material from a press and transfer it to another machine for fabrication. The one machine replaces 20 workers, and this is only one phase of the assembly operation. The results, when magnified throughout a plant, achieve considerable savings. At the same time, the new machine replaces older types of machines and causes a decline in demand in other industries. Technological change is not an unmixed blessing; yet improved productivity and automation are necessary if we are to survive in world markets against strong competition.

OTHER FACTORS. Other signs pointing to a worsening of the competitive position of an industry include excessive productive capacity and rising prices. The auto industry could possibly be in this position now. An industry that is no longer expanding will not need new plant and equipment. If the industry needs only 60 percent of its capacity to meet the demand for its product, it may be operating close to its breakeven point. The only course remaining will be to raise prices, or even seek government help or protection. The overcapacity suggests, too, that the growth of the industry is not keeping pace with the national economy. With unused capacity and rising costs, an industry has difficulty maintaining its competitive position.

INVESTMENT CLASSIFICATION OF INDUSTRIES

The discussion up to this point has been about the economic classifications of industries. Investment services provide basic industry information more closely related to our needs and concentrate more on companies within the industry. Most of the services discuss the economic significance of the industry and its future outlook. If an industry appears to offer attractive future benefits, we can easily translate this into the probability that a company's common stock will allow us to share in the industry's prosperity.

The investor must know the industry classifications used by the investment services. It is vital to learn in detail the characteristics, problems, and practices of each industry—its present and future development and operating features—in order to establish the proper perspective in attempting to determine the future of the industry and of a specific company within that industry. Moody's manuals classify industries as banking and finance, industrials, public utilities, and transportation. Standard & Poor's *Industry Surveys* use an index to industry classification that should be referred to, since it is available in most libraries. It was used below, where the S&P 500 Index industries were grouped under the GNP components. The effects of change in a given product can be analyzed without losing the significance of the change in a mass of combined data.

An example of division into major groups and subgroups is found in the drug and cosmetic industry, which is classified as an industrial by Moody's. As classified by Standard & Poor's, it consists of four basic parts: drugs, divided into ethical pharmaceuticals and proprietary drugs; cosmetics and toiletries; hospital chains; and hospital supplies and equipment. They are grouped in this way because of the method of distribution of these products. The insurance industry serves as another example: It is divided into a few basic groups—life insurance companies, multiline group, property liability group, and specialty insurers (private mortgage guaranty group). These are all part of the banking and finance industry. It is important that these subgroups be used in making a comparative analysis, even though a knowledge of the broad classifications is also necessary. Let us look briefly at the major industry classifications.

Banks and Finance

This major American industry supplies money to other segments of the economy, both private and public, to meet their long- and short-term capital needs. It also provides protection for individuals, and investment management for investors.

BANKING.   Banking deals with commercial banks. Commercials banks make loans primarily to business and depend on prosperous business conditions to support their growth. In recent years, commercial banks have become "department-store" banks. They now make mortgage and home-improvement loans and loans to consumers for the purchase of durable consumer goods. Banking has become more competitive, and banks now offer a wider range of services than in the past. Included in these subsidiary activities are short-term trusts, investment trusts, investment management, complete data-processing and record-keeping services, mortgage lending, insurance, travel, foreign branches, and management consulting and financial planning for both individuals and corporations. Banks have also increased the number and amount of term loans they extend to business. The success of a commercial bank depends first on its ability to invest or lend money profitably. The profitability of banking depends on the level of interest rates and the relative success of business.

SAVINGS AND LOAN ASSOCIATIONS.   Savings and loan associations, particularly through savings and loan holding companies, have expanded rapidly in the post-World War II era. Originally they only made mortgage loans, but their lending and investing activities have broadened. Many savings and loan associations have expanded into leasing, consumer loans, and other types of loans in the housing area, including home-improvement loans. Savings and loans are tied to the building industry and require large amounts of savings to meet the demand for loans. The industry was in severe difficulty in 1982 because of the high cost of funds and low rates earned on older mortgages, but conditions improved in 1983.

CONSUMER CREDIT. Consumer credit is the mainstay of the small-loan finance industry; it has grown twice as fast as disposable personal income. The industry expanded rapidly after World War II, because of the growth of instalment contracts to finance autos, home appliances, and other durable consumer goods. Continued growth is likely because of (1) projected increases in personal income, which reflect our ability to borrow; (2) population growth, with a higher proportion of younger families; (3) more emphasis on home and auto ownership; and (4) new applications of consumer credit.

PERSONAL LOANS. Personal loans have grown as fast as the general use of credit. These are nonautomobile and nondurable-goods types of loans. Growth of the industry has been steady and faster than the national economy.

INSURANCE COMPANIES. The insurance industry, including both life insurance and fire and casualty companies, has experienced a dramatic growth since World War II. Part of this growth is attributable to National Service Life Insurance, which was underwritten for members of the armed services in World War II by the U.S. government. Rising personal incomes have also contributed to the growth of the life insurance industry.

Fire and casualty companies have also grown by offering a wider range of policies and attractive rates. Disability income policies and medical and accident insurance are becoming commonplace. Major medical insurance is provided by many employers. Insurance companies now offer complete coverage to an individual in one policy, which encompasses auto, home, life, and accident and sickness insurance. Companies supplying one type of insurance are also tending to broaden their activities into other areas. In recent years, casualty companies have suffered severe restrictions in profits because of the inflationary-spiral effect on costs and lagging rate increases.

INVESTMENT COMPANIES. There are two kinds of investment companies—closed-end or investment trusts, and open-end or mutual funds. They offer the investor the opportunity for diversification and management, plus ease of reinvestment of dividends. Investment companies have grown substantially since the late 1940s. This growth was restrained by the dip in the stock market in 1962, but it moved back sharply with market improvement in 1963 and since then has been phenomenal. In the period 1972 to 1976, however, purchases of mutual-fund shares declined, reflecting a lack of confidence by the public in equity securities. Some mutual funds, although not all, have done exceptionally well, moving ahead of the stock market and the national economy.

The major growth in the mutual fund industry in 1982 has been in money market mutual funds. Index mutual funds have also been established by institutional investors to provide returns equal to the S&P 500 Index. (See Chapter 2)

Industrials

The industrials represent a broad collection of industries in manufacturing, mining, and merchandising. The growth pattern of these industries covers all phases of the industrial growth cycle. Some of them established outstanding growth records during the late 1970s and early 1980s. Some areas of the following industries had experienced growth equal to or greater than the national economy: aerospace, amusements, computers, health care, drugs and cosmetics, electronics, office equipment, publishing, and the retail trade.

Some industries have actually declined in economic importance. Coal, for example, has lost its competitive position to oil and gas. Leather and shoe production has not expanded sales significantly. Agricultural machinery, rail equipment, and textiles and apparel have not grown as rapidly as the national economy. Yet in the mid-1970s, there was renewed interest in coal as an energy source. Agricultural machinery has expanded production worldwide to meet the food requirements of a growing world population. Textiles and apparel have shown signs of growth because of a fashion-conscious world. Some companies in declining industrial classes have been exceptionally good investments and should not be ignored.

Public Utilities

The telephone and electric and gas utility industries showed substantial growth during the 1960s and early 1970s. Few industry groups have achieved the growth rates or stability that these have experienced in the past. At the same time, their service rates have been controlled by regulatory bodies, including the ICC, the FCC, and various state public utility commissions. Rate legislation aud the determination of a fair return rate on a fair investment are important to the public utility industry as a whole. Its future is clouded by its large capital requirements, ecology problems, lagging rate adjustment, and growing demands for service. The current scarcity of gas, the possibility of deregulation of gas prices by the FPC, and the lack of a clear-cut energy policy have created difficulties for the gas utilities. The electric utilities are plagued with rising costs. It seems that the telephone industry has performed the best. Some utilities offer excellent investment opportunities, however, including electric utilities.

Transportation

The transportation industry has been undergoing a tremendous change in its competitive position. The passenger-railroad industry as a whole has been unprofitable in the past decade. Conrail and Amtrak are trying to bring renewed vigor to the national and eastern roads. More than $4 billion of federal money has been committed to revive the eastern railroads. Some of the transportation companies, however, have maintained their competitive position. A few major long-haul freight railroads offer the investor secure and stable opportunities for investment. In examining this industry, the investor must make a clear distinction between freight and passenger transportation.

Shipping and shipbuilding have been heavily subsidized. They offer relatively attractive opportunities for investment dollars, now that defense expenditures are expected to increase.

The air transport industry, both passenger and freight, has shown substantial growth of sales, but expenses and capital costs have increased much more rapidly than revenues. Growth potential exists for this industry, but many problems must be solved first. Air freight offers good profit opportunities if the industry can solve some basic problems. Some passenger airlines appear to offer attractive investment opportunities.

The trucking industry has continued to grow at a rate faster than the national economy, and this growth is likely to continue in the future. The trucking industry consists of companies that transport freight for short hauls. The growth of containerized shipping and piggyback operations should provide a further stimulus for growth in this industry and should help the railroads as well.

Conglomerates

A conglomerate company is one that has grown by adding diverse or unrelated types of companies producing unrelated products. The economic basis for conglomerates is the economy of management and the financial leverage for the parent company. Textron, based in Rhode Island, is a good example of a successful conglomerate. Textron has brought together a wide array of successful component companies, such as Bostitch, Gorham, Bell Helicopter, Homelite, Sheaffer Pen, Speidel, Fafnir, Talon, and Pittsburgh Steel Foundry and Machine. Under one management, they represent a powerful source of earning power. Conglomerates should not be ignored as a way to financial success.

Significance of Industry Information

The comments made above are designed to indicate the nature of an industry and its relative growth position. The investor must become familiar with these industries in order to select companies that might become satisfactory investments. Standard & Poor's *Industry Survey* and *The Value Line Investment Surveys* provide excellent factual data about each industry. Each service uses different categories, but once the investor becomes familiar with these sources of information, this will not be a handicap.

SELECTING AN EXPANDING INDUSTRY

An understanding of the growth pattern of an industry and of the stages of growth—pioneering, expansion, and stagnation—as well as of the signs of obsolescence, should help us reach a solution to the problem of where to invest. As a matter of principle, the investor should select industries that are in the expansion stage of the growth cycle and should concentrate on these areas. Except for special circumstances brought about by individual portfolio needs, an investor should not invest in industries in the pioneering stage unless he or she is prepared to accept a great deal of speculative risk, comparable to that assumed by the innovator or speculator. By the same token, the investor should ignore industries that are in the stagnation stage or are actually declining in economic importance. Investors should invest in those industries that have developed a strong competitive position, and under little threat of obsolescence. A careful analysis of industries is important to determine which are competitively strong.

This recommendation does not suggest that the investor should ignore industries that are not growing more rapidly than the national economy. The "growth concept" may seem to suggest a rate of growth much greater than that of the national economy. But the recommendation that the investor invest during the expansion stage of the growth cycle refers not only to growth-type industries, but also to those that are growing at a rate equal to that of the national economy. The selection of an industry that is expected to maintain its competitive position on a par with the GNP is entirely consistent with the recommendation.

The growth concept can also be applied to cyclical stocks. Since the economy is cyclical in character, the investor would concentrate on depressed cyclicals when the economy is in a recession. At such a time, cyclical stocks have all the characteristics of a growth stock during the recovery phase.

Comparison of Industry Sales, Production, or Shipments with GNP

The competitive position of an industry can be measured in one of two ways: (1) by comparing the industry growth over time with the growth of the national economy, or (2) by measuring the growth rate of the industry itself. The first step would be to obtain reliable estimates of the physical output, shipments, or sales of the industry. This is relatively easy where the product involved is homogeneous and the data are available. The electronic computing industry is one for which it is relatively easy to obtain shipment figures. From these figures, annual percentage changes can be calculated to reflect the relative growth of the industry. Industry growth can then be compared with the growth of GNP, national income (NI), or disposable personal income (DPI), whichever is more appropriate for the industry in question. If an industry is growing at the same rate as or more rapidly than the GNP or other components, this will be apparent from a comparison. Table 12–1 provides an example of this type of comparison. The GNP in dollars and percentage change is compared with the shipments of the electronic computing equipment industry.

Care must be exercised in selecting the companies to make certain that they are truly representative of the industry under study. Often, data about total sales for an industry cannot be obtained. In this case, several companies that produce the product can be combined to represent the industry's growth. The relationship between industry sales and the GNP is clearly shown in Table 12–1. If the electronic computing equipment industry had grown at the same percentage rate as the GNP, the ratios in the "% of GNP" column would be a constant. If, on the other hand, sales were increasing faster than the GNP, the ratio would be increasing; if sales were decreasing, the ratio itself would be declining. The percentage relationship between the sales of an industry and GNP is as important as the trend: Is the percentage increasing, decreasing, or constant? The stability of the relationship is most important: Is it cyclical or countercyclical, or does it follow the trend of growth, with a high degree of stability?

TABLE 12–1

Comparison of Electronic Computing Equipment Shipments
to GNP, 1975–1982

	Value of Industry Shipments (billions of current $ and percentage change)		GNP (billions of current $ and percentage change)		Shipments as a Percentage of GNP
1982	$34.1	11.4%	$3,057	4.1%	.0115%
1981	30.6	17.7	2,937	11.8	.0104
1980	26.0	23.8	2,626	8.8	.0099
1979	21.0	28.4	2,414	12.0	.0087
1978	16.4	26.6	2,156	12.4	.0076
1977	12.9	24.4	1,918	11.6	.0067
1976	10.4	21.4	1,718	10.9	.0060
1975	8.6		1,549		.0055

*E, estimated.

SOURCE: *1981 U.S. Industrial Outlook for 200 Industries with P.ojections for 1984,* U.S. Department of Commerce, January 1983, p. 275.

In this case, shipments for the industry have grown substantially more than GNP, which is a sign of strength. Shipments as a percentage of GNP are increasing, which further demonstrates the growth characteristics of the industry.

The relationship between electronic computing equipment and the GNP is also seen in Figure 12–2. This type of relationship is helpful in predicting future growth of an industry, assuming there is an adequate and accurate forecast of the GNP. In comparing GNP with the electronic computing equipment industry, we can see that the growth of the industry is substantially higher and more stable than the growth of the national economy. The conclusions to be drawn from this comparison are these: First, the industry is classed as a growing industry, with a growth greater than the national economy; second, it does not have cyclical characteristics; third, this growth pattern will probably continue and will help in estimating future performance of the industry.

Forecasting Using Industry Growth Compared to GNP Growth

The relationship between industry growth and GNP growth as developed in Figure 12–2 can be used to estimate the future growth of the industry. Assume that the best estimate for GNP for 1983 is $3,491 billion; and for 1984, $3,841 billion. (A 10 percent growth rate is assumed to be the best estimate.) These figures were plotted on Figure 12–2. The estimated shipments for the electronic computing equipment industry can be estimated by reference to Figure 12–2. Industry shipments in 1982 would be estimated at $35 billion, in 1983 at $38 billion, and in 1984 at $48 billion. Obviously these are approximations of future shipments and are dependent on accurate forecasts of GNP. The process also assumes that the relationship between the industry and GNP will continue. More accurate regression and correlation analysis may be used, but

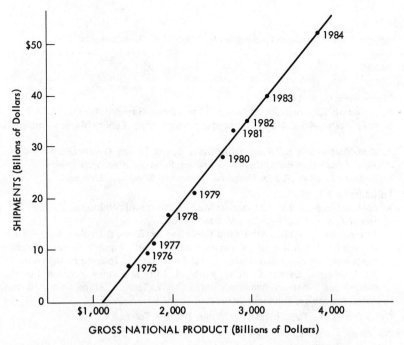

FIGURE 12–2

Relationship of Electronic Computing Equipment Shipments to GNP

SOURCE: Based on data in Table 12–1.

at least these tables and charts help investors understand the growth pattern of the industry.

Interpretation of Industry Growth for Investors

The relationship established between the growth of an industry and the growth of the national economy will be used in the investment decision process. First, it will identify industries that are growing faster than the national economy. Second, it will allow the investor to use the historical relationship to forecast the future growth of the industry. Third, it will set the stage for comparing the growth of the industry with the leading companies. Fourth, it will set the stage for portfolio decisions where the leading companies will be considered for a diversified portfolio.

Industry Stock Groups and the GNP Components

The GNP components can be identified with industry stock groups to translate the expected growth of the economy into the selection of specific industries. Table 12–2 lists some of the industries and companies that are included in the S&P 500 Index under the appropriate GNP component. Durables, for example, which are a major part of consumption expenditures, include motor vehicles and parts, furniture and appliances, and other durables which are a part of the S&P 500 Index industries.

In the analysis of the national economy, we learned that durables and services

TABLE 12–2

S&P 500 Industries and Companies Identified by Major GNP Components

I. Consumption
  A. Durables
    1. Motor Vehicles and Parts
       a. *Automobiles:* American Motors, Chrysler, Ford, General Motors.
       b. *Auto Parts—After Market:* Champion Spark Plug, Echlin Manufacturing, Genuine Parts.
       c. *Auto Parts—Original Equipment:* Dana, Eaton, Libbey-Owens-Ford, Timken.
       d. *Auto Trucks and Parts:* Cummins Engine, Fruehauf, Paccar, Signal.
       e. *Tire and Rubber Goods:* Firestone, Goodrich, Goodyear, Uniroyal.
    2. Furniture and Appliances
       a. *Electrical Household Appliances:* Maytag, Sunbeam, Whirlpool, Zenith.
       b. *Home Furnishings:* Kroehler, Mohasco, Roper.
       c. *Miscellaneous:* AT&T, Armstrong Cork, Bendix, Black & Decker, Borg-Warner, CPC International, Corning Glass, Eastman Kodak, FMC, Esmark, Gillette, Grace (W.R.), Honeywell Incorporated, International Telephone & Telegraph, Minnesota Mining, NL Industries, Owens-Corning, Polaroid, PPG Industries, Ralston Purina, Signal Companies, Sherwin-Williams, Singer, TRW, Timken, Fluor Corp., IC Industries, Litton Industries, Tenneco, Textron.
    3. *Other Durables—Toys:* Ideal Toy, Milton Bradley, Tonka.
  B. Nondurables
    1. Food and Beverages
       a. *Beverages (Brewers):* Anheuser-Busch, Coors (Adolph), Pabst Brewing, Schlitz Brewing.
       b. *Beverages (Distillers):* Heublein, National Distillers, Seagram, Walker (Hiram), Home.
       c. *Beverages (Soft Drinks):* Coca-Cola, Dr. Pepper, Pepsi, Royal Crown Cola, General Cinema.
       d. *Confectionery:* Hershey Foods, Wrigley.
       e. *Retail Stores (Drug):* Eckerd (Jack), Revco D. S., Rite Aid, Walgreen, American Stores.
       f. *Foods (Canned):* Campbell Soup, Heinz, Stokely-Van Camp.
       g. *Foods (Dairy):* Beatrice Foods, Borden, Dart & Kraft.
       h. *Foods (Meat Packing):* Esmark.
       i. *Foods (Packaged):* General Foods, Nabisco, Ralston Purina, Pillsbury, Carnation, General Mills, Gerber Products, Kellogg, Norton Simon, Quaker Oats, CPC International, Consolidated Foods.
       j. *Sugar Refiners:* Amalgamated Sugar, AMSTAR, Holly.
       k. *Retail Stores (Food Chains):* American Stores, Great A&P Jewel Companies, Kroger, Lucky Stores, Winn-Dixie, Safeway Stores.
    2. Clothing and Shoes
       a. *Retail Stores (Department Stores):* Allied Stores, Associated Dry Goods, Carter Hawley Hale Stores, Federated, Macy, Marshall Field, May Department Stores, Penney, Dayton Hudson.
       b. *Retail Stores (Mail Order & General Chains):* K-Mart, Woolworth, Penney, Sears.
       c. *Retail Shoes:* Brown Group.
       d. *Shoes:* Brown Group, Genesco, Interco, Melville.
       e. *Textiles (Apparel Manufacturers):* Blue Bell, Cluett Peabody, Levi Strauss, Hart, Schaffner & Marx, Jonathan Logan, V. F. Corporation.
       f. *Textiles (Synthetic Fibers):* Akzona, Celanese.
       g. *Textiles (Products):* Burlington Industries, West Point Pepperell, Cone Mills, Lowenstein, Reeves, Springs Mills, Stevens.

TABLE 12–2   (Continued)

3. Oil, Fuel Oil, Gasoline and Coal
   a. *Coal (Bituminous):* Eastern Gas & Fuel, Westmoreland, North American Coal, Pittston.
   b. *Oil (Integrated-Domestic):* Atlantic Richfield, Conoco, Standard Oil (Ohio), Phillips, Cities Service, Continental Oil, Getty Oil, Shell, Standard Oil (Indiana), Sun Company, Union Oil of California.
   c. *Oil (Integrated-International):* Exxon, Gulf, Mobil Oil, Royal Dutch, Standard Oil of California, Texaco.
   d. *Oil (Crude Producers):* General American, Louisiana Land & Exploration, Mesa Petroleum, Superior Oil, Texas Oil & Gas.
   e. *Off-Shore Drilling:* Global Marine, Reading & Bates, SEDCO, Western of North America.
4. Other Nondurables
   a. *Chemicals:* Allied Chemical, American Cyanamid, Dow, DuPont, Hercules, Monsanto, Union Carbide, Akzona, Celanese, FMC, Grace (WR) & Co., PPG, Stauffer Chemical.
   b. *Cosmetics:* Alberto-Culver, Avon, Chesebrough-Pond's, Faberge, International Flavors & Fragrances, Revlon.
   c. *Drugs:* American Home, Bristol-Myers, Lilly (Eli), Merck, Pfizer, Schering-Plough, SmithKline Beckman, Searle (G.D.), Sterling, Warner-Lambert, Squibb, Upjohn.
   d. *Fertilizers:* Beker Industries, First Mississippi, International Minerals & Chemical, Williams Companies.
   e. *Leisure Time:* AMF, Brunswick, Mandleman, Outboard Marine, Questor.
   f. *Paper:* Crown Zellerbach, International Paper, Kimberly-Clark, Mead, St. Regis, Scott, Union Camp, Westvaco.
   g. *Soaps:* Clorox, Colgate-Palmolive, Procter & Gamble, Purex, Unilever N.V.
   h. *Tobacco:* American Brands, Philip Morris, Reynolds Industries.

C. Services
1. Housing
   a. *Hotel:* Hilton Hotels, Holiday Inns, Ramada Inns.
   b. *Real Estate:* Equitable Life, First Union Real Estate, Mass-Mutual M & R, Mony Mtge Invest, Wells Fargo Mtge/Eqty.
2. Household Operation
   a. *Electricity (Electric Power):* American Electric Power, Baltimore Gas & Electric, Central & South Western, Consolidated Edison, Detroit Edison, Duke Power, Florida Power & Light, Middle South Utilities, Mohawk, New England Electric System, Niagara Mohawk, North States Power, Ohio Edison, Pacific Gas & Electric, Philadelphia Electric, Public Service & Gas, Public Service of Indiana, Southern California Edison, Southern Company, Texas Utilities, Virginia Electric & Power, Wisconsin Electric Power.
   b. *Natural Gas (Natural Gas Distributor):* American Natural Gas, Brooklyn Union Gas, Columbia Gas, Consolidated Natural Gas, Oklahoma Natural Gas, Pacific Lighting, Peoples Gas, Ensearch.
3. Transportation
   a. *Air Transport:* American Airlines, Delta Airlines, Northwest Airlines, Pan Am World Airways, UAL.
   b. *Air Freight:* Emery Air Freight, Tiger International, Federal Express.
   c. *Railroads:* Burlington Northern, Missouri Pacific, Norfolk & Western, Sante Fe Industries, Southern Pacific, Southern Railways, Union Pacific, CSX.
   d. *Truckers:* Consolidated Freightways, McLean Trucking, Roadway Express, Yellow Freight Systems.

TABLE 12–2 (Continued)

4. Hospital Management: American Medical International, Hospital Corporation of America, Humana, National Medical Enterprises.

5. Other

   a. *Telephone:* American Telephone & Telegraph, Central Telephone & Utilities, Continental Telephone, General Telephone & Electric, United Telecommunications.

   b. *Banks (New York City Group):* Bankers Trust, Chase Manhattan, Chemical New York, Citicorp, Manufacturers Hanover, Morgan (J.P.).

   c. *Banks (outside New York City Group):* Bank America, Continental Illinois, First Chicago, First International Bancshares, First Pennsylvania, First National Boston, Mellon National, NCNB, Northwest Bancorp, First Interstate.

   d. *Brokerage Firms:* Bache, Donaldson Lufkin & Jenrette, Edwards (A.G.), Hutton (E.F.) Group, Merrill Lynch, Paine Webber, Shearson Hayden Stone.

   e. *Life Insurance:* Jefferson-Pilot, NLT, Connecticut General, Lincoln National, Capital Holding.

   f. *Multiline Insurance:* Aetna Life & Casualty, American General Insurance, CNA Financial, Travelers.

   g. *Property-Casualty Insurance:* Chubb, Continental, INA, St. Paul Companies, SAFECO, U.S. Fidelity & Guaranty.

   h. *Savings and Loan Associations:* Ahmanson (H.F.) & First Charter Financial, Great Western Financial.

   i. *Finance Companies:* Heller (Walter E.) International, Transamerica, American Express.

   j. *Finance—Small Loans (Personal Loans):* Beneficial, Household Finance.

   k. *Entertainment:* Columbia, Disney (Walt), MCA, Metro-Goldwyn-Mayer, Warner Communications.

   l. *Publishing:* Harcourt Brace Jovanovich, Macmillan, Meredith, Scott, Dunn & Bradstreet, McGraw-Hill, Scott Foresman.

   m. *Radio-TV Broadcasters:* American Broadcasting, CBS, Capital Cities Communications, Cox Broadcasting, Metromedia, Taft.

   n. *Restaurants:* Denny's, Church's Fried Chicken, Gino's, Marriott, McDonald's, Pizza Hut.

   o. *Vending Food Service:* ARA Services.

II. Investment

   A. Fixed

      1. Nonresidential

         a. Equipment

            (1) *Aerospace:* Boeing, General Dynamics, Grumman, Martin Marietta, McDonnell-Douglas, Raytheon, Rockwell International, United Technologies.

            (2) *Aluminum:* Alcan Aluminum, Aluminum Company of America, Kaiser Aluminum, Reynolds Metals.

            (3) *Chemicals:* Allied, American Cyanamid, Dow, DuPont, Hercules, Monsanto, Union Carbide.

            (4) *Containers (Metal & Glass):* American Can, Continental Group, Crown Cork, National Can, Owens-Illinois.

            (5) *Containers (Paper):* Bemis, Diamond International, Federal, Maryland Cup.

            (6) *Copper:* Newmont Mining, Phelps Dodge, Asarco.

            (7) *Electrical Equipment:* Gould, Emerson Electric, Thomas & Betts, McGraw-Edison, Square D, Grainger (W.W.).

            (8) *Electrical-Electronics Major Company:* General Electric, RCA, Sperry Rand, Westinghouse Electric.

            (9) *Electronics:* AMP, Hewlett-Packard, National Semi-Conductor, SmithKline Beckman, Tektronix, Texas Instruments, Perkin Elmer, Motorola, Intel.

TABLE 12-2 (Continued)

(10) *Forest Products:* Boise Cascade, Champion International, Evans Products, Georgia-Pacific, Louisiana Pacific, Potlatch, Weyerhaeuser.

(11) *Gold Mining:* ASA Limited, Campbell Red Lake, Dome.

(12) *Steel:* Armco, Bethlehem, Inland, Interlake, National, Republic, U.S. Steel, Wheeling-Pittsburgh, Acme Cleveland, Brown & Sharpe, Cincinnati Milacron, Giddings & Lewis, Monarch Machine Tool.

(13) *Hospital Supplies:* American Hospital, Abbott Lab, Bard (C.R.), Baxter Travenol Laboratories, Becton Dickinson, Johnson & Johnson.

(14) *Lead & Zinc:* Hudson Bay-Mining, Amax, Homestake Mining, Inco, Phibro.

(15) *Machinery (Agricultural):* Allis-Chalmers, Deere, International Harvester, Massey Ferguson.

(16) *Machinery (Construction & Material):* Bucyrus-Erie, Caterpillar Tractor, Clark Equipment, Rexnord, Hyster.

(17) *Machinery (Industrial/Specialty):* Briggs & Stratton, Chicago Pneumatic Tool, Cooper Industries, Combustion Eng., Foster Wheeler, Ingersoll-Rand, Ex-Cell-O.

(18) *Machinery (Specialty):* Ex-Cell-O, Foster Wheeler, Joy Manufacturing.

(19) *Machinery (Oil Well Equipment & Services):* Baker International, Dresser, Halliburton, Hughes Tool Company, McDermott (J. Ray), Schlumberger.

(20) *Machinery (Steam Generating):* Combustion Engineering, Foster Wheeler.

(21) *Metal—Miscellaneous:* Amax, ASARCO, Homestake Minerals, Hudson Bay Manufacturing, INCO, Phibro.

(22) *Office & Business Equipment:* Burroughs, Control Data, Digital Equipment, International Business Machine, NCR, Pitney Owens, Sperry, Xerox, Wang Labs, Data General, Datapoint, Honeywell, Storage Technology.

(23) *Steel:* Armco, Bethlehem Steel, Inland, Interlake, National, Republic, U.S. Steel, Wheeling-Pittsburgh.

(24) *Pollution Control:* Browning-Ferris, Envirotech, Peabody Galion, Wheelabrator-Frye, Waste Management.

2. Structures

   a. *Natural Gas Pipelines:* El Paso Company, Northern Natural Gas, Panhandle Eastern Pipeline, Southern Natural Resources, Texas Eastern Transmission, Texas Gas Transmission.

   b. *Building Materials (Air Conditioning):* Fedders, Trane.

   c. *Building Materials (Cement):* Alpha Portland Industries, Lone Star Industries, Ideal Basic.

   d. *Building Materials (Heating & Plumbing):* American Standard, Crane, Masco.

   e. *Building Materials (Roofing & Wallboard):* Jim Walter, Johns-Manville, Masonite, National Gypsum, U.S. Gypsum.

3. Residential

   a. *Structure Building Materials (Air Conditioning):* Fedders, Trane.

   b. *Building Materials (Cement):* Alpha Portland Industries, Lone Star Industries, Marquette, Penn-Dixie.

   c. *Building Materials (Heating & Plumbing):* American Standard, Crane.

   d. *Building Materials (Roofing & Wallboard):* Jim Walter, Johns-Manville, Masonite, National Gypsum, U.S. Gypsum.

   e. *Forest Products:* Boise Cascade, Champion International, Evans Products, Georgia-Pacific, Louisiana Pacific, Potlatch, Weyerhaeuser.

   f. *Mobile Homes:* Fleetwood Enterprises, Redman Industries, Skyline.

   g. *Equipment:* American Telephone & Telegraph, Central Telephone & Utilities, Continental Telephone, General Telephone & Electronic, United Telecommunications.

   h. *Containers (Metal & Glass):* American Can, Continental Group, Crown Cork, National Can, Owens-Illinois.

TABLE 12–2 (Continued)

      i. *Containers (Paper):* Brown, Diamond International, Federal, Hoerner, Maryland Cup.

      j. *Electrical (Household Appliances):* Maytag, Sunbeam, Whirlpool, Zenith.

      k. *Home Furnishings:* Kroehler, Mohasco, Roper.

      l. *Miscellaneous:* American Telephone & Telegraph, Armstrong Cork, Bendix, Black & Decker, Borg-Warner, CPC International, Corning Glass, Eastman Kodak, FMC, Gillette, Grace (W.R.), Honeywell, International Telephone & Telegraph, Minnesota Mining, NL Industries, Owens-Corning, PPG Industries, Polaroid, Ralston Purina, Sherwin-Williams, Singer, TRW, Timken.

     m. *Paper:* Crown Zellerbach, International Paper, Kimberly-Clark, Mead, St. Regis, Union Camp, Westvaco, Scott Paper.

     n. *Soaps:* Clorox, Colgate Palmolive, Procter & Gamble, Unilever N.V., Purex.

  B. Change in Inventories

III. Exports*

IV. Imports*

V. Government

  A. Federal*
    1. National Defense
    2. Nondefense

  B. State and Local*

---

*It is assumed that all the above industries and related companies are involved in some form of importing and exporting, and are making sales to governments.

seemed to offer investment opportunities. By looking at industries and companies in these categories in Table 12–2 an investor might find attractive investments. As an example, beverages (brewers) was an industry thought by some investors to offer attractive investment opportunity. Some thought shoes to be attractive, and others thought that offshore drilling was attractive. In the services area of GNP, we would find banking, electric power, gas, and hospital management, which many investors considered attractive for future investment. The other category includes several industries that were considered to be attractive, including telephone, banks outside New York City, brokerage firms, entertainment, and restaurants. Under fixed investment in the GNP accounts we find several groups of companies that appeared attractive, including aerospace, electronics, hospital supplies, machinery (specialty), machinery (oil well equipment and services), office and business equipment, and pollution control.

The relationship between the stock groups and the economic areas in the GNP accounts should help in the selection of industries for investment. The investor must obtain information about the industries from a source such as *Industry Surveys* published by Standard & Poor's and *Value Line*. The goal of the analysis is to select industries that offer a high and stable real growth in the future. As a guide, we can use the expected growth rate of GNP. The reasoning is that strong industries will allow investors to profit from the purchase of the shares of companies in those industries, providing that the investor does not pay too much for shares of these competitive and profitable firms. A list of rapid growth industries appears in Table 12–3.

TABLE 12–3

Rapid Growth Industries and Growth Factors

	Industry Growth Factors	Compound Average Annual Growth Rates		New Products	Less Than Avg. Price Increase	Product Substitutions	Expanded Export Markets	Energy Related	Other
		1972–78	1979–85						
3674	Semiconductors and related devices	19.1	20.7	x	x	x	x		
3693	X-ray apparatus and tubes	19.1	6.5	x			x		
3832	Optical instruments and lenses	18.4	13.8	x			x		
3573	Electronics computing equipment	17.0	15.0	x	x		x		
3795	Tanks & tank components	15.7	15.7+						x
3574	Calculating and accounting machinery	13.6	10.0	x	x	x	x		x
2795	Lithographic platemaking services	12.8	4.0			x			x
3678	Electronic connectors	12.3	7.9	x			x		
2448	Wood pallets and skids	12.2	9.0		x	x			
3533	Oilfield machinery	12.2	8.4	x			x	x	
3951	Pens and mechanical pencils	11.4	5.0	x			x		
3497	Metal foil and leaf	11.3	5.5	x				x	
3823	Process control instruments	11.0	12.9	x	x	x	x	x	
2831	Biological products	10.9	4.0	x	x				x
3824	Fluid meters & counting devices	10.3	5.9	x					x
2843	Surface active agents	10.1	4.2	x		x	x		
3579	Office machines, n.e.c.	9.7	15.0	x		x	x		
3519	Internal combustion engines, n.e.c.	9.6	5.2+	x					
3713	Truck & bus bodies (incl. motor homes)	9.6	3.0						x
2035	Pickles, sauces, salad dressings	8.9	6.7	x		x			
3563	Air and gas compressors	8.6	3.8	x				x	
3829	Measuring and controlling devices, n.e.c.	8.4	10.6	x					
3498	Fabricated pipe and fittings	8.2	8.5					x	
3825	Instruments to measure electricity	7.9	8.8	x	x	x			
2833	Medicinals and botanicals	7.7	5.0	x			x		
2434	Wood kitchen cabinets	7.6	7.6						x
2873	Nitrogenous fertilizers	7.5	2.5						x
2047	Dog, cat, and other pet food	7.4	2.0	x					
3549	Metalworking machinery, n.e.c.	7.4	5.2	x					
3861	Photographic equipment and supplies	7.4	5.2	x					
3691	Storage batteries	7.2	3.5	x					
3425	Handsaws and saw blades	7.1	2.6	x		x		x	
3651	Radio and TV receiving sets	7.1	7.3	x	x				
3079	Misc. plastics products	6.9	4.5	x		x		x	x
3692	Primary batteries, dry and wet	6.9	3.5	x					
2439	Structural wood members, n.e.c.	6.8	9.0	x		x			
3679	Electronic components, n.e.c.	6.8	7.2	x	x	x			
3811	Engineering & scientific instruments	6.8	−1.0	x			x		
3296	Mineral wool	6.6	3.0					x	
3484	Small arms	6.5	4.0						
3822	Environmental controls	6.5	11.9	x				x	
2087	Flavoring extracts and syrups, n.e.c.	6.4	4.5	x					
3211	Flat glass	6.4	3.7					x	
3463	Nonferrous forgings	6.4	4.0					x	x
3843	Dental equipment and supplies	6.4	4.7	x					

SOURCE: 1983 U.S. Industrial Outlook for 200 Industries with Projections for 1987. U.S. Dept. of Commerce, Bureau of Industrial Economics, January 1983, p. xvii.

Industry Forecasts—The Department of Commerce

The Department of Commerce forecasts the expected growth of 200 industries in its publication, *1981 U.S. Industrial Outlook for 200 Industries with Projections for 1985.* Expected real growth rates through 1985 appear for each industry. From this list, investors could select industries for investment that offer above-average real growth (see Table 12–4). The conclusion from this type of analysis is that the following industries are attractive for investment: electronic components, computing equipment, instruments, metal-working machinery and equipment, consumer electronics, broadcasting, telephone and telegraph services, health and medical services, and medical and dental instruments and supplies and drugs.

Reason for the Analysis

The basic reason for determining the relationship between the growth rate of an industry and GNP or the appropriate component is to aid in predicting the future

TABLE 12–4

Selected Industries with Growth Rates Higher than GNP Growth,
Estimated 1981–1985

Industry and Subindustry	Average Annual Growth Rate of Sales or Shipment in 1972 Dollars (%)
Broadcasting	
Cable TV	16.6%
Telephone and telegraph services	
Telegraph services	16.0
Computing equipment	15.0
Electrical equipment and components	14.0
Metal-working machinery and equipment	
Machine tools	10.0
Industrial heating	9.5
Instruments for measurement, analysis, and control	9.0
Telephone and telegraph services	
Domestic and international telephone	8.0
Telephone and telegraph equipment	7.4
Metal-working machinery and equipment	
Tool and die industry	6.0–7.0
Consumer electronics	6.5
Medical and dental instruments and supplies	
X-ray and electromedical equipment	6.5
Surgical and medical instruments	5.6
Metal-working machinery and equipment	
Welding apparatus	5.3
Perishable metal cutting	5.2
Drugs	3.8

SOURCE: 1981 U.S. Industrial Outlook for 200 Industries with Projections for 1985, U.S. Department of Commerce, Bureau of Industrial Economics, January 1981.

growth of that industry. Economic forecasts are made in terms of GNP and components. If the sales of an industry vary directly with national income, then barring major changes, these relationships should continue in the future. This, like all forecasts, is not a certainty, but it does provide a way of obtaining an estimate of future industry sales.

We could also use per capita industry sales to estimate future sales of an industry. This would require two ingredients: (1) per capita industry sales, and (2) expected population. Thus, if per capita industry sales are about $143, as they were for the computer industry in 1981 (sales in 1981 were $32.8 billion of shipments, with a population of 230 million), and if we believe that the population will be almost 235 million by 1984 and that per capita shipments will rise to $185, then industry sales in 1984 will be $43.5 billion.

Since the investor's success is based on future sales and profits of an industry and a specific company, a reasonable estimate of future sales must be made and industries selected that offer the greatest growth of future sales and earnings. This type of estimate will help the investor compare a chosen company with the industry as a whole and forecast the company's earnings—a fundamental step in the valuation process.

SUMMARY

Investors should seek out strong industries for investment. Since industrial growth follows a pattern, it seems wise to invest in those industries beyond the pioneering stage but substantially before the stagnation stage. Investors are warned to beware of competitive latent obsolescence.

Industries are classified by investment services into broad groups. Investment services such as Standard & Poor's *Industry Surveys, Moody's Handbook*, and *Value Line* provide a practical guide to these classifications.

The notion of investing in expanding industries requires an estimate of sales for an industry to compare to the growth of the economy. The relationships between industry growth and GNP can be used as a forecasting tool to estimate future industry growth.

The industries that make up the S&P 500 Index were merged into the GNP components to identify industries in the strong sectors of the economy.

An analysis of the Department of Commerce's *U.S. Industrial Outlook* provides a list of industries which over the period 1981–85 should provide greater growth than the GNP in real or constant dollars. It seems wise to seek out the companies in these areas for successful investment.

SUMMARY OF PRINCIPLES

1. Investors should invest in industries that are in a strong competitive position.
2. Investors should invest in industries that are in the expansion stage of their life cycle.
3. Investors should avoid industries that are stagnating.
4. In order to identify the strong industries, it is necessary to analyze the subindustries.

1. Discuss what is meant by the term *industry*. Why is a knowledge of the industry concept so important in our analysis?

2. Explain the growth pattern of the typical industry.

3. Why do industries tend to grow at a decreasing rate? Discuss.

4. Explain the industry growth-cycle thesis.

5. In what phase of industry growth should investment take place?

6. Discuss possible limits to the growth-cycle thesis.

7. Should the investor invest in cyclical stocks? Explain.

8. What are the reasons for the decline in the competitive position of an industry as it enters the stagnation stage?

9. What is meant by the term *latent obsolescence*?

10. Explain how to determine the current phase of growth of an industry. Specifically, how do you determine if an industry is expanding?

11. What is the logic behind the investment classification of an industry?

12. Explain how the investor might forecast the future growth of sales and the competitive position of an industry.

PROBLEMS

1. Based upon the data in Chapter 12 and the data contained in Table 12–2, identify 10 industries (that is, subindustries) that appear to be strong and growing and good candidates for investment.

2. Compare the list in problem 1 above with the data in Tables 12–3 and 12–4. Which industries appear to be strongest?

3. Identify the companies in each subindustry that might be considered for investment.

4. Do the industries in problem 2 appear to be in the expansion phase of industry growth? Explain.

5. What factors of latent obsolescence does each industry face?

6. Identify three industries with a list of companies in the industry in which you would be willing to invest.

CASE

Katherine and John were at a social gathering and met a broker who advised them that money was to be made in Canadian oil stocks. They had $100,000 to invest and they wanted to make the right decision. They thought there were other industries in which to invest and they did not wish to put all their money into one industry. Advise them as to how they might make a decision and what industries they should consider.

SELECTED READINGS

Industry Outlook. U.S. Department of Commerce, Washington, D.C.

Industry Surveys. New York: Standard and Poor's.

PORTER, MICHAEL E. "Industry Structure and Competitive Strategy: Keys to Profitability." *Financial Analysts Journal,* July–August 1980.

INDUSTRY SOURCES OF INFORMATION

INDUSTRY STATISTICS AND TRADE-ASSOCIATION PERIODICALS:*

> *American Gas Association Monthly*
> *American Machinist*
> *American Petroleum Institute Statistical Bulletin*
> *Automotive Industries*
> *Baking Industry*
> *Best's Insurance Reports*
> *Broadcasting—Telecasting*
> *Business Executives of America*
> *Coal Age*
> *Directory of National Trade Associations*
> *Dodge Reports*
> *Electrical Merchandising*
> *Electrical World*
> *Engineering and Mining Journal*
> *Engineering News–Record*
> *Fibre Container and Paperboard Mills*
> *Implement and Tractor and Farm Implement News*
> *Industrial and Engineering Chemistry*
> *Iron Age*
> *Leather and Shoes*
> *Oil and Gas Journal*
> *Paper Trade Journal*
> *Polk's National New Car Service*
> *Printer's Ink*
> *Railway Age*
> *Rock Products*
> *Televison Digest*
> *Textile Organization*

GOVERNMENT PUBLICATIONS

> *Industry Outlook 1983, Department of Commerce*
> *Washington, D.C. (and future years)*

*Many of these sources were found in John W. Bowyer, *Investment Analysis and Management* (Homewood, Ill.: Richard D. Irwin, 1966), Chapter 8.

CHAPTER 13

COMPANY ANALYSIS
AND THE COMPETITIVE POSITION
OF THE COMPANY

The purpose of this chapter is to begin a discussion of the important variables that determine the return and risk expected from the purchase of the common stock of a company. The purpose of company analysis is to help investors make better decisions. The variables in the valuation equation are estimated, as well as the qualitative aspects of analysis that allow the investor to determine if the return is proportional to the risk.

The analysis of a company is begun by determining its competitive position within the industry. The leading drug companies in the drug and healthcare industry will be used as a case in which a complete analysis will be made and the expected return and risk determined.

THE VALUATION PROCESS

The valuation equation helps the investor to determine the return and risk expected from an investment in common stock. The return, r, and the variability of r must be estimated, using the equation:

$$P_0 = \sum_{t=1}^{n=3} \frac{D_0(1 + g_d)^t}{(1 + r)^t} + \frac{E_0(1 + g_e)^3(P/E)_3}{(1 + r)^3}$$

This requires an estimate of earnings and dividends over the next three years, and of price at the end of that period.

Risk is determined by the variability of future return, r. The greater the variability, the greater the risk. The major activity of investors is to make decisions based upon the risk and return.

The present value of future dividends and price will provide a total return rate, which will be judged satisfactory or unsatisfactory depending on the risks involved. In order to establish variability of returns, estimates of the future earnings, dividends, and price will be estimated within ranges, as is done in Chapter 18. The results will be averaged and the standard deviation of returns estimated to provide an estimate of risk. If a company has stable and certain earnings, is in a strong competitive position, has an excellent profit margin, has experienced an excellent operating rate, is in a strong current financial position, is adequately financed, has a capable and imaginative management, and provides 12 percent return with a 3 percent variability, its stock would be considered a very attractive investment.

Figure 13–1 depicts the valuation process. The balancing factor, the risk rate of return, will vary among investors. Some investors would consider the expected return of 12 ± 3 percent satisfactory. As the risk associated with the venture increases, the return required would, of course, increase too. A company that provides quality but an unacceptable return would be rejected.

FACTORS TO CONSIDER IN COMPANY ANALYSIS

In order to translate the valuation process into a concrete reality and determine the present and future amount and quality of earnings, and therefore return and its variability, several important variables must be examined. Figure 13–2 pictures the transition from valuation of common stock in Figure 13–1 to the subject of company analysis. The important variables that influence future earnings and dividends of the company and future price of the stock, and hence the estimate of future return and

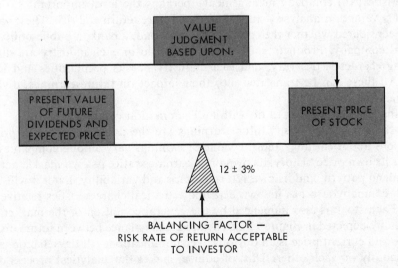

FIGURE 13–1

The Valuation of Common Stock

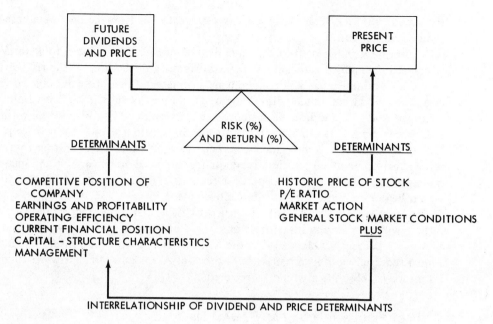

FIGURE 13–2

The Major Influences on Returns

the variability of the return (risk) expected from the common stock, are presented in Figure 13–2. These variables are (1) the competitive position of the company, based on the record and prospects of growth; (2) company profitability; (3) the operating efficiency of the company; (4) its current financial position; (5) the capital structure characteristics; (6) company management—perhaps the most important variable of all and (7) valuation analysis—an estimate of future return and risk. These variables must be considered whether the company is a railroad, a bank, a public utility, or an industrial company. Products and services produced in each industry are different. Operating characteristics vary, and each industry has its peculiarities and idiosyncrasies. All these can be translated into their impact on future earnings, dividends, and price.

The analysis process has to do with an examination of influences on the present price of the stock. Obviously, future earnings are the dominant force in price, yet expectations about earnings and the value of earnings vary among companies. Each stock has its own price history, its own price-earnings ratio, its own market action, its own dividend pattern, and its own return pattern and variability. Later it will be seen that each company also has its own beta and statistical characteristics relative to the market. Each stock is also influenced by the general condition of the market. These influences are depicted in Figure 13–2. The indicated balance between future dividends and price and current price is an obvious oversimplification. All these factors operate simultaneously on each other. This, of course, makes the analytical process difficult and complex.

FUNDAMENTAL ANALYSIS

The Competitive Position of the Company

The first variable that influences future earnings, in terms of both quantity and quality, is the competitive position of the company, or simply the company's past growth of sales, future expected growth, and position within the industry. What type of product or service is produced by the company, and what is the future demand for it? Is the company a leader in its industry, and does it have prospects for continued growth and leadership? How does the company compare in size and growth rate to leading competitors? A company in a strong competitive position will provide greater earnings with more certainty than will a company in a poor competitive position.

Company Earnings and Profitability

Generating a dollar of sales costs money. The expenses of operating the plant and of the raw materials used in the manufacturing process must be paid for before profits are achieved. Uncle Sam must also be paid, so taxes must be deducted. The expense and profitability relationships are used to determine the future earnings of the company and the expected variability of those future earnings. The higher and more stable the growth rate of earnings of the company, the greater and more stable is their value—and, since dividends are directly influenced by earnings, the greater are the future dividends, *ceteris paribus*. Profit margins have a great effect on future earnings. A company that enjoys a high profitability rate and growth of earnings is in a strong competitive position.

Operating Efficiency

Knowledge about a company's operating efficiency and ability to expand its plant provides further information about future earnings. Operating efficiency attempts to relate real input to real output. In the majority of cases, the operating efficiency of the company must be determined through an analysis of financial data. In recent years, high rates of inflation have distorted the "real" earnings and productivity of a company. An analysis of operating efficiency establishes the "real" growth of the company and helps to eliminate the inflationary bias.

The operating efficiency of a company is measured by its operating ratio and its breakeven point. The lower the operating ratio, the higher the earnings, other things being equal. The lower the breakeven point and the higher the level of operations in relation to plant capacity, the higher the profitability of the company. In addition, efficiency is measured by output per employee and output per dollar of invested capital.

Current Financial Position

A company should be in a good financial position in order to maintain its profitability and earnings for the common stockholder. The basic financial problem of corporate management is to maintain a balance between liquidity and profitability. Inability to meet current bills as they come due and to take advantage of discounts offered by suppliers immediately raises the possibility of failure. Too much cash or liquidity, on the other hand, does not help profits; idle funds are not productive funds. The ideal current financial position is one of balance. Current funds should be sufficient to meet the regular needs of the business, but cash should not be excessive. Several tests are available to help the investor decide what is an adequate cash and current financial position.

Capital Structure Characteristics

How a corporation raises funds to finance its needs and growth will have an impact on future earnings because of its effect on the amount and stability of earnings. Debt financing is a low-cost source of funds for the company, providing financial leverage for the common stock. As long as the earnings of the corporation are higher than the cost of the borrowed funds, the earnings per share of common stock are increased. Unfortunately, the use of large amounts of debt in the capital structure tends to make earnings unstable, and might result in financial failure if the earnings do not materialize. Thus, a judicious amount of debt in the capital structure is desirable for the greatest amount and stability of corporate earnings.

Management

Quality of management is essential to the future profitability of a business. Many investors consider the quality of corporate management the single most important factor influencing future earnings and overall success. Without good management, a company cannot maintain its competitive position or introduce new products. It cannot control costs of operation or maintain its earnings or financial position. Therefore, management's ability to direct the affairs of the company to a profitable future must be carefully assessed.

Valuation Analysis—Return and Risk

The investor must analyze carefully the price paid for a security to make certain that it will provide a satisfactory return. Return, of course, is dependent on future expected dividends and future anticipated price. Future earnings will affect the future price of the stock; therefore, a study of price cannot be made without a study and analysis of future earnings.

Other factors also influence the price of a stock at any given moment. There are any number of variables—some quantitative, some emotional. Here are a few:

1. The historic level of prices, including the price range.
2. The price–earnings ratio, and what might be a fair future ratio, as an acceptable measure of risk. We are interested in knowing what investors are paying for a dollar of earnings of the company, what they have paid in the past, and what they might be willing to pay in the future based upon these past relationships.
3. The market action of the stock. We ask: Is the price stable or unstable? Does it move with the stock market, or does it move against the market? That is, does the stock have a high or low beta?

4. The general level of the market and its future expected course. It is important that the investor understand that an individual common stock in the marketplace is only a part of the capital market. What happens to the price of a stock is influenced more by the general condition of the capital market than by the earnings and dividend behavior of the company. Most stocks move with the market, and it is unrealistic for an investor to expect that a stock will rise in a falling market. It is therefore imperative that the investor analyze the behavior of the capital market before embarking on an investment in a few individual common stocks or bonds.

5. The past return of the stock and its variability. The investor can't invest in the past. Nevertheless, the past return and risk of a stock can provide some insight into the future.

Once the investor has made an analysis of the quality of the company, the quality of earnings, and the price, has calculated the return expected, and has balanced these subjectively with the risks involved, he or she can determine whether the investment is satisfactory or not. It is wise to make a comparative analysis of several companies within the industry, since the investor is always dealing in relatives, not absolutes, in analyzing common stock. No one company at any given moment of time will necessarily be the best investment; there might be several that would satisfy the investor's requirements. One security in a specific industry might appear to be more attractive than another even though it is not the only satisfactory investment for *all* industries. In the analysis of a company and its common stock in the next several chapters, several of the strongly competitive, dominant companies will be selected from a strong industry. Then, analysis should indicate the company offering the best opportunity for investment success.

This method of company analysis will begin by examining the competitive position of the company within the industry. In subsequent chapters, the analysis will be completed and a decision reached about which company to select. The drug industry will be used in the case analysis from this chapter through Chapter 18. Chapter 19 will present a comprehensive case analysis of the electronics industry, demonstrating this suggested method of analysis.

THE COMPETITIVE POSITION OF THE COMPANY IN THE INDUSTRY

Major industries in the United States are composed of hundreds of individual companies. There are, for example, more than 42,000 businesses in the petroleum industry, excluding service stations. The chemical industry comprises more than 7,000 companies and the pharmaceutical industry more than 1,100. Most are small, are privately owned, and share a very small percentage of the market. The majority do not have securities outstanding, so investors are unable to share in their future. Their size alone, even if they were stock companies, would preclude them from consideration. Nor do they possess the amount, quality, and stability of sales we want for investment.

Within each industrial group, a few firms control the major portion of the output. In the chemical industry, 175 firms account for over 90 percent of the entire output. Seven firms are dominant—du Pont, Union Carbide, Allied Chemical, Monsanto,

Dow, Olin, and American Cyanamid. In the auto industry, three companies—Chrysler, Ford, and General Motors—dominate the passenger car market in the United States. Together with American Motors, these companies virtually control the domestic automobile market. Fewer than ten companies, led by U.S. Steel, dominate the domestic market for steel. Approximately eight companies have captured the bulk of the market for paper and allied products. With the exception of banking and finance, dominance by a few firms persists in virtually all industries in the United States.

As a matter of principle, the risk-averse investor should be interested in those companies that have reached positions of dominance. They are the largest companies in the industry and have been successful in meeting competition. They have demonstrated over time their ability to lead and have established their position by obtaining a significant share of the market for their products. They have demonstrated profit potential, too, having grown because they have been profitable. Once such companies obtain a position of leadership within an industry, they seldom lose it.

Selecting the Competitively Strong Company

The competitive position of a company within an industry can be determined by the use of several criteria: (1) the amount of annual sales, (2) the growth of annual sales, and (3) the stability of annual sales.

AMOUNT OF SALES OR REVENUES. The dollar amount of annual sales helps to determine a company's relative competitive position within an industry. The greater the annual sales, the more successful the company has been in meeting competition. In 1980, BankAmerica Corporation, Citicorp, and Chase Manhattan Coporation were first, second, and third in the banking business; IBM led in the computer industry; Exxon, Mobil, and Royal Dutch in the international oil group.

One problem faced when ranking companies by size is making certain the companies are comparable. Within an industry, companies must be compared by like-product groups. The paper industry, for example, is divided into several subindustry groups oriented around different products. The leading producers of sanitary tissues would be ranked together and the leading producers of corrugated board, rather than the leading producers of "paper and allied products." Otherwise, conclusions may be erroneous and lead to a poor selection for investment.

Size is an excellent guide to competitive position. The leading companies of today will most likely be leaders in the future; smaller companies might not survive the competition. General Motors has been the leader in its industry for decades. In selecting from among the largest firms in the industry, we are helping to reduce the business risk, which tends to reduce the variability of the return by reducing the variability of dividends and earnings. Once the leading companies of an industry are identified, they may be selected on the basis of their expected growth of sales and earnings. Hence, the first principle is to invest in a growing industry. The second is to select a growing company based on sales or revenues and profits from among the competitive leaders in the industry. The company need not be the largest. In fact, the largest company might not offer sufficient growth potential to make it attractive for investment.

GROWTH OF SALES OR REVENUES. In determining the competitive position of a company, size is not the only criterion; the annual rate of growth of sales is equally, if not more, important. A company with rapidly expanding annual sales and adequate financing would be in a better position to earn money for the stockholder than one large in size but with no prospects for growth. Ideally, the investor desires both size and rapidly expanding sales. The size of the company protects it from the vicissitudes of economic fluctuations. Growing sales give it growing profits. Growth is a relative concept, and the standard of growth is how one company in an industry compares with the others. Whether a company expands from within, by building new plants, or from without, by acquisition of existing plant capacity, is not important at this point. What is important is that the company demonstrate an ability to obtain a large share of the market, leading eventually to greater profits.

How do investors decide when a company is growing more rapidly than other companies in the industry? They usually compare its sales growth with that of the industry, in terms of both dollars and physical units. Investors want the company to grow not only in dollar terms, but also in real terms—in goods and services produced. The growth of a single company can also be compared with the growth of the national economy as measured by GNP, NI, and DPI. The investor should make certain that the appropriate index in the national income accounts has been selected for comparison. It is helpful to use a base period in sales and calculate an index of sales growth. Currently, 1972 is used as the base year for GNP accounts. A comparison with disposable personal income, for example, would be a good measure of growth in the retailing industry. The gross national product would be excellent for comparison with the industrial-construction industry. The FRB indexes would be appropriate for comparing growth in real terms. The comparison enables the investor to see readily how the company has grown in dollar terms, compared with the industry and the national economy.

The investor is also interested in the annual growth rate and would like a company that is growing at a rate faster than the industry in which it competes. In doing so, it will increase its share of the market over time and will be competitively stronger than the other companies. In a very rapidly expanding industry, a company might become larger and larger in importance, yet grow less rapidly than the industry. It is still profitable and still expanding, but not as fast as the industry. A company's sales can be computed as a percentage of industry sales. If the company is increasing its share of the market—IBM is a good example of this—the investor knows it is doing better competitively.

The reason for comparing growth both in dollar and in physical terms is to determine the degree of inflation. A company that is expanding in real units produced and in constant dollars of income received is much more attractive for investment than one that is not growing in real terms. An example of the process of determining rate of growth of companies will be demonstrated for companies in the "Health Care, Drugs and Cosmetics" group, as established by Standard & Poor's.

COMPANIES WITH DIVERSIFIED SALES. In reality, most companies produce many different items within a product classification, and some produce many unrelated goods. Procter & Gamble is a soap company, but it also produces packaged cake mixes and toothpaste. Coca-Cola leads in production of carbonated beverages, yet it has a big stake in the frozen-food industry through its Minute Maid division. Companies that produce in more than one industry must be examined in such a way that the investor knows the percentage of sales distributed by each industry. The SEC now requires a breakdown of sales by product line in the 10-K reports filed by companies.

Assume that a food company diversifies its productive activities by acquiring a drug company and a chemical company. In the first year after acquisition, we find that 38 percent of its sales are in drugs, 22 percent in chemicals, and 40 percent in food. The company is still predominantly a producer of food, but now 60 percent of its sales are contributed by other products in other industries. It is no longer a food company, but a food-drug-chemical company. It is necessary, then, to examine the growth characteristics of the company in all its classes. This will prevent the false assumption that the company is in only one industry. The competitive position in all phases of the company's activities must be examined.

Often, a company is producing so many different products that it is difficult to classify it according to a major product group.[1] This is particularly true of conglomerates such as Transamerica, ITT, and Textron. Then the only recourse is to examine the overall sales figures for the company without the benefit of an industry comparison, or to make an assumption as to what the primary activity of the company is and compare that with the comparable industry. If no single industry is discernible, the growth of sales can be compared to national income or gross national product. This will provide a standard of comparison to determine the relative growth position of the company in the national economy.

STABILITY OF SALES. The stability of sales is important, in addition to amount and rate of growth. A firm with stable sales revenues, other things being equal, will have more stable earnings. A wide variation in sales will not allow for the advantages of financial planning, expansion, plant utilization, or dividends to stockholders. Aggregate sales of different industries vary in their degree of stability. Company sales should follow the pattern of the industry. The revenues of all industries except railroads have generally been stable upward and have ranged from modest to rapid growth. Revenues of industries that provide a basic service or necessity goods tend to be more stable than those of other industries. Industries offering capital goods or high-cost durable consumer goods tend to have less stable revenues.

A Forecast of Sales

The analysis of the competitive position of the company assumes that a company that has been in a strong competitive position in the past and has demonstrated a superior rate of growth in sales, both in dollars and physical units, should continue this pattern in the future. But there is no certainty in this assumption; therefore, the investor must make the best possible estimate about future sales.

Five methods can be used to forecast company sales. First, the investor can fit

---

[1]Accountants recognize the problem of accounting for firms with diversified operations. Schachner suggests that assets and earnings be broken down by product line for easier analysis and understanding. Leonard Schachner, "Corporate Diversification and Financial Reporting," *Journal of Accountancy*, April 1967.

a trend line to past sales, either visually or mathematically, by using the least-squares method.[2] Second, company sales might be related to industry sales by percentage, by a line of average relationship, or by regression analysis. Third, the analyst might relate company sales to population growth; this would require an estimate of sales per capita. Fourth, the investor might analyze demand for the products of the company by analyzing the types of customers. In this case, the investor would consider military and nonmilitary demand, commercial, industrial, and consumer demand, and foreign and domestic sales, and would need to identify the product as a luxury or a necessity, durable or nondurable, and high- or low-priced, and then assess the impact these factors would have on demand for the product. Fifth, the investor can use estimates of sales provided by company economists, investment analysts, and management.

Since the estimates made will vary in their reliability, they must be used only as an approximation of the future. Where no estimates for the company exist, it might be assumed that its growth will parallel the growth of the industry. Hence, if it is anticipated that the industry will double its sales within the next decade, it can be assumed that the company under consideration will also double its sales if it has followed the growth of the industry in the past. The investor might compare growth of sales with the growth of the national economy, using past national economy–industry relationships to estimate the future. This is the real reason for developing these relationships. If we assume that the national economy is going to expand by $100 billion in the next decade, then an industry that obtains 0.6 percent of the GNP will increase its sales by $600 million in the next decade. A company that generates 10 percent of industry sales will, assuming its competitive position remains unchanged, achieve 10 percent of the growth of industry sales; thus, its sales in the example will increase by $60 million.

The investor need not use all these methods; each will serve to provide the necessary forecast. But all estimates of future growth of a company must be constantly revised. Its competitive position can deteriorate. The investor must periodically reappraise and be informed about the sales position of the company. The investor must learn to anticipate changes in demand for its products and services. These are not simple tasks, and judgment must be exercised.

Selecting the Competitive Firm—A Summary

In summary, several principles may be used as a guide to selecting the best company for investment. First, the investor should select a company that is dominant in the industry—one that is a leader, that has obtained a position of dominance, that is not likely to lose its position, and that offers size, stability, and growth of sales. Second, the investor should select a company that is expected to grow faster than its competitors. Third, a company should be competitive in all areas of its productive activity. A company that has a diversified specialty is perhaps better than one producing a large group of unrelated products. At this point, tentative decisions can be made, based on the competitive position of the company, that allow the investor to narrow the field of inquiry to the leading companies in an industry.

[2]The reader might review Frederick E. Croxton, Dudley J. Cowden, and Sidney Klein, *Applied General Statistics*, 3rd ed. (Englewood Cliffs, N.J.: Prentice-Hall, 1967), chap. 15, "Analysis of Time Series," particularly pp. 399–411, or a later edition of this text or other texts on statistics.

SELECTING THE LEADING COMPETITIVE COMPANIES
IN THE INDUSTRY—AN ACTUAL CASE IN MID-1981

The method of company analysis will be applied here to the health care, drug, and cosmetics industry. The analysis will begin by examining the leading competitive companies in the industry, and it will be continued in each of the following chapters until it is completed and an investment decision has been reached—to buy or not to buy shares in one or all of these leading companies in the industry.

The Health Care, Drug, and Cosmetics Industry

The health care industry has shown dramatic growth over the past two decades.[3] It is highly competitive and depends upon research and a high degree of technical and scientific knowledge for its existence. In 1980, about $245 billion was spent in the United States for health care products. Of that total, 40 percent was spent for hospital care; 18 percent for physicians' services; 7 percent for drugs and drug sundries; 9 percent for nursing-home care; 7 percent for dentists' services; 3 percent for construction; 5 percent for expenses for prepayment and administration, 3 percent for government public health activities; 2 percent for research; 2 percent for eyeglasses and appliances; and 2 percent for "all other."

The drug portion of the industry is divided into two main groups, ethical drugs and proprietary drugs. Ethical drugs are sold only by prescription, and advertising is directed toward the medical profession. Probably the most familiar ethical drugs are penicillin and other antibiotics, such as Aureomycin, Terramycin, and Bicillin. The best-selling prescription drugs of 1980 included Tagamet (anti-ulcer), Inderal (anti-hypertensive), and Naprosyn (anti-arthritic). Other familiar ethical drugs include hormones, prescription vitamins, hematinics, biologicals, cancer drugs, cardiovascular drugs, and polio vaccines.

Proprietary drugs are sold without prescription, mainly in drugstores. Advertising is directed to the consumer. The most familiar proprietary drugs are vitamins, cold remedies, analgesics, laxatives, and cathartics. The consumer knows proprietary drugs by their popular names, such as Anacin, Alka-Seltzer, Bufferin, Pepto-Bismol, Rem, and Hadacol.

Cosmetics and toiletries are considered usually part of the health care industry. Chesebrough-Pond's is a good example; it produces Vaseline and Pertussin, as well as Pond's Cold Cream and Prince Matchabelli and Simonetta perfumes. Avon Products, Fabergé, Max Factor, Gillette, and Revlon are companies in this group.

The broad health care industry group also includes hospital supplies and equipment. Representative companies in the group include American Hospital Supply; Baxter Travenol Laboratories; Becton, Dickinson; Ipco Hospital Supply; and Johnson & Johnson.

Hospital chains round out the industry group. Proprietary hospitals have gained acceptance and should grow in the future with the growth of the industry. Representative companies in this group include American Medical International, American

---

[3] Much of the data presented in this section were obtained from Standard & Poor's *Industry Survey— Health Care, Drugs and Cosmetics*, January 13, 1981.

Medicorp, Hospital Affiliates International, Hospital Corporation of America, and Humana, Inc.

The subindustry of drugs within the overall health care industry has been selected for analysis here, since it has grown more rapidly than the national economy. Based upon data presented in Chapter 12, annual growth for drugs in real terms will average 3.8 percent from 1981 to 1985. This is a higher rate than that expected for growth in the national economy for the same time period. The industry has also grown faster than disposable personal income. Its total sales have increased continually since 1957, and the industry increased its share of DPI from 1.48 percent in 1972 to 1.76 percent in 1980 (see Table 13–1). Industry growth in real terms was greater than that of all manufacturing companies. This dynamic growth record is the reason for selecting the drug industry.

TABLE 13–1

Index and Annual Growth Rate of Sales in Drug Industry Compared with Disposable Personal Income (1972 = 100)

Year	DPI Billion $	DPI Index	U.S. Drug Industry Sales* Billion $	U.S. Drug Industry Sales* Index	Annual % Increase in Drug Industry Sales	$ Sales of Drug Industry as a % of DPI
1980	$1,822	225	$32	266	14%	1.76%
1979	1,642	203	28	234	15	1.71
1978	1,463	181	24	203	15	1.67
1977	1,312	162	21	178	8	1.62
1976	1,194	147	20	164	10	1.65
1975	1,096	135	18	149	12	1.63
1974	998	123	16	133	17	1.60
1973	915	113	14	114	14	1.50
1972	810	100	12	100	—	1.48

*Net sales of 20 largest companies in the industry according to *The Value Line Investment Survey.*

SOURCE: *Economic Indicators,* Council of Economic Advisers, Washington, D.C., May, 1981, p. 6.

The Leading Companies in the Drug Industry

The leading companies in the ethical and proprietary drug industry are presented in Table 13–2, ranked according to 1980 sales. American Home is actually in both ethical and proprietary drugs. Many ethical drug companies have branched out into proprietary medicines, and the proprietary companies have moved into the ethical field. Little change occurred in the relative position of the companies in the ethical drug industry between 1978 and 1980. Marion Lab moved from fifth place to eleventh, Forest Labs from twelfth to eighth place, American Home Products moved to third, and SmithKline moved to number one.

The growth of sales in the drug industry has been excellent. Total sales were $12 billion in 1972 and $32 billion in 1980. If the trend continues, they may increase to approximately $60 billion in 1984 (see Figure 13–3).

TABLE 13–2

The Leading Ethical and Proprietary Drug Companies Ranked by Index of Sales and Size
(in millions) (Index 1972 = 100)

Company	Sales ($ millions)			Index 1972 = 100			Rank by Index of Sales			Rank by Amount of Sales		
	1980	1979	1978	1980	1979	1978	1980	1979	1978	1980	1979	1978
Ethical												
Forest Labs	$ 17	$ 13	$ 10	283	227	168	8	11	12	14	14	14
ICN	63	78	85	39	48	53	14	14	14	13	13	13
Eli Lilly	2,559	2,266	1,852	312	276	226	6	6	6	3	3	3
Marion Lab	116	120	117	227	236	230	11	9	5	12	12	12
Merck	2,734	2,385	1,981	285	248	207	7	8	10	2	2	2
Pfizer	3,029	2,746	2,362	277	251	216	9	7	7	1	1	1
A. H. Robins	432	386	357	259	232	214	10	10	9	10	10	10
Rorer-Amchem	313	269	220	188	161	133	12	12	13	11	11	11
Schering-Plough	1,740	1,434	1,083	342	284	215	5	5	8	6	6	7
Searle	1,082	898	848	397	330	312	3	3	1	8	8	8
*SmithKline	1,772	1,351	1,112	440	336	276	1	1	2	4	7	6
Squibb	1,658	1,453	1,516	179	157	164	13	13	11	7	5	4
Syntex	580	470	381	413	335	272	2	2	3	9	9	9
Upjohn	1,761	1,508	1,329	344	295	260	4	4	4	5	4	5
Proprietary												
American Home Products	3,799	3,401	3,062	239	214	193	3	4	4	1	1	1
Bristol Myers	3,158	2,753	2,450	263	229	204	2	2	2	3	3	3
Morton-Norwich	847	732	657	230	199	179	6	6	6	6	6	6
Vick Drugs	1,212	1,091	945	271	244	212	1	1	1	5	5	5
Sterling Drugs	1,701	1,500	1,315	236	208	182	4	5	5	4	4	4
Warner Lambert	3,479	3,217	2,879	234	216	194	5	3	3	2	2	2

*SmithKline merged with Beckman to become SmithKline Beckman in 1982.

SOURCE: The Value Line Investment Surveys, Drug Industry, Arnold Bernhard & Co., Inc., New York, 1981. Reprinted by permission.

The Three Leading Ethical Companies

The ethical drug industry was chosen for investment consideration because it has had a slightly faster rate of growth than the proprietary drug companies, based upon the data listed in Chapter 12. Three of the ethical drug companies listed in Table 13–2 will be selected for analysis based upon the competitive position or size of the company and the growth rate of sales. Which companies should we choose? If we select the top six companies based on size alone, as measured by 1980 actual sales, we would pick Pfizer, Merck, Lilly, SmithKline, Upjohn and Schering. If we made our decision on the basis of the growth rate of sales through 1980; we would have SmithKline, Syntex, Searle, Upjohn, Schering, and Eli Lilly. Actually determining the competitive position requires a great deal more analysis than just ranking companies by size and growth. However, since we wish to select the recognized industry leaders, we will start with size and growth.

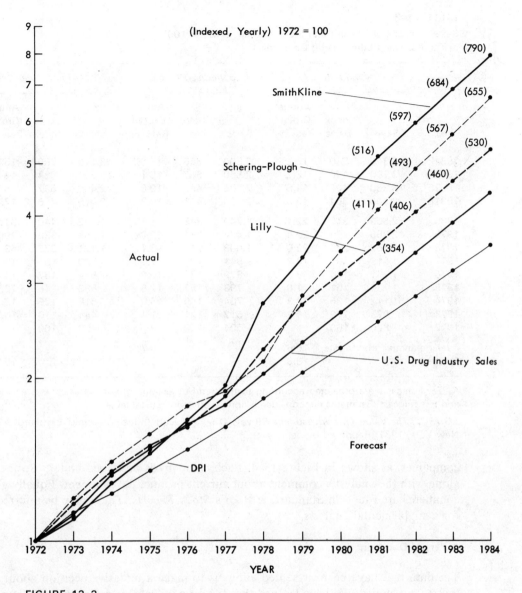

(Indexed, Yearly) 1972 = 100

(790)
(684)
(655)
SmithKline
(597)
(567)
(530)
(516)
Schering-Plough
(493)
(460)
(411) (406)
Lilly
Actual
(354)

U.S. Drug Industry Sales

Forecast

DPI

1972 1973 1974 1975 1976 1977 1978 1979 1980 1981 1982 1983 1984
YEAR

FIGURE 13–3

Drug Industry Sales, DPI, and Sales of Lilly, Schering-Plough, and SmithKline,
Actual 1972–80 and forecast, 1981–84

A defensive and conservative choice of companies designed to reduce the business risk suggests the elimination of Searle and Syntex as being too small on a relative basis, since we are trying to avoid risk. Based upon a combination of size and growth rate of sales, Eli Lilly, Schering-Plough, and SmithKline will be analyzed as investment candidates. Their growth of sales is seen in Table 13–3 and Figure 13–3. *The Value Line Investment Survey* provides concise and comprehensive data for these

TABLE 13–3

Sales (Millions of Dollars) and Index of Sales (1972 = 100)
of Three Leading Ethical Drug Companies

	Eli Lilly			Schering-Plough			SmithKline		
Year	Sales	Index Sales	Annual Growth Rate (%)	Sales	Sales Index	Annual Growth Rate (%)	Sales	Sales Index	Annual Growth Rate (%)
1984F	$4,340	530	15.2%	$3,300	655	15.5%	$3,175	790	15.5%
1983F	3,770	460	13.2	2,860	567	15.1	2,750	684	14.0
1982F	3,330	406	14.8	2,485	493	19.8	2,400	597	15.7
1981E	2,900	354	13.3	2,075	411	19.3	2,075	516	17.1
1980	2,559	312	22.4	1,740	345	21.5	1,722	440	31.2
1979	2,266	276	22.4	1,434	284	32.2	1,351	336	20.5
1978	1,852	226	22.0	1,083	215	13.1	1,121	276	43.7
1977	1,518	185	13.2	941	187	7.9	780	194	15.7
1976	1,341	164	8.7	872	173	10.0	674	167	14.4
1975	1,234	151	11.0	793	157	12.6	589	146	13.7
1974	1,112	136	14.3	704	140	15.0	518	129	16.7
1973	973	119	18.7	612	121	21.4	444	110	10.2
1972	820	100		504	100		402	100	
Average annual growth rate			16.6%			16.7%			20.8%
Forecast			13.8			18.0			15.8

NOTE: Forecasts are projected according to the trend of average growth in sales. E is estimated and F is forecast. Estimates are considered conservative and sustainable.

SOURCE: The Value Line Investment Survey, Drug (Ethical) Industry, Arnold Bernhard & Co., New York, 1981. Reprinted by permission.

companies, as shown in Figure 13–4. Each company is described under "Business," along with the analyst's comment about current product development. Equally good comments are found in Standard & Poor's *Stock Reports*. These may be referred to for a supplemental analysis.

A Partial Decision

The data that have been presented allow us to make a tentative decision about our investment choice. We have learned that the drug industry is growing faster than the national economy. The firms in the industry with both size and growth of sales have been found. From among these Lilly, Schering, and SmithKline were selected for several reasons. All have excellent growth rates, as shown in the projected growth figures in Figure 13–3 and Table 13–3. If this growth continues, the companies will increase their share of the market and maintain their competitive position. We would rank SmithKline, Schering and Lilly in that order based on the criteria established. This is a tentative decision. A final decision will be made only after all other factors have been examined. The relative position of the companies is summarized in Table 13–4.

LILLY (ELI) & CO. NYSE-LLY

RECENT PRICE	52	P/E RATIO	10.7 (Trailing: 10.9 Median: 21.0)	EARN'S YLD	9.3%	DIV'D YLD	5.0%	1262

| High→ | 28.8 | 39.0 | 51.8 | 54.5 | 64.3 | 80.0 | 92.5 | 82.8 | 79.8 | 60.0 | 48.3 | 54.0 | 63.9 | 63.8 | 68.8 | | | | 320 |
| Low→ | 21.9 | 24.0 | 34.5 | 39.0 | 49.3 | 54.9 | 69.8 | 55.8 | 49.5 | 43.0 | 32.6 | 36.6 | 47.1 | 45.8 | 45.3 | | | | 240 |

Insider Decisions 1981

	J A S O N D	J F M A M J J A S
to Buy	0 0 0 0 0 1	0 0 0 0 0 0 1 1 0
to Sell	0 4 3 3 1 3	1 0 0 2 5 1 2 0 0

25.0 × "Cash Flow" p sh

2-for-1 split

2-for-1 split

Options Trade On ASE

Relative Price Strength

Target Price Range

1984 1985 1986

Nov. 20, 1981 Value Line

TIMELINESS 3 Average
(Relative Price Performance Next 12 Mos.)

SAFETY 1 Highest
(Scale: 1 Highest to 5 Lowest)

BETA 1.05 (1.00 = Market)

1984-86 PROJECTIONS

	Price	Gain	Ann'l Total Return
High	140	(+170%)	31%
Low	115	(+120%)	25%

© Arnold Bernhard & Co., Inc.

Institutional Decisions

	2Q'80	3Q'80	4Q'80	1Q'81	2Q'81
to Buy	98	120	104	82	92
to Sell	81	94	78	87	88
Hldg's(000)	48001	47267	47676	48646	47947

Percent shares traded 3.0 2.0 1.0

1966	1967	1968	1969	1970	1971	1972	1973	1974	1975	1976	1977	1978	1979	1980	1981	1982	1983		84-86E
5.70	6.25	7.18	7.99	8.75	10.62	11.96	14.12	16.10	17.85	19.39	21.51	25.41	30.25	33.76	35.60	38.95		(A)Sales per sh	54.80
.93	.98	1.25	1.45	1.65	1.76	2.20	2.65	3.00	3.07	3.40	3.68	4.43	5.18	5.26	5.55	6.10		"Cash Flow" per sh	9.05
.77	.83	1.08	1.25	1.40	1.42	1.85	2.26	2.59	2.62	2.90	3.10	3.81	4.52	4.52	4.75	5.25		(B)Earnings per sh	7.95
.40	.40	.45	.53	.65	.70	.73	.79	.97	1.10	1.25	1.42	1.65	1.95	2.20	2.38	2.65		(C) Div'ds Decl'd per sh	3.60
.51	.68	.44	.82	1.14	.51	.48	.58	1.19	1.56	.96	1.11	1.23	2.37	3.04	3.00	3.50		Cap'l Spending per sh	5.00
3.77	4.28	5.02	5.89	6.73	7.53	9.02	10.60	12.29	13.86	15.60	17.12	18.99	21.54	22.92	25.10	27.65		Book Value per sh	38.80
64.37	65.30	66.81	67.23	67.66	68.11	68.56	68.88	69.03	69.12	69.13	70.58	72.89	72.91	75.78	76.25	76.50		Common Shs Outst'g	78.00
26.8	31.3	28.1	32.3	33.6	41.0	37.7	36.2	26.8	25.1	17.8	12.5	11.9	12.2	11.8	Bold figures are			Avg Ann'l P/E Ratio	16.0
3.7%	3.2%	3.6%	3.1%	3.0%	2.4%	2.7%	2.8%	3.7%	4.0%	5.6%	8.0%	8.4%	8.2%	8.5%	Value Line estimates			Avg Ann'l Earn's Yield	6.3%
1.9%	1.5%	1.5%	1.3%	1.4%	1.2%	1.0%	1.0%	1.4%	1.7%	2.4%	3.7%	3.7%	3.5%	4.1%				Avg Ann'l Div'd Yield	2.8%

CAPITAL STRUCTURE as of 3/31/81
Total Debt $255.6 mill. Due in 5 Yrs $216.3 mill.
LT Debt $39.3 mill. LT Interest $3.1 mill.
(2% of Cap'l)

Leases, Uncapitalized Annual rentals $17.7 mill.

Pension Liability $58 mill. in '80 vs. $58 mill. in '79

Pfd Stock None

Common Stock 75,956,239 shs. (98% of Cap'l)

819.7	972.6	1111.6	1233.7	1340.6	1518.0	1852.1	2205.8	2558.6	2715	2980	(A)Sales ($Mill)	4275
27.0%	28.6%	28.5%	27.3%	27.6%	27.6%	28.4%	27.8%	26.4%	24.3%	24.0%	Operating Margin	25.5%
24.7	26.8	28.1	31.0	35.0	41.4	45.1	48.3	56.7	62.0	68.0	Depreciation ($Mill)	85.0
126.3	155.5	178.8	181.3	200.2	218.7	277.5	329.5	342.0	362	400	Net Profit ($Mill)	620
35.7%	38.8%	40.9%	39.3%	41.3%	43.3%	42.5%	40.3%	42.1%	43.0%	43.0%	Income Tax Rate	42.0%
15.4%	16.0%	16.1%	14.7%	14.9%	14.4%	15.0%	14.9%	13.4%	13.3%	13.4%	Net Profit Margin	14.5%
285.5	369.8	459.6	510.8	614.0	713.9	711.0	770.9	800.5	940	1025	Working Cap'l ($Mill)	1250
10.9	6.5	5.6	11.5	19.6	--	4.7	4.1	32.9	45.0	50.0	Long-Term Debt ($Mill)	60.0
618.2	730.2	848.5	958.0	1078.6	1208.7	1384.1	1570.4	1736.7	1915	2115	Net Worth ($Mill)	3025
20.2%	21.2%	21.0%	18.7%	18.3%	18.1%	20.0%	20.9%	19.4%	18.5%	18.5%	% Earned Total Cap'l	20.0%
20.4%	21.3%	21.1%	18.9%	18.6%	18.1%	20.1%	21.0%	19.7%	19.0%	19.0%	% Earned Net Worth	20.5%
12.4%	13.8%	13.2%	11.0%	10.6%	9.9%	11.6%	11.9%	7.7%	9.5%	9.5%	% Retained to Comm Eq	11.0%
39%	35%	37%	42%	43%	45%	42%	43%	61%	50%	51%	% All Div'ds to Net Prof	45%

CURRENT POSITION ($Mill)

	1979	1980	3/31/81
Cash Assets	174.0	202.3	254.7
Receivables	459.4	544.7	676.1
Inventory (LIFO)(D)	605.4	672.5	648.0
Other	58.8	118.2	123.0
Current Assets	1297.6	1537.7	1701.8
Accts Payable	102.2	109.5	104.5
Debt Due	100.3	184.7	216.3
Other	324.2	443.0	467.9
Current Liab.	526.7	737.2	788.7

ANNUAL RATES

of change (per sh)	Past 10 Yrs	Past 5 Yrs	Est '78-'80 to '84-'86
Sales	14.0%	13.0%	11.0%
"Cash Flow"	13.0%	11.5%	10.5%
Earnings	13.0%	11.5%	11.0%
Dividends	13.5%	15.0%	10.0%
Book Value	13.5%	12.0%	10.5%

QUARTERLY SALES ($ mill.)

Calendar	Mar. 31	June 30	Sept. 30	Dec. 31	(A)Full Year
1978	492.8	457.0	427.9	474.4	1852.1
1979	613.0	542.0	509.4	541.4	2205.8
1980	717.6	599.9	601.6	639.5	2558.6
1981	812.6	624.6	623.8	654	2715
1982	885	680	680	735	2980

EARNINGS PER SHARE (B)

Calendar	Mar. 31	June 30	Sept. 30	Dec. 31	Full Year
1978	1.10	.98	.84	.89	3.81
1979	1.41	1.18	.96	.97	4.52
1980	1.47	.98	1.00	1.07	4.52
1981	1.65	1.00	1.04	1.06	4.75
1982	1.75	1.15	1.15	1.20	5.25

QUARTERLY DIVIDENDS PAID (C)

Calendar	Mar. 31	June 30	Sept. 30	Dec. 31	Full Year
1977	.355	.355	.355	.355	1.42
1978	.40	.40	.40	.45	1.65
1979	.45	.45	.525	.525	1.95
1980	.525	.525	.575	.575	2.20
1981	.575	.575	.575	.65	

BUSINESS: Eli Lilly and Co. mfrs. a broad line of medicines for human use; agric. chems.; cosmetics; animal health prods.; electronic medical instruments and implantable cardiac pacemakers. Antibiotics sales, 27% of total. Brand names include Darvon (analgestic); Keflin, Keflex, Kefzol, Mandol, Ceclor, Ilosone, Nebcin (antibiotics); Nalfon 600 (antiflammatory); Treflan (herbicide). Int'l business, 40% of sales (27% of pretax income); R&D, 8%; est'd labor costs, 30%. '80 deprec. rate: 4.4%. Est'd plant age: 10 yrs. Has 28,100 empls., 31,000 stkhldrs. 20% of stock closely held. Chrmn. & Pres.: R.D. Wood. Inc.: Ind. Address: 307 E. McCarty St. Indianapolis, Ind. 46285.

Lilly is slowly moving back on track. After posting flat earnings last year, the company reported a 7% year-to-year net profit advance in the first nine months, despite a 20¢ a share foreign exchange penalty. We estimate full-year earnings at $4.75 a share vs. 1980's $4.52.

The recession-resistant healthcare business is performing well. Worldwide pharmaceutical sales rose 18%, year to year, in the first nine months, thanks to Lilly's newer antibiotics, Mandol and Ceclor. Early signs indicate that combined worldwide sales of these compounds could hit $150 million this year (a 35% jump) with a bottom-line contribution of 40¢-50¢ a share. We expect growth to slow in 1982 to "only" 20% or so because of rising competition. Still, overall pharmaceutical sales should rise about 15%. New products, including Benoxaprofen for arthritis, will give volume a lift.

But nonhealthcare operations are another matter. Profits at Elizabeth Arden are off, due to slack demand for cosmetics, especially in foreign markets. And the agricultural business is in a deeper slump. Profits fell more than 20% in the first nine months, reflecting sharply reduced sales of Treflan, a high-margined herbicide. The U.S. recession and the lingering business hesitation abroad might preclude a strong upturn in agricultural and cosmetics sales before mid-1982.

Finances are in great shape. Long-term debt accounts for less than 5% of total capital, and virtually all that debt is at low, fixed interest rates. The absence of leverage makes Lilly's hefty returns on equity (about 20%) that much more impressive. The company probably will need little outside financing for capital expenditures over the next year.

Though year-ahead stock performance prospects may be only average for this top-quality issue, the longer view looks brighter. Once the recession is past, we expect the agricultural and cosmetics segments to recover. This, plus continued solid gains by healthcare products, could well give rise to double-digit profit growth and worthwhile share price appreciation over the next 3 to 5 years. R.C.C./N.R.W.

Restated Sales (and Pretax Margins) by Business Line

	1978	1979	1980	1981
Human Health	1063.9(28.5%	1183.5(24.9%)	1426.0(23.2%)	1625(24.0%)
Agriculture	600.4(28.2%)	795.9(30.2%)	871.7(27.4%)	805(18.5%)
Cosmetics	187.8(10.2%)	226.4(10.6%)	292.9(10.3%)	285(10.0%)
Company Total	1852.1(26.6%)	2205.8(25.3%)	2558.6(23.3%)	2715(20.1%)

(A) Incl. Elizabeth Arden from '71; IVAC from '77; Cardiac Pacemakers from '78; Physio-Control from '80. (B) Based on avg. shs. outst'g. Incl. pretax foreign currency exch. gains (losses): '78 (10¢); '79 (20¢); '80 (14¢). Next eps. rep't due late Jan. Est'd constant-dollar egs./sh.: 80, $3.68, (C) Next div'd meet'd about Dec. 15. Goes ex about Feb. 5. Div'd paym't dates: Mar. 10, June 9, Sept. 10, Dec. 10. (D) Switch to LIFO Dec. '80 penalized egs. 24¢/sh.

Company's Financial Strength	A++
Stock's Price Stability	85
Price Growth Persistence	30
Earnings Predictability	95

Factual material is obtained from sources believed to be reliable but cannot be guaranteed.

FIGURE 13–4(a)

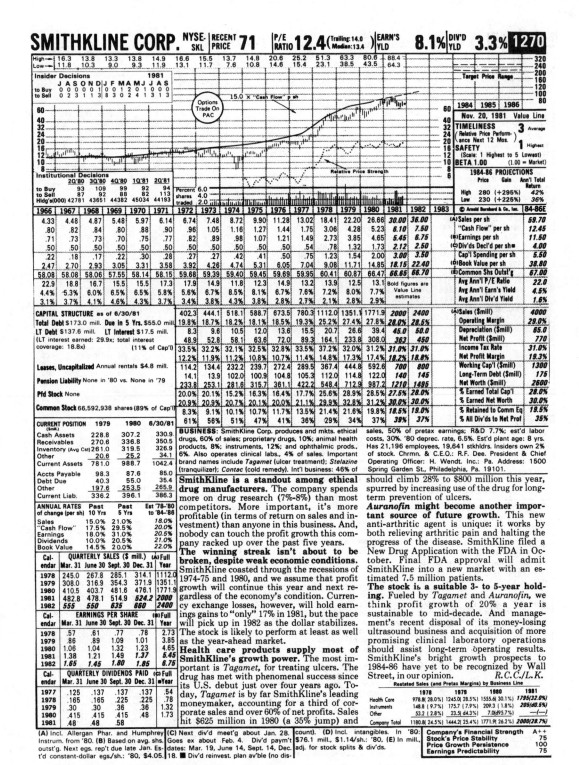

SMITHKLINE CORP. — Value Line report

NYSE-SKL			RECENT PRICE **71**			P/E RATIO **12.4** (Trailing: 14.0 / Median: 13.4)					EARN'S YLD **8.1%**		DIV'D YLD **3.3%**		**1270**			

| High → | 16.3 | 13.8 | 13.3 | 13.8 | 14.9 | 16.6 | 15.5 | 13.7 | 14.8 | 20.6 | 25.2 | 51.3 | 63.3 | 80.6 | 88.4 | | | |
| Low → | 11.8 | 10.3 | 9.0 | 9.3 | 11.9 | 13.1 | 11.7 | 7.6 | 10.8 | 14.6 | 15.4 | 23.1 | 38.5 | 43.5 | 64.3 | | | |

Insider Decisions 1981

	J	A	S	O	N	D	J	F	M	A	M	J	J	A	S
to Buy	0	0	0	0	1	0	0	1	2	0	1	0	0	0	0
to Sell	0	2	3	1	1	3	8	3	0	2	4	1	3	1	3

Options Trade On PAC

15.0 X "Cash Flow" p sh

Institutional Decisions

	2Q'80	3Q'80	4Q'80	1Q'81	2Q'81
to Buy	93	109	99	92	94
to Sell	87	92	88	82	113
Hldg's(000)	42781	43651	44382	45034	44193

Percent shares traded — 6.0 / 4.0 / 2.0

		1984	1985	1986

Target Price Range

Nov. 20, 1981 Value Line

TIMELINESS 3 Average (Relative Price Performance Next 12 Mos.)

SAFETY 1 Highest (Scale: 1 Highest to 5 Lowest)

BETA 1.00 (1.00 = Market)

1984-86 PROJECTIONS

	Price	Gain	Ann'l Total Return
High	280	(+295%)	42%
Low	230	(+225%)	36%

© Arnold Bernhard & Co., Inc.

1966	1967	1968	1969	1970	1971	1972	1973	1974	1975	1976	1977	1978	1979	1980	1981	1982	1983		84-86E
4.33	4.48	4.87	5.48	5.97	6.14	6.74	7.48	8.72	9.90	11.28	13.02	18.41	22.20	26.66	**30.00**	**36.00**		(A) Sales per sh	59.70
.80	.82	.84	.80	.88	.90	.96	1.05	1.16	1.27	1.44	1.75	3.06	4.28	5.23	**6.10**	**7.50**		"Cash Flow" per sh	12.45
.71	.73	.73	.70	.75	.77	.82	.89	.98	1.07	1.21	1.49	2.73	3.85	4.65	**5.45**	**6.75**		(B) Earnings per sh	11.50
.50	.50	.50	.50	.50	.50	.50	.50	.50	.50	.50	.54	.78	1.32	1.73	**2.12**	**2.50**		(C) Div'ds Decl'd per sh ■	4.00
.22	.18	.17	.22	.30	.28	.27	.27	.42	.41	.50	.75	1.23	1.54	2.00	**3.00**	**3.50**		Cap'l Spending per sh	5.50
2.47	2.70	2.93	3.05	3.31	3.58	3.92	4.26	4.74	5.31	6.05	7.04	9.08	11.71	14.85	**18.15**	**22.40**		(D) Book Value per sh	38.80
58.08	58.08	58.06	57.55	58.14	58.15	59.68	59.39	59.40	59.45	59.69	59.95	60.41	60.87	66.47	**66.65**	**66.70**		(E) Common Shs Outst'g	67.00
22.9	18.8	16.7	15.5	15.5	17.3	17.9	14.9	11.8	12.3	14.9	13.2	13.9	13.9	13.1	Bold figures are			Avg Ann'l P/E Ratio	22.0
4.4%	5.3%	6.0%	6.5%	6.5%	5.8%	5.6%	6.7%	8.5%	8.1%	6.7%	7.6%	7.2%	8.0%	7.7%	Value Line estimates			Avg Ann'l Earn's Yield	4.5%
3.1%	3.7%	4.1%	4.6%	4.3%	3.7%	3.4%	3.8%	4.3%	3.8%	2.8%	2.7%	2.1%	2.8%	2.9%				Avg Ann'l Div'd Yield	1.6%

CAPITAL STRUCTURE as of 6/30/81

Total Debt $173.0 mill. Due in 5 Yrs. $55.0 mill.

LT Debt $137.6 mill.   LT Interest $17.5 mill.

(LT interest earned: 29.9x; total interest coverage: 18.8x)   (11% of Cap'l)

Leases, Uncapitalized Annual rentals $4.8 mill.

Pension Liability None in '80 vs. None in '79

Pfd Stock None

Common Stock 66,592,938 shares (89% of Cap'l)

402.3	444.1	518.1	588.7	673.5	780.3	1112.0	1351.1	1771.9	**2000**	**2400**		(A) Sales ($mill)	4000
19.8%	18.7%	18.2%	18.1%	18.5%	19.3%	25.2%	27.4%	27.8%	**28.0%**	**28.5%**		Operating Margin	29.0%
8.3	9.6	10.5	12.0	13.6	15.5	20.7	26.6	39.4	**45.0**	**50.0**		Depreciation ($mill)	65.0
48.9	52.8	58.1	63.6	72.0	89.3	164.1	233.8	308.0	**363**	**450**		Net Profit ($mill)	770
33.5%	32.2%	32.1%	32.5%	32.8%	33.5%	37.2%	32.0%	31.2%	**31.0%**	**31.0%**		Income Tax Rate	31.0%
12.2%	11.9%	11.2%	10.8%	10.7%	11.4%	14.8%	17.3%	17.4%	**18.2%**	**18.8%**		Net Profit Margin	19.3%
114.2	134.4	232.2	239.7	272.4	289.5	367.4	444.8	592.6	**700**	**800**		Working Cap'l ($mill)	1300
14.1	13.9	102.0	100.9	104.8	105.3	112.0	114.8	122.0	**140**	**145**		Long-Term Debt ($mill)	175
233.8	253.1	281.6	315.7	361.1	422.2	548.4	712.9	987.2	**1210**	**1495**		Net Worth ($mill)	2600
20.0%	20.1%	15.2%	16.3%	16.4%	17.7%	25.6%	28.9%	28.5%	**27.5%**	**28.0%**		% Earned Total Cap'l	28.0%
20.9%	20.9%	20.7%	20.1%	20.0%	21.1%	29.9%	32.8%	31.2%	**30.0%**	**30.0%**		% Earned Net Worth	30.0%
8.3%	9.1%	10.1%	10.7%	11.7%	13.5%	21.4%	21.6%	19.8%	**18.5%**	**19.0%**		% Retained to Comm Eq	19.5%
61%	56%	51%	47%	41%	36%	29%	34%	37%	**39%**	**37%**		% All Div'ds to Net Prof	35%

CURRENT POSITION (($Mill.))	1979	1980	6/30/81
Cash Assets	228.8	307.2	330.9
Receivables	270.6	336.8	350.5
Inventory (Avg Cst)	261.0	319.5	326.9
Other	20.6	25.2	34.1
Current Assets	781.0	988.7	1042.4
Accts Payable	98.3	87.6	85.0
Debt Due	40.3	55.0	35.4
Other	197.6	253.5	265.9
Current Liab.	336.2	396.1	386.3

ANNUAL RATES of change (per sh)	Past 10 Yrs	Past 5 Yrs	Est '78-'80 to '84-'86
Sales	15.0%	21.0%	18.0%
"Cash Flow"	17.5%	29.5%	20.0%
Earnings	18.0%	31.0%	20.5%
Dividends	10.0%	20.5%	21.0%
Book Value	14.5%	20.0%	22.0%

Cal-endar	QUARTERLY SALES ($ mill.) (A)				Full Year
	Mar. 31	June 30	Sept. 30	Dec. 31	
1978	245.0	267.8	285.1	314.1	1112.0
1979	308.0	316.9	354.3	371.9	1351.1
1980	410.5	403.7	481.6	476.1	1771.9
1981	482.8	478.1	514.9	**524.2**	**2000**
1982	**555**	**550**	**635**	**660**	**2400**

Cal-endar	EARNINGS PER SHARE (B)				Full Year
	Mar. 31	June 30	Sept. 30	Dec. 31	
1978	.57	.61	.77	.78	2.73
1979	.86	.89	1.09	1.01	3.85
1980	1.06	1.04	1.32	1.23	4.65
1981	1.38	1.21	1.49	**1.37**	**5.45**
1982	**1.65**	**1.45**	**1.80**	**1.85**	**6.75**

Cal-endar	QUARTERLY DIVIDENDS PAID (C)				Full Year
	Mar. 31	June 30	Sept. 30	Dec. 31	
1977	.125	.137	.137	.137	.54
1978	.165	.165	.225	.225	.78
1979	.30	.30	.36	.36	1.32
1980	.415	.415	.415	.48	1.73
1981	.48	.48	.58		

BUSINESS: SmithKline Corp. produces and mkts. ethical drugs, 60% of sales; proprietary drugs, 10%; animal health products, 8%; instruments, 12%; and ophthalmic prods., 6%. Also operates clinical labs, 4% of sales. Important brand names include Tagamet (ulcer treatment); Stelazine (tranquilizer); Contac (cold remedy). Int'l business: 46% of sales, 50% of pretax earnings; R&D 7.7%; est'd labor costs, 30%. '80 deprec. rate, 6.5%. Est'd plant age: 8 yrs. Has 21,196 employees, 19,641 stkhldrs. Insiders own 2% of stock. Chrmn. & C.E.O.: R.F. Dee. President & Chief Operating Officer: H. Wendt. Inc.: Pa. Address: 1500 Spring Garden St., Philadelphia, Pa. 19101.

SmithKline is a standout among ethical drug manufacturers. The company spends more on drug research (7%-8%) than most competitors. More important, it's more profitable (in terms of return on sales and investment) than anyone in this business. And, nobody can touch the profit growth this company racked up over the past five years.

The winning streak isn't about to be broken, despite weak economic conditions. SmithKline coasted through the recessions of 1974-75 and 1980, and we assume that profit growth will continue this year and next regardless of the economy's condition. Currency exchange losses, however, will hold earnings gains to "only" 17% in 1981, but the pace will pick up in 1982 as the dollar stabilizes. The stock is likely to perform at least as well as the year-ahead market.

Health care products supply most of SmithKline's growth power. The most important is Tagamet, for treating ulcers. The drug has met with phenomenal success since its U.S. debut just over four years ago. Today, Tagamet is by far SmithKline's leading moneymaker, accounting for a third of corporate sales and over 60% of net profits. Sales hit $625 million in 1980 (a 35% jump) and

should climb 28% to $800 million this year, spurred by increasing use of the drug for long-term prevention of ulcers.

Auranofin might become another important source of future growth. This new anti-arthritic agent is unique: it works by both relieving arthritic pain and halting the progress of the disease. SmithKline filed a New Drug Application with the FDA in October. Final FDA approval will admit SmithKline into a new market with an estimated 7.5 million patients.

The stock is a suitable 3- to 5-year holding. Fueled by Tagamet and Auranofin, we think profit growth of 20% a year is sustainable to mid-decade. And management's recent disposal of its money-losing ultrasound business and acquisition of more promising clinical laboratory operations should assist long-term operating results. SmithKline's bright growth prospects to 1984-86 have yet to be recognized by Wall Street, in our opinion.   R.C.C./L.K.

Restated Sales (and Pretax Margins) by Business Line

	1978	1979	1980	1981
Health Care	978.8(28.0%)	1245.0(28.5%)	1555.6(30.1%)	1795(32.0%)
Instruments	148.8(9.7%)	175.7(7.9%)	209.3(1.8%)	205(d0.5%)
Other	53.2(2.8%)	23.5(d4.3%)	7.0(d95.7%)	—(—)
Company Total	1180.8(24.5%)	1444.2(25.1%)	1771.9(26.2%)	2000(28.7%)

(A) Incl. Allergan Phar. and Humphrey Instrum. from '80. (B) Based on avg. shs. outst'g. Next egs. rep't due late Jan. Est'd constant-dollar egs./sh.: '80, $4.05. (C) Next div'd meet'g about Jan. 28. Goes ex about Feb. 4. Div'd paym't dates: Mar. 19, June 14, Sept. 14, Dec. 18. ■ Div'd reinvest. plan av'ble (no dis- count). (D) Incl. intangibles. In '80: $76.1 mill., $1.14/sh.: '80. (E) In mill., adj. for stock splits & div'ds.

Company's Financial Strength	A++
Stock's Price Stability	75
Price Growth Persistence	100
Earnings Predictability	75

Factual material is obtained from sources believed to be reliable but cannot be guaranteed.

FIGURE 13–4(b)

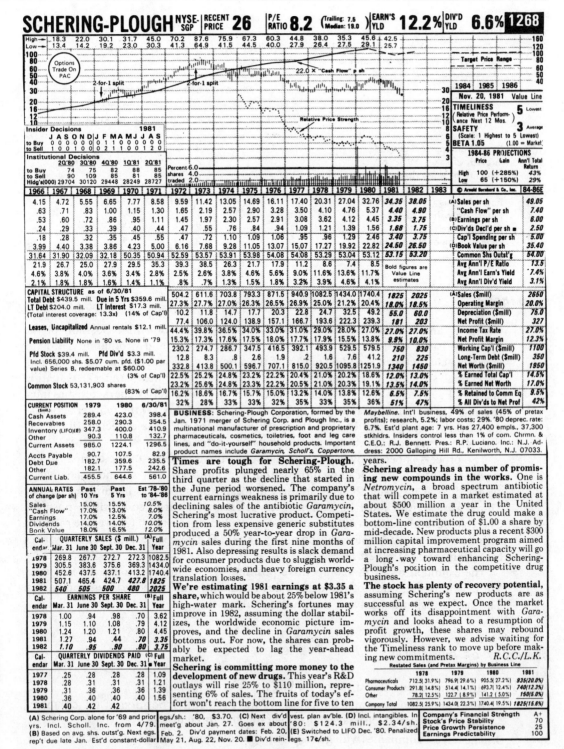

FIGURE 13–4(c)

TABLE 13–4
A Comparison of the Competitive Positions of Lilly,
Schering-Plough, and SmithKline

Characteristics	Relative Position or Company		
	Lilly	Schering	SmithKline
Size of company, 1980	1	2	3
Growth of sales, 1972–80	3	2	1
Stability of sales (based on variability of growth rate)	1	2	3
Foreign sales (rank and percent)	3 (40)	2 (46)	1 (47)
Future growth of sales	3	1	2
Product diversification	3	2	1
Overall competitive position	3	2	1

SUMMARY

Company analysis includes an examination of (1) the competitive position of the company based on past and future growth, (2) earnings and profitability, (3) the operating characteristics and efficiency of the company, (4) current financial position, (5) capital structure characteristics, (6) company management, and (7) valuation analysis. Each has an effect on earnings and price. Return and risk characteristics must consider (1) the past price range, (2) the price-earnings ratio, (3) the market action of the stock, (4) the general level of the stock market, and (5) the expected return and risk—the variability of return—and the beta characteristics.

The process is begun by examining the competitive position of the company. The investor wants, first, a leading firm within the industry, and second, one that is expected to grow faster than its industry domestically as well as in foreign markets. Third, all activities must be examined to determine the true competitive position. There are several methods of forecasting sales, including (1) trend, (2) average relationship between industry sales and company sales, (3) sales per capita, (4) analysis of customers, and (5) expert forecasts.

The examination of the competitive position of a company is only the first step. We began a case study of the drug industry and selected three leading companies. The final decision must await a complete analysis.

SUMMARY OF PRINCIPLES

1. Investors should invest in the leading firms in the industry.
2. Investors should examine all aspects of the competitive position of the company, including all products, as well as domestic and foreign sales.
3. The largest companies with good growth potential are usually the most competitive.

FUNDAMENTAL ANALYSIS

1. What factors must be examined in estimating the future earnings capability of a company?

2. Explain briefly what is meant by each of these terms:
   a. Competitive position.
   b. Company profitability.
   c. Operating efficiency.
   d. Current financial position.
   e. Capital structure characteristics.
   f. Management.
   g. Valuation

3. Why should the investor be concerned with the price of a common stock, and how does this relate to earnings?

4. How is the competitive position of a company within an industry determined?

5. Explain the significance of size, stability, and rate of growth of sales for an investor.

6. In defining the competitive position of a company, why is it so important to understand the nature and type of products produced?

7. How would you analyze a company that produced more than one major product? How would you analyze a company that did not have one major product?

8. What does the character of the product—that is, luxury or necessity, high-priced or low-priced—have to do with the competitive position of a company?

9. Explain how we might forecast a company's sales if we did not have an expert to tell us how they were expected to grow.

10. What conclusions do you draw from an analysis of the competitive position of the companies in the drug industry? Why were Lilly, Schering and SmithKline chosen for analysis?

PROBLEMS

This series of problems should be considered along with the problems at the end of Chapters 13 through 18 as a complete case in fundamental analysis.

1. Identify the leading companies in the industry analyzed in Problem 4 of Chapter 12.

2. Rank each company on the basis of dollar sales and sales in units of goods produced for 1972 and the most recent year for which figures are available.

3. Based on an index of dollar or physical sales using 1972 as 100, compare the overall growth between the base year and the current year for each of the leading companies. Select the companies that have shown the greatest competitive strength, as evidenced by growth of sales. Based on size and growth rate, select the three leading companies in the industry. Answer the same question on a subjective basis.

4. Compute an index of sales for the years 1972 to the present for each of the companies. Compare with the growth of the industry.
   a. Which company appears to have the highest rate of growth?
   b. Which company has the greatest stability of sales?
   c. Rank each of the companies according to these characteristics.

5. a. What products are produced by each of the three companies? Include in the answer the percentage composition of product sales of each company.
   b. Does the company produce a luxury or a necessity product?
   c. What percentage of sales are military and nonmilitary? foreign and domestic?
6. Forecast the sales for each company for the next three years. Use one of the methods presented in this chapter.
7. On the basis of this analysis, which company would you select? Use criteria comparable to those presented in the chapter in answering this question.

SELECTED READINGS

BAUMAN, W. SCOTT. "Investment Analysis: Science or Fiction?" *Financial Analysts Journal*, January–February 1976, p. 93.

BERNSTEIN, LEOPOLD A. "In Defense of Fundamental Analysis." *Financial Analysts Journal*, January–February 1975, p. 57.

BISSELL, GEORGE S. "Responsibility in Financial Forecasting." *Financial Analysts Journal*, May–June 1972, p. 73.

FARRELL, JAMES L. JR. "Homogeneous Stock Groupings." *Financial Analysts Journal*, May–June 1975, pp. 50–63.

MEYERS, STEPHEN L. "A Re-Examination of Market and Industry Factors in Stock Price Behavior," *The Journal of Finance*, June 1973, pp. 695–706.

NORBY, WILLIAM C., and FRANCIS STONE. "Objectives of Financial Reporting." *Financial Analysts Journal*, July–August 1972, p. 39.

PORTER, MICHAEL E. "Industry Structure and Competitive Strategy: Keys to Profitability." *C.F.A Readings in Financial Analysis*, 5th ed., p. 300. Homewood Ill.: Irwin, 1981.

SHAPIRO, ALAN C. "Exchange Rate Changes, Inflation, and the Value of the Multinational Corporation." *The Journal of Finance*, May 1975, pp. 485–502.

SHASHUA, L., and Y. GOLDSCHMIDT. "An Index for Evaluating Financial Performance." *The Journal of Finance*, June 1976, pp. 797–814.

SHOHET, RUBEN. "Investing in Foreign Securities." *Financial Analysts Journal*, September–October 1974, pp. 55–72.

TERBORGH, GEORGE. "Inflation and Profits." *Financial Analysts Journal*, May–June 1974, pp. 19–24.

CHAPTER 14

CORPORATE EARNINGS
AND PROFITABILITY

A strong competitive position helps ensure growth of earnings. However, before sales can be converted into earnings, certain costs and expenses must be met. A corporation must be able to produce goods or services cheaply and efficiently in order to convert sales into profits. Beyond this, new plants must be added to allow production and sales to expand. To determine how much a company can earn in the future and how profitably, the investor must analyze the expenses and costs required to generate profit and earnings per share from sales. Future earnings can be estimated only if we are aware of these relationships.

The analysis of the company is continued in this chapter by examining the relationship between earnings and sales, and how expenses might vary independently of sales. Methods of forecasting future earnings per share, using current statistical and analytical techniques, will be examined. As a matter of principle, the investor should invest in companies that provide a strong and stable growth of earnings in the future. A reliable estimate of future earnings makes it possible to estimate expected return and risk.

THE RELATIONSHIP BETWEEN SALES AND EARNINGS PER SHARE

The purchase of a common stock offers the investor the right to an uncertain amount of future earnings and dividends. The investor is interested in the amount, stability, and growth rate of these earnings—particularly their amount and when they will be received. If the investor knew for certain the future earnings per share, he or she could quickly estimate the future price and dividends and reach a decision as to whether the stock provided an acceptable return.

The investor usually tries to choose for investment those companies that have stable and growing sales, because it is assumed that earnings will follow the growth of sales. This assumption rests on several premises: first, that expenses will not vary—that is, that profitability, the relationship between sales and expenses, will remain constant; second, that there will be a constant utilization of plant and equipment above the breakeven point, so that the effects of operating leverage will be the same; third, that there will be no changes in debt in the capital structure; and finally, that the combination of products produced will remain the same. Obviously, if any of these variables change in the future independently of sales changes, earnings per share will change. That is why costs and expenses must be analyzed carefully in estimating future earnings.

Unfortunately, earnings do not always follow the path of sales. Sometimes they actually move in an opposite direction. The financial press frequently reports that a company's sales have increased but its earnings per share have declined. A few years ago, for example, Allied Paper announced that its new earnings per share would decline to about $1 from the previous year's $1.09, but that sales for the corresponding period would increase to about $50 million, up from $46 million—or about a 10 percent increase in sales with a 10 percent decrease in earnings per share. Obviously, this is not a desirable situation.

Another problem of analysis is the difference in the relative rates of growth of earnings and sales. The rate of change of earnings can be different from the rate of change of sales, depending on operating and financial leverage and changes in costs and expenses. Sales might, for example, increase 10 percent but earnings per share increase only 4 percent. There is a correlation between earnings and sales, but it is imperfect.

An even more frustrating situation occurs when earnings increase with a decreased volume of sales. Hallicrafters, a manufacturer of radios and electronic components, had this experience. During one period, sales decreased but earnings per share remained the same. In some cases, earnings per share have even gone up with a decrease in sales.

The illustrations dramatize the perplexing problems investors face in estimating earnings. It would be wrong to rely upon size and growth of sales without inquiring into the ability of the company to earn. It cannot be assumed that fixed relationships will always exist between sales and profits. Earnings must be carefully examined and their derivation understood if investors are to be reasonably certain of the future earnings capability of a company. The company's earnings should be compared to those of the industry and to the national economy. The basic problem is to determine whether companies selected for future sales growth will also be profitable and provide future earnings of sufficient amount, quality, and certainty.

AGGREGATE CORPORATE PROFITS AND THE NATIONAL ECONOMY

The relationship between corporate profits and sales and the national economy on an aggregate basis is helpful in providing background for discussion about the relationship between company sales and earnings per share. We know that the GNP and NI have expanded between 1978 and 1981. Intermittent periods of recession have occurred, however. At other times, industrial activity declined, resulting in a decrease in corporate earnings. Corporate profits after taxes, shown in Table 14-1, reflect these changes in business activity. Corporate profits have been cyclical in character. They increased sharply in 1979, followed by a decline of almost 4 percent for all of 1980. Corporate profits declined 5.5 percent in 1981, followed by a further decline in 1982. Corporate profits were expected to rise in the first half of 1983, followed by an increase as recessionary conditions abated. During the same period, cash dividends steadily increased.

Even in an expanding economy, the earnings of companies do not follow a consistent growth pattern. Profits are unstable and vary with the business cycle. Cash dividends tend to follow the secular growth of the economy, and retained earnings are most affected by the change in profitability.

TABLE 14-1
Corporate Profits and Their Distribution

Corporate Profits with Inventory Valuation and Capital Consumption Adjustments (billions of dollars and percentage change)	1978	1979	1980	1981	1981		1982		
					QIII	QIV	QI	QII	QIII
Corporate profits before tax $	223.3	255.4	245.5	232.1	233.3	216.5	171.6	171.7	180.3
% change		14.4	−3.9	−5.5		−7.2	−20.7	(NC)	5.0
Profits—tax liability $	83.0	87.6	82.3	81.2	82.4	71.6	56.7	55.3	60.9
Profits after tax $	140.3	167.8	163.2	150.9	150.8	144.9	115.0	116.3	119.4
% change		19.6	−2.7	−7.5		−3.9	−20.6	1.1	2.7
Dividends $	44.6	50.2	56.0	65.1	66.8	68.1	68.8	69.3	70.5
% change		12.6	11.6	16.3		1.9	1.0	7.3	1.7
Undistributed profits $	95.7	117.6	107.2	85.8	84.0	76.9	46.1	47.0	48.8
Inventory valuation adjustment $	−24.3	−42.6	−45.7	−24.6	−23.0	−17.1	−4.4	−9.4	−10.3
Capital consumption adjustment $	−13.5	−15.9	−17.2	−16.8	−17.1	−15.5	−10.1	−6.9	−3.8
Profits after tax with inventory valuation and capital consumption adjustments $	102.5	107.2	97.0	109.5	110.7	112.3	100.4	100.0	105.3
% change		4.6	−9.5	12.9		1.4	−10.6	−0.4	5.3

SOURCE: U.S. Department of Commerce, Bureau of Economic Analysis, *Third Quarter 1981 Corporate Profits Preliminary,* December 1982, Table 3.

DETERMINING CORPORATE EARNINGS

Aggregate corporate profits are presented only to provide a point of orientation. The basic problem in estimating the future earnings per share of a company's common stock is to establish the ability of the company to earn money. A careful examination of the profit and loss statement or operating statement will help in the analysis of earnings.

Sales and Operating Revenues

Simplified operating statements of two hypothetical companies—an industrial and an electric utility—are given in Table 14–2 to review how net income and earnings per share are computed. The operating statement of Industrial, Incorporated, is presented in two ways, both used by industrial companies. All three statements are typical of companies in their industry.

Individual items in the operating statement vary from industry to industry. Electrical, Incorporated, has only a service to sell. No tangible product is involved, so *operating revenues* rather than *sales* is the term used by water and gas companies, railroads, toll-highway companies, and the like to denote their major source of income. Commercial banks, which derive their income from interest on loans to

TABLE 14–2

Methods of Presenting Income Statement,
for Industrial and Public Utility Companies

Industrial, Incorporated, Operating Statement, May 31 (millions of dollars)

Alternate #1			Alternate #2		
Net sales		197	Net sales		197
Cost of goods sold		160	Other income		1
Gross profit on sales		37	Total income		198
Operating expenses:			Cost of goods sold		160
General administrative	10		Operating expenses		21
Selling	7		General administrative	10	
Depreciation	3		Selling	7	
Retirement funds	1		Depreciation	3	
Total		21	Retirement funds	1	
Profit from operations		16	Interest and other		
Other income		1	nonoperating expenses		5
		17	Total cost and		
Interest expense		5	expenses		186
Net income before taxes		12	Net income before taxes		12
Federal and state income					
taxes (50%)		6			
Net income after taxes		6	Federal and state		
			income taxes (50%)		6
Earnings per share (2,000,000		$3.00			
shares outstanding)			Net income after taxes		6
Cash earnings per share		$4.50*			
			Earnings per share		
			(2,000,000 shares		
			outstanding)		$3.00
			Cash earnings per share		
			(cash flow)		$4.50*

TABLE 14–2   (Continued)

Electrical, Incorporated, Operating Statement, December 31 (millions of dollars)

Operating revenues		655
Operating expenses:		
Operations	268	
Maintenance	62	
Depreciation	58	
Property taxes	118	
Total		506
Operating income		149
Nonoperating income		1
Gross income		150
Interest on debt		39
Net income before taxes		111
Federal income taxes		40
Net income after taxes		71
Earnings per share (10,000,000 shares outstanding)	$ 7.10	
Cash earnings per share	$12.90*	

*Net income after taxes, plus depreciation and other noncash expenses. Here we add only depreciation, because it is difficult to establish the amount of the other items.

business and interest on investments, usually refer to interest income as operating revenue. Insurance companies have two main sources of revenue or income—premiums from policyowners, and interest, dividends, and rents from investments. Manufacturing companies in a class similar to Industrial, Incorporated, sell a tangible product, and their revenues are referred to as sales, since the production of income requires that an actual good be sold.

Nonoperating Income

Most industrial companies receive, in addition to sales revenue, other income that is considered *nonoperating income*—usually interest from bonds, lease rentals, or dividends from securities of subsidiaries. These can be extremely important sources of revenue to some companies. The presentation of operating revenues or sales and operating and nonoperating income and expenses differs from company to company. Alternate #1 for Industrial, Incorporated, and the operating statement of Electrical, Incorporated, follow the same approach. First, they present operating income and operating expenses, then nonoperating income and expenses, and finally net income after federal income taxes.

Another way of presenting an operating statement is shown in Alternate #2 of Industrial, Incorporated. All sources of income are given; then all costs and expenses are deducted; then net income before and after taxes is established. Both methods lead to the same earnings per share.

An understanding of these methods will be useful later in the chapter when ways of measuring profitability are discussed. In addition, in making an analysis of a company, the investor must be familiar with the terminology used by the company being considered. A standard accounting pattern is followed in reporting income. The significance of each item in the statement and variations in accounting must be determined if successful results are to be obtained. As an illustration, the insurance industry uses terms that may not be familiar to the investor—for example, *premiums from policyowners*, and *policy proceeds left with the company*. Actually, "premium income" is quite easily understood; it represents payment for the life insurance benefits, which puts the insurance policy into effect and continues it in effect; when we pay life insurance premiums, they are income to the insurance company. "Proceeds left with the company" represents one option included in some life insurance policies, by which the beneficiary, when receiving the proceeds of the policy, can leave the funds with the company to earn interest at a guaranteed rate, rather than receive a life income or a lump sum.

Earnings per Share

Since the unit of measurement in investment is a share of stock, it is important that net income after taxes be converted into per share figures. Earnings per share are found by dividing the number of total outstanding shares into corporate net income after taxes, first deducting preferred dividends, if preferred stock exists. Earnings per share should not be confused with dividends per share. Dividends represent the amount actually paid to the shareowner. In the case of Industrial, Incorporated (Table 14–2), total earnings after taxes were $6 million. Since 2 million shares were outstanding, earnings per share amounted to $3. In actual practice, the corporation should use the average number of shares outstanding for the year. This is particularly important when a company issues new shares of stock during the year.

Cash Flow or Cash Earnings per Share

Today, increasing attention is being given to the cash flow of the business enterprise. The term *cash flow* is used to describe the funds, generated from operations, that remain after all cash expenses have been subtracted. The usual way of estimating cash flow per share is to add all noncash expenditures to net income after taxes, then divide by the number of shares outstanding. For most companies, the most important noncash expense—in many cases, the only one—is depreciation; all other items of expense are assumed to be cash items. Reference to Table 14–2 will show how cash flow or cash earnings are determined for Industrial, Incorporated. Net income after taxes was $6 million and depreciation expense $3 million, which provided a cash flow of $9 million, or $4.50 per share for the 2 million shares outstanding. The same computation was made for Electrical, Incorporated, which had a cash flow of $129 million, or $12.90 per share on the 10 million shares outstanding.

Cash earnings are significant because they give an estimate of the amount of discretionary funds over which management has control. Many corporate managements, when planning for the future, look upon depreciation—a noncash expense—as a source of funds. In reality, sales are the original source of funds, but depreciation expenses keep funds within the company. These depreciation funds, when consciously used to govern capital expenditure policy, may buy or build new plant and equipment or even increase working capital. Cash earnings, then, are a good guide to the availability of internally generated funds that can be used for expansion. By considering cash earnings or cash flow rather than net income, we can appraise more realistically the earning power of a company, as well as its future ability to earn. It is conceivable that a company with a small net income per share might have a sizable cash flow that would turn a seemingly unprofitable venture into a profitable one, using the term *profitable* broadly.

THE QUALITY OF CORPORATE EARNINGS

Much of the work that is done in analysis is based on information published by the company under study, or by an investment service. In the discussion on corporate earnings, it was assumed that the earnings reported by the company were accurate and a true reflection of profitability. Just what constitutes a "true" measure of earnings is difficult to determine. The investor wishes to know if the reported earnings figures are realistic or whether they have been influenced unduly by temporary changes in income or costs and expenses. The investor should be willing to pay full value for a dollar of quality and recurring earnings. A dollar of temporary, transitory earnings would not be worth very much, since the earnings will not occur in the future and will be of little benefit. In the analysis of earnings, therefore, income and costs and expenses must be examined to make certain they are accurate measures of the company's ability to earn. Depreciation policies and accounting practices must also be understood, since they might affect the current earnings report of the company. To the extent that it is possible, reported earnings should be adjusted either up or down to reflect permanent changes in earnings. Temporary influences on earnings resulting from changes in income or expense should be disregarded in estimating future earnings.

Opinions of the Old Accounting Principles Board
and the New Financial Accounting Standards Board

The American Institute of Certified Public Accountants, through its boards and committees, reviews corporate financial statements to improve their usefulness. In the past, the Accounting Principles Board would take a stand on a controversial item in order to clarify some problem confronting the accounting profession and the analyst. Several of the "Opinions" it issued in the past are of significance to investors and financial analysts.

The board found that net income should reflect all items of profit and loss recognized during the period, with extraordinary items segregated and shown separately in the income statement. It suggested the following presentation:

Income before extraordinary items

Extraordinary items
  (Less applicable income tax)

Net income[1]

[1] The American Institute of Certified Public Accountants, APB *Accounting Principles*, vol. I, current text, section 2010, paragraph 19.

The board strongly recommended that earnings per share be disclosed in the statement of income and approved of historical reporting of net income and earnings per share. It recommended that earnings per share be based on the average number of shares outstanding for the period. It also suggested that earnings per share reflect the potential dilution created by a convertible preferred stock or convertible bond issue outstanding, and potential dilution from warrants, stock options, and agreements for issuing new shares for little or no value.[2] The AICPA continues this work through its publication *Accounting Trends and Techniques*.

A new, independent seven-member body, the Financial Accounting Standards Board, was founded in 1973 to provide a new direction in the establishment of better accounting practices, and it replaced the APB. The investor should be aware of new methods and procedures promulgated by the FASB.

It is difficult if not impossible to record all generally accepted accounting practices (GAAP). However, the American Institute of Certified Public Accountants, through a report of the Study Group on the Objectives of Financial Statements, has clearly set forth objectives that are attainable in stages within a reasonable period of time. A summary of these objectives is as follows:[3]

1. Provide information useful for making economic decisions.

2. Serve primarily those users who have limited authority, ability, or resources to obtain information and who rely on financial statements as their principal source of information about an enterprise's economic activities.

3. Provide information useful to investors and creditors for predicting, comparing, and evaluating potential cash flows to them in terms of amount, timing, and related uncertainty.

4. Provide users with information for predicting, comparing, and evaluating enterprise earning power.

5. Supply information useful in judging management's ability to utilize enterprise resources effectively in achieving the primary enterprise goal.

6. Provide factual and interpretive information about transactions and other events that is useful for predicting, comparing, and evaluating enterprise earning power. Basic underlying assumptions with respect to matters subject to interpretation, evaluation, prediction, or estimation should be disclosed.

7. Provide a statement of financial position useful for predicting, comparing, and evaluating enterprise earning power. This statement should provide information concerning enterprise transactions and other events that are part of incomplete earnings cycles. Current values should also be reported when they differ significantly from historical cost. Assets and liabilities should be grouped or segregated by the relative uncertainty of the amount and timing of prospective realization or liquidation.

8. Provide a statement of periodic earnings useful for predicting, comparing, and evaluating enterprise earning power. The net result of completed earnings cycles and enterprise activities resulting in recognizable progress toward completion of incomplete cycles should be reported. Changes in the values reflected in successive state-

[2]See also Leopold A. Bernstein, Ph.D., CPA, "An Analysis of APB Opinion No. 9, Reporting the Results of Operations," *The New York Certified Public Accountant*, March 1967; and Frank T. Weston, CPA, "Reporting Earnings per Share," *Financial Analysts Journal*, July–August 1967.

[3]AICPA, Report of the Study on the Objectives of Financial Statements, "*Objectives of Financial Statements*," chap. 11, 1973. American Institute of Certified Public Accountants, Inc., New York.

ments of financial position should also be reported, but separately, since they differ in terms of their certainty of realization.

9. Provide a statement of financial activities useful for predicting, comparing, and evaluating enterprise earning power. This statement should report mainly on factual aspects of enterprise transactions having or expected to have significant cash consequences. This statement should report data that require minimal judgment and interpretation by the preparer.

10. Provide information useful for the predictive process. Financial forecasts should be provided when they will enhance the reliability of users' predictions.

Although the specifics behind each objective are not provided, the investor can gain some insight into the possible effect on accounting statements, including both the operating statement and the balance sheet.

It is imperative that the investor have comparable data to use in making estimates of the future earning power of a company. Some of the likely variations will be discussed under the analysis of earnings.

Variation in Income

A company's earnings can change sharply because of a nonrecurring change in sales. Assume, for example, that a company suffered a strike in a particular year, the first in its history. It caused a reduction in output and lower sales for the year, reducing earnings by $.50 per share. Now the strike has been settled; peaceful coexistence prevails. The influence on earnings was temporary. The investor would conclude that earnings ability had not been fundamentally impaired and would adjust the stated earnings to reflect the fundamental earnings of the company. On the other hand, if the strike that brought about the decline in earnings was an annual event for the company and brought to the surface a basic antagonistic difference in labor-management relations, the decrease in earnings could be expected again in the years ahead. Since the strike is recurring, the decline in earnings is recurring, and accordingly the investor would not adjust the earnings deficit by adding back the temporary decline in earnings. An investor would be unwilling to pay much for this stock, because of the high variability of earnings and because future earnings would be lower with recurring strikes. In an appraisal of earnings, therefore, the investor must take cognizance of the reliability and dependability of the major source of the company's revenues.

Often, the income of a company rises sharply because of a temporary increase in sales. The investor discounts a temporary decline in sales revenues, and should also discount a temporary increase in net income. The auto industry in 1981 reached new lows in sales levels. But this industry has cyclical earnings, and this should be considered exceptional—much worse than normal. The investor would have adjusted earnings upward in 1982 rather than accept them at face value, in order to estimate long-range earnings.

Variation in Expenses and Costs

The other cause of a change in earnings is changes in costs and expenses. To determine future earnings, each item of the expense account should be examined to ascertain whether the increase or decrease will have a transitory or a permanent impact on earnings. An example of this type of adjustment is that for CIT, a financial company. Its interest expense was expected to increase because of the increase in short-term interest rates. It was assumed that increased interest costs would result in a maximum decrease of $0.25 per share, so earnings were lowered from $4.35 to $4.10.

Other expenses not usually labeled in the operating statement have an impact upon corporate earnings. Many corporations must make engineering changes that reduce earnings. The crash of an airline plane costs the company substantial sums of money to determine its cause. Automobile recalls cost auto manufacturers large amounts. It would be logical to assume that such inordinately high expenses would be non-recurring and that earnings in such a year do not reflect future earning power.

Depreciation

A more familiar business expense that can raise or lower corporate earnings is depreciation. The investor must ask whether the method of computing depreciation expense, or changes in depreciation expense, will have a temporary effect on the company's net earnings. Since each company has a wide variety of assets that are depreciated over varying time periods under different rates established by the Internal Revenue Service, it is difficult to determine an overall depreciation rate for a company. However, through observation and evaluation, the investor can learn to determine the impact of depreciation accounting on the company's earnings.

Some oil companies, for example, capitalize their drilling expenses and write them off as an expense over the life of the asset; others write off all their drilling expenses as current expenses. The method used will have an effect on reported earnings. Assume that a company had drilling expenses of $1 million. Instead of writing off the expense this year, the company writes it off over a period of five or ten years. This would have the effect of reducing the drilling expenses in the first year as a charge to income. However, if drilling continued for a five- or ten-year period at the same rate, eventually the annual amount written off would equal the actual annual expenditure. The effect in the first years of this practice would be to overstate earnings. If a company changed from one method to the other—say, from the capitalization-of-earnings method to writing off the capital expenditure as current expense—it would reduce earnings because current expenses would be increased. This would be a permanent change in depreciation policy that would have the effect of temporarily reducing earnings.

The method chosen by the firm to depreciate its assets will affect reported earnings. The Economic Recovery Tax Act of 1981 addressed the concept of capital cost recovery to replace depreciation as a method to recover capital costs. ERTA of 1981 terminated the Asset Depreciation Range (ADR) system for recovery of assets placed in service after December 30, 1980. Under the new system, the cost of an asset is recovered over a predetermined period shorter than the useful life of the asset or the period the asset is used to produce income. Eligible assets can be recovered over a minimum of three, five, ten, or fifteen years, depending on the type of asset. Companies have the option of using the straight-line method of depreciation, a declining balance method at a rate up to 200 percent of the straight-line rate, or sum-of-the-years'-digits method for the appropriate recovery period. (See Chapter 11 for the details of the Economic Recovery Tax Act of 1981.)

Any form of accelerated depreciation tends to understate net income in early years and overstate it in later years. Where changes from one form of depreciation to another occur, we must adjust the earnings of the company accordingly. This would be particularly important when a corporation added large amounts of plant and equipment because of an expansion in services. Making these adjustments is necessary in order to be certain that two companies being compared are actually comparable even though their methods of depreciation are different.

Depletion

Some companies, notably those in the oil, mining, and forest products industries, are permitted to write off a portion or all the assets used in production. The theory of depletion is that a company loses its ability to produce in the future when it uses irreplaceable oil, gas, or minerals. The company using depletion is allowed to write off a fixed asset as a current expense. The rate of depletion, which is calculated as a percentage of gross income for oil and gas properties, is 22 percent. An increase in the percentage rate of depletion will have the same effect upon earnings. We must understand the method used in computing depletion allowances and assess the impact on earnings of depletion or of any impending change.

Inventory

The investor should be aware of the method used in accounting for the cost of goods sold, because a change in inventory policy could have a marked effect on earnings. The method used in computing inventory is usually explained in a footnote to the financial accounting section of a company's annual report. Few problems would exist in inventory-accounting practices if prices remained stable, but prices of inventory do vary. In the last decade there has been an upward trend in the price level.

Business, from time to time, has changed its method of costing inventory to adjust for changes in price level, and these changes have had an effect on earnings. Two methods of determining the cost of inventory are first-in, first-out (FIFO) and last-in, first-out (LIFO). The traditional practice is to use the FIFO method, which assumes that goods are sold in the order in which they are acquired, so that inventory on hand is assumed to be that most recently purchased. Thus, if a company purchased 200 units of inventory during the year and sold 100 units, the remaining 100 units would have a cost based upon the most recent price. If the company bought 100 units at $10 in the first part of the year and another 100 at $11 later in the year, the first 100 units sold would have a cost of $10, and the remaining 100 units would have a cost of $11.

The LIFO method assumes that the inventory going out bears a cost comparable to the *last* items of inventory purchased. Thus, in the illustration above, the inventory cost would be based on the price when the inventory was sold. If 100 units of inventory were purchased at $10 and another 100 units at $11 per unit, and then 100 units of inventory were sold, they would have a unit cost of $11. The next 100 units would have a cost of $10. The effect of LIFO inventory accounting is to raise costs when prices are rising and lower corporate income. The FIFO method, under the same circumstances, would tend to lower prices and raise net income, but to lower net income when prices are declining. The effect of using LIFO is to reduce the inventory profit. When inventory is purchased at $11 per unit and costed at $11 per unit, no inventory profit is achieved. However, when inventory purchased at $10 per unit is costed at $10 per unit with a market price of $11, there is a $1-per-unit gain or inventory profit that accrues to the company. In inflationary periods companies realized substantial gains or profits on inventory, which should not be considered a normal part of profits. As prices declined, some companies realized inventory losses that could not be considered permanent losses. Another way of costing inventory is to use an average-cost method. All these methods are acceptable in determining inventory cost for federal income tax purposes, but the method adopted must be used consistently and the effect on present and future earnings estimates established.

The valuation of inventory can be based upon one of the cost methods or upon cost or market price, whichever is lower. *Cost* is the price paid for the goods, and *market price* is the price at which the goods can be replaced. Cost is a realistic value for inventory, since it represents the cost of an actual transaction. Some accountants follow a more conservative approach and use market price if it is lower than cost. The lower-of-cost-or-market method uses the lower price for inventory, which tends to increase earnings. Thus, if prices are rising, FIFO as a cost method tends to increase net earnings. The combination of FIFO and lower-of-cost-or-market further increases net income. A change from one method to another, even though the new method will be used consistently, might result in a nonrecurring change in earnings that must be adjusted.

Replacement-Cost Accounting

On March 23, 1976, the SEC issued Accounting Series Release 190, which requires financial statement disclosure of the year-end replacement-cost inventories and property, plant, and equipment (both gross and net of depreciation), together with depreciation for the year based on the average replacement cost of properties, and cost of sales for the year based on the replacement cost of the goods at the time they were sold. ASR 190 applies to all SEC registrants whose inventories, property, plant, and equipment total more than $100 million and 10 percent of total assets at the beginning of the most recent fiscal year, as shown on the company's Form 10-K. The purpose of ASR 190 is to permit the analyst to estimate the effects of inflation of assets on the earnings of the company and to estimate the company's real earnings and asset position. This is an experimental attempt to develop techniques to implement replacement-cost theory. In any case, analysts should be aware of the impact of inflation on real earnings and adjust accordingly.

Wages

For many companies, labor costs are a significant portion of total operating costs. In making an analysis of the impact of labor costs on corporate earnings, the investor must consider the trend and the immediate impact of changes in wage costs, including those that result from automatic cost-of-living adjustments related to some price index. The impact of these changes will be more strongly felt by a company that has a large proportion of wage costs to total costs than by one that uses only a small amount of labor.

Generally speaking, the average hourly earnings of wage earners have increased over the last decade. Bureau of Labor Statistics figures indicate an upward trend of labor costs in the United States. But each company has its own peculiar wage-cost requirements and must be examined separately from the trend in the economy as a whole. The question usually asked is, What effect will a wage increase of $.40 per hour in the automobile industry, for example, have on operating costs and profits of companies in the industry? Or the broader question, What effect will an increase in the minimum wage have on industry profits? Changes of this type have a permanent effect on earnings, as well as the immediate effect. This assumes, of course, that the wage increase cannot be offset by a price increase.

Once direct labor costs and fringe benefits have been added to employee wages, they are seldom reduced. As long as a company grants wage increases to correspond to the productivity of the employee, a balance is maintained between profitability of earnings and costs. Should a company continue to grant wage increases beyond the scope of productivity, then the profits of the company will be in jeopardy and will decline. By cutting total wages and reducing the number of employees, wage costs can be reduced as a percentage of total costs and profitability can be improved.

Federal Income Taxes

Several areas in federal income tax accounting allow special adjustments that will either understate or overstate a company's earnings. Depreciation, already discussed, is one tax factor that has an impact on earnings. Another is the provision of the IRS Code that allows a company to carry back a loss incurred in one year to adjust the past three years' income and then, if necessary, to write off any remaining loss over the next five years. The loss carry forward or carryback provision tends to overstate the amount of earnings in previous and future years because of the tax credit for losses. It is possible that in a year when a company has earnings to carry forward, the provision will balance out the taxable earnings. No federal income taxes will be paid, and in that year earnings will be overstated by the amount of the tax credit. Obviously, this will not be continued in the future, and an appropriate adjustment must be made.

Examples of special tax treatment are found in some industries. Taxes in the oil industry are different from those in other industries because of the right to capitalize drilling expenses and write them off as depreciation or charge them as a current expense against income. Public utility companies often have a portion of their income taxed as a capital gain. Some also have switched from a practice of *normalizing* earnings to allowing the earnings to *flow through* to net income. Under the normalizing concept, public utilities are allowed a fast tax writeoff for capital expenditure purposes, but for rate-making purposes they actually average the amount of depreciation. The Ohio Public Utility Commission allows the flow-through method, which permits the fast tax writeoff to flow through and is used to determine the rate base. This tends to reduce taxes and net income, but it increases cash flow and has the impact of improving the profitability of the utility.

The items of income and expense and their variations are not all the possible factors an investor must consider. They are merely representative of a species of change that might affect corporate earnings. Before investors accept too readily the stated earnings of a company, they must make a judgment of the quality of the earnings and determine if they are recurring and permanent. If not, they should be adjusted so that they reflect the true earnings potential of the company.

An example of the type of change being discussed is demonstrated in Table 14–2. The items of expense for Industrial, Incorporated, appear to be normal. However, its annual report stated that operating expenses were $2 million above normal because of a temporary increase in costs associated with a plant expansion program. Thus, earnings after taxes are temporarily reduced by $1 million or $.50 per share (50 percent tax bracket is assumed). The earnings for that year, then, would have been closer to $3.50 per share than $3. The other expenses did not change and were considered normal. Adjustments of this type are not always as simple as this illustration, but they should be undertaken to improve the accuracy of reported earnings.

MEASURING PROFITABILITY

Measures of profitability permit investors to compare companies in an industry to determine which appear to be most profitable. All profitability measures relate profit to company sales or to assets. These ratios become a measure of the financial or earning efficiency of a company. They tell much more than the direction of earnings; they help show what will happen to earnings if sales or investment in operating assets is increased. The measures usually used in financial circles are PM, profit margin; earning power or ROI, return on investment; ROE, return on equity; and ROS, return on sales, which is sales divided into net income.

Profit Margin (PM)

The profit margin (PM) is found by dividing operating revenues or sales into operating profit. It is usually expressed as a percentage of operating revenues or sales and directs attention to the profitability of the sales or the revenue dollar. The operating profit represents the amount of money remaining from sales or revenues after all operating expenses and the cost of goods are subtracted. Income taxes, interest, and other non-operating expenses and income are not deducted. The operating statement of Industrial, Incorporated, in Table 14–2 will serve as an example of how the profit margin is computed. The company's operating profit was $16 million, and it had operating revenues of $197 million. The profit margin is 8.1 percent ($197 million divided into $16 million).

Asset-Turnover Ratio (TO)

The turnover of total assets (TO) employed in the business is helpful in understanding profitability. Although it is not a profit measure as such, it can be used as a measure of efficiency, which will be discussed in the next chapter. The asset-turnover ratio is calculated by dividing total assets into sales or revenues. For Industrial, Incorporated, this would be $110 million divided into net sales of $197 million, resulting in an asset-turnover ratio of 1.791. The asset-turnover ratio multiplied by the return-on-sales ratio is equal to the return-on-assets ratio. The higher the asset-turnover ratio, other things being equal, the higher the profitability of the firm.

Return on Investment (ROI)—Earning Power

Another way of measuring profitability is to divide total assets into net income after taxes. This measure is known as return on investment (ROI), and it provides a way of determining how profitable the use of assets of a company has been, based upon the net book value of the assets. It can be calculated by multiplying PM × TO. This measure takes into consideration the profitability of all assets related to all income after income taxes, expenses, and cost of borrowed capital. It reflects the economic return on assets employed. A direct relationship exists between investment in assets on the one hand, and sales and profits on the other. The higher the earning power and the higher the profit margin, the more profitable the company.

Table 14–3 presents the balance sheet for Industrial, Incorporated. Total assets are $110 million. Since the company's net income after taxes is $6 million (Table 14–2) and operating assets are $110 million, the earning power, or return on investment, is 5.45 percent. Whether this is a satisfactory rate of return is a function of a comparison to past performance and the return on investment of competitive firms.

TABLE 14–3
Typical Balance Sheet of an Industrial Company

Industrial Incorporated, December 31 (millions of dollars)

Current assets:			Current liabilities:		
Cash	$ 2		Trade accounts	$ 8	
Governments	2		Bank loan	2	
Receivables	8		Total		$ 10
Inventory	8				
Total		$ 20			
Fixed assets:			Debt:		
Plant (net)	60		Bond issues		40
Equipment (net)	20				
		80	Capital stock		40
Nonoperating assets		10	Retained earnings		20
		$110			$110

Nonoperating income is included in the ROI figure, since most corporations earn additional income from ownership of nonoperating assets or from temporary investment in short-term securities. These assets and investments are not the primary source of revenue, but for some companies they add a significant amount to corporate earnings.

Nonoperating expenses are considered in the figure for net income after taxes. Many companies have nonoperating expenses, such as interest on debt that must be paid each year, which can have a significant impact on earnings. The first effect of interest, for example, on operating expenses is that it reduces net income available for the shareowner. However, since the payment of interest represents low-cost capital and results in financial leverage, the income to the owner is actually increased.

Without a detailed explanation of this leverage process at this point, let's say capital is hired at 16 percent with an after-tax cost of approximately 8.64 percent. The money is then invested to earn 15 percent after taxes. This process is advantageous to the stockholder if it is not carried to extremes. If excessive debt is employed, it will have an unsettling impact on per-share earnings. More will be said about this subject when we analyze the capital structure of a company.

Return on Sales or Revenues (ROS)

Net income after taxes as a percentage of sales or revenues is another way to measure the profitability of a company. The higher the net income as a percentage of sales or revenues, the more profitable the company. Industrial, Incorporated, has a net-income-to-sales ratio of 3.05 percent. This figure, which would be considered low by business management, is found by dividing sales of $197 million into $6 million, the net income after taxes. This ratio, examined over time, gives us one more clue to the profitability of a company for investment.

Return on Equity (ROE)

Another profitability measure is return on equity. This is found by dividing the common stockowners' equity into the net income after taxes. The owners' equity for Industrial, Incorporated, is $60 million. Since net income after taxes is $6 million, the return on owners' equity is 10 percent ($6 ÷ $60). Other things being equal, the higher the ROE, the more profitable the company. In addition, the investor must compare trends over time.

Significance of Profitability Measures

The significance of the profitability measures can be determined only by an analysis of their behavior and direction. The profit margin focuses attention on the ability of a company to produce goods and services at a profit. But a high profit margin is only one part of the equation, particularly when the future is being forecasted. The investor must know what to expect from sales. A company that has a profit margin of 10 percent and prospects of its sales doubling in five years will be a better investment than a company with a 15 percent profit margin but no prospect of increased sales. It is desirable to invest in a company that has a growing profit margin and expanding sales, but this is not always possible. Under these conditions, the investor might select a company that has expanding sales with a stable profit margin.

The significance of ROI, ROE, and the ratio of net income to sales is similar in analysis of the profit margin. ROI recognizes a company's ability to earn profits on its assets. The ratio of net income to sales (ROS) provides a measure for determining the overall profitability of corporate sales. It is desirable to have an expansion of operating assets that will ensure future profitability. It is desirable to have an increasing ROI, ROE, and net income as a percentage of sales. However, these ratios themselves need not increase as long as sales are increasing. Large plant expenditures and greater sales will assure future profits for the shareholder even if the profitability measures are stable and turnover remains the same.

Perhaps the best way to determine the quality of the profit ratios is to compare one company with other leading companies within the industry. The investor can then make a value judgment as to which company has done best and what changes have occurred allowing comparative standards to be adjusted.

FUTURE EARNINGS

Future earnings are clearly the most important part of the valuation equation, and the most important consideration for management. No matter what has happened to a company in the past, future earnings and expectations about future earnings really determine the current value of its common stock. This does not mean that investors will necessarily act rationally about future earnings, but they will focus on the earnings capability of a company under investigation.

The impact of future earnings on price and the impact of change in expectation of future earnings on price are difficult to comprehend. Sometimes long-run and short-run changes do not seem to be rational. For example, a stock may drop 3 points on the announcement of a sharp increase in earnings. Is this rational? asks the investor. Shouldn't the price of the stock increase? Actually, the action of the stock is logical, because the investment community had foreseen a good earnings report; investors and probably some speculators had purchased the stock, anticipating a rise in price. The price did rise, and on the announcement date, the stock was sold by many owners for a short-term gain. Selling pressure forced the price down.

Texas Instruments, an electronics company, had a similar experience with its common stock. The company's earnings had increased, and because of expectations of continued growth, the price of the stock rose from 27 to approximately 240. Suddenly the price plummeted. At the time of the decline, current earnings were adequate. Why then should the stock drop in price? One important factor was a change in expectation about future earnings: Because of an upsurge in foreign competition, product prices were expected to decrease. The neophyte investor might conclude that this is irrational behavior; in reality, it is quite rational. Investors are simply reacting to a change in expectations about a company's earnings.

Thus, a careful analysis of a company will include an estimate of future earnings, using past behavior to provide a clue to a company's future. There are many methods of estimating future earnings. We will consider three: (1) a forecast of future earnings per share based on past earnings; (2) a forecast based on the past relation between sales and earnings, or the line of average relationship; and (3) an estimate based on profit margins and forecasted sales.

A Projection of Earnings per Share

The growth of future earnings may be estimated by fitting a trend line to the past earnings per share and extending it into the future. An example of this can be seen in Figure 14–1. The trend line results in estimated earnings per share between 1981

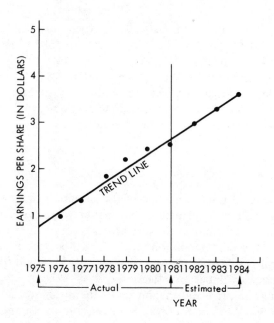

FIGURE 14-1

Projection of Future Earnings Based on a Trend Line Fitted to Past Years' Earnings per Share

and 1984. The danger of this approach is that the trend line might not actually describe the pattern of earnings per share. Earnings might decline or increase as a firm experiences internal or external changes that have not been a factor in past earnings. In this category might be a merger, the development of a revolutionary new product, or a major modernization and mechanization program that will reduce costs and increase earnings. Each time changes affect earnings, adjustments must be made in the trend line. The investor must be constantly aware of new developments that might change future earnings.

The investor might also achieve the same results by calculating the ten-year average growth rate of earnings and the standard deviation of those earnings. The average rate could be used as a trend estimate for the future. The standard deviation of the average could be used as upper and lower estimates of earnings growth rates. These estimates will be used in the valuation equation that helps the investor determine if the return is satisfactory compared to the risk.

Line of Average Relationship between Sales and Earnings

A second approach is to forecast earnings based on the expectation of growth in sales and the relationship between past sales and earnings. In the preceding chapter, a forecast of sales was made from which future earnings per share could be determined. Past earnings and sales are plotted as in Figure 14–2. A trend line is fitted to the data and projected until it intersects with the estimated sales line. Earnings per share are

FUNDAMENTAL ANALYSIS

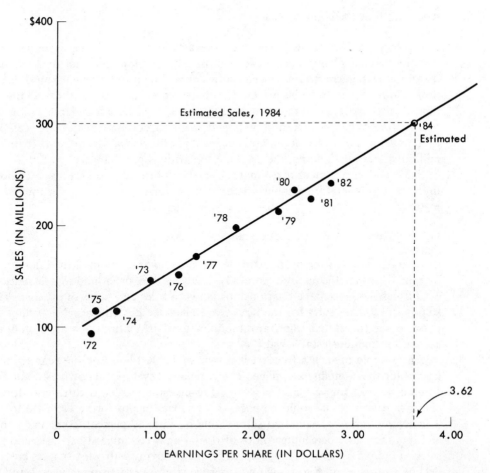

FIGURE 14-2

Line of Average Relationship between Sales and Earnings per Share as a Method of Estimating Future Earnings per Share

read from the bottom of the chart by dropping vertically to the horizontal axis. This method, as well as the one discussed above, is valid only for short-range forecasts in which the variables influencing sales and expenses are relatively constant. In investment analysis, the professional usually discusses earnings for the next year but refers only vaguely to the earnings potential over a longer period of time—say, three years. A three-year or longer forecast is quite difficult to make with any accuracy.

Since it is difficult to determine future sales with precision, it would be wise for the investor to establish two or three estimates for sales and then estimate earnings, in this fashion arriving at the best estimate. It is important to realize that any estimate of the future is only that, an estimate—and estimates are subject to error. In spite of this, the investor must estimate what the future earnings per share are expected to be; otherwise, an intelligent decision is impossible.

Sales and Profit Margin Forecast

In this method, the investor uses sales forecasts to estimate future earnings per share. Assume that sales three years hence will be $300 million, and that the average profit margin is 18 percent and has been quite stable. The profit margin from sales will be $54 million. Since this figure includes depreciation, interest, and taxes, these items must be deducted to obtain net income after taxes. Assume that depreciation requires a deduction of $17 million and interest $5 million. Assume the tax rate is 50 percent; thus, taxes will be $16 million, and net income after taxes $16 million. If there are 8 million shares outstanding, the estimate of earnings per share will be $2.

Sales and profit-margin estimates for the future are subject to variation. The investor must therefore establish a range of estimates of earnings in the use of this method.

Pro Forma Profit Estimates—An Example

In making pro forma profit estimates, a more complex form of the sales and profit-margin forecast, the analyst carefully analyzes the profit-and-loss statement and establishes the percentage relationships between sales and items of expense. The next step is to estimate sales for the next year. Then the percentage relationships are applied to the forecasted sales, any modifications in relationships are noted, and an earnings estimate is established.

An example of such a forecast is shown in Table 14–4. For the year 1, the actual figures for the company are given. The company developed its own estimate for year 1 and a forecast for year 2. If in year 1 the investor wanted a three-year forecast of earnings per share, it would be necessary to make a pro forma estimate for year 4. The assumption was made that sales would increase 10 percent from year 3 to year 4 and that the year 1 percentage ratios of operating costs, interest expense, and taxes to sales would persist into year 4. (Actually, the company estimated that its costs would decline and its profit margin would improve from year 1 through year 2 and year 3. This was assumed to be too optimistic.) It was also assumed that no new shares would be issued and there would be no extraordinary items. The analyst must adjust estimates of future earnings per share according to the number of shares to be outstanding in each of the forecast years. The year 4 forecast of earnings amounted to $2.18. Thus, in looking forward in year 1 to the next three years, the investor could expect earnings per share of $1.80 in year 2, $2.09 in year 3, and $2.18 in year 4.

Earnings Forecasts from the Investment Community

The financial analysts of large brokerage firms prepare estimates that may help the investor determine future earnings. Certainly, all analysts can look to these sources for help in determining the future level of earnings. Standard & Poor's provides estimates of next year's earnings in its publication *Earnings Forecaster*, a handy reference for such estimates. Included are estimates of many brokerage houses, along with the S&P estimate. Value Line provides earnings estimates for companies included in its surveys. Such data are helpful for comparison with the investor's own estimates. The I.B.E.S. estimates are also helpful.

         FUNDAMENTAL ANALYSIS

TABLE 14-4

A Company's Forecast of Earnings and a Pro Forma Forecast

Statement of Consolidated Income (Years Ended December 31, in $ thousands)

	Year 1 (Actual)		Year 2 (Estimated)	Year 3 (Forecast)	Year 4 (Forecast)
Net sales and revenues	100.0%	$366,557	$430,000	$484,000	$532,400
Operating costs and expenses	90.0	$331,072	$385,600	$431,600	$479,160
Interest expense	2.2	8,006	8,700	10,000	11,712
Total costs and expenses	92.2%	$339,078	$394,300	$441,600	$490,872
Operating income before taxes	7.5	$ 27,479	$ 35,700	$ 42,400	$ 41,528
Provision for income taxes	3.7	13,477	17,700	21,000	19,699
Net operating income	3.8	$ 14,002	$ 18,000	$ 21,400	$ 21,829
Extraordinary item		(3,500)*	—	—	—
Net income		$ 10,502	$ 18,000	$ 21,400	$ 21,829
Earnings per common and common equivalent share (8,541,000 shares in 1971, 9,500,000 shares in 1972 and 10,000,000 shares in 1973)†					
Net operating income		$1.59	$1.85	$2.09†	$2.18‡
Extraordinary item		(.41)	—	—	—
Net income		$1.18	$1.85	$2.09†	$2.18‡
Earnings per common share assuming full dilution (9,731,000 shares in 1971, 9,870,000 shares in 1972 and 10,000,000 shares in 1973)†					
Net operating income		$1.44	$1.80	$2.09†	$2.18‡
Extraordinary item		(.36)	—	—	—
Net income		$1.08	$1.80	$2.09†	$2.18‡

*Loss on the sale of a business.

†Earnings per share forecast for year 3 does not include shares which may be issued in either stock dividends or in acquisitions.

‡Assumes no change in number of shares outstanding.

SOME LEADING COMPANIES IN THE DRUG INDUSTRY— AN EARNINGS ANALYSIS

We will continue our actual company analysis by examining the amount and growth of past earnings and the magnitude of profit margins for Lilly, Schering-Plough, and SmithKline. We will also estimate future earnings, so that we may have this important variable for use when we apply the valuation model to each company in order to estimate expected return and risk.

Earnings

The adjusted earnings per share for each of these companies are presented in Table 14–5, along with the annual rate of growth of earnings. Schering-Plough demonstrated an exceptional growth rate of earnings for the ten-year period 1970–80 and was expected to continue that growth. Much of the growth can be explained by the merger of Schering and Plough, two complementary companies, in January 1973. Lilly has enjoyed an excellent growth of earnings, too, only slightly lower than Schering-Plough's, but the growth rate has been less stable. SmithKline has also demonstrated an excellent growth in earnings, which should sustain it well in the future. SmithKline would be ranked first in growth of earnings per share, followed by Schering-Plough and Lilly.

TABLE 14–5

Adjusted Earnings per Share, Year-End, for Lilly, Schering-Plough, and SmithKline
(In dollars, % change, and index 1972 = 100)

Year	Lilly			Schering-Plough			SmithKline		
	$	Index	Change	$	Index	Change	$	Index	Change
1980	$4.52	244	0%	$4.45	307	23%	$4.65	567	97%
1979	4.52	244	38	4.12	284	34	3.85	470	137
1978	3.81	206	38	3.62	250	38	2.73	333	151
1977	3.10	108	11	3.08	212	11	1.49	182	34
1976	2.90	157	15	2.91	201	29	1.21	148	18
1975	2.62	142	2	2.57	172	14	1.07	130	10
1974	2.59	140	18	2.30	158	22	0.98	120	12
1973	2.26	122	22	1.97	136	36	0.89	108	8
1972	1.85	100	23	1.45	100	23	0.82	100	7
1971	1.42	77	2	1.11	77	12	0.77	93	2
1970	1.40	75	7	0.95	65	6	0.75	91	6
Mean average % change		16.0%			22.5%			43.8%	
Standard deviation		13.7			10.9			56.3	

SOURCE: Value Line Investment Survey, August 21, 1981, pp. 1261, 1267, 1269. Copyright 1981 by Arnold Bernhard & Co., Inc. Reprinted by permission.

FUNDAMENTAL ANALYSIS

Profit Measures

Schering-Plough and Lilly have had a profit margin of similar magnitude, with Schering-Plough having a slight edge (Table 14–6). SmithKline would be first in this class with a rising profit margin.

TABLE 14-6
Profit Margin, Percent Earned on Total Capital, and Net Income as a Percent of Sales for Lilly, Schering-Plough, and SmithKline

Year	Profit Margin*			% Earned on Total Capital†			Net Income as a % of Sales‡		
	Lilly	Schering	SmithKline	Lilly	Schering	SmithKline	Lilly	Schering	SmithKline
1980	13.4%	13.8%	17.4%	19.4%	18.6%	28.5%	13.4%	13.7%	17.4%
1979	14.9	15.5	17.3	20.9	20.2	28.9	14.9	15.5	17.3
1978	15.0	17.9	14.8	20.0	21.0	25.6	15.0	17.9	14.8
1977	14.4	17.7	11.4	18.1	20.4	17.7	14.4	17.7	11.4
1976	14.9	18.0	10.7	18.3	22.2	16.4	14.9	18.0	10.7
1975	14.7	17.5	10.8	18.7	23.2	16.3	14.7	17.5	10.8
1974	16.1	17.6	11.2	21.0	24.8	15.2	16.1	17.6	11.2
1973	16.0	17.3	11.9	21.2	25.2	20.1	16.0	17.3	11.8
1972	15.4	15.3	12.2	20.2	22.5	20.0	15.4	15.4	12.2
Mean average	14.9	16.7	13.1	19.8	22.0	21.0	15.0	16.7	13.1
Standard deviation	0.8	1.5	2.7	1.2	2.2	5.4	0.8	1.5	2.7

*Operating earnings before deduction of depreciation, interest, and income tax as a percentage of sales.
†Net income after taxes as a percentage of total capital, common, preferred, and bonds.
‡Net income after taxes as a percentage of sales.
SOURCE: The Value Line Investment Surveys, August 21, 1981, pp. 1261, 1267, 1269. Copyright 1981 by Arnold Bernhard & Co., Inc. Reprinted by permission.

SmithKline had the highest return on total capital invested. Schering-Plough would be ranked third on the basis of return on capital. In 1980 and 1979, SmithKline had the best ratio of net income to sales; next was Schering, and then Lilly. It is apparent that these three firms have enjoyed an adequate and stable profit position over the years. In spite of the possibility of narrowing profit margins in the future, all three companies were expected to maintain their established profits growth over the next three years.

Estimating Future Earnings per Share

When we are expected to supply earnings per share estimates for the valuation equation

$$P_0 = \frac{D_0(1 + g_d)}{(1 + r)} + \frac{D_0(1 + g_d)^2}{(1 + r)^2} + \frac{D_0(1 + g_d)^3 + P_3}{(1 + r)^3}$$

we need to know what the growth rate of dividend is expected to be for the next three years as well as the amount of earnings in the third year. P_3 is found by multiplying the earnings expected in the third year by an expected P/E in the third year $(E_0(1 + g_e)^3 P/E_3)$. Certainly it is difficult to estimate future earnings, but to arrive at an estimate we can use accepted procedures. These include developing a regression equation between past sales and earnings per share, which is demonstrated in Figure 14–3. Another method is to use the historic average rate of growth to calculate earnings three years in the future, as shown in Table 14–5. An example of this for the three drug companies is found in Table 14–7. Once these estimates are obtained, they can be averaged and the amount and growth rate of future earnings is estimated. The results of these estimates appear in Table 14–7. This might not seem a very sophisticated system, but the approximations of earnings, revised frequently, can be very helpful.

SmithKline has had the highest overall rate of growth of earnings per share. These estimates will be used as a part of valuation analysis in Chapter 18, where we will relate present price to future expected dividends and price to learn if the security offers an acceptable return for the risks involved.

Although a three-year estimate of earnings is based on trend analysis, an analysis of next year's earnings should be based on a careful estimate of sales and expected expenses. The 1980–83 earnings estimates for Lilly, Schering-Plough, and SmithKline were obtained this way. Estimates of next year's earnings can also be obtained from Standard & Poor's *Earnings Forecaster*, from *The Value Line Investment Surveys*, and from I.B.E.S.

The important part of the analysis is to determine what changes are expected in future earnings, if any. Sales for Lilly rose almost 20 percent in 1981 due to the success of Mandal and Ceclor, new antibiotic drugs. Earnings for Schering-Plough are expected to decline somewhat due to weak sales of Garamycin, the company's most lucrative product. SmithKline is expected to continue the previous high growth in earnings. A final note about earnings estimates: All estimates must be accepted with some margin of error.

Summary of Analysis

The results of the analysis of earnings and profitability are summarized in Table 14–8. The stability of earnings and profitability refer to the variation of earnings around the trend line. If there is great variation in earnings or profitability, we can say that they are unstable. Stability is judged on the basis of past relationships. Instability is a sign of riskiness.

The tabular presentation only helps to show the relative positions of the companies. When later price is related to the quantity of future earnings, a decision will be possible about the desirability of investing in one of the companies. The beginning investor and analyst must recognize that these estimates are made at a given moment of time, are subject to errors of judgment, and must be continually revised to keep the future in perspective. On the basis of future earnings per share, SmithKline seems to be number 1. Our analysis will continue in the following chapters.

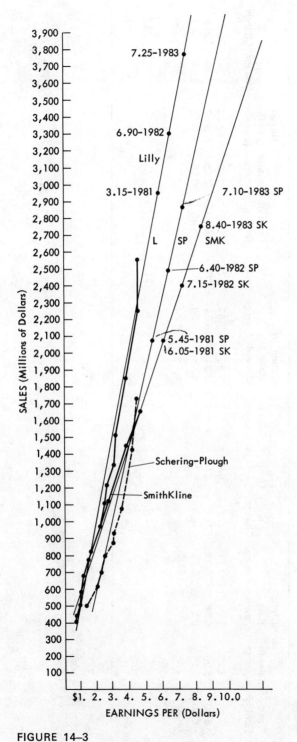

FIGURE 14–3

Estimated Future Earnings per Share for Lilly, Schering-Plough, and SmithKline Based on Sales to Earnings per Share Regression

TABLE 14–7

Estimated Earnings per Share for Lilly, Schering-Plough, and SmithKline

	Lilly					Schering-Plough					SmithKline				
Year	Trend of Earnings	Sales to Earnings	Historic Rate (average)	Average	% Change	Trend of Earnings	Sales to Earnings	Historic Rate (average)	Average	% Change	Trend of Earnings	Sales to Earnings	Historic Rate (average)	Average	% Change
1983	7.20	7.25	7.05	7.17	12.0	6.90	7.13	7.60	7.87	17	7.35	8.40	13.83	9.86	28.0
1982	6.30	6.90	6.08	6.43	21.0	6.00	6.40	7.84	6.74	26	6.30	7.15	9.62	7.69	27.0
1981	5.60	5.15	5.24	5.33	18.0	5.20	5.45	5.45	5.36	20	5.40	6.05	6.69	6.04	30.0
1980	(actual)			4.52					4.45					4.65	
Mean average					17.0					21.0					28.0
Standard deviation					4.0					4.6					1.5

TABLE 14-8

Companies Ranked by Past and Future Earnings per Share
and Profitability

Past and Future Earnings	Company by Rank		
	Lilly	Schering	SmithKline
Past earnings			
Amount per share, 1980	2	3	1
Rate of growth	3	2	1
Stability	2	1	3
Profitability			
Profit margin	2	1	3
% on capital	3	1	2
Net-income-to-sales ratio	3	2	1
Stability of profit margin	1	2	3
Future earnings per share			
Growth rate	3	2	1
Stability	3	2	1
Overall profitability	3	2	1

SUMMARY

The investment potential of a company is determined by its future expected growth of earnings. A company that has experienced a growth in earnings per share is desirable for investment. Stability and quality in earnings is a desirable feature of investment. The past growth and stability of earnings are guides to the future earnings of a company.

Future earnings and the expectation about them are the central theme of investment value. We attempt to assess the future earnings capability of a company by fitting a regression line to the past relationship between sales and earnings, or estimating earnings per share based on expected sales and profit margins. These methods should lead to satisfactory results in forecasting, but they are only estimates and must be changed when changes occur within the company. Some companies provide their own estimates of future earnings, at least for one year. This is controversial, but would be very helpful and has been recommended by some members of the SEC.

Companies that have adequate profit margins, earning power, and ratio of net income to sales will most likely maintain earnings per share. The company that has the best profitability ratios should provide the greatest profit to the investor as sales increase.

The reported earnings of a company are adjusted to reflect the recurring and permanent earnings and to eliminate the nonrecurring and temporary earnings. Each item of income and expense should be examined to determine as well as possible if it is temporary or permanent. When a company has temporary additions and deductions from earnings, we must make adjustments accordingly.

The basic problem is to compare several companies and to select the one that appears to offer the best earnings. This process was demonstrated with an actual case.

To guide the investor, we suggested that each company have:

1. Stability or growth of earnings compared with its competitors.
2. A high degree of permanency and quality of earnings.
3. Stable or improving profit margins, earning power, and net income as a percentage of sales.

Investors and analysts are cautioned about forecasting future sales and earnings per share. The margin of error is high, and the forecast requires evaluation and revision to be successful.

SUMMARY OF PRINCIPLES

1. The investor must estimate or forecast future earnings per share of a company before making an investment decision.
2. The investor must understand the generally accepted accounting principles, GAAP, to understand the nature of past and future earnings.
3. Stable earnings are generally considered to be more valuable earnings.
4. The investor must understand whether earnings have grown in real terms.
5. ROI is a powerful measure of a company's earning power.
6. A pro forma earnings forecast is an excellent way to estimate future earnings per share.

REVIEW QUESTIONS

1. Corporate earnings always follow the direction of sales. As sales increase, corporate profits increase; as sales decline, corporate profits decline. Should we agree with these statements? Why, or why not?
2. What has been the pattern of aggregate corporate earnings in the United States? Explain.
3. Is there any truth in the observation that dividends follow earnings? Comment.
4. Discuss the various ways we can compute earnings per share from sales and other income minus costs and expenses.
5. What is meant by the term *quality of corporate earnings*?
6. To what extent may we rely on earnings reported by the company in estimating the true earning power of the company?
7. List the major costs and expenses a corporation might report. To what extent might each of these vary and be recurring or nonrecurring, and hence reflect themselves in recurring or nonrecurring profits? Include in your discussion the following;
   a. Depreciation.
   b. Depletion.
   c. Inventory.
   d. Wages.
   e. Federal income taxes.

8. Explain the difference among profit margin, earning power, and net-income-to-sales ratio as measures of corporate profitability.

9. a. Discuss the methods by which we may forecast corporate earnings and arrive at a three-year estimate of future earnings.
   b. To what extent may we rely on these estimates?
   c. Can you suggest an improved technique for estimating earnings?
   d. How do we forecast earnings of companies that have a cyclical character?

10. Review the earnings, cash flow, profitability, quality of earnings and adjusted earnings, and forecasted earnings of the three drug companies presented for analysis. Comment on the analysis.

11. Based on the information presented about each company's profit position, do you agree with the relative ranking in the summary of analysis?

12. What position has the Financial Accounting Standards Board taken with respect to corporate reporting of earnings?

PROBLEMS

1. Obtain the earnings per share from 1975 until the present year for the three companies selected in the problems in Chapter 13.

2. Adjust the earnings per share of each company for any nonrecurring items of income or expense.

3. Add to earnings per share any noncash expenditures per share to arrive at an estimate of cash flow per share.

4. Plot the adjusted earnings per share of each company on semilog paper (3 cycle).

5. a. Which company appears to have the greatest rate of growth of earnings?
   b. Which has the greatest amount of earnings per share?
   c. Which appears to have the greatest stability of earnings per share?
   d. Rank each company in order of rate of growth of earnings, amount of earnings per share, and stability of earnings per share.
   e. Which company appears to be best?

6. Determine the profit margin, ROI, ROE, and net-income-to-sales ratio for each of the three companies from 1975 to the present.
   a. Which company has the highest profit margin?
   b. Which company has the highest earning power?
   c. Which company has the highest net-income-to-sales ratio?
   d. Which company has the greatest overall profit stability as measured by the three ratios of profitability?

7. Estimate future earnings per share based on forecasted sales and profit margins, the line of average relationship between sales and earnings, a trend-line projection of earnings, and pro forma analyses.
   a. Which company appears to have the expectation of the greatest amount and growth of future earnings?
   b. Which company has the greatest stability of earnings?
   c. Rank each company on the basis of stability and amount of future earnings.

8. Examine the product of each company. Are any developments under way that

might change these forecasts? Include in your answer developments in the domestic and foreign economy and in the military and nonmilitary sectors.

9. Based on this analysis and the relative ranking process, which company appears to be best for investment?

10. Record the earnings estimate for each company, since these will be used in the final valuation process.

SELECTED READINGS

ANDERSON, T. A. "Trends in Profit Sensitivity." In *Modern Developments in Investment Management*, 2nd ed. (New York: Dryden, 1978, p. 659.

BERNSTEIN, LEOPOLD A., and JOEL G. SIEGEL. "The Concept of Earnings Quality." *Financial Analysts Journal*, July–August 1979, p. 72.

GREEN, DAVID, JR., and JOEL SIEGEL. "The Predictive Power of First-Quarter Earnings Reports." In *Investment Classics*. Belmont, Calif.: Goodyear, 1979.

MORTIMER, TERRY. "Reporting Earnings: A New Appraoch." *Financial Analysts Journal*, November–December 1979, p. 67.

NIEDERHOFFER, V., and P. J. REGAN. "Earnings Changes, Analysts' Forecasts, and Stock Prices." In *Modern Developments in Investment Management*, 2nd ed., New York: Dryden, 1978.

PAKKALA, A. L. "Fixed Costs and Earnings Predictions." *Financial Analysts Journal*, January–February 1979, p. 46.

STICKNEY, CLYDE P. "Analyzing Effective Corporate Tax Rates." *Financial Analysts Journal*, July–August 1979, p. 45.

TREYNOR, J. L. "The Trouble with Earnings." In *Modern Developments in Investments*, 2nd ed. New York: Dryden, 1978.

CHAPTER 15

OPERATING EFFICIENCY

The earnings and profitability of a company are directly affected by the efficiency with which it conducts its business. Operating efficiency can be measured in terms of profit margins, earning power, and earnings per share, as was done in the preceding chapter. Or it can be measured by comparing revenues with expenses, or input (expenses) with output (the sales generated as a result of the expenditures). This measure, the operating ratio, helps to determine the relative degree of efficiency with which a company operates. Other measures, such as output per employee, output per dollar of plant, operating rate, and the breakeven point, help also to explain how efficient a company is in performing its tasks, which obviously has an influence on earnings per share.

THE OPERATING CHARACTERISTICS OF A COMPANY

The operating efficiency and the earnings of a company are influenced directly by the company's operating characteristics. A company that is constantly expanding its physical facilities and continues to operate at full capacity is more likely to produce profits and earnings in the future than one that is not utilizing all its operating capacity. A company that is expanding and is maintaining a high operating rate with a low breakeven point will be a profitable company; one that operates at a low level of capacity with a high breakeven point will be less profitable, or might even suffer a loss. A company with a stable operating rate will have more stable revenues than one with an unstable operating rate.

There is no magic about the source of revenues for any company. Income from sales is the result of the efficient use of capital assets combined with raw materials, labor, and management. If a company is to expand sales or revenues, it must also expand its capital-asset base. The assets will be purchased from funds generated internally through company operations or from the sales of debt, preferred stock, or common stock. The addition of new assets will affect the breakeven point of a company and its range of profitable operations. Expanding plant investment, for example, raises the breakeven point and, until sales expand, temporarily reduces profits. If the money to buy the assets came from the sale of additional common stock, then earnings per share might be reduced even further.

The discussion of operating efficiency will begin by examining what is meant by the operating capacity of a company, its operating rate, and its breakeven point. These concepts will then be related to earnings per share in the past and the future.

Productive Capacity

What is the capacity of a company to produce a product or service? This is an obvious question, but the answer is not simple. Many companies produce more than one product; therefore, when the investor asks what the productive capacity is, he or she must specify a product or a group of products produced together that utilize the existing plant and equipment. Some companies produce so many products that they cannot come up with any answer, except in broad dollar terms, such as, "With our present plant and combination of products, we have the capacity to produce $325 million worth of sales." Thus the capacity is measured in terms of dollars of output. In spite of the difficulty involved, however, the investor is interested in knowing the capacity of a firm to produce and how much it can earn if it operates at full capacity. Let us examine further the concept of plant capacity.

When a company produces one product, or a few that are homogeneous, plant capacity should be readily determined. Consider an electric utility, for example. The output is measured in kilowatt hours. Each company can produce a certain number of kilowatt hours of electricity, determined by the rated capacity of the generators used to produce the electricity. But even under these circumstances, it is difficult to determine the actual capacity to produce. Most generators can be operated safely above their rated capacity. Let us assume, for instance, that Cleveland Electric Illuminating has a generator with rated capacity of 100,000 kilowatts. It would be possible for CEI to generate 110,000 to 115,000 kilowatts of capacity for short periods of time without harm to the generator. Thus, the company could operate 10 to 15 percent above rated capacity.

The steel industry has occasionally operated at 104 or 105 percent of capacity. This is possible only because of the method used in determining the capacity of blast furnaces, which can be changed by a change in technology. In modern steel mills, oxygen is used in one phase of the production cycle. This increases the speed with which impurities are removed from the molten ore and speeds up the production cycle, which increases the output of the blast furnace far beyond its rated capacity. When making an estimate of capacity, these ancillary factors must therefore be considered.

The production capacity of companies in many other industries is more difficult to determine. What is the plant capacity of a drug company or department store, for example? The capacity of such a company to produce would depend upon the product being produced and in what portion of the total plant. Assume a simple case. A drug company produces products A and B. Its total capacity to produce will be different if 50 percent of the plant space is devoted to each product than if 40 percent of productive space is devoted to product A and 60 percent to product B. When plant capacity is estimated for this type of company, certain assumptions must be made about the balance of its productive facility between products.

A department store, with its many individual departments and products, would be forced to consider floor space, the number of square feet available, as its capacity to produce. Hence, the store having a greater amount of floor space would have a greater capacity to produce. The most efficient company, of course, would generate the most dollars of sales per square foot.

Some companies have no capacity limit other than the imagination or energy of their management and staff. What, for example, is the capacity of a life or casualty insurance company to produce? The average sales per employee for the industry could be multiplied by the number of people employed in the company, and this could serve as the capacity figure. But it would not be a satisfactory measure for a specific company.

The commercial bank, contrary to what might be expected, does have a limit (imposed by the capital-deposit ratio) to its capacity to lend. In banking, the typical capital-deposit ratio is close to 1 to 10. This is imposed by principles of conservative bank management and is not a federal or state reserve requirement. In order to expand plant, a bank must have more capital. If a bank operates below a 1-to-10 ratio, it is operating below capacity. If it operates above this ratio, more capital is probably needed.

If the unit of measurement is known, the capacity of a firm can be estimated through careful study. Where a measure of physical capacity is nonexistent or difficult to determine, the investor can substitute dollar figures for physical capacity. In this case, the capacity of a firm to produce might be estimated at $500 million. Before the company could expand its output beyond this amount, it would have to add to plant capacity or to sales personnel. Table 15–1 gives the units of measure for some industries. These can be used as an aid in determining plant capacity.

The Operating Rate

Manufacturing equipment is usually designed to be most profitable when operated at or close to full capacity. A high operating rate is so important for some companies that they do not earn a profit if they go below 95 percent of capacity.[1] Other companies become less efficient as they approach full capacity, because they must use inefficient equipment. One public utility, for example, uses its old equipment only when the demand for electricity exceeds normal demands. When this company increases its production from 95 percent to 100 percent of capacity, its increase in profit is less than if the more efficient, low-cost equipment were used. With many corporations,

---

[1]*Operating rate* is defined as output or production expressed as a percentage of plant capacity.

TABLE 15-1

Units of Measure for Selected Industries
to Aid in Establishing Plant Capacity

Containers	Tons
Utilities—gas	Thousand cubic feet (MCF)
Utilities—electric	Kilowatt hours (KWH)
Shoes	Number of pairs
Drugs and drug products	Pounds, gram units
Meats	Pounds
Passenger airlines	Passenger seats available on scheduled flights
Coal	Tons
Baking and milling	Pounds
Retail trade	Dollars
Liquor	Gallons
Textiles	Yards
Sugar	Tons
Metals	
Aluminum	Pounds
Steel	Tons
Paper	Tons
Rubber	Pounds
Electronics	$ and number of machines
Tobacco	Billions of cigarettes
Soft drinks	Cases
Candy	Pounds
Aerospace	$ and number of engines
Office equipment	$ and numbers of machines
Oil	Barrels × operating rate
Railroads	Ton miles
Insurance	Dollars
Banks	Dollars

profits increase with increased production only up to a point. Most companies are most profitable as they expand production and operate at a high level of capacity, but not necessarily when they operate at or above 100 percent of rated capacity. Operating characteristics differ, and the profitability level might be 60 percent of capacity for one company and 90 percent for another.

Investors are concerned about the operating rate because of its impact on earnings per share. This effect manifests itself in two ways. First, the higher the operating rate, the higher the per-share earnings. Second, a change in the operating rate of a company from one level to another differs in its effects. As a company moves toward full capacity, a given increase in output, other things being equal, will have a smaller effect on earnings. This makes it difficult to rely on percentage changes in earnings because of the leverage effect.

Our first concern is to learn what the historical operating rate of the company has been. Has the company been able to operate at a high level of capacity during both depression and prosperity? A knowledge of the operating characteristics of the industry is helpful in evaluating the operating rate of a company. Excellent operating data for many industries are reported regularly in the financial press. Refer to Table 11-2 for the capacity utilization rate of the manufacturing part of the national economy over a period of time.

To be considered a growing company, a company must have a favorable operating rate. It will expand its facilities to meet the growing demand for its product. It will probably operate close to full capacity. Growth is not limitless, but while the company is expanding, its level of operations will not be a problem. The biggest problem will be to keep up with the demand. The manufacturer of color television sets in the 1960s was a good example of expanding production in an expanding industry. The production of CB radios followed the pattern in mid-1976. The producers could not keep up with demand. Home computers had the same pattern in 1983.

Companies not in growth industries may experience a decline in demand for their product, will be plagued with unused capacity, and will operate well below productive capacity. Earnings, too, will decline. The alternative is to develop new products that will allow the plant to be used in a more profitable way; otherwise, the unused facilities will provide a low profit for the owners. Several small business investment companies (SBICs) were in this position early in 1964.[2] Only one-quarter to one-half their funds were invested profitably; the rest remained idle. The profitability of these companies was low. They were only partially productive and not operating at full capacity. Although not manufacturing plants with a fixed capacity, SBICs still have a total capacity to invest.

The problem of unemployed capital assets is not confined to an industry or to a company, but is a national problem. In the late 1950s, the national economy operated at around the 90 percent level, with a peak of 97 percent in 1955. In the 1960s, after billions of dollars had been spent on new plant and equipment, the operating level of industrial operations was between 85 and 90 percent; by mid-1973, it was at 84 percent but moving higher. In 1976, however, the operating rate had retreated below 75 percent, according to the FRB Index. The economy began to recover in 1977, and the operating rate increased to 82 percent of capacity. The operating rate for 1983 was below 70 percent of capacity.

As a principle, the investor should invest in those companies that maintain a high rate of production and employ their resources efficiently and to the fullest advantage. The most productive firms should be the most profitable for investment. The type of analysis that should be made is presented in Table 15-2. Operating capacity, output, and operating rate are presented for company A. Compared with the industry and company B, company A has enjoyed a higher and more stable operating rate. Based on this factor alone, we would consider company A a better-quality company. Unfortunately, data of this type are not available for all companies or all industries.

The Breakeven Point, Operating Capacity, and Leverage

The breakeven point is that place in the level of operations where revenues just equal total costs—fixed plus variable costs. The usual theoretical way of presenting the

---

[2]SBICs are mutual funds that specialize in raising capital for the small, growing company with the aid of government financing.

TABLE 15–2
Operating Capacity, Output, and Operating Rate, Compared with Operating Rate
of a Competitive Company and the Industry

| | Company A* | | | Company B* and Industry | |
Year	Operating Capacity (units)	Output (units)	Operating Rate (%)	Operating Rate (%)	
1981	450	425	94%	27%	92%
1980	400	380	95	90	93
1979	350	325	93	89	89
1978	315	300	95	91	91
1977	280	200	93	90	90
1976	250	240	96	92	92

*Companies are hypothetical.

breakeven point is shown in Figure 15–1. The vertical axis represents both dollars of revenue and dollars of expense. Usually, only the percentage of capacity or the number of units produced is shown on the horizontal axis. Some companies, however, do not produce a tangible product and do not have a well-defined capacity in units or percentage of output; the only figures available are dollars of sales. It must be assumed that at some dollar volume of sales, the company will break even. To accommodate companies of this type, dollars of revenue were put on the horizontal axis.

The revenue line in Figure 15–1 represents the amount of revenue received at each level of production or percent of capacity of the firm. If dollars of sales are used, obviously dollars will be on the horizontal as well as the vertical axis. The variable-costs line is the total of the variable costs as they change with total output. Ordinarily, these expenses are assumed to increase directly with output; in reality, they tend to increase at a slower rate than output because of the economies of large-scale production. The economies achievable with volume vary from company to company and depend a great deal on the size of the firm and its ability to benefit from such economies. Fixed costs are added to variable costs to establish the total costs of the firm. Fixed costs are constant and do not vary within the productive range of the firm. As output increases, however, they do decrease per unit. If new plant were added, fixed costs would increase, and the breakeven point would be changed. For example, an increase in fixed costs would, without any offsetting changes in volume of output or variable costs, tend to raise the breakeven point.

Only after the company moves beyond the breakeven point does it become profitable. Therefore, a company that has a low breakeven point and a consistently high operating rate will be a very profitable company. And if the company can maintain the high rate over a period of years, investors will have an attractive investment possibility. The importance of the operating rate is once again brought into focus.

The fact that a company is operating at a specific percentage of capacity is, how-

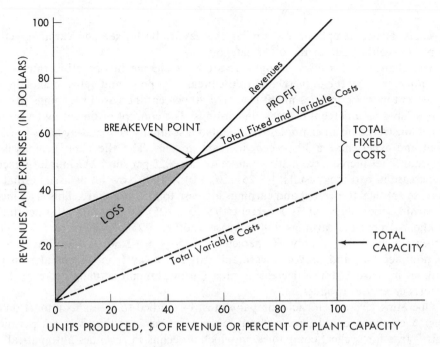

FIGURE 15–1

Typical Breakeven Chart for a Company

ever, only an indication of relative profitability. A company would probably be more profitable if it operated at 95 percent rather than 85 percent of capacity, but it cannot be said that one company, because it operates at 85 percent of capacity, is more profitable than another operating at 78 percent. The relative degree of profitability of the two companies depends not only on the operating level, but on the breakeven point. A firm operating at 78 percent of capacity with a 50 percent breakeven point will be more profitable than a firm operating at 85 percent of capacity with an 80 percent breakeven point. The operating rate must be related to the breakeven point to determine profitability; so it is important to try to estimate the breakeven point of the company and to assess its impact on earnings per share.

The determination of the breakeven point is not a simple task. The relative degree of profitability must be determined based on the existing levels of plant, price, and cost structure that remain fixed. The output of the company is then varied. Now it can be estimated at what volume of sales or at what percentage of capacity the company will cover all costs and break even. Unfortunately, prices vary, costs vary, and mixture of the products produced varies over short periods of time, making the task of calculating the breakeven point difficult. And there is another problem. The classification of fixed cost and variable cost is arbitrary, since some costs fall into both categories. Telephone expenses are a good example. The charge for basic service is fixed, but long-distance calls and calls beyond the basic number are additional and variable charges. Therefore, as the volume of business increases, so do telephone expenses. Hence, telephone and similar charges are both fixed and variable, yet must be put into either one or the other category.

The change in earnings brought about by a change in operating rate is called *operating leverage*. It can be related to the breakeven point and helps to explain why a 10 percent increase in sales might lead to a 20 percent increase in earnings per share, or possibly to a 5 percent decrease in earnings. The concept of operating leverage can be demonstrated by an example. Assume that a company is operating at its breakeven point and experiences a 10 percent increase in sales. The effect on earnings is phenomenal. They increase from $0 per share to, say, $.25 per share. An infinite percentage of increase in earnings results: $[(\$.25 - 0)/\$.0] \times 100$. Now let us assume that sales increase another 10 percent and earnings increase to $.50 per share. This is an increase in earnings per share of 100 percent: $[(\$.50 - .25)/\$.25] \times 100$. If sales increase another 10 percent, earnings will increase another $.25 per share to $.75, but the percentage increase is only 50 percent: $[(\$.75 - .50)/\$.50] \times 100$. Thus, as production increases and moves toward full capacity away from the breakeven point, earnings increase, but at a decreasing rate. Earnings might actually decrease if inefficiencies enter into production.

Operating leverage in each company must be studied to assess its impact on earnings. A company could have a sharp increase in earnings that was not permanent. This is true for cyclical companies, in which a decline in revenues automatically sets the stage for a sharp increase in earnings (after a sharp decrease) that might give the appearance of a growth situation or basic improvement. Assume, for example, that Company A's revenues declined by 10 percent because of a cyclical decline, that earnings dropped sharply, and that there was a greater percentage drop in earnings than in revenues. An analysis of the operating characteristics of Company A will help us anticipate what will happen to earnings based on changes in sales and operating revenues. The following year, however, business improves and so do the revenues of Company A. The improvement in business brings about a sharp increase in profits for Company A because of operating leverage. If one noticed only the increase in profits and ignored operating leverage, one might draw a wrong conclusion about the profit characteristics of the company.

Limits to the Use of Breakeven Point. Breakeven analysis is essentially static. It assumes that prices, wages, capital, and interest are constant over the range of production. Yet these variables do change. Once the breakeven point has been calculated, it might be found that the variables have changed, and this destroys the validity of the analysis. The relationships between revenues and expenses or costs are assumed to be linear, yet this might not be so simple. Previously it was said that variable costs might not change at the same rate, because of economies of large-scale production. If this is true, the profit forecasts will be inaccurate if a straight-line projection is used.

In spite of these limitations, breakeven analysis focuses attention on operating rates, profitability, and operating leverage. To the extent that it helps in approximating levels of profits, it has accomplished a good deal to help support the analysis and forecast of earnings per share.

In addition to the operating rate and the breakeven point, several other measures are available to establish the relative operating efficiency of a company. Three familiar measures are (1) operating ratio, (2) sales or profit per employee, and (3) sales or profit per dollar of plant investment. In addition to these ratios, each industry has its own measures, which can be used to advantage.

The Operating Ratio

The operating ratio is found by dividing operating revenues into operating expenses plus cost of goods sold. It is directly related to the profit margin: If the profit margin is subtracted from 100 percent, we have the operating ratio.

The operating ratio is a good measure of operating efficiency, for it relates costs and expenses directly to revenues. It is easily understood. The lower the operating ratio, the more efficient the company—and, of course, the more profitable. However, overall profitability and efficiency must also be related to operating assets. The fact that the operating ratio of a company is low and signifies operating strength is valid only for comparable corporations within the same industry. The operating ratio does change over time; it is important in any analysis to consider the direction of the change. An increasing operating ratio should be interpreted as a sign of weakness; a constant or decreasing operating ratio would be a sign of strength.

Sales and Earnings per Employee

Sales per employee, measured in terms of dollar sales or units of output, provide another indication of corporate efficiency. The greater the sales per employee, the greater the relative efficiency of a company. Profit or earnings per employee might also be used as a measure of efficiency: The greater and the more stable the earnings per employee, the greater the overall efficiency of the company. Earnings per employee is actually a financial ratio, but it can be used as an efficiency ratio. Both sales per employee and earnings per employee may be used as measures of the quality of a company. The higher the output and earnings per employee over time, the better the company.

Sales and Earnings per Dollar of Plant Investment

The same comments can be made about these measures of efficiency and profitability as about sales and earnings per employee. The greater the sales or earnings per dollar of plant investment, the better the company. These ratios are considered by some analysts as more important than net income to sales. They reflect the return derived from expenditures on new plant and equipment. In some industries, there is a direct relationship between investment in plant and sales. In the chemical industry, for example, a dollar of plant should produce a dollar of sales. A higher or lower ratio would reflect relative degrees of operating efficiency. A decrease in sales and profits per dollar of plant would indicate a weakness in the efficiency and profitability of the company.

CAPITAL EXPENDITURES

Future earnings depend upon the ability of management to invest new corporate funds wisely and to manage the old efficiently. The investment of corporate funds is referred to as a *capital expenditure*. Not all expenditures for plant and equipment will be equally profitable, but it can be assumed that the greater the expenditure for new plant and equipment and the improvement of old facilities, the better able the company will be to deliver future earnings. Therefore, capital expenditure can be used as one guide to determining the future profitability of a company.

A positive and definite relationship exists between capital equipment and sales and future earnings. There is a physical limit to a firm's ability to produce and sell. Once that limit is reached, the firm cannot expand without more expenditures for new plant and equipment or for improving old plant and equipment. The relationship between sales and plant is not the same for each industry. In the steel industry, for example, a dollar spent for plant has the potential of generating a dollar of sales; but a dollar spent for new plant by an electric utility might produce only $.20 of sales.

Perhaps more important than the magnitude of capital expenditures is the relationship between capital expenditures and existing plant. One company might spend $1 million on new plant, and a second company $10 million. The second company made the bigger expenditure. But if the expenditure made by the first company increased its fixed assets by 50 percent and that by the second company increased its assets by only 10 percent, we would conclude that the first company had made the larger relative expenditure. The first company actually had $2 million of plant and equipment to begin with, whereas the second company had $100 million. The relative impact on earnings would be greater in the first company.

Table 15–3 shows capital expenditures as a percentage of existing plant for several leading industries. These data will give some idea of what capital expenditure we can expect from individual companies in these industries. The impression given by Table 15–3 is that capital expenditures as a percentage of plant typically range from 5 to 36.3 percent, with an average of 18.5 percent. In the last analysis, what constitutes a large or a small capital expenditure depends on how the individual company compares with the industry in which it functions.

Capital expenditures undertaken by a company should reflect an increased demand for a product or an attempt to improve plant so that costs can be reduced, making the firm more competitive. Fully expensed annual capital expenditures also add to the stock of capital to make the firm more competitive. The needs of each corporation will vary, depending upon its competitive position. Capital expenditures made in anticipation of increased demand for a product must be analyzed carefully. If the anticipated demand does not materialize, the result will be excess capacity, a poor operating ratio, and impaired earnings and profitability. The initial capital expenditures, an evidence of strength, can become a sign of weakness because of incorrect anticipation of demand. This type of situation existed in the past in the aluminum,

TABLE 15–3

Capital Expenditures as a Percentage of Existing Plant
for Selected Industries, 1979

S&P Industry Survey	Industry	1979 Average
May 28, 1981	Aerospace	36.31%
October 1, 1981	Autos, autoparts	
	Automobiles	31.01
	Trucks, trailers, and parts	15.30
	Auto parts, after market	6.51
	Auto parts, original equipment	22.12
July 9, 1981	Containers	
	Metal and glass containers	22.21
	Paper containers	22.05
June 4, 1981	Electronics—electrical	
	Major companies	25.72
	Electronics (semiconductor/components)	35.12
	Electronics (instrumentation)	18.67
	Electrical equipment	30.06
	Electrical household appliances	9.76
July 16, 1981	Food processing	
	Foods	19.31
	Sugar refiners	4.97
January 1, 1981	Health care	
	Hospital supplies	13.06
	Cosmetics	13.06
	Drugs	9.47
May 21, 1981	Metals	
	Metal fabricating	17.93
	Aluminum	16.69
	Copper	11.92
	Metals—miscellaneous	15.94
	Gold mining	12.03
July 30, 1981	Office equipment	
	Computer services	24.71
	Office and business equipment	33.97
March 26, 1981	Telecommunications	
	Communication equipment manufacturers	9.07
	Telephone companies	16.46
June 18, 1981	Textiles	15.40
October 23, 1981	Utilities—natural gas	
	Distributors	15.83
	Pipelines	19.33

SOURCES: Standard & Poor's *Industry Surveys* in order presented : Aerospace, May 28, 1981, p. A30; Autos—Autoparts, October 1, 1981, p. A157; Containers, July 9, 1981, p. C135; Electronics—Electrical, June 4, 1981, p. E34; Food Processing, July 16, 1981, p. F35; Health Care, January 1, 1981, p. H31; Metals, May 21, 1981, p. M192; Office Equipment, July 20, 1981, p. O33; Telecommunications, March 26, 1981, p. T34; Textiles, June 18, 1981, p. T70; Utilities—Natural Gas, October 23, 1981, p. U76.

paper, and plywood industries, which suffered from excess capacity and temporary overexpansion. When we examine capital expenditures, we must realize that the threat of overexpansion exists.

AN ANALYSIS OF OPERATING EFFICIENCY APPLIED TO THE ETHICAL DRUG COMPANIES

Thousands of products are produced in the ethical and proprietary drug industry. Over $1.5 billion was spent for drug research in 1979, and 854 totally new pharmaceutical drugs were introduced between 1970 and 1979.[3] The amount of money spent for research has increased substantially in the last decade, but the number of new drugs introduced annually has not shown a consistent increase. These products differ to such an extent as to prohibit a definition of a single production or consumption unit. Any attempt to determine the operating capacity of the industry or of a particular company in physical units is impractical. Dollar figures of capital expenditures, sales, and operating ratio must be used as a guide to overall productivity.

The Operating Rate and Operating Capacity

Lilly, Schering-Plough, and SmithKline operated at full capacity during the period 1976–80. This is reflected in growth of sales and growth of plant. The gross plant (Table 15–4) of each company has expanded substantially. SmithKline has demon-

TABLE 15–4

Gross Plant and Capital Expenditures as a Percentage of Gross Plant
(Millions of dollars and precentage)

Company	Gross Plant (millions of dollars)					
	1975	1976	1977	1978	1979	1980
Lilly	$697	$760	$834	$908	$1,078	$1,276
Schering-Plough	332	385	428	473	594	732
SmithKline	224	255	294	355	476	609

Company	Capital Expenditures in Millions of Dollars and as a Percentage of Plant and Equipment										
	1975		1976		1977		1978		1979		1980
										$	%
Lilly	$108	15%	$67	9%	$78	9%	$90	10%	$173	16%	$N.A.	N.A.%
Schering-Plough	59	18	58	15	52	11	51	11	130	18	131	18
SmithKline	24	11	38	15	46	16	75	21	94	15	133	22

SOURCES: *Moody's Industrial Manual,* vol. 2 (New York: Moody's Investors Service, 1981), pp. 3801, 4211; and *Stock Report* (New York: Standard & Poors, July 1981), pp. 1354, 1986, 2050.

[3] Paul de Haen, in Standard & Poor's *Industry Surveys—Health Care, Drugs & Cosmetics,* January 13, 1981, p. H16.

FUNDAMENTAL ANALYSIS

strated the greatest growth and spent the greatest amount as a percentage of gross plant. If these companies had not demonstrated such dramatic growth, we would have examined their operating capacity more closely. The implication here is that the greater the growth in net plant, the better the company for investment. This assumes, of course, that a company can operate an expanded net plant profitably. It also assumes comparability in accounting practices and reporting of expenditures.

Operating Ratio

SmithKline enjoyed the lowest operating ratio of the three leaders in the ethical drug industry. Schering-Plough and Lilly also had excellent ratios. We notice (Table 15–5) that the operating ratio has been relatively stable. Schering-Plough had the highest, but all were below the figure for the drug industry as a whole.

TABLE 15–5

Operating Ratio for Lilly, Schering-Plough, and SmithKline

Company	1975	1976	1977	1978	1979	1980
Lilly	73	73	72	72	74	76
Schering-Plough	74	73	73	75	79	80
SmithKline	82	81	81	75	73	72

SOURCE: Value Line Investment Survey, August 21, 1981, pp. 1261, 1267, 1269. Copyright 1981 by Arnold Bernhard & Co., Inc. Reprinted by permission.

Operating Efficiency and Capital Expenditures

When we examine the operating efficiency of these companies in Table 15–6, we find that SmithKline appears to hold the position of leadership. It has the highest net income per employee, and the highest net income and sales per dollar of gross plant. Schering-Plough experienced the next best record for net income and sales per dollar of gross plant. Lilly was second in efficiency for net income and sales per employee in 1980.

TABLE 15–6

Sales and Net Income per Dollar of Gross Plant and per Employee, 1980

Company	Employees	Sales ($ millions)	Net Income ($ millions)	Gross Plant ($ millions)	Net Income per Employee ($ thousands)	Sales per Employee ($ thousands)	Net Income per $ of Gross Plant	Sales per $ of Gross Plant
Lilly	28,100	$2,559	$342	$1,296	$12.17	$91.07	$.26	$1.97
Schering-Plough	27,400	1,740	239	732	8.72	63.50	.32	2.38
SmithKline	21,196	1,772	308	609	14.53	83.60	.51	2.90

SOURCE: Moody's Industrial Manual, vol. 2 (New York: Moody's Investor Service, Inc., 1981), pp. 3807, 5461, 4211.

From Table 15–4 we learn that in 1980, SmithKline had the highest capital expenditure as a percentage of gross plant, followed by Schering-Plough and Lilly. Schering-Plough's percentage was highest in 1979.

Summary of Operating Characteristics

A summary of the observations about the relative position of each of the three companies appears in Table 15–7. The physical data about operations and operating efficiency augment our quantitative knowledge about these companies. The analysis

TABLE 15–7

Companies Ranked by Operating Characteristics,
Operating Efficiency, and Capital Expenditures

	Lilly	Schering-Plough	SmithKline
Operating Characteristics			
Productive capacity	1	2	3
Operating rate	1	1	1
Growth of plant	2	3	1
Operating margin (interest)	1	3	2
Overall	1	3	2
Operating Efficiency			
Sales per dollar of plant	3	2	1
Earnings per dollar of plant	3	2	1
Earnings per employee	2	3	1
Sales per employee	1	3	2
Overall	2	3	1
Capital Expenditures			
Total spent (1975–80)	1	2	3
Total spent as % of gross plant	3	2	1
Overall	3	2	1

suggests that SmithKline is a well-run company and first in operating characteristics, followed by Schering-Plough. The analysis reinforces our value judgment about the ability of each company to meet its future earnings estimate. The valuation appraisal will continue in the next chapter, where we will examine the current and long-term financial position of each company.

SUMMARY

A thorough analysis of a company requires an examination of operating characteristics and efficiency. One of the first steps in this examination is to learn the capacity of the firm to produce its product or services. Second, its operating characteristics and its historical operating rate should be understood. The third step is to establish the level of existing capacity and historic operating rate; this tells a good deal about the profit expectation of the company. Fourth, capital expenditures tell something about the firm's ability to expand and be more profitable in the future. Expanding plant capacity *should* reflect an increased profitability. The fifth step is to analyze the operating efficiency of the company. This is expressed in dollar terms and is used with the financial and profitability ratios. The ratios used are the operating ratio, sales and net income per employee, and sales and income per dollar of gross plant.

Investors want a company that has an expanding plant capacity and a high operating rate. These are indicative of profitability and help improve future earnings. The measures of operating efficiency are also indicative of profitability. The company with the lowest operating ratio, the highest sales and net income per employee, and the highest sales and net income per dollar of plant investment should be the best company. It is helpful when examining these ratios to compare them with those of other companies and, if available, comparable data for the industry. The analysis adds a qualitative dimension to the value analysis based on estimates of future profitability.

SUMMARY OF PRINCIPLES

1. Investors should choose companies that maintain a high rate of production.
2. Investors should choose firms that employ their resources efficiently and to the fullest advantage.
3. Investors should select companies that have stable production, well above the breakeven point.
4. Investors should select companies that have an above-average rate of capital investment.
5. Sales and profits per employee and sales and profits per dollar of plant investment are good measures of operating efficiency.

REVIEW QUESTIONS

1. What is the usual relationship between the operating efficiency of a company and its earnings? For example, as operating efficiency improves, do earnings improve? Comment.
2. How do we determine the productive capacity of a company? What are the problems in establishing productive capacity in companies in the following industries?
   a. Banking and finance.
   b. Industrial.
   c. Public utility.
   d. Transportation.
3. How would you measure the capacity of a company to produce if it made several different types of products? Explain.
4. Define what is meant by the term *operating rate*.
   a. Why is the historic operating rate of a company important?
   b. Why is a change in operating rate important?

5. Is it desirable for a company to operate consistently above its rated capacity? Explain.

6. Explain what is meant by the term *operating leverage*.

7. To what extent is breakeven analysis helpful in determining the earnings of a company? What are its limits?

8. Explain how operating ratio, sales or profits per employee, and sales or profits per dollar of plant investment are used as measures of operating efficiency.

9. Explain the extent to which capital expenditures are indicative of a growing company. Can level of capital expenditures be used as the sole criterion for estimating future growth of sales? Comment.

10. Review the analysis of the operating characteristics of the three drug companies. Do you agree with the results?

PROBLEMS

1. What is the physical capacity to produce for the three companies you selected for analysis in the previous chapters? If units of capacity are not available, use dollar sales as a measure of capacity.

2. Has operating capacity in physical units or dollars increased for each company between 1975 and the present?

3. a. How much did each of the companies spend annually on capital expenditures for the period 1975 to the present?
   b. What percentage of plant was the annual capital expenditure?
   c. Rank each of the companies. Which one was best?

4. a. What was the operating rate for each of the three companies from 1975 to the present?
   b. Rank each company on the basis of its operating rate. Which was best?

5. How do the operating rate and growth of capacity of the three companies compare with growth in the industry?

6. a. What has been the profit and sales per dollar of plant and per employee for each of the three companies?
   b. Which company appears to be best in this regard?

7. Based on this analysis, which company would you consider to be best?

8. Does the information given in this chapter change your valuation appraisal of the company?

SELECTED READINGS

DHAVALE, DILEEP, G., and HOYT G. WILSON "Breakeven Analysis with Inflationary Cost and Prices." *Engineering Economist* 25 (winter 1980), pp. 107–121.

GRITTA, RICHARD. "The Effect of Financial Leverage of Air Carrier Earnings: A Breakeven Analysis." *Financial Management* 8 (summer 1979), pp. 53–60.

JAEDICKE, ROBERT K., and ALEXANDER A. ROBICHEK "Cost-Volume-Profit Analysis under Conditions of Uncertainty." *Accounting Review* 39 (October 1964), pp. 917–26.

RAPPAPORT, ALFRED. "Measuring Company Growth Capacity during Inflation." *Harvard Business Review* 57 (January–February 1979), pp. 91–100.

RAUN, D. L. "The Limitations of Profit Graphs, Breakeven Analysis, and Budgets." *Accounting Review* 39 (October 1964), pp. 927–45.

SOLDOFSKY, R. M. "Accountant's versus Economist's Concepts of Breakeven Analysis." *N.A.A. Bulletin* 41 (December 1959), pp. 5–18.

CHAPTER 16

CURRENT AND LONG-TERM
FINANCIAL ANALYSIS

The function of current financial analysis is to determine a company's ability to pay current bills as they come due. This ability necessitates adequate liquidity, which is acquired through a regular conversion of inventories into sales, sales into accounts receivable, and receivables into cash. Liquidity implies adequate balances kept at the bank and funds invested in short-term government securities. The liquidity of a firm has obvious effects on its earnings. If current assets are not converted regularly into cash, or if cash or equivalent balances are not maintained, the company will not be able to pay its bills. Defaults on contracts and debts will result in the failure of the company. On the other hand, if the company has too much cash or too many government securities—in short, is too liquid—earnings will be lower than if assets were invested more profitably.

Long-term financial analysis determines the ability of the company to support or repay long-term debt. Borrowing money for working capital and plant expansion has obvious advantages for common stock earnings. But excessive long-term debt can have a disastrous impact on the company's future and, in fact, can result in corporate failure. The problem of financial analysis is to determine the short- and long-run financial solvency of the company. In this chapter, ratio analysis will be used to measure the current financial position of the company. Long-range solvency will be tested by an examination of long-term debt in the capital structure and its impact on the amount and stability of a company's earnings. The basic investment principle followed is that a company will be a good investment if its short-term and long-term financial position is strong.

FINANCIAL OBJECTIVES OF THE COMPANY

The basic financial objectives of a company are long-range profitability and short-run liquidity. Long-range profitability is achieved by investing money in productive and profitable business ventures. The source of this money is the sale of securities to investors, or funds generated internally through sales but kept as depreciation expenses and retained earnings. The liquidity function is performed by management, which makes certain that money is on hand to pay for raw materials, to finance credit sales, to pay salaries, and to repay current debt.

The problem of financial management is one of balance. If all money were kept on deposit at the savings bank, in a certificate of deposit, or in a checking account, the company would be completely liquid. However, this would not constitute a very profitable investment of funds. At best, the funds would earn $7\frac{1}{4}$ percent—not a very attractive rate of return for a business corporation. At the other extreme is investment of all funds in buildings, land, machinery, and equipment, leaving no working capital or cash to pay bills as they come due before receivables have been collected. The return on such investment could be 20 percent or higher, but the company could not function long without funds to meet operating expenses. Somewhere between the condition of all cash and no fixed assets and all fixed assets and no cash is the solution to the dilemma. Money is usually employed most profitably in both short-term investment and long-range projects.

To accomplish the objectives of profitability and liquidity, management engages in financial planning. This involves planning for short-term needs by use of the cash budget, as well as planning capital expenditures and acquisitions that require long-range budgeting. Often the company must obtain money—short-term or long-term, debt or equity—to meet its needs. It might borrow temporary cash from a commercial bank or possibly open-book credit from a supplier. This will increase short-term indebtedness. Occasionally, a company will raise funds for plant and equipment expenditures or for working capital from reinvested earnings or the sale of debt or equity securities. The investor should be concerned about whether the company can pay off its indebtedness, both short-term and long-term, and whether this can be done safely and in a method beneficial to the investor.

JUDGING THE SHORT-TERM FINANCIAL POSITION OF THE COMPANY

When we analyze the current financial position of a company, we raise a series of questions about overall liquidity and ability to pay its short-term obligations. Does the company have adequate current assets to pay its debts? Does it have sufficient cash to maintain a smoothly functioning organization that takes advantage of discounts and similar savings? Does the company have adequate working capital? Is inventory excessive? Are credit sales too high? Are accounts receivable exorbitant? Answers to these questions are obtained from a detailed examination of the balance sheet and income statement by using financial ratio analysis.

No company should be considered for investment unless it has a good current financial position. Let us examine the ratios used to determine the adequacy of that position. Data used in these ratios are supplied by the company through its annual report, in which explanations of variables and exceptions are also provided. Annual reports are usually issued at a time selected by the company, and discretionary variables are explained at the option of the company. A review of the information contained in an SEC prospectus or 10-K would be very helpful.

The Current Ratio

The current ratio helps the analyst determine the ability of a company to pay its short-term debts. Current ratio is found by dividing current liabilities into current assets, and it is expressed as, say, 2.5 to 1 or 3.5 to 1, meaning that the company has 2.5 or 3.5 dollars of current assets for every dollar of current liabilities. The American Widget Company's balance sheet and operating statement, presented in Table 16-1, will be used to show how the ratios are computed. American Widget has $220,000 of current assets and $100,000 of current liabilities. Its current ratio, therefore, is 2.2 to 1 ($220,000/$100,000). What does this mean? The purpose in comparing current assets with current liabilities is to determine whether sufficient current assets are available to pay current liabilities should they be presented for payment. The higher its current ratio, the better a corporation is able to pay its current debt; the lower the ratio, the less able. Often a 2-to-1 ratio is considered adequate; however, no single standard can be applied that will be the same for all companies. A public utility, for example, would have a much different current ratio from that of a manufacturing company.

American Widget's current ratio of 2.2 to 1 is better than the 2-to-1 standard, but rather than accept an arbitrary ratio, consider the extent to which current assets, when converted into cash, will pay current liabilities. In reality, this is a better and more basic test of corporate financial well-being. American Widget's inventory does not appear to be excessive. If the receivables are collectible, it would be concluded that the current ratio reflects a good current position. But if it were found, on closer inspection, that a high percentage of the current assets were not salable, or were reserved for compensating balances, then the 2.2-to1 ratio would not be really adequate. This is the type of value judgment that must be made.

The Acid-Test Ratio

The acid-test ratio is designed to focus attention on the liquid assets of the company. It ignores current assets that might not be easily converted into cash. The *acid-test ratio* is found by dividing current liabilities into cash plus short-term securities plus accounts receivable; in short, current liabilities are divided into current assets minus inventory. Inventory is excluded because its cash equivalent might not be available to pay short-term debts. If a company is having difficulty selling its product, then a large inventory that cannot be sold will not help the company pay off current debt. A high current ratio might result because of the large inventory, but the company still will not possess liquidity. The acid-test ratio, therefore, is a better indication of ability to pay current debts than is the current ratio.

If liquid current assets—current assets minus inventory—are equivalent to or exceed current liabilities, then, theoretically at least, the company has an excellent current financial position. Practically speaking, an acid-test ratio above 1 to 1 is

TABLE 16–1
American Widget Company Balance Sheet and Operating Statement,
December 31 (thousands of dollars)

Balance Sheet

Current Assets			Debt		
Cash	$ 10		*Short-Term:*		
Government securities	20		Accounts payable	$40	
Accounts receivable	70		One-year loan	60	
Inventory: Finished, 60			Total		$100
In process, 30			*Long-Term:*		
Raw materials, 30	120		6% mortgage loan		200
Total current assets		$220	Total debt		$300
Fixed Assets			Ownership		
Buildings and land:	$200		Common stock		150
Reserve for depreciation	50		Retained earnings		50 200
Net buildings & land		$150	Total debt & ownership		$500
Machinery & equipment:	$150				
Reserve for depreciation	20				
Net machinery & equipment		130			
Total fixed assets		280			
Total assets		$500			

Operating Statement

Sales		$1,000
Cost of goods sold		600
Gross profit on sales		400
Selling expenses	$150	
General expenses	50	
Depreciation	10	210
Net profit		190
Other income (interest income)	1	
Other expense (interest expense)	16	15
Net income before federal income taxes		175
Federal income tax (estimated)		85
Net income		$ 90

---

adequate only if receivables can be easily converted into cash. If accounts receivable include a large percentage of bad debts or uncollectible accounts, even the acid-test ratio would not adequately describe current liquidity. To be certain that current assets can pay off current debt immediately, the amount of the accounts receivable must be adjusted to eliminate bad accounts. Such detailed information about the accounts is usually unavailable to investors. It must also be assumed that the cash and equivalent in government securities and a reduced amount of receivables will be able to meet current liabilities.

The American Widget Company has a favorable acid-test ratio, according to the criterion that current assets minus inventory should equal or exceed liabilities. Cash, government securities, and accounts receivable total $100,000, compared to current liabilities of $100,000. The acid test ratio is 1 to 1 ($100,000/$100,000). The ratio is favorable because the most liquid of current assets equals the total of current liabilities. Even if the accounts receivable could not be collected, the company would be able to sell some inventory, which would probably be sufficient to meet current liabilities when combined with cash and government securities.

Composition of Current Assets

The composition of current assets is also important in determining the overall liquidity of a company. A very large proportion of inventory in current assets would suggest that the current assets were not as liquid as they should be. It might also indicate that management is following a poor inventory policy. Of course, some companies must maintain large inventories because of the nature of their operations. Tobacco companies, for instance, have an extremely high ratio of inventory to total current assets and to total assets. Actually, to the tobacco company, tobacco should be looked upon as a fixed investment.

On the other hand, a company might have a high percentage of current assets in cash and government securities. This might be a good policy, since it allows the company to take advantage of cash discounts and provides emergency funds for periods of distress. Adequate cash balances work to improve the company's credit rating and general good standing with commercial banks. A large cash balance and investment in government securities might mean that a company is building up funds to acquire new plant and equipment. Large balances are justified under these circumstances.

The American Widget Company appears to be in a favorable position with respect to the composition of its current assets. Cash represents about 4.5 percent of current assets, a low figure based on the rule of thumb, used in the past, that the amount of cash should equal at least 10 percent of current assets. The rule originated at a time when financial managers did not invest the company's funds directly. Today, many financial managers would not let this large an amount of cash remain idle and unproductive. Funds not needed, even for a short period, are invested in short-term securities to improve the company's earnings position. Therefore, in using the 10 percent cash rule today, short-term investment should be included for American Widget, as its cash and government-securities accounts equal 13.6 percent of total current assets, clearly above the 10 percent limit:

	Thousands of Dollars		Percentage of Total	
Cash	$ 10	} $30	4.5	} 13.6
Government securities	20		9.1	
Accounts receivable	70		31.8	
Inventory	120		54.6	
	$220		100.0	

The accounts-receivable position does not seem extraordinary at about 32 percent of current assets; 50 percent or more would be high. If American Widget had 70 percent of its current assets in accounts receivable, on the basis of reason alone, the amount would be too high. Inventories of American Widget are not excessive, either. A level of 50 to 60 percent can be expected. American Widget's ratio is 54.6 percent, which might be considered normal. However, inventory ratios vary from industry to industry, and a final conclusion would be made after comparing this ratio with those of other companies in the industry and over a period greater than one year.

Credit Sales Carried as Receivables

Receivables and inventory, respectively, vary with credit sales and total sales of the company. Therefore, for the limits of receivables and inventory to be established in a more logical way, they must be compared with sales figures. The investor can best determine whether receivables are excessive from the number of days credit sales are carried on the corporate books as accounts receivable. This is computed by dividing the average amount of daily credit sales into the average of accounts receivable on the books, as reflected in the balance sheet and operating statement of the company. In making an analysis of a company, the investor can use data from the annual reports, which do not usually provide credit-sales figures or the average amount of receivables carried. As a practical matter, the net-sales figure can be used in place of the credit-sales figure. Most corporate sales are done on open-book account; therefore, credit sales usually differ little from total sales. The receivables figures provided in the annual report are also used instead of the average accounts receivable carried, simply because the average figure is usually unavailable.

The American Widget Company had sales of $1,000,000 and receivables of $70,000 for the accounting period ending December 31. During the year, the company averaged about $2,780 of daily sales ($1,000,000/360). It had 25.2 days' sales on the books in the form of receivables ($70,000/$2,780) at the end of the year. This calculation can be expressed simply as $DSO = (R \times 360)/S$, where DSO is days' sales outstanding, R is the amount of accounts receivable on the books, and S is the credit sales, or simply the sales of the company. In the case of American Widget, this would be $DSO = (\$70,000 \times 360)/\$1,000,000 = 25.2$. The significance of this figure is established only when it is compared with the credit period extended by the company. If the credit period of American Widget is 30 days, we can conclude that the DSO are small in relation to what is expected. Assume, for the moment, that another company has 60 days' sales outstanding. Compared with American Widget, this is an extremely high ratio. It would be concluded that the other company was in a poorer credit position. Upon closer examination, however, it is learned that the credit period of American Widget is 30 days and that of the other company is 60 days. Relatively, American Widget is still in the better position, but only because it has fewer days' sales outstanding compared with the credit period, and not because it has less than half as many days' sales outstanding compared with the other company.

Net-Sales-to-Inventory Ratio

The net-sales-to-inventory ratio provides a way to determine whether a company's inventory is too high or too low. It is computed by dividing the inventory on the books into the annual net sales. The ratio for American Widget Company would be 8.33 to 1 ($1,000,000/$120,000). This ratio simply shows that, for each dollar invested in inventory, the company generates $8.33 of sales. The true significance of the ratio, however, can be ascertained only by noting its direction of change and how it compares with other companies. If the sales-to-inventory ratio were decreasing for American Widget and increasing for other companies in the industry, this would be a sign that American Widget suffered excessive inventory in relation to sales, or that sales were too low for the inventory carried. To be most efficient, a company should keep its sales-to-inventory ratio as high as possible consistent with the demands imposed by its competition.

Inventory-Turnover Ratio

Closely related to the net-sales-to-inventory ratio is the inventory-turnover ratio, computed by dividing finished-goods inventory into net sales at cost or cost of goods sold. This is somewhat difficult to compute, since in published data, the inventory is not always broken down by major components—finished goods, goods in process, and raw materials. Where figures are available, however, the ratio does provide a measure of efficiency on which to judge a company. The total inventory given in the annual report is usually used for the calculation. When a corporation sells $8 worth of a product for every dollar invested in finished-goods inventory, it is doing a better job than if it sells only $6 worth for every dollar of inventory. However, before any significance can be attached to the ratio, a comparison must be made with other companies in the industry.

The figures for the American Widget Company can be used as an example of how to use the inventory-turnover ratio. The finished-goods inventory of the company is $60,000, and the cost of goods sold is $600,000, which gives an inventory-turnover ratio of 10 to 1 ($600,000/$60,000). If this breakdown were not available, total inventory would be used—in this case, $120,000; then the inventory-turnover ratio would be 5 to 1 ($600,000/$120,000). Whether this turnover ratio is high or low will depend on a comparison with other companies in the industry and the previous experience of American Widget.

Net Sales to Net Working Capital

A ratio significant in determining the ability of the company to finance sales growth is the ratio of net sales to net working capital. The net working capital of a company is found by subtracting current liabilities from current assets. In the case of American Widget, working capital is $120,000($220,000 − $100,000), and the net-sales-to-working-capital ratio is 8.33 ($1,000,000/$120,000). Again, whether this is good or poor depends upon American Widget's position compared with that of other companies in the industry. It is desirable to maintain the level of working capital at a point where new sales can be financed easily. Many firms have a great deal of difficulty maintaining this working capital position. As sales expand, a company may be unable to finance, from bank loans and open-book accounts, all the growth of inventory and receivables needed to support the sales, so it must supply working capital to finance receivables and inventory. Working capital is supplied only by long-term capital in the form of retained earnings, the sales of common or preferred stock, and the sale of bonds. The prime consideration in the use of the ratio of net sales to working capital is whether it maintains a degree of stability and grows with sales. It tells the investor if a company has the ability to obtain adequate working capital to finance its sales and the future growth of sales. A declining ratio would indicate the need for a more efficient use of previously invested capital. A ratio that was too high would reflect that more working capital was needed.

Cash Budget

The cash budget has become a valuable tool of modern corporate and business financial analysis. Long- and short-range budgets are now used to help plan and control the future of well-managed companies. These budgets are invaluable guides to financial solvency. If such data are available, they can shed light on corporate financial affairs and make ratio analysis somewhat superfluous. Unfortunately, such data are not readily available to investors and analysts.

THE SIGNIFICANCE OF RATIO ANALYSIS

The neophyte investor or analyst can seldom immediately assess the value of the current ratio, the acid-test ratio, the number of days' credit sales outstanding, or the inventory-turnover ratio; nor can he or she readily assess their impact on earnings. A question often asked is, "What do I do with these ratios after I have computed them?" or, more simply, "What do they mean?"

Relative Comparison

The significance of the ratios rests in their performance over time and how they compare with those of other companies in the industry on a collective basis. These measures are all relative; the test of reasonableness must be added to them. The investor asks, "Is the ratio reasonable based on the objectives of the firm?" For example, would it be reasonable to have 90 percent of current assets in inventory, or 90 percent in accounts receivable, or, for that matter, 90 percent in cash and government securities? By the same token, it would not be a reasonable situation if cash represented only 2 percent of current assets, or if inventory or receivables each represented 10 percent of current assets—unless, of course, the company sold only for cash or produced not a tangible product, but a service that required little inventory. Thus, in making an analysis of the current position of a company, a sense of proportion and reasonableness must be maintained. This comes from experience and judgment by using and applying the ratios we have discussed.

Year-to-Year Change

A second criterion for judgment is what happens to the ratio from year to year. Actually, stability in the financial position, once the proper relationships have been established, is more important than growth or change. Once a corporation has obtained an adequate working balance in its current-assets position and between current assets and liabilities, this ratio should be maintained as sales and plant investment increase. An increase in the current ratio or acid-test ratio would indicate an increase in liquidity and an increase in working capital. An improvement in the working-capital position of the company might be temporary and a result of long-term financing in anticipation of growth in sales. It might mean an increase in liquidity, in which case funds would be available for investment, or even paid to the stockholders in the form of dividends. A decrease in the current ratio or acid-test ratio would indicate the need for long-term working-capital funds. Stability in the current ratio and acid-test ratio is expected and important.

Changes in the Ratios

Sharp changes in these relationships might be temporary, but they might also be indicative of long-range changes that forecast decreased earnings.

INVENTORY. An increase in inventory usually indicates that a company is not selling as much of its product as formerly. A company cannot profit from a buildup in inventory over time unless it is a temporary buildup in anticipation of increased sales volume. Most companies try to keep inventory in balance with sales so that available funds can be used effectively. A decline in inventory, on the other hand, might indicate an improvement in sales, a need for more productive capacity, or a basic internal change in inventory policy. A company can have too little inventory as well as too much. If it has too little, sales might be lost. If it has too much, earnings will be lost on unprofitable funds invested in inventory.

RECEIVABLES. An increase in receivables would indicate an increase in credit sales, or possibly a slowing down in the collection of receivables. The number of days' sales outstanding (DSO) is a good test for determining whether receivables are excessive. If credit sales increase, receivables on the books should increase in the same proportion. If, on the contrary, sales do not increase but an increase in receivables occurs, the company will be forced to increase its investment in receivables without an increase in profit. This, of course, is undesirable.

CASH POSITION. The cash position of a company can improve—that is, a company can acquire more cash and government securities as a percentage of current assets—but only within a well-defined range. Any company that has permanent excess balances in the commercial bank really has only two alternatives: (1) The money can be invested in more productive assets, or (2) it can be paid out to stockholders in the form of dividends. Here the problem is one of a balance between liquidity and profitability, and not of the actual amount of the cash balance.

SUMMARY. The comparisons involved in the analysis of the current position over time suggest that stability of relationships is more important than growth. The keynote of these comparisons is in balance of the various items. Therefore, it is not desirable to have a buildup of inventory or receivables or cash per se, but only if there is a corresponding increase in sales. The best the investor can expect from the current and long-term assets of the company is that they correspond directly with an increase or decrease in sales and that the company be in a position to finance any changes.

CURRENT ANALYSIS OF THE DRUG COMPANIES

A continuation of the study of the ethical drug industry will prove somewhat more rewarding than a hypothetical situation as an illustration of current financial analysis. The criteria established to test the current financial position are basically those of solvency and financial strength. The specific task we face is to determine if the drug companies have an adequate current financial position and if this enhances or reduces earnings.

A current analysis was made for the three companies we have been analyzing. The results are presented in Table 16–2. The leading companies were in an excellent liquid position, with a rather large average current ratio and acid-test ratio and a high percentage of the current assets in liquid assets. Lilly was close to conservative accounting in its ratios. Inventory, for example, was low in the three companies. The average days' sales outstanding suggests that credit term varied around 60 days among the leading companies. The net-sales-to-inventory ratio was stable, indicating good sales per dollar of inventory—a desirable trait. At the same time, net sales to working capital has declined, which indicates that the companies have more than adequate working capital in relation to sales. Overall, the companies were in a good current financial position.

TABLE 16–2

Current Financial Analysis of Lilly, Schering-Plough, and SmithKline

Ratio	Lilly		Schering-Plough		SmithKline	
	1980	1979	1980	1979	1980	1979
Current ratio	2.09	2.47	1.90	2.16	2.61	2.43
Acid test	1.17	1.32	1.28	1.40	1.80	1.66
Composition of current assets (%)						
Cash	13	13	34	29	34	34
Receivables	38	36	24	26	33	32
Inventory	45	46	33	35	31	31
Other	5	4	9	10	2	3
Number of days sales in receivables outstanding (DSO)	83	75	60	65	68	72
Net sales to inventory	3.80	3.67	4.35	4.13	5.55	5.15
Net sales to working capital	3.19	2.87	3.00	2.71	2.77	2.75

SOURCE: *Moody's Industrial Manual* (New York: Moody's Investor Service, Inc., 1981), pp. 3804, 4209, 5460.

SmithKline was the most liquid of the companies presented. Its current ratio had improved, whereas Lilly's and Schering's current ratio had deteriorated between 1979 and 1980. The summary ranking of the companies' current financial position is found in Table 16–3. It is clear that SmithKline is the best of the three, followed by Schering-Plough and Lilly.

TABLE 16–3

Companies Ranked by Current Financial Position

Comparative Current Financial Analysis	Lilly	Schering-Plough	SmithKline
Current ratio*	2	3	1
Acid-test ratio*	3	2	1
Composition of current assets†	3	2	1
DSO (days sales outstanding)‡	3	1	2
Net sales to inventory**	3	2	1
Net sales to working capital**	3	2	1
Overall liquidity	3	2	1

*Based on highest percentage.
†Based on greater of cash and equivalent.
‡Based on lowest-ranked first.
**Based on highest-ranked first.

CAPITAL STRUCTURE ANALYSIS

At the present time, debt financing is the cheapest way for a company to obtain capital. A heavy reliance on debt financing tends to raise the rate of return to the common stockholder. Of course, the funds must be invested profitably and at a higher rate than the interest paid for using them. Borrowing money at a low rate and investing it at a higher rate is referred to as *trading on the equity*. A large debt creates a high degree of financial leverage. If the revenues of the company are unstable, the presence of a large amount of debt tends to further increase the instability of earnings per share. Companies with a high degree of both operating leverage and financial leverage might have a high degree of earnings instability if revenues are unstable. If a company experiences a wide fluctuation of earnings because of its revenue pattern, it will experience an even wider and more unstable fluctuation of earnings if there is a large amount of debt in the capital structure.

The impact of debt in the capital structure on valuation and earnings is subject to a wide difference of opinion. Two views indicate the breadth of current thought. One group believes that capital structure can affect the aggregate market value of a company's securities apart from the tax impact. The second group thinks that, except for the tax factor, the capital structure has no effect on the total market valuation of a company's securities.

It is the author's view that an *optimum* amount of debt leads to both a tax advantage and an increase in total company value; that debt in the capital structure increases the risk of loss for the common stock owners; that with increased debt, the P/E ratio of common stock is lowered because of the additional risk; and that at the *optimum* debt level, the P/E ratio is lowered, but the percentage drop is less than the tax advantages and increase in value. It is therefore important for the investor to ascertain whether debt is excessive by an analysis of debt in the capital structure.

If a company depends solely on the sale of common stock to raise capital, the impact on earnings per share is somewhat different. Besides reducing earnings per share, the sale of additional common stock might also have the effect of reducing total value, because the advantages to the stock owners of having some debt in the capital structure are lost. Some debt is desirable, the optimum amount lying between the maximum leverage in earnings and the maximum amount of increase in risk. If, for example, the present rate of return earned on the common stock is 10 percent, and the new funds from the sales of additional common stock earn only 8 percent, the earnings of the existing shares have been diluted. Raising capital by the sale of common stock under these conditions reduces overall earnings on the common stock and thus reduces per-share market prices. It is undesirable from the point of view of management and of the investor to have a set of conditions that reduces earnings per share. If a company proposes to raise capital by selling common stock, we must examine and estimate the effect on per-share earnings.

Of course, capital raised in this way, although expensive, can be invested in such a way as to improve earnings per share for all outstanding shares. Money can be raised by sales to the public or to the existing stockholders. If there is a danger of dilution in earnings and assets when it is necessary to obtain funds, stock can be sold to the existing stockholders. In this way, the old shareholders, if they subscribe to the stock, will maintain their relative position in the company.

Often, a corporation will finance by the sale of common stock even though the use of borrowed funds might be more advantageous. This is done by the more conservative management, which does not wish to jeopardize corporate existence through the default of a bond issue and therefore engages only in equity financing. Companies that have widely fluctuating earnings, or companies that are new and somewhat speculative, also tend to finance through the sale of common stock. They are not unaware of the advantages and disadvantages of debt financing, but as a matter of policy they decide against it. Their position is such that the advantages of debt financing are outweighed by its disadvantages and by the advantages of equity financing.

The Capital Structure

The source of capital should enhance and improve the per-share earnings of the common stock. Steps must be taken to make certain that debt or preferred stock charges, both interest and dividends, are not excessive in relation to earnings and that debt alone is not excessive in relation to the total assets and capital of the company.

The *capital structure* is simply the sum of the net worth plus any outstanding long-term debt. The capital structure of Bristol-Myers in 1966, 1971, 1975, and 1980 is presented in Table 16–4 as an example of how one company has raised its long-term funds. Actually, all of Bristol-Myers's long-term funds in 1966 came from common stock, capital surplus, and retained earnings; 77.5 percent came from these in 1971,

TABLE 16-4

Composition of the Capital Structure of Bristol-Myers, 1966, 1971, 1975, 1980

	Million of Dollars				Percentage of Total			
	1966	1971	1975	1980	1966	1971	1975	1980
Long-term debt (corporate bonds)	$ 0	$122.7	$ 94.6	$ 111.9	0%	22.3%	11.9%	7.5%
Preferred stock	0	1.3	1.3	1.2	0	.2	.2	.1
Common stock	25.2	30.1	31.4	66.0	15.3	5.5	3.9	4.4
Capital surplus	6.6	56.7	63.5	61.9	4.0	10.4	8.0	4.1
Retained earnings	132.3	339.3	603.1	1,252.0	80.7	61.6	76.0	83.9
Total long-term capital	$164.1	$550.1	$793.9	$1,493.0	100.0%	100.0%	100.0%	100.0%

SOURCE: *Moody's Industrial Manual,* June 1967, p. 1267; June 1972, p. 696; June 1976, vol. 1, A-1, p. 211; 1981, vol. 1, A-1, p. 806.

87.9 percent in 1975 and 92.4 percent in 1980. Debt was increased in the fourteen-year period, but the amount of debt was modest, and the company was able to more than double its capital structure in a short period of time.

Preferred Stock in the Capital Structure

Preferred stock has never been a significant source of capital for the majority of corporations. It accounts for approximately 10 percent of the source of capital for railroads and public utilities, and about 5 to 6 percent for industrial companies. Although use of preferred stock has been somewhat limited, it was welcomed as a source of capital in previous periods of tight money. Its presence in the capital structure must be analyzed from the points of view of both the common and the preferred investor. Let us look briefly at each point of view.

THE VIEWPOINT OF OWNERS OF PREFERENCE SHARES. The owners of preferred stock are interested in knowing if the dividend is secure and if the preferred claims will be satisfied should the company fail. The preferred owner ascertains whether the earnings of the company, after taxes and after prior-interest claims have been paid, are sufficient to pay a dividend on the preferred, assuming normal as well as adverse or abnormal fluctuations in corporate earnings. The preferred owner also examines the nature of the company's assets and the claims on assets to learn if the preferred claims will be paid if the company should fail. Any other contractual obligations must also be satisfied, and the preferred stockholder must verify the certainty of these other conditions. Investors who buy ordinary preferred stock want stable revenues and security of principal.

THE VIEWPOINT OF THE COMMON STOCKHOLDER. The presence of preferred stock in the capital structure of a corporation, like the use of debt, leads to some degree of leverage of earnings. The leverage impact on common stock is not as great as that of debt, because the preferred dividends are not tax deductible except under special circumstances. They are paid out of net income or earnings, after taxes have been deducted. Nevertheless, if 15 percent can be earned on funds raised by the sale of a 10 percent preferred stock, then the common owners will receive the difference, and the per-share earnings will increase even after allowance from income taxes. A low-cost preferred, then, has a positive effect on the common earnings through the leverage effect if the trend of earnings is stable, higher than the dividend rate, and increasing.

An excessive amount of preferred stock in the capital structure tends, however, to create a situation of instability of earnings in the common stock if the earnings of the company fluctuate. Another limit imposed on the common stockholder by the preferred agreement is in the matter of dividend payments. Where earnings and working capital limits are not met or where dividends are in arrears, no dividends will be paid to the common stockholder. Preferred stock in this case would be detrimental to the common stockholder.

One other effect on the per-share common-stock earnings occurs in the special case of convertible preferred. The possibility of a conversion of preferred into common stock might dilute the earnings of common stock. When common stock is purchased from the company with a large amount of convertible preferred out-standing, the possible effect of conversion must be determined. The amount of stock converted might result in a sharp increase in the number of shares of stock outstanding and a sharp decrease in earnings per share, causing common prices to drop.

LIMIT TO THE USE OF PREFERRED STOCK.   No hard-and-fast rules exist for the use of preferred stock as a source of capital for the corporation. However, several comments can be made as a guide for a company analysis. First, when preferred stock is used, it should add to the financial strength of the company. Excessive use of preferred would impose a dividend burden that would be difficult to meet. Second, preferred dividends and bond interest should be adequately covered by the earnings of the corporation after taxes. Third, the use of preferred stock should enhance and maximize the earnings of the common stock, leading to stability rather than instability of earnings per share. Where earnings are already unstable, preferred stock should not be used in an amount that would add to this instability because of financial leverage. Fourth, the use of special types of preferred stock, such as convertible preferred, should not lead to the dilution of common stock in the corporation. Fifth and last, preferred stock and debt should not exceed the net tangible assets of the company. These general principles will serve as a guide in making an analysis.

Debt in the Capital Structure

Debt plays an important part in the long-term financing of most corporations. As previously noted, debt has certain advantages in terms of cost and market acceptability that make it attractive as a source of funds. The use of debt results in a form of earnings leverage that can be highly beneficial to common stock owners. On the other hand, leverage can be detrimental to common stockholders by causing a great deal of instability of earnings per share and can actually force a company into bankruptcy.

The leverage impact can be demonstrated by the following example: Assume that two companies have the same amount of sales and expenses, resulting in an identical profit margin of $20 million. Sales are $100 million and neither company has any other income, so that profit margin is 20 percent of operating revenues. One difference exists between the two companies: One company has a capital structure consisting entirely of common stock and retained earnings; the other has a capital structure consisting of 50 percent common stock and 50 percent debt with an interest rate of 5 percent. The capital structure of each company appears graphically in Figure 16–1.

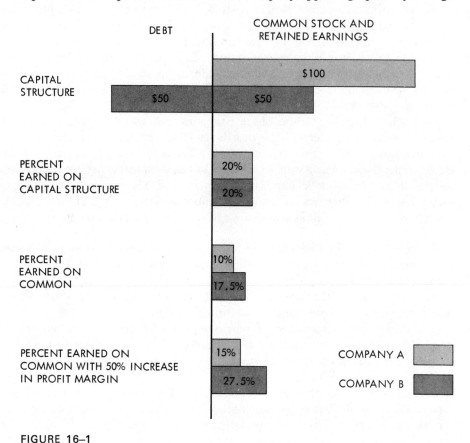

FIGURE 16–1

Percent Earnings on Common Stock of Two Companies with the Same Operating Profits but Different Capital Structures ($ millions)

Each company earned 20 percent before taxes on its capital structure ($20/$100). However, federal income taxes (assumed to be 50 percent) must be considered, and interest expense must be considered. When this is done, company A is found to earn $10 million after taxes, providing the common stockholder a return of 10 percent after taxes. Company B is in a somewhat different situation. Before taxes are paid, interest of $2.5 million (5 percent of $50 million) must be deducted. Taxable income, therefore, is $17.5 million, income taxes are $8.75 million, and company B has an income after taxes of $8.75 million. The rate of return on common equity is 17.5 percent ($8.75 million/$50 million). Therefore, two companies that have the same profit margin have two different rates of return on common equity, simply because one has used low-cost, tax-deductible debt and the other has used either common stock or retained earnings.

The leverage aspect is more dramatically demonstrated when a change in profit margin occurs. Assume that both companies experience an increase in profit margin to 30 percent, and in dollars from $20 to $30 million. This represents a 50 percent increase in the profit margin. What happens under these assumptions to the rate of return of common stocks? Company A pays a $15 million federal income tax on its profits, which leaves $15 million net income after taxes. This is a 15 percent rate of return on owners' equity. Company A, therefore, realizes a 50 percent increase in the return on the owners' equity with a 50 percent increase in its profit margin. The net income available for the common stockholder, however, increases dramatically. Taxable income is $27.5 million ($30 − $2.5 million), and net income after taxes amounts to $13.75 million ($27.5 − $13.75 million taxes). This amount is available to the owners and provides them with a 27.5 percent rate of return on their equity in the business. A 50 percent increase in the profit margin of company B, therefore, leads to a 57.1 percent increase in the return to the common stockholders. This is the leverage principle at work, as pictured in Figure 16–1.

The unfortunate part about leverage is that it also works when the profit margin declines. In a highly leveraged capital structure (one that employs a great deal of debt or fixed-payment preferred stock), the effect on earnings for the common stock will be great. With a given change of earnings up or down, the rate of return to the common stockholders will change more than the change in earnings. Just how damaging or beneficial a highly leveraged capital structure is depends not only on the amount of debt or preferred stock in the capital structure, but on the stability of earnings. Technically, a gas pipeline has a highly leveraged capital structure. Yet since its earnings are stable, the leverage has little effect on the earnings per share of the company. An industrial company that has 30 percent debt in its capital structure does not have excessive debt, although the company's earnings vary widely and the leverage effect brings about an accentuation of the variation of earnings per share. The leverage factor in the capital structure must be assessed in terms of stability or instability of revenues. Where revenues are stable and certain, as in the telephone or public utility industries, a large amount of debt can be carried and is beneficial to the stockholder. Where earnings fluctuate considerably, debt should be modest in relation to the capital structure, so that earnings fluctuation will not be reinforced to the detriment of the common stockholder. The investor should try to avoid situations where debt is excessive.

Debt Limits

The limits of debt that are imposed usually relate to the ability of the company to pay interest and the ability of the assets to repay the debt should the company default, as discussed in Chapter 4.

FIXED-ASSET LIMIT. The fixed-asset limit imposed on debt states that debt should bear some reasonable relationship to the assets of the company. It is usually suggested that long-term debt in the balance sheet of a railroad or public utility not exceed 50 percent of the fixed assets. Some analysts would limit debt to 40 percent for the railroads and 60 percent for public utilities as a group. The industrial company also follows the debt-to-fixed-asset limit; debt should not exceed 50 percent of fixed assets. In addition, a working capital limit is imposed which states that long-term debt should not exceed the working capital of the company.

INTEREST AND COVERAGE. The basic premise is that if a company has adequate income to pay the interest on the debt, it will be in a good financial position, interest will be secure, and failure is unlikely. The greater the number of times bond interest is covered by net income after taxes, the more secure the debt position of the company. The wider the margin of protection between income and interest, the safer the position of the bond issue. The common stockholder is in a better position too, since inability to pay the debt could result in the failure of the company. The number of times fixed charges are covered will vary from time to time because of the level of the interest rate. The suggested limit for total interest coverage in industrial companies is three times, and for public utilities and railroads two times. Thus, if the net income after taxes for industrials covers fixed charges (interest on debt) three times, this is adequate to protect the interest payment. The trend of interest coverage, as well as its future expected level, is also important in the analysis.

DEBT-TO-NET-WORTH RATIO. Debt to net worth is also used as a guide to whether a company's debt is excessive. *Net worth* includes all owners' equity. The word *debt* includes both long-term and short-term debt. This limit, usually imposed in the field of industrial financing, suggests that total debt should not exceed the net worth of the company. This is a realistic limit. It prevents lenders from supplying more long-term capital than the owners do. In a risk venture, the residual risk taken should be provided by the owners, not the creditors. Of course, situations exist where debt does exceed the net worth of the company. In cases like this, the debt must be justified by the peculiar circumstances surrounding the future growth and financial position of the company, or it would be wise to avoid the company.

CONVERTIBLE DEBT AND DEBT LIMITS. When convertible debt is used to raise capital for a company, two questions should be asked: Is debt excessive? What impact will the conversion of the debt have on the earnings of the common stockholders? The immediate impact of selling convertible bonds might be to increase earnings because of leverage and the profitability of the investment. After the bonds are issued, earnings might be diluted when the bonds are converted into common stock. Whether the debt is excessive under these circumstances can be judged by the ratios we have discussed. The result of conversion must be calculated, giving full effect to the change in level of corporate taxes as it might affect future earnings and the increase in common shares that will result.

RULE OF REASON AND DEBT. The investor must use reason in applying the debt limits that have been discussed. Under certain conditions, a company might seem to have excessive debt in its capital structure; yet when the financial position and growth prospects of the company are analyzed and understood, the debt may appear to be reasonable and an aid to growth. In fact, it might be a necessity for growth. Many public utilities are in this position. They are growing and need debt funds to finance their growth. However, even a small amount of debt, well below the limits suggested, might in some cases result in permanent damage to the long-range financial position of the company. In all matters of debt, the investor must use business and financial sense in deciding what is or is not excessive debt.

AN ANALYSIS OF THE CAPITAL STRUCTURE
OF THE DRUG COMPANIES

The capital structure of our three ethical drug companies is composed almost entirely of common stock and retained earnings. Except for SmithKline, long-term debt of these companies represents less than 3 percent of the capital structure. The bulk of the funds raised came from retained earnings. The industry has been conservatively financed, and little or no leverage existed; the earnings of the companies were not aided or disturbed, therefore, by large amounts of low-cost debt financing. The earnings of the industry should be relatively stable and vary only with variations in sales. Fluctuations should not be increased because of substantial financial leverage (Table 16–5).

TABLE 16–5

Long-Term Debt and Capital Structure Analysis of Lilly, Schering-Plough, and SmithKline, 1980 (In millions of dollars and percentage of total capital)

	Lilly		Schering-Plough		SmithKline	
Capital Structure						
Long-term debt	$ 33	2%	$ 41	3%	$ 121	11%
Preferred stock	—	—	—	—	—	—
Common equity	1,736	98	1,271	97	987	89
Total	$1,769	100%	$1,312	100%	$1,108	100%
Assets, interest and liabilities						
Gross plant	1,296		525		609	
Working capital	801		580		638	
Net worth	1,737		1,984		1,554	
Long-term debt	33		41		121	
Short-term debt	737		644		396	
Total debt	770		685		517	
Net income after taxes	342		239		308	
Debt interest charges	18		27		25	
Preferred dividend	—		3		—	
Common dividend	209		82		113	
Total charges	227		85		138	
Debt limits						
Times fixed charges earned	19.0		8.9		12.0	
Long-term debt to net worth	1.9		2.0		7.0	
Long-term debt to fixed assets	3.9		7.8		28.7	
Long-term debt to working capital	4.0		14.0		5.3	

SOURCE: *Moody's Industrial Manual,* vol. 2 (New York: Moody's Investor Service Inc., 1981), pp. 3804, 4209, 5460.

Fixed charges are more adequately covered for all companies and the debt-to-net-worth ratio is completely satisfactory. (Table 16–5). Debt to fixed assets and debt to working capital are not excessive in any of the companies, suggesting that their method of financing has been satisfactory. Some leverage exists in SmithKline, but not enough to cause alarm. The capital structure analysis of the three companies demonstrates a sound, conservative method of financing an industrial company. Based on the analysis, we could place each company in its relative position as in Table 16–7. The high rate earned on net worth (presented in Table 16–6) for SmithKline is aided by its use of debt.

TABLE 16–6

Rate of Return on Net Worth

Year	Lilly	Schering-Plough	SmithKline
1982E	19.0%	7.5%	19.0%
1981	19.0	6.5	18.5
1980	19.7	12.6	19.8
1979	21.0	13.8	21.6
1978	20.1	14.0	21.4
1977	18.1	13.2	13.5

SOURCE: *The Value Line Investment Survey,* November 20, 1981, pp. 1262, 1268. Copyright 1981 by Arnold Bernhard & Co., Inc. Reprinted by permission.

TABLE 16–7

Companies Ranked by Debt Limits

	Lilly	Schering-Plough	SmithKline
Times fixed charges earned	1	3	2
Long-term debt to net worth (lowest)	1	2	3
Long-term debt to fixed assets	1	3	2
Long-term debt to working capital	3	1	2
Rate earned on net worth	1	3	2
Overall capital position	1	3	2

Lilly and Schering-Plough are most conservatively financed, which would tend to reduce the risk of investment in these companies. Overall, Lilly would be first, in terms of the strength of capital structure, followed by SmithKline and Schering-Plough.

SUMMARY

As a matter of principle, investors should choose companies that are in superior financial condition, including current financial position and capital structure. There is more risk in the debt-laden company. The current financial position of the company is judged by the current ratio, the acid-test ratio, the composition of current assets, the number of days' sales outstanding (DSO), net sales to inventory, and net sales to working capital. The current ratio and acid-test ratio indicate the ability of the company to pay its current debts. The composition of current assets helps to determine whether the company possesses sufficient immediate liquidity to meet its debts. The number of days' sales outstanding indicates the effectiveness with which accounts receivable are collected. If the DSO compared with the credit period is high, the company is jeopardizing its liquidity. The net-sales-to-inventory ratio, as well as net sales to working capital, indicates liquidity and the ability of a company to finance sales growth with its funds. The basic concern in current analysis is to make certain the company can pay its bills and finance its sales growth easily and quickly.

No absolute standard will ensure success. Each company must be compared with the other companies in the industry and with its own position over time. Stability in these relationships is desirable, for a marked change in any ratio might indicate a weakness in the company that is a latent threat to future profits. Balance in the current financial position assures that earnings will not be reduced because of too little cash, which might result in failure, or too much cash, which will not contribute to maximum earnings. An adequate current financial position tends to reduce business risk.

The ability of a company to raise long-term funds often determines its future success. Expenditures for improvement in plant and equipment and for working capital also require adequate financing. How a corporation raises long-term capital has an impact on earnings. A large amount of debt or preferred stock in the capital structure tends to increase the per-share earnings of the common stockholder. However, it also tends to increase the instability of corporate earnings. This is particularly true in the case of industrial companies that have unstable operating conditions. As profits increase or decrease, the earnings per share on common stock fluctuate much more than the original change in profits. This phenomenon is referred to as *operating* or *financial leverage*. A company that has a large debt in the capital structure is said to have a high degree of financial leverage in its capital structure. Leverage has a greater impact on earnings per share if revenues of a company are unstable than if they are stable.

Debt in modest amounts is desirable. Excessive debt is to be avoided, as the long-range profitability of the company might be jeopardized. The tests of whether debt is excessive are (1) debt to fixed assets, (2) debt to net worth, (3) debt to working capital, and (4) an adequate coverage of interest charges and preferred dividends by net income after taxes.

SUMMARY OF PRINCIPLES

1. Investors should select companies for investment that are in a strong current financial position.
2. Investors should choose companies that have a strong capital structure; that is, ones in which both short-term and long-term debt are not excessive.
3. Some debt is desirable in the capital structure of a company, because the leverage that occurs increases earnings per share.

4. Companies with stable sales and higher profit margins can support a higher level of debt.

REVIEW QUESTIONS

1. What are the basic financial objectives of a company?
2. What is the significance of each of the following, and what does each indicate?
   a. Current ratio.
   b. Acid-test ratio.
   c. Percentage composition of current assets.
   d. Days' sales outstanding (DSO).
   e. Net sales to inventory.
   f. Inventory-turnover ratio.
   g. Net sales to net working capital.
3. What would a comparison of these ratios for a company reveal? What would a sharp change, either upward or downward, in each of the ratios reveal to the investor?
4. Can a company have too much cash or liquidity? Explain and indicate the significance of excess liquidity for earnings per share.
5. Review the analysis of the current position of the drug companies. Do you agree with the conclusions reached? Explain.
6. What impact might the source of funds for capital growth have on the common-stock earnings per share?
7. Explain what is meant by the term *capital structure*.
8. Does the use of preferred stock lead to leverage in the earnings on common stock?
9. What are the limits to the use of preferred stock in the capital structure?
10. a. Explain how the use of debt brings about financial leverage in the earnings on common stock.
    b. What are the advantages of leverage from the point of view of the common stockholder?
    c. What are the disadvantages of leverage?
11. Define and explain the significance of the following debt limits:
    a. Fixed asset.
    b. Earnings.
    c. Debt to net worth.
12. What effect would the conversion of convertible bonds have on leverage and future earnings on common stock?
13. What is meant by the *rule of reason* in debt analysis?
14. Review the analysis of the capital structure of the three drug companies. Do you agree with the results?
15. The percentage of debt in its capital structure has no impact on the valuation and earnings of a company. Comment.

PROBLEMS

1. Compute the following for each of the three companies you are analyzing, for the year 1975 and the present year:
   a. Current ratio.
   b. Acid-test ratio.
   c. Percentage composition of current assets in cash, receivables, inventory, other.
   d. Days' credit sales outstanding (DSO).
   e. Net sales to inventory.
   f. Net sales to working capital.

2. Are the companies in a good current financial position?

3. Which of the three companies appears to be in the best current financial position in each category of analysis?

4. If possible, compare the current financial position of each company with the industry's position.

5. Compute the percentage composition and dollar amount of the following items in the total capital structure for the three companies chosen for analysis, for 1975 and for the current year:
   a. Long-term debt.
   b. Preferred stock.
   c. Common stock.
   d. Capital surplus.
   e. Retained earnings.

6. Obtain the following figures in dollars for the three companies under analysis, for 1975 and the present year:
   a. Fixed assets.
   b. Working capital.
   c. Long-term debt.
   d. Short-term debt.
   e. Net worth.

7. Compute the following debt limits of the companies:
   a. Total debt to net worth.
   b. Long-term debt to fixed assets.
   c. Long-term debt to working capital.
   d. Times interest earned by income after taxes.
   e. Times preferred dividends and interest earned by income after taxes.

8. Is the debt of any company excessive? Explain.

9. Which company has the greatest leverage? Which has the most conservative capital structure? Explain.

10. If a company has convertible preferred stock or convertible bonds outstanding, indicate the effect on earnings of the common stock if the securities were converted.

11. a. Rank the companies in order of preference, as in Table 16–7.
    b. Based on the information above, which company would you select for investment?

CHAMBERS, R. J. "The Delusions of Replacement Cost Accounting." *Financial Analysts Journal*, July–August 1977, p. 48.

FALKENSTEIN, ANGELA and ROMAN L. WEIL, "Using Replacement Costs to Measure Income—Part I," *Financial Analysts Journal*, January–February 1977, p. 46.

———, and ———. "Using Replacement Costs to Measure Income—Part II," *Financial Analysts Journal*, March–April 1977, p. 48.

LASMAN, DANIEL A., and ROMAN L. WEIL. "Adjusting the Debt-Liquidity Ratio." *Financial Analysts Journal*, September–October 1978, p. 49.

PAGE, JOHN R., and PAUL HOOPER. "Financial Statements for Security Analysts." *Financial Analysts Journal*, September–October 1979, p. 50.

WOO, J. C. H., and S. B. SETH. "Replacement Costs and Historical Performance," *Financial Analysts Journal*, March–April 1978, p. 48.

CHAPTER 17

MANAGEMENT
AND
COMPANY ANALYSIS

It is not an easy task to determine the competence of a company's management, yet excellent management is paramount to investment success. An investment principle of the greatest importance is to seek out companies that have excellent management. Even though it may hold a substantial share of the market for its products, a corporation must still meet the competition of other companies. The investor's basic problem is to determine the quality of company management, and whether it is capable of maintaining the competitive position of the company and successfully running the company's affairs to produce a profit.

COMPANY OBJECTIVES AND MANAGEMENT FUNCTIONS

As one book on the subject of management states, "Management is a distinct process consisting of planning, organizing, actuating, and controlling, performed to determine and accomplish stated objectives by the use of human beings and other resources."[1] Although a primary objective of most companies is the maximization of the present value of the firm to the owners, this is not the only objective a company considers. Other objectives concern other groups of individuals both within and outside the corporate family. The employees and the public must be recognized, as well as the owners of the company.

Some of the more common objectives are (1) to provide good products and services,

[1] George R. Terry, *Principles of Management* (Homewood, Ill.: Irwin, 1972), p. 4.

(2) to remain ahead of competitive firms, (3) to provide for the needs and welfare of employees, (4) to maintain an orderly growth, (5) to be efficient in providing goods and services, (6) to assist society in the elimination of pollution of air and water, (7) to assist in the maintenance of our stock of public capital by protecting public property and keeping the roads and highways clean, and (8) assisting in the educational process by disseminating knowledge. At the same time, it is the basic objective of management to bring the stated objectives into a logical whole for the good of all people associated with the firm.[2]

The managers achieve their objectives through the careful performance of the fundamental management functions of planning, organizing, actuating, and controlling. If the overall objectives of the company are achieved, investors will have a profit. It might not be in the amount desired, but profit is only one of the goals of management and receives varying degrees of attention from it. Some companies are more profit-oriented than others. A management that ignores profits, however, might do more harm to the future of the company than one that overemphasizes them. If profits are not obtained, new capital will not flow to the enterprise, or capital will leave and the success of the company will end. It is imperative in the long run that the public, employees, and owners share in the fruits of their efforts.

The successful management will state as an objective the participation of each group in the success of the venture. Northern Illinois Gas is a good example of what a company can do to make its policies and objectives known to investors through its annual report. Northern Illinois's basic purpose "is to perpetuate [its] effort as an investor-owned, free enterprise company rendering a needed, satisfactory service and earning optimum, long-range profits."[3] The investors, customers, employees, and the public are considered individually, and a set of principles, purposes, and objectives is provided for each group. The statement made to investors is reproduced in part below:

INVESTORS

The Company will:

A. Strive to provide to its owners, the holders of its common stock, a growing per share value, measured in terms of both income and appreciation and to be the maximum, in the long run, consistent with the Company's responsibilities to its customers, employees and the public.

B. Seek to continue to hold the interest of its broad, diversified, well-balanced and stable family of shareholders, and to attract others who will maintain this balance.

C. Provide for its stock a ready, convenient and technically sound market to ensure optimum flexibility for its owners.

D. Keep present and potential investors in the Company and their representatives well informed about the Company and its prospects, in order that they may make their investment decisions with full knowledge and that the Company's securities will be appraised fairly.

E. Keep its books in accordance with accepted, conservative accounting principles and practices.

[2]Ibid., p. 43.

[3]Corliss D. Anderson, *Corporate Reporting for the Professional Investor* (Aubundale, Mass.: Corporate Information Committee of the Financial Analysts Federation, 1962), p. 18.

F.   Soundly employ, control and safeguard Company funds and property.

G.   Maintain a sound, conservative capital structure to support the quality of all its securities, assure its ability to attract new capital when needed, and provide good protection to the investors in its senior securities. Maintenance of a sound capital structure, coupled with strong earnings, should assure optimum preservation of the investments of both the shareholders and senior security holders.

H.   To develop strong earnings:
1.   Promote aggressively the sale of its product and of appliances and equipment utilizing its product.
2.   Maintain a close control over expenses, and constantly seek means to reduce them.
3.   Recover, as an operating expense, a realistic allowance for depreciation.
4.   Engage in and support research to improve the utilization of gas, develop new uses, provide a substitute when needed and find better ways to transport, store, deliver, measure, bill and collect for it.
5.   Provide capable, well-trained and enthusiastic managers, with adequate replacements ready when needed.
6.   Enter other phases of the energy business which have economic risks compatible with existing operations, which conform with the Company's Basic Purpose and supplement or complement its principal business.

I.   Pay to the holders of its common stock in dividends a reasonable proportion of the earnings. The dividend rate will be reviewed thoroughly at least once a year. Establishment of a rate that can be continued despite possible adverse economic, regulatory or other developments will be the goal.

J.   Promote private enterprise and endeavor to minimize municipal or other governmental ownership of business.[4]

Additional objectives and management principles are set forth for customers, employees, and the public.

THE QUALITIES OF GOOD MANAGEMENT

What is meant by the term *good management*? What qualities must a manager or the management of a company possess in order to be considered good, adequate, or excellent? There is no golden rule for determining management success, just as there is no trait or combination of traits in an individual that will ensure success. Koontz and O'Donnell suggest as special traits of management an ability to get along with people, leadership, analytical competence, industry, judgment, and ability to get things done.[5] Terry suggests that a successful manager possesses the following traits:

1. Intelligence
2. Initiative
3. Energy or drive
4. Emotional maturity
5. Persuasiveness
6. Communicative skill

[4]Anderson, *Corporate Reporting for the Professional Investor*, pp. 19–21.

[5]Harold Koontz and Cyril O'Donnell, *Principles of Management: An Analysis of Managerial Functions*, 5th ed. (New York: McGraw-Hill, 1972), p. 455.

7. Self-assurance
8. Perception
9. Creativity
10. Social participation[6]

Unfortunately, it is difficult to measure management by traits, and today greater emphasis is placed on an objective set of performance standards. A more promising approach is "the system of evaluating managerial performance against the setting and accomplishing of verified objectives."[7]

It is difficult enough to decide on just what traits lead to executive and company success. An even more imposing task is to learn if the executives of the company in which an investor is interested actually possess the desired traits and have accomplished their objectives. Many investors do not know who the president of their company is. Obtaining information about the officers and directors of a company, except for what is published in the annual report or available in public statements, is difficult. Such executives, and their abilities, are known to security analysts and other professionals. Therefore, most small investors depend upon the advice of professionals in making investment decisions and feel they do not need to know the management of the company, assuming in most cases that the management is good. Since greater proof of excellence of management is needed for analysis, the investor must investigate more thoroughly the qualities of management.

Determining Management's Ability

Two types of information are needed to understand the ability of management. First, something must be known about the men and women who manage. Who are they, and what is their background of experience and development? Second, some tests are needed to judge the management's ability and to determine how well management has done.

THE BACKGROUND OF MANAGEMENT. Some things can be learned about a manager from a sheet of vital statistics—the manager's age, educational background, advancement within the corporation, levels of responsibility achieved, and activities in social, cultural, civic, educational, philanthropic, and charitable organizations. Some of the personal data about management can be found in *Who's Who in Business*, *Who's Who in America*, or Dun's *Reference Book of Corporate Managements*. The information listed will be valuable clues to the person's intelligence and ability as a corporate executive. It will provide the investor with some idea of the manager's goals in society and sense of involvement, as well as how the manager has developed the needs of the corporation.

STRATEGIC PLANNING AND MANAGEMENT. Strategic planning "is the continuous process of making present entrepreneurial (*risk-taking*) *decisions* systematically and with the greatest knowledge of their futurity; organizing systematically the *efforts*

---

[6]Terry, *Principles of Management*, pp. 471–72.
[7]Koontz and O'Donnell, *Principles of Management*, p. 459.

needed to carry out these decisions; and measuring the results of these decisions against the expectations through organized, *systematic feedback*."[8]

Strategy is defined as "the objectives, purposes, or goals, and major policies and plans for achieving these goals, stated in such a way as to define what business the company is in or is to be in and the kind of company it is or is to be."[9]

Nine questions may be posed of any strategy, as follows:

1. Is the strategy identifiable and has it been made clear either in words or practice?
2. Does the strategy fully exploit environmental opportunity?
3. Is the strategy consistent with corporate competence and resources both present and projected?
4. Are the major provisions of the strategy and the program of major policies of which it is comprised internally consistent?
5. Is the chosen level of risk feasible in economic and personal terms?
6. Is the strategy appropriate to the personal values and aspirations of the key managers?
7. Is the strategy appropriate to the desired level of contribution to society?
8. Does the strategy constitute a clear stimulus to organizational effort and commitment?
9. Are there early indications of the responsiveness of markets and market segments to the strategy?[10]

An answer of "yes" to all these questions would be evidence of a strong company management.

THE RECORD OF MANAGEMENT. The facts about management and its abilities and qualities are in reality impressions, most of them based on individual and collective achievement. The comments in *Who's Who in Business* help to determine what the people have accomplished. A familiar statement, "We measure a person by deeds and not by years," seems to apply here. Investors want management to be intelligent, hardworking, socially oriented to groups, and interested in work, home, society, and religion. Investors also want it to achieve the objectives of the company by performing efficiently and effectively the functions of management—planning, organizing, actuating, and controlling. The investor hopes these objectives will be consistent with the objective of profits and will result in income and capital gain for the securities the investor owns.

What has the top management done during its tenure in office? Has it accomplished the goals of growth, diversification, profits, and benefits to society and employees alike? If management's record has been good, then the management has been good. If the record has been poor, then the conclusion must reflect this. There is no personal assessment here of moral aptitude; there is simply an assessment of management's ability to achieve its objectives.

The appraisal of the record of management covers many of the same topics already discussed. The competitive position of the company, capital expenditures, profits,

[8]Peter F. Drucker, *Management Tasks, Responsibilities, Practice* (New York: Harper & Row, 1973), p. 125.

[9]C. Roland Christensen, Kenneth R. Andrews, and Joseph L. Bawer, *Business Policy Text and Cases* (Homewood, Ill.: Irwin, 1973), p. 107.

[10]Ibid., pp. 114–17.

and financing are used as criteria to determine if management is capable. This might seem like circular reasoning, and to some extent it is. However, in modern-day business management, the officers of the company, acting as managers, make the decisions about what will be done as well as when, where, how, and why. They *are* in reality the company; to assess their activities is to assess the activities of the company. The record of accomplishment is used because it is difficult to find other information that will tell whether management is capable. Testing management might be possible for the personnel officer or the plant psychologist, but it is not suitable for the financial analyst or investor.

The appraisal of management over time assumes that the management has been stable and that the results can be tested. If management has not been stable and turnover has been high, it is impossible to judge "a" management. Instead, the management *system* imposed by the company is being tested.

ABILITY TO MAINTAIN THE COMPETITIVE POSITION OF THE COMPANY.   One of the first tests of the effectiveness of management is whether it has been able to maintain the competitive position of the company. If management can achieve a growth of sales superior to that of other companies in the industry, it can be concluded that it has done a good job.

A different criterion is imposed on the company whose stock is purchased not for growth but for its stability and regularity of yield. This type of company need not obtain a greater share of the market, as long as it maintains its relative position in the market. A railroad, for example, might be purchased because of income and yield. The railroad may not be increasing its sales every year, yet it may provide enough revenue to maintain adequate dividends and earnings. The management is meeting the objectives imposed and is considered to be successful.

ABILITY TO EXPAND.   A firm may expand from within, through expenditures for new plant and equipment, or externally, through the acquisition of other companies. Many firms have grown larger and have developed a stronger competitive base through merger—Textron, for example. Royal Little, former president of the company, led it to an impressive size; its current management continues its growth, both internally and through judiciously selected mergers. Whether profitable benefits are always achieved through mergers is a moot point. Merger or consolidation is one way in which an aggressive and capable management can direct the growth of a company. A more competitive management would use merger as an immediate step for improving its competitive position.

ABILITY TO MAINTAIN PROFIT MARGINS.   One important function of the financial and corporate management is to maintain cost levels and profit margins. In performing the selling function, management cannot and must not ignore costs. If a company can increase sales only by increasing costs and reducing profits, the management would not be very efficient. On the other hand, a management that increases sales and conserves costs without decreasing profit margins is doing a good job of controlling the company and maintaining profits.

The concept of earnings and profitability is relative to the company and the industry, including changes over time. If the profit margin for an entire industry is declining, one management cannot be condemned because it is unable to maintain its profit margins. However, if a company could reduce its operating expenses and costs and maintain or improve the profit margin at a time when profit margins were declining, this would demonstrate a real show of strength on the part of management.

There is another side to this story. The ability to reduce costs cannot always be considered an advantage. Suppose, for example, costs were reduced at the expense of new product development. This type of reduction in costs and expenses might reduce long-range profits far more than a temporary reduction in expenses would add to profits and earnings.

ABILITY TO MAINTAIN EFFICIENT PRODUCTION. Output per employee or operating efficiency as measured by the operating ratio can provide a basis for determining how well management has done in maintaining the company's productive efficiency. A management that is able to improve its output or sales per employee and maintain its operating efficiency is a good management. This is particularly important when the company is doing a better and more efficient job than its competitors. Another aspect of the question of efficiency is the ability of the company to operate at close to full capacity and to maintain its level of operations above the breakeven point. In the steel industry, Armco is a good illustration of a comapny that has typically operated at a rather high percentage of capacity and has done a somewhat better job in maintaining its level of operations than the industry as a whole.

ABILITY TO FINANCE THE COMPANY ADEQUATELY. Management must be able to finance the production and sales of its product. How it accomplishes the financing is a direct reflection on its ability. A company that maintains an adequate profit margin, retains a sufficient amount of profits within the enterprise, maintains adequate relations with commercial and investment bankers, and provides funds when needed can be considered a well-managed and well-financed company.

Companies differ as to their ability to provide adequate funds. The characteristics of each industry vary, so that a variation in the method of financing is to be expected. Companies with large profit margins are in a much better position to finance their operations; internally generated funds might satisfy the needs of such a company. A business that is not growing at a rapid rate has an easier job of financing than has a rapidly growing company. The important consideration is that the company's management provide funds when needed, regardless of the amount or timing of those funds.

The corporate management must maintain realistic dividend and capital-expenditure policies in relation to earnings. A dividend policy that requires an excessive payment of earnings can be harmful to a company, as can a policy of overexpansion. Conversely, a company that pays out little in dividends, spends little for plant expenditures, and builds up excessive liquid balances is not managing corporate funds adequately. Such a company is not as profitable as it could be, and management is not doing a good job.

Management must be able to finance the company's needs without resorting to excessive debt financing. One cause of corporate failure is inability to repay debt.

Debt has the unhappy faculty of coming due at the wrong time; many companies have gone into receivership because they were not able to pay their debt obligations. One airline company, for example, had borrowed heavily to finance the purchase of medium-range jets to improve service and stay ahead of the competition. The jets were not suitable for the company's operation, and revenues were not satisfactory. The debt burden was too great, and the company failed. A good management will have demonstrated over time an ability to manage debt successfully.

ABILITY TO WORK WITH EMPLOYEES AND UNIONS. The growth of unions and collective bargaining has forced management to recognize the employees—sometimes to the exclusion of other groups. Management must present the company's position strongly, so that the public, the owners, and management do not suffer as a result of benefits to labor. Therefore, good labor relations—a mark of good management—means that labor receives wages and fringe benefits in some relation to productivity and that a fair share of productivity goes to the owners, the management, and the public. A management that consistently gives in to labor demands that are not based upon increases in productivity is a weak management. A management that does not consider labor at all, or has poor working conditions and frequent strikes, is also inconsiderate of the overall objectives of the company and is doing a poor job. An inconsiderate management jeopardizes the long-range profitability of the company. A company that has good management will have good labor relations—that is, a relationship that is fair to the public, to the stockholder, and to the employees, in direct relation to each group's contribution to productivity.

ABILITY TO APPLY CONTEMPORARY MANAGEMENT METHODS. Managemement is much more complex than it was fifty years ago. Then, decisions were based on intuition, and little scientific methodology was used. Today's corporate manager has been trained through experience, through development programs, and through higher education to perform the task effectively and profitably. Computers aid in performing routine repetitive tasks, and office equipment is now being used to provide almost instant data to help management reach the best decision from among the alternatives. Cost controls have been and are being imposed by management, and time and motion studies are being undertaken to increase productivity while improving the compensation and working conditions of the worker. *Quality control* is a common term in industry, and more and more frequently the investor hears such words as *planning division*, *linear programming*, *organizational development*, and *psychological testing*. The truth of the matter is that a good management is using all the available tools of scientific management. These will, in the long run, provide generous benefits to all the groups within the corporate family.

ABILITY TO WORK WITH GOVERNMENT. Modern corporate management must be able to work with government officials in two important areas. One is in the complicated process of entering into contracts with the federal government to produce goods needed by civilian and military personnel. The second is in the area of antitrust suits brought by the Justice Department against illegal competitive practices.

Not all managements have the ability or the desire to negotiate and compete for government contracts. Many companies think that government business is unprofitable and do not care to engage in it. Others, hearing that several aerospace companies, for example, have been affected because of cutbacks in military appropriations, consider contracts with the government uncertain. The pitfalls of government contracts are many, and it takes an experienced management to understand this phase of business activity and operate within its environment. We as investors must determine, if the company is engaged in government business, what skills management has in this area.

The federal government has always been concerned with unfair competitive practices. The Justice Department attempts to carry out the letter if not the intent of the antimonopoly laws. The companies in which investors purchase stock must be large and stable, with growth possibilities, and the large corporations usually have a dominant position in the market. The leading companies might even collectively "control" the market for particular goods and services. This position can be profitable for the investors in these companies, but this monopolistic, or even oligopolistic, competition must be carried on without collusion, conspiracy, or fraud. Where there is restraint of trade and conspiracy, comparable to the situation in the electrical-equipment industry in the early 1960s the Justice Department has every right to bring the guilty party to terms so that the public will not suffer. It is the duty of management to maintain competitive conditions without collusion or conspiracy. A management that does not possess honor, integrity, and character is not worth the trust placed in it by the shareholders, and certainly such a company is no place for an investor's funds. A company involved in kickbacks to suppliers, bribes to foreign governments, or unlawful political contributions cannot be considered a place for the investor's dollars.

When management is accused wrongly by the federal government of unfair competitive practices, however, it should have the ability to pursue the charge until it has been cleared. Several important suits in recent years have been brought by the Justice Department against large corporations, where the department has found what it considers to be restraint of trade, or a material lessening of competition because of a merger. In these cases, management must use every fair, legal means available to repudiate the charge and defend its competitive practices. Thus, management is charged with the responsibility of not engaging in collusive activities and unfair competition, and the duty to protect the public, the employees, and the owners from unfair charges brought against them by the government. To the extent that it fulfills these obligations, it will be considered a good management.

Additional Tests of Management's Abilities

The quality of management can be judged by several additional yardsticks in the area of its activities. Does management, for example, engage in research and product development that will improve and ensure future profits? Is there a training program at all levels of management to keep and attract managerial talent? Does management take an active part in community projects, and does it foster and encourage questioning by the owners? These are yardsticks that are subject to wide variation in interpretation. They are intangibles, and yet an affirmative answer to each of these questions would suggest that management is capable and doing a good job.

RESEARCH AND PRODUCT DEVELOPMENT.   Many corporations are producing today, for mass consumption, products that did not exist ten years ago. We live in a day of invention and innovation. In order for a company to survive, it must constantly produce improved products to maintain its competitive position. A management that recognizes its responsibility to the shareowners will be in constant search of new and better products that will benefit and protect people and prove profitable for the company. The good management translates this responsibility into action by the expenditure of funds for product development and research. Without expenditures for new products, many firms will not exist in the future. A management that does spend efficiently for product development can be considered a good management.

EXECUTIVE DEVELOPMENT AND MANAGEMENT.   The management of a company has the obligation not only to manage well in the present, but to provide for the future. This means active recruitment of potential business executives from colleges, universities, and the school of experience. Most large corporations, with the cooperation of college placement bureaus, interview hundreds of likely management-trainee prospects each year to find men and women who will fill future positions of responsibility. Many companies have well-defined training programs designed to provide a wide range of experience for the newly hired person. Through exposure in several areas, the company hopes to develop the recruit so that he or she will eventually make a contribution to the company. The personnel department's task is to see that the training program is fruitful for the trainee and the company. Merrill Lynch, Pierce, Fenner & Smith, for example, has an excellent training program for aspiring sales executives and financial analysts. Each year, only a few out of the total number who apply for selection are taken. Those who succeed quickly learn many facets of the securities business. Industrial and utility companies such as AT&T, IBM, Procter & Gamble, Xerox, and Cleveland Electric Illuminating Company have excellent training programs.

Management must be concerned not only with younger executive trainees, but also with the development of middle and upper management. Many companies have their managers take part in executive-development programs. Harvard, Columbia, Stanford, the George Washington University, and many other schools of business in the United States have provided industry with programs designed to improve managers' abilities and capabilities to assume more important responsibilities in the corporation. Many corporations encourage their executives to take advantage of the educational opportunities within the community, both to broaden their vision and to enable them to do a specific task more easily. Some send their managers to three-month or one-year programs to freshen their perspective and exchange views with their contemporaries within and outside their own discipline in business.

All the programs mentioned lead to better-trained, better-informed, and more perceptive management. Some even provide the executive with a more liberal, socially oriented education. Bell Telephone, early in the 1950s, began a seminar program at the University of Pennsylvania. Aspen Institute in Colorado has been developed to broaden management's thinking ability and managerial leadership. These programs do not train managers to do a specific job, but help them understand the broad areas of their activities. The extent to which these programs prepare management to do a better job today, tomorrow, and in the future is beneficial for all groups within the corporation.

MANAGEMENT AND THE COMMUNITY. A good management accepts the responsibility of helping the community in which it lives. This help comes from the members of management as individuals as well as from the corporation. For example, the former chairman of Riggs Bank, Vincent C. Burke, contributes to local universities by chairing fund-raising committees. Marriott executives and the Marriott family have supported the fund-raising activities of the University of the District of Columbia. IBM has spent substantial sums for golf courses and recreation facilities that enhance the community of Endicott, N.Y.

Contrast this to companies that offer little in the way of assistance to community activities or growth. Some time ago, a report was published about a company that took no part in community activities. The stated company policy was complete *laissez faire*—let the community take care of its problems, we will take care of ours. The report discussed ways in which the company was cutting costs and improving its profit margin. We cannot help but think that the company might be profitable, but the management was not giving its full measure of time and effort to the broad social responsibilities it must share. This management could not be considered adequate in fulfilling its reasonable, long-range responsibility to society and the corporate owners.

LEARNING ABOUT MANAGEMENT'S ABILITY

Information about the qualities and abilities of management can be obtained from many sources, including published research in the *Financial Analysts Journal, Harvard Business Review*, Harvard cases, and research reports of brokerage houses. Several of the usual places where the investor can learn about management are listed below.

The Annual Report

The annual report usually presents information about the top executives—both the board of directors and the officers—of the corporation. The plans of management for the years to come are presented, and the events of the past year are examined. When significant management changes occur, they too are reported. In most annual reports, the officers' service to the company, education, and background are given.

The Financial Press

Often, information as to the excellence of management can be obtained from articles in the financial press and periodicals, such as *The Wall Street Journal, Barron's, Fortune, Business Week, US News & World Report*, and *Forbes. Fortune* magazine is a good source, even though it does glamorize the information. Each month it provides in its column "Businessmen in the News" a commentary on what the country's active businessmen are doing. *Forbes* presents excellent editorialized views of top management. *The Wall Street Journal* reports up-to-the-minute management changes, and *Business Week* frequently has feature articles about leading corporations, providing information useful for learning about management.

Analysts' Meetings and Public Comments

The caliber of management can often be inferred from public meetings with corporate executives. There is, of course, the possibility of bias against or for management. A dynamic corporate president might radiate optimism and well-being and leave the investor confident of success. Another executive, equally qualified, may not convey the same qualities of leadership, and a somewhat less flattering conclusion is drawn by the investor. Unless the analyst is somewhat knowledgeable about assessing the qualities of management, it might be better to judge not from a possible personal bias, but from performance.

Analysts' society meetings in recent years have served as a way for professional analysts to become acquainted with the qualities and abilities of management. Almost every day in New York City, and at least once a month in the major cities in the United States, the members of the analysts' societies meet to learn more about the companies they are recommending to clients. Usually, a report is given by members of the top management of a company and is followed by a question-and-answer period. Keen interest is shown in new products and services being developed and the anticipated level of earnings in the coming year. From meetings such as these and from personal contacts, the analyst becomes thoroughly informed over the years about the activities of companies and the quality of management. Only members and guests are admitted to these meetings, but investors can read the comments made by the officers who speak for the company. The talk is usually published and sent to other analysts and investors. *The Wall Street Transcript* presents major speeches of corporate executives and almost all speeches of the local chapter of the Financial Analysts Federation.

Personal Interviews

Personal interviews with management are of help in assessing its abilities. Direct and pertinent questions asked in good faith will usually be answered in the same way. Information that is confidential and might weaken the competitive position of the company will not, of course, be given.

Many companies follow a policy of providing information to analysts and investors. RCA, for example, involves itself in these activities with two fundamental objectives in mind:

> The first is to provide full, accurate and timely information to the investing public and their representatives in order to provide them with sound information and to minimize the chance of judgments formed on rumor or speculation.

> The second is to encourage the investment community to disseminate this information as broadly as possible among investors.[11]

[11]John A. Hearharg, "Corporate Management and the Analysts," *Financial Analysts Journal*, September–October 1967.

The success of the personal interview depends on the knowledge and skill of the person interviewing the officer of the company. If the interviewer has a good deal of background about the company before the meeting, a common ground is reached immediately. A wise course when planning an interview is to outline the questions that are to be asked; the time of the executive should not be wasted with questions that could be answered by reading the annual report. Emphasis should be placed on new developments.

Before visiting the company, the analyst should note the advice of one of the financial analysts' societies:

Do your homework. (This has become an overworked admonition in view of the improvement in the last decade. Many quality analysts do such a good job now that many of their remaining questions are the ones for which we all wish we knew the answer.)

Clearly identify yourself and your objectives to the company.

Keep the length of any interview within reasonable limits. (In an ideal situation, the amount of time management spends over a period of time with analysts would vary with the quality of the analysts' questions.)

Don't push for information the company is not prepared to make available to its share owners.

Have experience and maturity appropriate to the level of the management contact.[12]

When you get to talk with management, you might wish to focus on the organization of the management team and its planning role, which are vital to the success of the company.[13] Above all, be certain that "insider" information is not divulged to persons outside the company as a result of information obtained in the interview. Other things being equal, insider information is any data not readily available to all investors. The investor also might consider the following questions:

Can management make money when the economy has leveled off?

What does the analysis of trends reveal with respect to the quality of management?

Does the company use its own resources effectively?

Has the business a future?

Are the objectives clearly defined?

Is there sound planning to meet objectives?

Is the organization structure sound?

Does the company have vital leadership?

Is the chief executive timid or aggressive?

What are the qualities of those in top management positions, and how old is management?

Is there a sound executive-development program?

Does the company plan effectively for merger and growth?

Is management research-minded?

Does the company have modern systems of quality control?

Is management close to its market, to the public, and to its customers?

Does management have sound analytical controls?

Are facilities up to date?

[12] Ibid.

[13] William P. Hall, "Management Appraisal," *Financial Analysts Journal*, September–October 1967.

Does management do a good job with labor?

Finally, what do other managements think of the management?[14]

Many corporations have a planned program for visiting shareholders and investors, allowing each person to ask questions about the company and obtain valuable information in a short period of time. There are programs and supplementary data designed specifically for stockholders as well. General Mills holds mock regional shareholders' meetings to inform shareholders of the progress of the company. Other companies have had rather elaborate annual meetings where the shareholder was invited to attend and ask questions of management. Programs such as these allow the shareholder to meet management, as well as to obtain up-to-date information about the company. The investor will not be able scientifically to test management's ability at these gatherings, but impressions of excellence and ability can be obtained. All corporations hold annual meetings, but many do not encourage stockholders to attend.

In many corporations, the chief financial officer considers it a duty to keep the financial community informed about company developments. The financial vice-president holds meetings with analysts at the company's executive offices, and often he or she will visit the major financial centers and present the most recent developments of the company to the financial analysts and managers. Meetings of both types provide current information about a company and an opportunity for the financial community to judge the qualities of its top management. Special reports, in addition to annual reports, are also sent to financial analysts. In some companies, one person is responsible for public relations and deals with the financial community.

MANAGEMENT AND CHANGE

Secular Change

It has been said that companies fail because they do not have a product to sell or because the demand for the product has declined to a point where it can no longer be produced profitably. The idea is that management in such cases is capable, but factors external to the company and beyond management control bring about the failure. An example is the company that made wooden and metal propellers for aircraft. With the advent of the jet plane, the demand for propellers dropped sharply, presumably without warning, and the company was forced to close its doors. The village smithy, carriagemakers, and buggy-whip manufacturers could also be used as examples.

The examples, however, miss the whole point of the function of good management. Management must plan ahead and anticipate the change in demand for the product to assure the future of the company. Any reasonable manager of a buggy-whip company or propeller company should have been able to see new and competitive products being developed and to forecast a declining use for existing products. What should the manager do under these circumstances? New products should be found that can be manufactured with the facilities then owned by the company. Nothing would

[14]Harlow J. Heneman, "The Financial Analyst and Management," *Financial Analysts Journal*, September–October 1967.

prevent the companies in question from making new products for automobiles or for jet aircraft. W.T. Grant and Railway Express were companies that could not change to meet the changes in a competitive environment. The problems did not develop overnight; management did have time to change, but it seemed unable to change. Management has the responsibility, for the benefit of shareholders, of changing its product line to adjust to the economies and changes in demand of a given industry. If one product does not sell, then new products must be developed that will maintain the sales of the company. The tobacco industry is in a position today where product changes have been undertaken to ensure future profits. Good management and failure appear, therefore, to be inconsistent.

Many companies have failed because they did not change or were slow or unable to change. Officials of a watch company in the East did not wish to continue the development and improvement of their product; they were resting on the laurels of past product development. This conscious decision of management not to develop caused the company serious financial difficulty and eventual failure.

Cyclical Changes

The business cycle and its impact on corporate earnings cannot be ignored. Cyclical changes, another type of change with which management must cope, are not regular, but they may be periodic. The nature of most postwar recessions has been that of inventory adjustments. When inventory becomes excessive, production must slow down or stop until the inventory is brought in line with sales. The impact of this type of cyclical decline is not measured by change in gross national product or national income account figures, but by the Federal Reserve Board Index of Industrial Production. Usually, national income is maintained during the period of inventory liquidation, but industrial activity declines.

Management, in planning and controlling corporate activities, must be able to adjust easily to changes in business activity. Many industries are affected very little by the business cycle. Food, electricity, gas, and utilities are not cyclical, whereas autos, machinery, and building industries are. A good management operates satisfactorily during recessions and cyclical dips and manages its inventory in line with sales. If inventory is larger or smaller than needed and not managed adequately, then management is not doing a satisfactory job.

MANAGEMENT OF THE DRUG COMPANIES

Any study of the management of a company will be limited to the availability of information, and inferences must be made from the data. The drug industry is no exception. The comments below about the management of the three companies under analysis are not complete, but we can try to judge management from the things they do and say, and what the company has done in the past. Our comments are divided into two parts. The first part mentions the experience of the individual officers in each company; the second discusses the overall activities of the companies, which reflect the job management has done.

Management Background and Experience

The managements of Lilly, Schering-Plough, and SmithKline vary in background, but they have certain things in common. They have had a wide range of executive experience in and outside the company, they seem well educated, and they take part in fraternal, professional, cultural, benevolent, and social activities, in which they have held positions of leadership. The top officers of each company in 1981 were:

Lilly: Richard D. Wood, chairman of the board, president and chief executive officer

Schering-Plough: Richard J. Bennet, chairman of the board and chief executive officer; Robert P. Luciano, president and chief operating officer

SmithKline: Robert F. Dee, chairman of the board and chief executive officer; Henry Wendt, president and chief operating officer

A brief biography of each officer of these companies can be found in "Who's Who in America." In the last analysis, however, it is the performance of the company that will be the acid test of how well management has done.

Company Activities

LILLY. Eli Lilly & Co. is a leading producer of ethical drugs, and it also manufactures agricultural chemicals, which could eventually become the company's principal product line. In 1980, pharmaceuticals accounted for 46 percent of sales, agricultural chemicals for 20 percent, animal products for 14 percent, cosmetics for 10 percent, and industrial and miscellaneous products and packaging for 10 percent. Pharmaceutical and health, agricultural, and animal products contributed about 95 percent of net income, and cosmetics 5 percent. International operations accounted for 40 percent of sales and 26 percent of net income.

Major pharmaceutical products include Keflin, Mandel, Keflex, Nebcin, and several forms of penicillin. Other key pharmaceutical products are Darvon, Darvon combination analgesics, insulin, Nalfon, hormones, sedatives, and vitamins.

In agricultural chemicals, Treflan, a soybean-and-cotton herbicide, accounts for the bulk of sales. Other products in the areas of agricultural chemicals and animal health are Rumensin, a cattle feed additive, and Coban.

The Elizabeth Arden cosmetics line represents the primary thrust into consumer markets.

Overall, Lilly shows good product diversification and should continue to expand sales and earnings by over 10 percent per year, owing to its strong research and development program.

SCHERING-PLOUGH. Schering-Plough is a major producer of ethical pharmaceuticals and proprietary medicines (52 percent of 1980 sales), consumer products (40 percent), and other items (8 percent). International operations accounted for approximately 49 percent of 1980 sales.

The most important ethical drug is Garamycin antibiotic. Other pharmaceutical products include Valison, Fulvicin, Chlor-Trimeton, Coricidin, Di-Gel, St. Joseph aspirin, and Drixoril.

In consumer products, Maybelline is the leading seller in eye cosmetics. Other consumer products relating to cosmetics are Coppertone, QT, Solarcaine, and Sardo bath oil.

Other products included products which are led by the DAP line, which includes various home repair and improvement products. Finally, Schering-Plough operates six AM and six FM radio stations in the United States.

SMITHKLINE. SmithKline is a large producer of ethical and proprietary drugs (70 percent of 1980 sales), animal health products (8 percent of 1980 sales), instruments for industrial and medical applications (12 percent of 1980 sales), and opthalmic and optical-related products (10 percent of 1980 sales).

The most important ethical drugs produced by SmithKline include Tagamet and Combid, which are gastrointestinal compounds, Dexedrine and Dexanyl, which are amphetamines, and Ancef and Anspor, which are antibiotics. Proprietary drugs include Contac, Sine-Off, and Contac Nasal Mist. Animal health products include production of vaccines and veterinary pharmaceuticals.

Sales and earnings should continue to rise by over 15 percent due to a strong demand for the company's ethical drugs. Sales growth of 12 percent is expected as an aggressive acquisition program and marketing of new pharmaceuticals offset a declining market share for Garamycin.

Comparative Management Analysis

Table 17–1 provides a comparative rank of the managements of the three companies using objective criteria or attributes that have been developed in the last few chapters. The source of the information has not been identified by chapter, but is quite clear. Some of the rankings are close, particularly ability to maintain efficient production. All the companies have maintained satisfactory operating ratios, which indicate efficiency. The adequacy of government relations was difficult to discern. All the companies must deal directly with the government to introduce new products and are regulated by the FDA, so it is assumed that all have the ability to operate within the

TABLE 17–1

Comparative Rank of Company Management

	Company and Rank		
Management Attribute	Lilly	Schering-Plough	SmithKline
Ability to maintain competitive position	3	2	1
Ability to expand	3	2	1
Ability to maintain profit margin and earnings	1	2	3
Ability to maintain efficient production	3	2	1
Ability to finance growth	1	2	3
Ability to meet secular and cyclical change	2	2	
Expenditures on R&D (rank and % of sales)	1 (7.8%)	3 (5.7%)	2 (7.6%)
Overall capabilities	3	2	1

spectrum of the federal government's activities. It is also assumed that the companies have maintained good stockholder, employee, and community relations. Their past success suggests this. On an overall basis, SmithKline would be ranked first, and Schering-Plough would be ranked second, followed by Lilly.

SUMMARY

The basic function of management is to plan, organize, actuate, and control the activities of the corporation to meet the needs of the stockholders, the public, and the employees. Investors are interested in the profits that will come to them through good and capable management. To assess its qualities, they learn about management through information obtained in published sources, through the comments of others, and through interviews.

Management is judged by its past record, since few objective tests exist to tell if it is good. A management that has brought about increased sales at a profit, maintained a good financial position, and been able to raise long-term capital is a good one. In addition, a trained management that can change with secular and cyclical changes, that can maintain good community, employee, stockholder, and union relationships, and that can be flexible in its work with government can be considered a good management.

In the final analysis, a good management is one that can grow profitably, perpetuate excellence, and introduce new products to ensure continued and growing profitability. Management has the greatest impact on future earnings, which are at the center of the valuation and appraisal process.

SUMMARY OF PRINCIPLES

1. An investor should select a company that has excellent management.
2. Management can be judged on its record of accomplishment.
3. Management must be measured as successful if the company's competitive position has been maintained and it has been profitable, efficient, and adequately financed.
4. Successful management plans strategically, successfully solves its cyclical and secular problems, works compatibly with employees and government, and is responsive to societal problems.
5. The individual traits of a single manager do not ensure a company's success; rather. a strong management system leads to success.

REVIEW QUESTIONS

1. What are the basic objectives of a company's management? Is profit maximization its only objective? Discuss.
2. Explain why we should understand the stated objectives of a company with respect to employees, customers, the public, and investors.
3. What are the qualities of good management?

4. How do we go about determining the ability of management?
5. Explain what significance each of the following has in regard to a determination of management's ability:
   a. Competitive position of company.
   b. Ability of company to expand.
   c. Maintenance of profit margins.
   d. Maintenance of efficient production.
   e. Adequate financing.
   f. Harmonious and productive employee relations.
   g. Use of scientific management.
   h. Maintenance of harmonious government relations.
6. To what extent do research and product development indicate good management?
7. What do executive-development programs and community responsibility reflect about corporate management?
8. What can we learn about management's ability from annual reports and the financial press?
9. Explain the importance of meetings and public comments in assessing management's ability.
10. Explain how information might be obtained through personal interviews with the company treasurer and top management.
11. Management must demonstrate its ability to meet secular and cyclical change in demand for company products. Explain.
12. a. Review the analysis of management of the three drug companies in this chapter.
    b. Do you agree with the results?
    c. What information is missing? Explain.

PROBLEMS

1. What are the backgrounds of the chief executive officers of the three companies analyzed in past assignments? (For information, examine current issues of *Business Week*, *Forbes*, *Fortune*, and *The Wall Street Journal*.
2. How well has each company's management performed in the following areas?
   a. Ability to maintain profits and earnings.
   b. Sales expansion.
   c. Ability to finance the company adequately.
   d. Ability to apply scientific management techniques.
   e. Ability to develop new products.
3. What percentage of sales was spent on research and development in 1975 and in the present year?
4. What has been the ability of the company to build and maintain good community, employee, and owner relations?
5. Has management been able to meet the cyclical and secular trends of the industry? Explain.
6. After a thorough study of the companies, interview management about future prospects. What conclusions do you draw?

7. Which company has the best management? Explain.

8. Rank the companies on the basis of overall management ability.

SELECTED READINGS

FULLER, R. J., and R. W. METCALF. "How Analysts Use Management Forecasts." *Financial Analysts Journal*, March–April 1978.

HARRIS, D. GEORGE. "How National Cultures Shape Management Styles." *Management Review*, July 1982, p. 58.

OHMAE, KENICHI. "Foresighted Management Decision Making: See the Options Before Planning Strategy" *Management Review*, May 1982, p. 58.

PAULSON, ROBERT D. "The Chief Executive is Change Agent." *Management Review*, February 1982, p. 25

TREYNOR, JACK L. "The Financial Objective in the Widely Held Corporation." *Financial Analysts Journal*, March–April 1981.

WEIHRICH, HENRY. "How to Set Goals That Work for Your Company—and Improve the Bottom Line." *Management Review*, February 1982, p. 60.

CHAPTER 18

THE VALUATION
OF COMMON STOCK,
THE RETURN TO RISK RATIO,
AND THE INVESTMENT DECISION

The valuation of common stock is much more difficult than that of preferred stock and bonds, because far more uncertainty and instability surround common stock prices.

THE PROBLEM OF COMMON STOCK VALUATION

To determine the value of a common stock, three important variables must be dealt with that are not fixed. First, the amount of future earnings or when they will be earned is not known precisely. Second, the amount and timing of dividend income is uncertain. Third, the value that will be given to future earnings and dividends of the company by the investor is unknown and uncertain. Therefore, it is difficult to determine the future price. If all these variables were known—that is, with complete knowledge and certainty about future earnings, dividends, price, and risk associated with common stock investment—making a decision would be relatively easy. But since such certain knowledge is unavailable, an investment in common stock demands that future earnings, dividends, P/E ratio, and price be estimated. The risks involved must be determined and then weighed against the estimated return to determine whether the stock is overpriced, fairly priced, or underpriced; that is, whether the stock is over-valued, fairly valued, or undervalued.

In reaching a solution to the valuation problem, a "normal" level of risk for the company must be established, within an acceptable margin of error. Once the companies under consideration are ranked according to their risk characteristics, returns are estimated to determine whether they are commensurate with risks. Those projects that are extremely risky would require a high return. Conversely, if the risk were very small, a low return would be acceptable. The principle is to maximize return and minimize risk.

VARIOUS VALUATION MODELS AND THE VARIABLES

The value of any common stock is determined to be "fair" only by comparing the present price to future dividends and the price at some future time. The purpose of valuation is to determine whether the income and capital gains will provide a satisfactory return commensurate with the risk. If we know we can buy a common stock at $100 a share, sell it for $133 a share in three years, and also receive $3 per share in dividends, we have a way of determining if $100 is a fair price. We examine the risks involved and then assign the appropriate discount rate to compensate for risk. If we think the company is in the 10 percent risk category, we would consider the stock fairly priced if we could buy future dividends and price to return 10 percent. In this case, the present value of $133 at 10 percent is approximately $100, and the present value of $3 per year in dividends at 10 percent for three years is $7.46 (2.487, the present value of an annuity of $1 at 10 percent for three years, times 3). Hence, a fair price for the stock is $107.46 with a risk rate of 10 percent. At $100, the stock is underpriced or under-valued on a theoretical basis. In this case, the following valuation model was used:

$$V_0 = \frac{D_1}{(1 + k)^1} + \frac{D_2}{(1 + k)^2} + \frac{D_3 + P_3}{(1 + k)^3}$$

where D_1, D_2, and D_3 are dividends in years 1, 2, and 3; P_3 is the price in year 3; and k is the risk capitalization rate as determined by the judgment of the investor. In the example, D_1, D_2, and D_3 were $3, P_3 was $133, and k was 10 percent, or .10. The present value of the income stream was found in the present-value tables in the Appendix, A1.

All valuation models rely on some form of the basic capitalization or present-value equation. These were shown in the preceding chapters when yield on fixed-income securities was discussed. The equation above is a special form of the discount equation that uses estimates for the annual dividend, D_t; P_3, the estimated price in three years; and k, the estimated capitalization rate that reflects the risks involved with the investment as well as the reward expected. The general equation for this valuation can be written:

$$V_0 = \sum_{t=1}^{n} \frac{D_t}{(1 + k)^t} + \frac{P_n}{(1 + k)^n}$$

where n is the holding period in years; $n = 3$ is used throughout this chapter.

The focus of the valuation equation is on four variables—namely, future dividends, future price, time, and the capitalization rate. Price is some function of the expected growth and stability of company earnings, expressed as dollars per share. In addition, the price of shares in the market is a function of the expected growth of the national economy and the availability of money within the monetary system.

The price expected in the third year, P_3, can be estimated by using the equation $P_3 = E_3(P/E)_3$; where E_3 is the earnings per share expected in year 3, and $(P/E)_3$ is the price-earnings ratio expected in the third year. The P/E ratio is found by dividing current years earnings per share into the current price. $(P/E)_3$ is a function of the growth rate of earnings and dividends expected in all future years beyond the third year. It is appropriate to examine each of the variables common to all valuation equations and understand their influence on value and the part they play in the valuation process.

Expected Future Earnings

All methods of common stock valuation are based on or related to an estimate of expected future earnings. Although it may be impossible to forecast future earnings with precision, and despite the uncertainties involved, an estimate must be attempted by anyone who seeks to be successful in investment. This was done in Chapter 14, where we provided examples of how to estimate earnings.

The future expected growth rate is important in forecasting earnings for growth stocks and stocks of quality comparable to the Dow Jones Industrial Average. Special valuation techniques are necessary to evaluate growth shares, particularly where there is a strong possibility that growth rates might diminish in the future, as they tend to do. Will earnings grow at a constant rate, or will they grow cyclically? If no growth is anticipated, are earnings expected to be stable, or are they cyclical in character? Each pattern of earnings has its own effect on the valuation equation, not only in what E_3 or E_n will be, but in what dividend rate will be used, what capitalization rate and what price will be used in year 3 (or n), or what price-earnings multiple to use with earnings in year 3 (E_3) to arrive at P_3. Several other variations in the valuation model will consider the pattern-of-earnings effect in the application of the theories of valuation expressed in this chapter.

Expected Future Dividends

Future dividends, $D_1, D_2, \ldots, D_n$, are related to future expected earnings, the payout ratio, and the dividend policy established by management to provide maximum benefits to stockholders and the company. Most methods of valuation consider future dividends as partially or wholly the basis for the valuation of common stock. The dividends relate more closely to cash earnings (earnings per share plus noncash expenditures per share, such as depletion). Dividends also have patterns of growth of their own, independent of the growth rate of earnings. It cannot be assumed that dividends grow at the same rate as earnings, since management policy enters into the dividend decision far too much. Some companies, such as public utilities and railroads, do have a very stable payout ratio (the percentage of current earnings per share paid out). The growth industrial company does not. Company management should establish a dividend policy that attempts to maximize the present value of dividends to the owner; this might mean no dividends with large earnings, or large dividends with little earnings. The annual average growth rate of the dividends themselves is a good guide to the future growth rate.

Dividends are important in the valuation equation. They are also important in measuring the past profitability of an investment and the performance of a common stock.

The Capitalization Rate or Discount Rate

What rate (k) should be used to find the present value of the income stream? The appropriate rate will take into consideration the risks involved, which are influenced by the growth of earnings or dividends expected in the future, and the future expected price. In short, risk is a function of the variability of return. A higher discount rate will be employed where the risk is greater, and a lower one where risks are lower. A *minimum* capitalization rate would be equal to the yield on a higher-grade bond, assuming the risk is comparable.

Some years ago, Nicholas Molodovsky found the average return on common stocks since 1871, including dividends and price appreciation, to be slightly less than 8 percent.[1] This could be used as an average capitalization rate for all common stocks. In a subsequent ariticle, Molodovsky and others suggested 7 percent as an attainable rate usable as an average capitalization rate.[2] Fisher and Lorie found stocks returned 9 percent for the period 1926–60, giving another clue to what might be considered an average risk-capitalization rate for the valuation process.[3] Subsequent studies confirmed this 9 percent return.

The S&P 500 Index of stock prices, between 1972 and 1981, earned an average annual rate of return of 6.87 percent, a standard deviation of 13.18 percent.[4] Return was calculated by averaging the high and low price for the year, and then using the formula:

$$\frac{P_i - P_{i-1} + D_{i-1}}{P_{i-1}}$$

where P_i is the average annual price for year i; P_{i-1} is the average annual price for the base year; and D_{i-1} is the annual dividend rate in dollars. The average annual price is computed by using the equation $P_i = (H_i + L_i)/2$, where H_i represents the high and L_i the low price for the year. The annual returns were then averaged and the standard deviation calculated by the use of a computer program designed for the IBM 370.

For our purposes, we can assume that this rate is equal to a risk rate of capitalization (k). The standard deviation is calculated on the basis of ten average annual returns. It is appropriate to use market averages as a guide to the risk-capitalization rate, but k in the equation is a function of a determination of the risks involved in each company, and each company must be appraised separately around its own norm.

Does this then mean that the discount rate should be 6.87 percent? The answer is no, for two reasons. First, such a low discount rate would not compensate investors for the risk inherent in common stock, particularly when bonds yield 14 to 16 percent. Second, the discount rate reflects the future and not the past. Historic rates serve only

[1] Nicholas Molodovsky, "Stock Values and Stock Prices—Part I," *Financial Analysts Journal*, May–June 1960.

[2] Nicholas Molodovsky, Catherine May, and Sherman Chattiner, "Common Stock Valuation—Principles, Tables, and Application," *Financial Analysts Journal*, March–April 1965.

[3] Lawrence Fisher and James H. Lorie, "Rates of Return on Investments in Common Stocks," *Journal of Business*, January 1964.

[4] Frederick Amling and Associates, Washington, D.C.

as a guide to the capitalization rate, and one period alone is an insufficient guide to the future. Future expectation for the S&P 500 Index suggested that a capitalization rate of 16 to 18 percent was more appropriate. Such a rate would compensate for the risks of common stock and would be attractive compared to bond yields.

Price and P/E Ratio in the Valuation Equation

Price at any given moment in time is the sum of the present value of all future benefits in the form of dividends or future price, discounted at a present-value rate (k) that the investor is willing to accept in view of the risks involved. P_3 is thus the present value of all future income streams in years 4, 5, . . . n; or for a finite period. The present value of all future dividend income $(D_4, D_5, . . . , D_n)$ plus some future price, P_n, provides the value for P_3. The income stream beyond year 3 is discounted at a rate that reflects the risks involved in ownership of the stock.

An estimate of P_3 must be obtained. If the stock is to be held forever, it is unnecessary to find P_3. The present value of *all* future dividends is found using a capitalization rate, k, that fully compensates the investor for the associated risks. In short, all the investor receives is the dividend income. If, on the other hand, the stock is to be held for three years (or any other number of years), then P_3 as well as D_1, D_2, and D_3 must be estimated. This is realistic in view of the fact that the dividend income of the S&P 500 from 1972 to 1981 was 4.63 percent. Since the average return was 6.81 percent, 2.18 percent must be attributed to price appreciation.

In theory, P_3 can be estimated by considering it some function of $E_3 \times (P/E)_3$. Earnings in year 3 (E_3) can be calculated by using several different techniques, and $(P/E)_3$ is some function of the expected growth in earnings in years E_4 through E_n. A normal P/E ratio for the S&P 500 is 11.1, with an earnings growth rate of 10.85 percent and dividend growth rate of 9.20 percent. Therefore, if the S&P 500 were evaluated and P_3 were to be estimated, the historical data could be used. If earnings in year 0 were $14.80, then in year 3, at a 10.85 percent compounded rate, they would be 14.80×1.3621, where $1.3621 = (1.1085)^3$. The sum would be $20.16. P_3 then would be $20.16 \times 11 = 221.8$. If the growth rate is expected to increase, then E_3 would be increased, and perhaps $(P/E)_3$, also, if the increased earnings were expected to be permanent.

The principle to be followed is that the higher the expected growth rate of earnings, the higher the P/E ratio. This is why a common stock with an expected 20 percent growth rate of earnings will sell at a higher P/E multiple compared to the stock of a company that expects earnings to grow at 10 percent. There is a tendency for the marketplace to bid up the price of a stock so it sells at a price that reflects the appropriate risk-capitalization rate. For a growth stock, the reciprocal of the price-earnings ratio should not be used as the risk-capitalization rate. The only reason an investor would pay 20 times the current year's earnings for a share of stock is that earnings are expected to increase 20 percent a year in the future. The high P/E ratio relative to current earnings suggests a low risk. Yet the 15 to 20 percent growth rate indicates a high degree of risk. It would be wise to heed the risk inherent in the high growth rate of the earnings of a stock rather than the low risk suggested by a high P/E ratio.

Some Guidelines to the Use of the P/E Ratio

Some guidelines are necessary to establish the P/E ratio that will be used in the valuation equation. The P/E ratio used will be influenced by the following:

1. P/E ratios, for a group of companies, tend to change little from one period to the next. Therefore an investor cannot expect a dramatic change in future P/E ratios. The future level of the P/E ratio could be viewed as a function of the current P/E ratio or an average P/E ratio over some period of time.

2. The P/E ratio is a function of future expected earnings. The higher the growth rate of earnings expected, the higher the P/E ratio. An investor will be willing to pay a higher price for a dollar of current earnings if earnings are expected to grow at a much higher rate in the future.

3. Market P/E ratios of the DJIA have declined to the 11 level, but are relatively stable.

4. Inflationary expectations tend to reduce P/E ratios.

5. High interest rates tend to reduce P/E ratios.

6. It is difficult to determine a normal P/E for the market. A normal P/E ratio is established for each company, but it can be compared to the market P/E ratio to provide some idea of risk. The higher the P/E ratio relative to the market, the higher the risk. This is true in spite of the fact that investors are willing to pay more for a dollar of earnings of the company.

7. P/E ratios vary by industry.

8. An investor should examine the trend of P/E ratios over time for each company.

9. The level of P/E ratios is not an absolute value but a relative one. A relatively high P/E ratio in 1981 would be 15 compared to a market level of 11.

10. Speculative companies and cyclical companies have relatively low P/E ratios.

11. Growth companies tend to have higher P/E ratios.

12. Companies with a large portion of debt in the capital structure tend to have lower P/E ratios.

13. A company that pays a higher dividend tends to have a higher P/E ratio.

14. P/E ratios can change radically and suddenly because of a change in the expected growth rate of earnings. Therefore the greater the expected stability of the growth rate of earnings per share, the higher the P/E ratio.

The P/E Ratio as a Guide to Investment Decisions

How can the P/E ratio be used to aid in making an investment decision? First, obtain some idea of a reasonable price to pay for a stock by comparing the present P/E ratio to its past levels. What is a high and a low P/E ratio for the individual company can be estimated. Compare the P/E ratio of the company to that of the market to provide an estimate of the relative magnitude of the ratio. The average P/E ratio over ten years can be a guide to the proper ratio to use in the valuation equation. A high P/E ratio is 20 and above, an average P/E between 11 and 10, and a low P/E 5 or below.

Time and the Valuation Equation

The basic valuation equation under discussion uses a three-year future time. But why not one year, or two years, or five years, or forever? Some authorities do indeed suggest forever, by ignoring future price and simply focusing on the present value of all future dividends to be received over the next 80 to 100 years. A five-year model was used in previous editions of this book; but I have learned in the past few years that a five-year model looks too far into the future. A three-year model now appears to be more realistic, since it is long enough to eliminate market cycles and short enough to be predictable—or at least estimatable by the analyst.

The three-year forecast period is usually associated with growth stock. Cyclical stocks would have a completely different time horizon. In fact, with cyclical stocks, the holding period might be much less than three years. Since it is necessary to trade in cyclical stocks to maximize return, we must estimate the trading period carefully. An optimum holding period might be 12 or 18 months from trough to peak.

The stock would be purchased at the low of the market cycle, when earnings and prices were depressed, and then sold at the high and even perhaps sold short. Such trading activity increases risks, but if successful, it also increases returns, the reward of investment. The difficult task of trading in cyclical stocks is the selection of the time period for trading.

VALUATION MODEL FOR GROWTH STOCKS

The basic valuation model can be changed to reflect the conditions of a growth stock:

$$V_0 = \frac{D_0(1 + g_d)^1}{(1 + k)^1} + \frac{D_0(1 + g_d)^2}{(1 + k)^2} + \frac{D_0(1 + g_d)^3 + P^3}{(1 + k)^3}$$

where V_0 is the present value; D_0 is dividends in year 0; g_d is the annual growth rate of dividends; and P_3 is the price expected in year 3, which is some function of E_3 (earnings per share in year 3) times $(P/E)_3$ (price-earnings ratio in year 3 based on the growth of earnings in years 4, 5, 6, . . . , n). The equation for P_3 may be written $P_3 = E_0(1 + g_e)^3(P/E)_3$, where E_0 is the earnings per share in year 0; g_e is the expected growth rate of earnings per share, and $(P/E)_3$ is the price-earnings ratio expected in year 3. Then, the equation can be written:

$$V_0 = \sum_{t=1}^{3} \frac{D_0(1 + g_d)^t}{(1 + k)^t} + \frac{E_0(1 + g_e)^3(P/E)_3}{(1 + k)^3}$$

Assume, for example, that dividends are growing at the rate of 5 percent and earnings at the rate of 10 percent annually; the stock is selling at 11 times current year earnings, which is assumed to be a "fair" P/E ratio for a stock with an annual earnings-per-share growth of 10 percent. Assume further that D_0 is $1 and current year earnings are $3. Dividends in year 1 will be $1.05 ($1.00 × 1.05); in year 2, $1.10 [$1.00 × (1.05)²]; and in year 3, $1.16 [$1.00 × (1.05)³]. Price in year 3 is found by multiplying 10, which is the expected "fair" P/E ratio in year 3, by E_3, which will be $4. E_3 is found by multiplying earnings per share in year 0 (E_0) by the 10 percent growth rate for each of the next three years [$3.00 × (1.10)³]. Thus, the price in year 3 will be $44 (11 × $4). What then is the present value of the stock? The income stream expected is:

Year	Income ($)	Capital (P_3) ($)
1	$1.05	
2	$1.10	
3	$1.16	$44

The present value of this income at a 16 percent discount rate, or "fair" capitalization rate, is calculated thus:

$ 1.05	×	.862*	=	$ 0.905
1.10	×	.743	=	0.817
45.16	×	.641	=	28.948
				$30.670

*Appendix A1

Thus, if the assumptions of the "normative," "growth," "theoretical" model are correct, an investor would be willing to pay $30.67 for a share of stock. If it could be purchased at a lower price, it would be a bargain.

VALUATION MODEL FOR CYCLICAL STOCKS

Cyclical stocks do not have an ever-increasing stream of earnings and dividends. The earnings and dividends fluctuate with the industry cycle and the business cycle of the economy, and the price of the stock fluctuates with the variations in earnings. The valuation model must reflect these changes by a different relation to the variables in the equation.

Let's assume that a stock has a four-year business cycle from trough to peak to trough; that the stock pays a regular dividend; and that the investor is willing to trade in and out of the stock but, since the risks are great, must earn a 20 percent rate of return (k) rather than 10 percent. If the investor bought the stock at the low and sold it at the high, the equation would be:

$$V_0 = \frac{D_1}{(1 + k)} + \frac{D_2 + P_2}{(1 + k)^2}$$

where D_1 and D_2 are dividends, and P_2 is the expected price, including capital gains, at the top of the cycle. If D_1 and D_2 are $1, and P_2 is $80, then the present value of the stream of income at 20 percent is as follows:

Income	Capital	Total	20% PV	
$ 1.00		$ 1.00	.833	= $ 0.833
1.00	$80.00	81.00	.694	= 56.214
				$57.047
				= $57.05

Therefore, if the stock could be purchased at $57.05 or lower, it would provide the speculative investor with a return of 20 percent.

But what valuation model would be employed if the speculative investor wished to continue trading in shares, did not wish to sell short, and therefore was temporarily out of the market? Maybe the funds were used to purchase Treasury bills or placed in a savings account. The equation would be as follows:

$$V_0 = \frac{D_1}{(1+k)} + \frac{D_2 + CG_2}{(1+k)^2} + \frac{I_3}{(1+k)^3} + \frac{I_4}{(1+k)^4} + \frac{D_5}{(1+k)^5} + \frac{D_6 + P_6}{(1+k)^6}$$

where CG_2 is capital gains in year 2, I_3 and I_4 are interest income, and $D_1, \ldots, D_6$ are dividends. The equation covers a successful trade from the purchase of stock at the cyclical low, to a sale at the high and a move to a 5 percent savings account, then to a repurchase at the low, and a final sale at the peak in year 6. (Of course, transaction costs were ignored.) It is obvious that this is difficult to do in practice and that the cycle might be substantially shorter than six years. Let's see how this affects the income stream and present value of the previous example; but this time, it is assumed that the low price, the purchase and repurchase price, is $60.

Income		Capital Gains	Price
D	I		
$1.00			
1.00		$20.00 (CG)	
	$4.00		
	4.00		
1.00			
1.00			$80

Cash return and present value at 20 percent are as follows:

Cash Income	PV 20%		
$ 1.00	.833	=	$ 0.833
21.00	.694	=	14.574
4.00	.579	=	2.316
4.00	.482	=	1.928
1.00	.402	=	0.402
81.00	.335	=	27.135
			$47.188

Theoretically, the stock would provide a 20 percent yield if it could be purchased at $47.19. Since it was assumed that the stock was purchased and repurchased at $60, it would be considered an unattrative speculative investment—that is, unless the investor wished to lower k, the expected return. Note also that it would be unnecessary to purchase the stock at exactly $47.19 if the capital gain in year 2 and the final selling price were raised.

Obviously, the cyclical model is difficult to formulate even on a simple configuration, but it does point out the variables that must be considered. One additional point is that the longer the time period in the future, and the higher the discount rate, the more difficult it is to reach the investor's expected rate of return or discount rate (k). In the second cyclical model, substantial capital gains were obtained, but they were not great enough to provide a 20 percent return. The power of time and compounding is great, with high rates being difficult to achieve for long periods of time.

THE MOST IMPORTANT VALUATION EQUATIONS TO FIND EXPECTED RETURN

Investors are interested in the return they expect to receive from an investment as well as the risk. The valuation equation can be solved to find the expected returns, r, instead of solving for V_0. This is done by substituting P_0, the current price, for V_0 and then solving for r by trial and error until the present value or discount rate is found that equates the present value of the income stream to current price, P_0. The equation then becomes:

$$P_0 = \frac{D_0(1 + g_d)^1}{(1 + r)^1} + \frac{D_0(1 + g_d)^2}{(1 + r)^2} + \frac{D_0(1 + g_d)^3 + P_3}{(1 + r)^3}$$

or, as it is stated alternatively:

$$P_0 = \sum_{t=1}^{3} \frac{D_0(1 + g_d)^t}{(1 + r)^t} + \frac{E_0(1 + g_e)^3(P/E)_3}{(1 + r)^3}$$

where P_0 is the current price, E_0 is earnings per share in year 0, D_0 is dividends in year 0, and all are known; g_e, g_d, and $(P/E)_3$ are estimated. The equation is solved for r, the internal rate of return, or the discount rate, by trial and error.

An example of the first equation will demonstrate how a solution is reached. Suppose that a stock is selling at $100 in the marketplace and pays a dividend of $4. Dividends are expected to grow by 5 percent over the next three years, and the price expected in three years is $130. If an investor did purchase the stock at $100, what return could be expected? It is solved as follows:

Investment	$100.00
Income	
Year 1	$ 4.20
Year 2	4.41
Year 3	4.63
Year 3 (capital)	$130.00

Thus, a discount rate that equates the following income stream to $100, the current price, must be determined:

Year 1	=	$ 4.20
Year 2	=	4.41
Year 3	=	134.63

As a first approximation, it can be seen that $100 invested for three years that returns $134 is about a 10 percent investment. However, since dividends amount to 4 percent, the process might start with a discount rate of 14 percent, 10 + 4. The present value of $1 in the future at 14 percent is as follows:

Year 1	=	.877
Year 2	=	.769
Year 3	=	.675

Thus, the present value of the income stream at 14 percent is as follows:

Year 1	4.20	×	.877	=	$ 3.683
Year 2	4.41	×	.769	=	3.391
Year 3	134.63	×	.675	=	90.875
				=	$97.949

Since the present value is below $100, the first estimate of discount rate is too high. Therefore, a lower discount rate—say, 12 percent—is next used, as follows:

Year 1	$ 4.20	×	.893	=	$ 3.751
Year 2	4.41	×	.797	=	3.515
Year 3	134.63	×	.712	=	95.857
					$103.123

A 12 percent discount rate is too low. Now it is known that the return expected is between 12 and 14 percent. The exact return can be found by interpolation. The interval between the present-value rates of 12 and 14 percent is $103.123 − $97.949 = $5.174. Thus, to find the percentage, multiply:

$$\frac{\$103.123 - \$100}{\$5.174} \times 2\% = \frac{\$3.123}{\$5.174} \times 2\% = .604 \times .02 = .01208$$

or 1.208 percent, rounded to 1.21 percent. The 1.21 percent is then *added* to 12 percent, and the discount rate that is expected to be earned is 13.21 percent.

Thus, if the stock were purchased at $100 and sold at $130 three years in the future, a compounded rate of return, of 13.21 percent would be earned. Whether this is a satisfactory return is based on the investor's expectations and on the risk or variability of the investment return. Variability can be introduced by changing the expectations about the future and then once again calculating the expected return. If this were done several times, an average expected return of 12.8 percent might be found, plus or minus a standard deviation of 6.4 percent. This information establishes the level of the return and the level of risk.

The emphasis on the solution of the valuation equation for r is appropriate because the investor should focus on the returns and risk that are expected. The calculation of the r for the holding period for common stock then allows investors to compare the returns for each type of investment, including bonds and preferred stock. One question often asked about the use of valuation equations is this: "Where do I get the estimate of earnings growth rate, dividend growth rate, and the price-earnings ratio expected in year 3?"

Obviously, the answer to this question is not simple. Several approaches can be used to solve the equation. These will be identified as (1) trend, (2) trend-current, (3) ABE, and (4) random.

Trend

In every valuation model, the P_0, E_0, and D_0 are known. Estimates must be obtained for the unknowns g_e (expected earnings growth), g_d (dividend growth rate), and $(P/E)_3$. Using the TREND model, the investor reasons that the past trend of earnings growth, dividend growth, and P/E ratio will continue in the next three years. This model has been used successfully in the valuation of securities. The trend is based on the past ten years of experience, a period that is used to estimate the return for the next three-year holding period. The TREND analysis, as well as other methods, will be applied to the S&P 500 Index to demonstrate how they are used.

The S&P 500 Index was 125 at the end of 1981. In 1980, the index earned $14.79 per share and had $6.55 dividends per share. For the purposes of valuation, 125 is P_0, $14.79 is E_0, and $6.55 is D_0. For the ten-year period ending in 1980, the growth rate of earnings was 10.85 percent, the dividend growth rate was 9.2 percent, and the ten-year price-earnings ratio was 11. Therefore, $g_{e,10} = 10.85$ percent; $g_{d,10} = 9.20$ percent; and $(P/E)_{3,10} = 11$. Substituting these estimates into the valuation equation gives the following:

$$\$125 = \frac{\$6.55(1.092)}{(1+r)} + \frac{\$6.55(1.092)^2}{(1+r)^2} + \frac{\$6.55(1.092)^3}{(1+r)^3} + \frac{\$14.79(1.1085)^3 11}{(1+r)^3}$$

$$\$125 = \frac{\$7.15}{(1+r)} + \frac{\$7.81}{(1+r)^2} + \frac{\$8.53}{(1+r)^3} + \frac{\$221.60}{(1+r)^3}$$

$$\$125 = \frac{\$7.15}{(1+r)} + \frac{\$7.81}{(1+r)^2} + \frac{\$8.53 + \$221.60}{(1+r)^3}$$

$$\$125 = \frac{\$7.15}{(1+r)} + \frac{\$7.81}{(1+r)^2} + \frac{\$230.13}{(1+r)^3}$$

Then it is necessary to solve the equation for r by trial and error. After a series of tries, starting with an r of 24 percent that provided a present value of 131.44, then an r of 26 percent that provided a present value of 125.68, it was found that r, the return for the holding period, was about 26 percent.

The conclusion reached on the basis of this TREND valuation is that the investor would earn a return of 26 percent for the three-year holding period through the end of 1984. This would be compared with other investments to establish whether or not it was satisfactory for the investor. Actually, a return of 26 percent would be attractive and acceptable for most investors.

Trend-Current

The TREND-CURRENT equation uses the ten-year growth rate of earnings per share and dividends as the estimate for the future three-year holding period, but it uses the current P/E ratio for $(P/E)_3$. The S&P 500 Index will continue to be used in this equation. As it is used, the only change made in the equation is that the $(P/E)_3$ estimate is changed from 11 to 8, and the new valuation mode becomes:

$$\$125 = \frac{\$7.15}{(1+r)} + \frac{\$7.81}{(1+r)^2} + \frac{\$8.53}{(1+r)^3} + \frac{\$14.79(1.1085)^3 8}{(1+r)^3}$$

$$\$125 = \frac{\$7.15}{(1+r)} + \frac{\$7.81}{(1+r)^2} + \frac{\$8.53 + \$20.145 \times 8}{(1+r)^3}$$

$$\$125 = \frac{\$7.15}{(1+r)} + \frac{\$7.81}{(1+r)^2} + \frac{\$8.53 + \$161.16}{(1+r)^3}$$

$$\$125 = \frac{\$7.15}{(1+r)} + \frac{\$7.81}{(1+r)^2} + \frac{\$169.69}{(1+r)^3}$$

$$= \$126.82 \text{ at } 14\%$$

$$= \$123.78 \text{ at } 15\%$$

Again, in solving for r by trial and error, the r value is found to be between 14 and 15 percent. (It might be a good idea if the reader verified this calculation.)

The conclusion based on this set of estimates for the three-year future period is that the return is comparable to what the investor might earn with less risk on long-term bonds that were available in 1981. Based on these estimates, the investor would not rush into the market at the 125 level of the S&P 500 Index.

Analyst's Best Estimate (ABE)

ABE stands for analyst's best estimate. In this case, the estimates are based on what an informed analyst thinks will be earned in the future, what dividends will be paid, and what P/E multiple to assign in year 3 in the future.

The company analysis we have been engaged in for the past several chapters leads to the analyst's best estimate of what the growth rate of earnings and dividends is likely to be over the forecast period. The analyst also estimates the expected P/E ratio in the third year, which results in a price estimate. When the estimates from the analyst are put into the valuation equation, the expected annual return for the period is obtained.

In December 1981, one analyst expected the S&P 500 earnings to increase 10 percent annally from 1981 to 1984. That would mean that earnings per share would increase to $18.15 in 1982 from the estimated $16.50 per share in 1981. Earnings in 1983 and 1984 were estimated to be $19.97 and $21.96. And dividends would increase 9 percent per year over the forecast period. The 1981 dividend was $7.14. The analyst expected a P/E ratio of 11 in 1984. Based on these estimates, the equation is:

$$\$125 = \frac{\$6.55(1.09)}{(1 + r)} + \frac{\$6.55(1.09)^2}{(1 + r)^2} + \frac{\$6.55(1.09)^3}{(1 + r)^3} + \frac{\$16.50(1 + .12)^3 11}{(1 + r)^3}$$

$$\$125 = \frac{\$7.14}{(1 + r)} + \frac{\$7.78}{(1 + r)^2} + \frac{\$8.48}{(1 + r)^3} + \frac{\$23.18(11)}{(1 + r)^3}$$

$$\$125 = \frac{\$7.14}{(1 + r)} + \frac{\$7.78}{(1 + r)^2} + \frac{\$8.48 + \$255}{(1 + r)^3}$$

$$\$125 = \frac{\$7.14}{(1 + r)} + \frac{\$7.78}{(1 + r)^2} + \frac{\$263.48}{(1 + r)^3}$$

In solving the equation, again by trial and error, the return r is found to be 31.6 percent. Based on the analyst's best estimate, the S&P 500 at 125 would provide the investor 31.6 percent over the next three years. The 31.6 percent would be an excellent return over that period, given the risks involved and compared to long-term bonds.

The Random Valuation Model

The RANDOM valuation model begins with the premise that the next three years' growth of earnings, dividends, and price will be similar to those of the past ten years. This is similar to the TREND valuation equation for estimating r. In RANDOM, the ten-year growth rate of earnings and dividends is used, along with the ten-year P/E ratio. But instead of assuming that the ten-year rates will continue in the future, it is assumed that the rate is unknown but that it is likely to be within the value established by the ten-year mean value and the standard deviation around that mean value of the estimate. This applies to each variable that is to be substituted into the valuation equation to solve for r, the rate of return. Three variables must be estimated in the valuation equation to estimate r, the expected return. They are g_d, the expected dividend growth rate; g_e, the expected earnings growth rate, and P/E_3, the expected P/E ratio in the third year. In the previous valuation models we assumed that the rates for each variable were based on the trends of the past ten years or that the financial analyst could provide these values. Under RANDOM, we assume that we do not know what each rate will be. We assume that the value for each variable will be around the historic mean plus one standard deviation of the estimate.

As an example, the growth rate of earnings per share for the S&P 500 Index was 11 percent annually for the ten-year period 1972 to 1980. The standard deviation of this mean value was 12 percent. The dividend growth rate was 9.2 percent, with a standard deviation of 22 percent. The PE ratio averaged 11 with a standard deviation of 3.7 percent. This is depicted graphically as follows:

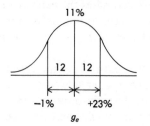

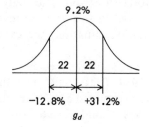

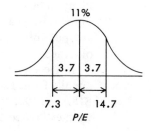

The assumption is made that these values are normally distributed around the mean, although this might not be the case.

RANDOM assumes that the future three years will yield growth rates within the limits and certainty assumed by the respective probability distributions. In applying RANDOM, it is understood that no one knows accurately what the future will bring, but it is assumed that the outcome will be within the specified statistical limits. The proxy for the unknown future is the random selection of each of the key variables in the valuation equation and the solution of the equation to find r, the rate of return. This process is done repeatedly, the results are averaged, and the standard deviation is calculated. The average r is the expected annual return for the next three years, and the standard deviation is the expected variation of return and represents risk.

Let us apply this to the S&P 500 Index. It is known that the past growth rates of earnings were 11 ± 12 percent; the past growth rates of dividends were 9.2 ± 22 percent; and the past P/E ratios were 11 ± 3.7. RANDOM is then found in the following way: An earnings growth rate is selected at random from the limits of -1 to $+23$ percent. Then a dividend rate is selected at random between -12.8 and 31.2 percent. Finally, a P/E ratio is selected at random between 7.3 and 14.7 percent. The equation is solved for $\tilde{r}$. A second set of variables is again selected at random within the limits of the data, and $\tilde{r}_2$ is calculated. This process continues until $\tilde{r}$ has been calculated 100 times, $\tilde{r}_{100}$. The resulting $\tilde{r}$ values are averaged and the standard deviation calculated. The average $\tilde{r}$ value becomes the estimate of the random return, and the standard deviation, the variability of random return, is the measure of risk. This process may be summarized as follows:

$\tilde{g}_e$	$\tilde{g}_d$	$\widetilde{P/E}$	$\tilde{r}$
$\tilde{g}_{e1}$	$\tilde{g}_{d1}$	$(\widetilde{P/E})_1$	$\tilde{r}_1$
$\tilde{g}_{e2}$	$\tilde{g}_{d2}$	$(\widetilde{P/E})_2$	$\tilde{r}_2$
$\cdot$	$\cdot$	$\cdot$	$\cdot$
$\cdot$	$\cdot$	$\cdot$	$\cdot$
$\cdot$	$\cdot$	$\cdot$	$\cdot$
$\tilde{g}_{e100}$	$\tilde{g}_{d100}$	$(\widetilde{P/E})_{100}$	$\tilde{r}_{100}$
			average $\tilde{r} \pm \tilde{\sigma}$

where $\tilde{g}_e$, $\tilde{g}_d$, and $\widetilde{P/E}$ are the first set of randomly selected variables, and $\tilde{g}_{e100}$, $\tilde{g}_{d100}$, and $(\widetilde{P/E})_{100}$ are the one-hundredth set of randomly selected variables. The 100 calculations of $\tilde{r}$ are then averaged and the variability of the $\tilde{r}$ values is calculated. The tilda indicates that the variables are randomly established.

The estimated average $\tilde{r}$ values from RANDOM do not differ substantially from TREND. The significant difference in the valuation methods is that RANDOM established the variability of return, which becomes an estimate of risk. In fact, this measure allows for the calculation of the return-to-risk ratio. The return-to-risk ratio is found by subtracting the risk-free rate of return from the estimated return divided by the standard deviation of the return. This is written $\tilde{r}_\mu - r_f \div \tilde{\sigma}_r$, where $\tilde{r}_\mu$ is the mean of the $\tilde{r}$ values, rf is the risk-free yield, and $\tilde{\sigma}_r$ is the standard deviation of the mean of the $\tilde{r}$ values. The return-to-risk ratio indicates the level of return to risk, which helps the investor establish the relative riskiness of an investment. A return-to-risk ratio of 1.0 or higher is acceptable; those less than 1.0 are unacceptable.

With a knowledge of the expected return $(\tilde{r}_\mu)$ and the estimate of the standard deviation $(\tilde{\sigma}_r)$ and the return-to-risk ratio $(\tilde{R}/\tilde{R})$, the investor has two excellent measures of investment attractiveness—return and risk.

Obviously, solving the valuation equation 100 times is time-consuming, and the process will not be replicated here. A computer program, Modesystem, has been written that provides these calculations, and it will be discussed shortly. The $\tilde{r}$ value from the computer output was 28.05 percent, with a standard deviation of 16.4. Thus, the expected return $(\tilde{r}_\mu)$ for the next three years using RANDOM was 28.05 percent, which suggests that the S&P 500 offered the investor an excellent return compared to historic standards. However, the return-to-risk ratio (.87) was a bit low, suggesting that there was slightly more risk for each unit of return. The return-to-risk ratio was $(28.05 - 12.0) \div 18.42 = .87$. But this was at an S&P 500 price of 122.5.

The use of the RANDOM model doesn't change the investment conclusion. The S&P 500 Index at 122.5 offers a fair return, but the risk and risk-free returns are relatively high, which would cause an investor to be cautious. The same conclusion was reached in the results of the other valuation models.

ADDITIONAL VALUATION MODELS

In addition to the variations on the present-value model, several other methods of valuation can be employed to estimate common stock value.

Capitalization of Earnings Method

The capitalization-of-earnings method focuses on estimating future earnings and the risk-capitalization rate. The formula is $V = E_a/k$, where V is the present value of the stock, E_a represents future anticipated earnings per share, and k is the risk-capitalization rate. If earnings are $1 per share and are expected to grow at 10 percent per year in the future, the earnings per share would be $2.59 in 10 years and $4.18 in 15 years (from compound interest tables in the Appendix). The annual average earnings per share for the 15-year period would be $(\$1.00 + \$4.18) \div 2 = \$2.59$. In this case, 15 years represents "all future earnings," and the average future earnings figure is found by adding the earnings at the end of the period to those at the beginning of the period and dividing by 2.

How shall the capitalization rate be established? Current evidence suggests that an 18 percent rate be used for all stocks. But a constant rate for all stocks would not be realistic, since the risks involved differ. A stock with great risk should have a much higher capitalization rate than a stock with low risk.

If this method were applied to the S&P 500 Index in December 1981, the following would be the result: Earnings of the S&P 500 in 1980 were $14.79, and the historic growth rate (10 years) was 11.0 percent. Therefore, in 15 years the earnings would be $14.79 \times 4.785 = \$70.77$. The average earnings would be $(\$14.79 + \$70.77) \div 2$

= \$42.78. Using a capitalization rate of 18 percent, the value would be \$42.78 ÷ .18 = \$237.67. Therefore, with the S&P 500 Index at 122.5 in 1981, had a capitalized value of \$237.67, and the index was underpriced.

Dividend Growth—The Gordon Model

The cost of equity capital is an integral part of corporate finance. In estimating the cost of equity capital, the equation $k_e = D_0/P_0 + g_d$ is used, where k_e is the discount rate or expected rate from common stock; D_0 is the current dollar amount of dividends; P_0 is the current price; and g_d is the growth rate of dividends, which is some function of the amount of reinvestment of dividends (b) times the rate of return to be earned on those dividends (r)[5].

Assume for the S&P 500 Index that dividends are going to grow at 9.2 percent and that the current dividend is \$6.55 and the current price is \$122.50. Then, $k_e = \$6.55/\$122.50 + 9.2 = 5.35 + 9.2 = 14.55$ percent. The investment in the S&P 500 at 122.5 provides an expected return of 14.55 percent. If the investor considers it satisfactory compensation for risk, then the return is acceptable.

The validity of the valuation model $k_e = D_0/P_0 + g_d$ depends on the company's ability to maintain a constant growth rate forever in the future, and on the prospect that the current dividends and price reflect the future accurately. It is clear that in a growth model such as this, the future rate of growth of dividends is much more important than the current yield. In fact, what is being expressed is a statement that in a growth situation, k_e is equal to the internal rate of return earned on reinvested earnings. A growth company would therefore reinvest all its earnings, and g_d would be equal to the internal rate of return. A modest growth stock would pay some dividends, and k_e would be equal to a combination of growth of dividends and the current dividend rate. This model has not been as successful with valuation for all types of common stock as has the present-value model demonstrated earlier.

THE PSYCHOLOGICAL ASPECTS OF VALUATION

A number of people say that the value of a stock is determined by the supply and demand for it and the psychological aspects related to it. Some investors think that demand and supply in the short run are the only considerations. Demand might or might not be an accurate reflection of value that considers only earnings. Institutional investors play an important part in this process, since institutions account for more than 70 percent of market activity. They must invest their funds in bonds or stocks, and since only a limited number of high-quality stocks are available for investment, these are bid up higher than normal. Demand exceeds supply, and the price goes up. In short, a stock moves up in price when the psychology of the market toward the stock is favorable. Historically, institutional investors were more cautious on the down side of the market and more often invested in fixed-income obligations than in stocks. In

[5]See M. J. Gordon and E. Shapiro, "Capital Equipment Analysis: The Required Rate of Profit," *Management Science*, III (October 1956), 104–6.

such a situation, when the psychology of the market suggests "Don't buy," demand subsides and prices fall, since relative supply is greater than demand.

These psychological aspects of supply and demand help to explain short-range cyclical market effects. From time to time, too much or too little demand in relation to supply causes excessive price fluctuations. An example of this is Texas Instruments common, which was bid up to an inordinately high price, approximately 151, in the early 1980s and then dropped back to the 70–80 price range. Countless other examples could be given: Litton's price was bid up to 92 in 1981 and subsequently fell to 36.

There is a limit to what can realistically be paid for common stock. An excessive price created by an artificial demand-supply relationship can lead only to excessive loss by the investor. Demand should be based on a realistic price for realistic earnings, dividends, and future price—not on extremely optimistic views of the future and a pie-in-the-sky philosophy. The value of a stock should be determined by future income and capital stream capitalized at a reasonable rate; that is, by the fundamental earnings and dividends position of and the risks inherent in the company.

Two principles are expressed in these comments: One is, *don't be the last optimistic buyer*. This means simply that an investor should not choose the favorites by paying a high price for the shares. An investor's eagerness to buy reminds me of the old adage —sin in haste and repent at leisure. The second principle relates to the *Ricardian rent theory*, which tells us that the price of a superior piece of land will be bid up to the point where only normal returns will be earned. Remember, a superior growth stock will be bid up in price to the point where only normal returns will be earned and not the returns indicated by the rate of growth of earnings or the rate of return on a company's equity.

VALUATION AND THE COMPUTER

The profession of investment analysis in the United States has been moving toward new frontiers in the use of the computer. In the future, there will be greater emphasis on the large computer throughout the entire investment process—in both analysis and management. The computer is obviously needed to assimilate the large quantity of data required for assessing changes in the prices and earnings of thousands of common stocks, in relation to their short- and long-range investment positions. With the computer, analysts can select from among seemingly attractive investment opportunities and put together the combination of securities offering maximization of reward. The valuation formula:

$$P_0 = \frac{D_0(1 + g_d)^1}{(1 + r)^1} + \frac{D_0(1 + g_d)^2}{(1 + r)^2} + \frac{D_0(1 + g_d)^3 + E_0(1 + g_e)^3(P/E)_3}{(1 + r)^3}$$

is well adapted to the computer if the investor is willing to accept the calculation of returns based on historical data. Certainly, projections that provide estimates of expected future earnings, expected future dividends, P/E multiples, and yields to maturity, and also provide clues to the earnings capitalization-rate multiplier, are helpful in the decision-making process and take much of the work out of valuation. Such projections are comparable with the ideas of valuation discussed by other financial and academic writers, like Bauman, Clendennin, Ferguson, Hayes, Malkiel, Molodovsky, Walter, and Wendt.[6]

If data can be provided quickly and accurately with a minimum of maintenance and updating, the investor, analyst, or portfolio manager has another valuable tool for analysis. The computer program presented here is applied to the valuation equation above.

The Computer Program

Figure 18–1 is MODE 1 for American Hospital Supply from a computerized investment system. The entire integrated system of investment analysis and portfolio

A AMERICAN HOSP.SPL.			B CUSIP = 26681		J
C YEAR	D HIGH	E LOW	F EPS	G DIV	PE STATISTICS
71	40.60	30.60	0.85	0.26	MEAN VALUES
72	55.40	37.90	0.99	0.27	10YR AVG: 23.83
73	52.80	36.40	1.13	0.28	STD: 13.98
74	41.40	18.80	1.28	0.30	MAX: 47.88
75	38.50	25.90	1.52	0.31	MIN: 9.90
76	37.80	28.13	1.78	0.39	YRLY FLACTUAT
77	31.00	22.00	2.09	0.52	10YR AVG: 9.58
78	32.75	22.63	2.47	0.65	STD: 5.46
79	35.75	23.63	2.91	0.77	MAX: 17.68
80	50.75	26.88	3.01	0.89	MIN: 4.10

RECENT PRICE: 34.75 H   CURRENT PE : 11.54 I

O PAST PERFORMANCE		Q GROWTH RATES		S ESTIMATED PERFORM	
DIV RETURN		DIV GRTH RATE		YLD TO MATURITY	
10YR AVG:	1.45	10YR AVG:	16.01	10/10:	53.12
STD:	0.82	STD:	10.66		
ANNUAL YLD				3YR SIML:	50.81
10YR AVG:	3.86	R EARN GRTH RATES		STD-RISK:	34.48
STD:	21.33	10YR AVG:	15.98	T	
BETA :	1.15	STD:	4.56	RWRD/RISK:	1.12
STD ERROR :	0.13	5YR AVG:	15.55		
ALPHA :	-0.04	STD:	5.74		
M PRICE STBL:	71.18	3YR AVG:	13.41	K EARN-81:	3.73
N EARNG STBL:	96.99	STD:	6.87	L DIVD-81:	0.95

P CURRENT DIVID RETURN: 2.56

FIGURE 18–1

Modesystem-Mode 1

SOURCE: Frederick Amling & Associates, Washington, D.C.

[6]John C. Clendennin, "Theory and Technique of Growth Stock Valuation," Occasional Paper No. 1, Bureau of Business and Economic Research, UCLA, 1957; W. Scott Bauman, "Estimating the Present Value of Common Stock by the Variable Rate Method," Michigan Business Reports No. 42, Bureau of Business Research, University of Michigan, 1963; Robert Ferguson, "A Monograph for Valuing Growth Stocks," *Financial Analysts Journal*, May–June 1961, pp. 29–34; Douglas A. Hayes, CFA, "Some Reflections on Techniques for Appraising Growth Rates," *Financial Analysts Journal*, July–August 1964; B. G. Malkiel, "Equity Yields and Structure Share Prices," *American Economic Review*, December 1963, pp. 1004–31; Molodovsky, May, and Chattiner, "Common Stock Valuation"; and James E. Walter, "Dividend Policy and Common Stock Prices," *The Journal of Finance*, March 1956, pp. 29–42.

management is called Modesystem. Figure 18–1 represents the output from MODE 1, which provides ten years of historical data, statistical analysis of key variables, and expected performance based on estimated return, using the most successful of the valuation models discussed previously.

Items marked A through H represent factual data that are supplied by the analyst. They are part of the computer data base, and become part of the output of MODE 1. Item A is the name of the company, and B is the cusip number that identifies the industry and subindustry classification of the company. Item C gives each year of the ten years of data, D is the high price and E the low price for each year, F is the reported earnings per share for each year, and G is the annual dividends per share for each of the ten years. Item H is the market price per share and I is the current P/E ratio. It is found by dividing 1980 EPS into the current price. The price in H is P_0 in the valuation equation.

The P/E computation from the data is recorded under item J. The first item under MEAN VALUES is the ten-year average P/E ratio. Following down the column are the standard deviation of the mean average P/E ratio (STD:); the maximum P/E ratio for the ten-year period (MAX:); and the minimum P/E ratio for the period (MIN:). The P/E information is particularly helpful for the analyst when an attempt is made to estimate what P/E ratio is to be used in the valuation equations under TREND, TREND-CURRENT, ABE, as well as RANDOM.

The second major category of information under P/E computations concerns the fluctuations of the P/E ratio. The ten-year average of the yearly fluctuations (10 YR AVG:) indicates the average fluctuation around the yearly high and low P/E ratio; then, the standard deviation (STD:), and the maximum, (MAX:) and minimum, (MIN:) deviation are provided. This information is very helpful in estimating the risk and stability of a stock. Essentially, the higher the fluctuations in the P/E ratio, the higher the risk.

It is helpful to know the P/E ratio related to historical trend and averages. If the current P/E ratio is below the historical average it would be considered favorable, assuming there are no changes in fundamentals. Other things equal, the lower the P/E ratio, the higher the risk. Stocks that historically sell at low P/E ratios are considered riskier than stocks selling at higher P/E ratios.

Item K is the best estimate of the expected earnings per share in the next year beyond the historical data reported in items D through H. This estimate can be based on the analyst's expectation of earnings per share in the year ahead, or on the consensus or market estimates as obtained from expert analysts and as reported in Standard & Poor's *Earnings Forecaster*, or I.B.E.S.[7]

Item L is an estimate of the dividends per share expected in the forecasted year, the year beyond the data represented in items D through H.

Price stability is given in item M. Generally, the closer the number is to 100, the more stable the price. The lower the price stability, the higher the risk of the stock. Price stability is a measure of market risk. The earnings stability in item N is also an indication of the risk inherent in a stock. Earnings stability is a measure of the business risk. The higher the earnings stability, the lower the risk involved with the stock.

[7]I.B.E.S., Institutional Brokers Estimate System, 1981, Lynch Jones and Ryan.

The performance of the dividend yield (DIV RETURN), and of the total annual return (ANNUAL YLD) of the stock, and the relationship of the individual stock to the market index, are provided in O. Under the dividend return is the ten-year average dividend rate (10 YR AVG) and the standard deviation of the dividend yield (STD). The annual dividend yield is found by dividing the average of the high and the low prices into the yearly dividend. This is calculated for each year, and the average and standard deviation are calculated. The average dividend yield and the standard deviation or variability give some indication of the riskiness of the investment and its suitability for income.

The current dividend rate, P, is found by dividing price, item H, into 1980 dividends, item G. It represents dividends earned in the current year.

Under ANNUAL YLD in item O, PAST PERFORMANCE, is found the percentage of average annual total return and the standard deviation of the annual total return. This represents the average annual return an investor would have earned if the stock had been held for the past ten years. The annual capital gain (or loss) plus dividend income represents the return, and into this was divided the average of the high and low prices.

The formula used for each year is as follows:

$$\frac{\dfrac{P_{1H} + P_{1L}}{2} - \dfrac{P_{0H} + P_{0L}}{2} + D_1}{\dfrac{P_{0H} + P_{0L}}{2}}$$

where P_{1H} is the high price for year 1, and P_{1L} is the low price; P_{0H} is the high price in year 0 and P_{0L} is the low price; and D_1 is the dividend per share in year 1.

This was done for each year. The average of the return for ten years was calculated and the standard deviation determined. The return and risk, thus calculated, become a measure of historical return and risk that helps the investor in the decision-making process.

It is important to know how the return of the individual stock compares to the return of the S&P 500. The beta, standard error of the estimate, and alpha, listed O in the column, are the variables involved in the regression of the annual return of a stock for a ten-year period against the annual return of the market index (S&P 500) for the same period of time. The basic regression equation is $Y = \alpha + \beta x + \epsilon$. The ϵ is the random error of the estimate. The β in the equation is the beta coefficient and is the slope of the regression line. The higher the β or beta, the more risky the stock relative to the market, and vice versa. Beta represents the systematic risk relative to the market. A beta of 1 indicates that the stock has the same risk as the market.

The alpha, α, represents the Y intercept and is referred to as the unsystematic risk along with ϵ, the unexplained error with a mean value of zero. The alpha and the epsilon represent the unsystematic risk of the market.

The standard error of the estimate represents the closeness of the fit around the regression line. A low standard error, STD ERROR, indicates a close relationship between the return of the stock and the return of the market. A stock that was identical to the market for a ten-year period would have a beta of 1.00, a standard error of the estimate of zero, and an alpha of zero. The combination of statistical measures helps the investor understand the characteristics of the return of the stock relative to the return of the market. This knowledge is very helpful in making investment decisions (see Figure 18–2).

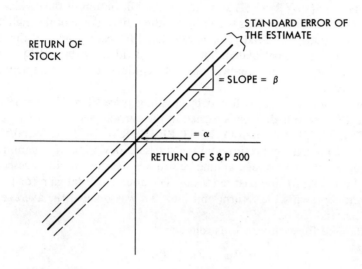

FIGURE 18–2

Regression Analysis

The price stability (PRICE STBL), M, and earnings stability (EARNG STBL), N, are measures that can be used to indicate risk. The more unstable the earnings and price, the greater the risk. Both measures are found by calculating the standard error of the estimate around the regression line fitted to the price and earnings data. The standard error is substracted from 1.00 and multiplied by 100 to establish the index. The lower the index, the more unstable the price or earnings and the greater the risk.

Item Q presents the average ten-year growth rate of dividends (10 YR AVG:) and the standard deviation of the dividend growth rate (STD:). The past earnings growth rates are provided in column R under EARN GRTH RATES. The investor can follow the trend of the earnings per share growth by examining the ten-year average growth rate (10-YR AVG:), the standard deviation (STD:) and the 5-YR and 3-YR averages. A constant average suggests that the company is sustaining its growth rate. These data are useful with the valuation equations, particularly with TREND, TREND-CURRENT, and RANDOM.

The ESTIMATED PERFORM for estimated performance over the next three years in item S, provides a solution for the *r* value for the TREND valuation equation YLD TO MATURITY (10/10:) and the RANDOM valuation equation (3YR SIML: and STD-RISK:). The *r* values indicate whether the investment annual average return expected for the next three years will adequately compensate the investor for the risk. The higher the expected return, *r*, the more attractive the investment, but also the more risky, for both 10/10 and 3YR SIML.

The 10/10 refers to the figures that are substituted into the valuation equation. The first 10 indicates that the ten-year average growth rate of dividends and earnings per share are used to estimate g_d and g_e in the valuation equation. The second 10 indicates that the ten-year average P/E ratio is used for P/E_3 in the equation.

The random simulated return ($\tilde{r}$) (3YR SIML) and the standard deviation (STD-RISK) provide an estimate of both return and risk. Thus, the investor may judge whether the return is proportional to risk. Risk increases with return, but the level of risk might exceed the level of return.

The equation for RANDOM can be restated as follows:

$$P_0 = \sum_{t=1}^{n=3} \frac{D_0(1 + \tilde{g}_d)^t}{(1 + \tilde{r})^t} + \frac{E_0(1 + \tilde{g}_e)^3 \widetilde{P/E}_3}{(1 + \tilde{r})^3}$$

This indicates that $\tilde{g}_d$, $\tilde{g}_e$, and $\widetilde{P/E}_3$ are randomly determined as demonstrated before—that is, that the variables are selected randomly from the mean value plus and minus the standard deviation. Remember this is done 100 times and 100 $\tilde{r}$s are obtained. The average and standard deviation become the 3YR SIML $\tilde{r}$ and the STD-RISK, which is $\tilde{\sigma}$.

The reward-to-risk ratio (RWRD/RISK:), T, is an indication of the proportionality of the investment reward to the investment risk. The higher the ratio, the more attractive the investment, given the same return. The reward-to-risk ratio or return-to-risk ratio is calculated by dividing the standard deviation (STD-RISK:) into the return (3YR SIML:), minus the risk-free return. For the purposes of this discussion, the risk-free return is assumed to be 85 percent of the yield on Treasury bills. The yield on Treasury bills was 14.34 percent, and 85 percent of this equals 12.2 percent. The reward-to-risk ratio may be written $(\tilde{r}_\mu - r_f) \div \tilde{\sigma}_r$, where $\tilde{r}_\mu$ is the mean value of the expected return, r_f is the risk-free return, and $\tilde{\sigma}_r$ is the standard deviation. The practical application of the reward-to-risk index to investment decisions has been most useful. The ratio is an extremely helpful tool in making investment decisions. A ratio above 1.0 is a positive indicator for investment.

ARE VALUATION MODELS RELIABLE?—SOME EVIDENCE

A Test of Trends and Trend-Current

Intuitively, valuation models or equations certainly seem helpful in making investment decisions, since they bring into focus the variables of most importance to the investor. Over the years, I have been interested in testing whether the results of valuation models are reliable. The focus has been on whether the returns (r's) expected in the future holding period (three years) have actually been obtained. In other words, if the valuation model projected an expected return of 12 percent, did the investor actually earn 12 percent from the investment? If so, it could be concluded that the valuation model was accurate.

One study conducted in the graduate business program at Miami University, Oxford, Ohio, was designed to test the validity and reliability of the return (r) figures generated by the output from Modesystem—MODE 1. The future holding period was five years instead of three, but the principles were the same.

The period covered in the study was 1916 through 1966. Four valuation models were used and applied to stocks in the Dow Jones Industrial Average. The models used were TREND and TREND-CURRENT, and two variations—a three-year growth rate of earnings and dividends and the current P/E ratio model, and the three-year growth rate of earnings and dividends and the ten-year P/E ratio model.

Each of the four models was employed to determine the individual stocks in the DJIA that had the highest estimated return (r) for the forecasted five years. These stocks would be assumed to be purchased, and their actual performance compared to the results. The values for each company were computed using Modesystem—MODE 1.

During the period 1916 through 1966, assuming that each of the 30 DJIA stocks was purchased and held for the period, the DJIA earned an average annual return of 14 percent. If only the most profitable stocks—those in the top 25 percent, based upon expected return—had been purchased and held for the entire period, the performance would be expected to be higher than 14 percent. The results of the study confirmed that.

A return of 16 percent would have been earned on the stocks chosen by the valuation model if the current P/E ratio and the three-year earnings and dividend growth rate had been used.

A return of 20 percent would have been earned based on the TREND-CURRENT model. In this model, the ten-year growth rate of earnings and dividends was used, along with the current P/E ratio.

A return 18 percent would have been earned if the ten-year P/E ratio and the three-year earnings growth rate had been used.

A return of 23 percent was earned using TREND, which used the ten-year growth rate of earnings and dividends and the ten-year P/E ratio.

It appears that TREND, at a 23 percent return, and TREND-CURRENT, at 20 percent, achieved results substantially above the 14 percent earned from all thirty DJIA stocks.

On the basis of the study, it can be concluded that stocks in the DJIA that were selected as being in the top 25 percent of profitability by expected returns (r) actually achieved returns above the average. It would seem, therefore, that valuation models and their resulting estimated returns would be helpful in investment decisions.

A Study of Random

Intuitively, the RANDOM simulated valuation equation appears to offer an excellent proxy for future expectations. The estimated mean $\bar{r}$ value and the standard deviation of the mean $\bar{r}$ value should represent a set of expectations that could be actually achieved by the investor. In 1975, a study was undertaken to determine if the estimated and expected returns and the variance ($\bar{\sigma}$) of the returns as simulated by the RANDOM model were actually obtained.[8] In other words, the study raised the question, "If a return of 10 percent plus or minus 5 percent, for example, is forecasted, to what extent are the expected returns achieved?"

The study concluded: "The expected return and the standard deviation of the Dow

[8]Spyridon C. Manolis, "Performance of Common Stock Portfolios Based on Simulated Risk-Yield Rates," unpublished master's thesis in Business Administration, The George Washington University, Washington, D.C., May 1975.

Jones Industrial Average as determined by the RANDOM simulation model were shown to accurately predict the true performance of the DJIA in the probabilistic sense expected from a normally distributed variable characterized by the given statistics."[9] In addition, the expected return and the standard deviation computed by RANDOM for each of the securities in the DJIA were predictive of the true performance of each of the securities.[10]

The study further concluded that "randomly selected portfolios as well as efficient portfolios at three levels of risk . . . structured on the basis of expected yield ($\bar{r}$) and standard deviation ($\bar{\sigma}$) generated by the simulation model RANDOM for each of the component securities were shown to have yields which were normally distributed within the range of their computed or expected yield and standard deviation. These portfolios were proven predictive in the probabilistic sense implied by the assumptions."[11]

Another conclusion of the study was that medium- and low-risk portfolios were far more profitable than the market, with the medium-risk portfolios returning 60 percent more yield with one-half the risk of the market, and low-risk portfolios returning the same yield as the market but with 40 percent of the risk.[12]

A study of the value of the reward-to-risk ratio in selecting securities that provided a higher return was undertaken in 1979.[13] The study found that stocks of the DJIA with a reward-to-risk ratio of .99 or higher earned significantly higher returns compared to stocks with a reward-to-risk ratio below .99. The period covered in the study was only the two-year period 1977 and 1978.

RETURN AND RISK ANALYSIS APPLIED TO THE THREE DRUG COMPANIES—THE ANALYSIS CONCLUDED

The final investment decision about each company should be made on the basis of the quality of the company and the expected return and risk. Table 18–3 provides a summary of the return and risk calculations for each of the drug companies under analysis. The price data are taken from data contained in Figure 18–3 as well as estimates for the TREND return and risk, the RANDOM return and risk, the reward-to-risk ratio, and the beta. The return calculated by the analyst (ABE) was taken from data in Tables 18–1 and 18–2.

The highest return is expected from Schering-Plough on both the TREND and RANDOM methods. Schering-Plough is also the riskiest based on the random standard deviation of the expected return. However, Schering-Plough does not have the highest risk based on the ten-year standard deviation of the annual return or the ten-year beta. The reward-to-risk ratio is highest for Schering-Plough and lowest for Smith-Kline. Based on expected returns and risk, either Schering-Plough or Lilly would be

[9]Ibid., p. 92.

[10]Ibid.

[11]Ibid., p. 93.

[12]Ibid.

[13]Frederick Amling, *Valuation Models, The Reward-to-Risk Ratio and Common Stock Performance* (S. E. Aids, 1979 American Institute for Decision Sciences Proceedings), p. 207.

LILLY,ELI&CO.   CUSIP = 532457

YEAR	HIGH	LOW	EPS	DIV	PE STATISTICS
71	64.30	49.30	1.41	0.70	MEAN VALUES
72	80.00	54.90	1.84	0.73	10YR AVG: 23.37
73	92.50	69.80	2.26	0.79	STD: 11.79
74	82.80	55.80	2.59	0.97	MAX: 41.28
75	79.80	49.50	2.62	1.10	MIN: 11.86
76	60.00	43.00	2.90	1.25	YRLY FLACTUAT
77	48.25	32.63	3.10	1.42	10YR AVG: 7.95
78	54.00	36.63	3.81	1.65	STD: 3.67
79	63.88	47.13	4.52	1.95	MAX: 13.64
80	63.75	45.75	4.51	2.20	MIN: 3.71

RECENT PRICE: 49.25   CURRENT PE : 10.92

PAST PERFORMANCE		GROWTH RATES		ESTIMATED PERFORM	
DIV RETURN		DIV GRTH RATE		YLD TO MATURITY	
10YR AVG:	2.36	10YR AVG:	14.36	10/10:	52.23
STD:	1.26	STD:	5.08		
ANNUAL YLD				3YR SIML:	48.15
10YR AVG:	2.82	EARN GRTH RATES		STD-RISK:	28.92
STD:	19.00	10YR AVG:	12.89		
BETA :	0.13	STD:	9.97	RWRD/RISK:	1.24
STD ERROR :	0.18	5YR AVG:	12.92		
ALPHA :	0.02	STD:	8.32		
PRICE STBL:	75.85	3YR AVG:	13.83	EARN-81:	5.42
EARNG STBL:	92.75	STD:	10.05	DIVD-81:	2.32

CURRENT DIVID RETURN: 4.47

FIGURE 18–3 (a)

SOURCE: Frederick Amling & Associates, Washington, D.C.

TABLE 18–1

Analyst's Best Estimate (ABE) of Return and Risk for Lilly, Schering-Plough, and SmithKline

	Lilly		Schering-Plough		SmithKline	
Year	Earnings	Dividends	Earnings	Dividends	Earnings	Dividends
1980	*4.51*	*2.20*	*4.44*	*1.56*	*4.63*	*1.73*
1981	5.33	2.50	5.30	1.80	6.04	1.95
1982	6.43	2.85	6.74	2.10	7.69	2.20
1983	7.17	3.25	7.87	2.43	9.86	2.50
g_e^a (%)	17		21		28	
g_d^b (%)	14		16		13	
P/E_3	11[c]		10[d]		14[e]	
P_0 ($)	49.25		28.50		70.25	
P_3 ($)	78.87		78.70		138.04	
r (%) (approx.)	22		45		28	

[a]Table 14–6, estimate.

[b]Figure 18–3. Figures were rounded to significant whole number.

[c]Current *P/E*, Figure 18–3.

[d]Estimated *P/E_3*. Trend *P/E* is too high and current *P/E* is too low.

[e]Ten-year average, Figure 18–3.

```
SCHERING-PLOUGH           CUSIP = 806605

YEAR    HIGH      LOW        EPS        DIV          PE STATISTICS
-------------------------------------------------   --------------------
71     45.00     30.30      1.14       0.44        MEAN VALUES
72     70.20     41.30      1.46       0.47          10YR AVG: 21.33
73     87.60     64.90      1.97       0.55               STD: 12.62
74     75.90     41.50      2.30       0.76               MAX: 38.90
75     67.30     44.50      2.57       0.84               MIN:  7.33
76     60.30     40.00      2.90       0.94        YRLY FLACTUAT
77     44.75     27.88      3.08       1.09          10YR AVG:  8.93
78     38.00     26.38      3.63       1.21               STD:  5.80
79     35.25     27.50      4.14       1.39               MAX: 19.79
80     45.63     29.13      4.44       1.56               MIN:  1.87

RECENT PRICE:     28.50                   CURRENT PE :   6.42


PAST PERFORMANCE          GROWTH RATES             ESTIMATED PERFORM
------------------        -------------------      --------------------
DIV RETURN                DIV GRTH RATE            YLD TO MATURITY
   10YR AVG:    2.30         10YR AVG: 15.74          10/10:  81.86
        STD:    1.48              STD:  8.58
ANNUAL YLD                                          3YR SIML:  81.33
   10YR AVG:    4.66      EARN GRTH RATES           STD-RISK:  34.01
        STD:   26.26         10YR AVG: 15.37
BETA     :      0.73              STD:  8.97        RWRD/RISK:  2.03
STD ERROR :     0.23          5YR AVG: 12.00
ALPHA     :    -0.00              STD:  4.37
PRICE STBL:    68.76         3YR AVG: 13.07         EARN-81:  5.59
EARNG STBL:    91.71              STD:  4.39        DIVD-81:  1.87

CURRENT DIVID RETURN:      5.47
```

FIGURE 18–3 (b)

TABLE 18–2

Present Value of Dividend and Price Stream for Lilly,
Schering-Plough, SmithKline, and Estimated Return r

Lilly

Price (P_0)	D_1		D_2		D_3		P_3
$49.25	$2.50		$2.85		$3.25		$78.87
PV discount at 22%*	.820		.672		.551		.551
ΣPV = $49.22 =	2.05	+	1.92	+	1.79	+	43.46

Schering-Plough

Price (P_0)	D_1		D_2		D_3		P_3
$28.50	$1.80		$2.10		$2.43		$78.70
PV discount at 45%*	.690		.476		.328		.328
ΣPV = $28.85 =	1.24	+	1.00	+	.80	+	25.81

SmithKline

Price (P_0)	D_1		D_2		D_3		P_3
$70.25	$1.95		$2.20		$2.50		$138.04
PV discount at 28%*	.781		.610		.477		.477
ΣPV = $69.90 =	1.52	+	1.34	+	1.19	+	65.85

---

*Appendix A1.

SMITH KLINE CORP.   CUSIP = 832377

YEAR	HIGH	LOW	EPS	DIV
71	14.88	11.88	0.77	0.50
72	16.63	13.13	0.82	0.50
73	15.47	11.72	0.89	0.50
74	13.72	7.57	0.98	0.50
75	14.75	10.82	1.07	0.50
76	20.63	14.63	1.21	0.50
77	25.19	15.38	1.49	0.54
78	51.25	23.06	2.72	0.78
79	63.25	38.50	3.84	1.32
80	80.63	43.50	4.63	1.73

PE STATISTICS

MEAN VALUES
  10YR AVG: 14.18
      STD: 2.09
      MAX: 17.90
      MIN: 11.80
YRLY FLACTUAT
  10YR AVG: 5.87
      STD: 2.13
      MAX: 10.36
      MIN: 3.67

RECENT PRICE: 70.25   CURRENT PE : 15.17

PAST PERFORMANCE

DIV RETURN
  10YR AVG: 3.22
     STD: 0.69
ANNUAL YLD
  10YR AVG: 24.72
     STD: 31.24
BETA   :   0.87
STD ERROR   :   0.28
ALPHA   :   0.17
PRICE STBL: 61.51
EARNG STBL: 79.10

CURRENT DIVID RETURN: 2.46

GROWTH RATES

DIV GRTH RATE
  10YR AVG: 13.17
     STD: 24.35

EARN GRTH RATES
  10YR AVG: 22.82
     STD: 23.15
  5YR AVG: 38.47
    STD: 25.10
  3YR AVG: 45.44
    STD: 25.91

ESTIMATED PERFORM

YLD TO MATURITY
    10/10:   15.12

  3YR SIML: 15.82
  STD-RISK: 23.08

  RWRD/RISK: 0.16

  EARN-81:   4.59
  DIVD-81:   2.10

FIGURE 18–3 (c)

TABLE 18–3

Price, Expected Return, Risk and Return-to-Risk Ratio for Lilly, Schering-Plough, and SmithKline

	Lilly	Rank	Schering-Plough	Rank	SmithKline	Rank
Price per share	$49.25	3	$28.50	2	$70.25	1
Return						
Expected annual average rate of return—next three years ABE (Table 18–2)	22	3	45	1	28	2
Expected annual return—Trend 10/10	52.23	2	81.86	1	15.12	3
Expected annual return—Random	48.15	2	81.33	1	15.82	3
Risk						
Last 10 years—standard deviation of annual return	19.00	3	26.26	2	31.24	1
Random standard deviation	28.92	2	34.01	1	23.08	3
Beta	.13	3	.73	2	.87	1
Return-risk ratio	1.24	2	2.03	1	.16	3

acceptable investments. A ranking on the basis of expected return and risk would suggest that Schering-Plough be ranked first and Lilly second, with SmithKline unacceptable.

The final investment decision is reflected in Table 18–4. Here all factors of fundamental analysis are summarized. The final decision would be for the investor to select Schering-Plough or Lilly. Both have attractive expected returns and are relatively low in risk. The final investment decision is based on a summary comparative analysis. The investor should therefore select the company that offers the highest quality and the highest returns with the lowest risk and the highest return-to-risk ratio.

TABLE 18–4
Summary of Fundamental Analysis of Lilly,
Schering-Plough and SmithKline

	Lilly	Schering-Plough	SmithKline
Competitive position	3	2	1
Profitability	3	2	1
Operating efficiency	3	2	1
Current financial position	3	2	1
Capital structure strength	1	2	3
Management	3	2	1
Return	3 (22)	1 (45)	2 (28)
Risk			
Beta (lowest)	1 (0.13)	2 (0.73)	3 (0.87)
Return-to-risk (highest)	2 (1.24)	1 (2.03)	3 (0.16)

SUMMARY

The valuation process focuses on the estimate of the expected return from an investment. The expected return is based on the growth rate of earnings (g_e), the growth rate of dividends (g_d), and the price earnings ratio (P/E_3) expected over the three-year forecast period. The analyst (ABE) or the computer (TREND over ten years and RANDOM) then provides estimates of the return and risk expected from the investment. It seems wise to use a ten-year P/E rate as a proxy for P/E_3 although the P/E ratio is influenced by many variables. The investor can measure risk by the beta, standard deviation of past annual returns and the standard deviation of expected annual returns.

In the last analysis, an investor should choose those securities that offer a reward-to-risk ratio of 1.00 or higher.

SUMMARY OF PRINCIPLES

1. The investor must estimate expected return and risk before making a decision and must relate the final decision to the reward-to-risk ratio.

2. An investor should invest in securities that offer a high return relative to risk—that is, a high reward-to-risk ratio. A R/R ratio of 1.00 or higher is acceptable.

3. Investors should purchase securities when P/E ratios are low relative to expected P/E ratios, but P/E ratios are stable from period to period.
4. Beta analysis helps to determine the risk level of the securitiy.
5. Markets are assumed to be somewhat efficient and fundamental analysis is worthwhile.
6. The random expected return and risk is a good proxy for an unknown future return and risk level.
7. Valuation models are helpful in determining the reward-to-risk characteristics of a common stock.
8. Don't be the last optimistic investor. SmithKline was a good example.

REVIEW QUESTIONS

1. Why is the valuation of common stock different from that of bonds or preferred stock, and what is the purpose of common stock valuation?
2. Explain the variables in the following equations:

a. $P_0 = \dfrac{D_1}{(1+r)} + \dfrac{D_2}{(1+r)^2} + \dfrac{D_3}{(1+r)^3}$

b. $P_0 = \dfrac{D_0(1+g_d)}{(1+r)} + \dfrac{D_0(1+g_d)^2}{(1+r)^2} + \dfrac{D_0(1+g_d)^3 + P_3}{(1+r)^3}$

c. $P_0 = \sum\limits_{t=1}^{n} \dfrac{D_0(1+g_d)^t}{(1+r)^t} + \dfrac{E_0(1+g_e)^n(P/E)_n}{(1+r)^n}$

3. What part do the growth rate of earnings, dividends, and the future P/E play in the valuation equation?
4. Explain and contrast:
   a. TREND valuation equation.
   b. TREND-CURRENT valuation equation.
   c. ABE valuation equation.
   d. RANDOM valuation equation.
5. What would be the main emphasis in valuing a cyclical stock?
6. Explain how you would adjust the valuation model for risk. (Explain variable by variable.)
7. Explain each item in the computer printout of MODE 1 of Modesystem in Figure 18–1.
8. Can one pay too much for a quality company?
9. What is the significance of the P/E ratio, and how can it help determine whether the current price of a stock is reasonable?
10. What has been the trend of the P/E ratios in the market over the past decade?
11. What is the relationship between the P/E ratio and risk?
12. a. Would the P/E ratio of a speculative company be expected to be high, low, or normal? Explain.
    b. What P/E would be expected from the growth company? Relate this to the discussion about the P/E ratio.
    c. What kind of P/E ratio would be expected for a company with a large amount of debt in its capital structure?

d. What kind of P/E ratio would be expected for a company with cyclical earnings?

e. Would a high or low P/E ratio be expected if the company had a stable dividend policy?

f. What are the dangers involved in purchasing a high P/E ratio stock?

g. The average P/E ratio permits a forecast of future price of the stock based on future estimated earnings. Discuss.

13. Explain how total return is estimated based on expected dividends over the next three years and expected price in three years. Can these estimates be relied on?

14. What is the beta factor of an individual stock, and how is it used?

15. Are individual betas reliable?

16. Explain the use of the return-to-risk ratio in the final investment decision.

PROBLEMS

1. Mrs. Hills can buy a stock that will pay $1 in dividends annually over the next three years. The earnings of the company are expected to grow, and the stock is expected to reach a price of $50 per share at the end of three years. This is a conservative investment, and Mrs. Hills expects a return of 15 percent. What price should Mrs. Hills pay for the stock if she wishes to earn 15 percent?

2. Mr. Clark is a conservative investor who demands 13 percent interest on his money market fund but 20 percent from his common stock investments. He has been considering the purchase of a stock that pays $2 in dividends this year and whose dividends are expected to grow 8 percent per year for the next three years. Earnings this year are $4 per share and are expected to grow at 10 percent for the next seven years. Stocks growing at this rate generally sell at 12 times earnings. What price should Mr. Clark pay for this stock?

3. Mr. Ross would consider investment in the common stock that Mr. Clark is interested in, but he thinks he should earn a yield of 15 percent rather than 20 percent. What price would Mr. Ross consider fair?

4. Mr. Anderson is suspicious of the estimates prepared by Mr. Clark and Mr. Ross. He has examined the company and thinks dividends will grow at 4 percent, earnings growth will be 9 percent, and the future P/E ratio will be 18. Like Mr. Ross, he thinks the discount rate should be 12 percent. What would Mr. Anderson pay for the stock?

5. Mr. Williams wants to buy stock in XYZ Company. It traded yesterday at 244. The company paid a dividend last year of $.24 per share. Dividends have grown at 11 percent per year, and earnings at 16 percent per year, for the last ten years. Earnings per share were $2.75 last year and are expected to be $3.50 this year. Earnings are expected to grow at a 20 percent rate next year and the year after, and the stock should enjoy a P/E ratio of 15. The company announced that the stock was to be split 2 for 1 shortly. Dividends should increase as they have in the past. What return would Mr. Williams earn from the investment if he purchased it at 244 and held it for three years?

6. Jefferson Pilot Corporation, a leading insurance company, was recommended for purchase by a leading brokerage firm. At a price of 24, would you agree? In order

to answer this question, you should use the following valuation equations:

a. TREND.
b. TREND-CURRENT.
c. ABE.
d. RANDOM.
e. Reward-Risk Ratio.

Based on valuation analysis, would you agree with the recommendation? Why or why not?

```
JEFFERSON-PILCT CORP      CUSIP = 475070

YEAR    HIGH       LOW        EPS        DIV          PE STATISTICS
--------------------------------------------------------    --------------------
 71     24.90      13.50      1.17       0.43         MEAN VALUES
 72     36.80      21.30      1.39       0.46            10YR AVG: 11.80
 73     40.90      26.90      2.13       0.50               STD:    4.64
 74     38.30      20.50      2.42       0.58               MAX:  19.78
 75     38.80      26.30      2.44       0.69               MIN:    6.40
 76     32.38      24.60      2.82       0.78         YRLY FLACTUAT
 77     32.38      26.38      3.29       0.89            10YR AVG:    5.09
 78     35.13      26.50      3.86       1.01               STD:    3.47
 79     38.00      28.75      4.52       1.16               MAX:  11.15
 80     31.50      22.88      4.20       1.35               MIN:    1.82

RECENT PRICE:     24.13                         CURRENT PE :   5.74


   PAST PERFORMANCE          GROWTH RATES              ESTIMATED PERFORM
   ----------------          ------------              -----------------
   DIV RETURN                DIV GRTH RATE             YLD TO MATURITY
      10YR AVG:    2.72         10YR AVG:   14.05          10/10:   60.53
           STD:    1.06              STD:    3.56
   ANNUAL YLD                                            3YR SIML:  58.88
      10YR AVG:    6.57       EARN GRTH RATES          STD-RISK:   25.56
           STD:   17.06         10YR AVG:   15.51
   BETA      :    0.23              STD:   15.53       RWRD/RISK:    1.83
   STD ERROR :    0.16          5YR AVG:   13.04
   ALPHA     :    0.05              STD:    9.58
   PRICE STBL:   74.94          3YR AVG:    9.31          EARN-81:    5.74
   EARNG STBL:   89.22              STD:   11.45          DIVD-81:    1.63

   CURRENT DIVID RETURN:     5.60
```

Source: Frederick Amling & Associates, Washington, D.C.

CASE

An investor was concerned that she had made the correct decision to buy Lilly and/or Schering-Plough. Review the analysis and learn if the decision was right. In reappraising each company one year later, Miss Queeny noted the following changes. The price of Lilly increased to 65. Schering-Plough rose to 45, and SmithKline to 75. The growth rate of dividends increased by 10 percent over the previous growth rate for each company, and the rate of earnings growth increased 5 percent. The P/E ratios remained the same. First, she wanted to know how her stock had performed over the year. And she wanted to know if she should continue to hold. Examine the changes and using the data in Figure 18–3, revalue each company and recommend what she should do.

Bower, Dorothy H., and Richard S. Bower. "Test of a Stock Valuation Model." *The Journal of Finance*, May 1970, p. 483.

Durand, David. "Growth Stocks and the Petersburg Paradox." *Journal of Finance* XII (September 1957), pp. 348–63.

Fama, Eugene F. "Stock Market Price Behavior, Efficient Capital Markets: A Review of Theory and Empirical Work." *The Journal of Finance*, September 1970, p. 383.

———. "Components of Investment Performance." *The Journal of Finance*, June 1972, p. 551.

Ferguson, Robert. "How to Beat the Index Funds." *Financial Analysts Journal*, May–June 1975, pp. 63–72.

Graham, Benjamin. "The Future of Common Stocks." *Financial Analysts Journal*, September–October 1974, p. 20.

Holmes, John R. "Growth, Risk, and Stock Valuation." *Financial Analysts Journal*, May–June 1976, pp. 46–55.

Joy, O. Maurice, and Charles P. Jones, "Predictive Value of P/E Ratios." *Financial Analysts Journal*, September–October 1970, p. 61.

Kaplan, R., and R. W. Roll. "Accounting Changes and Stock Prices." *Financial Analysts Journal*, January–February 1973, p. 48.

Keenan, W. Michael. "Toward a Positive Theory of Equity Valuation." *The Journal of Finance*, March 1968, p. 197.

Levy, Robert A. "Beta as a Predictor of Return." *Financial Analysts Journal*, January–February 1974, p. 61.

———. "On the Safety of Low P/E Stocks." *Financial Analysts Journal*, January–February 1973, p. 57.

Miller, Merton H., and Franco Modigliani. "Dividend Policy, Growth and the Valuation of Shares." *The Journal of Business* XXXIV (October 1961), pp. 411–33.

Murphy, Joseph E., Jr., and J. Russell Melson. "Stability of P/E Ratios." *Financial Analysts Journal*, March–April 1969, p. 77.

Niederhoffer, Victor, and Patrick J. Regan. "Earnings Changes, Analysts' Forecasts, and Stock Prices." *Financial Analysts Journal*, May–June 1972, pp. 65–71.

Pinches, George E., and William R. Kinney, Jr. "The Measurement of the Volatility of Common Stock Prices." *The Journal of Finance*, March 1971, p. 119.

Reilly, Frank K. "Stock Price Changes by Market Segment." *Financial Analysts Journal*, March–April 1971, p. 54.

Robichek, Alexander A., and Marcus C. Bogue. "A Note on the Behavior of Expected Price/Earnings Ratio over Time." *The Journal of Finance*, June 1971, p. 731.

Wendt, Paul F. "Current Growth Stock Valuation Methods." *Financial Analysts Journal*, March–April 1965, pp. 91–103.

Whitbeck, Volkert S., and Manown Kisor. "A New Tool in Investment Decision-Making." *Financial Analysts Journal*, May–June 1963, pp. 55–62.

Williams, John Burr. *The Theory of Investment Value.* Cambridge, Mass.: Harvard University Press, 1938.

CHAPTER 19

INVESTMENT ANALYSIS

A Case Study
of the Electronics–Electrical Industry

The method of analysis presented in the preceding chapters will now be applied to the electronics-electrical industry circa Fall 1981 to make certain that the principles of analysis are fully understood. It does take a good deal of time to obtain the information and summarize the data; yet the method used in making a comparative analysis of different companies provides a clearly organized path for the investor to follow in reaching a decision.

In the analysis of the electronics industry, each factor will be examined and a conclusion will be reached. Every effort will be made to indicate why the conclusion was reached. It is possible that a company carefully analyzed and studied might not turn out to be a good investment. Perhaps the qualitative and quantitative conditions will change, so that the original conditions of analysis no longer apply. Obviously, the investor or analyst must keep abreast of competitive conditions, and take appropriate action because of a change in fundamental values or market prices, or both.

It is also possible that errors of judgment will be made. No one can forecast the future with certainty. If a mistake is made, the best course of action is to sell the stock as soon as possible and make a better decision the next time.

One other point must be made about the possibility of poor judgment. The investor does not buy only one company or one security. By investing in several common stocks and fixed-income securities from several different companies, the investor is able to reduce the risk. The act of diversification reduces variability and possible loss in the selection or timing of the purchase of one security. This subject will be discussed at greater length in the chapter on portfolio management theory and principles.

The word "electronics" was not in our vocabulary in 1940.[1] It was not until the early 1950s that the industrial classification, "electronics industry," was identified. Perhaps Edison, Marconi, and DeForest could be considered the fathers of the electronics industry. Glover and Lagai, in their book *The Development of American Industries*, had no such classification; their listing was "The Electrical Industry," and included in that listing were some of the devices, such as the radio and phonograph, that are now regarded as part of the electronics industry.[2]

The industry has changed and it has grown. In 1950, it had half a billion dollars in sales, thirty times as much as in 1940. Its most recent growth is revealed in Table 19–1. The factory sales of the industry increased from an index of 100 in 1972 to an estimated 228 for 1981. The factory sales growth has actually lagged behind the growth of GNP, which reached an index of 244 in 1981. It is seen (Table 19–1) that factory sales as a percentage of GNP have increased steadily since 1975, and real growth adjusted for inflation has been superior.

Expectations about the industry suggested that the electronics industries would

TABLE 19–1

Factory Sales of Electrical Equipment Compared to FRB Index and Gross National Product (1972 = 100)

Year	Total Factory Sales ($ billions)	Sales Index (1972 = 100)	FRB Index (1972 = 100)	GNP ($ billions)	Index	Total Factory Sales as % of GNP
1983E*	$87.0	275	150	$3,425	292	2.54%
1982E	79.0	250	142	3,132	267	2.52
1981E	72.2	228	135	2,856	244	2.53
1980	66.4	210	128	2,626	224	2.53
1979	59.3	188	133	2,369	202	2.50
1978	51.8	164	127	2,128	182	2.43
1977	45.9	145	119	1,900	162	2.42
1976	41.4	131	109	1,702	145	2.43
1975	36.4	115	99	1,529	131	2.38
1974	35.9	114	108	1,413	121	2.54
1973	34.4	109	110	1,171	100	2.70
1972	31.6	100	100	1,171	100	2.70
1971	27.8	88	93	1,063	91	2.62
1970	26.7	84	93	982	84	2.72

*E, estimate.

SOURCE: Standard & Poor's *Investment Survey, Electronics-Electrical,* October 29, 1981, p. E11; *Value Line Investment Survey, Electrical Equipment Industry,* November 13, 1981, p. 1001. Tables 19–1, 5, 6, 7, 10, and 11: copyright 1981 by Arnold Bernhard & Co., Inc. Reprinted by permission.

[1] F. Hoch Haworth, "Electrical and Electronics," *Financial Analysts Journal,* January–February 1961, p. 95.

[2] John C. Glover and Rudolph L. Lagai, *The Development of American Industries,* 4th ed. (New York: Simmons-Boardman Publishing Corp., 1959).

TABLE 19–2

U.S. Factory Shipments of the Electronics–Electrical Industry by Subindustry
(Millions of dollars; index 1972 = 100)

Year	Consumer Products ($)	Index	Communication Equipment ($)	Index	Industrial Products ($)	Index	Electronic Components ($)	Index	Government Products ($)	Index	Total
1983E*	$10,389	160	$27,921	260	$42,240	400	$30,916	438	$30,740	290	$141,486
1982E	9,415	145	27,707	258	39,600	375	27,231	395	28,620	270	132,573
1981E	9,090	140	26,096	243	36,432	345	24,818	360	26,076	246	122,512
1980E	8,800	136	24,300	226	33,300	315	27,700	329	28,000	226	89,100
1979	9,274	143	22,732	212	29,691	281	18,910	274	20,150	190	80,607
1978	9,303	143	20,514	191	25,162	238	15,567	226	17,650	167	70,546
1977	8,119	125	18,503	172	21,676	205	13,033	189	15,300	144	61,331
1976	6,921	107	15,243	142	17,889	169	10,884	158	12,750	120	50,937
1975	4,955	76	13,997	130	15,139	143	9,286	135	11,500	106	43,377
1974	6,274	97	12,797	119	15,118	143	10,403	151	11,150	105	44,592
1973	6,934	107	11,702	109	12,577	119	9,900	143	10,150	102	41,119
1972	6,493	100	10,739	100	10,560	100	6,894	100	10,000	100	34,686
1971	5,331	82	9,800	91	7,854	74	5,774	83	10,700	101	28,759

*E, estimate.

SOURCE: Standard & Poor's Industry Survey, Electronics-Electrical, August 28, 1980, p. 11.

grow in the future at a real rate of growth greater than the national economy. Real growth has been greater than that of the national economy. Table 19–2 reveals that the industrial products group, as a subindustry of the electronics-electrical industry, has grown faster than the national economy and faster than the other subindustry groups. Furthermore, Table 19–3 indicates that the industrial products group has grown steadily on a per capita basis. Per capita sales of industrial products have increased each year since 1976. The per capita data were used to provide the estimates of industry growth in Table 19–2, which were based on a constant population growth of 1.6 million people per year from 1981 through 1984. The consumer products subindustry was expected to expand cyclically as it had in the past. This estimate assumed that per capita sales would expand in 1984, which could be a year of growth. Industrial products were expected to continue the pattern of past growth. Government products and replacement components were expected to maintain their historic pattern, and the future per capita estimates reflect that pattern.

TABLE 19–3

Per Capita Dollar Sales of the Electronics–Electrical Industry
by Subindustry

Year	Population (millions)	Consumer Products	Industrial Products	Government Products	Total
1984E*	230.2†	$46.8	$198.6	$144.6	$654.9
1983E	228.6†	45.4	184.8	134.0	618.9
1982E	227.0†	41.5	174.4	126.1	584.0
1981E	225.4†	40.3	161.6	115.7	543.5
1980	223.8	39.3	148.8	125.5	400.4
1979	220.1	42.1	134.9	91.6	363.5
1978	218.5	42.6	115.2	80.6	322.9
1977	216.9	37.4	89.9	70.5	282.8
1976	215.2	32.2	83.1	59.2	236.7

*E, estimate.

†Assumed annual growth rate of 1.6 million persons.

SOURCE: U.S. Department of Commerce.

The estimates of the total growth of the industry are reflected in Table 19–2. The results show that the consumer products group declined in 1980. The industrial products group maintained a more constant growth rate through 1982. The estimated growth rate is 9.52 percent in 1981, 8.70 percent in 1983, and 6.67 percent in 1983. It would seem that this growth rate could be sustained for a longer period of time. By definition, the industrial products group is in the stage of investment maturity with some elements of the pioneering stage present, as will be seen.

THE PRODUCTS OF THE INDUSTRY

Some of the products produced in the electronics industry are easy to envision and understand. We know what a radio is, or a television set, or CB radio. Some of the other products are somewhat difficult to comprehend. What, for example, is a transistor, or a transducer, or a tunnel diode? These products form the basis for a multi-million-dollar industry, but relatively few people know their functions. Below is a list of definitions of terms frequently used in the electronics industry. This might help to identify some of the products of the industry and their uses. The source of these data was Standard & Poor's *Industry Surveys—Electronics-Electrical*. Although the list of terms is no longer carried in the *Electronics Survey*, a review of a current *Survey* would be helpful in understanding the industry.

Capacitor—A device consisting of two conductors carrying equal but opposite electric charges, which are separated from each other by a nonconductor. The primary function of a capacitor is the storage of electrical energy.

Diode—An electron tube or semiconductor material with two electrodes that is most commonly used to convert alternating current into direct current.

Electron—The elementary unit of a negative electrical charge.

Fuel cell—An electrochemical device that converts chemical energy directly into electrical energy.

Hybrid circuit—An assemblage of passive and active subminiature devices on an insulating substrate to perform a complete circuit function.

Infrared—That portion of the frequency band that is above microwaves and below the lowest frequency (the color red) of visible light. Infrared radiates from and is absorbed by all materials.

Integrated circuit—A complete functional circuit consisting of transistors, diodes, capacitors, and resistors all constructed within or on the surface of a monolithic chip of silicon.

Laser—A device for the amplification or generation of coherent light signals (*L*ight *A*mplification by *S*timulated *E*mission of *R*adiation).

Magnetron—A high-vacuum tube capable of producing high power output in the microwave region of the frequency spectrum.

Maser—A device for the amplification or generation of microwave signals (*M*icrowave *A*mplification by *S*timulated *E*mission of *R*adiation).

Microwaves—Very short electromagnetic waves lying between the television and infrared bands in the frequency spectrum. Microwaves are finding increasing usage in the communications field.

Monolithic—A semiconductor integrated circuit that is complete on one chip or piece of substrate.

Rectifier—A device, either vacuum-tube, semiconductor, gaseous, or electrolytic, used primarily to convert alternating current into direct current. The basic method of operation of rectifiers and diodes is identical, with various types and sizes of one often overlapping the other. Generally, the main point of difference is that rectifiers usually have a larger current capacity than do diodes.

Relay—An electrically operated switch, usually composed of an electromagnet, an armature, and one or more contact springs, used to open or close an electric circuit.

Resistor—An electrical component that restricts the flow of current into a circuit, thereby permitting control of the voltage across it.

Semiconductor—A material whose ability to conduct a flow of electrons is intermediate between that of a conductor (such as copper, which freely permits passage of an electric current when a difference of potential is applied to it) and that of an insulator (such as glass, which allows only a small amount of current to pass through it).

Solar cell—A device used to convert electromagnetic radiation from the sun into electrical energy.

Solid-state devices—Elements that can control current without moving parts, heated filaments, or vacuum gaps. Semiconductors are the best-known solid-state devices.

Sonar—Apparatus or techniques that employ underwater sound waves to locate and track objects below the surface of the water.

Telemetry—That field of instrumentation dealing with the transmission or measurement of data from a remote location to a more convenient location and the reproducing of this data in a form suitable for display, recording, or insertion into data-processing equipment.

Thermoelectricity—The direct conversion of heat to electricity and the reciprocal use of electricity to create the effect of heat or cold.

Transducer—A device used to change one form of energy into another. For example, a loudspeaker is a transducer that changes electrical energy into acoustical energy.

Transformer—An electric device that, by electromagnetic induction, transforms electric energy from one or more circuits to one or more other circuits at the same frequency, usually with changed values of voltage and current.

Transistor—A semiconductor device with three or more electrodes, commonly used to amplify or switch electric current.

Standard & Poor's divides the electronics–electrical industry into five groups, as shown in Table 19–2: (1) consumer products, (2) communication equipment, (3) industrial products, (4) electronic components, and (5) government products. The *Value Line* classifies the subindustries somewhat differently; in addition to the classifications provided by Standard & Poor's it includes electrical equipment, electronics, office equipment–computers, and instruments.

Consumer Products

Consumer products include black-and-white and color television using solid-state components, radios, videodisc players, citizens' band radios, cable TV, calculators, digital watches, phonographs, audio components, videotape recorders and players, and many other products—including electric guitars, hearing aids, electronic controls for the home, smoke alarms, intercoms, telephone answering devices, microwave ovens, and personal computers.

In the consumer products group also are electrical products such as kitchen appliances, home laundry appliances, room air conditioners, small electrical appliances, floor-care equipment, electrical personal-care items, and electric water heaters. Many of these products have enjoyed substantial growth.

Industrial Products

The industrial products segment has grown more rapidly than any other in the industry, because of the automation of office equipment and increased use of computers. This area overlaps that of the office equipment industry. The automation of all phases of industry offers great hopes for this segment of the electronics industry.

Government Products

Missiles;. The category of government products includes electronic equipment for missiles—for example, missile-testing equipment, flight-control apparatus, and missile communication equipment—as well as peacetime products used in space exploration. An impressive array of antimissile equipment is also being developed.

AIRCRAFT. The electronic content of manned aircraft has increased tremendously in recent years. Electronic equipment for aircraft accounts for more than 30 percent of its cost. The equipment performs the functions of navigation, communications control, and identification. Manned aircraft is the biggest single item in the military budget. Continued defense expenditures should generate substantial revenues in the years ahead, along with aircraft aid to foreign governments.

COMMUNICATION, SPACE PROGRAMS, INFRARED, AND MICROWAVES. The demands of the free world suggest a growing need for communications now and in the future satellite projects. The space program today uses millions of dollars worth of electronic equipment. Additional dollars will be spent for this purpose, but at a decreasing rate. Expenditures will continue for the space shuttle and space station programs.

The infrared segment of the industry should experience remarkable growth. All applications of infrared are based on the principle that infrared—the frequency band that lies between the microwave and visible light bands—radiates from and is absorbed by all materials. Its uses include (1) identification of substances by analysis of their frequency-absorption spectrum; (2) determination of the temperature and location of objects by detection of their infrared radiation; and (3) provision of large quantities of radiation for heating, drying, and curing processes.

The work with infrared by the military is classified. Its application in the area of automatic detection of missiles holds a great deal of promise for its future and the expansion of the electronics industry. It shows promise for application in nonmilitary areas such as temperature measurement and control, analytical instrumentation, industrial photography, transportation, food processing, space heating, and cooking and baking.

Microwave transmission also offers a great deal of expansion possibilities. It costs less over long distance and rough terrain than the lower-frequency transmission.

Electronic Components

Electronic components are the building blocks used to construct the electronic devices produced for the government, industry, and the consumer. They represent a major area of the electronics industry. The segment comprising passive components, those containing no energy source, represents about 13 percent of the market. The active component segment, which includes conventional tubes, semiconductors, and transistors, makes up 43 percent of this division. The other component segment makes up the remainder of this division. High growth is expected to continue in semiconductors. Integrated circuits, which account for 75 percent of total U.S. semiconductor shipments, is the fastest-growing segment of semiconductor industry. Integrated circuits are used as memory devices for computers.

Communications Equipment

Communications equipment includes videotape recorders for television broadcasters, land mobile radios, and mobile telephones. Telecommunications equipment is also included under this category. Areas of growth in this huge market include electronic switching, digital data systems, fiber optic transmission, and satellite communications.

New product development and competition in telecommunication is expected to increase dramatically over the next several years.

COMPETITIVE POSITIONS OF THE LEADING COMPANIES

The leading companies in the electronic products–electronics group are listed in Table 19–4, ranked according to 1981 sales and growth in the lower portion of the table. This is a growth industry, and we must use the criterion of growth rather than income to select companies for investment consideration.

Hewlett-Packard demonstrated the highest growth of sales from 1972 through 1981, increasing its size by 700 percent. Tektronix was second in growth rate for the same period. Fairchild was third in growth of sales but was deemed a bit small for investment consideration by a risk-averse investor. Litton was the largest company, but its growth rate diminished. Texas Instruments was the second largest company and maintained a growth rate in the middle of the group. The companies selected for analysis were chosen on the basis of size and growth. Hewlett-Packard (HWP) and Tektronix (TEK) were selected for their strong growth rate even though they were not the largest in the industry. Texas Instruments (TXN) was selected because of its relative size and growth rate. Litton was rejected because of relatively lower earning growth.

The companies' past growth of sales is shown in Table 19–5, and data about each company in Figure 19–1. The company information in Figure 19–1 should be read to obtain a background about the companies.

Hewlett-Packard (HWP)

Hewlett-Packard sales are expected to more than double from 1978 through 1982, and profits to increase almost threefold. HWP designs, manufactures, and markets a broad line of precision electronic instruments and systems for measurement, analysis, and computation. Approximately 3,400 of its products are used in industry, science, education and medicine.[3]

Test and measuring instruments, accounting for 37 percent of sales, include oscilloscopes, electronic counters, frequency and time standards, communications test equipment, microwave equipment, and power supplies. Electronic data products account for 50 percent of sales, medical electronics equipment for 7 percent, and analytical instrumentation 5 percent. Products include microwave diodes, light-emitting diodes, and high-frequency transistors in the components group. In computer systems, the products produced are digital computers, minicomputer systems, and related peripheral equipment and software.

HWP produces calculators, medical equipment, and analytical instrumentation used by the chemical, agricultural, and petroleum industries. The small Hewlett-Packard calculator has improved in the marketplace. HWP has enjoyed a 25 percent five-year average growth rate of earnings, and the rate has increased to 30 percent in recent years. Foreign sales accounted for 51 percent of sales in 1980, and government sales for 10 percent.

[3]Standard & Poor's *Stock Reports*, September 23, 1976, p. 1137.

TABLE 19-4
Sales Index for Leading Electronics Companies, 1972–1982 (1972 = 100)

Year	AMP, Inc.	Beckman Instruments	Fairchild	General Instruments	Hewlett-Packard	Litton	Motorola	Sanders	Tektronix	Texas Instruments	Varian Associates
1982E	480	483	548	344	919	217	322	299	716	498	368
1981	412	417	596	290	747	200	287	244	647	445	333
1980	385	371	393	259	647	171	266	189	592	432	303
1979	335	289	311	225	493	165	233	112	480	341	241
1978	265	228	232	173	360	148	191	101	365	270	197
1977	210	193	173	158	284	139	159	97	277	217	173
1976	173	189	114	146	232	136	129	132	224	176	168
1975	135	163	95	117	204	139	113	121	206	145	153
1974	159	154	109	131	184	122	118	109	165	167	144
1973	138	109	103	133	138	100	124	114	121	136	118
1972	100	100	100	100	100	100	100	100	100	100	100
1972 sales ($ millions)	$302	$148	$224	$219	$479	$2,245	$1,163	$149	$164	$944	$204
1981 rank	6	10	5	8	3	1	4	11	7	2	9
1981 sales ($ millions)	$1,245	$618	$1,370	$925	$3,580	$4,943	$3,335	$365	$1,062	$4,200	$680
Rank by growth of 1981 sales	6	5	3	8	1	11	9	10	2	4	7
1982E sales	$1,450	$2,985	$1,228	$1,097	$4,402	$4,872	$3,745	$446	$1,174	$4,701	$750

SOURCE: Value Line Investment Survey—Electrical Equipment Industry, November 13, 1981, pp. 1040, 1050, 1052, 1069, 1071, 1074; November 24, 1981, p. 1401; December 2, 1981, p. 154; October 23, 1981, pp. 558, 576.

Tektronix, Inc.

NYSE Symbol TEK   Put & Call Options on CBOE

Price	Range	P-E Ratio	Dividend	Yield	S&P Ranking
Aug. 5'81 54¾	1981 63¼–49½	13	0.92	1.7%	A–

Summary

Tektronix, a leader in the electronic test and measurement instruments industry, is the world's leading producer of cathode ray oscilloscopes. The graphic computer terminals business has also shown rapid growth. With a prospective improvement in economic conditions, earnings should recover in fiscal 1981–2. Long-term prospects appear favorable.

Current Outlook

Earnings for the fiscal year ending May 31, 1982 are projected at about $5.10 a share, versus fiscal 1980–1's $4.34.

Dividends should continue at a minimum of $0.23 quarterly.

Orders for test and measurement instruments and information display products have been relatively weak. However, with improved economic activity in prospect, orders should pick up. Most of the expected improvement in shipments, margins and earnings should take place in the second half of fiscal 1981–2. Over the long term, the steady spread of electronics technology usage will continue to increase the need for test and measurement instruments, and prospects for information display products are bright.

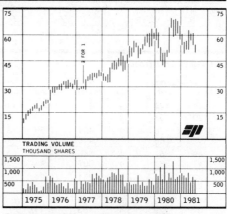

Net Sales (Million $)

Period:	1980–1	1979–80	1978–9	1977–8
12 Wks. Aug......	233	208	159	120
12 Wks. Nov......	249	222	180	140
16 Wks. Mar......	311	286	238	178
12 Wks. May	270	256	211	160
	1,062	971	787	599

Sales for the fiscal year ended May 30, 1981 (preliminary) rose 9.3%, year to year. Margins narrowed, and pretax income was down 3.3%. After taxes at 39.4%, against 37.9%, net income declined 5.8%. Share earnings were $4.34, versus $4.66, including a $0.28 nonrecurring gain in fiscal 1980–1 from the sale of the portable patient monitor business.

Common Share Earnings ($)

Period:	1980–1	1978–9	1978–9	1977–8
12 Wks. Aug.......	0.92	1.02	0.79	0.67
12 Wks. Nov.......	0.96	1.17	1.02	0.76
16 Wks. Mar.......	1.29	1.14	1.28	0.93
12 Wks. May	1.17	1.33	1.19	0.83
	4.34	4.66	4.28	3.19

Important Developments

Jul. '81—Orders for the fiscal year ended May 30 totaled $1.04 billion, down 0.9% from the $1.05 billion a year earlier. Backlog at May 30 was $295 million, down 6.9% from $317 million a year earlier. For fiscal 1980–1, sales of test and measurement products rose 5.0%, year to year; information display products increased 22%.

Next earnings report due in late September.

Per Share Data ($)

Yr. End May 31 [1]	1980	1979	1978	1977	1976	1975	1974	[2] 1973	1972
Book Value	NA	26.17	22.13	18.20	15.47	13.14	11.53	10.05	9.03
Earnings[3]	4.34	4.66	4.28	3.19	2.49	1.71	1.52	1.23	0.96
Dividends	0.90	0.79	0.60	0.48	0.22½	0.12	0.10	0.10	0.10
Payout Ratio	21%	17%	14%	15%	9%	7%	7%	8%	10%
Prices[4]—High	70¼	64	50½	40	34⅜	22¾	23⅞	28¼	32¾
Low	41⅝	46⅞	32½	28¼	22⅛	9	9	14⅞	16⅜
P/E Ratio—	16–10	14–10	12–8	13–9	14–9	13–5	16–6	23–12	34–17

Data as orig. reptd. Adj. for stk. div(s). of 100% May 1977. **1.** Of fol. cal. yr. **2.** Reflects merger or acquisition. **3.** Bef. spec. item(s) of +0.02 in 1971. **4.** Cal. yr. NA-Not Available.

Standard NYSE Stock Reports
Vol. 48/No. 154/Sec. 17

August 12, 1981
Copyright © 1981 Standard & Poor's Corp. All Rights Reserved

Standard & Poor's Corp.
25 Broadway, NY, NY 10004

FIGURE 19–1 (a)

Income Data (Million $)

Year Ended May 31[1]	Revs.	Oper. Inc.	% Oper. Inc. of Revs.	Cap. Exp.	Depr.	Int. Exp.	Net Bef. Taxes	Eff. Tax Rate	[4]Net Inc.	% Net Inc. of Revs.
1979	971	179	18.4%	116	30.7	16.0	[3]137	37.9%	85.1	8.8%
1978	787	143	18.2%	100	21.7	6.4	[3]127	39.1%	77.2	9.8%
1977	599	110	18.3%	42	15.5	4.3	[3] 96	40.8%	56.9	9.5%
1976	455	90	19.7%	22	13.2	4.1	[3] 76	41.9%	44.0	9.7%
1975	367	70	19.1%	19	12.2	4.8	[3] 55	45.5%	30.1	8.2%
1974	337	61	18.0%	32	9.7	4.8	[3] 47	43.8%	26.3	7.8%
[2]1973	271	47	17.1%	24	8.1	1.2	[3] 39	44.5%	21.4	7.9%
1972	198	33	16.8%	7	7.3	0.7	[3] 28	44.8%	15.7	7.9%
1971	164	25	15.5%	5	6.9	0.7	[3] 20	44.8%	10.8	6.6%
1970	146	22	15.3%	6	6.3	1.2	[3] 16	40.5%	9.3	6.4%

Balance Sheet Data (Million $)

May 31[1]	Cash	Current Assets	Current Liab.	Ratio	Total Assets	Ret. on Assets	Long Term Debt	Common Equity	Total Cap.	% LT Debt of Cap.	Ret. on Equity
1979	57.1	541	194	2.8	842	11.4%	136	483	644	21.2%	19.1%
1978	41.8	429	153	2.8	643	13.5%	62	403	484	12.8%	21.0%
1977	66.2	358	108	3.3	491	12.5%	37	327	380	9.8%	18.8%
1976	95.0	310	84	3.7	415	11.5%	40	274	328	12.1%	17.3%
1975	70.5	248	61	4.1	345	9.2%	39	232	284	13.6%	13.8%
1974	36.3	217	64	3.4	307	9.4%	30	202	243	12.3%	13.9%
1973	18.7	176	68	2.6	251	9.2%	1	175	183	0.3%	12.8%
1972	27.2	146	49	3.0	200	8.5%	1	150	151	0.6%	11.0%
1971	26.8	117	33	3.5	169	6.7%	1	134	135	0.8%	8.4%
1970	7.8	99	29	3.4	153	6.1%	2	122	124	1.4%	7.9%

Data as orig. reptd. **1.** Of fol. cal. yr. **2.** Reflects merger or acquisition. **3.** Incl. equity in earns. of nonconsol. subs. **4.** Bef. spec. item(s) in 1971.

Business Summary

Tektronix is one of the two largest test and measurement instrument companies. Test and measurement products accounted for 71% of fiscal 1980-1 sales, while information display products, mainly graphic computer terminals accounted for 29%. Foreign business provided about 41% of sales.

In order of contribution to total sales, major customer markets include electronic and electrical equipment manufacturers, the computer industry, Government, education, television, the instrumentation industry, and other including petroleum, chemical, transportation, medical, and printing and publishing markets. Primary foreign markets are the United Kingdom, France, Germany, and Japan.

Tektronix' major product is the cathode-ray oscilloscope. Other test and measurement products include modular plug-in instrument systems, spectrum analyzers, pulse generators, amplifiers, logic analyzers, microprocessor development aids, cable testers, power supplies and physiological monitors.

Information display products include graphic computer terminals that display not only words and numbers but also maps, diagrams and other pictorial content in black and white or color; graphic computing systems, which function as desktop computers or interact with a host computer; hard-copy units, which make paper copies of the CRT screen contents; display monitors, and digital plotters.

Dividend Data

Dividends have been paid since 1972.

Amt. of Divd. $	Date Decl.	Ex-divd. Date	Stock of Record	Payment Date
0.23	Sep. 29	Oct. 6	Oct. 10	Nov. 3'80
0.23	Dec. 1	Jan. 19	Jan. 23	Feb. 9'81
0.23	Mar. 26	Apr. 10	Apr. 17	May 4'81
0.23	Jun. 25	Jul. 13	Jul. 17	Aug. 3'81

Next dividend meeting: late Sep. '81.

Capitalization

Long Term Debt: $146,143,000.

Common Stock: 18,534,160 shs. (no par). Institutions hold about 49%; H. Vollum owns about 20%. Shareholders: 7,973.

Office—4900 S. W. Griffith Dr. (P.O. Box 500), Beaverton, Ore. 97077. **Tel**—(503) 644-0161. **Pres & CEO**—E. Wantland. **Secy**—R. A. Leedy, Jr. **Treas**—K. H. Knox. **Investor Contact**—F. Chamberlain (503) 643-8181. **Dirs**—H. Vollum (Chrmn), P. E. Bragdon, J. B. Castles, J. D. Gray, L. Laster, L. B. Perry, W. D. Walker, E. Wantland, F. M. Warren. **Transfer Agents**—United States National Bank of Oregon, Portland; Morgan Guaranty Trust Co., NYC. **Registrars**—First National Bank of Oregon, Portland; Citibank, NYC. **Incorporated** in Oregon in 1946.

Information has been obtained from sources believed to be reliable, but its accuracy and completeness are not guaranteed.   S.P.

FIGURE 19–1   (b)

Texas Instruments

2208

NYSE Symbol TXN   Put & Call Options on CBOE

Price	Range	P-E Ratio	Dividend	Yield	S&P Ranking
Aug. 21'81 87⅝	1981 126¼–87⅝	13	2.00	2.3%	A

Summary

Texas Instruments is the leading producer of semiconductor products, and has important representation in other segments of the electronics industry, in geophysical exploration, and in specialty metal products. Earnings for 1981 will be penalized by adverse market conditions, rising expenses, write-offs, and negative foreign currency translations. However, long-term prospects are enhanced by an impressive new products program and the trimming of low-margin products.

Current Outlook

Earnings for 1981 are expected to be in the range of $4.40–$4.60 a share, down from 1980's $9.22.

Dividends should continue at $0.50 quarterly.

Sales should increase moderately in 1981, with gains from Government electronics and geophysical exploration. Earnings, however, will be penalized by extremely weak pricing in memory components, increased depreciation and R&D expenses, phaseout costs and severance payments in the second quarter, and adverse effects from foreign currency translations. Long-term prospects are enhanced by TXN's impressive new products program and the trimming of its low-margin products.

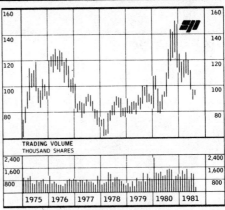

Net Sales (Million $)

Quarter:	1981	1980	1979	1978
Mar.	1,063	956	721	558
Jun.	1,056	1,007	784	615
Sep.		1,024	813	644
Dec.		1,087	906	733
		4,075	3,224	2,550

Sales for the six months ended June 30, 1981 rose 7.9%, year to year. Profitability was hampered by higher operating costs, a loss from the phaseout of certain product activities ($27.6 million), costs associated with employment reductions ($9.0 million), and negative effects from foreign currency translations. Pretax income fell 59%. After taxes at 42.0% against 44.0%, net income was down 58%. Share earnings were $1.91, versus $4.60.

Common Share Earnings ($)

Quarter:	1981	1980	1979	1978
Mar.	1.47	2.20	1.68	1.35
Jun.	0.44	2.40	1.95	1.50
Sep.		2.30	1.92	1.56
Dec.		2.32	2.03	1.74
		9.22	7.58	6.15

Important Developments

Jul. '81—Backlog of unfilled orders at the end of the 1981 second quarter was $2.136 billion, up from $2.037 billion a year earlier.

Jul. '81—Capital expenditures for 1981 were estimated at $405 million, down 25%, year to year. R&D expenses (TI-funded) are expected to total $220 million, up 16%, year to year.

Next earnings report due in late October.

Per Share Data ($)

Yr. End Dec. 31	1980	1979	1978	1977	1976	1975	1974	1973	1972	1971
Book Value	50.08	41.75	37.12	32.64	28.89	25.53	23.67	20.61	16.67	14.87
Earnings	9.22	7.58	¹6.15	¹5.11	¹4.25	¹2.71	¹3.92	¹3.67	¹2.17	¹1.52
Dividends	2.00	2.00	1.76	1.41	1.08	1.00	1.00	0.72½	0.41½	0.40
Payout Ratio	22%	26%	29%	28%	25%	37%	26%	20%	19%	26%
Prices—High	150¾	101	92½	102¼	129¾	119⅜	115¾	138⅞	95	64½
Low	78⅝	78	61⅜	68⅝	93⅛	61	58¾	74⅜	58⅝	39¾
P/E Ratio—	16-9	13-10	15-10	20-13	31-22	44-23	30-15	38-20	44-27	42-26

Data as orig. reptd. Adj. for stk. div(s). of 100% May 1973. **1.** Ful. dil.: 7.52 in 1979, 6.12 in 1978, 5.10 in 1977, 4.23 in 1976, 2.70 in 1975, 3.91 in 1974, 3.64 in 1973, 2.16 in 1972, 1.52 in 1971.

Standard NYSE Stock Reports
Vol. 48/No. 166/Sec. 26

August 28, 1981
Copyright © 1981 Standard & Poor's Corp. All Rights Reserved

Standard & Poor's Corp.
25 Broadway, NY, NY 10004

FIGURE 19–1 (c)

Income Data (Million $)

Year Ended Dec. 31	Revs.	Oper. Inc.	% Oper. Inc. of Revs.	Cap. Exp.	Depr.	Int. Exp.	Net Bef. Taxes	Eff. Tax Rate	Net Inc.	% Net Inc. of Revs.
1980	4,075	676	16.6%	¹542	257	44.3	379	44.0%	212	5.2%
1979	3,224	507	15.7%	435	187	19.5	309	44.0%	173	5.4%
1978	2,550	385	15.1%	311	131	8.4	257	45.5%	140	5.5%
1977	2,046	319	15.6%	200	108	9.2	211	44.7%	117	5.7%
1976	1,659	250	15.1%	138	87	8.3	178	45.3%	97	5.9%
1975	1,368	207	15.1%	71	92	10.8	116	46.4%	62	4.5%
1974	1,572	257	16.3%	150	87	10.7	163	45.0%	90	5.7%
1973	1,287	205	15.9%	127	60	6.7	146	42.8%	83	6.5%
1972	944	131	13.9%	54	48	5.7	85	43.2%	48	5.1%
1971	764	110	14.4%	35	51	6.5	59	43.3%	34	4.4%

Balance Sheet Data (Million $)

Dec. 31	Cash	Current Assets	Current Liab.	Ratio	Total Assets	Ret. on Assets	Long Term Debt	Common Equity	Total Cap.	% LT Debt of Cap.	Ret. on Equity
1980	140	1,299	971	1.3	2,414	9.7%	212	1,165	1,376	15.4%	19.9%
1979	117	1,083	882	1.2	1,908	10.1%	18	953	970	1.8%	19.2%
1978	115	915	637	1.4	1,518	10.1%	19	845	864	2.2%	17.7%
1977	257	815	467	1.7	1,255	9.8%	30	745	774	3.8%	16.6%
1976	294	783	418	1.9	1,128	9.4%	38	660	698	5.5%	15.7%
1975	267	663	302	2.2	941	6.5%	48	585	633	7.5%	11.0%
1974	155	656	342	1.9	965	10.0%	73	541	614	11.8%	17.7%
1973	179	590	283	2.1	828	11.3%	68	469	537	12.6%	19.6%
1972	196	470	188	2.5	634	7.9%	71	370	441	16.2%	13.7%
1971	186	415	153	2.7	580	6.1%	95	329	423	22.4%	10.7%

Data as orig. reptd. 1. Net of curr. yr. retirement and disposals.

Business Summary

Texas Instruments produces a variety of electrical and electronics products for industrial, consumer and government markets. Contributions by industry segment in 1980 were:

	Sales	Profits
Components	44%	52%
Digital products	24%	13%
Government electronics	18%	17%
Metallurgical materials	3%	5%
Services	11%	13%

Operations outside the U.S. accounted for 34% of sales and 45% of operating profits.

Components include semiconductor integrated circuits (microprocessors, memories and digital and linear circuits), semiconductor discrete devices (transistors, diodes and optoelectronic products), assembled modules (microprocessor and memory printed circuit boards), and electrical and electronic control devices.

Digital products include minicomputers, electronic data terminals and peripherals, geophysical and scientific equipment, electronic calculators, home computers, learning aids and other products.

Government Electronics products include radar, infrared surveillance systems and missile guidance and control systems.

Services mainly consist of the collection and electronic processing of seismic data in connection with petroleum exploration.

Metallurgical materials primarily involve clad metals which are used in variety of applications.

Employees: 89,875.

Dividend Data

Dividends have been paid since 1962.

Amt. of Div. $	Date Decl.	Ex-divd. Date	Stock of Record	Payment Date
0.50	Sep. 26	Sep. 30	Oct. 6	Oct. 27'80
0.50	Dec. 19	Dec. 26	Jan. 2	Jan. 26'81
0.50	Mar. 13	Mar. 24	Mar. 30	Apr. 20'81
0.50	Jun. 22	Jun. 26	Jul. 2	Jul. 27'81

Next dividend meeting: late Sep. '81.

Capitalization

Long Term Debt: $213,200,000.

Common Stock: 23,530,905 shs. ($1 par). Institutions hold about 66%. Shareholders: 28,370.

Office— 13500 North Central Expressway, Dallas, Texas 75265. **Tel**— (214) 995-3773. **Chrmn & CEO**—M. Shepherd, Jr. **Pres**—J. F. Bucy. **VP-Secy**—W. J. Roche. **VP-Treas**—M. L. Lane, Jr. **Investor Contact**—M. Post. **Dirs**—J. F. Bucy, E. G. Fubini, S. T. Harris, E. R. Kane, P. F. Lorenz, P. W. McCracken, F. Seitz, M. Shepherd, Jr., B. F. Smith, C. J. Thomsen, J. M. Voss, J. M. Walker. **Transfer Agents & Registrars**—Republic National Bank, Dallas; Morgan Guaranty Trust Co., NYC. **Incorporated** in Delaware in 1938.

FIGURE 19–1 (d)

Hewlett-Packard

NYSE Symbol HWP   Put & Call Options on CBOE

Price	Range	P-E Ratio	Dividend	Yield	S&P Ranking
Oct. 6'81 41⅞	1981 53⅞-38⅜	17	0.24	0.6%	A+

Summary

This electronics concern is the largest manufacturer of electronic test and measurement instruments, and the second leading producer of minicomputers. The upward trend in earnings should be maintained over the intermediate term, but the rate of improvement may be reduced in fiscal 1981, partly as a result of slower economies overseas. The shares were recently split 2-for-1.

Current Outlook

Earnings for fiscal 1982 are projected at $3.20 a share, up from the $2.55 a share estimated for fiscal 1981.

Dividends should continue at the recently increased rate of $0.06 quarterly.

Revenues should continue to advance at a strong pace through fiscal 1982, although the strong gains of the past several years may not be repeated. The advance should be aided by a large order backlog (up 25%, year to year, at July 31, 1981, despite some third-quarter weakness in order rates). Price adjustments, close control of expenses and employment levels, and efficient asset management are expected to help maintain margins while commitments to research and development are increased. The potential productivity improvements offered by HWP's products should help sustain rising demand over the longer term.

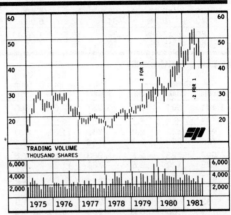

Net Sales (Million $)

Quarter:	1980-1	1979-80	1978-9	1977-8
Jan.	775	664	505	368
Apr.	867	754	555	415
Jul.	936	810	620	428
Oct.		871	681	517
	3,099	2,361	1,728	

Sales for the nine months ended July 31, 1981 rose 16%, year to year, reflecting gains in all four segments. Operating expenses were fairly well controlled, but with R&D expenditures up 28%, the gain in pretax income was held to 12%. After taxes at 47.3%, versus 49.1%, net income advanced 15%, to $1.78 a share from $1.58.

Common Share Earnings ($)

Quarter:	1980-1	1979-80	1978-9	1977-8
Jan.	0.53	0.46	0.38	0.29
Apr.	0.60	0.55	0.43	0.31
Jul.	0.66	0.58	0.45	0.29
Oct.		0.66	0.47	0.44
		2.24	1.72	1.32

Important Developments

Sep. '81—HWP entered into negotiations to acquire Software Management Corp., a private producer of software products with fiscal 1981 sales of $1.6 million, for an undisclosed amount of stock. The acquisition of Information Resources Ltd., a software development firm, is still pending.

Aug. '81—HWP introduced its first desk-top computer, the HP 125, priced from $7,500.

Next earnings report due in mid-November.

Per Share Data ($)
Yr. End Oct. 31

	1981	1980	1979	1978	1977	1976	1975	1974	1973	¹1972
Book Value	NA	12.85	10.44	8.64	7.22	6.02	5.06	4.17	3.23	2.67
Earnings²	NA	2.24	1.72	1.32	1.07	0.81	0.76	0.77	0.48	0.35
Dividends	0.22	0.20	0.17½	0.12½	0.10	0.07½	0.06⅜	0.05	0.05	0.05
Payout Ratio	NA	9%	10%	9%	9%	9%	8%	6%	11%	14%
Prices³—High	53⅞	48½	31½	23¼	21⅞	29½	30¼	23⅛	25¼	22⅛
Low	39	25⅝	21	15½	17⅛	20	14⅛	13	17⅞	11½
P/E Ratio—	NA	22-11	18-12	18-12	20-16	36-25	40-19	30-17	53-38	61-31

Data as orig. reptd. Adj. for stk. div(s). of 100% Jul. 1981, 100% Jul. 1979. 1. Reflects merger or acquisition. 2. Bef. spec. item(s) of +0.01 in 1972, +0.01 in 1971. 3. Cal. yr. NA-Not Available.

October 14, 1981

Standard & Poor's Corp.
25 Broadway, NY, NY 10004

FIGURE 19-1   (e)

Investment Analysis

Hewlett-Packard Company

Income Data (Million $)

Year Ended Oct. 31	Revs.	Oper. Inc.	% Oper. Inc. of Revs.	Cap. Exp.	Depr.	Int. Exp.	Net Bef. Taxes	Eff. Tax Rate	[4]Net Inc.	% Net Inc. of Revs.
1980	3,099	616	19.9%	297	93.0	NA	523	48.6%	269	8.7%
1979	2,361	470	19.9%	191	72.0	NA	[3]398	49.0%	203	8.6%
1978	1,728	335	19.4%	159	56.0	6.00	[3]296	48.3%	153	8.9%
1977	1,360	267	19.6%	116	47.6	4.20	[3]229	47.0%	122	8.9%
1976	1,112	192	17.3%	103	39.5	4.12	[3]161	43.5%	91	8.2%
1975	981	178	18.1%	66	35.3	2.19	[3]149	43.7%	84	8.5%
1974	884	176	19.9%	86	31.5	8.50	[3]144	41.8%	84	9.5%
1973	661	110	16.7%	81	22.9	5.06	[3] 95	46.3%	51	7.7%
[1]1972	479	85	17.7%	39	16.7	1.76	[3] 70	46.7%	37	7.8%
[2]1971	375	56	15.0%	19	15.1	1.24	[3] 43	47.3%	23	6.1%

Balance Sheet Data (Million $)

Oct. 31	Cash	Assets	Current Liab.	Ratio	Total Assets	Ret. on Assets	Long Term Debt	Common Equity	Total Cap.	% LT Debt of Cap.	Ret. on Equity
1980	247	1,491	691	2.2	2,337	12.6%	29.0	1,547	1,646	1.8%	19.2%
1979	248	1,269	599	2.1	1,900	12.0%	15.0	1,235	1,301	1.2%	18.0%
1978	189	952	415	2.3	1,462	11.6%	10.0	1,002	1,047	1.0%	16.6%
1977	173	752	292	2.6	1,158	11.5%	12.1	824	866	1.4%	16.1%
1976	107	597	223	2.7	933	10.6%	7.6	677	711	1.1%	14.6%
1975	78	499	179	2.8	768	11.7%	4.9	561	588	0.8%	16.3%
1974	14	417	179	2.3	654	13.5%	2.9	458	475	0.6%	20.7%
1973	9	395	221	1.8	580	10.5%	2.2	349	359	0.6%	15.9%
1972	20	263	96	2.7	383	10.9%	1.9	284	288	0.7%	14.3%
1971	11	194	60	3.2	294	8.1%	1.3	233	234	0.5%	10.4%

Data as orig. reptd. 1. Reflects merger or acquisition. 2. Reflects accounting change. 3. Incl. equity in earns. of nonconsol. subs. 4. Bef. spec. item(s) in 1972, 1971. NA-Not Available.

Business Summary

Hewlett-Packard produces a broad range of electronic instruments and systems for measurement, analysis and computation. Business segment contributions in fiscal 1980 were:

	Sales	Profits
Electronic Test & Measurement Products......	39%	44%
Electronic Data Products	49%	46%
Medical Electronic Equipment..........................	7%	6%
Analytical Instrumentation	5%	4%

Operations in Europe provided 37% of sales and 24% of operating income in fiscal 1980. Foreign activities outside Europe amounted to 14% and 9%, respectively.

Test and measurement instruments evaluate the operation of electrical equipment against predetermined standards and produce, measure or display electronic signals.

Electronic data products include computers, data terminals, printers, disc memories, and calculators.

Medical electronic equipment acquire, display, record, store and analyze bio-medical signals.

Analytical instrumentation include gas and liquid chromatographs and gas chromatograph/mass spectrometers.

Employees: 57,000.

Dividend Data

Dividends have been paid since 1965.

Amt. of Divd. $	Date Decl.	Ex-divd. Date	Stock of Record	Payment Date
0.10	Dec. 5	Dec. 18	Dec. 24	Jan. 15'81
0.10	Jan. 23	Mar. 19	Mar. 25	Apr. 15'81
2-for-1	May 15	Jul. 20	Jun. 17	Jul. 17'81
0.06	May 15	Jun. 11	Jun. 17	Jul. 8'81
0.06	Jul. 16	Sep. 17	Sep. 23	Oct. 15'81

Next dividend meeting: early Dec: '81.

Capitalization

Long Term Debt: $23,000,000.

Common Stock: 122,000,000 shs. ($1 par). Institutions hold about 47%; W.R. Hewlett & D. Packard families control some 35% (in part held by institutions).
Shareholders: 33,854.

Office—1501 Page Mill Rd., Palo Alto, Calif. 94304. Tel—(415) 857-1501. Pres & CEO—J. A. Young. Secy—S. T. J. Brigham III. VP-Treas & Investor Contact—E. E. van Bronkhorst. Dirs—D. Packard (Chrmn), L. W. Alvarez, E. C. Arbuckle, G. F. Bennett, R. L. Boniface, R. M. Brown, W. P. Doolittle, R. C. Ely, Jr., R. J. Glaser, H. J. Haynes, W. R. Hewlett, J. D. Hodgson, A. T. Knoppers, D. O. Morton, T. P. Pike, W. E. Terry, E. E. van Bronkhorst, J. A. Young. Transfer Agent & Registrar—Crocker National Bank, San Francisco. Incorporated in California in 1947.

Information has been obtained from sources believed to be reliable, but its accuracy and completeness are not guaranteed. J.R.L.

FIGURE 19-1 (f)

TABLE 19-5
Sales for Hewlett-Packard, Tektronix, and Texas Instruments
(Millions of dollars; index 1972 = 100)

Year	HWP Sales	HWP Index	HWP % Change	TEK Sales	TEK Index	TEK % Change	TXN Sales	TXN Index	TXN % Change
1982E	$4,402	919	23%	$1,175	716	11%	$4,700	498	12%
1981	3,580	747	15	1,062	647	9	4,200	445	3
1980	3,099	647	31	971	592	23	4,074	432	27
1979	2,361	493	37	786	480	31	3,224	341	26
1978	1,728	360	26	589	365	39	2,549	270	30
Average rate of growth 1978–82		26			23			20	
Standard deviation		9			13			12	

SOURCE: Value Line Investment Survey—Electrical Equipment Industry, November 13, 1981, pp. 1052, 1069, 1071.

Tektronix, Inc. (TEK)

Tektronix is the leading producer of precision cathode-ray oscilloscopes, which show a visual presentation of electrical wave forms on the screen of a cathode-ray tube similar to that of a TV receiver. TEK's markets include electronic and electrical equipment manufacturers, computer manufacturers, government, education, TV broadcasting, and "other"—petroleum, chemicals, transportation, printing, publishing, and medicine.[4]

Foreign sales amounted to 41 percent of sales in 1980. This company has grown at 23 percent per year on the average for the last five years, although the growth rate was only 9 percent in 1981.

Texas Instruments (TXN)

Texas Instruments is the world leader in the semiconductor industry. It also has important representation in minicomputers, electronic systems, geophysical services, calculators, digital watches, and other electrical products. Semiconductor products account for about 44 percent of sales, and 18 percent comes from government. The overseas market accounted for 34 percent of sales in 1980. The company groups consist of semiconductor products, government electronic products, distributed computing products, materials and electrical products, and geophysical services.[5]

Summary of the Competitive Positions

On the basis of the past, we would rank HWP as the most competitive firm, Texas Instruments next, and then Tektronix. Unfortunately, past competitive practices have changed. There is some doubt about the ability of HWP to maintain its past growth

[4]Standard & Poor's *Stock Reports,* August 2, 1976, p. 2195.
[5]Standard & Poor's *Stock Reports,* August 27, 1976, p. 2208.

rate. *The Value Line* estimates of future sales suggest that growth will be greatest for HWP (21 percent), followed by TEK (16 percent), and then TXN (15 percent). The competitive position of the companies may be summarized as follows:

	HWP	TEK	TXN
Size	1	3	2
Sales growth 1978–81	1	2	3
Sales growth 1981–84	1 (21%)	2 (16%)	3 (15%)
Sales stability, 1978–81	1	3	2
Product development	1	3	2

EARNINGS AND PROFITABILITY

The growth of earnings per share for the three companies is presented in Table 19–6. HWP has had the highest average growth rate of earnings, with a lower growth rate in 1982. TXN has had a 23 percent growth rate, and earnings per share increased by 66 percent in 1982. TEK (Tektronix) has experienced the lowest rate of growth (22 percent) for the ten-year period, but earnings increased by 13 percent in 1982.

TABLE 19–6

Earnings per Share and Annual Percentage Change for Hewlett Packard, Tektronix, and Texas Instruments

Year	HWP		TEK		TXN	
	EPS	% Change	EPS	% Change	EPS	% Change
1983E*	$4.23	43%	$7.15	46%	$11.95	71%
1982E	2.95	18	4.90	13	7.00	65
1981	2.50	12	4.34	(7)	4.25	(54)
1980	2.24	30	4.66	9	9.22	22
1979	1.72	30	4.28	34	7.58	23
1978	1.32	23	3.19	28	6.15	20
1977	1.07	32	2.49	45	5.11	20
1976	0.81	7	1.72	13	4.25	57
1975	0.76	(1)**	1.52	23	2.71	(31)
1974	0.77	64	1.24	27	3.92	7
1973	0.47	34	0.98	40	3.67	69
1972	0.35	59	0.67	10	2.17	60
Average (1972–82)		28		22		23
Standard deviation		20		6		39

*E, estimate.   **Negative.

NOTE: Estimates for 1983 are based on an average of 1982 and 1984–86 estimates.

SOURCE: *Value Line Investment Survey—Electrical Equipment Industry,* November 13, 1981, pp. 1052, 1069, 1071.

FUNDAMENTAL ANALYSIS

Unfortunately, TXN has had the most unstable earnings. HWP was the second least stable, and TEK enjoyed the most stable earnings for the period.

The profit margin on the average was highest for HWP, followed by TEK. TXN had the lowest average profit margin. These relationships are summarized in Table 19–7.

TABLE 19–7

Profit Margin, Percent Earned on Capital, Net Income as a Percent of Sales for Hewlett-Packard, Tektronix, and Texas Instruments

Year	Net Income as a Percent of Sales			Percent Earned on Capital			Profit Margin		
	HWP	TEK	TXN	HWP	TEK	TXN	HWP	TEK	TXN
1982E	7.4	7.7	3.5	10.0	12.5	11.0	20.0	17.5	14.0
1981	4.3	7.6	2.4	5.5	17.6	7.5	12.0	17.0	17.5
1980	11.3	8.8	5.2	16.6	14.2	16.5	27.2	18.3	16.6
1979	11.7	9.8	5.5	25.7	16.7	17.9	29.0	18.1	15.7
1978	11.1	9.5	5.5	21.6	16.0	16.4	27.6	18.3	15.1
1977	11.2	9.7	5.7	21.3	14.4	15.2	28.0	19.6	15.6
1976	11.2	8.2	5.9	23.0	11.7	14.2	27.0	18.9	15.1
1975	11.9	7.8	4.5	21.9	11.7	10.2	27.9	18.0	15.1
Average	10.0	7.5	4.8	18.2	13.7	13.6	24.8	18.2	14.9
Standard deviation	2.7	2.8	1.2	1.3	1.9	3.6	5.9	7.9	1.2

SOURCE: *Value Line Investment Survey—Electrical Equipment Industry,* November 13, 1981, pp. 1052, 1069, 1071.

Hewlett-Packard earned the highest percentage profit on total capital of the three companies. On the other hand, the average net income as a percent of sales was highest for Hewlett-Packard, second was TEK, and third was TXN. On an overall basis, HWP has an edge over TEK, with TXN in third position.

The profit and earnings position of the three companies is summarized as follows:

	HWP	TEK	TXN
Magnitude of earnings per share (EPS)	3	2	1
Rate of growth of EPS	1	2	3
Stability of EPS	2	1	3
Magnitude of profit	1	3	2
Percent earned on capital	1	2	3
Net income to sales	1	2	3
Overall profitability ratios	1	2	3

ESTIMATED FUTURE EARNINGS

A summary of estimated earnings for HWP, TEK, and TXN appears in Table 19–8. Three methods of estimating future earnings were used. The trend-of-earnings method represented an extension into the future of the past earnings growth rates. The second

TABLE 19–8

Earnings per Share Estimates for Hewlett-Packard, Tektronix, and Texas Instruments (1981–1984)

HWP

	Trend of Earnings* $	Sales to Earnings† $	Pro Forma Estimate‡ $	Average Estimate (Change) $	%
1984	4.83	4.00	5.76	4.86	24
1983	3.78	3.45	4.58	3.93	26
1982	2.95	3.00	3.64	3.12	24
1981				2.50	
				AV	25

	Shares Outstanding	Sales, $	PM, %	P, $
1984	121.2	6,989	25	1,747
1983	121.0	5,546	25	1,387
1982	120.8	4,402	25	880
1981	120.6			

TEK

	Trend of Earnings* $	Sales to Earnings† $	Pro Forma Estimate‡ $	Average Estimate (Change) $	%
1984	7.29	6.65	7.09	7.01	18
1983	5.98	6.00	5.78	5.92	17
1982	4.90	5.50	4.74	5.05	16
1981				4.34	
				AV	17

	Shares Outstanding	Sales, $	PM, %	P, $
1984	18.8	1,778	18	320
1983	18.7	1,445	18	260
1982	18.6	1,175	18	212
1981	18.5			

TXN

	Trend of Earnings* $	Sales to Earnings† $	Pro Forma Estimate‡ $	Average Estimate (Change) $	%
1984	10.59	7.35	12.64	10.19	20
1983	8.61	6.20	10.62	8.47	22
1982	7.00	5.00	8.92	6.97	64
1981				4.25	
				AV	35

	Shares Outstanding	Sales, $	PM, %	P, $
1984	24.1	6,748	15	1,015
1983	23.9	5,640	15	846
1982	23.7	4,700	15	705
1981	23.5			

*HWP = 28%, TEK = 22%, TXN = 23%.

†Based upon trend growth of sales to earnings per share. HWP growth of sales to earnings = 28%, TEK = 23%, and TXN = 20%. The net-income-to-sales ratio for HWP was 10.0%, TEK was 7.5%, and TXN was 4.2%.

‡These are based on the figures in the bottom half of the table. PM is profit margin and P is profit. Sales, shares, and profits are in millions.

method was the relationship between sales and earnings per share. A sales forecast was made based on past relationships and extended into the future. The results of this forecast appear in Figure 19–2. The third method was to estimate earnings on the basis of pro forma analysis. Future sales were estimated, and the average net income as a percent of sales was used to estimate net income after taxes. This figure was obtained from Table 19–7. The net income estimate was then divided by the number of shares outstanding. Since the number of shares outstanding for each company has tended to increase each year, it was necessary to estimate the number of new shares that would be outstanding in each future year. These estimates are found in Table 19–8. All three estimates were averaged to provide an estimate of the future growth of earnings per share.

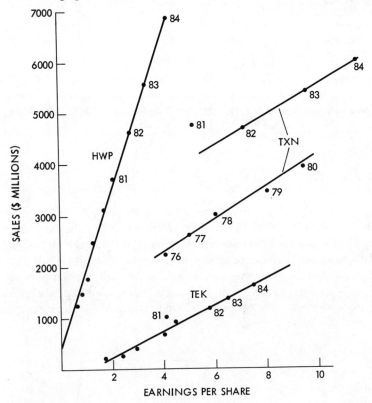

FIGURE 19–2

Sales Forecast for Hewlett-Packard, Tektronix, and Texas Instruments

A summary of the estimates of future earnings suggests the following ranking of the companies:

	HWP	TEK	TXN
Amount of future earnings per share	3	2	1
Future growth rate of earnings per share	2	3	1
Stability of future earnings per share	2	1	3

TABLE 19-9

Operating Ratio, Sales per Employee, Net Income per Employee, Sales per Dollar of Plant, Net Income per Dollar of Plant, and Capital Expenditures as a Percent of Gross Plant, 1981, for Hewlett-Packard, Tektronix, and Texas Instruments

	HWP	TEK	TXN
Operating Ratio	73	82	83
Employees	52,000	23,900	89,875
Sales ($ millions)	3,099	971	4,075
Sales per Employee ($)	59,598	40,268	45,341
Net Income ($ millions)	269	85	212
Net Income per Employee ($)	5,173	3,696	2,359
Net Plant ($ millions)	789	277	1,097
Gross Plant ($ millions)	1,161	403	1,723
Sales per Dollar of Gross Plant ($)	3.93	3.51	3.71
Net Income per Dollar of Gross Plant ($)	.34	.31	.19
Capital Expenditures, % of Gross Plant	38	42	49

SOURCES: *Value Line Investment Survey,* November 13, 1981, pp. 1051, 1069, 1071; Moody's *Industrial Manual,* 1981, vol. I, p. 2406, vol. II, pp. 5553, 5561.

OPERATING EFFICIENCY

The ratios of operating efficiency are presented in Table 19–9. As you study this table, you will note that HWP had the lowest operating ratio but the largest amount of sales per employee based on 1980 data. In addition, HWP had the highest income per employee. This suggests that the company is the most efficient. HWP also had the greatest sales per dollar of gross property, as well as the highest amount of net income per dollar of gross property. TXN spent the greatest amount for capital expenditures as a percent of gross property. The operating characteristics of the three companies may be summarized as follows:

	HWP	TEK	TXN
Productive capacity	2	3	1
Growth of property	2	3	1
Operating ratio	3	2	1
Sales per dollar of gross plant	1	3	2
Sales per employee	1	3	2
Net income per dollar of gross plant	1	2	3
Net income per employee	1	2	3
Capital expenditures as a percent of gross plant	3	2	1
Overall operating characteristics	2	3	1

CURRENT FINANCIAL POSITION

Table 19–10 summarizes the current financial position of these three major companies in the electronics industry. Each company operates under a different set of financial constraints. If liquidity is a virtue, then HWP would be first, since it has the highest

TABLE 19–10

Current Financial Analysis of Hewlett-Packard, Tektronix, and Texas Instruments, 1972, 1976, 1980

Ratio	HWP			TEK			TXN		
	1972	1976	1980	1972	1976	1980	1972	1976	1980
Current ratio	2.7	2.7	2.5	3.2	4.1	2.7	2.5	1.9	1.4
Acid-test ratio	1.5	1.6	1.5	1.7	2.5	1.3	1.9	1.4	.9
Composition of current assets:									
Cash (%)	7.5	18.0	28.0	20.2	28.2	8.0	41.7	38.0	5.0
Receivables (%)	45.1	39.2	40.0	29.4	28.2	36.0	33.4	36.0	53.0
Inventories (%)	45.2	39.9	20.0	48.3	39.9	51.0	21.9	25.0	34.0
Other (%)	2.2	2.9	12.0	2.1	3.7	5.0	3.0	1.0	8.0
Receivables outstanding (daily credit sales divided into receivables)	90.0	77.0	62.0	80.0	70.0	70.0	88.0	62.0	54.0
Net sales to inventory	4.0	4.7	8.6	2.8	3.7	3.6	9.2	8.4	10.3
Net sales to working capital	2.9	3.0	2.9	1.9	2.0	2.9	3.3	4.9	12.5

SOURCE: Figure 19–1, Standard & Poor's *Stock Reports,* and *The Value Line Investment Surveys,* February 18, 1977, p. 1066; April 8, 1977, pp. 187, 198; November 13, 1981, pp. 1052, 1069, 1071.

acid-test ratio and a high liquid cash position. TXN has the lowest amount of receivables outstanding related to sales, and the highest ratio of net sales to inventory. The current financial position of all three companies is adequate. The current financial analysis may be summarized as follows:

	HWP	TEK	TXN
Current ratio	2	1	3
Acid-test ratio	1	2	3
Liquidity (cash)	1	2	3
Receivables outstanding (days' sales)	3	2	1
Net sales to inventory	2	3	1
Net sales to working capital	2	3	1
Overall liquidity	2	1	3

CAPITAL STRUCTURE ANALYSIS

Table 19–11 reveals that HWP has the simplest capital structure and the smallest amount of debt as a percentage of the capital structure. It also has the highest interest-coverage ratio, the smallest amount of debt to net worth, and the least amount of debt to gross property and working capital. TEK, by contrast, has the highest amount of debt in its capital structure, the highest-debt-to-net-worth ratio, and the highest debt to gross property and working capital. Even though the debt is relatively high,

TABLE 19–11

Capital Structure and Debt Limits of Hewlett-Packard, Tektronix, and Texas Instruments

Capital Structure	1972		1976		1980	
	Dollars in Millions	% of Total	Dollars in Millions	% of Total	Dollars in Millions	% of Total
Hewlett-Packard						
Long-term debt	2	1	8	1	26	1
Preferred stock	0	0	0	0	0	0
Net worth	283	99	677	99	1810	99
Total	285	100	685	100	1836	100
Tektronix						
Long-term debt	1	1	39	14	146	21
Preferred stock	0	0	0	0	0	0
Net worth	134	99	232	86	558	79
Total	135	100	271	100	704	100
Texas Instruments						
Long-term debt	21	4	38	5	213	14
Preferred stock	2	1	0	0	0	0
Net worth	444	95	660	95	1260	86
Total	467	100	698	100	1473	100

Debt Limits	HWP			TEK			TXN		
	1972	1976	1980	1972	1976	1980	1972	1976	1980
Number of times fixed charges earned, after taxes	22.0	180.0	27.0	—	19.4	8.2	21.4	54.0	6.1
Number of times preferred charges earned, after taxes	—	—	—	—	—	—	16.7	—	—
Total debt to capitalization (%)	31.0	1.0	1.0	1.0	14.0	21.0	4.0	5.0	15.0
Long-term debt to working capital (%)	1.2	2.0	2.5	1.0	18.0	26.0	25.0	11.0	16.0
Rate of return on equity (%)	13.0	13.0	16.0	8.0	13.0	14.4	13.0	15.0	8.0
Rate of return on capital (%)	13.0	13.0	16.0	8.0	12.0	12.6	12.0	14.0	7.5

SOURCE: *Value Line Investment Survey—Electrical Equipment Industry,* November 13, 1981, pp. 1052, 1069, 1071.

it is not excessive. TXN is adequately financed and its debt adequately secured by assets, equity, and net income. A summary of the capital structure analysis would be as follows:

	HWP	TEK	TXN
Debt as a percent of capital structure	1	3	2
Times fixed charges earned	1	2	3
Times preferred charges earned	—	—	—
Debt to capitalization	1	3	2
Debt to working capital	1	3	2
Overall debt position	1	3	2

MANAGEMENT

The management of the three companies under analysis reflects a background of high-level competence and attainment. Yet some problems have occurred for all the companies. We now look at the strategies of the top managements of HWP, TEK, and TXN.

Hewlett-Packard

David Packard[6] was chairman of the board of directors and J. A. Young[7] was president of Hewlett-Packard. Their record is the best guide to their accomplishments. Management has stressed research and development and brought the company to the position of the world's largest maker of electronic measuring instruments.

Management's emphasis on R&D and foreign growth suggests further growth for the company, especially in electronic data products. The company was expected to introduce a large number of measurement instruments which are computer controlled, with the goal of increasing productivity in this area. Management has achieved success through close control of expenses and employment levels and efficient asset management, as well as a commitment to R&D.

Tektronix, Inc.

Tektronix's management has made the company the world's leading producer of cathode-ray oscilloscopes and has expanded the product line to include other products using a graphic display. Further growth is anticipated because of the company's recognized technological abilities. Management has increased sales 600 percent since 1972, substantially increased net income, and increased shareholder's equity; and at the same time, it has maintained liquidity. Tektronix's strategy is to increase market share in CRT oscilloscopes by introducing a new line aimed at the low-price end of the market. This approach is devised to meet strong competition from Japan. The president of Tektronix is E. Wantland and the chairman is Howard Vollum.

[6] *Who's Who in America*, 39th ed. (Chicago: Marquis—Who's Who, 1981–1982).
[7] Ibid.

Texas Instruments

Texas Instruments' management has brought it to the point where it is the leading producer of semiconductor products. The company's leadership in microelectronics and the emphasis on R&D make long-term prospects for the company attractive.

In 1981 revenues of the semiconductor division had been falling due to a poor European market and reduced domestic orders. Price competition had been strong. However, increased defense spending, starting in 1981, meant higher sales and earnings for the government electronics division.

Over the past decade, TXN had increased sales almost five times, had increased property almost the same amount, and had quadrupled net income. Earnings per share have increased but they have been cyclical, reflecting the competitive nature of the semiconductor industry. The new products and production methods have kept this company a leader in a rapidly changing industry.

Management's Attainments by Objective Standards

The management background of the companies suggests success. However, we must use objective criteria to judge how well they have done. This may be summarized as follows:

	HWP	TEK	TXN
Ability to maintain competitive position	1	3	2
Ability to expand	2	3	1
Ability to maintain profitability	1	2	3
Ability to finance growth	1	3	2
Ability to expand R&D	1 (9%)*	2 (8%)*	3 (5%)*
Ability to meet secular and cyclical changes	1	3	2
Overall management	1	3	2

*Percentage of sales.

It would appear that on an objective basis, HWP would be first, followed by TXN as a close second and TEK as a close third.

PRICE ACTION, RETURN, RISK, BETA, AND FUTURE EXPECTED RETURN

HISTORIC RETURN.   A great deal of financial data presented in Table 19–12 will help us make a final decision about the three companies. We also have a comparison with the S&P 500 Index. All companies have been more profitable than the S&P 500 Index. We notice that TEK earned the highest average annual return, 18.07%, compared to 18.04% for HWP and 11.63% for TXN. TEK also had the highest absolute risk with a reward-to-risk ratio of .15. HWP had the highest historical R/R, .16, and TXN was last with —.08. On a historical basis, therefore, HWP seems to have been the most profitable and least risky investment.

TABLE 19–12

Historical Financial Data and Forecasts for Hewlett-Packard, Tektronix, and Texas Instruments

	HWP	TEK	TXN	S&P 500
Historic return, %	18.04	18.07	11.63	7.51
Historic reward-to-risk ratio	.16	.15	−.08	−.44
Earnings stability	85.35	86.69	81.85	93.00
Price stability	66.34	64.01	67.43	83.40
Dividend growth rate, %	18.53	34.18	21.21	9.20
Beta	1.12	1.64	1.01	1.00
P/E ratio	9.54	12.56	8.21	8.28
Earnings growth rate, %	26.01	25.96	18.94	10.85
Expected return, $\bar{r}$, %	79.51	40.93	58.73	28.05
Expected risk and variability of return, %	46.15	30.46	38.27	18.42
Total return 10/10 trend, %	81.87	48.68	69.92	28.02
Analyst's best estimate of return, %	16.00	12.00	30.00	n/a
Estimated return-to-risk ratio	1.46	.74	1.05	.86

SOURCE: MODE I of Modesystem, Frederick Amling & Associates, Washington, D.C.

EARNINGS STABILITY. TEK has enjoyed the highest earnings stability, with an index of 86.69, compared to 85.32 for HWP and 81.85 for TXN. Notice, however, that all three were below the earnings stability of the market.

DIVIDEND GROWTH RATE. TEK had the highest dividend growth rate, 34.18 percent. TXN had an excellent dividend growth rate of 21.21 percent, and so did HWP, with 18.53 percent.

REWARD-TO-RISK RATIO. The RANDOM valuation model output "3YR SIML" and "STD-RISK" allow for the calculation of the reward-to-risk ratio, "RWRD/ RISK." TXN and HWP had acceptable ratios at 1.05 and 1.46. On this basis the investor would choose one of them.

BETA ANALYSIS. The ten-year beta figures indicate that all three companies have betas higher than the market, and that TXN has the lowest beta volatility. This means that TXN is less risky compared to the market than HWP and TEK.

P/E RATIOS. All the companies are selling well below their ten-year trend P/E ratios. This suggests a good deal of pessimism expressed toward the companies, if you accept the thesis that a low P/E indicates a lack of confidence. It might also mean that these stocks are relatively cheap.

PRICE STABILITY. TXN has had the highest statistical price stability, 67.43, compared to second-place HWP with 66.34 and TEK with the lowest, 64.01.

EARNINGS GROWTH RATE. HWP enjoyed the highest growth rate of earnings, with a 26.01 percent ten-year rate. This was higher and more stable than TXN, although TEK was a close second.

EXPECTED RETURN. The expected return generated by the computer for both TREND and RANDOM indicates that HWP is the most attractive, followed by TXN and then TEK. On the basis of expected return alone, HWP would be the investor's choice.

VALUATION METHOD, ANALYSTS' BEST ESTIMATE (ABE). The ABE is another way to estimate the return we will receive. Here we will use again the present-value equation:

$$P_0 = \sum_{t=1}^{n=3} \frac{D_0(1 + g_d)^t}{(1 + r)^t} + \frac{E_0(1 + g_e)^3(P/E)_3}{(1 + r)^3}$$

and solve for r, the present value of return, using ABE. In the equation, the following price and growth rates are used for each company:

	HWP	TEK	TXN
Earnings 1980, E_0, $	2.24	4.66	9.22
Dividends 1980, D_0, $	.20	.86	2.00
Earnings growth rate (%) EST.	28	22	23
Earnings in 3 years ($) AV.	3.93	5.92	8.47
Dividend growth rate (%) EST.	20	19	12
P/E ratio, 3 yr	18	12	21
Present price ($)	47	54	83
P_3—price in 3 years ($EPS_3 \times (P/E)_3$), $	71	71	178

The present-value calculations based on these numbers are as follows:

	Dividend Income ($)	× PV Factor	= Present Value ($)
HWP		(16%)	
1981	.24	.862	.21
1982	.29	.743	.22
1983	.35	.641	.22
Price 1983 (P_3)	71.00	.641	45.51
Total PV			46.16
Present price (P_0)			47.00
TEK		(12%)	
1981	1.02	.893	.91
1982	1.22	.797	.97
1983	1.45	.712	1.03
Price 1983 (P_3)	71.00	.712	50.55
Total PV			53.46
Present price (P_0)			54.00
TXN		(30%)	
1981	2.24	.769	1.72
1982	2.51	.592	1.49
1983	2.81	.455	1.28
Price 1983 (P_3)	178.00	.455	80.99
Total PV			85.48
Present price (P_0)			83.00

The r value or total return calculated above was not an exact rate but an approximate one. HWP, on the basis of this estimate, was expected to return 16 percent, TEK slightly less than 12 percent, and TXN slightly more than 30 percent. The analysis suggests that HWP, and TXN are investment candidates.

The ranking of each company on the basis of the price trend, and the return to risk ratio as in Table 19–12, is as follows:

	HWP	TEK	TXN
Market-price trend	1	2	3
Price stability	2	3	1
P/E ratio, highest	2	1	3
Dividend return, highest	3	2	1
Total return 10/10 Trend (computer output)	1	3	2
Random expected return, $\bar{r}$	1	3	2
Analysts' best estimate (ABE), r	3	2	1
Historic annual return, R	2	1	3
Risk and variability of return, lowest	3	2	1
Beta (10 year), lowest	2	3	1
Return-to-risk ratio	1	3	2
Overall	1	3	2

SUMMARY OF ANALYSIS AND DECISION

The Summary

As is always the case in the art of investment analysis, there are conflicts and counter-vailing forces. The analysis undertaken was designed to be done by the investor without the benefit of outside opinion. It was designed to have the person look at the information and make a decision in spite of the seemingly limited amount of data. An investor's judgment cannot be sharpened unless he or she "does it alone." A quick summary of the factors in our analysis will help to "put it all together";

	HWP	TEK	TXN
Competitive position	1	3	2
Earnings and profitability	1	2	3
Operating efficiency	2	3	1
Current financial position	2	1	3
Capital structure and debt	1	3	2
Management	1	3	2
Historic total return	2	1	3
Return-to-risk	1	3	2
Expected total return (computer)	1	3	2
Expected highest total return (ABE)	3	2	1
Beta	2	3	1
Overall ranking	1	3	2

The Decision

It appears, then, on an overall basis, we would rate Hewlett-Packard first in terms of investment attractiveness, Texas Instruments next, and Tektronix, third. Hewlett-Packard offered an excellent return for the investor if the forecasts of earnings growth and price were achieved. The expected earnings growth and price were not certain, however; substantial variability of price and earnings is expected in the future, and market risk equal to the S&P 500 Index is associated with investment in HWP. In spite of this note of caution, Hewlett-Packard and Texas Instruments would have been the stocks to purchase, and would have been combined with other investments to form the investor's portfolio.

SUMMARY

The comparative analysis allowed us to come to a logical conclusion and decision about which company to purchase. The analysis was accomplished through a logical method from relatively available data. It raised important questions that must be answered before investment takes place. It also incorporated the newer, quantitative techniques of analysis such as total return, variability, and expectations. And they have helped. Analysis is only a part, however, of a rational thought process. We must still add experience and judgment to the final decision.

This analysis should serve as a guide to the application of the principles established in the analysis of the economy, the industry, and the company in Chapters 13 through 18.

SUMMARY OF PRINCIPLES

1. Select a company that is a competitive leader.
2. Select a company that offers future growth, stability, and predictability of earnings.
3. Select a firm that is efficient.
4. Select a firm that is in a strong current financial position.
5. Select a firm that has a strong capital structure.
6. Select a firm that has strong management.
7. Select a firm that at the current price offers an attractive total return relative to risk.
8. Select stocks that have a favorable reward-to-risk ratio.

REVIEW QUESTIONS

1. Review the analysis of the electronics industry.
   a. What has been the pattern of growth of the industry compared to the national economy?

FUNDAMENTAL ANALYSIS

b. What are the basic divisions of the electronics industry? Indicate the products included in each division.

c. What are the leading companies in the industry? Should Hewlett-Packard, Tektronix, and Texas Instruments still be chosen, based on the data presented, as the leading three companies in the industry?

d. Which of the companies in the industry appears to be best in respect to each of the following?
 (1) Competitive position.
 (2) Present and future earnings.
 (3) Operating capacity and efficiency.
 (4) Current financial position.
 (5) Capital structure.
 (6) Management.
 (7) Total return and risk.

e. Which company appears to be most reasonably priced in relation to present price and P/E ratio?

f. Which company appears to offer the greatest growth of earnings and dividends?

g. What total return could one expect to earn annually over the next three years on the basis of the forecasts we made?

h. In terms of total return and risks, qualitative and nonqualitative factors, which company would you select for investment?

PROBLEMS

1. Bring the analysis of the electronics industry up to date. Based on new data, select three leading companies. Indicate why you would consider these companies for investment.

2. Based on the following criteria, which of those companies should you consider for investment?
 a. Competitive position.
 b. Earnings and future earnings.
 c. Operating characteristics.
 d. Current financial analysis.
 e. Capital structure analysis.
 f. Management.
 g. Expected total return and risk.

3. What companies would you select, based on your analysis? Indicate your conclusion and your decision.

4. Write a report to present your findings.

CHAPTER 20

RETURN AND RISK
IN THE STOCK MARKET
AND TECHNICAL ANALYSIS

A thorough fundamental analysis provides the investor with an estimate of expected returns for a three-year future period and an estimate of the variability of that expected return. These estimates of the future allow the investor to estimate the return-to-risk ratio for each stock, which helps to determine if the stock is fairly valued in the marketplace, offering a return proportional to the estimated risk.

As a matter of principle, the investor should attempt to estimate the expected return and risk for the major market indexes, including the DJIA and S&P 500 Index. It is important to do this because most individual stocks behave in a similar way to the market. Few stocks behave exactly like the market, because historic price betas range from .5 to 1.5. However, if it can be determined that the market index is under- or overvalued, this will help the investor decide which stocks to include in a portfolio.

In this chapter, the indexes used to determine the level of the entire market will be identified and analyzed. Estimates of past market returns and risks will be provided, along with estimates of future returns and risks. Economic and technical indicators will be examined, as they help to interpret the movement of the market. The random-walk hypothesis will be examined in relationship to the ability of technical indicators to forecast stock prices.

THE INDEPENDENCE OF THE STOCK MARKET

The stock market as a whole may not act rationally and consistently in terms of the fundamentals we have studied. Often, the market for a stock behaves contrarily to what fundamental economic conditions suggest. The economic position of a company and the national economy might be strong, and yet the stock market might drop in price. By contrast, the fundamental position of the economy might be weak, and yet the stock market as a whole might be strong. When this happens, some writers suggest, it is because the technical position of the market is weak. That is, many weak or small stockholders were selling; or market speculators are selling because of a short-term swing in the market; or only a small amount of stock is available to be purchased; or traders are covering their short sales in the market.[1] In short, the stock market as a whole may behave differently from what might be expected from a fundamental investment analysis.

Our analysis of the national economy included the stock market as a leading indicator. Therefore, the stock market indexes must be watched carefully because they can help determine if the economy will continue to expand in the future. The DJIA dropped in the first quarter of 1980, correctly predicting a business trough. The average rose in mid-1980 to forecast correctly the upturn in the economy in late 1980. A decline in the market in early 1981 correctly predicted the recession in late 1981, extending into 1982. The market recovered to new historic highs in 1983, anticipating a modest recovery in 1983 and 1984.

The stock market has its likes and dislikes, and these may run contrary to the trend of the market or the national economy as a whole. Investors and speculators tend to favor certain securities in certain industries. This suggests not only that market movements are independent of fundamental economic forces, but that certain stocks, perhaps a minority, can cause changes that accentuate the movements of the market. This action is usually a short-term phenomenon, and investors or traders should not become blinded to the economic realities of the trend of the stock market. When sharp technical changes occur in the market, it is possible to pay too much for a security and it is possible to find bargains.

The market as a whole also acts independently of the realities of the business and economic world. The trend of the market may lead economic conditions, but its cyclical movements react to temporary technical, psychological, and emotional events that can be seen but might be unforeseen. The strength of these cyclical activities is apparent from the studies that have been made about the relationship between individual prices and the stock market as a whole. Although some stocks have much greater volatility than the market and some have substantially less, the movement of the market as a whole is responsible for probably two-thirds of the movement of the price of an individual stock. In the major movements, or under conditions where there is a strong upswing in the market, the movement of the market accounts for an even greater amount of stock price change. Market movements follow a distinct pattern. The quality issues move up first. When the rise continues, the weaker issues begin to move up. In the latter phase, most of the price increase in individual stocks is carried along by the general movement of the stock market. When the market movement is downward, the same pattern prevails.

[1]A short sale, in essence, is the sale of borrowed stock in the hope that the price will decline. If the price does decline, the trader buys back the stock and returns it to its owner. The transaction is facilitated by the stockbroker who has arranged to buy the shares. When a person sells stock short, he is said to take a short position in the stock. Stock purchases for investment are assumed to be long—that is, the investor buys the securities outright and owns them as an investment. The investment concept suggests a long-term period.

Stock market analysis is simply an extension of one of the factors of investment analysis. Timing of the purchase of securities to put the investor in the best possible position for obtaining capital gains is an important part of portfolio management. Often, timing makes the difference between a successful investor and an unsuccessful one. Some error of judgment is expected in the analysis; but it is far better to make errors of judgment about the stock market than to make no estimate or forecast at all, or to ignore the condition of the market. Without a great deal of emphasis on timing of purchases and the level of the stock market, there is no real portfolio management at all.

MEASURING THE MOVEMENT OF THE MARKET

The general movement of the stock market is usually measured by a stock market average or index consisting of a group of securities that is supposed to reflect the entire market. One such, based on the principles of weighted index construction, is Standard & Poor's 500 Index. This is used as a standard of performance for many mutual funds, as recommended by the SEC. The Dow Jones Averages are indexes of securities that have been selected historically as being representative of the market as a whole, with no attention given to weighting.

It is assumed that if the price index or average goes up, the market as a whole goes up. One could compute the daily movement of the stock market by adding the total dollar value of all the shares traded each day and dividing into this figure the total number of shares. This would provide a weighted average price of the shares traded and would reflect the condition of the stock market. In some ways this method might be superior to the averages and the indexes, but it would be difficult, expensive, and time-consuming to compute. It would also be inaccurate for comparison, since different shares are traded each day, so there would be little uniformity in the average. Such a method would ignore the practical qualities and advantages of sampling theory, which attempts to describe the average behavior of a time series or a market by using a small number of items rather than a large number. Many stock market averages or indexes have been constructed to indicate the movement of the stock market as a whole. The best known, which are the Dow Jones Averages and the Standard & Poor's Index of Stock Prices, will be examined here in detail; the New York Stock Exchange Indexes and the NASDAQ OTC Index will also be mentioned.

Dow Jones Averages

The Dow Jones Averages are among the oldest and most familiar of indexes. They are published in *The Wall Street Journal* and include the Dow Jones Industrial Average (DJIA), the Dow Jones Transportation Average (DJTA), and the Dow Jones Utility Average (DJUA). Since *The Wall Street Journal* is the leading daily financial newspaper and one of the best dailies in the United States, and since the Dow Jones Averages are quoted over radio and television, they are widely followed by investors.

The Dow Jones Industrial Average consists of 30 stocks that cover a broad group of industries. The companies are considered to be market-tested companies in their respective industries and representative of their industrial classes. The stocks in the DJIA are these:

Allied Corp.	General Foods	Owens-Illinois
Aluminum Co.	General Motors	Procter & Gamble
Amer Brands	Goodyear	Sears Roebuck
Amer Can	Inco	Std Oil of Calif
Amer Express	IBM	Texaco
Amer Tel & Tel	Inter Harvester	Union Carbide
Bethlehem Steel	Inter Paper	US Steel
Du Pont	Merck	United Technologies
Eastman Kodak	Minnesota Mining and	Westinghouse
Exxon	Manufacturing	Woolworth
General Electric		

The DJIA is computed by adding the prices of the securities included in the averages and dividing by a denominator adjusted periodically to reflect changes such as stock splits and stock dividends. In the case of a 2-for-1 stock split, for example, the average would drop if no adjustments were made, since half the price of the security would be subtracted. On April 7, 1983, the divisor used in computing the DJIA was 1.292.

The securities in the DJIA are changed from time to time to reflect changes in the representative character of the averages. They represent the market as a whole but do not include all types of securities.

The 20 stocks in the Dow Jones Transportation Average (DJTA) now include eight railroads, eight airlines, and four trucking companies.

AMR Corp	Norfolk Southern	Southern Pacific
Burlington Northern	Northwest Airlines	Transway International
Canadian Pacific	Overnite Transport	Trans World
Carolina Freight	Pan Am World Airways	UAL Inc
Consolid Freight	Rio Grande Ind	Union Pacific Corp.
CSX Corp	Santa Fe Indust	US Air Group
Delta Airlines		
Eastern Air Lines		

The divisor, as of April 7, 1983 was 1.574.

The Dow Jones Utility Average (DJUA) consists of 15 growth and income securities that encompass both gas and electric utilities and represent all parts of the United States. Again, these companies tend to be representative of the leading firms within their classification. On April 7, 1983, the divisor was 2.709. The companies included in the list were these:

Am Elec Power	Consol Nat Gas	Panhandle Eastern
Cleveland Elec Ill	Detroit Edison	Peoples Energy
Colum Gas Sys	Houston Indus	Phila Elec
Comwlth Edison	Niag Mohawk P	Pub Serv E&G
Consol Edison	Pacific Gas & El	Sou Cal Edison

The fourth of the Dow Jones Averages is the 65 composite average, made up of the 30 industrial, 20 transportation, and 15 utility companies in the other averages. The combined average provides an overall view of the direction of the market for the better-quality securities and does not reflect the action of securities traded on the over-the-counter market. The DJAs are charted and quoted in *The Wall Street Journal*. The divisor for the 65 stocks in the WSJ was 5,820 on April 7, 1983.

Standard & Poor's Index

Standard & Poor's Index of Stock Prices is a base-weighted aggregate showing the relative changes in the stocks it includes compared to a base year, in this case, 1941–43 = 10.

Stock Price Index Formula

The formula, adopted by Standard & Poor's after much testing, is generally defined as a "base-weighted aggregative" expressed in relatives with the average value for the base period (1941–1943) equal to 10. This method of computation has two distinct advantages over most index number series: (1) It has the necessary flexibility to adjust for arbitrary price changes caused by the issuance of rights, stock dividends, splitups, etc., and (2) the resultant index numbers are accurate and have a relatively high degree of continuity, which is especially important when long-term comparisons are to be made. Certain modifications to the basic formula have been necessary to maintain the best possible representation over the years. The character of the stock market is subject to gradual but continuous shifting, and it is only by periodic checks of coverage that true representation can be maintained.

WEIGHTING—Each component stock is weighted so that it will influence the index in proportion to its respective market importance. The most suitable weighting factor for this purpose is the number of shares outstanding. The price of any stock multiplied by the number of shares outstanding gives the current market value for that particular issue. This market value determines the relative importance of the security.

BASE VALUES AND GROUP INDEXES—Market values for individual stocks are added together to obtain their particular group market value. These group values are expressed as a relative, or index number, to the base period (1941–1943) market value. As the base period market value is relatively constant, subject to change only as described in this text, the index number reflects only fluctuations in current market values.

BASE PERIOD—The base value for any group is the average of the weekly group values for the period 1941–1943. The current group value is expressed as a relative by dividing it by its base period value and multiplying the resulting quotient by 10. In this relative form, an index number attains its maximum usefulness for statistical purposes.

FORMULA—The formula for the base-weighted aggregative index is

$$\text{Index} = \frac{\Sigma P_1 Q_1}{\Sigma P_0 Q_0} \times 10$$

where P_1 represents the current market price, P_0 the market price in the base period, Q_1 the number of shares currently outstanding, and Q_0 the number of shares outstanding in the base period, subject to adjustment when necessary to offset changes in capitalization. Σ is the Greek letter sigma, which always indicates addition, or the sum of, and in this instance indicates the addition of the market values of the individual companies comprising the group.[2]

Standard & Poor's Composite Average combines 500 stocks. Included are 400 companies from 85 industrial groupings; 40 commercial banks, savings and loan associations, and insurance, casualty, and finance companies; 20 air transport,

[2]Standard & Poor's *Trade and Securities Statistics, Security Price Index Record*, 1981, p. 2.

railroad, and trucking companies; and five utility groups, including telephone, comprising 40 companies. The index is broken down further into the various industry segments, facilitating comparison of the market actions of individual companies. Standard & Poor's 500 Index has the added advantages of being widely known, broad in scope and representativeness, and fairly sensitive to market change. The S&P 500 Index has become the basic standard of the direction of the stock market.

COMPOSITION OF WEIGHTINGS OF S&P 500 INDEX.   Table 20–1 provides the present weighting by industry groups for the first and second quarters of 1981. The companies in the S&P 500 Index are found in the appendix to this chapter.

The groups are important to professional investors who operate index funds. An index fund could use the S&P 500 Index average as an index of the market. In this case, the fund manager would diversify the fund using the same weights provided in the average.

New York Stock Exchange Common Stock Index

In July 1966, the New York Stock Exchange began the publication of its own common stock index. This index measures the price trends of the 1570 common stocks listed on the Big Board. In addition to the total, all-inclusive common stock index, separate indexes are calculated for finance, transportation, utility, and industrials. The Finance Index includes 223 issues of closed-end investment companies, savings and loan holding and investment companies, and companies in commercial and installment finance, banking, insurance, real estate, and related fields. The Transportation Index is based on 65 issues representing railroads, airlines, shipping, motor transport, and other operating, leasing, and holding companies in the transportation field. The Utility Index includes 189 separate stocks of operating, holding, and transmission companies in gas, electric power, and communications. The biggest and broadest index is the Industrial Index, comprising 1,093 listed stocks on the NYSE not included in the other indexes.[3]

The indexes are computed by multiplying the price of each stock by the number of its listed shares. It is therefore a capitalization-weighted index, and companies with the largest capitalization, such as GM, Exxon, AT&T, IBM, and du Pont, will have the greatest impact on the index. Every half hour, the change in average price is reported in dollars and cents and in index form, with the number of points' change from the previous day's close. On the hour, the same information is presented for all the indexes, plus the reported volume.[4]

December 31, 1965, is the base date, and the base was set at 50.00. The base market values are adjusted for stock splits and dividends, rights for the purchase of additional shares, rights to subscribe to other issues, and mergers or acquisitions that change the base values. If the index moves up substantially owing to a rise in market values, it will be readjusted or "split" by the NYSE. The method of computing changes appears

[3]New York Stock Exchange *Fact Book 1981*, p. 32.
[4]Ibid., p. 5.

TABLE 20–1

A Breakdown of Market Capitalization by Industry Groups

	S&P 500: Market Value Weightings (% of 500)				
	I Q81	II Q81		I Q81	II Q81
Aerospace	1.99%	1.92%	Miscellaneous	4.65%	4.34%
Aluminum	.78	.67	Mobile homes	.05	.05
Automobiles	2.07	2.13	Office and business equipment	6.03	6.02
Auto parts—after market	.17	.17	Offshore drilling	.44	.36
Auto parts—original equipment	.67	.70	Oil—crude producers	1.30	1.33
Auto trucks and parts	.15	.16	Oil—integrated domestic	8.87	8.04
Beverages—brewers	.28	.29	Oil—integrated international	9.14	8.83
Beverages—distillers	.55	.61	Oilwell equipment	4.16	3.76
Beverages—soft drinks	.87	.89	Paper	1.14	1.07
Building—A/C	.06	.06	Pollution control	.18	.18
Building—cement	.10	.12	Publishing	.57	.61
Building—diversified	.16	.28	Publishing news	.62	.73
Building—roofing and wallboard	.26	.27	Radio—TV Broadcasters	.53	.58
Chemicals	2.51	2.65	Railroad equipment	.23	.24
Chemicals—misc.	1.04	1.03	Restaurants	.44	.48
Coal—bituminous	.20	.20	Retail dept. stores	.69	.75
Communications—equipment/mfg.	.38	.40	Retail drug stores	.25	.26
Computer services	—	.27	Retail stores—food chains	.45	.45
Conglomerates	2.15	2.02	Retail stores—general	1.18	1.31
Containers—metal and glass	.38	.39	Shoes	.24	.26
Containers—paper	.13	.12	Soaps	1.02	1.10
Copper	.47	.28	Steel	.94	.85
Cosmetics	.63	.64	Sugar refiners	.04	.04
Drugs	4.17	4.09	Textile apparel mfg.	.32	.27
Electric equipment	.68	.73	Textile products	.17	.19
Major electric companies	2.12	2.03	Tire and rubber goods	.30	.30
Electric—household appliances	.21	.23	Tobacco	1.39	1.45
Electronics—Instruments	.92	.96	Toys	.03	.03
Electronics—Semicond/Components	.99	.95	Electric companies	3.09	3.46
Entertainment	.79	.76	Natural gas distributors	.76	.74
Fertilizers	.34	.28	Natural gas pipelines	.86	.80
Foods	2.49	2.56	Telephone	4.90	5.62
Forest products	1.33	1.28	Air freight	.19	.21
Gold	.31	.27	Air transport	.38	.41
Home furnishings	.01	.02	Railroads	2.17	1.93
Home building	.12	.11	Truckers	.18	.20
Hospital management	.52	.58	Banks (New York City)	.96	1.15
Hospital Supplies	1.65	1.68	Banks (outside NYC)	1.17	1.27
Hotel/motel	.25	.28	Life insurance	.59	.57
Leisure Time	.12	.14	Multi-line insurance	1.04	1.14
Machine tools	.15	.16	Property—Casualty insurance	.68	.77
Machinery—agricultural	.45	.39	Savings and loan companies	.15	.14
Machinery—const. Material Hndlg.	.77	.79	Personal loans	.14	.14
Machinery—indus./spec.	.79	.74	Financial—Misc.	.53	.58
Metals—misc.	1.70	1.54			

SOURCE: Drexel/Burnham Lambert.

TECHNICAL ANALYSIS

in Figure 20–1. The NYSE Common Stock Index has been linked statistically to the weekly SEC index of common stocks from 1939 to 1964. The NYSE Index has been computed on a daily basis since May 28, 1964, and the four indusrry-group indexes since December 31, 1965.[5]

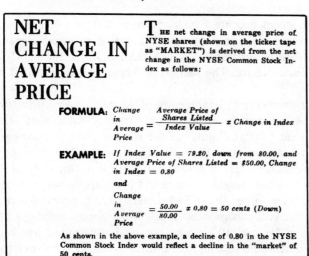

FIGURE 20–1

Method of Computing Changes in the NYSE Index

SOURCE: *Banking*, August 1966, p. 5.

The reaction to the introduction of the NYSE Common Stock Index by the professionals in Wall Street was unfavorable. Many felt that it was another index that was too broad and wouldn't show a thing. However, "seven months and one major market reversal later, Wall Street's technical analysts—whose main concern is the exegesis of charts—are looking on the Big Board's market yardstick with all the respect of gypsies fondling a potent new deck of tarot cards."[6] The reason for this changed feeling was the signal of a bullish market given by the NYSE Index in mid-November 1966. The Dow Jones Industrial Averages didn't break out above the 820 barrier with a confirmation of the Industrial Index and the Transportation Index until the second week in January 1967. The NYSE indexes do not have "history" or "lore," but they are good indicators of market behavior. Students of investment would be wise to watch them with care.

NASDAQ OTC Index

The National Association of Securities Dealers Automatic Quotation system, called NASDAQ, presents an excellent index of stocks traded in the OTC market. The computer-based system not only provides accurate quotes on these stocks; it now provides an index of the price behavior of the market itself through the NASDAQ Index, which includes a composite index as well as industrial, insurance, and bank-

[5]Ibid.

[6]"New Indexes Get There First," *Business Week*, February 25, 1967, p. 124.

stock indexes. The NASDAQ OTC Index is quoted in daily newspapers and in *The Wall Street Journal.*

The Two-Tier Market

In 1973, the two-tier-market concept became a major force in the securities market. It was said that the market was divided into two tiers. The first or upper tier was represented by a limited number of institutionally favored stocks, including IBM, Sears, Eastman Kodak, 3M, and Xerox. The second or lower tier represented all other stocks.

The creation of the two-tier market is a phenomenon of the institutional investors, intent on reducing the market risk and investing in only quality issues that other institutions can buy. Invest in the "vestal virgins" of the market place, they suggest by their actions, to reduce risk and protect their clients. However, the concept is really being tested in the marketplace today. There is danger in investing only in the upper-tier stocks. The risk to investors might be increased if an upper-tier company loses its glamour. Who will be there to buy the sullied sinners? The concept of investment quality is a good one, but you can pay too much for a good company. The concern for investing in only a favored 100 stocks out of 1,500 traded has been expressed in legislative action that would restrict institutional investors from investing in only a few stocks and force them to broaden their investment base. Additional regulations would be unfortunate, but there are obvious dangers in the concentration of funds in only a few companies.

Those interested in the two-tier concept might compare the behavior of the DJIA, representing as best it can the upper-tier stocks, and the NASDAQ Index, S&P 500 Index, and New York Stock Exchange Index, representing the second-tier stocks.

Which Average Should Be Used?

The average to use should be the one that is most familiar and available. People who read *The Wall Street Journal* will find the Dow Jones Averages the most convenient. These averages reflect conditions in securities traded on a national, registered exchange. They do not, however, include securities in the over-the-counter market. These are found in the National Quotation Bureau Average, an index of over-the-counter market stocks, which follows the pattern of the other averages satisfactorily, since the cyclical highs and lows of the averages tend to come at about the same time, as do the monthly highs and lows. The Dow Jones Averages tend to be a good indication of what is happening in the established cyclical companies. It is the emotional index of Wall Street professionals.

The Standard & Poor's 500 Index would be used as the market index "to beat" by professional investment fund managers. It is used by mutual fund managers to determine performance, and it is used in setting up an index fund. It tends also to be more stable and less cyclical than the DJIA. It would seem that if the investor had to use only one index to measure the behavior of the stock market, it would be the S&P 500 Index.

MEASURING MARKET RETURN AND RISK

Historic Return

The historic return of the S&P 500 is presented in Tables 20–2 and 20–3. Table 20–2 indicates that from 1972 through 1983, the return of the S&P 500 Index was 6.87 percent, with a risk (standard deviation) of 13.18 percent. The return was found using the formula $(P_1 - P_0 + D_1)/P_0$. The P_1 and P_0 represent averages of the high and low price for the base year (P_0) and the succeeding year (P_1). The annual returns are averaged and the risk is calculated from these averages.

TABLE 20–2

Past Return and Risk of the S&P 500 Index, and Estimated Return and Risk Based on Trend and Random Valuation Methods and Reward to Risk Ratio, 1972–1983

	Past Return and Risk			Valuation—Expected Return and Risk			
Recent Price (January 1983)	Return	Risk	Beta	Trend Return	Random Return	Risk	Reward to Risk Ratio
151.26	6.87	13.18	1.00	17.46	17.63	16.38	.62

SOURCE: Modesystem, MODE 1, Frederick Amling & Associates, Washington, D.C.

A more precise measure of the historic return of the S&P 500 is presented in Table 20–3 for the period 1976 through June 1981. The variability and the magnitude of the average return for each period of ownership are impressive. The quarterly and annual returns of the S&P 500 appear, as well as the cumulative return for the period 1976–82. The return was calculated by using the month-end price of the S&P 500 average and the quarterly dividend. The formula used is as follows:

$$\text{Return } \% = \frac{P_1 - P_0 + D_q}{P_0}$$

The annual returns were found using the same equation, except that the annual dividend was used.

Expected Return and Risk

The expected return and risk of the market are much more important than the historic return. The data in Table 20–2 provide estimates of expected return and risk along with the return-to-risk ratio. The valuation methods are the same as those discussed in Chapter 18, where individual securities were valued. The basic equation used is

$$P_0 = \sum^{n=3} \frac{D_0(1 + g_d)^t}{(1 + r)^t} + \frac{E_0(1 + g_e)^3(P/E)_3}{(1 + r)^3}$$

TABLE 20–3
Returns of S&P 500 (1977–1982), %

Year and Month	Month-end Price	Quarterly Dividend	Quarterly Return, %	Annual Return, %
Jan. 1977	102.03			
Feb. 1977	99.82			
Mar. 1977	98.42	1.05	(7.44)	
Apr. 1977	98.44			
May 1977	96.12			
June 1977	100.48	1.09	3.20	
July 1977	98.85			
Aug. 1977	96.77			
Sept. 1977	96.53	1.13	(2.81)	
Oct. 1977	92.34			
Nov. 1977	94.83			
Dec. 1977	95.10	1.17	(.27)	(7.37)
Jan. 1978	89.25			
Feb. 1978	87.04			
Mar. 1978	89.21	1.20	(4.93)	
Apr. 1978	96.83			
May 1978	97.24			
June 1978	95.53	1.23	8.46	
July 1978	100.68			
Aug. 1978	103.29			
Sept. 1978	102.54	1.26	8.66	
Oct. 1978	93.15			
Nov. 1978	94.70			
Dec. 1978	96.11	1.27	(5.03)	6.28
Jan. 1979	99.93			
Feb. 1979	96.28			
Mar. 1979	101.59	1.30	7.05	
Apr. 1979	101.76			
May 1979	99.08			
June 1979	102.91	1.34	2.62	
July 1979	103.81			
Aug. 1979	109.31			
Sept. 1979	109.32	1.38	7.57	
Oct. 1979	101.82			
Nov. 1979	106.16			
Dec. 1979	107.94	1.41	.03	17.96
Jan. 1980	114.16			
Feb. 1980	113.66			
Mar. 1980	102.09	1.45	(4.08)	
Apr. 1980	106.29			
May 1980	111.24			
June 1980	114.24	1.49	13.36	
July 1980	121.67			
Aug. 1980	122.38			
Sept. 1980	125.46	1.52	11.15	
Oct. 1980	127.47			
Nov. 1980	140.52			
Dec. 1980	135.76	1.54	9.44	31.33
Jan. 1981	129.55			

TABLE 20-3 (Continued)

Year and Month	Month-end Price	Quarterly Dividend	Quarterly Return, %	Annual Return, %
Feb. 1981	131.27			
Mar. 1981	136.00	1.57	1.33	
Apr. 1981	132.81			
May 1981	132.59			
June 1981	131.21	1.60	(2.35)	
July 1981	130.92			
Aug. 1981	122.79			
Sept. 1981	116.18	1.63	(10.21)	
Oct. 1981	121.89			
Nov. 1981	126.35			
Dec. 1981	124.00	1.66	8.16	(3.90)
Jan. 1982	115.74			
Feb. 1982	113.47			
Mar. 1982	112.97	1.68	(7.5)	
April 1982	115.72			
May 1982	113.11			
June 1982	110.14	1.70	(1.0)	
July 1982	111.42			
Aug. 1982	119.51			
Sept. 1982	121.97	1.71	12.29	
Oct. 1982	135.28			
Nov. 1982	133.88			
Dec. 1982	141.24	1.72	17.21	19.40

Summary: Annual, Cumulative,* and Average Annual Return for the Holding Period 1976–1982

Year	1976	1977	1978	1979	1980	1981	1982
1976	23.40						
1977	14.65	(7.37)					
1978	21.27	(3.69)	6.28				
1979	40.42	14.25	24.43	17.96			
1980	77.93	45.72	59.99	53.15	31.33		
1981	72.05	40.79	54.42	47.63	26.42	(3.90)	
1982	98.72	63.17	79.71	72.66	48.70	13.81	19.40
Average Annual Return for Holding Period	14.10	10.53	15.94	18.17	16.23	4.96	19.40

$^*[(P_N - P_0) + \Sigma D_N] \div P_0$. The Annual Returns are underlined and the cumulative total return is read down the column.

for TREND. RANDOM uses the same equation, but the variables, as described previously, are selected at random, and the $\tilde{r}$ values selected and calculated are then averaged to obtain the variability of the expected return or risk.

The TREND and RANDOM valuation methods indicate that the investor would receive a substantial return of about 18 percent. With a return-to-risk ratio of .62, the S&P 500 Index must be interpreted as a hold or sell, as these stocks are not an attractive investment opportunity. The return-to-risk ratio should be 1.00 or higher.

THE ECONOMIC AND MONEY MARKET INDICATORS OF THE STOCK MARKET

To determine the position of the stock market and its future course, investors, speculators, and market analysts have used many methods. Some, for example, use sunspots and the phases of the moon to forecast the market. Such methods are less than satisfactory as tools of market analysis. However, a small element of truth exists in the basic premise underlying them, and although they should be put aside as incomplete guides to market action, they cannot be ignored.

The more conventional methods of estimating the market and determining its level are (1) economic indicators, and (2) money market indicators. Each indicator can be helpful to the investor in determining the present and future position of the market, although neither is considered a panacea for all problems of prediction. They are considered aids to market analysis, not dogma.

Economic Indicators and the Stock Market

Economic indicators of the stock market, such as the Federal Reserve Board Index of Industrial Production, and gross national product, national income, and disposable income estimates, were discussed earlier, where it was pointed out that a healthy economy is a prerequisitie for a healthy and profitable industry or company. In addition to these aggregate measures, more specific indicators of economic activity are used to help forecast the stock market, such as auto production, steel production, and housing starts.

Changes in the aggregate and specific indicators are used to predict changes in the stock market and determine return and risk. The essential ingredient is an accurate forecast of the indicator, whether it is aggregate output or that of a specific area, such as housing. With a forecast of economic activity, a person could determine within reasonable limits the present position of the market and make a reasonably accurate estimate of what could be expected of it in the future. Some members of the financial community reverse the procedure and use the stock market as a forecaster of business activity. (The stock market is a leading indicator in the *Business Conditions Digest's* Composite Leading Indicator Series.) They reason that if the market goes down cyclically, business will be poor six to nine months ahead.

However, economic activity is more often used as an indicator of the future level of the stock market. Assuming a forecast of improved economic conditions and corporate profits, and low interest without inflation, the stock market should be strong or improve. Given a condition of weakness in economic conditions, high inflation, higher interest rates, and rising unemployment, the market should decline. Thus, the investor should use the forecasts of the GNP. FRB Index, NI, corporate profits, interest rates, inflation, and other measures of economic activity as indicators of what might happen to the stock market. There is some indication (not conclusive proof) that economic activity expected six months to a year in the future determines the current level of the stock market. For example, if business is expected to improve in six months, the present level of the stock market should be high. If a decline in business activity six months from now is forecasted, then the stock market should be low.

In 1981, the economy was in a recession. Economic activity was expected to improve late in 1982, with full recovery in 1983 and 1984. Real economic growth was expected to be between −1.0 and 1.0 percent. Interest rates and inflation were expected to decrease through the first half of 1982 and then rise modestly. The prime rate had fallen from the 20 percent level in mid-1981 to the 15.75 percent level by the end of 1981. The prime rate was expected to decline in the first half of 1982, and interest rates in general were expected to decline during 1982. Auto production and housing starts were expected to improve later in 1982 and reach normal levels by 1983 and 1984. Corporate profits were expected to have their biggest drop in the fourth quarter of 1981, decline modestly in the first half of 1982, and then increase to normal trend levels in 1983 through 1985.

What should the investor expect from the performance of the stock market in this environment? The market (DJIA) had fallen from above 1,000 to the 830 level in November 1981 and had rebounded to the 880 level. With interest rates declining, and with relatively low stock prices, the market was thought to be attractive below the 850 level. Longer-term bonds were also thought to be attractive, with yields ranging from 13 to 17 percent. Only modest amounts of money would be kept on reserve. Only if we feared a complete collapse of the U.S. economy would we be heavily invested in short-term, fixed-income securities.

Anyone working with economic forecasts as a basis for the expectation of market activity must realize the error involved in prediction. The estimates must be adjusted for the possibility of error and revised continuously for the best success. The investor using the economic indicators as a guide to market activity must consider them rough tools for trend and cyclical forecasting, but not useful in predicting daily movements of the stock market. It is also assumed that investors will not trade frequently but will buy or sell from portfolios on the basis of fundamental and major swings, rather than temporary and transitory changes, in the stock market.

Stock and Bond Yields, Money Market Indicators, and the Stock Market

A close relationship exists between the money market, the bond market, and the stock market, although it is sometimes difficult to observe. The term "money market" usually refers to the market for short-term debt instruments of both private and government corporations or political units. The bond market is the market for long-term debt of private and government corporations or political entities. Many forces have an impact on the bond market and the money market, including changes in the stock market. One effect, in its simplest form, is the movement of money between the markets. If, for example, stocks are sold, the funds from the sale can be held in cash, used to purchase other stocks, or used to buy long- and short-term debt instruments. The purchase of debt securities would be most likely when yields on bonds are high relative to the "total" return on common stocks. Cash would be held if equity prices were expected to decline. On the other hand, when funds were needed for the stock market, they could come from idle balances, sales of other stocks, or from the sales of long- and short-term debt securities. The effects of the shift of funds between the money market and the stock market are apparent. A sale of stock or long-term bonds tends to result in an increase in the supply of securities, which tends to decrease price and increase yields. The purchase of debt or equity securities tends to increase their price, and the return decreases. A purchase of stock and a sale of bonds tends to improve the price of stocks and reduce their return, and to decrease the price of bonds and increase bond yields. There are times, however, when relative demand results in lower stock *and* bond prices. This condition occurs when the money and capital markets are extremely tight and yields are increasing rapidly to compensate for the inflation or price-level risk, as occurred in 1980 and 1981. Inflation was extremely high. Federal Reserve Board policy was extremely tight. Under these conditions, the prime rate went above 20 percent, long-term bond yields went above 17 percent, and DJIA stock prices declined to a low of 730 in 1980 and 820 in 1981. However, later in 1981 interest rates declined and stocks began to rise. In this case, the change was favorable for stock prices. Needless to say, inflation does not help to increase equity or bond prices.

The relationship between yields on bonds and returns on common stock is the foundation for several indicators that help to forecast the future of the securities markets. As we discuss several of these money market indicators, keep in mind the mobility of funds between the money market and the stock market, and the impact of the flow of funds on yields.

CURRENT STOCK YIELDS AS A MARKET INDICATOR. One method of forecasting the stock market and determining if it is high or low is through the dividend yields on high-grade common stocks. Using current stock yields as a guide to the height of the market is quite simple. If stock yields are low, the stock market is high, and if stock yields are high, the stock market is low. The premise on which this concept is based relates to the price of the stock. As stock prices go higher, the yield moves lower. When yields are low, the investor earns much less on common stocks than from other securities. Common stocks become an unattractive investment. The investor sells common stocks to purchase other, more attractive securities. When yields on common stocks are high, on the other hand, the investor is enticed away from other investments that offer lower yields. Thus the investor is in a position to benefit from better yields on stocks and has the possibility of earning capital gains.

What is high or low depends on the relative condition of the money market and the level of the stock market. A study made by the Cowles Commission covering the period 1871–1937 concluded that stock prices were high when average yields were below 3 percent, and the market was low when yields were above 8 percent.[7] Only four times has the composite yield of Standard & Poor's Stock Price Index been above 8 percent: in 1931 and the first quarter of 1938 (both depression years), and in the last quarter of 1941 and the first quarter of 1942 (the beginning of World War II).

The conclusion we can draw from the stock-yield concept is this: Buy stock when the current yields are relatively high, and sell stock when current yields are relatively

[7]Cowles Commission for Research in Economics, "Common Stock Indexes, 1871–1937," Monograph No. 3, 2d ed. (Bloomington, Ind: Principia Press, 1939), p. 47.

low. Relatively high would be 5 percent, historically, and relatively low would be 3 percent. Even this hypothesis has serious limitations, since the investor would be required to move into and out of the market frequently. Based on the composite yields of Standard & Poor's averages, the investor sold stock in 1964 and 1965, purchased in 1966 and 1967, sold in 1968, purchased in 1970, and sold in 1972. With the market generally falling in 1973 and 1974, common stock yields rose well above 3 percent. The entire time period 1974–76 represented a buying market. The average dividend yield on the S&P 500 Index from 1977 to 1981 was 5.18 percent. These data would suggest a buying opportunity in 1979, 1980, and 1981, according to this simple dividend indicator model and historic dividend yield averages.

These comments are based on the yields of industrial common stocks in Standard & Poor's 500 Index and the composite yield, which includes industrial, rail, and utility securities. It is possible that several more times since 1930, the yields on the average of all stocks moved above or fell below the limits suggested by the Cowles Commission. However, a current yield below 3 percent or above 8 percent is an extreme case.

STOCK YIELD–BOND YIELD DIFFERENTIAL AS A MARKET INDICATOR. The stock yield–bond yield differential concept is used to determine the position of the market and to some extent forecast the market level by examining the difference in yields. When current yields on stocks are higher than yields on bonds and the difference between them is large, common stock should be purchased. When the yields on common stocks are equal to or lower than the yields on bonds or when the differential between them is slight, common stocks should be sold.

In 1938, industrial common stocks in Standard & Poor's Daily Price Index yielded 8.86 percent, compared to 3.20 percent for AAA bonds in the industrial, rail, and utility group of the Standard & Poor's series. The differential was large enough to suggest the purchase of common stocks. The industrial yields in 1936 and early 1937 were much lower—between 3.10 and 4.02 percent. The AAA bond yields in 1937 were 3.30 percent, resulting in a small differential between bond and stock yields. According to these figures, stock should have been sold in 1937 and not purchased again until the differential had improved, as the low differential would have forecasted a market decline.

The data in Table 20–4 tell us that yearly average common stock dividend yields have not been above annual average yields on corporate bonds since at least 1964. The fact that bond yields were well above stock yields should have signaled a drop in the market. The market did drop in 1980 and 1981, which suggests that bonds should have been purchased during this period. The greatest value of the stock yield–bond yield differential would be to aid the investor in determining whether the market is relatively high or low for assistance in buying and selling common stock on major swings. However, it would be difficult for the inexperienced investor or speculator to use in market trading. It has not been successful in forecasting all movements of the stock market. Current market yields indicate that both stocks and bonds are offering yields well above historic norms. The present differential of −10.55 percent is large enough to warrent serious consideration of bonds as an investment. This indicator becomes confusing in current conditions, because yields on both types of investments are significantly above previous standards.

TABLE 20–4
Stock–Bond Yield Differential

Year	Yield on Corporate Bonds (%)	Dividend Yield on Common Stocks (%)	Differential, Bond and Stock Yield (%)
1982	14.94	5.81	−9.13
1981	15.06	5.20	−9.86
1980	12.75	5.25	−7.50
1979	10.12	5.46	−4.66
1978	9.07	5.28	−3.79
1977	8.43	4.56	−3.87
1976	9.01	3.77	−5.24
1975	9.57	4.31	−5.26
1974	9.03	4.47	−4.56
1973	7.80	3.06	−4.74
1972	7.63	2.84	−4.79
1971	7.94	3.14	−4.80
1970	8.51	3.83	−4.68
1969	7.36	3.24	−4.12
1968	6.51	3.07	−3.44
1967	5.82	3.20	−2.62
1966	5.34	3.40	−1.94
1965	4.64	3.00	−1.64
1964	4.57	3.01	−1.56

SOURCE: *Federal Reserve Bulletin,* June 1968, pp. A31, A32; June 1976, p. A34; January 1976, p. A28; January 1978, p. A27; October 1981, p. A27; February 1983, p. A23.

STOCK PRICES AND MONEY RATES.   Three market indicators that relate directly to the movement of the stock market have at one time or another had some validity. All are based on the relationship between the movements of short-term money rates, long-term money rates, and the yields on common stock. These indicators assume that the movement of money rates precedes the movement of stock prices.

Movement of Short-Term Rates.   The first indicator has to do directly with the movement of the short-term money rates. In prosperity, as more and more business borrowing takes place, an increase in money rates is likely to occur, particularly in the later phases of the market cycle. The sharp rise in money rates precedes a decline in stock prices. As Grodinsky stated, "The culmination of an upward move in the stock market and the beginning of a downward movement was invariably signaled by a sharp advance in money rates."[8] This relationship existed until the 1929 market crash.

Sharp increases in money rates that occurred in 1980 and early 1981 resulted in a corresponding decline in the stock market during the same period. Money rates declined in the third quarter of 1981 as a recession eased the demand for short-term credit. The market declined in late 1981 due to high money rates. By late 1982,

[8]Julius Grodinsky, *Investments* (New York: Ronald Press, 1953), p. 410.

many economists and financiers expected short-term rates to decline before the economy moved upward. This was expected to pull the stock market up again, after the earlier decline in mid-1982.

Bond Prices and Stock Prices. A second indicator, relating to bond and stock prices, is almost identical in logic to the relationship between short-term money rates and stock-market prices. Under conditions of prosperity, businesses borrow more and more heavily. The demand for long-term funds forces the cost of money higher. At such a time, common stock becomes more profitable and investors favor it. This adds to the supply of funds for common stock but takes funds away from the bond market. Thus, in prosperous periods, bond prices fall and stock prices tend to rise. Later in the prosperous periods, borrowing becomes less profitable for businesses, borrowing stops, business becomes less profitable, common stocks are less attractive, and stock prices drop. All this activity begins with a decline in bond prices, which precedes the decline in stock prices.

Commercial Bank Loans. The third indicator relates to the investment practices of commercial banks. Commercial banks are in business to make loans to businesses, real estate borrowers, and consumers. When business and economic conditions are poor, the banks build up excess reserves. If they cannot make loans to business, they lend to the government by the purchase of government bonds. When business improves, the banks sell the government securities and make more loans to business. As the prosperity phase of the cycle continues, more and more demands are made for business loans and less money is invested in government bonds. Therefore, a decrease in the bond accounts of the commercial banks is an indication that the market is reaching a peak. Conversely, an increase in these bond accounts indicates that the market is relatively low. As a market indicator, this tells the investor to sell stock when bond accounts of commercial banks are small and buy stocks when they are large.

There is an element of truth in each of these market indicators. The assumptions on which they rest, however, are that we enjoy an orderly and free money market; that complete freedom of movement of funds exists between the money market, the bond market, and the stock market; and that the movement in interest rates and stock yields is determined by funds moving from bonds into stocks—a sign of strength for stocks—and from stocks into bonds—a sign of weakness. But this is only a part of the total money market. Since World War II, the central bank policy through the Federal Reserve Board and fiscal policy through the Treasury have had a much greater impact on the money market than the movement of money from common stocks to bonds and vice versa. Before predicting the direction of the stock market from money market indicators, we would carefully analyze all the forces operating in the money market. This would require particular attention to Federal Reserve and Treasury policies as they affect money market conditions.

FEDERAL-FUNDS RATE, MONEY SUPPLY, AND FEDERAL RESERVE POLICY AS MARKET INDICATORS. The yield on federal funds—loans from one commercial bank to another, used for settling reserve balances—is thought to be a good barometer of stock prices. When the federal funds rate is high and rising, stock prices should decline.

If the federal funds rate is low and stable, this is a favorable sign for equity prices. The federal funds rate is reported in the *Federal Reserve Bulletin* and in *The Wall Street Journal* on a daily basis. The rate has varied as follows:

1971	4.66
1972	4.44
1973	10.00
1974	10.51
1975	5.82
1976	5.05
1977	5.54
1978	7.93
1979	11.19
1980	13.36
1981	15.08
1982	12.26
1983 (Jan.)	8.44

Using this measure, stocks would have been purchased in 1971–72. Rates moved above 10 percent in mid-1973, which was a bearish indicator, except for the reasons cited above. At the end of October 1976, the funds rate was 5.00 percent, which would indicate that equities should be bought. (Interestingly, the market was thought underpriced at 940 based on the use of the valuation equation.) During 1982 and 1983, close analysis of the funds rate, which is controlled by the open-market committee of the Federal Reserve Board, indicated that when the rate declined, stock prices increased; when the rate increased, stock prices declined.

It pays to watch the changes in the amount of money in circulation as an indicator of the direction of the securities market. Generally speaking, a growing money supply and a rising securities market are synonomous. That is, as the money supply increases, equity prices tend to rise; when money supply decreases or declines in its growth rate, stock prices decrease. However, if the money supply expands more than the Federal Reserve Board thinks necessary for the stable growth of the economy, the rapid rise will lead to a tight-money policy, a rising fed-funds rate, and lower stock market prices.

Late in 1981, the growth rate of M1B and M2 were within the guidelines established by the Federal Reserve Board. The target rate for M1B was 3 1/2 to 6 percent and for M2, 6 1/2 to 9 1/2 percent. In the last few months of 1982, the Fed eased back from a position of monetary restraint and reduced the discount rate from 10 to 8.5 percent. Interest rates had moved lower, with the prime rate declining from 13.5 to 11.0 percent. The decline in the discount rate, along with the slower rate of growth of the money supply, suggested that interest rates would continue to decline and stock prices might rise.

The current definitions of money supply are:

M1: Averages of daily figures for (1) currency outside the Treasury, Federal Reserve Banks, and the vaults of commercial banks; (2) traveler's checks of nonbank issuers; (3) demand deposits at all commercial banks other than those due to domestic banks, the U.S. government, and foreign banks and official institutions less cash items in the process of collection and Federal Reserve float; and (4) negotiable order of withdrawal (NOW) and automatic transfer service (ATS) accounts at banks and thrift institutions, credit union share draft (CUSD) accounts, and demand deposits at mutual savings banks.

M2: M1 plus savings and small-denomination time deposits at all depository institutions, overnight repurchase agreements at commercial banks, overnight Eurodollars held by U.S. residents other than banks at Caribbean branches of member banks, and balances of money market mutual funds (general purpose and broker/dealer).

M3: M2 plus large-denomination time deposits at all depository institutions and term RPs at commercial banks and savings and loan associations and balances of institution-only money market mutual funds.

L: M3 plus other liquid assets such as term Eurodollars held by U.S. residents other than banks, bankers acceptances, commercial paper, Treasury bills and other liquid Treasury securities, and U.S. savings bonds.[9]

NEW OFFERINGS OF STOCK AS A MARKET INDICATOR. One aspect of the capital market that bears directly on the stock market is the underwriting of new issues of common stock. When business is expanding and in need of additional capital, new firms resort to the equity market for funds, and existing firms take the opportunity to raise capital. From 1980 through 1982, as seen in Table 20–5, the market for new

TABLE 20–5

New Issues of Corporate Common Stock by Years
(millions of dollars)

1963	$1,011	1970	$7,240	1977	$ 8,135
1964	2,679	1971	9,291	1978	7,526
1965	1,547	1972	8,318	1979	7,751
1966	1,939	1973	7,642	1980	16,858
1967	1,959	1974	3,994	1981	23,522
1968	3,946	1975	7,405	1982E*	24,373
1969	7,714	1976	8,305		

*E, estimate.

SOURCE: Federal Reserve Bulletin, December 1963, p. 1965; June 1968, p. A44; January and June 1973, pp. A46 and A48; February 1977, p. A36; October 1981, p. A36.; February 1983, p. A36.

issues of common stock was extremely good, and many companies resorted to the capital markets for funds. When the number of new issues is increasing and they are being taken off the market by support from investors, this is a sign of strength in the stock market. This was the case in 1983. However, if the new issues decline in volume and are difficult to market, this is a sign of weakness, which was the case in 1981. If after a market rise new stock issues are sold only at prices below their offering price, this is a sign that the market is too high and will probably decline. An investor using the change in volume of new security issues as a guide to market activity would heed such a market warning and establish a more defensive investment policy. As the market rose in 1982 and 1983, the issuance of common stock increased to a level much higher than previously obtained. This was a bullish sign. Volume in 1981 was lower, which was a bearish sign.

[9] Federal Reserve Bulletin, February 1983, p. A3.

The whole conceptual fabric of this book rests on the assumption that a thorough fundamental analysis of a company or the market will allow the investor to estimate the future level of earnings, dividends, and price. Further, the analysis will permit the investor to determine the estimated return from the investment, and to estimate the variability of expected return.

On the other hand, the stock market "technician" assumes that the stock market has a life of its own, independent of the fundamental attributes of investment value possessed by the individual companies that constitute the market.[10] Collectively, the market acts and reacts to news about business and government, as does an individual stock. The technical position of the market is important, since a market can be too high or too low, overbought or oversold. There are technical indicators or theories that attempt to establish the relative height of the market through an examination of its technical aspects rather than fundamentals. Most of the theories assume that the movement of the market tells all—or, as the professional states it, "the market discounts everything." Some people, known as "tape readers," concentrate on the stock ticker and make their decisions only on the basis of the price and volume figures they observe on the tape carrying the transactions of the New York Stock Exchange and the American Exchange. Others are "chartists," or point-and-figure experts, who interpret and forecast by the use of price movements of the stock. Those who read tapes and charts are, for the most part, speculators in the stock market.

Technical theory can be summarized as follows:

1. Market value is determined solely by the interaction of supply and demand.
2. Supply and demand are governed by numerous factors, both rational and irrational. Included in these factors are those that are relied upon by the fundamentalists, as well as opinions, moods, guesses, and blind necessities. The market weighs all these factors continually and automatically.
3. Disregarding minor fluctuations in the market, stock prices tend to move in trends that persist for an appreciable length of time.
4. Changes in trend are caused by the shifts in supply-and-demand relationships. These shifts, no matter why they occur, can be detected sooner or later in the action of the market itself.[11]

Levy states: "The basic assumption of technical theorists is that history tends to repeat itself."[12] The market technician assumes that past price action predicts future price behavior. The technician relies on the dependence of successive price changes.

The fundamentalist believes that each security has an intrinsic value based on earnings, particularly expected future earnings, and that future prices revolve around those earnings and intrinsic values. This process, in short, allows the investor to determine or estimate future price.[13] A value judgment is made that "in fact, there is

[10]See Robert A. Levy, "Conceptual Foundations of Technical Analysis," *Financial Analysts Journal*, July–August 1966.

[11]Robert D. Edwards and John Magee, *Technical Analysis of Stock Trends* (Springfield, Mass.: John Magee, 1958), p. 86.

[12]Levy, "Conceptual Foundations."

[13]Ibid.

is little justification for denying that properly performed fundamental analysis is superior to technical analysis."[14]

In spite of the claim of the superiority of fundamental analysis over technical analysis, it is important for the investor to be aware of technical market indicators and theories that help technicians understand the short-term aspects of the market. After the discussion of technical market indicators, the random-walk hypothesis will be mentioned again in relation to technical analysis. This hypothesis states that past prices cannot be used to predict future prices in the short term because, statistically, past prices are completely independent of future prices. And this, of course, makes it difficult to accept technical analysis.

The Dow Theory

The Dow theory is one of the oldest theories, and probably the most widely followed, about the technical action of the stock market. Part of the reason for its popularity is the widespread use of *The Wall Street Journal* and *Barron's*, both of which are publications of Dow Jones & Company, founded in 1882. Part of the reason, too, is the success that has been attributed to the theory by the Dow theorists.

The Dow theory was first presented by Charles H. Dow, who founded Dow Jones & Company. Later, he was the first editor of *The Wall Street Journal* and subsequently the publisher of *Barron's* magazine. Charles Dow never published a formal treatise on his theory; most of the Dow theory comes to us from the students of the market who followed Dow's interpretation of the stock market in 1901 and 1902. One of these was W. P. Hamilton, former editor of *The Wall Street Journal* and at one time (1903–29) the most prominent Dow theorist. Hamilton wrote a column on the theories of Charles Dow, and later wrote a book on the Dow theory.[15] Another student of the market, Robert Rhea, wrote *The Dow Theory* in 1932, and G. W. Bishop, Jr., wrote *Charles H. Dow and the Dow Theory* in 1960.[16] The best-advertised modern practitioner of the Dow theory was E. George Schaefer.[17] Dow was also considered an economist and followed the thinking of Wesley C. Mitchell.[18]

Most of the modern practitioners and interpreters of the Dow theory have added little except refinements, but they have eliminated some of the errors. Dow and his followers considered the stock market an excellent barometer of business but did not consider his theory a method of providing market tips.

THE MOVEMENT OF THE MARKET. The Dow theory is based on the movements of the DJIA and the DJTA. The movements of the market are divided into three major classifications: the primary movement, the secondary movement, and the daily fluctuations. The primary movement is the trend of the market, which lasts from one

[14]Ibid.

[15]W. P. Hamilton, *The Stock Market Barometer* (New York: Barron's, 1922).

[16]Robert Rhea, *The Dow Theory* (New York: Barron's, 1932); George W. Bishop, Jr., *Charles H. Dow and The Dow Theory* (New York: Appleton-Century-Crofts, 1960).

[17]E. George Schaefer, "Hold Stocks for Final Market Upsurge," *Forbes*, December 1, 1962, pp. 38–49.

[18]George W. Bishop, Jr., *Charles H. Dow: Economist* (Princeton, N.J.: Dow Jones Books, 1967).

year to 28–33 months or longer. The trend of the market is either bullish (up) or bearish (down). The bear markets historically have lasted a shorter period of time than the bull markets. The determination of the primary movement or trend of the market is the basic objective of the Dow theory.

The secondary movement of the market is shorter in duration than the primary movement, and it is opposite in direction. The secondary movement usually lasts from three weeks to three months and usually retraces one-third to two-thirds of the previous advance in a bull market or the previous decline in a bear market. Secondary movements frequently end in dullness in stock market activity.

Day-to-day fluctuation is not a part of the Dow theory interpretation of the stock market. Since the daily movements go to make up the longer movement in the market, however, they must be studied along with the primary and secondary movements.

FORECASTS AND THE DOW THEORY.   The forecasts of the Dow theory are based on the primary and secondary movements of the market. It is assumed that the movements of the market discount everything. All we must do is watch the averages; they will help to determine the direction of the market.

It is also assumed that the averages cannot be manipulated. Manipulation of the stock market was a grave problem prior to 1933. It was possible for "bear" pools to force a stock below its fair value, or for "bulls" to force a price higher and higher and then unload the stock on the public, causing a sharp drop in price. These manipulative practices have been curbed by the various Securities Acts, so this part of the theory is somewhat meaningless in today's economy.

The Dow theory's purpose is to determine where the market is, but it also indicates where the market is going, although not how far or high. The theory, in practice, states that if the cyclical swings of the stock market averages are successively higher and the successive lows are higher, the market trend is up and we are in a bull market. Contrarily, if the successive highs and successive lows are lower, the direction of the market is down and we are in a bear market.

In order for us to be certain that the primary trend is up or down, the industrial averages and the transportation averages must confirm the same market action. Figure 20–2 shows how the Dow Theory might be used. The trend of the market from P_1 to P_3 is bullish, because P_2 is higher than P_1 and P_3 is higher than P_2, and also because T_2 is higher than T_1 and T_3 is higher than T_2. The transportation averages confirm the movements of the industrial averages. When the trend of the market changes, we notice that T_4 is lower than T_3 and P_4 is lower than P_3. When this information is coupled with the successively lower bottoms of the transportation averages, we find confirmation of a bear market with a primary trend downward.

One problem with the Dow theory is that the confirmation of the market does not come until after a substantial rise or fall. In Figure 20–2, the points of confirmation of the bull market are A and A_R. Until these points are reached, the Dow theorist does not know if the market is in a primary trend upward or beginning a secondary movement downward. This is illustrated when the market reaches T_3. At this point, the market could continue down and, by going below T_2, might indicate the beginning of a primary movement in the bear market. However, the bear market cannot be confirmed until the market moves to P_4, turns around, and goes to point X and below.

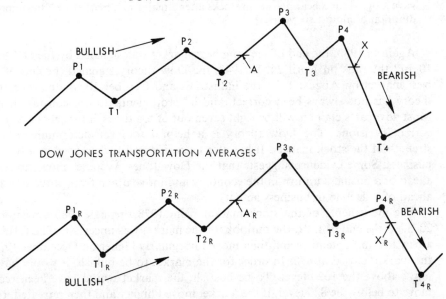

FIGURE 20–2

Determining the Direction of the Market Using the Dow Theory and the Dow Jones Averages

At point X, a bear market is in the process of development, but it must be confirmed by the movement of the transportation average to point X_R. The investor would move out of the market at point X, missing the top of the market, P_3, but preventing a further market loss. The upturn in a bear market would be similar to the movements traced for a bull market.

THE LINE MOVEMENT. In addition to the major movements of the market, the line movement is used as a part of the Dow theory. A line movement in the stock market is a trading range where the Dow Jones Averages fluctuate within a narrow price range of about 5 percent of the amount of the averages. The line might last several weeks or longer and is looked upon as a period of accumulation or distribution of stock. If both the DJIA and DJTA break out of the range on the upside, this is an indication that the market will move up. It is then assumed that the period was one of accumulation. If the averages move down and break through the trading range, it would be considered a period of distribution and would indicate a continued downward movement in the average. If both the averages do not confirm the breakthrough of the line movement, then the direction the market will take is in doubt.

THE SUCCESS OF THE DOW THEORY. The Dow theory was successful in showing the turn of the big bull market in October 1929. The industrials gave the signal on October 22, and the rails confirmed on October 23:

On the late Charles H. Dow's well-known method of reading the stock market movement from the Dow Jones Averages, the twenty railroad stocks on Wednesday, October 23, confirmed a bearish indication by the industrials two days before. Together the average gave a signal for a bear market in stocks after a major bull market with the unprecedented duration of almost six years.[19]

Again in 1933, the end of the long bear market was signaled by the DJIA on April 10 and the rails on April 24. In 1949, the Dow theory signaled the end of the 1946 bear market on August 1 for the industrials and October 10 for the rails. The Dow theory has not always been correct, and its proponents do not consider it infallible. Most advocates claim it will be right seven out of ten times, an excellent percentage of correct decisions. The Dow theory is a helpful tool for determining the relative strength of the stock market. It has also been successful when used as a barometer of business. Some evidence suggests that the Dow Jones Averages move up six months ahead of a business upturn in the economy and move down from three to six months ahead of a decline in business activity.

The movements of the stock market from 1978 through 1983 appear in Figure 20–3. At the end of 1981, the outlook for the market was uncertain. The DJIA reached a new low in September and then moved irregularly higher on December 19, 1981, as the market closed at 876. In order for the market to be bullish, it would have had to move above the 1020 level. To be bearish, the market would have been required to move to below the 820 level. If the market moved higher and then retreated, the action would represent a primary market that was bearish. A bear market was confirmed as

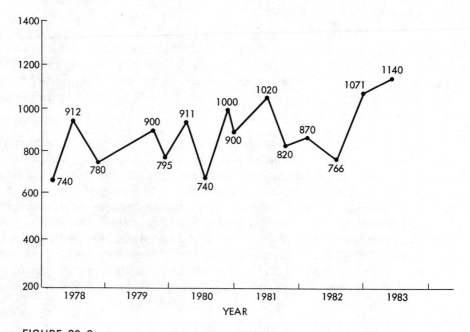

FIGURE 20–3

The Actual Direction of the Market in 1978–1983, Indicated by the Use of the Dow Jones Industrial Averages and the Dow Theory

[19]*The Wall Street Journal*, October 25, 1929, p. 1.

TECHNICAL ANALYSIS

the DJIA moved below 820 in 1982. A bull market was confirmed when the market moved above $970 and then to new records signalling a bull market in 1983.

Breadth Index

Some market traders and investors criticize the Dow theory because it does not reflect the movement of all stocks in the market; that is, the Dow Jones Averages are not representative of the market, since not all stocks move in the same direction at the same time as the Dow Jones Averages. Some chartists now consider the NYSE Index a better guide to the market. There is some validity in this criticism. In view of the fact that shares of more than 1,100 companies are traded on an active day, it is clear that the DJIA may not reflect the entire movement of the market. In order to overcome this weakness, some market analysts use an index that covers all securities traded and hence is called a *breadth index*.

The breadth index is computed by dividing the net advances or declines in the market by the number of issues traded. The information is obtained from *The Wall Street Journal*, in the "Market Diary" statistics for the New York Stock Exchange. This section of the *WSJ* also lists the "Dow Jones Closing Averages" and "Other Market Indicators," along with trading activity. The AMEX-Composite Transactions and the over-the-counter markets have a similar set of statistics. As an example, the number of companies whose shares were traded on Wednesday, December 9, 1981, was 1,943. Of these, 751 companies' shares increased in price, 717 decreased, and 475 remained unchanged. The net advances numbered 34 (751 − 717), and the breadth-index ratio on that day was 1.75 percent (34/1943). The number of companies whose shares were traded on the preceding Tuesday was 1,955. Of these, 471 increased in price, 1,039 decreased in price, and 445 remained unchanged. The net declines numbered 568, and the breadth index ratio on that day was a minus 29.1 percent (568/1,955).

The figures obtained in this way are then combined in a moving average of 150 days, or they are used for comparison with a base year. Today, the base year could be 1972 or a later date. The resulting figures are compared to the Dow Jones Averages. The breadth index supports or is contrary to the movement of the Dow Jones Averages. If it does not support them, this is considered a sign of technical weakness in the market—a sign that the market will move in a direction opposite to the Dow Jones Averages. If, on the other hand, the breadth index should confirm the movement of the Dow Jones Averages, this is interpreted as a sign of technical strength. In other words, strength is indicated if the market moves up or down and the breadth index parallels this movement; weakness, if the breadth index and Dow Jones Averages move in opposite directions. The breadth index on December 9, 1981 was a sign of strength, since the DJIA advanced 6.47 points. This was a sign that the market showed strength on the plus side, so the conclusion would be that the market was technically strong.

Volume of Trading

The volume of shares traded in the market serves as another guide to technical strength or weakness. The volume-of-trading concept suggests that an upward or downward movement of the stock market accompanied by a large volume of trading is a sign of strength, a movement without volume a sign of technical weakness. The volume concept has a very short-term impact on the market. It is usually associated with a turn in the market. Assume that the stock market begins to move up after a period of decline; investors are hopeful that the upward movement is an indication that the market has changed its course. However, it is observed that the market rise was accompanied by a relatively small volume. This would indicate that the market is technically weak. and investors should not expect a continued rise. If the upward movement were accompanied by a large volume of trading, investors could assume that the market was technically strong. There is no assurance, however, that the movement will continue upward. The volume concept is best used with another market indicator, such as the Dow theory.

The Odd-Lot Volume—Public Participation

Who is buying or selling is also a technical indicator of market strength or weakness. It is generally thought that the professional investor is the astute and informed or strong investor and that the public is the weak or emotional investor. If the professional investor dominates the stock market, then the market is technically strong. On the other hand, if the public is in the market, this is a sign of technical weakness, since public buying is concentrated at the top of the market cycle and public selling at the bottom. The quantity of odd-lot purchases and sales is the indication of the extent of public participation in the market, because the assumption is made that small investors do not buy in round lots; so the greater the volume of odd lots, the greater the public participation. If the odd-lot volume increases in sales or purchases, this is interpreted as a sign of technical weakness. The data about odd lots are readily found in *The Wall Street Journal*.

According to this concept, one should be quite apprehensive about a rise in public participation and consider the market technically weak. In defense of the public, it can be stated that public participation cannot generally be used as an indication of market weakness. Several studies have indicated that the public in general does not move into the market at the peak and move out at the bottom. Often just the reverse is true, and it can be concluded that the public is just as sophisticated about investment matters as professional investors.

Confidence Index

The confidence index is used by some market analysts as a guide to the technical strength of the market and as a method of trading or timing the purchase and sale of stock. Some analysts use it as a forecasting device, to determine the turning points of the market. The *confidence index*, which is found in *Barron's*, is computed by dividing the yield on *Barron's* best-grade bonds into the yield on *Barron's* intermediate-grade bonds. On a certain day, for example, the best-grade bonds yield was 12.84 percent and the yield on the intermediate-grade bonds was 11.58 percent, providing a confidence index of 88.1 percent. The rationale of the confidence index is that investors will buy lower-grade bonds if their confidence is high. This tends to increase the demand for lower-grade bonds and lowers the demand for high-grade bonds. The effect is to decrease the yields on the low-grade bonds and increase those on the high-grade bonds, thus increasing the confidence index.

Therefore, if the confidence index moves up, the market is technically strong, and if the confidence index moves down, it is a sign of technical weakness. As long as the index is above 88, there is unusual confidence in the market. If it falls, or if it is around 70, this is a sign of depressed conditions and a severe lack of confidence in the market. This index is not perfect and will not forecast accurately, nor will it determine the duration of the strength of the market. However, it is a specific factor that helps the investor judge the timing of the relative height of the market when making an investment decision.

Point-and-Figure Charts

Point-and-figure charts are used by market technicians to "predict" the extent and direction of the movements of the stock market. The charts are drawn on ruled paper, as seen in Figure 20–4. The numbers to the left in the figure represent the price of the

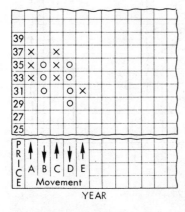

FIGURE 20–4

Part of a Two-Point Point-and-Figure Chart

stock at 2-point intervals, but the interval of price change can be 1, 2, 5, or 10 points, where 1 point equals $1, depending on the time-period orientation of the investor. An investor would be interested in a 5- or 10-point unit and a trader in a 1-point unit. If the price of the stock is high, a 5- or 10-point unit may be used; a 1-point unit or less will be used on low-priced stock. Only whole-number prices are recognized. In Figure 20–4, the initial price of 33 was entered in column A as an *X*. Only if and when the stock moves up to 35 will another *X* be placed in column A. As long as the price continues to move up, the *X*s are placed in the same vertical column—in this case, column A. The stock price in Figure 20–4 moved up from 33 to 37. If and when the price declines to a lower box or level, the chartist records the change by placing the *O* in the next column. In this case, the stock moved down to 35 and *O* was placed in column B at 35. No time is indicated on the point-and-figure chart, since price is recorded on the vertical axis and direction on the horizontal axis.

The simple rules followed by the chartist are these: Put an *X* on the chart for a price rise to or through a whole number, and an *O* if the price falls to or through a whole number; boxes are filled in only when price changes occur, and a new column is begun each time the direction of price is reversed.

The movements are then interpreted. Figure 20–5 is an example of chart interpretation. As long as the market action is between points *A* and *B*, there is little indication of market action. As the price breaks out of the upper resistance point *B*, this is a bullish sign and a signal to buy. The price continues to move up; new highs are made on the chart by the price action, and the new lows are higher than the previous lows. The stock moves to a higher level, and two new resistance points are made at *C* and *D*. The price finally moves through point *C*, indicating that the stock should be sold, since there has been a breakout.

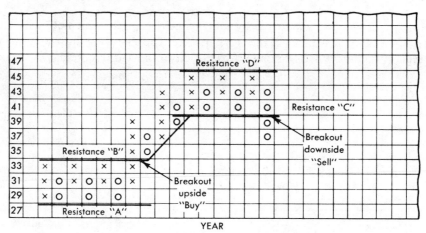

FIGURE 20–5

Use of Point-and-Figure Chart for Buying and Selling

This is an oversimplification of the point-and-figure chartist's activities. The charts are helpful in interpreting the market price movement of a stock and should be consulted to improve the timing of an investment. Dine's Technical Market Service, for example, is based on point-and-figure techniques.

Short Sales as a Market Indicator

The volume of short sales (short interest) in the stock market is also an indication of the technical strength or weakness of the market. A short sale involves the sale of borrowed stock. When a short sale is made, there is an increase in the supply of stock on the market, tending to reduce the price. When a short sale is completed, the purchase of the stock tends to increase the price. Those who follow and use the volume of short sales as an index of strength of the market say that as short sales rise, strength is indicated, and when short sales decline, technical weakness is shown. A large short interest in a rising market is a particularly strong indication of strength: first, because the market has absorbed the additional supply of stock, and second, because if the market should begin to decline, the short interest will help to support the price of the stock. As the market drops, the speculators will buy at lower prices, make a profit, and support the market.

As a technical indication of market strength, the short-interest concept is excellent when used with a general theory of the market such as the Dow theory. Figures on the volume of short interest in the market can be obtained from *Barron's* or *The Wall Street Journal.*

INTERPRETING CHARTS AND TECHNICAL ANALYSIS—
AN EXPLANATORY NOTE

Technical analysis "is the science of recording . . . the actual history of trading in a certain stock . . . and then deducing from that pictured history the probable future trend."[20] Technical analysts contend that the real value of a share is determined solely by the interaction of supply and demand, which are reflected in transactions consummated in the different exchanges. The market price reflects not only the statistics the fundamental analyst studies, but also other factors such as the "opinions of many orthodox security appraisers . . . the hopes and fears and guesses and moods, rational and irrational, of hundreds of potential buyers and sellers, as well as their needs and resources . . . in total, factors which defy analysis and for which no statistics are obtainable, but which are nevertheless all synthesized, weighed and finally expressed in the one precise figure at which a buyer and seller get together and make a deal."[21] Changes in demand and supply therefore force price changes. Prices in turn result in trends and continue to do so until another change in the demand-supply balance occurs. More important, certain formations appear on the charts which have a meaning and can be interpreted in terms of future trend developments. Therefore, prices and volume are the factors most closely watched by the technical analyst in arriving at an investment decision.

Charts are the main tool of the technical analyst. It is the chart that depicts the stock's historical price movements and gives the chartist a clue to probable future price movement:

> On the charts, price fluctuations tend, with remarkable consistency, to fall into a number of patterns, each of which signifies a relationship between buying and selling pressures. Some patterns, or formations, indicate that demand is greater than supply, others suggest that supply is greater than demand, and still others imply that they are likely to remain in balance for some time.[22]

Charts have been developed in many forms and styles—they may be monthly, weekly, or daily charts, point and figure or bar charts, and constructed on arithmetic, logarithmic, or square-root scales. All, however, are attempts to come up with a graphic history of price movements that will give the analyst a signal (or a warning) of a changing trend. A good source of charts is found in William L. Jiler's book, *How*

[20]Edwards and Magee, *Technical Analysis of Stock Trends*, p. 3.

[21]Ibid., p. 5.

[22]William L. Jiler, *How Charts Can Help You in the Stock Market* (New York: Trendline, 1967), p. 21.

Charts Can Help You in the Stock Market. These are daily, vertical-line (or bar) charts and have the advantage of being easily understood as well as containing the most important information—the highest, lowest, and closing prices, as well as the number of shares traded.

Trends

Prices tend to move in a certain direction for a considerable time. This tendency to move in a definite pattern along an imaginary straight line is one of the most extraordinary characteristics of chart movements.[23] Time is of no importance—a trend may continue a matter of minutes or years—what is important is that the trend is assumed to be intact until it actually reverses. In order to spot a trend, a minimum of three points are needed to confirm. An *uptrend* is a series of ascending highs and lows that can be connected with a line which points up. The opposite is implied and true for a *downtrend*. In practice, the uptrend line is drawn by connecting the lower points of a movement, while a downtrend line is drawn by connecting the higher points.

Channels

Once a particular trend has been established, one can usually draw parallel lines to the trend lines. The result is what chartists call *channels* through which prices move as they go up and down a trend line. Channels are useful in suggesting at what price a person may buy and sell a stock, if a decision concerning what action to take has been made. It must be noted, however, that a break in the trend line on the downside does not necessarily mean that the stock should be sold. Trend lines tend to decelerate and then form into what is called a *fan*. A fan develops when an established trend line is broken, resulting in another price trend in the same direction. This second line is broken again and results in a third line in the same direction. A break in the third line is usually a signal that a major turn is imminent. A fan formation is illustrated in Figure 20–6.

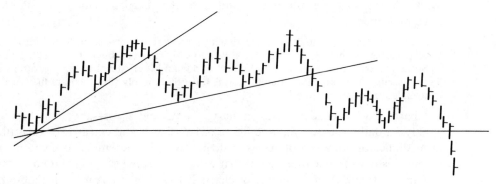

FIGURE 20–6

A Fan Line

[23] Ibid., p. 27.

Volume

"The volume is a measure of the intensity of buying and selling pressure—the conviction behind a move."[24] Generally speaking, therefore, a greater volume implies a more significant price movement. In an uptrend, volume increases when prices rise from the trend line and decreases when prices move back to the trend line. In a downtrend, volume is usually greater when prices drop than when they rally.

Support and Resistance Levels

A *support level* exists at a price where a considerable demand for that stock is expected. It is a level where a sufficient demand for a stock exists to halt a downtrend temporarily, or even reverse it. By the same token, a *resistance level* exists at a price level where an excess supply of that stock is expected.

Support and resistance levels usually come about whenever the turnover of a large number of shares tends to be concentrated at several price levels. When a stock's price touches a certain level and then drops, this is called a resistance. Conversely, whenever a stock's price reaches down to a certain level and then rises, there exists a support. It is important to note that these levels constantly switch roles from support to resistance and from resistance to support; once a support level has been penetrated, any subsequent rise to that former level becomes a resistance, and vice versa.

Reversal Patterns—Head and Shoulders Formation

One of the best known of all chart formations, the head and shoulders, portrays three successive rallies and reactions with the second rally reaching a higher point than either of the others. The third rally's failure to equal the second peak is a sign that a former trend will reverse itself. A head and shoulders top pattern is considered to be a bearish formation and is illustrated in Figure 20–7. The head and shoulders bottom formation is exactly the same as the head and shoulders top except that it is upside down (Figure 20–8). This formation is considered to be a bullish formation that marks the end of a downtrend. The volume pattern is usually different in both formations. No head and shoulders pattern must be regarded as complete until the neckline is broken.

Measurement of the Price Action Following a Breakout/Breakdown

In predicting the objective of a breakout/breakdown in this formation, one measures the difference between the top of the head and the neckline. This difference is added to (in the case of the head and shoulders bottom) or subtracted from (in the head and shoulders top) the neckline. This, as technical analysts contend, is where the last optimistic and last pessimistic investor will drive the price.

[24]Ibid., p. 32.

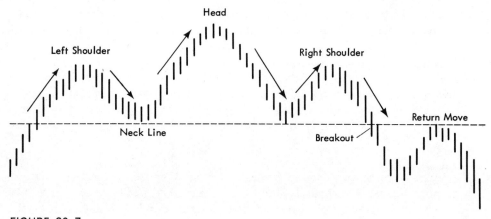

FIGURE 20–7

Head and Shoulders Top

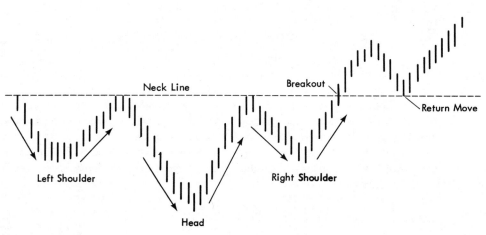

FIGURE 20–8

Head and Shoulders Bottom

Double Tops and Bottoms

A double top formation is completed whenever "a stock advances to a certain level with unusually high volume at and approaching the top figure, then retreats with diminishing activity, then comes up again to the same price level as before with some pick-up in volume but not as much as on the first peak, and then finally turns down a second time for a major or consequential intermediate decline."[25] A double bottom is, of course, the mirror image of the double top. It is important to note that, as in all formations, the investor must wait until the pattern is completed (until a breakout or breakdown is achieved) before taking a position or selling the stock. A breakout or breakdown in this formation usually suggests a move to the previous top (or bottom) price level achieved.

The Coil (or Triangle) Formations

A triangle formation is composed of a series of price fluctuations where each top (or bottom) is followed by progressively lower (higher) rallies. There are basically three types of triangle formations.

The first is where the top can be characterized by a downward-sloping line while the bottom being defined by an upward-sloping line. This is a *symmetrical* triangle. The *ascending* triangle is characterized by a similar resistance level (the top line being horizontal) and an upward-sloping bottom line. The *descending* triangle is the reverse of the ascending triangle; the bottom line is horizontal and there is a downward-sloping upper line (see Figure 20–9).

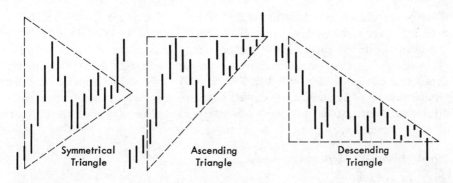

FIGURE 20–9

Triangle Formations

Prices may break out or break down from the symmetrical triangle. In this formation, the market is uncertain and one cannot predict whether prices will move up or down until the price moves out of the formation. The ascending triangle is considered to be a bullish formation; the descending triangle, a bearish formation. Volume usually decreases during the formation and increases on the breakout or breakdown. One would add the height of the triangle to the breakout/breakdown point to measure the price objective.

Many formations are used by the technical analyst. Other formations include the saucer, island, flag, pennant, wedge, and diamond. Their descriptions are readily available from any of the books cited. What is important is that the use of technical

[25]Edwards and Magee, *Technical Analysis of Stock Trends*, p. 129.

analysis is another tool in the investment decision process. It enables the investor to determine trend reversals in stocks.

INVESTMENT FORECASTING SERVICES

The future outlook for the stock market is so important to so many institutions and individuals that specialized forecasting advisory services were bound to develop. *Buying Power vs. Selling Pressure* and *The Value Line Investment Surveys* are two of the prominent services that provide forecasts of the stock market. In recent years, a host of new services have been established that advertise regularly in the Sunday *New York Times*. The services offer the promise of nearly perfect market forecasts, with the implication that a subscription to the service will lead to instant riches. One source points out that it selects a group of stocks set for a turnaround. Another asks, "The Dow 30: Buy? Hold? Sell?" A third tells about five stocks in the public eye. One discusses the CATV industry; another provides a major reappraisal of 64 growth favorites; still another gives 35 items to analyze in predicting the stock market.

Market analysis is important to the investor; it is wise for investors to orient themselves to the stock market before they make commitments, and there are times when market analysis will indicate an obviously high position. However, the ads describing these forecasts or projections are designed to sell a service. Many of them are valuable and helpful to the investor, but point-and-figure charts, chart reading, and market analysis are not services. The practice of market forecasting will not always lead to success, and market analysis is not a panacea for investment decisions. An investor would be wise to sample the market letters of writers such as Dines and Granville, advertised in *The New York Times*, to understand the type of service offered. The services discussed here are older and more fundamental. They do not necessarily offer any great advantage to the investor, but are only examples of what is available.

Buying Power vs. Selling Pressure

A service that attempts to forecast the movement of the market from the volume of purchases and sales is *Buying Power vs. Selling Pressure*, published by Lowry's Reports, Inc. This service bases its forecasts on stock market data and uses momentum theory, which considers both price and volume. In the buying power–selling pressure system, buying power is defined as demand, and selling pressure as supply. Buying power is determined by dividing the total number of shares traded in a day into the dollar value of the gains in those shares that have increased in price. Selling pressure is found by dividing the total number of shares traded into the dollar value of the losses of those shares that decreased in price. If buying power moves up and selling pressure moves down, this is an indication of strength. If buying power moves down and selling pressure moves up, this is an indication of weakness. A sell signal is given when, after a market rise, there is an increase in selling pressure. *Buying Power vs. Selling Pressure* does not attempt to predict the length or magnitude of the price trend. It does indicate the technical strength of the market, which is helpful to the investor in timing the purchase of quality stocks.

The Value Line Investment Surveys

The Value Line Investment Surveys, basically an information service, attempts to forecast both the prices of individual securities and the market trend. The forecasts of the market are usually short run and are based on fundamentals rather than the technical position of the market. The regular company reports of *The Value Line* attempt to be predictive and to anticipate changes in the market, but they do warn that not every stock will perform in accordance with its ratings. Reference to a current issue will indicate the basic nature of its predictions.

Standard & Poor's *The Outlook*

The Outlook provides forecasts of the stock market for its subscribers. The forecasts, which are short run and must be written to cover a broad group of investors, are based on the technical condition of the market, but fundamentals are given major attention. A sample of *The Outlook*'s technique of commenting about the market can be obtained from a current issue.

THE RANDOM-WALK HYPOTHESIS

The basic assumption in our discussion of technical analysis was that, since history tends to repeat itself, the stock market could be predicted if only the investor could select the correct variables—the keys that would open the door to the future of the stock market. This is the major premise on which point-and-figure charting is founded. The chartists claim that a certain behavior of the charts allows prediction of the next level of the price of the market or of an individual stock. There is a body of knowledge, however, that refutes the predictability of the stock market. In fact, the *random-walk hypothesis* states that the behavior of stock market prices is unpredictable and that there is no relationship between the present price of a stock and its future price.

The random-walk theorists assume that efficient markets exist—markets with a large number of rational investors and speculators who are trying to maximize profits by predicting future earnings, dividends, and values of the securities.[26] Information is known to all and is freely and instantaneously transmitted to the marketplace to establish prices. The price established tends to be a "fair" price. Given this type of market, the adjustment process tends to allow prices to vary randomly around the competitive norm. As new information is learned, prices move. Because of the adjustment process, the movement will be up or down, depending on the stimulus. Since the investor or speculator overreacts, the adjustment process becomes random in character. And as new events occur, they too are transmitted to a marketplace that has no memory—one where each price is independent of the previous price. This suggests that the chartists are wrong. In fact, the conclusion is that stock prices randomly determined in the short run are unpredictable.

[26]Eugene F. Fama, "Random Walk in Stock Market Prices," *Financial Analysts Journal*, September–October 1965. See also Seymour Smidt, "A New Look at Random-Walk Hypothesis," *Journal of Financial and Quantitative Analysis*, September 1968, pp. 235–61; Paul H. Cootner, "Stock Prices: Random vs. Systematic Changes," *Industrial Management Review*, Spring 1962, pp. 24–45; and Michael A. Godfrey, Clive W. J. Granger, and Oskar Morgenstern, "The Random-Walk Hypothesis of Stock Market Behavior," *Kyklos*, 1964, pp. 1–29.

There is enough evidence historically of the validity of the random-walk hypothesis that prices are independent and unpredictable, at least in the short term. However, in the long run, economic and trend analysis helps to determine the future direction. Anticipations of trends far enough in the future make it unnecessary to use technical analysis, except as a partial aid to timing. The predictive function of economic value analysis lessens the impact of the random-walk hypothesis and makes charting only an avocational and academic subject in making real investment decisions (see Table 20–6).

TABLE 20–6
Summary: Indicators*

Technical Indicator	Level	Recommendation for Purchase of Common Stock
Dow theory	876	Indeterminate
Breadth index	1.34% to 19.61%	Buy
Trading volume	32,424,200	Indeterminate
Odd-lot volume	107,730	Buy
Short sales	1,421	Indeterminate
Confidence index	88.1	Buy
Point-and-figure chart	—	Indeterminate
Valuation		
Trend (reward to risk)	.86	Sell
Random (reward to risk)	.86	Sell
Current stock dividend yield (%)	5.45	Buy
Stock yield–bond yield differential (%)	−9.92	Buy
Money rates	Decreasing	Buy
Bond prices	Increasing	Buy
Stock prices	DJIA 876	Indeterminate
Commercial bank loans	Decreasing	Sell
Fed-fund rate	12.26	Buy
Money supply	Expansive	Buy
Fed policy	Expansive	Buy
New common stock offerings	$1.2 million (est.)	Buy

*As of December 1981.

SUMMARY

As a matter of principle, the investor should estimate the expected return and risk for the major stock market indexes. This will help in making judgments about individual securities, since two-thirds of the price movement of a stock is related to the movement of the market. The stock market is a leading indicator of the economy and is independent of the economy, but it is intimately a part of the capital markets. The S&P 500 average is one of the best guides to the action of the stock market. The expected return of the market can be estimated by use of the valuation equation:

$$P_0 = \sum_{t=1}^{n=3} \frac{D_0(1 + g_d)^t}{(1 + r)^t} + \frac{E_0(1 + g_e)^3(P/E)_3}{(1 + r)^3}$$

TREND, RANDOM, and ABE methods may be used in estimating return and risk over a three-year holding period. A reward-to-risk ratio can be useful in determining if the market is underpriced or overpriced. Historic return and risk help the investor to understand the desirability of an investment in the market.

Money market indicators such as fed-funds yields, Federal Reserve Board policy, money supply, new offerings of common stock, and the movement of short-term rates, bond prices, and commercial loans are helpful indicators of the direction of the market.

The basic concept of this book is to use traditional analysis to estimate return and risk characteristics of an individual stock. Technical analysis assumes that supply and demand are the only determinants of market price. Supply and demand are influenced by fundamentals, opinions, moods, and blind necessities that are factored into the market. Prices tend to move in trends, and changes are caused by shifts in supply and demand. Future stock prices are a function of past behavior, because history tends to repeat itself. The best-known technical form of analysis is the Dow theory. The breadth index, volume of trading, odd-lot volume, short sales, confidence index, and point-and-figure charts are technical indicators of the level of the market.

Research done by Fama, Cootner, Godfrey, Granger and Morgenstern, Levy, Sharpe, Lintner, Pogue, Pinches, Reilly, and others suggests that prices are independent and the market is efficient—which leads to the random-walk hypothesis. Even so, technical analysis forces the investor to analyze the market carefully, which can be helpful in assessing the relative level of the market.

SUMMARY OF PRINCIPLES

1. Fundamental analysis can be used to estimate the return and risk of the market as measured by the DJIA, the S&P 500 Index, or a similar index.
2. The stock market, a major part of the capital market, behaves independently of of the economy but is related to it as a leading indicator.
3. Estimating the trend of bond yields and money market yields is helpful in estimating the direction of the stock market.
4. Tight money affects stock prices adversely, and easy money affects stock prices favorably.
5. According to the random-walk hypothesis, stock prices are random in character and basically unpredictable, which makes present prices independent of future prices.
6. Fundamental analysis is superior to technical analysis.

REVIEW QUESTIONS

1. The stock market acts rationally, and therefore can be predicted with a little effort. Comment.
2. The stock market has a life of its own and acts independently of what basic economics or the so-called fundamentals might suggest. Comment.
3. What do we usually mean when we use the term *position of the stock market*?
4. What are the qualitative, quantitative, and technical differences among the Dow Jones Averages, the NASDAQ/OTC Index, Standard & Poor's Stock Price Index, and the New York Stock Exchange Indexes?

5. Is there one best average that can be used by the investor as an indicator of the market as a whole?

6. What are the assumptions of fundamental analysis in attempting to predict the direction of the stock market?

7. How do money market indicators attempt to predict the stock market?

8. What are the technical indicators of the stock market?

9. Explain in detail the Dow theory and how it might be used to determine the direction of the stock market.

10. Explain how the breadth index, volume of trading, odd-lot volume, short sales, and confidence index may be used to determine the direction of the market.

11. What is an efficient market?

12. What is a point-and-figure chart, and how is it used?

13. What is the random-walk hypothesis?

14. If we accept the random-walk hypothesis, should we attempt to estimate the market?

15. Are future stock market prices predictable on the basis of past price behavior?

CASE

Joe, who recently inherited $100,000 from his grandfather's estate, is thinking of investing in the stock market. He has completed a comprehensive fundamental analysis of return and risk of the market as measured by the DJIA index. This analysis suggested the market will experience substantial growth for the coming year. Based on an analysis of technical indicators as of today, would it be wise for Joe to invest in the market now or wait? A summary list of technical indicators is given below.

March 15, 1982

Indicator	Level
Dow theory, DJIA	797
Breadth index	−.29
Trading volume	52,960,000
Odd-lot volume	161,399
Short sales	1,346
Confidence index	89.3
Valuation models	
Trend, Return to risk	1.01
Random, Return to risk	1.05
Stock dividend yield % DJIA	6.75
Yield differential	−6.67
Money rates	Down—Volatile
Bond prices	Up—Volatile
Stock prices	Down
Commercial bank loans	Up Slightly
Fed funds rate 13–15%	Up—Volatile
Money supply	Up—Volatile
Fed policy	Restrictive
Common stock offerings	$49,838,000

ARNOTT, ROBERT D. "Cluster Analysis and Stock Price Movements." *Financial Analysts Journal*, November–December 1980.

BABCOCK, GUILFORD C. "The Roots of Risk and Return." *Financial Analysts Journal*, January–February 1980.

BEAVER, WILLIAM, and DALE MORSE. "What Determines Price-Earnings Ratios?" *Financial Analysts Journal*, July–August 1978.

BENNINGTON, GEORGE A., and MICHAEL C. JENSEN. "Random Walks and Technical Theories: Some Additional Evidence." *Journal of Finance*, May 1970.

BUTLER, H. L., JR., and J. D. ALLEN. "Dow Jones Industry Average Re-examined." *Financial Analysts Journal*, November–December 1979.

COOTNER, PAUL H. "Stock Market Indexes: Fallacies and Illusions." *Commercial and Financial Chronicle*, September 1966.

FAMA, EUGENE F. "Efficient Capital Markets: A Review of Theory and Empirical Work." *Journal of Finance*, May 1970.

————, LAWRENCE FISHER, MICHAEL C. JENSEN, and RICHARD ROLL. "The Adjustment of Stock Prices to New Information." *International Economic Review*, February 1969.

————, "Brownian Motion in the Stock Market." *Operations Research*, March–April 1959.

LEVY, ROBERT A. "Conceptual Foundations of Technical Analysis." *Financial Analysts Journal*, July–August 1966.

LINDAHL-STEVANS, MARY. "Redefining Bull and Bear Market." *Financial Analysts Journal*, November–December 1980.

LORIE, JAMES H., and MARY T. HAMILTON. "Stock Market Indexes." In *The Stock Market: Theories and Evidence*, Homewood, Ill.: Travia Inc., 1973.

MILLER, EDWARD M., JR. "How to Win at the Loser's Game." *The Journal of Portfolio Management*, Fall 1978.

MURPHY, THOMAS T., and STEVE WEST. "Caveats for Market Technicians." *Financial Analysts Journal*, September–October 1978.

ROBERTS, HARRY V. "Stock Market 'Patterns' and Financial Analysis: Methodological Suggestions." *Journal of Finance*, March 1959.

RUDD, ANDREW T. "The Revised Dow Jones Industry Average." *Financial Analysts Journal*, November–December 1979.

APPENDIX: STOCKS IN THE S&P "500" PRICE INDEX[27]

400 INDUSTRIALS

AEROSPACE—Boeing; General Dynamics; Grumman; Martin Marietta; McDonnell Douglas; Raytheon; Rockwell Intl.; United Technologies.

ALUMINUM—Alcan Aluminum; Aluminum Co. of Amer.; Kaiser Aluminum; Reynolds Metals.

AUTOMOBILE—Amer. Motors; Chrysler; Ford; Gen. Motors.

AUTO PARTS (After Market)—Champion Spark Plug; Echlin Mfg.; Genuine Parts.

AUTO PARTS (Original Equip.)—Bendix

[27]As of December 31, 1982.

Corp.; Dana; Eaton, Lib.-Owens-Ford; TRW Inc.; Timken Corp.

AUTO TRUCKS & PARTS—Cummins Engine; Fruehauf; Paccar Inc.

BEVERAGES(BREWERS)—Anheuser-Busch; Coors (Adolph); Heilman (G) Brewing; Pabst Brew.

BEVERAGES (DISTILLERS)—Brown-Forman Distillers; Natl. Dist.; Seagram Ltd.; Walker.

BEVERAGES (SOFT DRINKS)—Coca-Cola; Dr. Pepper; General Cinema; PepsiCo Inc., Royal Crown Cos.

BUILDING MATERIALS (AIR CONDITIONING)—Fedders; Trane.

BUILDING MATERIALS (CEMENT)—Ideal Basic; Kaiser Cement; Lone Star Indus.

BUILDING MATERIALS (DIVERSIFIED)—Amer. Standard, Crane; Masco Corp.

BUILDING MATERIALS (ROOFING & WALLBOARD)—Jim Walter Corp.; Masonite; Natl. Gypsum; U.S. Gypsum.

CHEMICALS—Dow; Du Pont (E.I.); Hercules; Monsanto; Stauffer Chem.; Union Carbide.

CHEMICALS (MISC.)—Allied Corp.; American Cyanamid; Celanese Corp.; FMC Corp.; Grace (W.R.) & Co.; PPG, Inc.; Rohm & Haas.

COAL (BITUMINOUS)—Eastern Gas & Fuel; No. Amer. Coal; Pittston; Westmoreland.

COMMUNICATIONS—EQUIP./MFRS.—M/A-Com Inc.; Northern Telecom.; ROLM Co.; Scientific Atlanta.

COMPUTER SERVICES—Automatic Data; Computer Sciences; Electronic Data Systems; Tymshare.

CONGLOMERATES—Gulf & Western; IC Indus.; Int'l. Tel. & Tel.; Litton Indus.; Northwest Indus.; Teledyne; Tenneco Inc.; Textron.

CONTAINERS (METAL & GLASS)—Amer. Can; Contl. Group; Crown Cork; Natl. Can; Owens-Ill.

CONTAINERS (PAPER)—Bemis Co.; Stone Container; Federal; Maryland Cup.

COPPER—ASARCO Inc.; Newmont Mining; Phelps-Dodge.

COSMETICS—Alberto-Culver; Avon; Chesebrough-Pond's; Faberge Inc.; Intl. Flavors & Fragrances; Revlon.

DRUGS—Amer. Home; Bristol-Myers; Squibb Corp.; Lilly (Eli); Merck; Pfizer; Schering-Plough; Searle (G. D.); Smith-Kline Beckman Corp.; Sterling; Upjohn Co.; Warner-Lambert.

ELECTRICAL EQUIPMENT—Emerson

Electric; General Instrum; Grainger (W. W.); McGraw Edison; Square D; Thomas & Betts.

ELECTRONICS MAJOR COS—Gen. Elec.; RCA, Westinghouse Elec.

ELECTRICAL HOUSEHOLD APPLIANCES—Maytag; Sunbeam; Whirlpool; White Consol Inds; Zenith.

ELECTRONICS (INSTRUMENTATION)—Gould; Hewlett-Packard; Perkin-Elmer; Tektronix.

ELECTRONICS (SEMICONDUCTORS/ COMPONENTS)—AMP Inc.; Intel Corp.; Motorola; Nat'l Semiconductor; Texas Instruments.

ENTERTAINMENT—Disney (Walt); MCA; Metro-Goldwyn-Mayer Film Co.; Warner Communications.

FERTILIZERS—Beker Inds.; First Miss. Corp.; Intl. Minerals & Chem.; Williams Cos.

FOODS—Amstar Corp.; Archer-Daniels-Midland; Beatrice Foods; Borden; CPC Int'l.; Campbell Soup; Carnation; Consolidated Foods; Dart & Kraft Inc.; Gen. Foods; Gen Mills; Gerber Prod.; Heinz (H.J.); Hershey Foods; Kellogg; Nabisco Brands Inc.; Norton Simon; Pillsbury; Quaker Oats; Ralston Purina; Stokely-Van Camp; Wrigley (Wm.).

FOREST PRODUCTS—Boise Cascade; Champion Intl.; Evans Products; Georgia-Pacific; Louisiana-Pac.; Potlatch Corp.; Weyerhaeuser.

‡**GAMING COS.**—Bally Mfg.; Caesars World; Resorts Int'l (Cl, A); Webb (Del. E.).

GOLD MINING—ASA Ltd.; Campbell Red Lake; Dome; Homestake Mining.

HOME FURNISHINGS—Bassett Furniture; Mohasco Corp.; Roper.

HOMEBUILDING—Centex Corp.; Kaufman & Broad; U.S. Home Corp.

HOSPITAL MANAGEMENT—Amer. Med. Int'l; Hospital Corp. of Amer.; Humana Inc.; Nat'l Med. Enter.

HOSPITAL SUPPLIES—Abbott Lab.; Amer. Hospital; Bard (C. R.); Baxter Travenol Lab.; Becton, Dickinson; Johnson & Johnson.

HOTEL-MOTEL—Hilton Hotels; Holiday Inns; Ramada Inns.

LEISURE TIME—AMF Inc.; Brunswick; Handleman; Outboard Marine.

MACHINE TOOLS—Acme Cleveland; Brown & Sharpe; Cincinnati Milacron; Cross & Trecker; Monarch Machine Tool.

MACHINERY (AGRICULTURAL)—Allis Chalmers; Deere; Intl. Harvester; Massey Ferguson.

‡Not included in 400 industrials.

MACHINERY (CONSTRUCTION & MATE-RIALS HANDLING)—Bucyrus-Erie; Cater. Trac.; Clark Equip.; Hyster Co.; Rexnord Inc.

MACHINERY (INDUSTRIAL/SPECIALTY)—Briggs & Stratton; Chicago Pneumatic; Combustion Eng.; Cooper Indus.; Ex-Cell-O; Foster Wheeler; Ingersoll-Rand; Joy Mfg.

METALS MISC.—Amax Inc.; Hudson Bay Mng.; INCO Ltd.; Phibro Corp.; Salomon Inc.

MISCELLANEOUS—ARA Services; AT&T; Apple Computer; Armstrong World; Black & Decker; Borg-Warner; Corning Glass; Eastman Kodak; Esmark; Fluor Corp.; Gillette, Harris Corp.; Honeywell Inc.; MCI Comm.; Minnesota Mining; Owens-Corning; Polaroid; Sherwin-Williams; Signal Cos.; Singer; Snap On Tools; Stanley Works; Tandy.

MOBILE HOMES—Fleetwood Enterprises; Redman Inds.; Skyline.

OFFICE & BUSINESS EQUIPMENT—Burroughs; Control Data; Data General; Datapoint Corp.; Digital Equip.; Intl. Bus. Mach.; NCR Corp.; Pitney-Bowes; Sperry Corp.; Storage Tech.; Wang Lab Cl B; Xerox Corp.

OFFSHORE DRILLING—Global Marine; Reading & Bates; SEDCO; Western Co. of North America.

OIL (CRUDE PRODUCERS)—Gen. Amer.; Louisiana Land & Exploration; Mesa Pet.; Superior Oil; Texas Oil & Gas.

OIL (INTEGRATED-DOMESTIC) — Atl. Richfield; Getty Oil; Occidental; Phillips; Shell; Stand. Oil Ind.; Standard Oil Ohio; Sun Co.; Union Oil of Cal.

OIL (INTEGRATED-INTERNATIONAL)—Exxon Corp.; Gulf; Mobil Corp.; Royal Dutch; Stand. Oil Calif.; Texaco.

‡CANADIAN OIL & GAS EXPLORATION—Dome Petroleum; Gulf of Canada; Husky Oil; Imperial Oil Ltd.

OIL WELL EQUIPMENT AND SERVICES—Baker Intl.; Dresser; Halliburton; Hughes Tool; McDermott Inc.; NL Industries; Schlumberger.

PAPER—Crown Zell.; Int'l Paper; Kimb-Clark; Mead; St. Regis; Scott; Union Camp; Westvaco.

POLLUTION CONTROL—Browning-Ferris; Peabody Int'l.; Waste Management Inc.; Wheelabrator-Frye; Zurn Ind.

PUBLISHING—Dun & Bradstreet; Harcourt Brace Jovanovich; Macmillan; McGraw-Hill; Meredith; SFN Co.; Time Inc.

PUBLISHING(NEWSPAPERS)—Dow Jones; Gannett Co.; Knight Ridder Newspapers; Times Mirror.

RADIO-TV BROADCASTERS—American; CBS Inc.; Capital Cities Comm.; Cox Broadcasting; Metromedia; Taft.

RAILROAD EQUIPMENT—ACF Ind.; Amsted Indus.; Gen. Sig.

RESTAURANTS—Church's Fried Chicken; Denny's Inc.; Marriott; McDonald's Corp.; Wendys Intl.

RETAIL STORES (DEPT. STORES)—Allied Stores; Associated; Carter Hawley Hale Stores; Dayton Hudson; Federated; Macy; May Dept.; Merchantile Stores.

‡RETAIL STORES (DISCOUNT STORES)—KDT Ind.; Vornado; Zayre.

‡RETAIL STORES (DRUG)—Eckerd (Jack); Revco D.S., Inc.; Rite Aid; Walgreen Co.

RETAIL STORES (FOOD CHAINS)—Amer. Stores Co.; Great A. & P.; Jewel Companies; Kroger; Lucky Stores; Safeway; Winn-Dixie.

RETAIL STORES (GEN. MDSE. CHAINS)—K Mart. Penny (J.C.); Sears; Wal-Mart Stores; Woolworth.

SHOES—Brown Group; Genesco; Interco; Melville Corp.

SOAPS—Clorox; Colgate-Palmolive; Procter & Gamble; Unilever N.V.

STEEL—Armco; Beth.; Inland; Interlake; National; Republic; U.S. Steel; Wheeling-Pittsburgh.

SUGAR REFINERS—Amalgamated Sugar; Amstar Corp; Holly.

TEXTILES (APPAREL MFRS.)—Blue Bell; Cluett, Peabody; Hart Schaffner & Marx; Jonathan Logan; Levi Strauss; V.F. Corp.

TEXTILE PRODUCTS—Burlington Indus.; Collins & Aikman; Cone Mills, Lowenstein; Reeves; Springs Ind.; Stevens; West Point-Pepperell.

TIRES & RUBBER GOODS—Firestone; Goodrich; Goodyear; Uniroyal.

TOBACCO—Amer. Brands Inc.; Philip Morris; Reynolds Indus.

TOYS—COLECO Inc.; Mattel Inc.; Milton Bradley; Tonka Corp.

40 PUBLIC UTILITIES

ELECTRIC POWER—Amer. El. Pwr., Balt. G. & E.; Cent. & So. West. Corp.; Comm. Ed.; Con. Ed.; Detroit Ed.; Duke Power; Fla Power & Light; Middle So. Util.; New Eng. Elec. Sys.; Niagara Mohawk; No. States Pwr.; Ohio Ed.; Pac. G. & E.; Phila Elec.; Pub. Serv. E. & G.; Public Service of Indiana; So. Calif. Ed.; Southern Co.; Texas Utils.; Va. E. & P.; Wisc. El. Pwr.

NATURAL GAS DISTRIBUTORS—Bklyn. Union; Columbia; Consolidated Natural; ENSERCH Corp.; Oneok Inc.; Pac. Light; Peoples Energy.

NATURAL GAS PIPE LINES—American Natural Resources; El Paso Co.; Inter North Inc.; Panhandle Eastern; Sonat Inc.; Texas East. Corp.; Texas Gas Trans.

TELEPHONE—*AT & T; Central Tel. & Util.; Contl. Tel.; General Tel. & El.; United Telecommunications.

20 TRANSPORTATION

AIR FREIGHT—Emery Air Freight; Federal Express; Tiger International.

AIR TRANSPORT—AMR Corp.; Delta; Northwest; Pan Am; UAL, Inc.

RAILROADS—Burlington Northern Inc.; CSX Corp.; Norfolk Southern Corp.; Santa Fe Industries; So. Pac.; Union Pac. Corp.

TRUCKERS—Consol. Freightways; Overnight Transportation; Roadway Express; Yellow Freight Sys.

TRANSPORTATION (MISC.)—Leaseway Transportation; Ryder System.

40 FINANCIAL

BANKS (NEW YORK CITY)—Bankers Trust New York; Chase Manhattan; Chemical; Citicorp; Manufacturers Hanover; Morgan (J.P.) & Co.

BANKS (OUTSIDE NEW YORK CITY)— Bank America; Cont'l Ill. Corp.; First Chic. Corp.; First Intl. Bancshares; First Interstate Bancorp.; First Natl. Bost.; First Penn.; Mellon Natl.; NCNB Corp.; Northwest Bancorp.

LIFE INSURANCE—Capital Holding; Jefferson Pilot; Lincoln National Corp.; US Life.

MULTI-LINE INSURANCE—Aetna Life & Cas.; American Int'l Group; American General; Cigma; CNA Financial; Travelers.

PROPERTY-CASUALTY INSURANCE— Chubb Corp.; Continental Corp.; St. Paul; Safeco Corp.; USF & G Corp.

SAVINGS & LOAN HOLDING COS.— Ahmanson (H.F.); First Charter; Great Western.

PERSONAL LOANS—Beneficial; Household Int'l Inc.

FINANCIAL-MISC.—American Express; Heller (Walter E.); Merrill Lynch; Transamerica Corp.

**BROKERAGE FIRMS—Donaldson Lufkin Jenrette; Edwards (A.G.); Hutton (E.F.) Group; Paine Webber, Inc.

**INVESTMENT COMPANIES—Adams; Gen. Amer.; Lehman; Madison; Tri-Cont.

**INVESTMENT COS. (Bond Funds)— American General Bond; Intercapital Inc. Sec.; John Hancock Inc. Sec.; Mass Mutual Inc. Inv.; Montgomery Str. Inc. Sec.

**REAL ESTATE INVEST.—Equitable Life; First Union Real Estate; Mass-Mutual Mtge & Realty; Mony Mtg.; Wells Fargo Mortge. & Equity.

*Not included in Utility composite.

**Not included in Financial composite.

SOURCE: Standard & Poor's *Stock Market Encyclopedia of the S & P "500"* (New York: Standard & Poor's Corporation, 1983).

CHAPTER 21

MODERN PORTFOLIO THEORY— WITH IMPLICATIONS FOR PRACTICE

The fundamental approach to investment tells us that investors will analyze individual securities and, based on in-depth knowledge, select those which will meet their investment objectives. The details of this analysis were covered in Chapters 10 through 19. Fundamental analysis covered the analysis of the national economy, the analysis and selection of industries, the company analysis, and finally the selection and valuation appraisal of the company. A final decision was then made based on company analysis and estimates of expected return and risk. The assumption was made that each investor would make a thorough analysis of all industries and select those that appeared to offer the best opportunities. Then the companies in each industry that appeared to be the competitive leaders would be selected. Finally, the companies that seemed to offer the highest return with the lowest risk would be identified. Investors would choose from the companies that met their investment objectives. Essentially the combination of stocks is based on intuitive judgment and the notion that it is a good idea to diversify, since investors really do not know what will happen in the future. The assumption is made that risk will be reduced by owning more rather than fewer securities. But the fundamental diversification process might lead to a portfolio of from 7 to 50 stocks. And it might lead to equal amounts being invested in each stock (naive diversification) or varying amounts based on the investor's preception of return and risk.

Analysts go through the following process, which is simplified for illustrative purposes. Analysts select three industries with four companies each for investment consideration. This provides an array:

Industry A	Company 1, 5, 7, 9
Industry L	Company 3, 12, 19, 21
Industry O	Company 2, 7, 9, 10

The analyst then intuitively says, "I will invest 40 percent of my money in industry A, 35 percent in L, and 25 percent in O. Then the investor must decide how much to invest in each company. This decision is based on the informed judgment of the analyst-portfolio manager, relying on the fundamental analysis described in the previous chapters. The final amount invested in each security is thus a function of the analyst's judgment about the future.

Technical analysis makes the assumption that securities will be selected based on the technical strength of a particular company. Technical analysis seems to be silent about diversification. The assumption is made that the securities selected will result from the analytical process and that they will be few in number. There is a notion in technical analysis that the investor-speculator should concentrate on fewer stocks, trade more frequently, and follow market conditions more closely than the fundamental investor.

Modern portfolio theory, on the other hand, provides a solution to the diversification of risky securities in the portfolio. In its simplest terms, modern portfolio theory provides a method of diversification that allows an investor to minimize the risk of the portfolio. It also allows an investor to select the most efficient set of portfolios with the lowest risk. In this chapter, the development of MPT will be presented, along with its implications for the practice of portfolio management.

MODERN PORTFOLIO THEORY

Assumptions

The assumptions underlying modern portfolio theory are several. The first is that the marketplace is efficient. That is, everything is known or knowable about each stock. Fundamental analysis assumes that the market is inefficient and that superior returns can be obtained by finding undervalued securities through analysis.

The second assumption is that investors are risk-averse, that is, they do not like risk. Risk is measured by the variability of the rate of return, which reflects the possible loss of income or principal.

The third assumption is that investors prefer a higher rate of return to a lower rate of return. A related assumption is that the marginal utility of the return declines as more and more return is earned.

The fourth assumption is that all decisions will be made on the basis of the expected rate of return and the expected standard deviation of the rate of return. The annual expected rate of return is measured by the purchase price divided into the income per year plus the annual capital gain. Theory states that a rate of return and standard deviation of the rate of return must be known.

Fifth, the way in which securities returns are correlated to each other must be known. This was of critical importance to the portfolio theory developed by Markowitz.[1] By knowing the coefficient of correlation of one stock to the other, it would be possible to determine the combination of assets that would produce the lowest risk.

Sixth, the rate of return and risk are calculated for a single time period.

Seventh, the investment units are perfectly divisible; a risky security can be added or subtracted from a portfolio in any dollar amount.

Eighth, investors attempt to maximize returns and minimize risk from a portfolio. Investors will try to obtain the highest return per unit of risk. They will attempt to maximize return for a given level of risk and will attempt to minimize risk for a given level of return.

Ninth, it is assumed that the higher the return, the higher the risk, and the lower return, the lower the risk.

Tenth, it is further assumed that to reduce risk, an investor must add some amount of another security to the portfolio. This also reduces the return. The risk and return are increased as the number of securities is reduced.

Eleventh, the investor's task is to determine the efficient set of securities that will provide the portfolios that meet the above assumptions—portfolios that have the highest return for each level of risk.

Markowitz Diversification and Portfolio Theory

Markowitz[2] indicated that three variables were necessary to determine the efficient set of portfolios from among several stocks: return, the standard deviation of return, and the coefficient of correlation of each security to every other security. With these data and a computer, the expected return and the expected risk of the portfolio could be determined, and from this the efficient set of portfolios could be established. The model Markowitz used was a full covariance model.[3] The model generated the efficient portfolio set between the limits of zero and infinity of the return to risk tradeoff for investors (see Figure 21–1).

The standard deviation of the portfolio is the square root of the variance formula. The variance equation includes variance and covariance. The equation for a two-security portfolio is written:

$$\sigma_p = \sqrt{W_i^2\sigma_i^2 + W_j^2\sigma_j^2 + 2W_iW_j\rho_{ij}\sigma_i\sigma_j}$$

The σ_p^2 is equal to variance V of the portfolio. The part of the equation representing covariance is

$$2W_iW_j\rho_{ij}\sigma_j$$

where W_i and W_j are the weights of securities i and j. ρ_{ij} is the coefficient of correlation of security i to security j, and $\sigma_i\sigma_j$ is the standard deviation of security i times the standard deviation of security j. The first part of the equation represents the

[1]Harry M. Markowitz, "Portfolio Selection," *The Journal of Finance*, March 1952, p. 89.
[2]Ibid.
[3]Ibid.

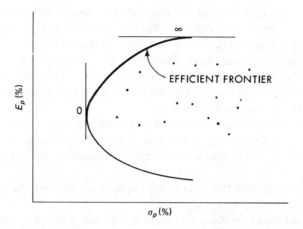

FIGURE 21–1

Efficient Portfolios between 0 and ∞

variance measured by the weight squared (W_i^2) of the security i times the standard deviation (σ_i^2) of security i plus the weight squared of security j (W_j^2) times the standard deviation squared (σ_j^2).

The basic purpose of the quadratic program is to find the combination of securities where the σ_p of the portfolio is a minimum. In a two-security portfolio the program develops that combination of two securities where σ_p is a minimum. In a general sense the basic purpose of the quadratic program is to develop all combinations of portfolios that have the lowest risk for each level of expected return between the limits of 0 and ∞, as seen in Figure 21–1. The slope of the efficient frontier of securities in Figure 21–1 marked 0 means that the slope of the line at that point is 0. This is the point of lowest risk. The slope of the efficient frontier at ∞ is so labeled because the slope at that point is infinite. The slope is represented by the symbol λ. For every λ there is a specific return (E_p) and risk σ_p. The purpose of the quadratic program is to find those values for every point or λ on the efficient frontier. The value established at each point is referred to as the objective function, ϕ.

The objective function is found by finding the minimum σ_p for every level of E_p. The equation is written $\phi = \lambda E_p - \sigma_p$, where ϕ the function is to be maximized at every point (λ) in the efficient frontier for each E_p where σ_p is minimized. The quadratic program makes these calculations. The principles at work can be demonstrated by the process where two securities are to be combined into an efficient combination of portfolios. Such a case is described below.

PORTFOLIO THEORY APPLIED TO A TWO-SECURITY PORTFOLIO

Five securities are listed to provide insight into the problems associated with portfolio theory. The securities have the following expected return, standard deviation, and return-to-risk ratio:

MODERN PORTFOLIO THEORY AND INVESTMENT PRACTICE

	Expected Return (%)	Standard Deviation (%)	Return to- Risk Ratio	Risk- free Return (%)
Anaconda (A)	10.0	1,110.0	—	
Bethlehem Steel (BS)	12.0	38.0	.2	
Commonwealth Edison (CWE)	14.0	9.0	1.0	5
Eastman Kodak (EK)	12.0	7.0	1.0	
United States Steel (X)	8.0	12.0	.2	

Then, asked to select from among the five the one security that is best, and applying the theory that the stock offering the highest expected return with the lowest expected standard deviation should be selected, the investor would choose Commonwealth Edison. It offers the highest return with the lowest risk, and it offers the highest reward-to-risk ratio. The reward-to-risk ratio is calculated by subtracting the risk-free return from the expected total return and dividing by the standard deviation. In this example the risk-free return used was 5 percent. But how does the investor decide on the second stock and in what combination with the first?

The second stock that would be considered acceptable would be EK, for it has the lowest risk and the second-highest return, 12 percent. Clearly, BS is unacceptable since its risk is very high, with a standard deviation of 38 percent. Anaconda (A) is too risky as well as less profitable than BS, CWE, and EK. U.S. Steel (X) is less profitable than any other security and has a relatively high risk.

These two securities have been selected without respect to how the returns of all stocks were correlated. For the moment, the correlation of returns will be ignored. Graphically, the relationships appear as in Figure 21–2. Two stocks, EK and CWE, are clearly suitable for investment, along with risk-free securities, r_f. It is observed

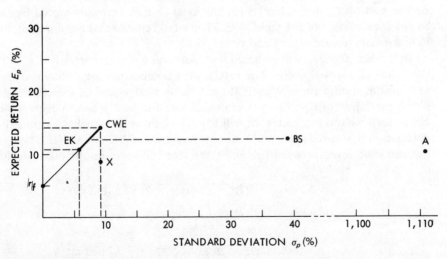

FIGURE 21–2

Two Security Efficient Frontiers

that BS and A are clearly unsuitable, since they have substantially more risk than CWE and a lower expected return. Stock X is also unattractive, since it offers an expected return lower than CWE but with the same amount of risk. As will be seen subsequently, stocks EK and CWE are said to be "efficient" and the reward is proportional to risk. Therefore, the investor might choose between securities EK and CWE or a combination of the two securities, represented by the line EK-CWE.

A two-security portfolio invested 50-50 in EK and CWE will have an average return of 13 percent. This was found using the basic equation $r_p = w_i r_i + w_j r_j$, where r_p equals the expected return of the portfolio, w_i is the weight of security i, r_i is the expected return of security i, w_j is the weight of security j in the portfolio, and r_j is the expected return of security j. In this case, w_i is .5 EK and w_j is .5 CWE. Therefore, the equation is $r_p = .5r_{EK} + .5r_{CWE} = .5(12.0) + .5(14.0) = 13.0$ percent.[4]

The standard deviation of the portfolio return is calculated by the equation:

$$\sigma_p = \sqrt{w_i^2 \sigma_i^2 + w_j^2 \sigma_j^2 + 2w_i w_j \rho_{ij} \sigma_i \sigma_j}$$

where σ_p is the standard deviation of the portfolio; w_i and w_j are the weights of stocks i and j; σ_i and σ_j represent the standard deviation of the expected returns; ρ_{ij} is the coefficient of correlation of the return of security i to that of security j; and $\sigma_i \sigma_j$ is the covariance of security i to j. Since security i is EK and security j is CWE, the equation is written as follows:

$$\sigma_p = \sqrt{(.5)^2(7)^2 + (.5)^2(9)^2 + 2(.5)(.5)(1)(7)(9)}$$
$$= \sqrt{.25(49) + (.25)(81) + 31.50}$$
$$= \sqrt{12.25 + 20.25 + 31.50}$$
$$= \sqrt{64.00} = 8.0$$

Thus, the expected return of the portfolio is 13.0 percent and the standard deviation 8.0 percent. The portfolio has a return-to-risk characteristic of approximately 1.00 ($[13.0 - 5.0]/8.0$), which is the same as the return-to-risk ratio of the stocks that make up the portfolio. Since return is proportional to risk, investors would be indifferent to any combination of EK and CWE. They would choose that combination that meets their attitude toward return and risk.

In the case above, it was assumed that there was a perfect correlation of 1.0 between the yields of EK and CWE. The results of diversification are different if the returns are correlated differently. We still do not know what would happen to the portfolios if the coefficient of correlation were calculated for each stock to every other stock, but at least we can find out what will happen to these two stocks. Assume there is no correlation (the correlation is 0) between the return of EK and CWE. Then, if a 50-50 balance is achieved between EK and CWE, the following results occur in calculating σ_p:

$$\sigma_p = \sqrt{(.5)^2(7)^2 + (.5)^2(9)^2 + 2(.5)(.5)(0)(7)(9)}$$
$$= \sqrt{(.5)^2(7)^2 + (.5)^2(9)^2} \qquad \uparrow$$
$$= \sqrt{.25(49) + .25(81)}$$
$$= \sqrt{12.25 + 20.25} = \sqrt{32.50} = 5.7 \text{ percent}$$

[4]The basic analysis is found in Jack Clark Francis and Stephen H. Archer, *Portfolio Analysis* (Englewood Cliffs, N.J.: Prentice-Hall, 1971).

Note that the only change in the equation noted above (↑) is the change in the correlation coefficient from 1 to 0.

Therefore, with 50 percent of EK and CWE and a zero correlation of return, the σ_p declines from 8.0 to 5.7 percent. This results in a reward-to-risk ratio of 1.40. Since the expected return remains the same but risk is reduced, the portfolio with zero correlation between the securities offers the lowest risk and would be preferable to the portfolio with a correlation of 1.0, which is perfectly positive.

Assume now that the returns of securities EK and CWE are perfectly negatively correlated, -1. The σ_p equation is written:

$$\sigma_p = \sqrt{(.5)^2(7)^2 + (.5)^2(9)^2 + 2(.5)(.5)(-1)(7)(9)}$$
$$= \sqrt{(.25))9 + .25(81) + 2[.25(-1)(63)]}$$
$$= \sqrt{(.25)(49) + .25(81) - 2(.25)63}$$
$$= \sqrt{12.25 + 20.25 - 31.5}$$
$$= \sqrt{1.0}$$
$$= 1.0$$

Therefore, the σ_p is 1.0 percent when there is a negative correlation between the returns of securities EK and CWE. The return-to-risk ratio increases to 8.00, which makes it the most attractive among the three alternatives.

The pattern of the returns and risks discussed above is depicted in Figure 21–3. This shows the efficient portfolio set for the two securities based on three different assumptions of the correlation of returns. If the returns of the two securities are negatively correlated, the efficient portfolio offers one set of alternatives for the investor.

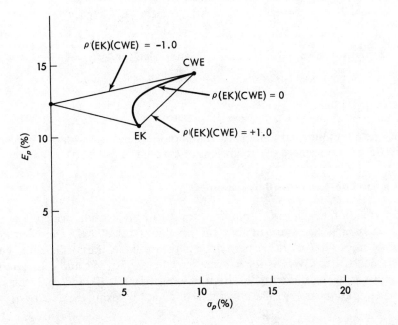

FIGURE 21–3

It is how the returns are correlated that determines the various combinations of securities where the risk or standard deviation for each expected return is a minimum.

The investor faced with this combination of alternatives would choose one from the set that offered the highest return at each level of risk. The investor would benefit from diversification more if the returns were negatively correlated, or if there were a small degree of correlation among the securities in the portfolio. In the case above, the investor would be better off with two securities that were negatively correlated.

But we have not arrived at the point where the standard deviation of the portfolio is the lowest under the assumption of negative correlation. If the two stocks EK and CWE were negatively correlated, we know from Figure 21–3 that there was a point where risk is a minimum, in this case zero as indicated in the line CWE, 0, EK. We could determine this point by trial and error, but there is an easier way to find the point where risk or σ_p is a minimum. This can be accomplished by using the standard calculus optimization techniques for determining the minimum variance weights. The variance of the portfolio of EK and CWE is given by the following equation:

$$V = (\rho_{EK+CWA})^2 = w_{EK}^2 \sigma_{EK}^2 + w_{CWE}^2 \sigma_{CWE}^2 + 2w_{EK}w_{CWE}\sigma_{EK,CWE}$$

$$\text{where } \sigma_{EK,CWE} = \rho_{EK,CWE}\sigma_{EK}\sigma_{CWE}$$

$$= w_{EK}^2 49 + w_{CWE}^2 81 + 2w_{EK}w_{CWE}(-1)(7)(9)$$

$$= w_{EK}^2 49 + w_{CWE}^2 81 + 2w_{EK}w_{CWE}(-63)$$

$$= 49w_{EK}^2 + 81w_{CWE}^2 - 126w_{EK}w_{CWE}$$

$$= 49w_{EK}^2 + 81(1 - w_{EK})^2 - 126w_{EK}(1 - w_{EK})$$

$$(\text{since } w_{CWE} = 1 - w_{EK})$$

$$= 49w_{EK}^2 + 81(1 - 2w_{EK} + w_{EK}^2) - 126w_{EK} + 126w_{EK}^2$$

$$= 49w_{EK}^2 + 81 - 162w_{EK} + 81w_{EK}^2 - 126w_{EK} + 126w_{EK}^2$$

$$= 256w_{EK}^2 - 288w_{EK} + 81$$

To minimize the variance, set $dV/dw_{EK} = 0$, and solve for w_{EK}:

$$dV/dw_{EK} = 512w_{EK} - 288 = 0$$

$$512w_{EK} = 288$$

$$w_{EK} = 56.25 \text{ percent}$$

Therefore, the minimum variance is at that point where $w_{EK} = 56.25$ percent and $w_{CWE} = 43.75$ percent, where the coefficient of correlation is -1.

Calculating the Coefficient of Correlation

Since the correlation coefficient is important to the diversification principle of investment, a discussion is necessary of how the ρ value is calculated. The coefficient of correlation of stock i to j or, as has been done in the example, the coefficient of correlation (ρ) of stock EK to CWE, is $\rho_{ij} = \sigma_{ij}/\sigma_i \sigma_j$, where σ_i is the standard deviation of security i (EK), σ_j is the standard deviation of security j (CWE), and σ_{ij} is the covariance of security i to security j. The covariance is found by using the equation:

$$\sigma_{ij} = \sum_{t=1}^{n} P_t\{[r_{it} - E(r_i)][r_{jt} - E(r_j)]\}$$

where P_t is the probability of occurrence of a return. If ten years of price data are used, as were used in the valuation model in Chapter 18, then nine annual rates of return are calculated. If each has an equal probability of occurrence, then the probability is .11 for the nine annual rates of return.

The term r_{it} is the return of the *it* security in each year.

$E(r_i)$ is the mean average rate of return. It is the average for the nine-year period. Since the past is expected to persist in the future, it is also the expected rate of return and is labeled $E(r)$.

The term r_{jt} is the rate of return for the *jt* security in each year, and $E(r_j)$ is the expected return of security j, which is the nine-year average rate of return.

The equation can be written:

$$\sigma_{ij} = \sum_{t=1}^{9} \frac{1}{9} [r_{EK} - E(r_{EK})][r_{CWE} - E(r_{CWE})]$$

The calculation of the covariance is as follows:

	CWE		EK		Prob-abilities	Products
	r_{it}	$[r_{it} - E(r)]$	r_{jt}	$[r_{jt} - E(r)]$	$P_t = 1/m$	$(P_t) [r - E(r_i)]$ $[r - E(r_j)]$
1966						
1967	.088	.082	.134	.062	.11	.00056
1968	(.019)	(.025)	1.38	.066	.11	(.00018)
1969	(.031)	(.037)	.000	(.072)	.11	.00029
1970	(.152)	(.158)	(.047)	(.119)	.11	.00207
1971	.206	.200	.228	.156	.11	.00343
1972	(.024)	(.030)	.429	.357	.11	(.00118)
1973	(.053)	(.059)	.065	(.007)	.11	.00004
1974	(.150)	(.156)	(.298)	(.370)	.11	.00635
1975	.191	(.185)	.011	(.061)	.11	(.00124)
Mean	.006		.072		1.00	$\sigma_{ij}\Sigma_{EK \cdot CWE}$ =.0101
Stan. Dev.	.123		.189			
$E(r_{CWE})$ = .006				$E(r_{EK})$ = .072		

The coefficient of correlation (ρ) may now be calculated:

$$\rho_{EK \cdot CWE} = \frac{\sigma_{EK \cdot CWE}}{\sigma_{EK}\sigma_{CWE}} = .0101 \div (.123)(.189) = .0101 \div .02325$$

$$= .43$$

There is approximately a 43 percent correlation—comparatively little—between EK and CWE.

Based on the knowledge that the coefficient of correlation between the two securities is .43, what then is the weight or amount of each security that will provide the investor with a minimum amount of risk? The only item that must be changed is the correlation coefficient, from -1 to .43, in the equation used to determine the minimum variance weights. The equation is changed to:

$$V = W_{EK}^2 49 + W_{CWE}^2 81 + 2W_{EK}W_{CWE}(.43)(7)(9)$$

$$= W_{EK}^2 49 + W_{CWE}^2 81 + 2W_{EK}W_{CWE}(30)*$$

$$= 49W_{EK}^2 + 81W_{CWE}^2 + 60W_{EK}W_{CWE}$$

$$= 49W_{EK}^2 + 81(1 - W_{EK})^2 + 60W_{EK}(1 - W_{EK}) \text{ [since } W_{CWE}^2 = 1 - W_{EK}]$$

$$= 49W_{EK}^2 + (81 - 162W_{EK} + 81W_{EK}^2) + (60W_{EK} - 60W_{EK}^2)$$

$$= 70W_{EK}^2 - 102W_{EK} + 81$$

To minimize the variance, we set $dV/d_{W_{EK}} = 0$, and solve for W_{EK}:

$$dV/d_{W_{EK}} = 140W_{EK} - 102 = 0$$

$$140W_{EK} = 102$$

$$W_{EK} = \frac{102}{140} = 72.8 = 73 \text{ percent}$$

Therefore the optimum combination for minimum risk between the two stocks is 73 percent of W_{EK} and 27 percent of W_{CWE}. This will give the combination of the two stocks that have the lowest risk. This can be done for the two securities as follows:

$$\sigma_p = \sqrt{(.73)^2(7)^2 + (.27)^2(9)^2 + 2(.73)(.27)(.43)(7)(9)}$$

$$= \sqrt{(.53)(49) + (.07)(81) + (.39)(.43)(7)(9)}$$

$$= \sqrt{26 + 6 + (.39)(.43)63}$$

$$= \sqrt{26 + 6 + 11\dagger}$$

$$= \sqrt{43}$$

$$= 6.5$$

With the 73 percent invested in EK, which earns a 12 percent return, and 27 percent in CWE, which earns a 14 percent return, the return of the portfolio at minimum risk is $(.73)(12) + .27(14) = 8.76 + 3.78 = 12.54$ percent. Thus in the diversification process, by combining the two securities to the point of minimum risk, the risk is reduced from 9 percent to 6.5 percent. This represents approximately a 27 percent reduction in risk. Return is reduced from 14 percent to 12.54 percent, which is approximately an 11 percent reduction in return. If the investor is willing to accept the lower return, this type of diversification seems to make sense.

Figure 21–4 charts the investment options available to the investor. The investor will invest in CWE or some combination of EK and CSW between the point CWE-EK and CWE. The investor would not invest between CWE-EK and EK, since return would be reduced and risk increased. Actually the investor has another option, which is investing in risk-free assets that provide a return of 10 percent and a risk of zero. Therefore the investor will invest some place on the line from r_f to the point where it

*Actually 29.62 rounded to 30.
†Rounds

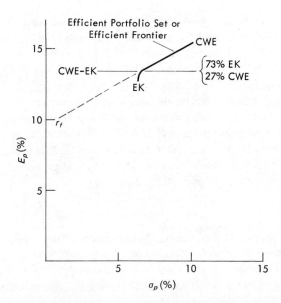

FIGURE 21–4

Efficient Portfolio Set for EK and CWE with an r of .43

meets the efficient frontier of the combination of CWE and CWE-EK at minimum risk and maximum risk. The investor will combine assets at r_f with assets on the efficient frontier line at tangency that meets the investor's attitude toward reward and risk. The heavy line in Figure 21–4 between CWE-EK and CWE is the efficient frontier or efficient portfolio set.

It becomes apparent that when more than two securities are to be put together to form efficient portfolios, the process becomes quite complicated if the investor must calculate the expected returns and standard deviation for each stock and for each portfolio, and also estimate how the return on each security correlates to the return on every other security. It takes a substantial amount of time to calculate an optimum combination of stocks in a portfolio of only two stocks; think how long it would take to solve the statistical problem for 30 securities. This type of exercise has been done on an IBM 370 computer, and it took 14 minutes. It would take a mathematician a lifetime to make the same calculations.

The principles expressed in the discussion and plotted in Figures 21–3 and 21–4 represent an example of the effects of Markowitz's diversification[5] and the work done by William Sharpe.[6]

This discussion so far suggests three principles to guide investors: First, securities must be included in the portfolio that are efficient—that is, possessing the highest expected return with the lowest expected risk. Second, in order to reduce risk, the investor should select securities not merely with the highest return but with returns that

[5]H. Markowitz, "Portfolio Selection," *The Journal of Finance*, March 1952, p. 89.

[6]William Sharpe, "Capital Asset Prices: A Theory of Market Equilibrium under Conditions of Risk," *The Journal of Finance*, September 1964.

are negatively correlated or that have a low positive correlation rather than a high positive correlation of 1.0. This will result in achieving the highest possible return with the lowest possible risk. Third, after the securities are chosen, the portfolio that offers the highest return and lowest risk can be obtained by shifting the weights of the stocks in the portfolio. As a principle, it is important to have not only the correct (efficient) stocks in the portfolio, but also the correct amount of each stock; the correct weights are determined by the way in which the stocks work together to establish the return and risk of the portfolio. The standard deviation and coefficient of correlation will determine the combination with minimum standard deviations. The basic emphasis in portfolio management is to make certain that risk is as low as possible for every possible return for one security or a portfolio of securities.

The Efficient Frontier

The Markowitz Full Covariance Model,[7] which has been described in the two-security portfolio, states that the purpose of portfolio management is to minimize variance for every possible level of E, the expected return. This may be stated $\phi = \lambda E - V$, where V is the variance of return, λE is every combination of return from the securities, and ϕ is the objective function that is to be maximized.

In the general case where there are a large number of securities, E, the expected return of the portfolio, may be written as E_p and V as V_p. The expected returns of the portfolio are found by using the equation $E_p = \Sigma_i X_i E_i$, where X_i represents the weight or amount of the ith security or all combination of securities in the portfolio, and E_i represents the expected return from the ith security or all securities in the portfolio.

The variance of the portfolio is found by using the equation $V_p = \Sigma_i \Sigma_j X_i X_j C_{ij}$ where $X_i X_j$ represents the efficient combination of all securities in the portfolio, designed to provide a minimum variance for every E and C_{ij} represents the covariance of each stock total return to each other stock total return.[8] The efficient set of portfolios obtained by this process is represented by Figure 21–5. Notice that the standard deviation, which is the square root of variance, is used.

The concept of the efficient frontier[9] in the general case is basic to the understanding of portfolio theory. Assume that in the marketplace, there are a fixed number of common stocks in which we can invest. Each of the securities has its own expected return and standard deviation. Many securities with the same expected return have different standard deviations; others have the same standard deviation but vary in expected return. The investor will select the security that offers the highest return

[7]Markowitz, "Portfolio Selection."

[8]See William F. Sharpe, "A Simplified Model for Portfolio Analysis," *Management Science*, January 1963, pp. 277–93. The article may also be found in Edwin J. Elton and Martin J. Gruber, *Security Evaluation and Portfolio Analysis* (Englewood Cliffs, N.J.: Prentice-Hall, 1972), pp. 448–63.

[9]See Harry M. Markowitz, "Portfolio Selection"; "The Optimization of a Quadratic Function Subject to Linear Constraints," *Naval Research Logistics Quarterly*, March and June 1956, pp. 111–33; and *Portfolio Selection: Efficient Diversification of Investments* (New York: Wiley, 1959). Sharpe, "A Simplified Model for Portfolio Analysis"; and *Portfolio Theory and Capital Markets* (New York: McGraw-Hill, 1970). William J. Baumol, "An Expected Gain—Confidence Limit Criterion for Portfolio Selection," *Management Science*, October 1963, pp. 174–82. John Lintner, "Security Prices, Risk, and Maximal Gains from Diversification," *The Journal of Finance*, December 1965, pp. 587–615.

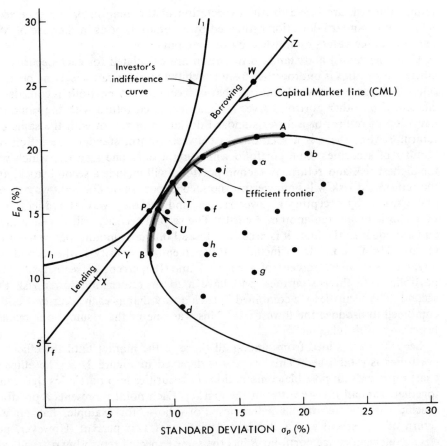

FIGURE 21–5

Ingredients of Portfolio Theory—Efficient Frontier, Market Line, and Indifference Curve without Short Sale Contraints

and lowest standard deviation. Thus, if the return is 8 ± 3 percent, it means that the average return is 8 percent, but two-thirds of the time it ranges from 5 to 11 percent. The ±3 represents a standard deviation around the mean of 3 percent. If three securities were each expected to return 50 percent, the one selected would have the lowest variability as measured by the standard deviation. If one stock had a standard deviation of 75 percent, another 70 percent, and a third 50 percent, the one with 50 percent would be chosen. The return range is stated then as 50 percent ±50 percent, or a return of 50 percent and a standard deviation of 50 percent, in absolute terms.

It is assumed that investors try to minimize risk by minimizing the deviations from the expected return, and this is done by means of portfolio diversification. The investor would rather have a portfolio furnishing 10 percent return with a 2 percent standard deviation than one that provided a 10 percent return with a 4 percent standard deviation; and would prefer a 12 ± 3 percent portfolio to a 15 ± 7 percent portfolio. In short, investors enjoy stability of return, and the higher the better.

All securities, then, are ranked on the basis of risk and return characteristics. The return and risk are based on the expectation of the analyst, or the expected future return and standard deviation estimated by an analyst, or as in the case of Modesystem, by source values established by the computer.

Once the return and standard deviation are calculated for each security, a set of efficient portfolios is put together from which the investor can select one portfolio that offers the degree of reward and risk that is acceptable. A portfolio is considered to be efficient if no other portfolio gives a higher expected return with the same standard deviation of return, or a lower standard deviation of return with the same expected return.[10] Also, there is a relationship between return, standard deviation, and the number of securities. One portfolio will contain only one security, which will offer the highest risk and return. A second portfolio will include a second stock, and both the return and risk will be lower on the second portfolio. The only way to obtain a lower risk is by accepting a lower return, and the only way of reducing risk in a portfolio is by adding another security. The second security will not be added in an amount equal to the first; it is necessary to add only an amount that reduces risk and reward. The first portfolio includes 100 percent of security 1; the second portfolio might consist of 90 percent of security 1 and 10 percent of security 2. The third portfolio, with three securities, will have a lower return and lower risk than the second. The securities are combined in such a way that as each security is added, it is combined to produce the lowest risk. This was one of the assumptions made in the beginning of the chapter.

Securities are added from among all those in the market until the efficient set of portfolios is established. This process is depicted in Figure 21.5. The ellipse in the chart represents all possible combinations of securities into portfolios that can be put together from all the securities in the market. Each point represents a portfolio with specific risk and return characteristics. Portfolio e, for example, has an expected return of 11 percent and a standard deviation of 12.5 percent. However, portfolio e is not efficient, since portfolio B has the same expected return but a standard deviation of only 8 percent. Portfolio h has a higher return and the same risk as portfolio e. It is more attractive than portfolio e but not efficient, since portfolio f has a still higher return with the same degree of risk as e and h.

Portfolio A is a single-stock portfolio that has the highest return and risk; in no way can you improve on its return-to-risk ratio. If you move to the right on the curve, return decreases and risk increases; if you move to the left on the curve, return decreases and risk decreases. You are therefore on the efficient frontier, which is shown by the shaded area of the parabola. It represents all possible portfolios that are "efficient" as you move to the left and down.

In the calculation of portfolio return and risk, the coefficient of correlation (ρ) of one stock to another is calculated along with the variance of one stock to another. The efficient frontier in Figure 21–5 represents all possible combinations of portfolios A, T, and B. The other dots on the efficient frontier represent other portfolios with "efficient" return-to-risk characteristics.

[10]Sharpe, "A Simplified Model," p. 278.

Certain assumptions are made in the calculation of the efficient set of portfolios from any number of securities. From among all the securities, there will be one that has the highest return and the lowest risk. This means, of course, that the one stock from among, say, 30 stocks, will become a single-stock portfolio. There will be no other security or portfolio that will offer a higher return with a lower risk.

In order to reduce risk and obtain the second efficient portfolio on the efficient frontier, another security must be added. The stock selected will be chosen from among the other 29 stocks. The second stock added to the first portfolio will be combined in such a way, based upon weights, that it reduces the return and the risk of the portfolio. Once the new return (or E_p) is found, all combinations of the two securities will be calculated until the minimum standard deviation is obtained. Before this is determined, however, the return and standard deviation and covariance must be calculated for every security, because not only do the expected return and standard deviation vary, but so does the coefficient of correlation of one security to every other security. This process continues until all the returns and variances of the stocks in the portfolio have been calculated and the efficient frontier of portfolios has been established.[11]

Therefore, the only way the investor can obtain a higher return on the efficient frontier is to accept a higher amount of risk. The only way the investor can reduce risk is by adding another security to the portfolio, thereby diversifying and accepting a lower return.

WHERE TO INVEST ON THE EFFICIENT FRONTIER.   Which of the portfolios should the investor choose? Should portfolio A be chosen, with an expected return of 22 percent and a risk of 18 percent (and a reward-to-risk ratio of .94)? Or should it be portfolio T, with 17.5 ± 11 percent (reward to risk equals $[17.5 - 5] \div 11 = 12.5 \div 11 = 1.14$), or portfolio B, with 12 ± 8 percent and a reward-to-risk ratio of .88? The risk-free return of 5 percent is for illustrative purposes only. The rate varies in practice with the yields on Treasury bills.

Actually, the investor would invest somewhere on the line $r_f TZ$, which represents all possible combinations of portfolio T and risk-free securities. This is similar to the portfolio combination in the two-security cases, but now there are many more portfolios. By combining the securities in portfolio T with risk-free securities at r_f, the investor would actually reduce risk more than the reduction in return. The reduction of risk makes the combination of securities of T and r_f more attractive at point P than an all-common-stock portfolio at U. The portfolio at P on the market line, consisting of 70 percent of portfolio T and 30 percent of risk-free securities, r_f, has the same return as but lower risk than portfolio U and therefore would be more acceptable to the investor, or more efficient.

That part of the capital-market line from r_f to T is called a *lending portfolio*, in that the investor is willing to buy riskless securities or lend a portion of the total portfolio at the risk-free yield. The investor can invest all funds in portfolio T, all

---

[11] Markowitz, "Portfolio Selection."

funds in portfolio r_f, or some combination of T and r_f; for example:

Point on MCL	Portfolio Combination (%)		Approximate Return (%)	Approximate Standard Deviation (%)	Reward-to-Risk Ratio
	r_f	T			
r_f	100	0	5.0	0.0	—
X	50	50	11.25	5.5	1.15
Y	40	60	12.5	6.6	1.14
T	0	100	17.5	11.0	1.14
W	(−20)	125	21.875	13.75	1.14
Z	(−33)	150	26.25	16.5	1.14
A	(−50)	200	36.00	19.25	1.14

Or the investor could invest at the segment of the capital market line (CML) between T and Z, which represents a *borrowing portfolio*. The investor would buy the securities in portfolio T and would borrow money at the riskless rate to purchase more of the stocks in portfolio T. A practical limit on the amount of money borrowed is 50 percent of the value of portfolio T. Portfolio Z on the MCL represents 150 percent of portfolio T and a loan of 50 percent of the value of the equities. Portfolio W on the MCL represents approximately 125 percent of portfolio T, with the amount borrowed representing 25 percent of the value of the equities. The maximum amount borrowed would be 100 percent, where 200 percent was invested in the portfolio at T.

Think of this segment of the capital-market line as 125, 150 or 200 percent of portfolio T as you move up and to the right on the line. If the investor can borrow at a risk-free yield and invest in portfolio T, then the move would be to point Z on the capital-market line, when the reward would be proportional to the risk rather than less proportional, as a point A on the efficient frontier for common stocks. Therefore, in theory, it pays investors to borrow and buy stock of an efficient portfolio, since it improves the reward-to-risk ratio so that reward and risk are proportional.

The Capital-Market Line
and the Investor's Indifference Curve

Where investors operate on the capital-market line depends on their attitudes toward risk and return. Investors must determine their own preferences for risk and return by way of an indifference curve, such as curve I_1I_1 in Figure 21–5. Actually, indifference curve I_1I_1 is only one of many such curves. (Imagine a whole set of curves moving up and to the left of curve I_1I_1 similar to the illustration in Chapter 1.) In theory, the investor will invest in the combination of securities found at that point where the highest indifference curve just touches the capital-market line. That is portfolio P in Figure 21–5. Investors might have higher return and lower risk goals, but they can obtain those combinations only on the capital-market line, and will invest at some point that gives the combination of return and risk that allows them to maximize net worth and make a satisfactory investment.

MODERN PORTFOLIO THEORY AND INVESTMENT PRACTICE

APPLYING MARKOWITZ DIVERSIFICATION TO THE ART AND PRACTICE OF PORTFOLIO MANAGEMENT

The principles illustrated by the Markowitz concept of modern portfolio theory can be applied with the help of the computer to the practice of portfolio management. This has been done by using the values obtained from Modesystem for the expected return and the standard deviation of the expected return. In Chapter 18, we showed how the expected rate of return was calculated by the use of the RANDOM model. The RANDOM model also provided a standard deviation of expected returns. If you recall, these values were based on ten years of price data that provided annual returns for nine periods. These values have been found to be very helpful in the investment decision process. The return-to-risk ratios calculated using the RANDOM values have been extremely useful in establishing attractive investment opportunities. In fact, in several empirical tests, it was found that stocks having a reward-to-risk ratio of 1.00 or higher outperformed securities that had a reward-to-risk ratio lower than 1.00. You might wish to review the data provided in Modesystem in Chapter 18 to identify the values of RANDOM return $\bar{r}$ and RANDOM risk $\bar{\sigma}$.

The coefficient of correlation of the annual returns of one stock to the annual returns of all other securities is calculated using the nine years of annual return data, as was one with stocks EK and CWE in the two-security illustration. This too is a part of the efficient frontier generator of Modesystem.

Thus we have the ingredients that Markowitz thought necessary to develop the efficient portfolio set: the expected return, the expected risk as measured by the standard deviation of the annual returns, and a way of calculating the coefficient of correlation of one stock to every other stock. This allows us to determine the lowest risk level of each of the portfolios, taking into consideration the covariance effect established by Markowitz. The computer program used is a quadratic program similar to the one used by Markowitz.

In the case to be described below, the 30 Dow Jones Industrial Average stocks were used to calculate the efficient portfolio set. The computer program was run in mid-1981 using current prices of the 30 stocks in the DJIA group. The computer generated the efficient portfolio set. The results are summarized in Table 21–1. Across the top of the table is listed each efficient portfolio of stocks. The left column identifies each stock. Under the efficient portfolio heading is found the percentage of each stock in each portfolio. At the bottom of the table is found the expected return of each portfolio, the expected risk (standard deviation), and the return-to-risk ratio. Notice also how the standard deviation declines as the return declines. In addition, the return-to-risk ratio rises. The efficient frontier is presented in graph form in Figure 21–6.

The program was run with one constraint, and that was there shall be no more than 12.5 percent of any one stock in the portfolio. The program rounded this to 13 percent. Notice how a few stocks dominate each portfolio. It is thought that in practice an investor might achieve the same results by buying only the dominant stocks in the portfolio.

What DJIA portfolio from Table 21–1 should the investor choose? And what combination of risk-free and risky assets should be selected? These questions must

TABLE 21–1

Efficient Portfolio Set for DJIA, May 1981 (13 percent maximum for each stock)* Based on Markowitz's Quadratic Computer Program

Portfolio Number and Percentage of Each Stock

Stocks in DJIA	1	2	3	4	5	6	7	8	9	10	11	12	13	14	15	16	17	18	19	20	21	22	23	24	25	26	27	28	29	30	DJIA INDEX	S&P 500
Allied Chemical																															4	
Alcoa	13	13	13	13	13	13	13	12	11	9	7	7	6	5	4	4	3	3	2	2	2	2	2	2	3	13	13	13	13	13	2	
American Brands	13	13	13	13	13	13	13	13	13	13	13	13	13	13	1	1										2	1	1	1	1	3	
American Can	13	13	13	13	13	13	13	13	11	10	10	10	9	5	1	1	6	7	9	10	12	11	11	10	11	8	8	7	7	4	3	
AT&T	13	13	13	13	13	13	13	13	13	13	13	13	13	13	13	13	13	13	13	13	13	13	13	13	13	13	13	13	13	13	4	
Bethlehem Steel																							1	1	1			1	1	2	2	
DuPont																							1	1	1		1	1	1	1	4	
Eastman Kodak																															6	
EXXON																															5	
GE																															5	
General Foods	13	3	3	8	3	3	3	3	2	7	7	8	8	9	9	9	10	10	11	12	12	12	12	12	12	11	11	11	11	11	2	
GM	3	3	3	8	3	3	3	3	3	1	1	1	1	9																	4	
Goodyear																															1	
Inco																															2	
IBM	13	13	13	13	13	13	13	13	13	13	13	13	13	13	13	13	13	11	9	8	8	7	6	6	5	3	1	1	1	1	4	
International Harvester	13	13	13	13	13	13	13	11	11	8	7	6	6	4	4	4	2	2	2	2	2	2	2	1	1	1	1	1	1	1	1	
International Paper	13	13	13	13	13	12	12	11	11	8	7	7	7	5	5	5	4	3	3	3	3	3	3	3	3	2	2	2	2	2	2	
Johns Manville																												1			1	
Merck	10	13	13	13	13	13	13	13	13	13	13	13	13	10	12	13	13	13	13	13	13	13	13	13	13	13	13	13	13	13	7	
MMM		13	13	13	13	13	13	13	13	13	13	13	13	10	9	9	7	7	7	6	6	6	6	6	6	5	5	5	5	5	4	
Owens Illinois																														1	2	
Procter & Gamble	13	13	13	13	13	13	13	13	13	13	13	13	13	13	13	13	13	13	13	13	13	13	13	13	13	13	13	13	13	13	5	
Sears																													5	5	1	
Standard Oil (Calif.)	13	13	13	13	13	13	13	13	13	13	13	13	13	13	13	13	13	13	13	13	13	13	13	13	13	13	13	13	13	13	3	
Texaco			13	8	8	9	10	11	11	7	8	8	7	5	5	5	3	4	4	4	4	4	4	4	4	3	3	3	3	2	3	
Union Carbide								1	1	1	1	1	1	1	2	2	2	3	3	3	1	1	1	2	3	1	3	1	2	2	4	
U.S. Steel	13	13	13	13	13	13	13	13	13	13	13	13	13	13	13	13	13	13	13	13	13	13	13	13	13	13	13	13	13	13	2	
United Technologies																															4	
Westinghouse	13	13	10	5	2	2	1	1	1	1	1	1	1	1																	2	
Woolworth																															3	
Total (%)	100	100	100	100	100	100	100	100	100	100	100	100	100	100	100	100	100	100	100	100	100	100	100	100	100	100	100	100	100	100	100	
Expected return E_p (%)	59	58	57	56	55	54	54	53	53	50	48	47	47	44	43	43	40	40	39	38	38	38	37	37	34	28	27	27	26	24	32	25
Dividend return (%)	7.2	7.2	7.2	7.2	7.4	7.4	7.4	7.3	7.3	7.5	7.5	7.4	7.3	7.0	6.9	6.9	6.9	6.9	6.9	6.9	6.9	6.9	6.8	6.8	6.8	6.4	6.3	6.3	6.2	5.9	5.7	5.0
Risk σ_p (%)	43	42	37	32	29	29	38	38	27	25	24	23	23	23	21	21	20	20	19	18	17	17	17	16	16	14	14	14	14	13	35	18
Return-to-risk ratio	1.02	1.16	1.31	1.31	1.37	1.37	1.37	1.37	1.38	1.42	1.41	1.41	1.40	1.39	1.38	1.37	1.31	1.32	1.33	1.33	1.33	1.33	1.33	1.33	1.23	.93	.89	.88	.84	.72	.51	.56

*Maximum was 8 stocks, but computer rounds from 12.5 to 13 percent.

NOTE: Risk-free return = 14.6 percent.

SOURCE: A Security Valuation and Portfolio Management Program, THE MODESYSTEM, School of Government and Business Administration, The George Washington University, June 11, 1981.

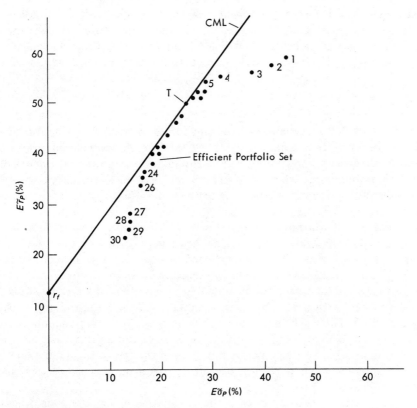

FIGURE 21–6

Chart of Efficient Frontier of DJIA Stocks, mid-1981

SOURCE: Table 21–1.

be answered by the investor. Yet the investor will choose a point somewhere on the capital-market line (CML), which is drawn from risk-free (r_f) to the point of tangency to the efficient portfolio set (T). Investors who are completely risk-averse will put 100 percent of their assets in risk-free assets at point r_f. Those who are risk-takers will invest all their assets in the portfolio at T. Those who are willing to accept maximum risk will borrow money up to 100 percent of the money available to buy securities in portfolio T. The reason for the 100 percent limit is because of the 50 percent margin requirement established by the Federal Reserve Board which was in effect in 1981. This means that the investor with $10,000 would borrow $10,000 and buy $20,000 of securities of portfolio T.

A note about the efficient portfolio set generated in Table 21–1. All the portfolios through portfolio 25 have a return-to-risk ratio that is acceptable. Portfolios 26 through 30 are unacceptable because of a low return-to-risk ratio. This conclusion is based on research results previously cited in the text. If an investor decided to "buy the market"—to invest money in each of the stocks in the DJIA average where the DJIA is the market—the investor would have a beta of 1.00, which indicates the risk level of the market. The investor would also earn the return of the market. If an investor did diversify in this fashion, the results as seen in Table 21–1 would not be very good. The return-to-risk ratio is far too low. Even the dividend yield is lower than any of the portfolios that are considered efficient. The DJIA is even less efficient than the S&P 500 Index. The better portfolios, from a return-to-risk basis, are in numbers 10 to 13.

Implications for Investment Practice

The efficient portfolio set generated by the quadratic program provides an investor with the portfolio with the minimum risk. The use of the program eliminates the problem of how to diversify among risky assets. It eliminates the notion that naive diversification (equal amounts in each security) is a sound way to select risky securities. It still leaves the decision about the balance between risky and riskless assets up to the investor.

The application of Markowitz principles to portfolio management assumes that the estimates of expected return and risk are accurate measures of the actual returns and risks of a portfolio and its securities. This is an assumption difficult to accept. It is unlikely that a historical set of data will repeat itself in the future.

It is also difficult to accept the notion that the coefficient of correlation is an accurate reflection of future relationships. Certainly these values change for each security over time. The work the author has done with Spiro Manolis indicates that the portfolio management based on the Markowitz quadratic program can lead to performance that is 2 percentage points higher than the return of the market. These results are improved when portfolios are created from among stocks that have a return-to-risk ratio of 1.00 or higher.

Still another weakness is that a sophisticated and complex computer program is required to generate the portfolio set.

Still another practical problem is that investors are asked to buy securities that are negatively correlated to each other to achieve the best results. This means that the investor should buy a stock with the return expected to decline in one year combined with a stock that will earn a high return. Unfortunately, most investors don't like to buy stocks that are expected to show a low rate of return.

In spite of these weaknesses, the Markowitz concepts provide us with excellent principles to follow in portfolio management.

1. The risk of each stock and its covariance with each other stock determines its weight in a portfolio.
2. A small amount of diversification can result in substantial reduction in risk.
3. The focus of the investor's decision is based on the correct variables expected return, expected risk, and the relationship of one security's return to another.
4. It suggests that under certain circumstances investors can borrow money to buy stocks.

Establishing Artificial Diversification Limits
Using the Markowitz Principles

Often investors will put their own constraints on the amount of money to be invested in each security in a portfolio. Some will say that no more than 10 percent of a portfolio should be committed to one stock. Others might even state that no more than 5 percent of a portfolio should be invested in a single stock. The Markowitz principles suggest that securities should be put in a portfolio based on their return, risk and covariance characteristics, not on the basis of arbitrary, naive practice. To demonstrate the correctness of this statement, the Markowitz quadratic program was employed to calculate the efficient frontier of portfolios based on the assumption that there were no limits on diversification, that there was a 10 percent limit and a 5 percent limit. Figure 21–7 indicates graphically the effect on the efficient frontier of portfolios (EF) and the capital-market line (CML) based on the different assumptions.

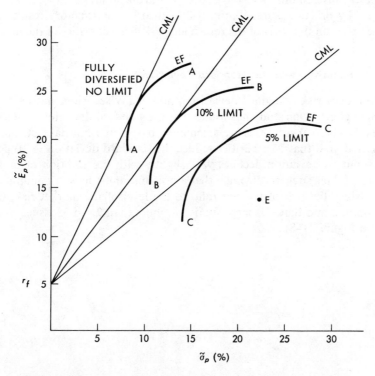

FIGURE 21–7

The Effect of Arbitary Diversification Rules on Risk and Reward, Using the Markowitz Full Covariance Model

SOURCE: Frederick Amling & Associates, Washington, D.C.

The efficient frontiers *AA*, *BB*, and *CC* are generated by the computer using the Markowitz full covariance model. From the 65 Dow Jones Average stocks, the 30 with the highest return and the lowest risk were chosen, and these became the universe from which securities were to be selected. The efficient frontier *AA* represents the selection of an efficient set of portfolios from among the 30 stocks without any arbitrary weight constraints. Any stock could be 100 percent of the portfolio, or a large portion of it. Efficient frontier *AA* would be considered fully efficient. However, efficient frontier *BB* was constructed with a 10 percent diversification limit—that is, no more than 10 percent of the portfolios could be invested in any one stock. The efficient set of portfolios CC represents the results of the imposition of a 5 percent diversification limit.

The result of this simulation suggests that when you impose artificial weight limits for an investment portfolio from a limited set of securities, as the amount of diversification increases, the return, $\tilde{E}_p$, decreases, and the risk, $\tilde{\sigma}_p$, tends to increase. Therefore, overdiversification can lead to a lower return and greater risk. Only when a portfolio manager held portfolio E in Figure 21–7 would it be more efficient to have a 5 percent or 10 percent diversification limit. Obviously, a fully efficient diversified portfolio is best. This demonstrates the notion that artificial limits imposed on investment managers by practice or regulation will lead to less satisfactory results than a portfolio diversified on the basis of the return and risk characteristics of the individual stocks.

The Number of Securities and the Standard Deviation

If we wish to reduce risk (standard deviation), how many securities must we add to have a sufficient effect? One study has found that the standard deviation is reduced to acceptable levels when 10 securities are assembled, based on a normal distribution of securities selected, and that 15 securities reduce the standard deviation to 10 percent, after which standard deviation declines very slightly with the addition of more and more securities.[12] This suggests strongly that a portfolio must have a minimum of 10 securities to reduce the risk of the portfolio to the level of the market risk, that 15 would be optimum, and that, for large funds, no more than 25 to 35 issues would be necessary, (see Figure 21–8).

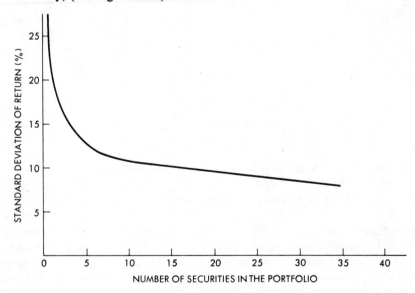

FIGURE 21–8

Relationship of Number of Securities to Standard Deviation of Return

[12]See J. L. Evans, "Diversification and the Reduction of Dispersion: An Empirical Analysis," National Association of Investment Companies, Washington, D.C.

MODERN PORTFOLIO THEORY AND INVESTMENT PRACTICE

This also demonstrates another principle. If the curve in Figure 21–8 is drawn properly, the greatest reduction in risk comes about with the addition of the first five securities. As additional securities are added, the risk is reduced only slightly and the return declines only slightly. This suggests that investors might wisely reduce the number of securities in a portfolio to the range of five to seven. In this way risk is reduced to near market levels, yet return is retained at well above market levels.

MODERN PORTFOLIO THEORY WITH BETA ANALYSIS

The application of the Markowitz diversification principles requires the use of a complex computer model because of the calculation of the variance of each stock to every other stock as part of the portfolio selection process. Sharpe[13] argued that it was unnecessary to calculate the variance for each stock. He reasoned that similar results could be achieved if the investor knew how the annual returns of each stock related to the annual returns of the market, as represented by the S&P 500 Index. His approach was to apply regression analysis to the data to determine the risk characteristics of each stock. Once investors knew the risk characteristics of each stock, they could combine the stocks into a portfolio that would have the risk and return characteristics the investor was willing to accept. The way in which this relationship is established is by the use of the regression equation $Y = a + bX + \epsilon$. In the general form Y is the dependent variable, X is the independent variable, a is the Y intercept, b is the slope of the regression line and is measured by dividing ΔX into ΔY, and ϵ is the error factor, which has an average of zero and is measured from the vertical distance between the regression line and a data point. These relationships are seen in Figure 21–9.

When regression analysis is applied to securities, it uses the returns of the stock R_s compared to and plotted against the returns of the market R_m, where the market is usually the S&P 500 Index. Therefore, as we did in Chapter 1, the annual returns of a stock for ten years are regressed against the annual returns of the S&P 500 Index for ten years. They are then plotted as was done in Figure 21–9, and a regression line is fitted. Those investors who have a somewhat sophisticated hand calculator or a small computer can fit a trend line to the data using the least squares method with little difficulty.

The points that are being regressed in Figure 21–9 represent the relationship between the annual return of the stock and the annual return of the market. Point 3, representing year 3 in Figure 21–9, tells us that in year 3 the return of the market (S&P 500 Index) was approximately 5 percent and the return of the stock was 5.5 percent. In this case, ten years of data were regressed. Year 10, at point 10, shows a market return of 14 percent and a stock return of 14.25 percent.

Once the regression line is fitted to the data, the relationship of the annual return can be explained. In this case only 10 points were used. Often 60 points are used, based on monthly returns, which is a more reliable comparison. Several statisticians have suggested that 100 data points are necessary to provide reliable statistical relationships. The relationship may be expressed in the form of the regression equation,

[13]Sharpe, "A Simplified Model for Portfolio Analysis."

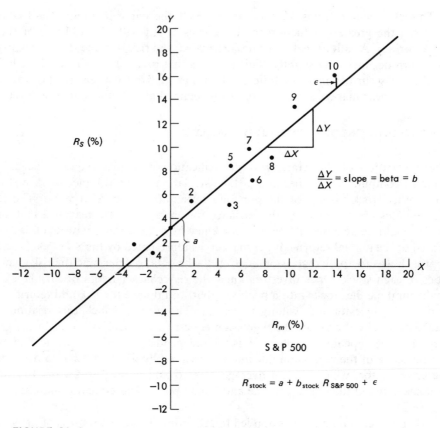

FIGURE 21–9

$R_s = a + bR_m + \epsilon$, where a is the Y intercept, b is the slope, R_m is the return of the market, and ϵ is the error factor. The values must be found to be substituted into the equation. The alpha, a, is 3.5 percent. The slope $\Delta y/\Delta x$ is $2.5/2.8 = .89$. And the ϵ (by visual reference) appears to be approximately 1.0. The equation therefore can be written:

$$R_s = 3.5 + .89R_m \pm 1.0$$

What does the equation tell us about the stock relative to the market? First, we must know that b or beta represents the systematic risk of the stock relative to the market. The a or alpha and the ϵ error factor represent the unsystematic risk of the market. If the systematic risk as measured by beta is higher than 1.00, the stock is said to be riskier than the market. If the beta is lower than 1.00, the stock is less risky than the market. If the alpha is positive, the stock has performed better than the market. If it is negative, the stock has performed worse than the market. If the ϵ is higher then the unsystematic risk is high, and vice versa.

The regression equation that explains the relationship between the stock (R_s) and the market (R_m) in Figure 21–9 may be explained as being less risky than the market with a beta of .89. It has a positive alpha, which is good, and it has a relatively small error factor. Let's see how this stock behaves if the return of the market (R_m) is 12 percent. Substituting in the equation, we obtain the following:

$$R_s = 3.5 + .89(12) \pm 1.0$$

$$R_s = 3.5 + 10.68 \pm 1.0$$

$$R_s = 14.18 \pm 1.0$$

Therefore when the market earns 12 percent, the stock should average 14.18 percent, with a range of 13.18 to 15.18 percent. If the stock performed exactly like the market, it would have earned a return of 12 percent; but it earned 14.18 percent. With a beta of .89, the stock should have earned $(.89 \times 12) = 10.68$ percent. Therefore, the stock really outperformed the market because of the positive alpha and the small ϵ factor. The performance of the stock was better because of the positive unsystematic forces.

If the market earned a return of -3.6 percent, as the S&P 500 Index did in 1981, what would you expect the stock to have earned? Substituting in the equation, we have:

$$R_s = 3.5 + .89(-3.6) \pm 1.0$$

$$R_s = 3.5 - 3.2 \pm 1.0$$

$$R_s = .3 \pm 1.0$$

$$\text{Range 1.3 to } -.7$$

Thus the security earned a positive return and again did better than the market.

The interpetation of the relationship between the market index and the stock in the regression equation is summarized in Table 21–2.

TABLE 21–2
Guides to Beta Analysis

Variable	Magnitude of Relationship to Market	Relationship to the Market Interpretation
a (alpha)	Positive	Better
	0	Same
	Negative	Worse
b (beta)	Higher than 1	More Risky
	0	Same
	Lower than 1	Less Risky
ϵ (epsilon)	0	Same
	Higher than 0	Worse

Thus a stock with a positive alpha and beta of 1 and an ϵ of zero is expected to do better than the market index. If the market is expected to rise, the best set of variables would be for a positive alpha, a beta higher than 1, and an ϵ of zero. If the market is expected to fall, the investor would want a positive alpha, a lower beta, and a zero ϵ. And if the investor wanted a stock to perform exactly like the market, the equation would have a zero alpha, a beta of 1, and an ϵ of zero.

In summary, a positive alpha and zero ϵ are to be desired. A high or low beta must be judged on the expectation of the market. If the market is expected to rise, then a high beta is desirable; if it is expected to fall, then a low beta stock is desirable. In addition, both the alpha and epsilon for stocks relative to the market tend to be low. A high alpha for stocks would be desirable but difficult to obtain.

Beta Analysis in Prediction

The regression equation of a stock is used to predict future returns for stocks. What if you knew that the relationship between a stock and the S&P 500 Index was $R_s = 1.0 + 1.1R_m \pm .5$. And further, you expect a 15 percent rate of return for the market. What return would you expect from the stock? The return expected would be $1.0 + 1.1(15.0) \pm .5$. This equals $1.0 + 16.5 \pm .5$, and finally the return equals $17.5 \pm .5$ percent.

Unfortunately, it is easy to calculate the return; the question is, how reliable is it? The answer is not very! Individual betas, alphas, and epsilons are not reliable. Betas are unstable, and stocks have a different beta in a rising market than in a falling market. Therefore the investor must do something to overcome this weakness. And this is diversify. It has been found that a group of stocks in a portfolio tend to have a stable beta and other regression relationships. So the investor's job is to put several stocks into a portfolio. Through diversification, the investor can reduce epsilon to zero as well as alpha. Then a sufficient number of stocks with beta of 1.00 will provide a partfolio that provides the risk of the market—a beta of 1.00 and no unsystematic risk, since a and ϵ are zero. The number of different shares necessary to achieve this goal is perhaps 25 to 35 different common stocks. In the process, the unsystematic risk is diversified away, leaving only the systematic risk of the market.

If an investor is willing to assume more risk, then stocks with higher betas can be

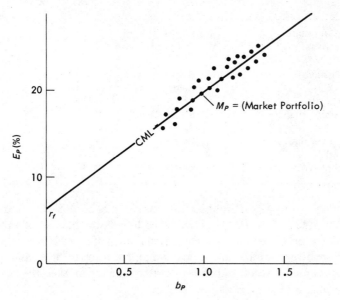

FIGURE 21–10

chosen for the portfolios. Figure 21–10 provides a chart of what an investor would expect if many portfolios were ranked by their portfolio betas. Portfolio betas are stable, remember. The point Mp on the capital-market line (CML) represents the beta of the S&P 500 Index, which is 1.0 with a return of 17 percent. If an investor wanted a market portfolio, this portfolio would be chosen. If a riskier portfolio were chosen, the investor would move to the right, farther out the line. If the investor wanted less risk, two choices are available. A stock portfolio to the left and lower down the CML line could be purchased. Or the investor could invest in the market portfolio (M_p) and then adjust for risk by adding a certain percentage of risk-free assets at r_f. This way the investor could lower the return and the risk. The equation that explains the relationship is as follows:

$$E_p = rf + b_p(E_m - r_f);$$

where E_p is the expected return of the portfolio, r_f is the risk-free return, b_p is the beta of the portfolio, and E_m is the expected return of the market. Assume that E_m is 15 percent. The beta on the portfolio (b_p) is 1.2 and r_f is 11 percent. A further assumption is that the unsystematic risk is zero. To determine what return to expect from the portfolio, it would be necessary to substitute these variables into the regression equation:

$$E_p = a + b_p E_m \pm E$$

$$= 0 + (1.2)(15) \pm 0$$

$$= (1.2)(15)$$

$$= 18 \text{ percent}$$

Thus an investor should expect a return of 18 percent.

Assume that the investor has chosen the portfolio with a beta of 1.2 and an expected return of 18 percent. But the investor would like to reduce the risk to a level equal to that of the market and earn a return equal to the market. This could be accomplished by using the equation:

$$E_p = (W_{r_f})r_f + (W_{b_p(E_m)})b_p(E_m)$$

where W_{r_f} is the amount invested in risk-free assets and $W_{b_p(E_m)}$ is the amount invested in the risky assets of the portfolio where $W_{b_p(E_m)} = 1 - W_{r_f}$. The equation would then become

$$15 = (W_{r_f})11 + (W_{b_p(E_m)})18.$$

The amount to be invested in r_f would be 11/29 and the amount in $b_p(E_m)$ would be 18/29. Thus 62.1 percent would be invested in $b_p(E_m)$ and 27.9 percent would be invested in r_f. This portfolio would have the same risk level as the market portfolio.

The Use of Beta Analysis in Portfolio Management

Usually, investors who rely on beta analysis and modern portfolio theory make several assumptions:

1. They assume that stock prices are independent and cannot be used to forecast future prices.

2. They assume that since prices cannot be predicted, it is difficult to beat the market. Since all knowledge is reflected in the stock price, everything is known about the stock and, on average, it is difficult to outperform the market, although some analysts have superior knowledge and intellect and can do better than the return of the market.

3. They assume that the transaction costs of trading shares will wipe out any additional gains from trading. Therefore they follow a buy and hold philosophy.

4. Since individual stock betas are unstable but properly diversified portfolio betas are stable, they structure a portfolio (diversify) so that they can earn the return of the market (a beta of 1), or they select an acceptable risk level, a beta of higher than 1 or lower than 1, by selecting a large enough number of shares to assure they will achieve the desired level of risk. As we indicated before, this requires that from 35 to 50 securities be purchased.

5. In the diversification process, the unsystematic risk of alpha and epsilon is reduced to zero. Thus only the risk of the market or some percentage of the market risk is faced. The systematic risk of the market remains and is measured by beta.

The MPT theorists are saying, in practice, if you can't beat the market, join it!

Limits of MPT with Beta Analysis

Those investors who employ beta analysis are willing to accept the returns of the market. In fact, the purchase of 35 to 50 securities in a portfolio almost guarantees the return of the S&P 500 Index or close to it. This acceptance denies investors of ever doing better than the market.

Beta analysis denies selectivity and the ability of analysts to discern superior investments. Much of the evidence of empirical research says that about half of all investors do worse than the market and half do better. And these are the professional investors, not amateurs. But there is evidence that suggests superior research will lead to superior investment results.

Richard Roll suggests that the S&P 500 Index does not really reflect the market for all stocks. In fact, he suggests that an investor's portfolio might do as well as the S&P 500 Index but might not earn the return of the "real" marketplace.

Edward Miller also states that to buy stocks without regard to price level and return just doesn't make sense. Miller thinks that emotional investors and speculators tend to bid prices too high relative to future dividends and earnings. That is, when a stock is perceived to be attractive, investors bid prices up. They bid prices up so high that it is difficult to earn a fair return on the investment. Miller presents the notion of the last optimistic investor. The last optimistic investor typically buys at the top of the market and ends up with a loss. Conversely, there is the last pessimistic seller. The last pessimistic seller holds a stock until it reaches bottom. Fully and thoroughly disappointed and disillusioned, the investor decides to sell. Both activities result in losses for investors and contrasts with modern portfolio theory, which assumes that the market for stocks is in equilibrium, and that investors have homogeneous expectations about stocks.

Last, modern portfolio theory denies the ability to obtain superior results through buying and selling securities at a profit. But timing the purchase and sale of stocks can improve investment performance substantially.

THE USE AND APPLICATION OF MODERN PORTFOLIO THEORY

INVESTMENT RESEARCH. Modern portfolio theory is being applied in two ways. One is through research undertaken by large brokerage houses and provided to their investment clients. Part of the research effort of Kidder Peabody, a national and international brokerage and investment banking firm headquartered in New York, for example, is devoted to modern portfolio theory. It has developed a body of knowledge explaining portfolio theory to institutional investors much like the discussion in this chapter. And it provides a list of securities with the expected returns which is based on regression analysis. Figure 21–11 provides such a list of securities. Notice that if a company provides a 19 percent expected return and the market return is 17 percent, the investor can assume that the stock has a beta of approximately 1.1, if $a = 0$. This means the stock is 10 percent riskier than the market index. Several national brokerage firms use MPT concepts, but their use is not widespread. The entire industry has been influenced by MPT, but its exclusive use and application is limited to about 10 percent of the investment industry.

INDEX FUNDS. Index funds in the mutual fund industry apply MPT exclusively. The typical index fund is a no-load fund that invests in all the stocks of the S&P 500 Index. The amount of each stock in the portfolio is based on the percentage the stock represents of the value of the S&P 500 Index stocks. The way this is calculated can be illustrated by an example. Assume that there is a two-stock market index. Stock A sells at a price of $50 per share, and the company has 100 shares outstanding. Stock B sells at $70, and has 200 shares outstanding. The total market value of the companies is $50(100) + $70(200) = $5,000 + $14,000 = $19,000. Stock A represents 26.3 percent of the two-stock index ($5,000/$19,000), and stock B represents 73.7 percent of the market index ($14,000/$19,000). In following the index fund principle, an investor would invest 73.7 percent in stock B and 26.3 percent in stock A in order to perform exactly like the index. An example of the weighting system used is found in Figure 20–1. A mutual fund practicing as an index fund would diversify the portfolio using these weights. As new money came in it would be invested to keep the weightings equal to the weighting in the index. Such an investment strategy should earn the return of the market, with the risk of the market.

INTERNATIONAL FUNDS. The same procedures are being followed in international mutual funds. The World Index is used as the basis. Approximately 50 percent of the stocks are American. The remainder are in the United Kingdom, Germany, Switzerland, France, Italy, Belgium, Japan, and Australia. Japan accounts for 19.5 percent of the fund; Europe and Britain account for 16 percent.

RANK BY EXPECTED RETURN*

		VALUATION INPUTS														VALUATION RESULTS					
		Current Fiscal Year			Near-Term Period			Plateau Period			Trans-ition Period	Steady-State Period		FRE		Expected Return*			Risk-Adjusted Expectations		Rank in Univ
	Price	Est EPS	Est Div	Est Yield	Earns Growth Rate	Div Growth Rate	Yrs	Earns Growth Relative	Div Payout Relative	Yrs	Yrs	Earns Growth Relative	Div Payout Relative	Value	Rank in Univ	Pct	Rank in Univ	Alpha	Zero-Alpha Price	Implied Price Change	
HEALTH CARE																					
Lifemark Corp.	31.000	$1.80	$0.40	1.3%	27.0%	32.7%	10	1.80	0.95	10	23	1.24	1.18	1.26	341	21.2%	20	2.9%	$60	92%	8
American Medical Int'l	44.875	3.50	0.85	1.9	26.5	27.4	9	1.80	0.78	9	25	1.20	1.20	1.19	290	20.2	39	2.1	77	71	13
Humana, Inc.	37.500	3.10	1.00	2.7	23.1	21.0	10	1.80	0.70	10	23	1.24	1.10	1.20	301	19.6	65	1.5	55	46	30
Richardson-Vicks	26.250	3.75	1.48	5.6	14.1	13.5	6	1.35	1.00	6	11	1.13	1.24	1.07	163	19.2	84	1.6	34	30	62
Schering-Plough Corp.	26.000	3.95	1.75	6.7	9.4	10.9	5	1.10	1.13	5	3	1.05	1.25	1.08	176	19.1	99	1.4	31	20	104
Squibb Corp.	28.625	2.40	1.22	4.3	19.0	18.6	10	1.27	1.16	10	9	1.10	1.24	1.09	184	18.9	111	1.2	35	21	97
Cordis Corp.	15.375	2.90	0.00	0.0	NC	NC	8	1.24	0.50	8	22	1.24	0.76	1.41	399	18.5	112	0.2	16	4	195
Hospital Corp. America	42.000	2.20	0.34	0.8	25.1	30.3	9	1.70	0.63	10	9	1.20	1.20	1.12	215	18.5	141	0.7	51	21	98
MortonNorwich Products	33.875	4.40	1.70	5.0	13.6	15.9	9	1.30	1.13	9	9	1.12	1.16	1.07	160	18.5	143	0.8	38	14	132
Amer. Hospital Supply	36.375	2.95	1.15	3.2	16.2	17.2	8	1.60	0.94	8	18	1.20	1.05	1.06	147	18.3	162	0.7	42	16	124
Servicemaster Ind.	26.000	1.22	0.80	3.1	21.1	20.1	10	1.40	1.63	10	10	1.24	1.24	0.99	80	18.0	189	0.6	29	11	147
Pfizer, Inc.	45.500	3.60	1.70	3.7	20.2	22.6	5	1.30	1.25	5	7	1.12	1.17	0.96	63	17.9	195	0.6	50	11	149
Rorer Group Inc.	19.125	2.15	0.95	5.0	13.0	13.0	5	1.30	1.13	5	9	1.10	1.13	1.06	150	17.7	225	0.1	19	1	210
Marion Laboratories, Inc.	24.375	1.00	0.70	2.9	33.9	23.7	8	1.20	1.00	8	5	1.10	1.13	1.06	152	17.7	231	0.0	24	0	218
Lilly (Eli) and Co.	52.750	4.70	2.30	4.4	12.1	15.3	8	1.10	1.38	8	7	1.10	1.50	0.94	49	17.6	236	0.4	56	6	179
Community Psychiatric Center	35.625	1.75	0.45	1.3	21.1	25.1	10	1.60	0.85	10	15	1.24	1.24	1.14	246	17.6	237	-0.3	33	-8	268
Baxter-Travenol Labs	62.875	3.95	0.88	1.4	19.6	22.7	10	1.60	0.75	10	18	1.20	1.24	1.08	168	17.5	242	-0.2	60	-4	243
Abbott Laboratories	28.125	2.00	0.72	2.6	16.8	18.3	10	1.40	1.00	10	7	1.24	1.15	0.96	58	17.5	248	0.2	29	5	187
Sterling Drug Inc.	22.125	2.00	1.00	4.5	15.6	15.7	10	1.10	1.20	10	4	1.08	1.35	0.95	57	17.4	259	0.1	23	2	208
Medtronics	33.500	3.00	0.64	1.9	17.4	30.3	8	1.24	1.00	8	0	1.24	1.00	1.13	232	17.3	271	-0.6	30	-12	288
Becton-Dickinson	44.750	4.16	1.16	2.6	14.8	16.5	8	1.50	0.83	8	13	1.20	1.20	1.06	145	17.0	298	-0.6	38	-14	302
Warner-Lambert Co.	20.000	2.00	1.34	6.7	10.9	5.2	10	1.15	1.13	10	4	1.08	1.24	1.05	132	16.8	308	-0.8	18	-12	289
Johnson & Johnson	36.375	2.25	0.90	2.5	15.9	16.1	10	1.50	1.00	10	20	1.10	1.15	0.90	40	16.6	324	-0.5	33	-11	280
American Home Products	36.875	3.15	1.90	5.2	11.9	11.9	10	1.10	1.40	10	1	1.08	1.35	0.81	24	16.6	328	-0.2	35	-4	239
Searle (G.D.) & Co.	33.500	2.40	0.57	1.7	26.9	38.3	5	1.30	1.00	5	10	1.10	1.13	1.08	174	16.5	333	-1.2	27	-20	323
Bristol-Myers Co.	55.250	4.55	1.78	3.2	13.5	15.4	10	1.25	1.20	10	8	1.10	1.28	0.94	47	16.4	341	-0.9	47	-16	308
Syntex Corp.	59.125	6.25	1.60	2.7	12.5	14.6	5	1.30	0.88	5	4	1.20	1.24	1.19	292	16.3	345	-1.7	42	-30	358
Merck & Co., Inc.	79.875	5.40	2.60	3.3	13.5	12.9	5	1.20	1.25	5	5	1.10	1.38	0.94	48	15.8	369	-1.4	60	-24	336
SmithKline Corp.	70.500	5.45	2.30	3.3	13.1	16.4	8	1.10	1.25	8	3	1.05	1.38	0.98	71	15.6	372	-1.8	52	-27	346
Robins, A.H. Co.Inc.	11.625	1.45	0.52	4.4	15.2	14.6	7	0.90	1.00	7	11	0.90	1.13	1.00	89	15.6	374	-1.9	9	-24	333
Upjohn Company	49.000	5.40	1.95	4.0	8.5	18.9	8	1.30	1.13	8	10	1.10	1.25	1.03	119	15.6	376	-2.0	36	-27	348
Intermedics Inc.	32.500	1.65	0.00	0.0	22.8	NC	10	1.43	0.40	10	8	1.24	0.76	1.17	277	15.1	395	-2.9	12	-62	407
National Medical Care	11.625	1.30	0.34	2.9	7.8	11.3	10	1.00	0.83	10	25	1.00	1.20	1.27	345	13.7	412	-4.6	5	-60	405
MULTI-INDUSTRY																					
RCA Corporation	17.125	$1.50	$1.80	10.5%	19.2%	0.0%	5	1.00	1.15	5	10	1.00	1.00	1.20	298	19.6%	66	1.5%	$20	18%	115
Raytheon Company	40.250	3.85	1.20	3.0	16.7	12.8	10	1.70	0.75	10	13	1.24	0.90	1.16	263	18.3	161	0.3	44	8	164
Northwest Industries, Inc.	60.500	9.20	2.68	4.4	21.5	15.8	4	1.20	0.75	4	12	1.00	0.88	1.15	252	17.2	277	-0.7	54	-10	278
Dover Corporation	29.000	2.85	0.66	2.3	19.6	20.3	5	1.50	0.63	5	11	1.24	0.76	1.02	105	16.5	334	-1.0	23	-22	328
TECHNOLOGY																					
GenRad	13.500	$-0.10	$0.10	0.7%	NC	41.5%	2	2.10	0.30	2	25	1.10	1.13	1.45	404	20.2%	37	1.3%	$18	37%	45
Loral Corp	29.250	2.35	0.72	2.5	19.8%	20.1	3	2.20	0.75	3	25	1.10	1.13	1.28	355	19.7	52	1.4	39	34	50
Lynch Communications Sys.	12.000	0.60	0.10	0.8	NC	36.6	5	1.80	0.60	5	25	1.20	1.00	1.19	294	19.7	56	1.6	17	45	32
Augat, Inc.	29.125	1.50	0.40	1.4	29.2	34.1	2	2.30	0.75	2	25	1.20	1.13	1.19	297	19.6	59	1.6	41	41	43
Wang Laboratories	32.125	1.80	0.16	0.5	37.5	41.1	1	2.50	0.40	1	25	1.20	0.75	1.31	363	19.5	68	1.1	43	33	52
Paradyne Corp.	43.125	1.35	0.00	0.0	43.9	NC	5	3.00	0.02	5	25	1.24	0.76	1.46	407	19.5	69	0.6	53	23	85
M/A-Com Inc.	28.625	1.50	0.15	0.5	31.9	33.5	5	2.80	0.25	5	25	1.20	0.76	1.35	385	19.5	71	0.9	38	32	58
Prime Computer	24.500	1.28	0.00	0.0	17.4	NC	5	2.50	0.40	5	25	1.20	0.76	1.46	405	19.4	77	0.5	28	13	136
NCR Corporation	44.500	8.30	2.20	4.9	12.1	12.1	7	1.50	0.65	7	20	1.10	1.00	1.16	268	19.2	88	1.3	56	25	78
Sperry Corp.	32.750	4.60	1.92	5.9	10.5	12.2	7	1.50	0.80	7	20	1.10	1.00	1.18	287	19.2	89	1.2	40	21	95

FIGURE 21–11

SOURCE: Kidder, Peabody & Co., *Monthly Valuation Data*, November 1981, p. 13.

Modern portfolio theory assumes that an efficient marketplace will establish a price that reflects everything known about the stock. Theory assumes that an investor need know only the expected return from a stock E, the risk as measured by σ, and how the returns are correlated to each other, since the degree of correlation changes the covariance of the return. Markowitz provided a quadratic program that would combine securities into portfolios and the efficient set of portfolios would be determined. The efficient portfolio set then establishes the efficient frontier of portfolios. The first efficient portfolio has the highest return and the lowest risk. The second efficient portfolio on the frontier adds one security or a portion of the security to the first, and the minimum risk is determined. This is best illustrated with a two-security portfolio. In the general case, the process is continued until the entire frontier is established. Then the investor must decide from among risk-free investments and risky assets determined by a line drawn to the point of tangency on the efficient frontier from the return on the risk-free asset. The investor invests in risk-free assets, risky assets, or is a borrower and buys more risky assets, depending on attitude toward risk.

Usually the estimates of return are based on historic relationships that are assumed to hold in the future. The RANDOM model used in Modesystem seems to be a reliable valuation model to use in developing portfolios. The strength of the Markowitz model is in its focus on risk as the determinant of what stocks are to be included in a portfolio. And it points out how diversification can reduce risk by the use of only a few securities because of the covariance effect. The weakness is in the complexity of the program and the negative aspects of adding securities whose returns might decline. Nonetheless, the notion is valid that a few stocks added together will reduce risk relatively more than the return.

Beta analysis and its application to modern portfolio theory assumes that the beta of the stock is a good guide to risk. Adding many stocks with a beta of 1.00 together changes the unstable stock relationship beta into a stable portfolio beta. A group of 35 to 50 stocks results in a beta that is stable and the unsystematic risk of alpha, a, and epsilon, ϵ, is reduced to zero.

Investors can also combine stocks into portfolios with betas of more or less than one. Investors then will choose a portfolio of risk-free assets and risky assets from portfolios along the capital-market line (CML) to meet their investment objectives. MPT followers believe in the notion that prices are independent; a buy and hold philosophy is preferred; and they are willing to accept the returns and risks of some market index.

Unfortunately, the beta approach to MPT ignores selectivity based on analysis, and tends to ignore timing of buy and sell decisions. There is a feeling that beta analysis leads to incorrect decisions because the market indexes used do not reflect the market returns and risk. In addition, it ignores the tendency to bid prices too high in buying and drop the price too low in the negative aspects of selling. Accordingly, the last optimistic investor and the last pessimistic seller dominate the market.

Modern portfolio theory is applied by some leading national brokerage firms and index mutual funds. Some international funds employ the principles of MPT and indexing. Generally, MPT-dominated funds are no-load funds.

1. The risk of a stock determines its weight in a portfolio.
2. A small amount of diversification can result in a substantial reduction in risk.
3. Investors should select efficient stocks from which portfolios will be constructed.
4. Investment decisions should be based on the return and risk relationship of a security in a portfolio.
5. Investors prefer more to less.
6. The higher the return, the higher the risk.
7. Investors are risk-averse.
8. One security may dominate a portfolio, which is opposite in view to naive diversification.
9. As numbers of securities in a portfolio increase, risk declines.
10. Wide diversification tends to reduce unsystematic risk; the systematic risk of the market remains.
11. A high, positive alpha is desirable.
12. Large returns can be obtained from a small selection of risky assets.
13. Individual investors tend to underdiversify and institutional investors tend to overdiversify.
14. In theory, an investor may borrow money to invest in an efficient portfolio.

REVIEW QUESTIONS

1. List the assumptions on which modern portfolio theory (MPT) rest.
2. Explain how the efficient frontier is determined using the Markowitz approach. Use a two-security approach.
3. In the general theory, where does the investor invest on the capital-market line (CML)?
4. What are the strengths and weaknesses of the Markowitz process?
5. Explain how the regression equation is used in security and portfolio management in MPT.
6. What assumption do beta theorists make in their solution to portfolio management problems?
7. Explain each of the variables in the regression equation.
8. Are individual stock and portfolio betas stable and reliable?
9. From what you know about foreign securities, would they be beneficial in a portfolio in the Markowitz sense?
10. What is the difference between systematic and unsystematic risk?
11. Explain the strengths and weaknesses of MPT using beta as the measure of risk.
12. What are the criticisms of beta analysis?
13. Does the S&P 500 Index reflect the entire stock market?
14. Should an investor, in theory, borrow money to buy risky securities?

15. If a portfolio has a beta of 1.2 and earns 18 percent and the market return is 15 percent, has it outperformed the market?

PROBLEMS

1. Select the two most efficient stocks for inclusion in an investment portfolio from among the following:

	E	σ
ABC	10%	5%
DBF	12	7
XYZ	17	9
AA	19	15
XX	10	7

2. Two stocks are available for inclusion in a two-stock portfolio. The stocks are ABC, with an E of 15 and a σ of 5, and XYZ, with an E of 12 and a σ of 3.5.
   a. Assuming a coefficient of correlation of 1, what would be the most efficient two-stock portfolio?
   b. Assuming an ρ of zero, what would be the most efficient two-stock portfolio?
   c. Assuming an ρ of -1, what would be the most efficient two-stock portfolio?

3. In problem 2 above, plot the efficient frontier of portfolios for a two-stock portfolio for each asset.

4. Assuming that the risk-free yield is 5 percent, construct a capital-market line for the one- and two-security portfolios in problem 3.
   a. Explain where an investor would invest if he or she were a lender and risk-averter.
   b. Explain where an investor would invest if he or she were a risk-taker and borrower.

5. Three stocks and the S&P 500 Index have had the following annual returns for the past ten years:

		Stocks		
Year	S&P 500 Index	A	B	C
1	.8	1.0	(.5)	1.0
2	1.2	1.5	(1.0)	1.0
3	1.9	1.7	2.0	1.0
4	(2.0)	(1.0)	3.0	2.0
5	1.8	3.0	.5	2.0
6	.9	1.0	.5	2.0
7	.3	.5	1.0	2.1
8	.5	1.0	1.0	2.2
9	(1.0)	(.5)	(4.0)	(2.3)
10	.5	1.0	.5	1.5

a. What was the ten-year average annual return for each stock and the S&P 500 Index?
b. What was the standard deviation of each stock and of the S&P 500 Index?
c. Rank each stock on the basis of its total return and risk.
d. Find the beta for each stock, by finding the regression equation for the line $Y = a + bX + \epsilon$, or by plotting the data on a graph and fitting a line to the data.
e. Rank each stock by its beta.
f. Rank each stock by its alpha.
g. Which stock is most volatile, and why?

6. Using the three companies in problem 5, combine them in a group of portfolios that are efficient and meet the risk and return preferences of an investor, under the following conditions:
   a. Use Markowitz principles, assuming that the past reflects the future and solve for a two-security portfolio.
   b. Use the principles established by beta analysis, assuming that the past reflects the future.
   c. What is the beta characteristic of each portfolio selected in (b)?
   d. If you were told that the market was expected to earn a total return of 20 percent in the next year, what would you expect to earn from each of the portfolios selected?

CASE

Vince and Mary have had their retirement funds invested in an index fund for the past ten years. The market return (S&P 500) for the period was 8.0 percent, with a standard deviation of 14. Their index fund earned 7.2 percent, with a standard deviation of 10. Their fund had a beta of .9.

Using standard deviation as a guide, was their fund more risky than the market? Based on beta analysis, was their fund more risky than the market? Did the index fund do its job? Why or why not? What should they expect from the index fund in the future?

SELECTED READINGS

BLACK, FISHER. "Random Walk and Portfolio Management." *Financial Analysts Journal*, March–April 1971, p. 16.

BLOCK, FRANK E. "Elements of Portfolio Construction." *Financial Analysts Journal*, May–June 1969, p. 123.

FAMA, EUGENE F. "Components of Investment Performance." *Journal of Finance*, in press.

FERGUSON, ROBERT. "Performance Measurement Doesn't Make Sense." *Financial Analysts Journal*, May–June 1980.

FRANCIS, JACK CLARK, and STEPHEN H. ARCHER. *Portfolio Analysis.* Englewood Cliffs, N.J.: Prentice-Hall, 1971.

FRANKFURTER, GEORGE M., H. E. PHILLIPS, and J. P. SEAGLE. "Performance of the Sharpe Portfolio Selection Model: A Comparison." *Journal of Financial and Quantitative Analysis*, June 1976, p. 195.

HELRUS, GARY B. "Toward Bridging the Gap." *Financial Analysts Journal*, January–February 1978.

HODGES, S. D., and R. A. BREALEY. "Portfolio Selection in a Dynamic and Uncertain World." *Financial Analysts Journal*, March–April 1973.

JACOB, NANCY L. "A Limited Diversification Portfolio Selection Model for the Small Investor." *The Journal of Finance*, June 1974, p. 847.

KLEMKOSKY, R. C., and J. D. MARTIN. "The Effect of Market Risk on Portfolio Diversification." *The Journal of Finance*, March 1975, p. 147.

KRIPKE, HOMER. "Inside Information and Efficient Markets." *Financial Analysts Journal*, January–February 1980.

MARKOWITZ, HARRY M. "Markowitz Revisited." *Financial Analysts Journal*, September–October 1976, p. 47.

———, "*Portfolio Selection.* New Haven, Conn.: Yale University Press, 1959.

———. "Portfolio Selection." *Journal of Finance*, March 1952.

MILLER, EDWARD M. "Counter Example to Random Walk." *Financial Analysts Journal*, July–August 1979.

MODIGLIANI, FRANCO, and GERALD A. POGUE. "An Introduction to Risk and Return." *Financial Analysts Journal*, March–April 1974.

RENSHAW, EDWARD F. "Short Selling and Financial Arbitrage." *Financial Analysts Journal*, January–February 1977.

SHARPE, WILLIAM F. *Portfolio Theory and Capital Markets.* New York: McGraw-Hill, 1970.

———. "Capital-Asset Prices: A Theory of Market Equilibrium under Condtions of Risk." *The Journal of Finance*, September 1964.

———. "Adjusting for Risk in Portfolio Performance Measurement." *Journal of Portfolio Management*, winter 1975.

———. "Evolution of Modern Portfolio Theory." *C. F. A. Readings in Financial Analysis*, 1981.

———. "A Simplified Model for Portfolio Analysis." *Management Science*, January 1963.

———. "Risk, Market Sensitivity and Market Diversification." *Financial Analysts Journal*, January–February 1972.

SOLNICK, BRUNO H. "Why Not Diversify Internationally?" *Financial Analysts Journal*, July–August 1974, p. 48.

TREYNOR, JACK L. "How to Rate Management of Investment Funds." *Harvard Business Review*, January–February 1965.

———, and FISCHER BLACK. "How to Use Security Analysis to Improve Portfolio Selection." *The Journal of Business*, January 1973.

VERTIN, JAMES R. "The Design and Control of Large Portfolios." *C.F.A. Readings in Financial Analysis*, 1981.

WAGNER, W. H., and S. C. LAU. "The Effect of Diversification on Risk." *Financial Analysts Journal*, November–December 1971, p. 48.

WEST, RICHARD R. "Two Kinds of Market Efficiency." *Financial Analysts Journal*, November–December 1975, p. 30.

WILSON, PAUL N., and ROBERT J. CUMMUNS. "Security Management and Transaction Costs." *Financial Analysts Journal*, March–April 1977.

CHAPTER 22

PORTFOLIO MANAGEMENT GOALS AND OBJECTIVES, AND ESTABLISHING THE INCOME PORTFOLIO

In Chapter 1 it was pointed out that an investor should choose securities or assets that provide a rate of return and risk level that is acceptable. The risks were clearly pointed out. In subsequent chapters we learned about the availability of investment bonds, and progressed to the more complex and risky securities, such as common stock. Mutual funds were considered, as well as investment in selected real assets. It was also suggested that investors consider foreign securities; since these securities are not highly correlated to the U.S. market, they could be profitable and the investor might benefit from the increase in the price of foreign currency. In fact, one way to provide international investment diversification is to buy foreign currency. If an investor thought the Japanese yen was going to increase in value, then dollars would be used to buy yen. Or investors could buy short-term commercial paper or Japanese government securities that would provide interest income and the possibility of sharing in the increased value of the yen.

A detailed discussion was provided of fundamental analysis, which is the way, right or wrong, that the majority of investment decisions are made in the investment community. Technical analysis was presented as a way to augment fundamental analysis, or as some investors use it, as the basis for all investment decisions. MPT was presented as an alternative method of putting together a portfolio of risky securities. Sufficient securities would be chosen to give the investor the risk of the market or some proportion of the market risk and keep the unsystematic risk at zero. Then the investor would select the combination of risk-free assets and risky assets that would meet his or her goals and objectives. At this point, we are going to discuss the process by which the investor puts together a list of investments into a portfolio.

THE PORTFOLIO MANAGEMENT PROBLEM

The basic problem of portfolio management is to establish an investment goal or objective and then decide how best to reach that goal with the securities available. This has been stated as an attempt by the investor to obtain maximum return with minimum risk. In order to do a proper job of portfolio management, the investor must be aware of the management process. The problem may be summarized as follows:

1. The investor must know the ingredients of portfolio management.
2. The investor must know the objectives of portfolio management.
3. The investor must understand himself or herself and how he or she reacts to risk.
4. The investor must not only have funds to invest, but must be in a sound financial position to accept the risks of investment.
5. The investor must be familiar with the returns and risks of the various securities and assets that are available.

THE INGREDIENTS AND OBJECTIVES OF PORTFOLIO MANAGEMENT IN PRACTICE

Both the ingredients and the objectives of portfolio management tend to focus on averting risk or obtaining a proper return according to good theory. Portfolio management, in total, includes the planning, supervision, timing, rationalism, and conservatism involved in the selection of securities to meet objectives. We will examine each phase and then the objectives an investor might establish in managing a portfolio.

Ingredients of Portfolio Management

Most investors first become aware of the need for investment information and knowledge when confronted with the need to invest a substantial sum of money suddenly under their control—or when they first learn about securities investment and develop a desire to build their wealth.

PLANNING FOR GOALS. The first essential ingredient in portfolio management is planning. This means thought and preparation in establishing a list of securities to meet the needs of the investor. If an investor needs capital growth now and income in later years, the plan must reflect these needs. When investments are made without regard to any plan, the investor may suddenly find he or she owns a group of securities that do not meet objectives. In investing this way, the investor could make errors that would lead to a financial loss.

To handle the problem intelligently, the investor must have objectives clearly defined and a plan established to meet them. It might be wise to write out the investment objectives and then originate a plan for meeting them. In this way, nothing is haphazard; a well-defined course of action is determined in advance.

Planning is a part of the risk-aversion process. The investor must determine how much risk is to be taken and then plan how to achieve these goals. Later we will talk about investment objectives. Goals and objectives may be considered together. The Economic Recovery Tax Act of 1981 provided for expanded IRA and Keogh investment. Millions of Americans were forced to plan how they would save and invest to meet their retirement goals. Everyone does not have money to invest. Therefore, an investment plan might begin with a small amount of money set aside from income to purchase securities later. Part of the plan might be to put $25 or $50 a month into a savings account or super money market fund until a sufficient amount of money is available for investment. Or, an individual might put $2,000 a year into an IRA account to provide financial independence at retirement.

TIMING. Another ingredient necessary for investment success is timing. This is also considered when the investment plan is being undertaken. The market fluctuates according to the economic and political climate. Individual stocks vary in price, in time establishing a price range. In the process of analysis, the investor must decide when a stock is high or low. We know we cannot always buy stocks at their low price and sell them at their high price, but we can tell within limits when a stock appears to be underpriced or overpriced. We should therefore try to purchase stock close to its low price, or at least at an attractive price consistent with its own price movement and future expectations.

If stocks are too high in price, they might be sold. If money is available for investment but stocks are overpriced, the investor will wait until prices decline. In this case, the money will be invested in short-term fixed-income investments. An example of this might make our position clear about timing. In planning a portfolio for an individual, a manager decided that AT&T would be a desirable stock to have. But at 65, it was thought to be overpriced in relation to its earnings. The price range for the stock was between 50 and 65. The conclusion was that AT&T would be a buy at 50. An order was placed to acquire the stock at that price. The market did react downward, and the stock was acquired.

Investors should not assume that because they have money to invest, good opportunities will be available. Often it is good advice to wait for the right time to buy. There is no relationship, necessarily, between the availability of funds and the attractiveness of stock prices. In fact, as each investment is considered, the investor should decide what will be done if the price drops 20 percent or rises 20 percent. Maybe stock should be bought if the price declines 20 percent or sold if it rises 20 percent.

CONSERVATISM AND RATIONALISM. The investor should be conservative and act rationally when making investment decisions. The concept of conservatism is extremely important. One of the essential aspects of investment is to minimize risk. The investor wishes to accept risk consistent with gains, but not beyond. It would be imprudent to accept risk beyond what is necessary. Risk and gain are correlated. It is wise to accept reasonable risk for reasonable gain, rather than undue risk for a strong possibility of gain and loss.

SUPERVISION. Portfolio management assumes periodic supervision of the securities in the portfolio. Some people advocate a buy-and-hold philosophy, whereby stocks are purchased and held forever. MPT suggests this action. In our competitive society and in view of the fluctuation of the stock market, this is not a very prudent, conservative, or rational plan of action for sound portfolio management. A stock may be bought and held for a lifetime—but it should not be ignored. The investor should frequently analyze the company and the security to make certain that it meets needs. The professional investment-fund manager, for example, will examine each client's account once a month. If a change is suggested by research and analysis, the necessary action will be taken. Changes will be made if the fundamental position of the investment has changed.

In theory and practice, it is important that the investor calculate quarterly returns and compare them to the market to make certain that the results are consistent with objectives. The discussion of the theory of performance can be applied directly to estimating performance. Most institutional investors provide their clients with detailed performance measures.

Objectives of Portfolio Management

The emphasis of portfolio management varies from investor to investor. Some want income, some capital gains, and some a combination of both. In spite of these variations, several objectives should be considered as basic to a well-executed investment program. These guiding principles establish the indifference curve of risk versus return for the investor.

SECURITY OF PRINCIPAL. The first consideration in establishing investment objectives is the security of principal—the preservation of the value of the investment account for the sake of future income and growth. There are two kinds of people to whom this principle should be especially emphasized. One is the investor with a small fund who says, "I'm interested in quick growth, and it really doesn't make any difference if I lose my entire investment, because I don't have too much to lose." This thinking can lead to unwise decisions and the acceptance of unnecessary risk, with the inevitable result that the investor may lose all the capital.

The other investor is the wealthy person with the large investment account. This person's position is the same as the small investor's, but for a different reason. This investor rationalizes, "I'm wealthy; therefore I can afford to lose some of my principal." This thinking may also lead to undue risk, resulting in a large capital loss that would be difficult to replace. Perhaps the wealthy person can assume more risk with a portion of the investment fund, but this thought process should not govern the entire fund.

Protection of principal should be the *dominant force* in portfolio management. Without capital, investment cannot take place, and capital is difficult to raise. It seems unwise to save for years to build an investment fund of $20,000 or more and then lose it in one careless, risky venture. Some people think that investors purchasing Treasury bills to yield 13 percent are cowards. "Go for common stocks," they will say, "that's where you can earn 25 percent." This would have been good advice in 1980. Many common stocks earned over 25 percent, and the S&P 500 Index from the beginning to the end of the year earned 32 percent. In 1981, the same index lost approximately 4 percent. Over long periods of time the market has earned 9 percent, with wide changes in returns. There is nothing wrong with a 13 percent TB yield that allows your principal to remain intact. Next year you will have $113,000 to invest. Even if you are in the 50 percent tax bracket, you will have $106,500 to invest at the end of the year. And that amount is certain. Obviously, the level of interest rates will make a difference in the conclusions drawn. Anyone is foolish to keep money in a savings account at 5 3/4 percent unless there are other good reasons for doing so.

Security of principal means more than just maintaining the original fund. It means the protection of the purchasing power of the fund. The purchasing-power risk is a very real risk assumed by investors, because of inflation. The necessary steps must be taken to maintain the purchasing power of the fund by buying common stocks that are expected to increase in value if the purchasing power of the dollar declines. Common stocks are not a perfect hedge against inflation, but they can be better at the task than fixed-income securities such as bonds or preferred stocks.

STABILITY OF INCOME. In establishing an investment fund, an investor should attempt to achieve stability of income as a practical goal. Income received in the form of dividends and interest is somewhat more valuable than a promise of future dividends and interest. Stability of revenues allows the investor to plan more accurately and logically, whether the goal is reinvestment or consumption. Stability of revenue is also more valuable than sporadic, unstable, or uncertain income.

Stability of income is obviously most important for the income investor, but it is equally important for the growth investor. Reinvested income is one way to achieve capital growth. This point is amply demonstrated by those who have invested small amounts regularly in tax-exempt Keogh or IRA accounts. Money invested in such accounts is exempt from income taxes. Therefore money invested in liquid money market funds will grow rapidly when the investment is compounded tax-free at rates ranging from 8 to 16 percent. Current IRS rules allow a person to invest a maximum of $15,000 a year, or 15 percent of income, in a Keogh plan. The value of $15,000 invested every year at 12 percent compounded amounts to $117,920 at the end of five years. Compounding at high rates can turn income into capital in a short time.

CAPITAL GROWTH. As a general rule, growth of capital is a desirable objective of portfolio management. This does not mean that every investor must invest in growth stocks; this would be inconsistent with many investors' needs. A fund can be built up from reinvested income as well as through the purchase of growth shares, as was illustrated above. A large fund does provide more income for the investor than a small fund. Many investors have increased the capital value of their funds through reinvested dividends and interest income. Capital growth is necessary to improve the long-range security of the investor, to maintain purchasing power, and to offer flexibility of management. Unfortunately, the search for capital growth by increase in share price is risky.

MARKETABILITY. Another desirable objective of a sound investment portfolio is marketability. Marketability refers to whether a security can be bought or sold easily and quickly. It is a function of price and the size of the market for a given stock. The size of the market is determined in turn by the size of the company, the number of shareholders, and general public interest in the stock. High-priced stocks, for example, are less marketable than low-priced. It is logical to expect that the marketability for a stock at the $400 level is less than for stock selling at $40.

The place where a stock is traded also has some impact on marketability. Stocks listed on the New York or the American Stock Exchange provide greater marketability and more information for the investor than those traded on local exchanges or in the over-the-counter market. However, the NASDAQ system has improved the marketability of OTC stocks, which makes where a stock is traded somewhat less important. A centralized market would add further liquidity.

Stocks of small companies tend to have less marketability than those of larger companies, simply because the larger companies have a greater number of shares outstanding. The increased number of shares traded allows a continuous market for the stock. The concept of continuous marketability refers to the number of transactions and the close relationship in price between one sale and the previous sale.

The size of the company influences marketability in another way. The larger companies tend to be more stable and of higher quality; and size, stability, and quality tend to make their stocks more marketable than those of smaller companies that often lack these investment characteristics.

LIQUIDITY. As stated before, one problem for the investor is to balance liquidity with profitability. Liquidity, or nearness to money, is desirable in the portfolio because it offers the investor an opportunity to take advantage of attractive opportunities that arise—such as lower prices or special situations. Conservative portfolio management suggests that some liquidity be maintained, either by setting aside a portion of the investment fund for such purposes or by arranging to use interest and dividends to purchase new shares.

DIVERSIFICATION. There is really one main reason for diversification—reduction of the risk of loss of capital and income. Investors face an unknown and uncertain future. Since no one can predict the future most investors diversify their investments. There are many ways to diversify investments. A list of ways to diversify includes:

1. Debt vs. equity
2. Maturity
3. Industry
4. Company
5. Nation
6. Time
7. Real or Physical Assets

Most of the diversification forms are obvious but an explanatory word seems in order.

Debt and equity diversification is quite common. Debt provides income with some debt securities, selling at a discount, also providing capital gains. Common stocks provide income, growth of income and capital gains. They are combined to compliment each other since bond yields and returns are not highly correlated to returns on common stocks.

Maturity diversification of bonds reduces the risk of loss created by rising yields. Usually short term yields are lower than long term yields. In cases of extreme monetary restraint, however, short term rates rise well above long term rates. Long term bonds will decline in price as market yields rise; therefore, in conditions of rising yields investors should invest in short term bonds. In periods of falling yields investors should invest in long term bonds. The problem, of course, is to determine which way yields are going. To avoid the problem investors invest in a range of maturities to maintain income and protect capital.

Industry diversification suggests that several industries be selected for investment consideration. This was discussed in Chapter 12.

Company diversification among risky securities suggests that a few securities be purchased to reduce risk. Technical analysis suggests that investors focus on a few securities. Fundamental analysis suggests selectivity and only a few stocks. After all an investor can buy more, over time, of each security. Modern portfolio theory suggests a large enough number of issues of common stocks to reduce the risk to the level of market risk or some multiple of the market risk. The market risk is measured by beta.

Nation. As the world competitive environment changes, industry leadership can move to other countries. The shift in world auto dominance from Detroit to Japan is a case in point. The competitive leader is not always found in the United States. Therefore, some foreign securities might be part of an investment portfolio. In addition, a gain in return might be achieved because of the increased value of the foreign currency.

Time. It doesn't make investment sense to put money into risky assets all at once. If an investor were to inherit $100,000, should all the money be committed to risky assets? Absolutely not. This first step would probably be to buy short-term commercial paper or Treasury bills while figuring out where and in what assets to invest. The notion of not putting your assets to work at the same time is a corollary to "don't put all your eggs in one basket."

Real Assets. Investors might consider real assets. In 1981 real investment assets (gold, diamonds, collectibles) were the worst investment. Yet that doesn't mean they will always be bad. In fact, some future years might be years of good performance for real assets. It wouldn't hurt to keep informed.

These forms of diversification will help the investor avoid risk or accept risk. Knowledge of these forms will let investors know their risk position.

FAVORABLE TAX STATUS. One factor of importance in the management of investment portfolios is the tax position of the investor. Many financial decisions in today's society are governed by federal income taxes. The problem is how to keep as much of the income and capital gains as possible. With progressive tax rates on ordinary income, it is difficult to keep a dollar of income. The investor invests in tax-free bonds or buys securities that pay no dividend income but offer the promise of future rewards in the form of capital gains. Long-term capital gains on the sale of a capital asset owned for one year or longer are taxed at the maximum rate of 20 percent under the Economic Recovery Tax Act of 1981 (ERTA). Short-term capital gains are taxed as ordinary income. (A current tax schedule can be obtained from the IRS or your local post office.) It is wise, therefore, for a person in the 50 percent or higher tax bracket to consider capital gains, or to invest in tax-exempt municipal bonds. In principle, this applies to any person who pays a relatively high marginal tax rate.

Not only is the high rate of federal income taxation a concern, but states are increasingly imposing income taxes on their residents that make it vital for wealthy investors to protect themselves from taxation and stay in a favorable tax position. In 1983, California income tax rates were as high as 10 percent, and New York state taxes went as high as 15 percent.

We learned in our discussion on municipal bonds that they are free from federal income taxes on the interest received. A person in the 50 percent tax bracket who buys a 13 percent tax-exempt bond receives, in effect, a 26 percent before-tax yield.

The tax position of the investor must not be ignored. One recent case demonstrates the difficulties involved in considering the tax factor when making decisions. An investor wanted a portfolio based on a growth objective to reduce income taxes. The investor was in the 50 percent tax bracket. However, the portfolio had no tax-exempt bonds, and several of the common stocks owned were income rather than growth stocks, with a high dividend rate. The portfolio policy did not reflect the tax position. The investor should have attempted to maximize investment returns by minimizing federal income tax liability. Or consider the wealthy industrialist, in a top income tax bracket, who had invested almost $200,000 in savings bonds over the years. He was keeping a very small amount of the interest after taxes.

The investor can minimize the tax liability in one or all of the following ways:

1. Purchase tax-exempt bonds, whose interest is free from federal income taxes.
2. Purchase bonds with a tax-free covenant. In this case, the corporation agrees to pay the tax for the bondholder directly.
3. Purchase bonds with a tax-refund clause. In this case, the bondholder pays the tax but is then reimbursed by the company.
4. Purchase securities that offer long-term capital gains, taxed at a maximum of 20 percent of the gain. Long-term capital losses can be offset against short-term capital gains to minimize income taxes.
5. When purchasing and selling assets, look for a possibility of exchanging assets. This exchange is referred to as a *tax swap*. In this situation, the investor trades an investment owned for another productive asset owned by another investor. A person who owns an apartment house, for example, might wish to trade with an investor who has a list of diversified securities of equal value. No income taxes are paid on the transactions, and the tax base follows the asset that is exchanged. In this way, a capital gains tax is postponed until the investor actually sells the asset.
6. Postpone income until retirement, when current income is lower and taxed at a lower rate. Or invest in an IRA account, where the tax is deferred until retirement.

Anyone working can "shelter" up to $2,000 of income. This money can be invested in a wide range of plans, depending upon the sponsoring financial institution.

7. Maximize long-term gains and minimize short-term gains. Long-term gains are taxed at a maximum of approximately 20 percent. Short-term gains are taxed as ordinary income at a maximum of 50 percent. This method would include writing off short-term losses against long-term gains.

8. Some states, such as Ohio, levy a personal-property tax on securities. Productive assets—those paying dividends or interest—are taxed at a lower rate than unproductive assets. Therefore, where appropriate, invest in productive assets rather than unproductive assets, because they are taxed at a lower rate.

9. Take advantage of tax-deductible annuities that allow income to be deferred until retirement and Keogh plans.

10. Consider companies whose dividends are taxed partially as capital gains. Investment companies and some public utilities are in this category. And some preferred-stock dividends are tax-free to certain corporate owners.

11. Consider the possibility of establishing a short-term trust to minimize taxes on income.

12. Invest in utilities' common stock. Public utility common stock has become attractive because of a provision of ERTA 1981. A dividend exclusion has been provided for taxpayers who choose to receive utility dividends in common stock rather than cash. This dividend reinvestment plan allows public utility stockholders to exclude up to $750 in such dividends each year from 1982 through 1985. The amount is $1,500 if you are filing a joint return. The shares must be registered in the shareholder's name and cannot be in the name of the broker. The investor should use the IRS reinvestment form and notify the utility that dividends are to be reinvested.

PORTFOLIO OBJECTIVES AND THE PERSONAL CHARACTERISTICS OF THE INVESTOR

In order to achieve the objectives that minimize risk and maximize reward, the investor must have personal qualifications to achieve these goals. One's financial position determines to a great extent one's ability to assume risk and gain the perspective for investment success. A strong financial position tends to minimize risk and maximize the opportunity for rewards in the future.

The Concept of a Strong Financial Position

A strong financial position is mandatory before investment takes place, particularly before risky assets are purchased. In order to meet the financial prerequisites of investment, an investor should

1. Have adequate life or term insurance—four to five times annual income at age 35.

2. Have a plan for the purchase of a home or own a home.

3. Maintain a control over consumer credit and instalment debt—no more than 10 to 20 percent of income over a two-year period.

4. Maintain adequate savings and checking balances—between four and six months of annual salary.

Meeting these conditions will put the investor in an excellent position to consider investment in risky assets.[1]

[1]See Frederick Amling and William G. Droms, *The Dow Jones Irwin Guide to Personal Financial Planning.* (Homewood, Ill.: Dow Jones–Irwin, 1982).

Attitude will determine the indifference curve that establishes investment preferences. Usually, a young, wealthy, healthy single person is best able to accept the risks of common stock investment. If youth, health, and single status all disappear, then money alone will allow the investor to accept the risk of common stock ownership.

THE AGE OF THE INVESTOR. It is difficult to make generalizations about this variable, but in general, the younger the investor, the more the interest in growth investments, and the older the investor, the more interested in income. But there are always exceptions. A gentleman in his late seventies came to see a broker about buying stock. The broker suggested a well-diversified income portfolio. The elderly gentleman said in astonishment, "I don't want income stocks, I want something with growth potential." Obviously, he was not investing to meet his own current needs. Younger investors usually tend to be less cautious than older ones. This might be because of willingness to accept risk, but it also might be because of lack of experience. No one should take unnecessary risks.

MARITAL STATUS AND FAMILY RESPONSIBILITIES. The marital status of the investor has an impact on investment needs. Married persons must provide for the physical and educational needs of the family, tending to make them more conservative and less likely to speculate. The investment needs of single persons are much simpler, usually because their financial needs are less complex. The financial commitments of the married investor are much greater, other things being equal, than those of the single person. The cost of establishing a home often makes investment difficult for the family, other than investment in real estate.

THE HEALTH OF THE INVESTOR. The health of investor and family also affects investment policies. An investor in poor health will be in a position in which income is in jeopardy, so demands for current income will be great, precluding investment for growth. A healthy family's investment decisions can be determined by more important investment criteria.

PERSONAL HABITS. The personal habits of an individual also influence investment needs. A frugal person will have no problem establishing a fund. Current and future financial needs will be minimal, suggesting a growth policy. Of course, the very frugal person will have less need for future income as well. At the other extreme is the spendthrift, who needs more current income. Current income demands might be so great that part of capital in addition to income is spent. Obviously, this investor must follow an investment program that maximizes current income. However, to ensure the maintenance of the investment fund, it might be wise to limit expenditures.

WILLINGNESS TO ACCEPT RISKS. The emotional makeup of a person will dictate the ability to assume the risks of investment. The risks are real; we must understand their nature and significance, we must be willing to accept them and provide against them. People vary as to their willingness to assume the purchasing-power risk, market risk, business risk, or money-rate risk. Some eagerly accept risk and are not alarmed if they actually lose large sums of money. These people are prepared financially and emotionally to invest. Others are so security-conscious that they could not risk the loss of a single penny. They are emotionally unable to accept the risk of loss, and should stay out of the stock market.

One of the important points to remember about investment is that while we can usually obtain results consistent with our objectives, there is no place for greed in the investment equation. If we are motivated by greed, we will often take unnecessary risks to achieve unrealistic goals unconnected with economic reality.

THE MONEY PSYCHOLOGY OF THE INDIVIDUAL. The overriding question the investor must ask is, "What is my psychological attitude about money?" Some people just can't bear the thought of parting with a dollar, even if they have more money than they will ever need. Such people could not buy stocks. A college professor once asked me if a certain mutual fund was a good and safe investment. Until this time, he had never owned a common stock. The mutual fund he mentioned was a good one, and I recommended purchase. Two months later, my friend approached me again. He said he would never again invest in the stock market, because he had lost money. I had not watched the price action of the mutual fund, so I inquired about the loss. He said he had "lost" $.51 a share during the two months he had owned the fund and thought he had been cheated. Obviously, this man is not psychologically attuned to the possible loss of money and should not own common stock.

By the same token, a person should not be so careless about money that he or she actually tries to lose. Psychopathic gamblers, as an extreme case, are hell-bent for financial and personal destruction. Anyone with this psychological attitude toward stocks should stay away from the market. A person needs a sound psychological attitude toward money in order to make money. Few are outstandingly successful and shrewd when it comes to money matters. The books *Bulls, Bears and Dr. Freud* and *The Money Game* will shed some light on this question of the psychological attitude of investors.[2] Before anyone begins an investment program, he or she must find out about his or her money psychology.

The Investor's Needs

Whether theory or practice is followed, it must be recognized that when money is invested for an individual, needs must be met. Some of the needs will be financial, some will be emotional and psychological. Certainly, the primary motive for investment is profit. It might be for retirement, for education, to improve one's standard of living, or to be benevolent and leave something for one's alma mater; nonetheless, the goal is profit.

A university professor died some years ago and left his estate to the university. He had taught chemistry and had never earned more than $5,000 a year. He lived close to the university; he married late in life and had no children; his wife preceded him in death. When we say his needs were modest, we overestimate his standard of living. He seemed as poor as a church mouse; his students once took up a collection to buy

[2]Albert Haas, Jr., and Don D. Jackson, *Bulls, Bears and Dr. Freud* (New York: World, 1967); and "Adam Smith," *The Money Game* (New York: Random House, 1968).

him a new pair of shoes, and although his old shoes were held together with rubber bands, he refused the offer. He invested his funds. He had faith in the Chicago Furniture Mart and bought this stock continuously, reinvesting all the profits to let the fund grow. His life and his happiness were given to him by the university; he asked only that he be allowed to work in the chemistry lab and teach. It is not strange for a professor to leave an estate to his university; the strange part is that he left over $1,000,000. His was an act of charity. He invested only for the benefit of others.

Other motives are equally strong for some people. The wealthy frequently want power, and they continue investing simply to maintain economic power and control over assets for their own benefit. Some people invest for status, so they can tell their friends they own stock. Others invest for educational reasons; Baldwin Wallace College and the University of Toledo, for example, have student investment funds, the purpose of which is to educate students in the art of investment analysis and management.

The point is that the investor must know himself and therefore know his own needs—financial, emotional, and psychological—in order to determine his own requirements for risk and reward.

Articulation of Goals and Objectives

It is extremely important that investors be as specific as possible about their goals and attitudes if they hope to meet them and be comfortable with their investments. In fact, investors should articulate their objectives by being specific about the rate of return and the amount of risks they expect. An investor should state, "I need a 10 percent return with little or no risk and stability of income." The statement should be written down and reviewed periodically. If an investor knows that risk-free assets, Treasury bills, offer a yield of 13 percent, longer-term bonds offer 14 to 17 percent yield and/or return with a standard deviation of 6 percent, and common stock offers returns of 18 to 23 percent with a standard deviation of 14 percent, he or she can determine where to invest funds.

If an investor says, "I need at least 10 percent with no risk," this could be achieved with investments in Treasury bills. There is no certainty that Treasury bills will always provide a yield of 10 percent (we may get lucky and have yields drop to 8 percent). In that case, the investor knows that longer-term bonds or income stock will be needed. The investor can combine Treasury bills with longer-term bonds and income common stocks to make up a portfolio of: 20 percent Treasury bills, 50 percent bonds, and 30 percent income common stocks. The combined portfolio would have a current return of 12.9 percent, with a risk level of less than a standard deviation of 6 percent. There would be some possibility of capital growth from the common stock. The dividend income would be stable and could grow modestly because of the ownership of common stock.

Even when investors seek help from the professional community, they must be able to tell their investment manager, counselor, or broker what they require. A trust company under a trust agreement, common trust fund, short-term trust, or investment management account must be able to work in terms of specific goals, and client-investors must be able to articulate their aims. This is also true when an investor opens a Keogh or IRA account. An investor must understand the retirement goals and the types of securities that will help meet those goals. Communication between investment management and customer is critical.

PORTFOLIO MANAGEMENT POLICIES

Some of the more common policies that might be followed in the management of an investment fund are income, growth, and a combination of the two. This way of classifying portfolio policy stresses whether returns to the investor will be in the form of current income or capital gains.

The income fund places emphasis on the maximization of current income. Capital gains and growth are given minimum significance in the income portfolio. The securities that provide income are the medium-grade bonds, preferred stocks, dividend-paying common stocks, and, for investors in a high tax bracket, tax-exempt securities.

The growth portfolio emphasizes the capital growth of the investment fund. The purpose of the growth fund is to postpone current income so that the fund increases in value. The increased value will allow the investor to improve income and growth at a later date. Investors interested in growth would buy stocks that offer appreciation potential and a low cash dividend.

The income-growth fund attempts to balance current income with some growth. The investor desires some current income, yet wishes to build the value of the fund. The problem is whether to balance the securities in the fund between income securities and growth securities, or to choose a security that possesses both growth potential and income—sometimes referred to as a straddle stock. A good example would be the common stock of American Telephone & Telegraph. It has paid some dividends each year since 1881, and it has growth potential. A well-diversified list of comparable stocks would make an excellent combination income and growth portfolio.

The remainder of this chapter will be devoted to the discussion of the portfolio management principles applied to an income fund.

THE INCOME PORTFOLIO

Income securities provide virtually all the income in the form of current yield, whether it is income from bond interest or dividend income from preferred or common stock. The income portfolio would attempt to minimize risk, as measured by the standard deviation of return. The ideal income common stock would be one with a high current-income level associated with low risk. High-yield preferreds and bonds would fit the description of an income investment.

The main function of the income portfolio is to provide maximum current income for the investor. The income obtained from the investment fund represents either a portion or all of the investor's income. It may supplement a relatively low income or represent the only source of income the investor possesses. The income portfolio, however, is not confined to the person who has modest means, or to the widow-and-orphan class. Someone with a large estate may desire, as an investment objective, the maximization of current income. The income portfolio is dictated by the relative need of the individual investor, not absolute needs.

There are two possible extremes in the management of the income portfolio. The first is the case in which the investment fund is not large enough to meet current demands for income. Even if safety were ignored and speculative bonds and high current yield common stocks were purchased, there would be insufficient income to satisfy the investor. The solution to this problem must rest outside the portfolio; that is, additional help must come from family, friends, or the state. Or the fund itself must be given up. In this case, a portion of principal and income is returned to the investor periodically until it is used up, or the fund is used to purchase a fixed-income annuity, which might or might not be able to provide an adequate standard of living for the investor.

At the other extreme is the income portfolio of the wealthy person with a large fund to invest who requires stability of income. The fund is managed with the object of maximizing current income but, of necessity, giving proper consideration to the investor's tax position. In this case, there is no need to reduce the requirements of safety. The income from a $500,000 fund will, even at relatively low yields, provide a fairly substantial income. A $250,000 investment in 15 percent AA bonds would provide $37,500 of income before federal income taxes. An investor with $37,500 of security income would be in the 37 percent marginal tax bracket, assuming that the standard deduction is taken plus two exemptions. The taxable income would be $32,250; the marginal rate above $32,000 based on 1981 rates was 37 percent, in the special tax category under joint returns. The investors could have invested in tax-exempt bonds to yield 13 percent to maturity, in which case they would have had a full $32,500 of income after taxes; with the fully taxable 15 percent bonds, the income after taxes would have been $23,485. The investor would have been in a better position with tax-exempt bonds yielding 13 percent.

People between the tax-rate extremes make up the majority of income investors. This group is neither extremely wealthy nor desperately dependent upon the income from the fund to sustain themselves and their families.

Securities for the Income Investor

The securities that meet the needs of the income investor stress safety of principal and current icome. Such securities are corporate bonds, Baa and above in rating; tax-exempt municipals; U.S. government bonds; preferred stock; and common stocks that pay a high dividend and have stability of earnings. A prospect for continued or increased dividends from the common stock increases the attractiveness of this type of income security.

SPECIFIC SECURITIES TO MEET INCOME REQUIREMENTS. Securities that would provide the investor with a high current yield appear in Table 22-1. These common stocks would provide safety, income, and the potential for appreciation. Most of them appear in the master lists of well-known investment services. Many of them are the leading companies in their industry. Obviously, these stocks will change, and their yield characteristics will have to be reexamined. Current yields on investment securities may be found in Standard & Poor's *Stock Guide*.

TABLE 22-1

Selected Income Stocks with Approximate Current Yield and Some Price Appreciation Potential

Company	Price 1/82	Dividend	Current Yield	Price 1/83	Dividend	Current Yield
AT&T	58	5.40	9.2	67	5.40	8.1
Exxon	30	3.00	9.8	31	3.00	9.7
Florida Power and Light	28	3.04	10.8	38	3.28	8.9
Royal Dutch Petroleum	32	2.62	8.2	37	2.92	7.9
Tenneco, Inc.	32	2.60	8.0	35	2.63	7.7

SOURCE: Standard & Poor's *Stock Guide*, November, 1981 and March 1983; *The Wall Street Journal*, January 19, 1982, and March 14, 1983.

Stability and regularity of income must be stressed when the income portfolio is established. The income must be regular and certain in amount, because the income investor must rely heavily on it to meet the expenses of daily living. The long-term securities of the U.S. government offered attractive yields which might satisfy income investors. A selected list of government securities appears in Table 22–2. Corporate

TABLE 22-2

A Selected List of Government Bills, Notes, and Bonds for Income and Safety, as of January 18, 1982, and March 14, 1983

Security	1982 Yield	1983 Yield
90-day Treasury bills, new	12.50	8.48
26-week Treasury bills, new	13.10	8.72
1-year Treasury note or bond	14.65	8.83
2-year Treasury note or bond	14.48	9.29
3-year Treasury note or bond	14.69	9.89
4-year Treasury note or bond	14.69	9.90
5-year Treasury note or bond	14.22	10.12
6-year Treasury note or bond	14.50	10.66
7-year Treasury note or bond	14.74	10.42
8-year Treasury note or bond	14.44	10.94
9-year Treasury note or bond	14.44	10.94
10-year Treasury note or bond	14.74	10.57
15-year Treasury note or bond	14.17	10.71
20-year Treasury note or bond	14.56	10.92
25-year Treasury note or bond	14.28	11.01

SOURCE: *Wall Street Journal*, January 19, 1982, pp. 39, 45; and March 14, 1983, p. 52.

bonds of individual companies of excellent quality could also be purchased on an attractive yield basis. Investors interested in income could select, from among a wide range of companies, many secure bonds and preferred stocks to provide a current yield above 8 percent.

BALANCE IN THE PORTFOLIO. The balance between bonds (defensive securities) and stocks (aggressive securities) will depend on the outlook for the stock market and the political, economic, and cultural climate. It will also depend on the yield offered by the various securities. Some bonds offered yields of 14 percent or higher, well above yields of common stock. In order to increase current income, it is usually necessary to have a portion of bonds in a portfolio. Not only is such a portfolio balanced in terms of risk and reward; it is balanced in regard to fixed-income securities and equities. A list of a few corporate bonds appears in Table 22–3 and a selected list of preferred stocks in Table 22–4. A selected list of tax-exempt bonds appears in Table 22–5. All these securities are useful for the income investor.

TABLE 22–3

A Selected List of Bonds for the Income Investor

| | | | | 1982 | | 1983 | |
| | | Coupon | | Approx. | Yield | Approx. | Yield |
Rating	Company	(%)	Maturity	Price ($)	(%)	Price ($)	(%)
AAA	AT&T	8.75%	2000	$63	14.0%	$80	11.0%
AA	Detroit Edison	9.15	2000	55	17.0	71	13.0
A+	PPG Industries	9.00	1995	65	15.1	84	11.0
AAA	Exxon	6.50	1998	50	14.3	67	9.7
A	Pacific T&T	8.75	2006	56	15.8	73	12.0
A	Kennecott Copper	7.87	2001	49	16.7	71	11.0

SOURCE: Salomon Brothers, New York, and *The Wall Street Journal*.

TABLE 22–4

Income Preferreds

Company	Price 1/15/82	Dividend ($)	Approximate Yield (%)	Price 3/14/83	Dividend ($)	Yield (%)
AT&T	61	4.00	12.0	70	4.00	5.7
Cincinnati Gas & Electric	30	4.75	16.0	39	4.75	12.0
Consolidated Edison	34	5.00	15.0	45	5.00	11.0
Consumers Power	27	4.50	17.0	35	4.50	13.0
General Motors	37	5.00	13.0	50	5.00	10.0
New York State Electric	13	2.12	16.0	18	2.12	12.0
Niagara Mohawk Power	23	4.10	14.0	34	4.10	12.0
RCA	22	3.65	16.0	29	3.65	13.0

SOURCE: *The Wall Street Journal*, January 19, 1982, and March 14, 1983.

TABLE 22–5

A Selected List of Tax-Exempt Bonds

Issue	Coupon	Maturity	Price, 1982	Yield	Price, 1983	Yield
Florida Turnpike Authority	4 3/4	2001	$68	7.55%	$ 85	6.0%
Louisiana Offshore Terminals	6 1/2	2006	55	10.7	74	8.8
Municipal Assistance Corporation of New York	10 5/8	2008	80	12.6	82	12.5
New York State Power Authority	9 1/2	2001	79	11.8	103	9.2
Valdez	5 1/2	2007	52	9.7	69	8.0

SOURCE: *The Wall Street Journal*, January 19, 1982, and March 14, 1983.

Establishing the Income Portfolio

In setting up an income portfolio, investors face all the investment risks, including business risk, credit risk, money-rate risk and market risk and the purchasing-power risk. Investors also must try to minimize risk.

A solution to the business and credit risk is to confine investments to high-quality income securities, including government bonds.

A solution to the money-rate and market risks is to diversify by maturities.

A solution to the purchasing-power risk is to obtain yields that compensate for an inflation rate of 6 to 9 percent or higher, and to invest in common stocks that provide income and growth.

As a solution to high tax rates, an investor can seek tax-exempt securities that also provide protection from the other risks of investment.

An example of how this might be accomplished is found in Table 22–6. The securities in Table 22–6 were selected from the securities in Tables 22–1, 22–2, and 22–3.

TABLE 22–6
A Sample Income Portfolio That Compensates for Investment Risks, January 1982

Issue	Percentage of Portfolio (%)	1982 Approximate Yield (%)	1983 Approximate Yield (%)
Treasury bills, 90 day	10	12.50	8.48
Treasury bills, 6 months	10	13.00	8.72
1-year Treasury notes	10	14.65	8.83
3-year Treasury notes	10	14.69	9.89
5-year Treasury notes	10	14.22	10.12
10-year Treasury notes	10	14.74	10.57
Income common stocks with growth	30	10.00	9.00
20-year AT&T bonds	10	14.00	11.00
Total	100	12.78 (average)	9.46 (average)

Income preferreds were not selected because the additional income provided was insufficient for the additional risk. Government securities were selected because of their high yield and high quality. Some common stocks were included because they added the prospect for future growth and offered a satisfactory amount of current income. If the investor were in a high tax bracket, some tax-exempt securities would have been included.

The bulk of the portfolio was invested in relatively short maturities because of the fear that interest rates might rise in the future. As the securities mature, they can be reinvested in higher-yielding securities. Yet half of the portfolio was invested in securities with maturities of ten years or longer and in income common stock. Thus the investor had a portfolio that diversified the investment risks and provided reasonably stable income with some growth.

Diversification, Risk, and Management of the Income Portfolio

The income portfolio in Table 22–6 was diversified based on the analyst's perceived notion of risk. Virtually all the securities are low-risk securities; there is a low variability of expected yield or return. The riskiest portion of the portfolio is the 30 percent invested in common stocks and the 10 percent invested in long-term bonds. Since the investor is interested in income, which will be stable, it is assumed that the investor will hold these securities until maturity and can ignore the fluctuation of the price of the investment. Of course, the investor can expect the price of the assets to vary.

In the management of the portfolio, the investor will reinvest the Treasury bills every 90 days and 6 months. If interest rates rise during the period, this money could be invested in longer-term bonds to take advantage of higher interest rates. Assume, for example, that government bond yields rose to 17 percent. The investor might then buy longer bonds to "lock in" the higher yield. In the process, the price of the longer-term bonds in the portfolio will drop. But the investor, anticipating this possibility, will hold until the bonds mature. At that time, the investor will decide where the money should be invested. If rates decline as in 1983, you have the income and a sizable capital gain.

If rates are low, the investor should stay relatively short in the fixed-income portion of the portfolio. If interest rates are very high, the investor should increase the length of maturity.

There is no perfect solution to the management of the income portfolio. Interest rates fluctuate, and it is difficult to forecast their future level. The best approach is to diversify as was done in Table 22–6 and be patient.

The most important point to remember is to keep up to date on the securities one might include in an income portfolio. We said earlier in the chapter that the investor must be familiar with investments to meet a specific portfolio objective. In this case, we had a list of income securities available that would meet the investor's goal of earning maximum income and yet diversifying against all or most of the investment risks. The list of investment alternatives will be discussed in more detail in Chapter 23.

SUMMARY

Investors must be in a strong financial position before investment begins. Investors who manage their own funds and institutional investors who manage portfolios for clients must understand the need for financial security before taking risks. Investment goals are established by the investor. The best way to establish goals is to state them in terms of income or growth, and with a specific return and risk level in mind. Once these goals are established, the investor will take an active part in portfolio management. This includes planning to meet investment goals with objectives of security of principal, income, growth of principal, liquidity, marketability, and a favorable tax status. Diversification of an investment portfolio is done to reduce the risk to the investor. The risks faced are the market risk, business and credit risk, the money-rate risk, and the risk of loss associated with inflation. Diversification takes the form of nation, industry, security, and time. The overriding goal is to protect principal and then obtain income or growth.

Once the portfolio is established, it must be managed to meet the investor's goals. The income portfolio must be managed to protect the investor from the money-rate risk and inflation. The current high returns on income securities, and the selection of some income stocks with growth and diversification by maturity, seem to solve the risk problems of the income investor. As the fixed-income investments reach maturity, they will be reinvested in the securities that best meet the investor's needs.

SUMMARY OF PRINCIPLES

1. The investor must have a list of securities with an estimate of return and risk.
2. The investor must plan an investment program to meet specific goals stated in terms of return and risk.
3. The portfolio must be managed.
4. Portfolio management objectives include security of principal, stability of income, capital growth, marketability, liquidity, diversification, and a favorable tax status.
5. The investor must be in a strong financial position to invest.
6. The age, marital status, health, attitudes, and needs of the investor determine the basic objective for portfolio management.
7. The income portfolio emphasizes current income but must diversify against the money-rate risk by having a balance between short-term and long-term securities and the purchasing-power risk.
8. Growth should not be ignored in the income portfolio.

REVIEW QUESTIONS

1. What is meant by planning portfolio objectives?
2. What is meant by management?
3. Why is diversification important, and what form does it take?
4. Why should income investors seek growth?
5. Can an income investor ignore safety of principal?
6. Why should an investor diversify between short-term and long-term securities?
7. Why is knowledge of tax status important for the investor?
8. What is the major objective of the income portfolio, and what types of securities would have the qualifications to meet these objectives?
9. Discuss the process and principles employed in setting up the income portfolio.
10. Is it difficult in today's market to obtain a generous income from an investment portfolio without sacrificing quality? Explain.
11. Explain how expected return and standard deviation, are used to establish the risk level in an income portfolio.

1. The income portfolio in Table 22–6 was established in January 1982. In June 1982, the portfolio changed in price and yields. Price each security in the portfolio and indicate the yield, remembering that each bond in the portfolio has one year less to maturity. Indicate the changes a portfolio manager would have made over the year. What would you have done to change the portfolio in mid-1983?

2. Based on the information in the chapter, set up a portfolio for an investor who is in the 50 percent tax bracket and who wants a high income after taxes and some growth of income. Assume that interest rates are expected to fluctuate and inflation is expected to be at 8 percent for the next few years.

CASE

Let's make the income portfolio more meaningful by an example—by setting up a $67,200 portfolio for the widow of a U.S. businessman who lost his life in a plane crash. Mrs. Black received the money as proceeds of a life insurance policy in 1976. She had three small children, was in her early thirties, and was working but needed more income with the possibility of capital growth. Since she was not completely dependent on the income from the portfolio for her livelihood, she wanted an income-growth portfolio.

The securities in the table below were selected for Mrs. Black, based on their indicated current yields, which averaged 7.20 percent for the fixed-income securities, 7.41 percent for the common stocks, and an overall yield of 7.15 percent. This amount was lower because of the $1,675 in cash.

The balance in the portfolio was kept at 50 percent bonds and 50 percent stock, to reduce the risks of common stock ownership. Because of the uncertainties surrounding interest rates, it was decided to invest only in short- and intermediate-term bonds. As these matured, the money from them would be invested in fixed-income securities based on the investment realities at the time.

The common stocks in the portfolio were selected from among the stocks in the Dow Jones Composite 65 Average. The first criterion for selection was low risk. Second, the stocks selected had to have an attractive total return and a dividend that would grow. Once the securities had been selected on a preliminary basis, the list was refined to include those stocks that offered the highest expected return. Industry diversification was also considered. Included in the portfolio was a tobacco and food company, a telephone company, an oil company, two gas companies, and two electric utilities.

The number of shares of each stock purchased—the weight—was designed to emphasize those stocks that had highest return with the lowest risk. Certainly the portfolio has risk. But it will be monitored to make certain the investments are doing their job. In the meantime, Mrs. Black is receiving almost $5,000 annually to help her raise her family.

Mrs. Black's portfolio was brought up to date in 1982, as the table shows. The G. D. Searle 8s of 1981 were called in 1981 and the proceeds put into a money market fund that yielded 11 percent, but with prospects for yields to increase. During the

An Income Portfolio for Mrs. Black

	1976						1982				
	Price November 1976	Number of Shares	Value	Dividends or Interest	Total Income	Maturity	Price January 1982	Number of Shares	Value	Dividends or Interest	Total Income
Cash or money market			$ 1,675						$11,675*	11.00	$1,284
Fixed-income securities											
Short-term 1-year Treasury notes, 5/77	101.10	10	10,110	6.75%	$ 675	1/83	99.00	10	9,900	13.625	1,363
Intermediate-term 2–5 year											
Treasury notes, 5/78	102.15	10	10,215	6.857	686		80.16	12	9,660	9.00	1,090
Commercial credit 8.875s 86	101.00	5	5,050	8.875	444	2/87	77.00	5	3,850	8.875	444
G. D. Searle 8s 81	104.5	10	10,450	8.00	800		called		—	—	0
Total fixed income			$35,825		$2,605				$35,085		$4,181
Common and preferred stock											
American Brands	41	200	$ 8,200	$2.76	$ 552		36	400	$14,400	3.25	$1,300
AT&T	59	50	2,950	$3.50	175		58	50	2,900	5.40	270
Texaco	27	50	1,350	$2.10	105		31	50	1,550	2.70	135
Columbia Gas System	25	200	5,000	$2.14	428		31	200	6,200	2.20	440
Consolidated Natural Gas	28	100	2,800	$2.30	230		18	100	1,800		
Houston Ind.	26	200	5,200	$1.64	328		21	200	4,200	2.16	432
Pacific Gas & Electric	21	200	4,200	$1.96	392		21	200	4,200	2.72	544
Total			$29,700		$2,210				$35,250		$3,121
Total portfolio			$67,200		$4,815				$70,335		$7,302
Return				7.16%							10.4%

*Included $10,000 from called Searle bonds.

SOURCE: Frederick Amling & Associates, Washington, D.C.

period, all the income was paid to Mrs. Black. Analyze the portfolio and determine what the performance was for the five-year period and whether it met Mrs. Black's goals. How could the portfolio be modified or changed?

SELECTED READINGS

COHN, R. A., W. G. LEWELLEN, R. C. LEASE, and G. G. SCHLAIBAUM. "Individual Investor Risk Aversion and Investment Portfolio Composition." *The Journal of Finance*, May 1975, p. 605.

GARGETT, DAVE R. "The Link between Stock Prices and Liquidity." *Financial Analysts Journal*, January–February 1978.

GOLDSMITH, DAVID. "Transactions Costs and the Theory of Portfolio Selection." *The Journal of Finance*, September 1976, p. 1127.

GOOD, WALTER R. "Short Term Clients and Long Term Performance." *Financial Analysts Journal*, November–December 1978.

GRAY, WILLIAM S. "The Major Shortfall of ERISA." *Financial Analysts Journal*, July–August 1977.

JENSEN, MICHAEL C. "The Performance of Mutual Funds in the Period 1945–64." *Journal of Finance*, May 1968.

KORSCHOT, BENJAMIN C. "Prudence Before and After ERISA." *Financial Analysts Journal*, July–August 1977.

REILLY, F. K., and E. F. DRZYCIMSKI. "Alternative Industry Performance and Risk." *Journal of Financial and Quantitative Analysis*, June 1974, p. 423.

ROLL, RICHARD. "Investment Diversification and Bond Maturity." *The Journal of Finance*, March 1971, p. 51.

SPIGELMAN, JOSEPH H. "What Basis for Superior Performance?" *Financial Analysts Journal*, May–June 1974, p. 32.

WALLICH, HENRY C. "Investment Income during Inflation." *Financial Analysts Journal*, March–April 1978.

CHAPTER 23

THE GROWTH PORTFOLIO

We continue our discussion of portfolio management with a consideration of the growth portfolio. The goal of the growth portfolio is to increase the future value of the portfolio. This is done by placing greater emphasis on capital gains than on current income. Young investors trying to build an estate would be interested in growth of capital. Investors attempting to become financially independent in their retirement years would be interested in capital growth. At some future time, the goal can be changed and the larger amount of capital can be used to produce income. Individuals in the 50 percent tax bracket are interested in capital gains, since long-term capital gains (over one year) are taxed at a maximum rate of 20 percent.

Ordinarily, the growth-oriented investor will reinvest dividend income to build capital. In fact, the IRA account is an excellent way to shelter income from taxes and build capital for retirement. When an investor can invest $2,000 a year at 8 to 15 percent on which no income tax is paid, it doesn't take too long to build a sizable amount of capital. Income securities under these circumstances can be considered a growth portfolio.

THE GROWTH CONCEPT AND SELECTING GROWTH STOCKS

The fundamentals of portfolio management must be applied vigorously if success is to be achieved in the management of the growth-stock portfolio. The growth concept assumes that a return substantially higher than the market will be sought with a low amount of current income. Therefore, great care must be taken in the selection of stocks for the portfolio. The principle of diversification cannot be ignored, since too few securities in a portfolio will result in too much risk, and too many securities will provide insufficient return.

The growth investor is very interested in selecting stocks that are efficient—those that have a high return and a low risk relative to the market. The growth investor is focusing on the future growth of the portfolio, since the objective is to increase the value of the portfolio some time in the future. Current income is not needed, but long-term capital gains are sought. Many growth investors are in a high tax bracket and wish to avoid paying a high tax rate on current income. Other investors with a small amount of capital are trying to increase capital in the future to make them financially independent. The criteria for the selection of growth stocks include the following:

1. Substantial growth in earnings and dividends.
2. Very stable earnings growth rate.
3. Low dividend payments.
4. High expected return.
5. A relatively low variability of expected return.

In addition, the fundamentals of analysis must be stressed. In-depth analyses must be undertaken of product demand, competitors' positions, and the competitive position, operating characteristics, and management of the company. The primary emphasis, however, is on the growth and stability of earnings per share over time. Certainly, the identification of growth industries would be helpful, although the final selection must be based on the individual companies.

The selection of growth stocks might very well come from a list of industries. However, two points must be made about the selection of growth stocks. The process suggested in the text is to choose the leading companies in the leading industries of an economy that is growing or is expected to grow in the future. But our focus must still be on value and high return to risk, not on just a rapid increase in sales of a new product related to research, or on high depreciation charges, stock dividends, able management, and rapid growth of earnings.

The fundamental approach is ideally suited to the selection of stocks for a growth portfolio. The idea is to invest in companies in strongly competitive industries. Several industries were identified in Chapter 12 as strongly competitive industries which an investor might consider. Table 23–1 provides a list of those industries and some companies that are competitive leaders in the industry. Since not all leading firms will be selling at an attractive price, the investor should select those companies that have an attractive return-to-risk ratio. Companies that seem to be attractive on a return-to-risk basis are also listed in Table 23–1. The growth investor can select stocks from this list to meet investment objectives.

If an investor were to have set up a growth portfolio from among these securities, which would be selected? What criteria would be used?

First and foremost, the investor would look at expected return—in this case, focusing on the return expected by the analyst, according to knowledge of the company and its future growth prospects. The investor would also want a company whose stock was selling at an attractive return-to-risk ratio.

TABLE 23-1

Industries and Companies That Appear Attractive for Investment
from among the S&P 500 Common Stocks,* 1982

Industry/Subindustry	Companies in Industry/Subindustry	Current S&P 500 Listing	Reward-to-Risk Ratio (Companies with R/R ≥ 1.00)
Broadcasting—cable TV	Teleprompter Corporation†		
	Storer Broadcasting Company		
	Cox Incorporated	x	−0.23
	Capital Cities Communications, Inc.	x	
Telephone & telegraph— telegraph services	Western Union Corporation		
	Graphic Scanning Corporation		
Computing equipment	IBM	x	1.42
	Burroughs Corporation	x	1.26
	Control Data Corporation	x	
	Data General Corporation	x	
	Digital Equipment Corporation	x	
	NCR Corporation	x	0.07
	Prime Computer, Incorporated		
	Sperry Corporation	x	1.52
	Storage Technology Corporation		
	Wang Laboratories, Incorporated	x	
	Xerox Corporation	x	1.20
Electronic equipment and components	Conrac Corporation		
	Emerson Electric Company	x	1.08
	General Electric Company	x	1.12
	Gould Incorporated	x	
	Itek Corporation		
	McGraw-Edison Company	x	0.11
	Oak Industries, Incorporated		
	Plantronics, Incorporated		
	Ranco, Incorporated		
	Robertshaw Controls Company		
	Scientific-Atlanta, Incorporated		
	Square D Company	x	0.98
	Thomas & Betts Corporation	x	0.85
	Westinghouse Electric Company	x	0.24
Semiconductors	AMP Incorporated	x	0.61
	Intel Corporation	x	
	Motorola Incorporated	x	0.35
	National Semiconductor	x	
	Texas Instruments	x	1.77

*Those checked are the S&P 500 companies. The reward-to-risk ratios underlined are the securities considered attractive for investment. A reward-to-risk ratio was not available for all companies. Reward to risk and return to risk are synonymous terms.

†Largest.

TABLE 23–1 (Continued)

Industry/Subindustry	Companies in Industry/Subindustry	Current S&P 500 Listing	Reward-to-Risk Ratio (Companies with R/R $\geq$ 1.00)
Metalworking machinery and equipment			
(a) Machine tools	Acme-Cleveland Corporation	x	
	Brown & Sharpe Manufacturing Company	x	
	Cincinnati Milacron Incorporated	x	0.71
	Giddings & Lewis, Incorporated	x	
	Monarch Machine Tool Company	x	0.78
	Kennametal Incorporated		
	Ex-Cell-O Corporation	x	1.05
	SPS Technologies, Incorporated		
(b) Industrial heating	Condec Corporation		
Instruments for measurement, analysis, and control	Honeywell, Incorporated	x	1.46
	Beckman Instruments, Incorporated	x	0.84
	Hewlett-Packard Company	x	1.46
	Perkin Elmer Corporation	x	
	Teletronix Incorporated	x	
	General Signal Corporation		
	Varian Associates, Incorporated		
Telephone and telegraph equipment	ITT	x	0.18
	ATT	x	1.37
	Harris Corporation	x	
	MA Communications	x	
	Northern Telecommunications	x	
	Rolm Corporation	x	
	Scientific Atlanta	x	
	GTE		0.29
	General Instrument Corporation		
	United Telecommunications		0.90
Metalworking machinery and equipment—tool and die industry	Allied Products		
	Gleason Works		
	Norton Company		
Consumer electronics	Craig Corporation		
	E. F. Johnson Company		
	North American Philips		
	RCA	x	0.59
	Superscope		
	Wurlitzer Company		
	Zenith Radio Corporation	x	−0.05
	Maytag Company	x	0.45
	Sunbeam Corporation	x	0.13
	Whirlpool Corporation	x	0.47

TABLE 23–1   (Continued)

Industry/Subindustry	Companies in Industry/Subindustry	Current S&P 500 Listing	Reward-to-Risk Rato (Companies with R/R $\geq$ 1.00)
Medical and dental Instruments			
(a) X ray and electronic equipment	Cordis Corporation		
	Flow General Incorporated		
	Medtronic, Incorporated		
	Narco Scientific Incorporated		
	(Others from analytical electronics group)		
(b) Surgical and medical instruments	American Sterilizer Company		
	CR Bard, Incorporated	x	0.21
	Bausch & Lomb		
	Becton, Dickinson & Company	x	0.84
	Cooper Labs		
	U.S. Surgical Corporation		
Metalworking machinery			
(a) Welding apparatus	Harsco Corporation		
	Cooper Industries	x	0.57
	Dover Corporation		
(b) Metal cutting	Mesta Machine Company		
Drugs	American Home Products Corporation	x	
	Bristol Myers Company	x	0.37
	Lilly Eli & Company	x	1.24
	Merck & Company	x	1.16
	Pfizer & Company	x	
	Schering-Plough Corporation	x	
	Searle G. D. & Company	x	
	SmithKline	x	0.16
	Squibb	x	
	Sterling Drug Incorporated	x	0.61
	Upjohn	x	
	Warner Lambert Company	x	0.75

The investor would be interested in diversification, but would be selective and focus on a relatively few issues. Time diversification would be considered. To do this, the investor would choose common stocks based upon the expected growth in the market. If market prices are low, then virtually all the money would be invested in common stocks. If prices are high, the investor would reduce the holdings of common stock substantially.

The above comment implies that the investor will be willing to trade—that is, be willing to sell stocks when they are perceived to be overpriced and buy when they are underpriced. Therefore there will be times when the investor has 100 percent of the portfolio in common stocks. There will also be times when the investor has the bulk of investments in defensive securities, such as Treasury bills or money-market securities.

The amount of money invested in each stock will be a function of the investor's knowledge of the return and risk attributes of each company. Those that are considered more attractive will represent a higher percentage of the portfolio. There is no need to have equal amounts of each stock in the portfolio.

The amount invested in stocks which are risky assets and risk-free assets such as Treasury bills must be decided by the investor. If the market is overpriced, then the stock portion should be reduced and the defensive portion increased. Money market securities should be increased. If the market is underpriced, then the percentage of equities will be relatively high. This assumes that the securities in the growth portfolio have the same attributes as the cyclical market. Some growth stocks do tend to increase in price over time, and these stocks should be held for long-term growth. The investor's attitudes about a defensive or aggressive investment posture are reflected in Figure 23–1.

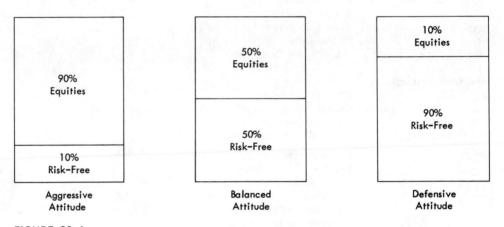

FIGURE 23–1

Diversification Examples Based on Aggressive and Defensive Investor Attitudes

Which companies would be chosen? Companies in growth industries would be selected because a growth industry should provide an atmosphere favorable for investment. Then common stocks that offered the possibility of a substantial return based primarily on the expected growth rate of earnings and the P/E ratio three years in the future and stocks with a reward to risk ratio of 1.00 or higher would be chosen.

INVESTMENT RISKS AND THE GROWTH PORTFOLIO

The growth investor faces all the investment risks. The growth investor attempts to solve the inflation risk by investing in securities that provide a higher return than the rate of inflation plus some real return. The emphasis on capital growth is designed to accomplish this.

The business risk is minimized by selecting strongly competitive companies, just as was done in the company analysis section of the book.

PORTFOLIO MANAGEMENT AND PERFORMANCE

The market risk and the money rate risk associated with fluctuation of stock prices are compensated for by attention to the timing of the purchase and sales of securities.

Thus the emphasis in the diversification process is to minimize these risks. The stock selection by industry and company compensates for the business risk. Timing the purchase minimizes the market risk.

Setting Up the Growth Portfolio

It is important for the growth investor to estimate the possible direction of the market and interest rates before setting up a growth portfolio. This is done to minimize the market risk. In January 1982 the market as measured by the DJIA was low and interest rates were rising. Economic recovery was expected later in 1982, with full recovery expected in 1983 and 1984. Low common stock prices suggested an aggressive investment attitude. Rising interest rates suggested a defensive policy with emphasis on short-term fixed-income securities. The portfolio, therefore, would emphasize equities. A suggested balance would be 30 percent money market securities and 70 percent equities. Stocks selected from Table 23–1 would make up 70 percent of the portfolio. A possible solution to the growth investor's problem appears in Table 23–2.

TABLE 23–2
Suggested Diversification of a Growth Portfolio, 1982

Security	Percentage of Portfolio
Short-term fixed income	
Treasury Bills	30%
Common Stock	70
Aerospace—Boeing	
Communications—AT&T	
Computer—IBM	
Defense—Litton	
Electronics—Texas Instruments	
Health care—Schering-Plough	
Oil service—Schlumberger	
Total	100%

The amount of money invested in each stock will be a function of the investor's attitude toward expected reward and risk. All the companies are selling at a price that provides a favorable reward-to-risk ratio. This is based on the result of the valuation models discussed under company analysis in Chapter 18. It is unnecessary to use a computer to make the reward-to-risk calculation. All the investor needs are these data:

1. An estimate of the expected rate of return.
2. An estimate of the risk-free rate of return.
3. The standard deviation of past returns.

The estimate of the expected return is based on expected price in some year in the future. Next the dividends are estimated. Then the return expected on the current price is estimated (see Chapter 18). The risk-free return is equal to the yield on Treasury bills. If Treasury bill yields are 13 percent, the risk-free return is 13 percent. To obtain the standard deviation of past returns, calculate the annual return for each of the last ten years. Calculate the average return from the data and then calculate the standard deviation around the average. When these three estimates are obtained, the reward-to-risk ratio is calculated by subtracting the Treasury bill rate from the expected return and dividing by the standard deviation.

AT&T in the portfolio had an expected return of 27 percent at a price of 59. The riskfree return was 13.5 percent. The standard deviation of AT&T's annual return was 9.4. The reward to risk ratio is therefore $(27 - 13.5) \div 9.4 = 13.5 \div 9.4 = 1.44$. Based on several studies, a reward-to-risk ratio of 1.00 or higher is satisfactory.

Strategy: Planning the Next Move

When putting the growth portfolio together, the investor should plan the future course of events. For example, what should the investor do if the price of a stock drops? What should the investor do if prices rise? It would seem wise for the investor to develop a strategy for each stock. This is done because no one is certain if a stock will rise or fall in price. AT&T may be used as an example. The price is 59, and the stocks were a good buy at 50. The stock seems to be unattractive on a reward-to-risk ratio at 70. As a strategy, the investor would try to buy at 50 and sell at 70. The investor would continue to hold until one of these events takes place. The strategy for the stocks in the growth portfolio is summarized in Table 23–3.

TABLE 23–3
Strategy for the Growth Portfolio

Company	Buy Price	Sell Price
Boeing	$25	$ 40
AT&T	50	65
IBM	50	75
Litton	50	82
Texas Instruments	75	125
Schering-Plough	30	45
Schlumberger	50	120

A Growth Portfolio from the Dow Jones Industrial Averages

Often the investor is overwhelmed with the job of selecting growth stocks, since the universe of securities is so great. Therefore, let's limit the number of securities from which to choose to those in the Dow Jones Industrial Average, which includes 30 stocks. By reducing the universe of stocks, the investor is better able to identify growth stocks. Stocks that have a reward-to-risk ratio greater than 1.00 should be selected, along with stocks that have a high earnings growth rate and dividend growth rate. A growth portfolio using these criteria was selected and is summarized in Table 23–4.

TABLE 23–4

A Conservative Growth Portfolio Selected from the DJIA

Company	Approximate Price January 1982	Dividend			Earnings Growth Rate (10 Years)†	Expected Return‡
		$	%	Rate*		
Eastman Kodak	70	3.00	4.3	9	10	14.3
Esmark	48	1.84	3.8	17	22	25.8
General Electric	59	3.20	5.4	10	12	17.4
Minnesota Mining & Manufacturing	55	3.00	5.5	14	12	17.5
Procter & Gamble	83	4.20	5.1	11	11	16.1
Standard Oil of California	35	2.40	6.9	13	18	25.9
S&P 500	115	6.55	5.35	9	11	16.2

*Ten-year growth rate.

†Annual average rate of return for period 1971 to 1980.

‡Growth rate of earnings plus dividend used as an alternative to the valuation equation rate of return.

The stocks selected, for the most part, had a reward-to-risk ratio greater than 1.00. The stocks had a substantial expected return. They had experienced a growth of earnings higher than that of the S&P 500 Index, and the dividend growth rate on the average was quite high. The stocks in the portfolio were chosen because of the high expected returns, low dividend return, and attractive reward-to-risk ratio. The amount of an individual stock in the portfolio is at the discretion of the investor.

Thus we have a growth protfolio that was established using statistical principles and reward-to-risk analysis. The number of stocks in the portfolio is relatively low, yet it represents a way in which an investor can construct a reasonably efficient portfolio using rudimentary statistical knowledge and fewer stocks. The emphasis is on reward, risk, and growth.

The investor would manage the portfolio on the basis of what happens in the market. As long as the expected return is satisfactory, stocks would be held. If the expected return declined and the reward-to-risk ratio dropped significantly below 1.00, the stock would be sold. Under this plan, the investor would change the portfolio infrequently.

Obviously, the relatively few securities in the growth portfolios presented represent the individual investor's position. If it were a growth portfolio of a large institution, the number of issues would increase. In the process, the expected returns probably would decline, since selectivity declines. Yet this is a practical problem associated with large portfolios. In spite of the fact that a few securities can provide superior returns with only small additional risk, it is impractical to invest a billion-dollar portfolio in only seven stocks.

Timing and the Growth Portfolio

The dollar amount invested in securities in the growth portfolio can be used to purchase additional risky assets if prices can become attractive. By the same token, when risky securities become overpriced (if they do), they can be sold. The proceeds can be used to add to risk-free assets (Treasury bills) or to buy risky assets that appear to be underpriced. More will be said about this subject in Chapter 24.

International Diversification

Since the world competitive environment is changing, investors might wish to consider investment in foreign securities for growth. Such investments allow investors to gain from changes in currency values. As of 1982, the dollar was strong, but other currencies increased in value relative to the dollar. Economic growth was expected to be strong in Japan in 1982, so a selection of Japanese companies in a growth portfolio might be appropriate. Table 23–5 provides a list of international companies that might be considered for a growth portfolio. The amount purchased will be a function of the investor's knowledge about the expected return-and-risk trade off.

TABLE 23–5
Selected International Stocks for Capital Gains

Company	Country	Price ($)
Marks & Spencer	Great Britain	$ 2.38
Schering	Germany	127.80
Asahi Glass	Japan	3.05
Canon	Japan	4.35
Fujitsu	Japan	3.20
Nippon Steel	Japan	0.82

Some growth was expected in selected companies in other countries as well. Germany and Great Britain are also represented in Table 23–5. These are not the only foreign stocks that might be considered, but they serve as examples.

Table 23–6 provides a forecast of returns expected in various foreign markets for the six-month period as of November 1981. In addition to Japan, the United Kingdom, and Germany, Hong Kong and Netherlands equity are expected to provide excellent total returns for the period. Companies in these countries may also be considered for investment opportunities for growth.

If an investor cannot find individual companies that are attractive, he or she might select an international mutual fund. KIF is an example of an international mutual fund that might be considered. There are some other international funds:

G. T. Pacific Fund

New Perspective Fund

Putnam International Equities Fund

Rowe Price International Fund

Scudder International Fund

Templeton World Fund

TABLE 23–6

A Forecast for International Equity Markets

Country	% of Index (9/81)	Market Index (11/3/81)	6-Mo. Forecast	Capital Apprec., %	6-Mo. Yield, %	Total Return, %	Exchange Rate (11/3/81)*	6-Mo. Forecast*	Currency Gain/Loss, %	Total Return, % (US$)
USA	52.1	117.9	125.0	+6.0	2.5	+8.5	—	—	—	+8.5
Japan	19.5	321.5	360.0	+12.0	0.8	+12.8	227.15	210.00	+7.6	+20.4
U.K.	7.2	173.4	190.0	+9.6	3.1	+12.7	1.8655	1.95	+4.3	+17.0
Germany	3.6	84.1	90.0	+7.0	2.9	+9.9	0.4490	0.47	+4.7	+14.6
Canada	4.3	206.1	205.0	—	2.0	+2.0	0.8300	0.83	—	+2.0
Australia	2.3	98.9	100.0	—	2.3	+2.3	1.1431	1.14	−0.3	+2.0
Switzerland	1.8	80.8	85.0	+5.2	1.7	+6.9	0.5532	0.58	+4.8	+11.7
Hong Kong	1.5	870.7	1,200.0	+37.8	1.3	+39.1	0.1718	0.18	+4.8	+39.1
Netherlands	1.1	87.0	100.0	+14.9	3.0	+17.9	0.4077	0.43	+5.5	+23.4
Singapore	0.7	496.0	540.0	+8.9	1.0	+9.9	0.4826	0.48	−0.5	+9.4
World	100.0	143.7	160.1	+11.4	2.7	+14.1	—	—	—	+14.1

*U.S.$ per local currency, except yen, which is yen per U.S.$.

SOURCE: Keystone International Fund (KIF), Boston, Massachusetts, as of November 4, 1981.

WORLD STOCK MARKETS

Here's a recap of the performance of eighteen stock markets in leading countries around the world as of November 30, 1981 based upon data supplied by Capital International Perspective of Geneva. It should be noted that the percentage changes are in local currencies and are calculated from Capital International's market indexes.

Rank		3 months % change	6 months % change	9 months % change	12 months % change	Price/ earnings ratio	Yield
1	SINGAPORE	19.1%	−13.9%	−10.1%	10.0%	22.0	2.0
2	SWEDEN	13.5	36.4	49.0	73.3	8.9	4.2
3	UNITED STATES	2.9	−3.8	−4.0	−10.0	8.0	5.6
4	DENMARK	2.1	11.6	27.2	43.5	8.6	4.5
5	NORWAY	1.2	20.9	0.8	−10.5	5.6	5.1
6	FRANCE	0.8	9.7	−14.9	−21.8	6.0	8.6
7	MEXICO					3.8	7.1
8	BELGIUM	−1.4	−2.2	−16.2	−17.5	9.7	17.3
9	SWITZERLAND	−2.9	−3.5	−10.0	−10.6	10.7	3.5
10	NETHERLANDS	−3.0	−0.1	−9.0	−10.9	5.5	7.6
11	AUSTRIA	−3.3	−8.4	−14.5	−17.3	22.7	3.7
12	GERMANY	−3.4	0.6	4.8	−0.6	9.0	6.1
13	UNITED KINGDOM	−3.8	3.0	4.0	0.8	8.4	6.0
14	AUSTRALIA	−7.6	−20.0	−12.6	−25.6	9.9	4.9
15	SPAIN	−8.1	9.5	20.6	31.9	15.4	10.4
16	JAPAN	−8.2	−2.8	14.9	18.7	17.3	1.8
17	CANADA	−8.6	−15.3	−8.2	−15.9	8.9	4.5
18	ITALY	−12.4	−26.8	−12.8	18.9	Loss	1.7
19	HONGKONG	−15.3	−17.7	−6.3	−3.6	13.4	3.7
	THE WORLD INDEX	−1.6	−4.0	−0.3	−4.2	9.3	4.9

WORLD BOND MARKETS

Listed below are yield and return data for the world's major international and domestic bond markets, as calculated by *InterSec Research Corp.*, New York, from its proprietary intermediate-term indexes.

Debt markets	Yield to maturity (compounded annually) 11/30/81	8/31/81	11/30/80	Cumulative index value Loc. cur.	U.S. $	from 10/31/81 Loc. cur.	U.S. $	from 8/31/81 Loc. cur.	U.S. $	from 5/31/81 Loc. cur.	U.S. $	from 11/30/80 Loc. cur.	U.S. $	Index characteristics at 11/30/81 weighted average coupon	maturity
U.S. dollar															
— Domestic*	14.0	16.4	13.6	151.9	151.9	9.8	9.8	15.3	15.3	9.4	9.4	11.9	11.9	10.8%	8.5
— Yankee	16.1	16.7	13.7	138.9	138.9	7.1	7.1	6.1	6.1	5.0	5.0	0.9	0.9	11.4	8.0
— Euro	14.4	16.1	13.4	157.3	157.3	10.9	10.8	12.2	12.2	9.5	9.5	7.9	7.9	12.2	8.6
British pound															
— Domestic	15.6	15.2	12.7	211.0	176.1	5.1	12.0	2.1	8.4	1.5	−3.9	1.8	−15.6	11.5	8.3
— Euro	15.7	16.1	13.9	NA	NA	8.0	15.0	5.9	12.4	3.9	−1.6	5.9	−12.2	12.0	8.5
Canadian dollar															
— Domestic	15.7	16.9	13.3	144.3	121.6	10.5	13.2	9.9	12.4	6.1	8.5	2.6	3.6	9.9	7.8
Dutch guilder															
— Domestic	11.1	11.9	10.0	179.1	239.8	6.0	8.9	8.0	21.6	8.6	16.2	6.3	−8.1	10.3	8.6
— Euro	11.8	11.8	10.3	172.9	231.4	2.1	4.9	4.7	17.9	6.1	13.5	4.8	−9.4	10.9	6.4
French franc															
— Domestic*	15.8	16.4	14.0	NA	NA	2.2	3.8	5.9	11.2	11.8	11.1	4.7	−15.9	10.4	8.2
— Euro	17.6	18.0	13.8	168.4	155.5	1.8	3.4	5.4	10.7	3.4	2.7	−2.2	−21.4	12.4	7.0
German mark															
— Domestic*	9.7	10.8	8.7	186.9	270.4	4.2	6.2	9.1	20.9	12.2	17.9	3.0	−10.2	8.6	8.2
— Euro	9.7	10.6	9.1	160.8	232.6	4.1	6.1	7.9	19.6	10.8	16.5	4.6	−8.9	8.9	8.7
Japanese yen															
— Domestic*	8.3	8.9	9.1	187.3	262.9	3.1	11.9	4.3	11.8	4.6	9.2	11.0	12.1	7.8	8.3
— Foreign	9.0	9.4	9.3	191.7	268.9	4.0	12.9	4.7	12.2	7.0	11.6	11.2	12.2	7.6	8.4
Swiss franc															
— Domestic*	5.6	6.0	4.7	NA	NA	3.8	8.1	4.7	26.6	5.8	23.7	1.3	−0.5	5.4	8.7
— Foreign	6.9	7.5	5.7	157.5	336.4	3.4	7.8	5.9	28.2	6.8	24.8	−1.5	−3.2	5.3	8.3
Global bond index					184.2		9.9		13.3		9.7		0.5		
Non-North American bond index					222.4		8.9		14.3		9.8		−5.1		

Notes: The indexes measure the combined effects of price movement, interest income and reinvestment of interest income. Bonds included in the indexes are seasoned, prime-quality supranational and government issues of common maturity, normally seven to ten years. Calculations are made from monthly prices. (The U.S. dollar domestic index is based on Merrill Lynch's Index No. 80 — government and federal agency issues of intermediate term.) Shown also are the weighted average coupon and maturity for each index, as well as its cumulative index value in both local currency and U.S. dollar terms since inception on December 31, 1972. All bonds are free from withholding tax for most international investors, except as noted by *. NA — Index does not date back to December 31, 1972. Source: InterSec Research Corp.

FIGURE 23–2

The Behavior of World Stock and Bond Markets

SOURCE: *Institutional Investor*, January 1982, p. 26.

Figure 23–2 provides data on the performance of leading world stock markets and bond markets. Notice that the United States market was third in performance for the three-month period. Swedish stocks would have been most attractive for investment for growth over the period covered.

SUMMARY

The concept of growth is familiar to almost all investors. The growth company is one that is growing in sales and earnings faster than the national economy and whose rate of growth is expected to continue in the future. Another characteristic of the growth company is its largely noncash dividend policy, since money is needed for reinvestment within the business to provide for the necessary expansion of facilities. The returns on such investments are usually better than returns that could be earned elsewhere. The investor who purchases growth shares is interested in future income and capital gains, not present returns. The investor in a high income tax bracket or one who wishes to build an estate would be interested in a growth company. Securities with a high expected return, low risk, and low dividend rate would be selected. The valuation of growth shares was explained in Chapter 18. The problem is one of estimating future return and standard deviation of returns (risk).

Examples of companies for potential growth were presented, as well as a few portfolios that demonstrated the position of various growth investors. Of particular importance is the list of companies for inclusion in a growth portfolio. The criteria for selection are important for the growth investor, in addition to the logic of the thought process and the investment decision.

Some investors might consider international companies for growth. Some companies were indicated as examples of foreign investment opportunities. A list of international mutual funds was provided for investors who find it difficult to select individual companies for investment.

SUMMARY OF PRINCIPLES

1. A growth portfolio emphasizes stocks that are efficient; that is, stocks that have the highest return and lowest risk.
2. A growth stock will have a growth of earnings and dividends greater than the S&P 500 Index, but will have a lower dividend payout.
3. The growth investor avoids current income in the hope of greater principal growth in the future.
4. The growth portfolio must be diversified to reduce risk.
5. The investor will be defensive by shifting between common stock and risk-free securities, depending upon expectations of the future.
6. A growth investor is wise to develop a strategy about each stock included in the portfolio.

1. What do we generally mean by the term *growth stock*?
2. Explain what a *growth investor* is.
3. What part do expected return and risk and beta play in the establishment of a growth portfolio?
4. Explain the thought process of making decisions for the growth portfolio.
5. Explain how stocks are selected for the growth portfolio.
6. Explain how the weights in a growth portfolio should be established.
7. Explain why an investor might wish international diversification in a growth portfolio.

PROBLEMS

1. Based on the discussion in the text, set up a growth portfolio that would meet the needs of a growth investor. Assume that the conditions described in the text are applicable. Be sure to determine the proportion in each security and the balance between risky and risk-free assets.
2. If you were to set up an international investment portfolio, in what countries would you invest and why? Refer to Table 23–6. How would you balance the portfolio between risky and risk-free assets?
3. Bring Table 23–4 up-to-date. How did the portfolio do?

CASE

In May of 1982, Dr. Martin owned the growth portfolio listed below. She hasn't paid much attention to the portfolio for several years and needs advice. She is still interested in growth, but is concerned about the economy. Find the current value of the portfolio and advise Dr. Martin.

Company	Price May 2, 1977	Number of Shares	Total Value	Dividend Income Per Share	Total
CBS	58	150	$ 8,700	$2.00	$ 300
La–Pacific	15	500[a]	7,500	.20	100
U.S. Gypsum	24	300	7,200	1.60	480
American Cyanamid	27	200	5,400	1.50	300
American Hospital Supply	23	150	3,450	.56	84
Johnson & Johnson	63	50	3,150	1.40	70
CIT	35	150	5,250	2.40	360
Borden	35	250	8,750	1.56	390
Norton Simon	36	205[b]	7,380	.50	102
Carrier	20	300	6,000	.64	192

[a]Split 2 for 1 in 1973.
[b]2 1/2% stock dividend declared in 1975.

Aetna L & C	33	200[c]	6,600	1.20	240
Philadelphia Life	13	210[d]	2,730	.25	52
U.S. F & G	36	150	5,400	2.48	372
Continental Oil	36	400[e]	14,400	1.40	560
Goodyear	20	200	4,000	1.10	220
Dart Industries	36	206[f]	7,416	1.00	206
Holiday Inns	12	200	2,400	.46	92
Total			$105,726		$4,120
S&P 500 Index	99				

[c]Split 2 for 1 in 1974.

[d]5% stock dividend declared in 1976.

[e]Split 2 for 1 in 1976.

[f]3% stock dividend paid in 1976.

SOURCE: *The Wall Street Journal* and Standard & Poor's *Stock Guide,* May 1976.

SELECTED READINGS

ANDREWS, JOHN R. "The Case for Investing in Growth." *Financial Analysts Journal,* November–December 1970, p. 55.

BABCOCK, GUILFORD C. "When Is Growth Sustainable?" *Financial Analysts Journal,* May–June 1970, p. 108.

DURAND, DAVID. "Growth Stocks and the Petersberg Paradox." *Journal of Finance,* September 1957.

HODGES, STEWARD D., and RICHARD A. BREALEY. "Dynamic Portfolio Selection." *Financial Analysts Journal,* November–December 1972, p.58.

HOLMES, JOHN R. "Growth, Risk, and Stock Valuation." *Financial Analysts Journal,* May–June 1976, p. 46.

JAHNKE, WILLIAM W. "The Growth Stock Mania Revisited." *Financial Analysts Journal,* January–February 1975, p. 42.

PRICE, LEE H. "Growth or Yield: The Choice Depends on Your Tax Rate." *Financial Analysts Journal,* July–August 1979.

CHAPTER 24

PORTFOLIO PERFORMANCE AND MANAGEMENT

According to the investment principles established in the preceding chapters, the investor should purchase a combination of stocks that provides the highest return with the lowest risk, and individual stocks with a satisfactory reward-to-risk ratio. But continual supervision of the portfolio must be conducted. Investors must be quickly responsive to market changes, and when expected return is too low or the risk too high in relation to return, action must be taken. The investor must take advantage of situations in which stocks are over- or underpriced.

Investors find it difficult to time the purchase and sale of securities correctly. Since no one can foresee the future, various methods and strategies have been developed to solve the dilemma of when to buy and sell.

TIMING THE PURCHASES OF SECURITIES

For the majority of people who invest, quality is the first consideration in the selection on investment securities. But after selecting quality companies, one must recognize the importance of timing in their purchase. When we examined the subject of potential return we found that a stock of excellent quality might still provide a return that was unsatisfactory. The timing concept, very simply, gives recognition to the cyclical characteristics of the securities market. Many examples can be given to dramatize the importance of the timing of stock purchases of quality companies. During 1980–82, high-technology, oil, defense, and oil service stocks became highly overpriced and then later in the period became underpriced.

Many long-term investors, however, invest on the assumption that it makes no difference what price you pay for a stock. In the long run, they reason, the good company will succeed; the price of its stock will go up and will eventually be higher than the purchase price. The buy-and-hold philosophy may be valid if they buy and hold the right stock. However, return can be improved with a fully timed and managed portfolio. With thought, patience, and experience, and without predicting the exact highs and lows of the market, investors can still be successful.

Another point that must be brought out in a discussion of timing is that urgency in investment decisions is often unwarranted. An investor is never required to buy a stock at a specific time. The *must-invest* concept has no part in the intelligent process of investment analysis and management. We are always faced with other alternatives—for example, putting funds into bonds or fixed-income securities, or simply holding cash and not making purchases of common stock. This is why investment "tips" are so incongruous with the investment decision-making process.

Price Strategies, Timing, and Management

One way to handle the problem of the timing of securities purchases would be to establish price goals for each stock and try to buy the stock at the predetermined price. Then, after the stock is purchased, a selling price and a holding period are determined. This process was discussed previously. This process requires a great deal of patience and presents the danger that one might miss out on some potentially excellent investment securities. Assume, for example, that an investor decides to buy a stock at 45. The current market price is 60. But the stock never goes down to 45; it continues up to 100. In this case, the goal was impossible, or at least unlikely to occur.

Another danger of waiting for a specific price to be reached is that a change may occur in the fundamental position of the company. A new analysis might reveal that the company was no longer desirable at the original price that was set. This again points up the need for continuous analysis of a company and the portfolio.

An example might help to clarify the good features of the process of price setting as a solution to the timing problem. Assume that an investor wishes to invest $100,000, most of which was the proceeds from life insurance and not previously invested. How should the investment program begin and what weight and consideration should be given to timing? The first step would be to place the funds in a liquid and marketable investment until the investment policy was established. Second, the person's investment objectives should be determined. Third, a portfolio should be constructed to meet the person's investment needs, considering the risks that the person can assume. Fourth, the securities to meet the portfolio requirements should be determined; and fifth, the securities should be acquired over the next six months or longer at attractive prices when and if they occur, to meet the yield and return the investor desires. If the stock market is low, it would be possible to invest more quickly. This process emphasizes selection and timing, and it offers one solution to the timing problem.

An actual case will demonstrate how this method works in practice. Some years ago, David Ganes inherited the tidy sum of $20,000. After considering Mr. Ganes's investment needs, the investment counselor decided he should have as his objective a combination of income and growth and his portfolio should be defensive in character, because of the uncertainty in the stock market. The market had dropped sharply and had established something of a resistance level around 560 of the DJIA. In order to achieve Mr. Ganes's objectives, it was decided that $10,000 of his funds should be put into a building and loan association to earn 5 percent. The remaining $10,000 was to be invested in a well-selected list of common stocks with both income and growth potential. Temporarily, all the money was kept in the bank while the portfolio was being established. The common stock portion was to be invested in telephone companies, public utilities, and industrial stocks.

Between the counselor and Mr. Ganes, a tentative list of securities was considered for purchase. On June 21, two stocks were purchased, and three more on June 22. These purchases put 70 percent of the common stock fund to work. Three additional companies were decided upon, but since it was thought that the current price was too high, a limit order was placed for them. The order for one of them was entered at 35 and was exercised when the market moved downward in October. Subsequently, in November and December of that year, the other orders were exercised at favorable prices.

The portfolio was put together over a period of eight months. The prices paid for the securities were much more attractive than the prices that had prevailed when the money was received by Mr. Ganes. The $10,000 in savings would be used as a protective fund, and a portion of it would be used to acquire additional common stock at favorable prices. If Mr. Ganes and his counselor had acted in haste and invested the funds immediately, he would have suffered a loss. Patience and price setting can be an excellent way to provide one solution to the timing problem. Ganes is a fictitious name for our investor, but the historic results portrayed were authentic.

PORTFOLIO MANAGEMENT AND PERFORMANCE

The best way to manage the investment portfolio is to monitor the portfolio closely to make certain it is meeting the established objectives. Portfolio management can be demonstrated by reference to the portfolio in Table 24–1. Only three securities were included to provide an example; the number of securities in actual practice would be higher. The portfolio was established with a certain price strategy in mind. The beginning portfolio had $19,000 in common stocks and $9,675 in Treasury bills, reflecting a defensive posture. The prices of the securities at the end of the quarter reflected substantial price changes. AT&T increased 10 points, Texas Instruments declined 10 points, and Schlumberger dropped 6 points. The net result was a $600 decline in the portfolio. The dividend income for the period was $205, so the portfolio suffered a net loss of $395. The rate of return on the portfolio was minus 2.1 percent. The S&P 500 Index, however, showed a return of 3.1 percent.

The portfolio did not do as well as the S&P 500 Index. What should the investor do? Based on the indicated strategy, the investor would use some of the money in Treasury bills to buy more of Texas Instruments and Schlumberger. Or the investor would review the other common stocks that were considered possible investment candidates and purchase stocks from that group. Or the investor might decide not to do anything. However, strategy would dictate that stocks should be purchased.

The results of one quarter's activity are inconclusive, but management would

TABLE 24–1
Portfolio Performance

Strategy	Stock	Pur- chase Price ($)	Number of Shares	Pur- chase Value ($)	Annual Divi- dend ($)	Price End of First Quarter ($)	Value End of First Quarter ($)	Quarterly Dividend Share ($)	Quarterly Dividend Total ($)	Quarterly Value Gain or Loss ($)	Quarterly Return ($)	Quarterly Return (%)
Sell above 65 Buy below 55	AT&T	$50	100	$5,000	$5.40	$60	$6,000	$1.35	$135	$1,000	$1,135	22.7%
Sell above 130 Buy below 90	Texas Instruments	85	100	8,500	2.00	75	7,500	0.50	50	(1,000)	(950)	(11.2)
Sell above 70 Buy below 55	Schlumberger	55	100	5,500	0.80	49	4,900	0.20	20	(600)	(580)	(10.5)
Total				$19,000			$18,400		$205	($600)	($395)	(2.1)%
S&P 500		116	1	116	6.55	118	118	1.63	1.63	2	3.63	3.1
Treasury bills		9,675	1	9,675	13.00	10,000	10,000		365	365	365	3.8

TABLE 24-2
Quarterly Performance of Portfolio (Rate of return, %)

	Year 1				Year 2				Year 3				Quarterly Return Average (%)	Quarterly Return Standard Deviation (%)	Ratio Portfolio Return S&P 500	Ratio Portfolio Risk to S&P 500 Risk
	Q_1	Q_2	Q_3	Q_4	Q_1	Q_2	Q_3	Q_4	Q_1	Q_2	Q_3	Q_4				
Portfolio	(2.1)	10.2	5.0	3.0	(2.0)	5.0	2.0	5.0	2.0	(3.0)	3.0	5.0	2.76	3.385	1.82	1.60
S&P 500	3.1	3.1	2.0	2.0	(2.0)	(1.0)	3.0	5.0	1.0	1.0	(2.0)	3.0	1.52	2.114	—	—

continue with growth as a goal. As each quarter developed, the investor would measure the performance and make changes to meet goals. As the quarterly returns of the portfolio are calculated, they are compared to the returns of the S&P 500. This was done in Table 24–2. It was assumed that the investment manager made changes in the portfolio based on strategy. The results are therefore clearly shown. In most of the quarters, the portfolio did better than the S&P 500. In fact, the average quarterly return for the portfolio was 2.76 percent compared to the return of the S&P 500 Index of 1.52 percent. Clearly, the portfolio earned a higher return and outperformed the S&P 500 Index with a 1.82 ratio.

The portfolio returns were less stable than the returns of the S&P 500 Index. The standard deviation of the portfolio was higher than that of the market, indicating higher risk. However, the portfolio risk to S&P 500 Index risk was 1.6. Thus the portfolio had 60 percent more risk than the S&P 500 Index. The portfolio enjoyed a return that was 82 percent higher. On a risk-adjusted basis, the portfolio provided a higher return with a higher risk, but the additional risk was lower than the additional rate of return.

The quarter-to-quarter performance of the portfolio is depicted in Figure 24–1, where the quarterly returns are charted. The chart clearly shows that the portfolio outperformed the S&P 500 Index. In the analysis of other portfolios, if the investor finds the percentage gain or loss always equal to the market, then the portfolio is exactly like the market. If the results are always less than the market, then the portfolio

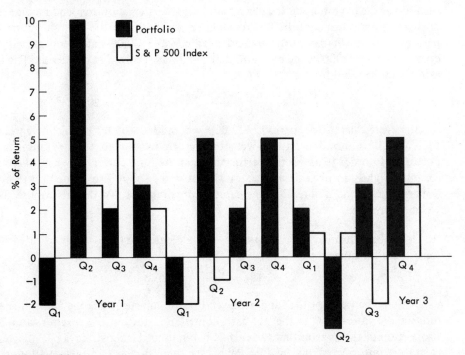

FIGURE 24–1

Quarterly Returns of Portfolio vs. Returns of S&P 500 Index

has done worse than the market. If the portfolio always does better than the market (higher gains and smaller losses), then the performance of the portfolio is superior to that of the market.

MEASURING THE RETURN OF THE PORTFOLIO

It is important to understand just what is to be measured in calculating the return of the portfolio. Conceptually, it would be wise to compare the return of the fund on a unit basis, just as mutual funds must do. They calculate the value of their shares twice each day, and the flow of money into and out of the fund is automatically compensated for in the daily calculations. It is also important to measure return flows into and out of the fund. Adjustments of the time value of money are easily made, and annual returns can be obtained by linking the returns together. Finally, a return formula must be used that accurately reflects the return of the portfolio.

INTERNAL METHOD—DOLLAR-WEIGHTED. The internal, or dollar-weighted method, calculates the total return of the portfolio without regard to the flow of funds. The basic equation is this:

$$R_{dw} = \frac{P_1 - P_0 + I}{P_0}$$

where P_1 represents the value of the fund at the end of the period, P_0 is the value of the fund at the beginning of the period, and I is the interest or dividend income received during the period or month. The formula simply tells you the internal return for the period. Assume that a portfolio had a value of $100,000 at the beginning of the quarter and $120,000 at the end, and that $300 was received in dividends. The internal rate of return would be:

$$\frac{\$120,000 - \$100,000 + \$300}{\$100,000} = \frac{\$20,300}{\$100,000} = 20.3\%$$

However, during the period, $12,000 was added to the portfolio from outside sources. The internal or dollar-weighted return overstated the profitability of the portfolio. In order to assess the performance of the fund correctly, we must change the formula slightly to provide an accurate measure of the return earned on the original dollars invested as well as the new capital contributions. To do this we use the time-weighted method.

TIME-WEIGHTED RATE OF RETURN. To calculate the time-weighted rate of return, we use the formula:

$$R_{tw} = \frac{P_1 - (P_0 + C)}{P_0 + (T \times C)}$$

where P_1 is the value of the fund at the end of the quarter, P_0 is the value at the beginning of the quarter, C is the net cash contributed during the quarter, and T is the proportion of the quarter that the cash is being used. Using 90 days per quarter, if the cash were put to work on the 45th day of the quarter, the T in the equation would be 45/90, or 1/2. Assume that the fund in the example above received $12,000 in contributions as well as $300 in dividends that must be reinvested. The contribution and dividends were received on the 45th day of the quarter; therefore, the cash flow was $12,300 and the time was 1/2. Substituting in the equation, we have:

$$= \frac{\$120,000 - (\$100,000 + \$12,300)}{\$100,000 + (1/2 \times \$12,300)}$$

$$= \frac{\$120,000 - \$112,300}{\$100,000 + \$6,150}$$

$$= \frac{\$7,700}{\$106,150}$$

$$= .0725$$

The quarterly return, therefore, was 7.25 percent. If this same rate continued for a year, we would link the returns together to find the annual return, as follows:

$$1.0725 \times 1.0725 \times 1.0725 \times 1.0725 = 1.3231$$

$$1.3231 - 1.00 = .3231 = 32.31 \text{ percent}$$

Thus the return for the year was 32.31 percent. This method is accurate when funds come in regularly, outside the control of the fund manager, and must be invested.

TIME-WEIGHTED METHOD—TESTING MANAGEMENT. In order to test the performance of management, the time-weighted return is found by calculating the return of the fund each time cash is put in or taken out. This provides a series of rates of return that can be linked together. Long periods are obviously weighted more heavily than short periods. This gives an exact time-weighted rate of return. The time-weighted rate is preferable to the dollar-weighted rate, but it is costly to calculate. The Bank Administration Institute (BAI), however, has provided an inexpensive computer program that allows these calculations to be made at relatively low cost.

Let us see how the manager might influence the results of the portfolio. Assume that the investment period is one quarter, as before. In the preceding case, the manager was required to invest the funds. This time, let's assume that the manager can invest the money or hold it, as he or she sees fit. Let's also assume that the value of the fund at the end of the quarter was $120,000 as before. The return for the investment period would be the same as our time-weighted example—.0725, or 7.25 percent. Now let's assume that the manager decided not to invest the $12,300 at the middle of the quarter because the market was thought to be overpriced.

We assume that the market moved up in the first half of the quarter and then decreased in the second half. Therefore, instead of investing the $12,300, the manager held the funds in Treasury bills. In the previous situation, it is assumed that the value of the portfolio was $115,000 at the middle of the quarter. Then $12,300 was added, and the portfolio dropped to $120,000 at the end of the period. The drop in the portfolio value was from $127,300 to $120,000, or $7,300/$127,300 = 5.7 percent. Now, with $12,300 in reserve in the checking account, the common stock value of the portfolio dropped 5.7 percent, from $115,000 to $108,445, because of the general drop in the market. And the value of the fund at the end of the period is $120,745 ($108,445 + $12,300). Therefore, because of good management, the portfolio has earned an extra $745. But let's see what it did to the return. The return was:

$$\frac{\$120{,}745 - \$100{,}000 + \$12{,}300}{\$100{,}000 + (1/2 \times \$12{,}300)} = \frac{\$8{,}445}{\$106{,}150} = 7.95\%$$

By good management, the fund manager improved the return of the fund from 7.25 percent for the period to 7.95 percent. The assumption is made that the returns in Table 24–2 were adjusted for the flow of money into the portfolio.

REGRESSION ANALYSIS—THE BETA AND ALPHA OF THE PORTFOLIO

The performance of the portfolio can be measured by the regression equation

$$Y_{port} = a + bX_{S\&P\ 500} + \epsilon$$

where Y_{port} is the return of the portfolio, a or alpha is the Y intercept, b or beta is the slope of the regression equation, and e epsilon is the error of the estimate. This was explained in Chapter 20. The values of the equation are found by fitting a line to the data. This was done for the portfolio in Table 24–2 and is depicted in Figure 24–2. The equation for the line is as follows:

$$Y_{port} = a + bX_{S\&P\ 500} + \epsilon \quad \text{where } Y_{port} = 1.37 + .74X_{S\&P\ 500} \pm 3.85.$$

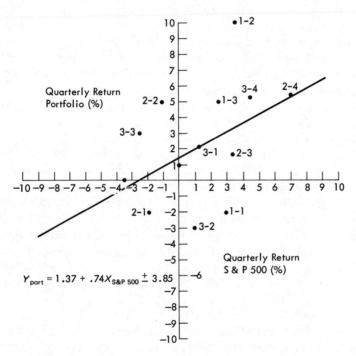

FIGURE 24–2

Regression Analysis—The Beta and Alpha of the Portfolio

PORTFOLIO MANAGEMENT AND PERFORMANCE

The portfolio has a positive alpha, which is good. The portfolio also has a beta lower than 1.00, which indicates less than market risk. The epsilon was relatively high, which is an indication of high unsystematic risk in the portfolio. The performance was better than the market, with less systematic risk, but the unsystematic risk was high. Portfolio performance was good.

Alpha and Beta

Those familiar with statistics know that the equation for the diagonal line is $Y = a + bX + \epsilon$. The X in the equation is the return of the market, and the Y is the return of the fund. The a in the equation represents that point where the diagonal line crosses the vertical axis; the b represents the slope of the diagonal line. The ϵ represents the unexplained variance. Thus, if the S&P 500 return increases by 1.0 percent and the return of the fund increases by .8 percent, the b, or beta, is .8/1.0, or .8. A beta of 1.5 or higher is said to be volatile, since as the market return increases 1.0 percent, the return of the fund would increase 1.5 percent; or if the return of the market declines 1.0 percent, the return of the fund declines 1.5 percent. It would be wise to have a high-beta portfolio or be in more volatile stocks as the market rises, and to be in low-beta stocks or in cash when the market declines. Beta explains the systematic risk and alpha and epsilon the unsystematic risk in the return of the fund.

A HIGH ALPHA OR A HIGH BETA? So what do we want, a high beta or a high alpha? Actually, we want a return that is stable, unvarying, and independent of the market. Hence, if returns on bonds went to 12 percent annually—or 3 percent quarterly—and the stock market continued to fluctuate, we would have a perfectly horizontal line explaining the relationship between the quarterly return of the S&P 500 and the return of the bond. This is shown in Figure 24–3. The equation would be $Y = 3.0$,

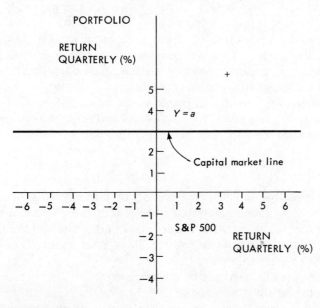

FIGURE 24–3

Capital-Market Line of a Fixed-Income Portfolio

since the beta has no relationship to the bond yield and is zero. So no matter what happens in the marketplace, the yield is positive and suggests the best alternative for the investor. As a matter of investment policy, we should strive to increase alpha through management and earn a high enough return to make us uninterested in seeking the market return only. If long-term bond yields did move to 12 percent, we certainly could expect the S&P 500 to reverse its return.

On the basis of a similar comparison, wouldn't we rather have 12 percent certain rather than a 15 percent return with a variability of plus or minus 14 percent that we could earn on stocks?

The only assumption that makes this analysis correct is that the bond is held to maturity and the investor has no plans to sell. Price changes are ignored. Unfortunately, the price does change, and the variation of bond return might be very close to the variation of the return of the S&P 500 Index. In that event, the b, or beta, might be close to 1.0, the a, or alpha, would be lower, and the correlation coefficient would be higher.

Correlation Analysis and Return

The other problem associated with the relationship of the return of the portfolio and the return of the S&P 500 is correlation. A perfect correlation, ρ, means that the return of the fund changes exactly as does the return of the market. Therefore, a .99 ρ means the fund return and the S&P 500 return are almost perfectly correlated. A zero correlation means there is no relationship between the return of the S&P 500 and the fund, as in the case of the 12 percent bond-investment yield. But which do we want, a high correlation to the market, or a high return with no correlation to the market (essentially a high alpha and a zero beta)? As before, we will accept readily a high return independent of the market (high alpha and low ρ) or a high beta and an opportunity to move to cash as the market peaks and buy stock at the market lows. Which we choose is realistically determined by what we can get in the marketplace, and obviously the high-beta stock to cash procedure is riskier than buying a 12 percent bond but, if it works, it is substantially more profitable.

The capital-market line of a portfolio of bonds would be as in Figure 24–4. The equation for this line is $Y_{port} = .66 + .3X_{S\&P\ 500} + .005$. The ρ (rho) is very low, indicating little correlation to the S&P 500 Index.

Beta Theory

Performance, or beta, is usually calculated on a monthly or quarterly basis for a period of three years or longer. Some even suggest that a five-year monthly beta is necessary to measure the relationship of the return of the portfolio to the return of the market. But why should we be interested in the past relationship of fund returns to returns of the market (the S&P 500)? After all, beta in this case concerns only part of the return of the portfolio as it relates to the return of the same market index; a beta of 2.0 means only that when the return of the market is 1.0 percent, the return portion *of the beta of the fund* is 2.0 percent. So why are we so interested in beta?

First, we are interested in the past beta because the portfolio beta changes slowly.

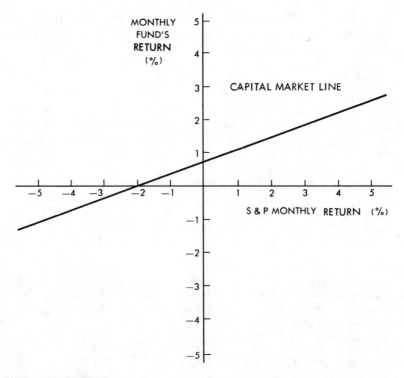

MONTHLY
FUND'S
RETURN
(%)

CAPITAL MARKET LINE

S & P MONTHLY RETURN (%)

FIGURE 24–4

Capital-Market Line of Bond Portfolio—.66 Percent Alpha and .3 Beta

Therefore, if a portfolio had a high beta in the past, it will probably have a high beta in the future. If this is the case, and if the market is expected to rise, then the high-beta stocks should move higher than the market. In short, beta analysis helps in prediction. We might not be able to predict the market precisely, but if the market moves up, we can expect the portfolio to increase in relation to the beta. This relationship was established in work done by Robert A. Levy of Computer Directions Advisers in Washington, D.C.[1] He demonstrated that high-beta stocks do move higher than the market when the market rises, and the return of the fund declines more than the return of the market when the market falls.

The second reason for beta analysis is that it allows the portfolio manager an opportunity to analyze portfolio policy and the individual securities, and to improve performance in the future. Without this type of analysis, little can be done to improve management.

Some criticism has been made of beta analysis. In retrospect, the criticism appears valid. Too much effort has gone into the relationship of the portfolio return to the market return in a relative sense. Not enough attention has been given to the search for high returns independent of the market, although some work has been done in

[1]Robert A. Levy, "Betas as Predicters of Return," *Financial Analysts Journal*, January–February 1974, p. 61.

the area of alpha analysis. Theoretically, however, we might follow the general portfolio policy of keeping our alpha up and our beta down and then search for common
stocks that will outperform the market.

Performance

INSTITUTIONAL PORTFOLIO PERFORMANCE. One mutual fund keeps track of its
performance in two ways. One is to compare the return of the fund to the return of a
market index and other funds. Table 24–3 provides such a comparison. The Keystone

TABLE 24–3

Comparative Performance of International Funds, November 1981

Fund	1981 YTD	LATEST 12 MO.	Since Inception (9/29/79)
G.T. Pacific Fund	+5.30%	+11.85%	
Keystone International Fund	−1.27	−4.49	+22.70%*
New Perspective Fund	+1.72	+1.09	
Putnam International Equities Fund	−0.99	−1.54	
Rowe Price International Fund	−4.56	−4.81	
Scudder International Fund	−5.80	−7.23	
Templeton World Fund	+5.34	+2.52	
Capital International World Index, (CIWI)	−5.19	−6.71	+18.45%†

*KIF since inception includes dividends paid November 79, November 80, and November 81.
†CIWI returns based on change in index and estimated yield.
SOURCE: For 1981 YTD and LATEST 12 MO.: Lipper Mutual Fund Performance Analysis,
November 12, 1981; all return figures assume the reinvestment of all capital gains distributions
and income dividends for the indicated period.

International Fund did better than the CIWI in 1981. So did G. T. Pacific, New
Perspective, Putnam, Rowe Price, and Templeton. The portfolio is also compared to
the CIWI, as seen in Figure 24–5. An index of 1.000 would indicate the KIF portfolio
earned a return relative to the market. Since its inception, the KIF portfolio has earned
the return of the market or higher.

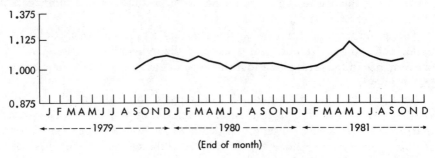

FIGURE 24–5

KIF Cumulative Performance Relative to CIWI (9/30/79–10/30/81)

MARKET LETTERS, MUTUAL FUNDS, AND PERFORMANCE.   More and more is being written about the performance of professional analysts. Usually, an average institutional investor cannot do better than the market. The notion that half do better than the S&P 500 Index and half do worse seems to be realistic. Figure 24–6 lets the investor

HULBERT'S 1981 PERFORMANCE RATINGS			
Newsletter	Dollar Value of Portfolio	Clarity (1)	Percentage Gain or Loss
The Boswell Report	$10,373	B	+ 3.7
Cabot Market Letter	10,509	A	+ 5.1
The Dines Letter			
Short-Term Trading Port.	9,083	B	− 9.2
Model Portfolio	5,923	B	−40.8
Supervised Long-Term			
#1. Good Grade	7,796	B	−22.0
#2. Speculative	11,549	B	+15.5
#5. Precious Metals	5,605	B	−43.9
#6. Short Sales	10,536	B	+ 5.4
Dow Theory Forecasts			
Income Stocks	8,756	B	−12.4
Investment Stocks	9,452	B	− 5.5
Growth Stocks	10,603	B	+ 6.1
Speculative Stocks	9,414	B	− 5.9
Dow Theory Letters	11,028	A	+10.3
Granville Market Letter	10,289	A	+ 2.9
Green's Commodity M.C.	11,709	A	+17.1
Growth Stock Outlook	11,157	A	+11.6
Harry Browne's S.R.	9,456	A	− 5.4
Heim Investment Letter	11,089	A	+10.9
Holt Investment Advisory	11,402	B	+14.0
Intl. Harry Schultz Letter	8,494	B	−15.0
Market Logic			
Aggressive Stocks	10,886	A	+ 8.9
Conservative Stocks	10,448	A	+ 4.5
Special Situations	10,885	A	+ 8.9
Myers Finance & Energy	9,350	A	− 6.5
Standard & Poor's Outlook			
Foundation Stocks	10,634	A	+ 6.3
Growth Stocks	11,781	A	+17.8
Speculative Stocks	10,127	A	+ 1.3
Income Stocks	10,788	A	+ 7.9
Professional Investor			
NYSE Scan	9,643	B	− 3.6
AMEX Scan	9,485	B	− 5.1
OTC Scan	9,403	B	− 6.0
Investment Grade Stocks	10,993	B	+ 9.9
Professional Tape Reader	10,686	A	+ 6.9
RHM Survey	5,152	B	−48.5
Ruff Times	9,739	B	− 2.6
Smart Money	8,541	B	−14.6
Speculator	9,328	B	− 6.7
United Business Service			
Growth Stocks	9,062	B	− 9.4
Cyclical Stocks	8,823	B	−11.8
Income Stocks	10,041	B	+ 0.4
Value Line OTC Survey	7,897	B	−21.0
Wellington Financial Letter			
(Stock)	10,390	A	+ 3.9
World Market Perspective	9,192	A	− 8.1
Zweig Forecast	13,777	A	+37.8

(1) Hulbert ranks newsletters in three grades according to their specificity and completeness.

HOW SIX INDEXES FARED LAST YEAR		
Dow Jones Industrials	$9,077	− 9.2
NYSE Composite	9,133	− 8.7
AMEX Market Value Index	9,198	− 8.0
S&P 500	9,028	− 9.7
NASDAQ OTC Composite	9,681	− 3.2
Wilshire 5000	9,247	− 7.5

FIGURE 24–6

Market Performance, Newsletter Writers

SOURCE: Barron's, January 18, 1982.

know how the newsletter writers performed relative to the market indexes. The market indexes were based on price changes only and did not include dividend income.

The results for the market indexes would have been better. The best performers, according to Hulbert, were Green's Commodity M. C.; S&P's Outlook, Growth Stocks; and Zweig Forecast. The worst performers were Dines Model Portfolio, Supervised Long-Term-Precious Metals, RHM Survey, and Value Line OTC Survey. But next year the outcome will be different, so don't bet on the winning jockeys. Figure 24–7 provides information on the performance of mutual funds relative to the market indexes. The DJIA had performed better than the other market indicators. The balanced funds seemed to do the best. None of the funds on the year to date or weekly data did well. And Figure 24–8 provides performance data for selected mutual funds, insurance company funds, and bank pooled funds.

FIGURE 24–7
Lipper Mutual Fund Investment Performance Averages (March 17, 1983)

Lipper Fund Indices				*Average Fund Performances*			
		Percentage Change				*Percentage Change*	
	Close	Year to Date	Weekly	No.	Type of Fund	Year to Date	Weekly
Growth Funds	196.12	+ 8.93	−0.87	66	Capital Appreciation	+10.35	−1.12
				158	Growth	+ 9.00	−1.12
Growth Income	291.16	+ 8.99	−0.78	20	Small Co. Growth Fds	+14.09	−1.00
				87	Growth & Income	+ 7.28	−0.90
Balanced Funds	246.66	+ 6.73	−0.47	27	Equity Income	+ 7.17	−0.28
				358	Average Performance	+ 8.99	−1.00
Other Market Indicators				24	Balanced	+ 5.95	−0.60
D. J. Industrial	1,116.96	+ 6.73	−0.35	27	Income	+ 5.26	+0.02
				7	Natural Resources	+ 1.97	−4.42
S. & P. 500	149.59	+ 6.36	−1.46	13	Specialty	+ 9.67	−1.19
				7	Gold	− 7.36	−8.77
S. & P. 400	167.54	+ 6.29	−1.64	13	International	+ 6.19	+0.04
				11	Option	+ 4.35	−1.00
N.Y.S.E. Comp.	86.22	+ 6.41	−1.63	119	Fixed Income	+ 4.35	+0.19
				579	Average Performance	+ 7.33	−0.79
Amex Index	379.11	+11.31	−2.00	579	Median Performance	+ 7.23	−0.60

Data supplied by Lipper Analytical Services. Year to date and weekly percentage changes on Thursday for mutual funds include reinvestment of income dividends and capital gains distributions, other market indicators do not. Only funds in existence for the entire period covered are included. Total number of funds, by objective, may include funds with net asset values unavailable at compilation time.

SOURCE: Barron's.

TIMING THE SALE IS CRITICAL

Selection of securities is of primary and paramount importance in portfolio management. Next in importance is buying and selling the securities. This is handled as part of the investor's strategy. The solution is complete management of the portfolio, which

The following three tables indicate how various funds are faring. The first table shows the rankings of the ten best performing mutual funds. The second table is a cross section of insurance funds and the third, a cross section of bank pooled funds.

MUTUAL FUNDS (As of 10/31/81)

1981 Rank	Fund name	Performance* 1981 to date % change	Performance* 12 months to date % change	Objective	Fund size as of 10/31/81 (millions)
1	Oppenheimer Target Fund	38.85%	**	Capital appreciation	$ 7.1
2	Lindner Fund	30.34	33.41%	Growth†	26.0
3	Quest for Value Fund	23.96	24.05	Capital appreciation	2.6
4	Lindner Fund for Income	19.90	21.55	Income fund	0.7
5	Delta Trend Fund	18.08	25.55	Capital appreciation	9.8
6	Mutual Qualified Income	17.57	24.76	Capital appreciation	4.3
7	Magnacap Fund	16.30	16.30	Growth	5.6
8	Century Shares Trust	15.75	18.28	Insurance stock fund	64.8
9	FH & Z Tax Managed Fund	15.57	28.45	Growth	1.1
10	Sequoia Fund	15.32	14.05	Growth	110.8
	Dow Jones Industrial Average				
	Standard & Poor's 500				

* Performance calculations include capital gains and income distributions and assume that these are reinvested when distributed.

** Fund not in existence for period covered.

† Denotes incentive management fee arrangement.

Source: Lipper Analytical Distributors, New York City. The survey from which this information is extracted covers 492 funds.

INSURANCE COMPANY FUNDS (As of 10/31/81)
(Common stock funds)

| | Number of funds | Assets in millions | Per cent change | | | |
			Latest quarter	Year to date	Latest three years	Latest five years
Less than $10 million	15	$ 58	−3.4%	−2.7%	57.6%	60.1%
$10-25 million	7	107	−6.5	−4.0	42.8	62.1
$25-50 million	5	188	−2.8	−0.8	66.3	83.3
$50-100 million	10	679	−4.5	−3.7	64.3	78.6
More than $100 million	14	15,447	−5.4	−5.4	55.7	57.1
Total	51	16,481	−5.4	−5.2	56.1	58.5
S&P 500			−5.6	−6.3	53.1	52.4

Source: Insurance Company Funds, published monthly by Computer Directions Advisors, Silver Spring, Maryland. The numbers represent time-weighted rates of return with all distributions reinvested; within each group, funds are weighted for asset size.

BANK POOLED FUNDS (As of 10/31/81)
(Common stock funds)

| | Number of funds | Assets in millions | Per cent change | | | |
			Latest quarter	Year to date	Latest three years	Latest five years
Less than $10 million	145	$ 600	−2.5%	−1.0%	55.1%	59.2%
$10-25 million	62	1,022	−3.6	−3.5	58.5	63.7
$25-50 million	33	1,204	−4.3	−2.7	61.8	65.4
$50-100 million	20	1,394	−3.4	−3.1	58.1	61.0
More than $100 million	18	11,430	−5.2	−5.7	58.8	57.0
Total	278	15,649	−4.6	−4.6	58.8	59.1
S&P 500			−5.6	−6.3	53.1	52.4

Source: Bank Pooled Funds, published monthly by Computer Directions Advisors, Silver Spring, Maryland. The numbers represent time-weighted rates of return with all distributions reinvested; within each group funds are weighted for asset size.

FIGURE 24-8

Mutual Funds, Insurance Company Funds, and Bank Pooled Funds

SOURCE: Institutional Investor, January 1982, p. 21.

includes a recognition of economic trends and of the market cycle as a phenomenon of its own. In our discussion of timing, we emphasized the timing of purchases of securities. Now we will emphasize the management problems involved with when to sell securities.

Here, we assume that we are managing our portfolio completely, selecting quality issues and buying them at the proper price. Now we will consider when we should sell the securities we have purchased. The concept of timing suggests not only that securities be purchased when they are relatively low, but that they be sold when they are relatively high. If the concept of timing has any validity, the idea of selling a security if it appears to be too high is just as reasonable as saying that the stock is low in price and should be purchased.

The solution to the matter of proper timing of the sale rests on expectations about the future. If, based on a reasonable and complete analysis, the present price is excessive compared to future returns from these earnings, then the security should be sold. On the other hand, if expectations about future earnings and return result in a present value that is sufficiently higher than the present price, the investor should consider holding the stock. Future returns should provide the clue of when to buy and sell.

Essentially, we must take advantage of the major movements of prices in the marketplace. We must sell securities when they are overpriced relative to future expected earnings, dividends, and price. We must purchase stocks when they are low and hence offer a high return. The only way an investor can "beat" the S&P 500 Index is by managing assets to take advantage of the market—by selling when it is overpriced and buying when it is underpriced. I myself have found the reward-and-risk analysis presented in the computer programs that are a part of Modesystem to be extremely useful in judging when the stock market and individual stocks are over- or underpriced. A stock is usually overpriced when it is selling at a low return and a low reward-to-risk ratio and offering a low or negative expected return based on the analysts' expected return and risk estimates.

When the S&P 500 Index reached the level of approximately 120 in December 1972, the expected return was 2 percent. This suggested that the market was overpriced. The index dropped to 101 in July 1973, and the return rose to 11 percent, indicating that the market was fairly priced by historical standards. In 1975, the reward-to-risk ratio for the S&P 500 was 1.46, offering an expected return of 21 percent. The market at that time was at approximately 90 and was considered a bargain. In November 1980, the S&P 500 Index was at 130 and overpriced, and attractive at 115 in 1982.

Guides to Timing the Sale of Securities

The first guide to follow in timing the sale of a security is to sell when the security no longer meets the objectives that were originally established. Investment needs frequently change, calling for a change in the type of security that should be held in the portfolio. Assume, for example, that an investor has followed an income-portfolio policy. Later, income needs are satisfied and current income is no longer required. Portfolio policy would shift to an emphasis on growth. This would require the sale of the income shares and purchase of growth shares. The same example could be given for the growth investor who now needs income and must sell growth stocks.

A second sign that indicates a time to sell is when the stock market as a whole has moved up to a historic high and the stock itself is selling at an extremely high price. So the investor must judge whether the market is high or low.

A third guide in timing the sale of a stock relates to the expectations about the return from the security, as discussed above. When a specific security no longer offers the investor the expectation of a satisfactory return and there is a sharp difference between the analysts' expectations and what can be reasonably obtained, the stock should be sold.

The fourth guide to selling under a completely managed portfolio is based on competitive alternatives. The investor should consider selling the stocks held—after all factors are considered, including risk, quality, and taxes—when a compelling alternative investment offers greater returns comparable to risks.

The stock should also be sold when the return is low and the reward-to-risk ratio is unattractive.

Tax Selling—An Important Consideration in Selling

No job of portfolio management can ignore taxes. Occasional selling of securities will realize capital gains or losses for the investor for tax purposes. This is referred to as *tax selling*. Tax switches would require, for example, that one stock be sold to establish a tax loss and a comparable security purchased to replace it in the investor's portfolio. This is really a technical trade to establish a loss or gain. The stock sold can be repurchased after 30 days and the long-term investment position maintained. In accordance with tax law, one must wait 30 days after selling a stock before repurchasing it, to be able to declare the gain or loss. If stock is repurchased before 30 days, it is considered a *wash sale*, and the IRS treats the transaction as if no sale were made, so the gain or loss cannot be claimed for tax purposes.

ALTERNATIVE SOLUTIONS TO TIMING

Many investors do not believe they have the ability to trade stocks and profit. They stress quality and selectivity and develop ways to minimize the effects of timing. Typical solutions to the timing problem are (1) stock-price averaging or dollar-cost averaging; (2) the formula plan, and (3) indexing.

Stock-Price Averaging

One way to solve the problem of the timing of portfolio purchases is to average the purchase price of the stock. The concept of averaging recognizes people's inability to judge accurately when a stock is high or low. Therefore, it suggests that we should ignore any attempt to predict the price of a stock. Instead, we are asked first to select quality stocks, and then, not to buy a security just once and put it away for safekeeping, but to buy it two or three times. If we do this, it is assumed that we will pay a much more realistic price for the stocks we purchase and, since we are investing for the long run, we will be better off with averaging than with only one purchase of a given stock for our portfolio.

A good example of averaging can be taken from a recent case. Margaret Winslow had purchased twenty shares of Procter & Gamble at 92. She realized that the company would provide her with an excellent long-term investment. However, the stock dropped to 64. She was concerned and wondered what should be done. She had an additional $1,000 that she wished to invest, thus adding to her problems. The solution, according to averaging, would be for Mrs. Winslow to purchase more of P&G at 64, to reduce the average cost of the shares she owned. With $1,000, Mrs. Winslow could buy an additional fifteen shares of P&G. The effects of the purchase (ignoring commissions and taxes) were as follows:

	Shares	Price per Share	Value
1st purchase	20	$92	$1,840
2nd purchase	15	64	960
Total	35	$80 (averaged price)	$2,800

Thus, Mrs. Winslow would have 35 shares of Procter & Gamble at an average price of $80 per share. The average price of $80 is much better than a price of $92. It puts Mrs. Winslow in a much better position as a long-term investor.[2]

Many well-known investment counselors and institutional investors recommend this system for purchasing stock. They suggest that investors buy quality stocks— stocks they would be willing to buy when they went down in price—and keep them in the portfolio as long-term investments. They also suggest that the stocks be bought at lower prices, to allow a lower average price.

The simple assumption on which the averaging concept rests is much like that of price setting. What is really being said is that we cannot predict the highs and lows and we do not know with complete assurance what is a fair price. Therefore, securities are purchased more than once, and in this way an average price will result that will be more realistic than any single price. The low and the high price will not be achieved, but paying an average-of-the-market price would be better than buying the stock at the high of the market.

The astute reader will raise the question of what happens if you had been able to buy the stock at the low of the market. You have actually paid more for the stock by averaging than by buying it at the low. This is true. However, we should be willing to trade the possible gains we might receive from buying the stock at its low point for the losses we would sustain from buying it at the height of the price movement. In essence, we are compromising our investment position.

DOLLAR-COST AVERAGING. Dollar-cost averaging is considered to be a better averaging technique, because it involves buying stock at a price lower than the average of the trend of the market, even though the market moves upward in a cyclical fashion.

[2]The question is often raised of what happens if the price of the stock continues to drop and finally goes to zero. In this case, the investor loses all the money invested in the stock, whether by making only one purchase for the total investment or by dollar averaging. If it does happen, dollar averaging still has the advantage. The investor loses all the money, but loses less per share!

With dollar averaging, the investor buys the same dollar amount of stock at regular time periods. As the market price declines, the investor is able to buy more shares of stock with a fixed number of dollars. If the stock moves up in price, the investor will buy a smaller number of shares. The effect of these transactions is to lower the cost below the average of the market. Assume, for example, that a person buys $1,000 worth of a stock at three different prices, as follows:

		Price	Number of Shares
(1)	$1,000	$ 50	20
(2)	1,000	40	25
(3)	1,000	100	10
Totals	$3,000		55

The average price per share is $54.54 ($3,000/55). If the investor had purchased the same number of shares at each of the prices shown, the average purchase price per share would have been $63.33, the average of the market price. Under dollar-cost averaging, the average price would have been lower than the average of the market price. Dollar-cost averaging is particularly attractive to smaller investors who are putting regular sums of money into the purchase of quality common stocks.

ADVANTAGES OF AVERAGING. The major advantage of averaging or of dollar averaging is that it takes the pressure from the investor in timing stock purchases. The concept works in a rising or in a declining market, although it works best when stock is acquired in a declining market. The dollar-averaging or averaging-down process reduces the average cost per share and improves the possibility of gain over the long term.

Another advantage of the averaging process is that it forces the investor to plan an investment program more thoroughly than if a commitment were made at one time. A final advantage is that it provides the periodic and continuous review of the investor's portfolio and objectives. The process of averaging or dollar averaging tends to eliminate the cyclical characteristics of a stock but retains the trend of growth over time.

DISADVANTAGES OF AVERAGING. The disadvantages of averaging might in some cases outweigh the advantages. The first disadvantage is the cost involved in purchasing the stock at several different times rather than at one time. This is particularly important for the investor with a modest fund who might be able to buy one round lot of stock but could not buy several round lots.

A second disadvantage is the inability or unwillingness of an individual investor to carry out an averaging program. It is very possible that the following situation might develop: Mr. Jones buys 25 shares of AT&T at 52. The stock begins to drop and finally reaches 40. Originally Mr. Jones was going to buy more stock, but when the price reaches 40, he decides not to purchase it because he thinks it will go lower. On the other hand, assume that Mr. Jones buys the stock at 40 and it moves to 52. He decides not to buy at 52 because he thinks the price is too high, and yet the stock moves to 58. The net result is that he does not buy additional shares to average or dollar-average; he has ignored the timing problem and the advantages that might be achieved by an averaging program.

A third disadvantage is that averaging attempts to provide a solution to the problem of the timing of purchases, but it does not call attention to the problem of when to sell the securities that have been purchased. Dollar averaging simply assumes that stock, once purchased, will be sold only infrequently, and that the selling of the stock is only incidental to the entire investment process. There is an advantage in selecting quality companies for long-term investment and then holding the securities. But the financial and economic affairs of a company do change. We should recognize a company's change of basic status in the industry, and once the change is recognized, we should act.

Formula Plans

By not telling the investor when to sell, dollar-cost averaging or averaging does not emphasize sufficiently the fundamental problem of the investment-management equation—bluntly stated as the *buy low–sell high* concept. If investors were perfect in their judgment of the market and market conditions, they would buy low and sell high. This process requires a great deal of patience and fortitude. It is full of pitfalls and errors in judgment. However, if we are to be successful, we must follow a path that allows us to buy securities when they are cheap and sell them when they are dear.

The buy low–sell high concept is excellent but difficult to employ, particularly for the small investor. A system is needed that will produce results comparable to those a skilled investor would achieve by good judgment on buying low and selling high; yet the system must be automatic, so that once it is established, the person with only a modest skill in investment timing will be able to carry out the program successfully. Programs that provide an automatic timing device for guiding the buy-and-sell transactions of the investor on a prearranged plan to approximate good management are referred to as *formula plans*.

ASSUMPTION; UNDERLYING A FORMULA PLAN. The first assumption on which the formula plan is based is that a certain percentage of the investor's portfolio will be invested in fixed-income securities or cash, and a certain percentage in common stocks. The exact amount invested in each depends on the height of the stock market at the time the investor begins the plan. It is not uncommon for an investor to follow a balanced-fund approach when the formula plan is established. The balanced-fund concept might require that, initially, 50 percent of the fund be invested in bonds and 50 percent in common stocks, or some other proportion. At the time the portfolio is established, an attempt should be made to determine the relative height of the stock market. If the market is relatively high, a greater percentage of the investment fund should be in fixed-income types of securities and cash, perhaps a ratio of 70 percent fixed and 30 percent stock. If, on the other hand, the market is low, then one could reverse proportions. This requires a judgment about the height of the stock market and calls essentially for a timing decision. A balance of 50-50 between common stocks and bonds is the most advantageous ratio for a constant-ratio plan.

The second assumption on which the formula plan is based is that as the market moves higher, the proportion of common stock in the portfolio either remains constant as a percentage of the total, or it declines. When the market declines, common stock becomes either an increasing percentage of the total, or it remains the same. One type of formula plan, for example, requires that as the stock market moves up, common stock is sold to keep the dollar amount of common stock equal to the amount of debt. A second plan requires a decline in the amount of stock as a percentage of the total portfolio when the market is high and an increase in the amount of stock as the market declines. These changes simply recognize that a portfolio should be more aggressive when the market is low and more defensive when the market is high.

A third premise on which a formula plan rests is that stock will be bought and sold when a significant change occurs in the price of the securities owned by the investor. A significant change in the level of the market as measured by a leading stock market index, such as the Dow Jones Industrial Average, or Standard & Poor's 500 Index might also signal a change. The time period between purchase and sale will depend on the movement of the market or the securities owned.

A fourth assumption is that the investor will adhere to the formula plan once it has been established. He or she will buy and sell according to a prearranged plan, and will not abandon the program once it has begun.

A fifth requirement is that the investor select quality stocks that move with the stock market. They will have the risk and reward characteristics of the market, and will have a beta of 1.0 and a p of close to 1.00. These securities will be carefully selected to meet the standards of financial and investment analysis. Essentially, a company whose stock is bought will possess sound earnings, a good financial position and capital structure, a good management, a dominant position within the industry, and a relatively attractive price and price-earnings ratio.

The last condition associated with formula plans is that they allow the investor to take advantage of the cyclical swings in the market, so that the benefits from the swings will accrue to the investor.

EXAMPLE OF A FORMULA PLAN.   The following example will demonstrate how we might be better off financially by using a formula plan. Assume that stock is sold when the value of the investment fund moves up 25 percent, and stock is bought when the value moves down 20 percent. The value of the stock amount will be kept at $1,000, and the total fund will be $2,000. When the fund moves up or down, the stock account will be adjusted to the $1,000 level. This is illustrated in Table 24–4, where we follow through two cycles of transactions. The fund's value moves up 25 percent and down 20 percent twice. In step 1, when the stock fund moves up 25 percent, the stock is sold and bonds are purchased. When the stock drops 20 percent, bonds are sold, and stock is purchased to bring the amount up to $1,000. The formula-plan method produces a profit of $100, and we end up with a $2,100 fund. Without the formula plan, we finish with the same amount we began with—$2,000. Under the formula plan, we

TABLE 24–4

Example of Financial Advantage of Formula Plan

Beginning position	Formula Plan			Buy-and-Hold Plan		
	Value of Stock	Value of Cash or Bonds	Total Value	Value of Stock	Value of Cash or Bonds	Total Value
(1) 25% increase	$1,000	$1,000	$2,000	$1,000	$1,000	$2,000
Sell stock	250	1,000	2,250	1,250	1,000	2,250
Buy bonds	1,000	1,250	2,250	1,250	1,000	2,250
(2) 20% decrease	800	1,250	2,050	1,000	1,000	2,000
Buy stock	1,000	1,050	2,050	1,000	1,000	2,000
(3) 25% increase	1,250	1,050	2,300	1,250	1,000	2,000
Sell stock	1,000	1,300	2,300	1,250	1,000	2,250
(4) 20% decrease	800	1,300	2,100	1,000	1,000	2,000
Buy stock	1,000	1,100	2,100	1,000	1,000	2,000

are 5 percent better off. Even if we added on the cost of buying and selling the stock, we would be slightly better off with a formula plan than without.

TYPES OF FORMULA PLANS. No single formula plan is used by individual and institutional investors. Rather, there are three basic formula plans that follow the pattern described above. The first is the *constant-dollar stock plan*, which begins with a fixed amount of money invested in stock and in cash or bonds. As trades are made, the investment in stock is kept at a fixed amount, based on the original amount invested in common stock. The second plan is the *constant stock–bond ratio plan*, which is based on a fixed relationship between amounts of bonds and stock. Once the ratio is established, it is kept constant based on the indicated changes in the market. If a 50-50 ratio between stocks and bonds had been established, then this ratio would be maintained as the market moved up or down by 25 percent. The third is the *variable stock–bond ratio plan*, which allows the investor to adjust the portfolio between stocks and bonds based upon the relative height of the stock market. When the market moves up, instead of maintaining a constant ratio between stocks and bonds, a ratio is adopted that decreases the emphasis on common stock and increases the amount of bonds in the investment account.

SOME ADVANTAGES OF FORMULA PLANS. The major advantage of the formula plan is its automatic character. Once the plan is established, we are free from making emotional decisions based on the current attitudes of investors in the stock market.

The second advantage is related to timing the sale of stock. Most effort and discussion about timing is concerned with buying securities. The formula plan stresses both buying and selling.

A third advantage of the formula-plan method as a solution to timing is its versatility. It recognizes the defensive and aggressive characteristics of an investment portfolio. As the market moves up, the formula plan results in an increasingly defensive position. When the market declines, the portfolio automatically becomes more aggressive.

SOME DISADVANTAGES OF FORMULA PLANS. One disadvantage of the formula plan is that we must make a value judgment as to the relative height of the stock market for the variable-ratio formula plans. A second disadvantage, related to the first, is that over a sustained market rise, we would be better off in common stock than in a combination of bonds and common. A third possible criticism is that we might choose securities that do not move with the market. After all, the beta characteristics of common stocks are not entirely stable. A fourth disadvantage of a formula plan is that it offers only modest opportunity for capital gains. A fully managed fund will offer a greater potential for gain, even though we might not achieve this goal.

Indexing

Many people think that they must do as well as or better than the market if they are to be successful investors. Unfortunately, it is difficult to do better than the market. In fact, half of all investors perform better than the market and half perform worse. Therefore, many investors would be willing to do as well as the market by earning the return of the market and accepting the risk of the market. This is the notion of the modern portfolio theorists.

"The market" is usually some market index, such as the S&P 500 Index. In order to "get the market," an investor would purchase all the stocks in the index based on the proportion of each in the index. Usually, the proportion of the stock in the index is determined by multiplying the number of shares of stock the company has outstanding by the market price of the shares. The total market value of each stock is then added to those of all the other stocks that make up the index. The percentage of each stock in the index is the weight. If an investor is to have the same portfolio as the "market" index, the percentages held in the portfolio must equal those of the index.

An example will explain how indexing works. Assume there are three stocks in the index, with numbers of shares outstanding and price per share as follows:

	Shares Outstanding (millions)	Share Price ($)	Value ($ millions)	Percentage
Company A	6.2	60	372.0	55.53%
Company B	4.5	35	157.5	23.51
Company C	7.8	18	140.4	20.96
Total			669.9	100.00%

An investor who wished to do exactly as well as the market index would invest 55.53 percent of her funds in company A, 23.51 percent in company B, and 20.96 percent in company C. For example, a woman with a $10,000 portfolio would invest $5,553 in company A, $2,351 in B, and $2,096 in C; this would give approximately 93 shares of company A, 67 shares of company B, and 116 shares of company C.

The unfortunate part about indexing is the number of companies an investor must own to obtain the results of the market average. There are 30 DJIA stocks and 500 stocks in the S&P Index. Some investors could diversify to obtain the results of the DJIA index, but only the largest institutions would be able to do so based on the popular S&P 500 Index. Therefore, indexing appears to be a weak alternative for the investor with limited funds. Besides, it violates the emphasis on analysis, quality, value, return, risk, and reward-to-risk principles presented in this text.

In addition, there is a cost involved in maintaining the same stocks in the portfolio as in the index. Transaction costs are a handicap, so even when the proper weighing is obtained, the portfolio might not perform as well as the index because of the transaction costs.

SUMMARY

Investors must measure the performance of their portfolios to make certain their objectives are being met. Changes in the portfolio are made based on performance— price changes—and strategy. Performance is measured by the percentage change in the portfolio relative to some market index such as the S&P 500 Index. Measuring the return on the funds invested accurately is important. Regression analysis helps understand the behavior of the portfolio.

The portfolio-management problem includes the timing of the purchase and sale of a security. Several rules help the investment manager to make a decision about the proper time to sell. Stocks are sold (1) when they no longer meet the needs of the investor; (2) when the price of the market and the securities is at a historic high; (3) when future expectations no longer support the price of the stocks, or when returns fall below the satisfactory level; (4) when other alternatives are more attractive than the securities held; and (5) when there is a tax advantage in the sale for the investor. The most important time to sell is (6) when the expected return is low, the risk high, and the reward-to-risk ratio significantly lower than the market and substantially less than 1.0.

Many investors recognize that they cannot accurately time the purchase and sale of securities. One solution is to time the purchase of stocks so that they can be bought at the lowest price. This solution requires patience and sound judgment, but it ignores the problem of when to sell. Another solution is dollar averaging, in which the investor buys stock several times and eliminates the cyclical aspects of the price movement, hoping that the increasing trend of stock prices will eventually lead to investment success. This solution, however, also does not consider when to sell. Another solution to the timing problem is some form of formula plan. Finally, indexing is a possible alternative to the timing problem.

The best solution to the timing problem still remains in the hands of the experienced manager, who, with the aid of the tools presented in the text, and with discretion, makes the decision of when and what to buy and sell based upon a predetermined strategy. Investors with proper education and experience can become competent in the management of investment accounts and avoid being the last optimistic investor.

SUMMARY OF PRINCIPLES

1. Expected return, risk, and the reward-to-risk ratio should govern the purchase and sale of securities in the portfolio.
2. Portfolio management is a continuous process of reevaluation to make certain that the securities combined in the portfolio continue to meet the investor's expectations.
3. Price strategy is an important part of intelligent portfolio management.
4. Regression analysis helps in the management of a portfolio.

REVIEW QUESTIONS

1. What is meant by the timing problem in securities investment?
2. One solution to the timing problem is to establish a price we consider to be attractive and then wait until that price is reached. Comment about the advantages and disadvantages of this approach to timing.
3. Explain the concept of dollar averaging and how it might be used in solving the problem of investment timing.
4. What are the basic advantages and disadvantages of dollar averaging?
5. Explain how formula planning can be used as a tool to solve the timing problem.
6. What are the solutions to the difficult problem of when to sell a security? Elaborate.
7. Explain how expected return may be used as a tool in making a decision concerning when to buy and when to sell.
8. What is the relationship of the beta factor to the problem of selling and buying common stock?
9. What part does the coefficient of correlation play in the purchase and sale of common stock?
10. Explain why the expected return and the reward-to-risk ratio are so important in making portfolio decisions.

The portfolio below was held by an investor in early January 1982. At the beginning of 1983, the stock prices and the S&P 500 Index had changed. Find the value of the portfolio at the end of each quarter in 1982. What was the portfolio return at the end of each quarter compared to the S&P 500 Index? Indicate at the end of each quarter whether the portfolio should be changed and how. Prices and dividends can be obtained from back issues of *The Wall Street Journal* or *The New York Times*. Explain how the return and risk of the portfolio relates to the S&P 500 Index. Did the portfolio outperform the market? Comment.

Company	Price
AT&T	$ 59
IBM	67
Eastman Kodak	68
MMM	54
S&P 500 Index	$116

CASE

Two sisters, Laura and Susan, inherited $1,000,000 at the end of 1979. At the time they were in graduate school and looked forward to a rewarding and satisfying career in business. They worked part-time and had adequate income to meet their current living expenses. One provision of the will required that the funds be managed by a trustee and that the goal of the fund was growth. The income from the fund was distributed to Susan and Laura to help with their expenses. Any capital gains from the fund were to be reinvested.

At the end of 1981, they asked the investment officer managing the portfolio to provide them with a performance report. The officer said she would be glad to furnish the usual performance measure. The report received by Laura and Susan is found in the table that follows, which was accompanied by this letter:

January 15

Dear Laura and Susan,

The performance report you asked for is enclosed. You will see that your portfolio has generally followed the pattern of the S&P 500 Index. The rate of return of your portfolio, R_p%, has generally followed the rate of return of the S&P 500 Index, R_m%. We are pleased that you have earned a dividend yield of 7.5 percent for the period and a capital gain of 2.27 percent. This has provided you with a total rate of return of 9.77 percent. And we have met your objectives of growth.

If we can be of service in the future, please do not hesitate to call or write. Sincerely yours,

Mary

Do you agree with the report and the letter?

Growth Portfolio Performance of Laura and Susan's $1 Million Portfolio

Number of Shares	12/31/79 P ($)	12/31/79 D ($)	3/31/80 P ($)	3/31/80 D ($)	3/31/80 Value Shares ($)	3/31/80 Value of Dividend ($)	6/30/80 P ($)	6/30/80 D ($)	6/30/80 Value Shares ($)	6/30/80 Value of Dividend ($)
S&P 500	$107.94	$1.41	$102.09	$1.45	$102.09	$1.45	$114.24	$1.49	$114.24	$1.49
2,432* Abbott	41 1/8	0.25	36 5/8	0.30	89,072	730	42 1/8	0.30	102,448	730
1,918 AT&T	52 1/8	1.25	48 5/8	1.25	93,263	2,398	52 1/2	1.25	100,695	2,398
1,975 Boeing	50 5/8	0.34	35 1/2	0.30	70,113	593	35	0.30	69,125	593
2,899 Coca-Cola	34 1/2	0.49	31 1/2	0.54	91,319	1,565	33	0.54	95,667	1,565
1,691† Hewlett-Packard	59 1/8	0.10	62 7/8	0.10	106,322	169	62 3/8	0.10	105,476	169
1,553 IBM	64 3/8	0.86	55 3/4	0.86	86,580	1,336	58 3/4	0.86	91,239	1,336
1,674 Eli Lilly	59 3/4	0.525	50 3/8	0.525	84,328	879	40	0.525	82,026	879
1,067‡ Schlumberger	93 3/4	0.275	106 1/4	0.33	113,369	352	115 1/2	0.33	123,239	352
1,670 Tektronix	59 7/8	0.21	49 1/4	0.21	82,248	351	49 3/4	0.21	83,083	351
1,136 Texas Instruments	88	0.50	82 3/4	0.50	94,004	568	92	0.50	104,512	568
Total market value	$1,000,000				$910,618	$8,941			$957,510	$8,941

R_m % (4.1) (13.4%)

R_p % (8.0) 6.1

Total capital gain (loss) over 2-year period 2.27%

Dividend yield (75,257) = 7.5%

Total return = 9.77%

*2-for-1 split, 6/30/81.

†2-for-1 split, 6/30/81.

‡3-for-1 split, 9/15/80 and 6/30/81.

SOURCE: Graduate Research Project, Laura Avrick and Susan Hodges, The George Washington University, Washington, D.C.

TABLE (Continued)

Number of Shares		9/31/80				12/31/80				3/31/81			
		P ($)	D ($)	Value Shares ($)	Value of Dividend ($)	P ($)	D ($)	Value Shares ($)	Value of Dividend ($)	P ($)	D ($)	Value Shares ($)	Value of Dividend ($)
	S&P 500	$125.46	$1.52	$125.40	$1.52	$135.76	$1.54	$135.76	$154	$136.00	$1.57	$136	$1.57
2,432*	Abbott	51 1/2	0.30	125,248	730	56 1/2	0.30	137,408	730	60	0.36	145,920	876
1,918	AT&T	51 7/8	1.25	99,496	2,398	47 7/8	1.25	91,824	2,398	51 1/2	1.35	98,777	2,589
1,975	Boeing	38 1/2	0.30	76,038	593	44 1/8	0.30	87,147	593	35 1/8	0.35	69,372	691
2,899	Coca-Cola	32 1/4	0.54	93,493	1,565	33 3/8	0.54	96,754	1,565	36 7/8	0.58	106,901	1,681
1,691†	Hewlett-Packard	74 7/8	0.10	126,614	169	89 1/2	0.10	151,345	169	92 1/2	0.10	156,418	169
1,553	IBM	64 1/8	0.86	99,586	1,336	67 7/8	0.86	105,410	1,336	62 3/8	0.86	96,868	1,336
1,674	Eli Lilly	51 3/8	0.575	86,002	963	63 3/4	0.575	106,718	963	64 3/8	0.575	107,764	963
1,067‡	Schlumberger	142 7/8	0.37	152,453	400	176	0.37	187,792	400	152	0.37	162,184	400
1,670	Tektronix	64 3/8	0.23	107,515	384	61 1/8	0.23	102,087	384	53 3/4	0.23	89,763	384
1,136	Texas Instruments	130 7/8	0.50	148,680	568	120 3/4	0.50	137,172	568	116 3/4	0.50	132,628	568
	Total market value			$1,115,125	$9,106			$1,203,657	$9,106			$1,166,595	$9,657
	R_m %	11.2%				9.4%				1.3%			
	R_p %	17.4%				8.8%				(2.3%)			

TABLE (Continued)

		6/30/81				9/30/81				12/31/81			
Number of Shares		P ($)	D ($)	Value Shares ($)	Value of Dividend ($)	P ($)	D ($)	Value Shares ($)	Value of Dividend ($)	P ($)	D ($)	Value Shares ($)	Value of Dividend ($)
	S&P 500	$131.21	$1.60	$131.21	$1.60	$116.18	$1.63	$116.18	$1.63	$124.00	$1.66	$124.00	$1.66
2,432*	Abbott	63	0.36	153,216	876	52	0.36	126,464	876	54	0.36	131,328	876
1,918	AT&T	56 1/4	1.35	107,888	2,589	57 7/8	1.35	111,004	2,589	58 3/4	1.35	112,683	2,589
1,975	Boeing	30 5/8	0.35	60,484	691	24 1/8	0.35	47,647	691	22 1/2	0.35	44,438	691
2,899	Coca-Cola	34 3/4	0.58	100,740	1,681	33 3/4	0.58	97,841	1,681	34 3/4	0.58	100,740	1,681
1,691†	Hewlett-Packard	95 1/4	0.12	161,068	203	84	0.12	142,044	203	79 1/4	0.12	134,012	203
1,553	IBM	57 7/8	0.86	89,880	1,336	54 1/8	0.86	84,056	1,336	56 7/8	0.86	88,327	1,336
1,674	Eli Lilly	61	0.575	102,114	963	47 1/8	0.575	80,143	963	56	0.65	93,774	1,088
1,067‡	Schlumbergr	142	0.45	151,152	480	117 1/2	0.45	125,400	480	125 5/8	0.45	134,100	480
1,670	Tektronix	55	0.23	91,850	384	48 1/8	0.25	80,377	418	55	0.25	91,850	418
1,136	Texas Instruments	97	0.50	110,192	568	82 7/8	0.50	94,152	568	80 1/2	0.50	91,448	568
	Total market value			$1,128,944	$9,771			$989,128	$9,805			$1,022,670	$9,930
	R_m %	(2.3%)				(10.2%)				8.2%			
	R_p %	(2.4%)				(11.5%)				4.4%			

BLACK, FISCHER. "The Investment Policy Spectrum: Individuals, Endowment Funds and Pension Funds." In James Lorie and Richard Brealey, *Modern Developments in Investment Management*, 2nd ed. Hinsdale, Ill.: Dryden Press, p. 397.

BLUME, MARSHALL E. "On the Assessment of Risk." *The Journal of Finance* XXVI (March 1971), pp. 1–10.

DIETZ, PETER O. "Measurement of Performance of Security Portfolios, Components of a Measurement Model: Rate of Return, Risk and Timing." *The Journal of Finance*, May 1968, p. 267.

FAMA, EUGENE F. "Components of Investment Performance." In James Lorie and Richard Brealey, *Modern Developments in Investment Management*, 2nd ed. Hinsdale, Ill.: Dryden Press, p. 448.

FARRELL, JAMES L., JR. "Homogenous Stock Groupings." *Financial Analysts Journal*, May–June 1975, p. 50.

JACOB, NANCY L., and KEITH V. SMITH. "The Value of Perfect Market Forecasts in Portfolio Selection." *The Journal of Finance*, May 1972, p. 355.

LEVITZ, GERALD D. "Market Risk in Institutional Portfolios." *Financial Analysts Journal*, January–February 1974, p. 53.

LEVY, ROBERT A. "Stationarity of Beta Coefficients." *Financial Analysts Journal*, November–December 1971, p. 55.

PRICE, LEE N. "Growth or Yield: The Choice Depends on Your Tax Rate." *Financial Analysts Journal*, July–August 1979.

SCHNEIDER, THEODORE H. "Measuring Performance." *Financial Analysts Journal*, May–June 1969, p. 105.

SHARPE, WILLIAM F. "Are Gains Likely from Market Timing?" *Financial Analysts Journal*, March–April 1975, p. 60.

———. "Imputing Expected Security Returns from Portfolio Composition." *Journal of Financial and Quantitative Analysis*, June 1974, p. 463.

TREYNOR, JACK L. "How to Rate Management of Investment Funds." *Harvard Business Review* 43 (January–February 1965).

———. "How to Use Security Analysis to Improve Portfolio Selection." *The Journal of Business* 46 (January 1973).

———. "Long-Term Investing." *Financial Analysts Journal*, May–June 1976, p. 56.

VERTIN, JAMES R. "The Design and Control of Large Portfolios." The Financial Analysts Federation, Annual Conference, May 1978.

APPENDIX

APPENDIX A1

Present value of $1 Received at the End of Year

PRESENT VALUE OF $1 RECEIVED AT THE END OF YEAR

Years Hence	1%	2%	4%	6%	8%	10%	12%	14%	15%	16%
1	0.990	0.980	0.962	0.943	0.926	0.909	0.893	0.877	0.870	0.862
2	0.980	0.961	0.925	0.890	0.857	0.826	0.797	0.769	0.756	0.743
3	0.971	0.942	0.889	0.840	0.794	0.751	0.712	0.675	0.658	0.641
4	0.961	0.924	0.855	0.792	0.735	0.683	0.630	0.592	0.572	0.552
5	0.951	0.906	0.822	0.747	0.681	0.621	0.567	0.519	0.497	0.476
6	0.942	0.888	0.790	0.705	0.630	0.564	0.507	0.456	0.432	0.410
7	0.933	0.871	0.760	0.665	0.583	0.513	0.452	0.400	0.376	0.354
8	0.923	0.853	0.731	0.627	0.540	0.467	0.404	0.351	0.327	0.305
9	0.914	0.837	0.703	0.592	0.500	0.424	0.361	0.308	0.284	0.263
10	0.905	0.820	0.676	0.558	0.463	0.386	0.322	0.270	0.247	0.227
11	0.896	0.804	0.650	0.527	0.429	0.350	0.287	0.237	0.215	0.195
12	0.887	0.788	0.625	0.497	0.397	0.319	0.257	0.208	0.187	0.168
13	0.879	0.773	0.601	0.469	0.368	0.290	0.229	0.182	0.163	0.145
14	0.870	0.758	0.577	0.442	0.340	0.263	0.205	0.160	0.141	0.125
15	0.861	0.743	0.555	0.417	0.315	0.239	0.183	0.140	0.123	0.108
16	0.853	0.728	0.534	0.394	0.292	0.218	0.163	0.123	0.107	0.093
17	0.844	0.714	0.513	0.371	0.270	0.198	0.146	0.108	0.093	0.080
18	0.836	0.700	0.494	0.350	0.250	0.180	0.130	0.095	0.081	0.069
19	0.828	0.686	0.475	0.331	0.232	0.164	0.116	0.083	0.070	0.060
20	0.820	0.673	0.456	0.312	0.215	0.149	0.104	0.073	0.061	0.051
21	0.811	0.660	0.439	0.294	0.199	0.135	0.093	0.064	0.053	0.044
22	0.803	0.647	0.422	0.278	0.184	0.123	0.083	0.056	0.046	0.038
23	0.795	0.634	0.406	0.262	0.170	0.112	0.074	0.049	0.040	0.033
24	0.788	0.622	0.390	0.247	0.158	0.102	0.066	0.043	0.035	0.028
25	0.780	0.610	0.375	0.233	0.146	0.092	0.059	0.038	0.030	0.024
26	0.772	0.598	0.361	0.220	0.135	0.084	0.053	0.033	0.026	0.021
27	0.764	0.586	0.347	0.207	0.125	0.076	0.047	0.029	0.023	0.018
28	0.757	0.574	0.333	0.196	0.116	0.069	0.042	0.026	0.020	0.016
29	0.749	0.563	0.321	0.185	0.107	0.063	0.037	0.022	0.017	0.014
30	0.742	0.552	0.308	0.174	0.099	0.057	0.033	0.020	0.015	0.012
40	0.672	0.453	0.208	0.097	0.046	0.022	0.011	0.005	0.004	0.003
50	0.608	0.372	0.141	0.054	0.021	0.009	0.003	0.001	0.001	0.001

APPENDIX A1 (continued)

Present Value of $1 Received at the End of Year

PRESENT VALUE OF $1 RECEIVED AT THE END OF YEAR

18%	20%	22%	24%	25%	26%	28%	30%	35%	40%	45%	50%
0.847	0.833	0.820	0.806	0.800	0.794	0.781	0.769	0.741	0.714	0.690	0.667
0.718	0.694	0.672	0.650	0.640	0.630	0.610	0.592	0.549	0.510	0.476	0.444
0.609	0.579	0.551	0.524	0.512	0.500	0.477	0.455	0.406	0.364	0.328	0.296
0.516	0.482	0.451	0.423	0.410	0.397	0.373	0.350	0.301	0.260	0.226	0.198
0.437	0.402	0.370	0.341	0.328	0.315	0.291	0.269	0.223	0.186	0.156	0.132
0.370	0.335	0.303	0.275	0.262	0.250	0.227	0.207	0.165	0.133	0.108	0.088
0.314	0.279	0.249	0.222	0.210	0.198	0.178	0.159	0.122	0.095	0.074	0.059
0.266	0.233	0.204	0.179	0.168	0.157	0.139	0.123	0.091	0.068	0.051	0.039
0.225	0.194	0.167	0.144	0.134	0.125	0.108	0.094	0.067	0.048	0.035	0.026
0.191	0.162	0.137	0.116	0.107	0.099	0.085	0.073	0.050	0.035	0.024	0.017
0.162	0.135	0.112	0.094	0.086	0.079	0.066	0.056	0.037	0.025	0.017	0.012
0.137	0.112	0.092	0.076	0.069	0.062	0.052	0.043	0.027	0.018	0.012	0.008
0.116	0.093	0.075	0.061	0.055	0.050	0.040	0.033	0.020	0.013	0.008	0.005
0.099	0.078	0.062	0.049	0.044	0.039	0.032	0.025	0.015	0.009	0.006	0.003
0.084	0.065	0.051	0.040	0.035	0.031	0.025	0.020	0.011	0.006	0.004	0.002
0.071	0.054	0.042	0.032	0.028	0.025	0.019	0.015	0.008	0.005	0.003	0.002
0.060	0.045	0.034	0.026	0.023	0.020	0.015	0.012	0.006	0.003	0.002	0.001
0.051	0.038	0.028	0.021	0.018	0.016	0.012	0.009	0.005	0.002	0.001	0.001
0.043	0.031	0.023	0.017	0.014	0.012	0.009	0.007	0.003	0.002	0.001	
0.037	0.026	0.019	0.014	0.012	0.010	0.007	0.005	0.002	0.001	0.001	
0.031	0.022	0.015	0.011	0.009	0.008	0.006	0.004	0.002	0.001		
0.026	0.018	0.013	0.009	0.007	0.006	0.004	0.003	0.001	0.001		
0.022	0.015	0.010	0.007	0.006	0.005	0.003	0.002	0.001			
0.019	0.013	0.008	0.006	0.005	0.004	0.003	0.002	0.001			
0.016	0.010	0.007	0.005	0.004	0.003	0.002	0.001	0.001			
0.014	0.009	0.006	0.004	0.003	0.002	0.002	0.001				
0.011	0.007	0.005	0.003	0.002	0.002	0.001	0.001				
0.010	0.006	0.004	0.002	0.002	0.002	0.001	0.001				
0.008	0.005	0.003	0.002	0.002	0.001	0.001	0.001				
0.007	0.004	0.003	0.002	0.001	0.001	0.001					
0.001	0.001										

SOURCE: Reprinted with permission from R. N. Anthony, *Management Accounting: Text and Cases* (Homewood, Ill.: Irwin, 1960), p. 658.

APPENDIX A2

Present Value of $1 Received Annually at the End of Each Year for N Years

PRESENT VALUE OF $1 RECEIVED ANNUALLY AT THE
END OF EACH YEAR FOR *N* YEARS

Years (N)	1%	2%	4%	6%	8%	10%	12%	14%	15%	16%
1	0.990	0.980	0.962	0.943	0.926	0.909	0.893	0.877	0.870	0.862
2	1.970	1.942	1.886	1.833	1.783	1.736	1.690	1.647	1.626	1.605
3	2.941	2.884	2.775	2.673	2.577	2.487	2.402	2.322	2.283	2.246
4	3.902	3.808	3.630	3.465	3.312	3.170	3.037	2.914	2.855	2.798
5	4.853	4.713	4.452	4.212	3.993	3.791	3.605	3.433	3.352	3.274
6	5.795	5.601	5.242	4.917	4.623	4.355	4.111	3.889	3.784	3.685
7	6.728	6.472	6.002	5.582	5.206	4.868	4.564	4.288	4.160	4.039
8	7.652	7.325	6.733	6.210	5.747	5.335	4.968	4.639	4.487	4.344
9	8.566	8.162	7.435	6.802	6.247	5.759	5.328	4.946	4.772	4.607
10	9.471	8.983	8.111	7.360	6.710	6.145	5.650	5.216	5.019	4.833
11	10.368	9.787	8.760	7.887	7.139	6.495	5.988	5.453	5.234	5.029
12	11.255	10.575	9.385	8.384	7.536	6.814	6.194	5.660	5.421	5.197
13	12.134	11.343	9.986	8.853	7.904	7.103	6.424	5.842	5.583	5.342
14	13.004	12.106	10.563	9.295	8.244	7.367	6.628	6.002	5.724	5.468
15	13.865	12.849	11.118	9.712	8.559	7.606	6.811	6.142	5.847	5.575
16	14.718	13.578	11.652	10.106	8.851	7.824	6.974	6.265	5.954	5.669
17	15.562	14.292	12.166	10.477	9.122	8.022	7.120	6.373	6.047	5.749
18	16.398	14.992	12.659	10.828	9.372	8.201	7.250	6.467	6.128	5.818
19	17.226	15.678	13.134	11.158	9.604	8.365	7.366	6.550	6.198	5.877
20	18.046	16.351	13.590	11.470	9.818	8.514	7.469	6.623	6.259	5.929
21	18.857	17.011	14.029	11.764	10.017	8.649	7.562	6.687	6.312	5.973
22	19.660	17.658	14.451	12.042	10.201	8.772	7.645	6.743	6.359	6.011
23	20.456	18.292	14.857	12.303	10.371	8.883	7.718	6.792	6.399	6.044
24	21.243	18.914	15.247	12.550	10.529	8.985	7.784	6.835	6.434	6.073
25	22.023	19.523	15.622	12.783	10.675	9.077	7.843	6.873	6.464	6.097
26	22.795	20.121	15.983	13.003	10.810	9.161	7.896	6.906	6.491	6.118
27	23.560	20.707	16.330	13.211	10.935	9.237	7.943	6.935	6.514	6.136
28	24.316	21.281	16.663	13.406	11.051	9.307	7.984	6.961	6.534	6.152
29	25.066	21.844	16.984	13.591	11.158	9.370	8.022	6.983	6.551	6.166
30	25.808	22.396	17.292	13.765	11.258	9.427	8.055	7.003	6.566	6.177
40	32.835	27.355	19.793	15.046	11.925	9.779	8.244	7.105	6.642	6.234
50	39.196	31.424	21.482	15.762	12.234	9.915	8.304	7.133	6.661	6.246

Present value of $1 Received Annually at the End of Each Year for N Years

PRESENT VALUE OF $1 RECEIVED ANNUALLY AT THE
END OF EACH YEAR FOR *N* YEARS

18%	20%	22%	24%	25%	26%	28%	30%	35%	40%	45%	50%
0.847	0.833	0.820	0.806	0.800	0.794	0.781	0.769	0.741	0.714	0.690	0.667
1.566	1.528	1.492	1.457	1.440	1.424	1.392	1.361	1.289	1.224	1.165	1.111
2.174	2.106	2.042	1.981	1.952	1.923	1.868	1.816	1.696	1.589	1.493	1.407
2.690	2.589	2.494	2.404	2.362	2.320	2.241	2.166	1.997	1.849	1.720	1.605
3.127	2.991	2.864	2.745	2.689	2.635	2.532	2.436	2.220	2.035	1.876	1.737
3.498	3.326	3.167	3.020	2.951	2.885	2.759	2.643	2.385	2.168	1.983	1.824
3.812	3.605	3.416	3.242	3.161	3.083	2.937	2.802	2.508	2.263	2.057	1.883
4.078	3.837	3.619	3.421	3.329	3.241	3.076	2.925	2.598	2.331	2.108	1.922
4.303	4.031	3.786	3.566	3.463	3.366	3.184	3.019	2.665	2.379	2.144	1.948
4.494	4.192	3.923	3.682	3.571	3.465	3.269	3.092	2.715	2.414	2.168	1.965
4.656	4.327	4.035	3.776	3.656	3.544	3.335	3.147	2.752	2.438	2.185	1.977
4.793	4.439	4.127	3.851	3.725	3.606	3.387	3.190	2.779	2.456	2.196	1.985
4.910	4.533	4.203	3.912	3.780	3.656	3.427	3.223	2.799	2.468	2.204	1.990
5.008	4.611	4.265	3.962	3.824	3.695	3.459	3.249	2.814	2.477	2.210	1.993
5.092	4.675	4.315	4.001	3.859	3.726	3.483	3.268	2.825	2.484	2.214	1.995
5.162	4.730	4.357	4.033	3.887	3.751	3.503	3.283	2.834	2.489	2.216	1.997
5.222	4.775	4.391	4.059	3.910	3.771	3.518	3.295	2.840	2.492	2.218	1.998
5.273	4.812	4.419	4.080	3.928	3.786	3.529	3.304	2.844	2.494	2.219	1.999
5.316	4.844	4.442	4.097	3.942	3.799	3.539	3.311	2.848	2.496	2.220	1.999
5.353	4.870	4.460	4.110	3.954	3.808	3.546	3.316	2.850	2.497	2.221	1.999
5.384	4.891	4.476	4.121	3.963	3.816	3.551	3.320	2.852	2.498	2.221	2.000
5.410	4.909	4.488	4.130	3.970	3.822	3.556	3.323	2.853	2.498	2.222	2.000
5.432	4.925	4.499	4.137	3.976	3.827	3.559	3.325	2.854	2.499	2.222	2.000
5.451	4.937	4.507	4.143	3.981	3.831	3.562	3.327	2.855	2.499	2.222	2.000
5.467	4.948	4.514	4.147	3.985	3.834	3.564	3.329	2.856	2.499	2.222	2.000
5.480	4.956	4.520	4.151	3.988	3.837	3.566	3.330	2.856	2.500	2.222	2.000
5.492	4.964	4.524	4.154	3.990	3.839	3.567	3.331	2.856	2.500	2.222	2.000
5.502	4.970	4.528	4.157	3.992	3.840	3.568	3.331	2.857	2.500	2.222	2.000
5.510	4.975	4.531	4.159	3.994	3.841	3.569	3.332	2.857	2.500	2.222	2.000
5.517	4.979	4.534	4.160	3.995	3.842	3.569	3.332	2.857	2.500	2.222	2.000
5.548	4.997	4.544	4.166	3.999	3.846	3.571	3.333	2.857	2.500	2.222	2.000
5.554	4.999	4.545	4.167	4.000	3.846	3.571	3.333	2.857	2.500	2.222	2.000

SOURCE: Reprinted with permission from R. N. Anthony, *Management Accounting: Text and Cases* (Homewood, Ill.: Irwin, 1960), p. 657.

APPENDIX A3
Compound Sum of $1

COMPOUND SUM OF $1

Year	1%	2%	3%	4%	5%	6%	7%
1	1.010	1.020	1.030	1.044	1.050	1.060	1.070
2	1.020	1.040	1.061	1.082	1.102	1.124	1.145
3	1.030	1.061	1.093	1.125	1.158	1.191	1.225
4	1.041	1.082	1.126	1.170	1.216	1.262	1.311
5	1.051	1.104	1.159	1.217	1.276	1.338	1.403
6	1.062	1.126	1.194	1.265	1.340	1.419	1.501
7	1.072	1.149	1.230	1.316	1.407	1.504	1.606
8	1.083	1.172	1.267	1.369	1.477	1.594	1.718
9	1.094	1.195	1.305	1.423	1.551	1.689	1.838
10	1.105	1.219	1.344	1.480	1.629	1.791	1.967
11	1.116	1.243	1.384	1.539	1.710	1.898	2.105
12	1.127	1.268	1.426	1.601	1.796	2.012	2.252
13	1.138	1.294	1.469	1.665	1.886	2.133	2.410
14	1.149	1.319	1.513	1.732	1.980	2.261	2.579
15	1.161	1.346	1.558	1.801	2.079	2.397	2.759
16	1.173	1.373	1.605	1.873	2.183	2.540	2.952
17	1.184	1.400	1.653	1.948	2.292	2.693	3.159
18	1.196	1.428	1.702	2.026	2.407	2.854	3.380
19	1.208	1.457	1.754	2.107	2.527	3.026	3.617
20	1.220	1.486	1.806	2.191	2.653	3.207	3.870
25	1.282	1.641	2.094	2.666	3.386	4.292	5.427
30	1.348	1.811	2.427	3.243	4.322	5.743	7.612

Year	8%	9%	10%	12%	14%	15%	16%
1	1.080	1.090	1.100	1.120	1.140	1.150	1.160
2	1.166	1.188	1.210	1.254	1.300	1.322	1.346
3	1.260	1.295	1.331	1.405	1.482	1.521	1.561
4	1.360	1.412	1.464	1.574	1.689	1.749	1.811
5	1.469	1.539	1.611	1.762	1.925	2.011	2.100
6	1.587	1.677	1.772	1.974	2.195	2.313	2.436
7	1.714	1.828	1.949	2.211	2.502	2.660	2.826
8	1.851	1.993	2.144	2.476	2.853	3.059	3.278
9	1.999	2.172	2.358	2.773	3.252	3.518	3.803
10	2.159	2.367	2.594	3.106	3.700	4.046	4.411
11	2.332	2.580	2.853	3.479	4.226	4.652	5.117
12	2.518	2.813	3.138	3.896	4.818	5.350	5.936
13	2.720	3.066	3.452	4.363	5.492	6.153	6.886
14	2.937	3.342	3.797	4.887	6.261	7.076	7.988
15	3.172	3.642	4.177	5.474	7.138	8.137	9.266
16	3.426	3.970	4.595	6.130	8.137	9.358	10.748
17	3.700	4.328	5.054	6.866	9.276	10.761	12.468
18	3.996	4.717	5.560	7.690	10.575	12.375	14.463
19	4.316	5.142	6.116	8.613	12.056	14.232	16.777
20	4.661	5.604	6.728	9.646	13.743	16.367	19.461
25	6.848	8.623	10.835	17.000	26.462	32.919	40.874
30	10.063	13.268	17.449	29.960	50.950	66.212	85.850

APPENDIX A3 (continued)

Compound Sum of $1

COMPOUND SUM OF $1

Year	18%	20%	24%	28%	32%	36%
1	1.180	1.200	1.240	1.280	1.320	1.360
2	1.392	1.440	1.538	1.638	1.742	1.850
3	1.643	1.728	1.907	2.067	2.300	2.515
4	1.939	2.074	2.364	2.684	3.036	3.421
5	2.288	2.488	2.932	3.436	4.007	4.653
6	2.700	2.986	3.635	4.398	5.290	6.328
7	3.185	3.583	4.508	5.629	6.983	8.605
8	3.759	4.300	5.590	7.206	9.217	11.703
9	4.435	5.160	6.931	9.223	12.166	15.917
10	5.234	6.192	8.594	11.806	16.060	21.647
11	6.176	7.430	10.657	15.112	21.199	29.439
12	7.288	8.916	13.215	19.343	27.983	40.037
13	8.599	10.699	16.386	24.759	36.937	54.451
14	10.147	12.839	20.319	31.691	48.757	74.053
15	11.974	15.407	25.196	40.565	64.359	100.712
16	14.129	18.488	31.243	51.923	84.954	136.97
17	16.672	22.186	38.741	66.461	112.14	186.28
18	19.673	26.623	48.039	85.071	148.02	253.34
19	23.214	31.948	59.568	108.89	195.39	344.54
20	27.393	38.338	73.864	139.38	257.92	468.57
25	62.669	95.396	216.542	478.90	1033.6	2180.1
30	143.371	237.376	634.820	1645.5	4142.1	10143.

Year	40%	50%	60%	70%	80%	90%
1	1.400	1.500	1.600	1.700	1.800	1.900
2	1.960	2.250	2.560	2.890	3.240	3.610
3	2.744	3.375	4.096	4.913	5.832	6.859
4	3.842	5.062	6.544	8.352	10.498	13.032
5	5.378	7.594	10.486	14.199	18.896	24.761
6	7.530	11.391	16.777	24.138	34.012	47.046
7	10.541	17.086	26.844	41.034	61.222	89.387
8	14.758	25.629	42.950	69.758	110.200	169.836
9	20.661	38.443	68.720	118.588	198.359	322.688
10	28.925	57.665	109.951	201.599	357.047	613.107
11	40.496	86.498	175.922	342.719	642.684	1164.902
12	56.694	129.746	281.475	582.622	1156.831	2213.314
13	79.372	194.619	450.360	990.457	2082.295	4205.297
14	111.120	291.929	720.576	1683.777	3748.131	7990.065
15	155.568	437.894	1152.921	2862.421	6746.636	15181.122
16	217.795	656.84	1844.7	4866.1	12144.	28844.0
17	304.914	985.26	2951.5	8272.4	21859.	54804.0
18	426.879	1477.9	4722.4	14063.0	39346.	104130.0
19	597.630	2216.8	7555.8	23907.0	70824.	197840.0
20	836.683	3325.3	12089.0	40642.0	127480.	375900.0
25	4499.880	25251.	126760.0	577060.0	2408900.	9307600.0
30	24201.432	191750.	1329200.	8193500.0	45517000.	230470000.0

Index